# STATS BASEBALL SCOREBOARD 2000

John Dewan, Don Zminda, Jim Callis, Editors

Thom Henninger, Jim Henzler,

Chuck Miller, Tony Nistler, Assistant Editors

Published by STATS Publishing
A division of Sports Team Analysis & Tracking Systems, Inc.

Cover by Marc Elman, Ben Frobig and Chuck Miller

Cover photo by Scott Jordan Levy
Inside photos by Larry Goren

STATS™ Baseball Scoreboard 2000. Copyright © 2000 by STATS, Inc. All rights reserved. Printed in the United States of America. No part of this book may be used or reproduced in any manner whatsoever without written permission except in the case of brief quotations embodied in critical articles and reviews. For information, address STATS, Inc., 8130 Lehigh Ave., Morton Grove, IL 60053

STATS is a registered trademark of Sports Team Analysis and Tracking Systems, Inc.

First Edition: March, 2000

ISBN 1-884064-77-9

# Acknowledgments

The process of putting together the *Baseball Scoreboard* takes a full major league season and some postseason work. We'd like to thank everyone who contributes to this effort.

STATS CEO John Dewan and President Alan Leib are leading us into the new millennium. Helping them stay on course is Jennifer Manicki, who provides invaluable assistance to both of them. Two vice presidents, Sue Dewan and Bob Meyerhoff, play critical roles in our company's future, directing our Research & Development/Special Projects teams. Sue works with Jim Osborne and Andy Tumpowsky. Bob teams with Athan Arvanitis and Joe Sclafani.

The members of the Publishing Products Department handled a majority of the writing and editing responsibilities, under the direction of vice president Don Zminda. Jim Callis, Thom Henninger, and yours truly oversaw the production of this book, while Jim Henzler ably wrote and manipulated the programs for it. Chuck Miller laid out the pages and John Grimwade again supplied the entertaining illustrations. Thanks also to Taylor Bechtold and Marc Carl, who stat-checked a majority of this manuscript, as well as to Steve Schulman and Mike Murphy, who each contributed an essay to this year's edition.

Getting the word out about the *Baseball Scoreboard* and all other STATS Publishing ventures depends on Marc Elman and his promotions group. Marc works with Ben Frobig, Mike Janosi, Antoinette Kelly and Mike Sarkis. Ben, our graphics man, designed this book's cover.

The wonderful statistics that hold this book together were gathered by our Data Collection Department. Allan Spear heads the group, which includes Jeremy Alpert, Scott Berg, Michelle Blanco, Jon Caplin, Jeff Chernow, Mike Hammer, Derek Kenar, Tony Largo, Jon Passman, Jeff Schinski, Matt Senter, Bill Stephens and Joe Stillwell. With a vast reporter network making statistical collection possible, Jeff Chernow oversaw the compilation of MLB data during the 1999 season.

The Commercial, Fantasy and Interactive Products and Sales departments are key components of the STATS family. Vince Smith heads our Commercial Products staff, which includes Ethan D. Cooperson, Dan Matern and David Pinto. Steve Byrd oversees the Fantasy Department, which consists of Bill Burke, Sean Bush, Jim Corelis, Dan Ford, Brian Hogan, Stefan Kretschmann, Walter Lis, Marc Moeller, Mike Mooney, Oscar Palacios, Jim Pollard, Corey Roberts, Eric Robin, Jeff Smith, Yingmin Wang and Rick Wilton. Rick also contributed an essay for this year's edition. Michael Canter leads an active Interactive group that includes Dave Carlson, Jake Costello, Joe Lindholm, Will McCleskey, Dean Peterson, Pat Quinn, John Sasman, Meghan Sheehan, Morris Srinivasan and Nick Stamm. Jim Capuano directs a Sales team comprised of Greg Kirkorsky and Jake Stein.

Our Financial/Administrative/Human Resources/Legal Department keeps the office running smoothly and efficiently at our Morton Grove, Ill., home. Howard Lanin oversees the financial and administrative concerns of the company with assistance from Kim Bartlett, Mary Ellen Gomez and Betty Moy. Susan Zamechek assists in finance and keeps the office functional on a day-to-day basis. Tracy Lickton is in charge of human resources while Carol Savier aids with legal matters. Art Ashley provides programming support throughout the building.

—Tony Nistler

To Lisa Fenn,
who always asks a creative question.

—David Pinto

# Table of Contents

**Foreword by Gary Carter**   1

**Introduction**   3

**I. TEAM QUESTIONS**   5

    **Anaheim Angels:** Can Percival Come Back? ...............................6

    **Baltimore Orioles:** Is Mussina on Track For the Hall of Fame?....9

    **Boston Red Sox:** Did Martinez Deserve the MVP Award?..........12

    **Chicago White Sox:** Will the Youngest Soon Be the Best?.........15

    **Cleveland Indians:** Are Teams That Dominate Their Division at a Disadvantage in the Postseason?..............................................17

    **Detroit Tigers:** Will the Gonzalez Trade Pay Off?......................19

    **Kansas City Royals:** How Good Was Beltran's Rookie Season? ................................................................................................22

    **Minnesota Twins:** Was Milton's No-Hitter a Sign of Things to Come?..............................................................................................25

    **New York Yankees:** Were They the Sports Franchise of the Century?..........................................................................................27

    **Oakland Athletics:** Were They the Ultimate Sabermetric Team? ................................................................................................29

    **Seattle Mariners:** Does Safeco Field Really Cut Down on Homers? ..........................................................................................31

    **Tampa Bay Devil Rays:** Is It Smart to Load Up on Old Sluggers?..........................................................................................34

    **Texas Rangers:** Will Palmeiro Post Cooperstown Numbers? ......36

**Toronto Blue Jays:** Is a Great Rookie Season a Good Sign For a Closer?..................................................................................38

**Arizona Diamondbacks:** Why Can't Hitters Bank on Bank One?...............................................................................................40

**Atlanta Braves:** Can Galarraga Come Back?...............................42

**Chicago Cubs:** Is Sosa the King of the Also-Rans? ......................45

**Cincinnati Reds:** Did They Overwork Their Bullpen?..................48

**Colorado Rockies:** Can Cirillo Replace Castilla? ........................50

**Florida Marlins:** Has Anyone Had a Ground Game Like Castillo's?......................................................................................52

**Houston Astros:** How Underrated Is Biggio?................................54

**Los Angeles Dodgers:** Is Brown the Best Travelin' Pitcher Ever? ...............................................................................................56

**Milwaukee Brewers:** Can Burnitz Become Their Biggest Basher Ever? ..................................................................................58

**Montreal Expos:** Can You Win Without Walking? ......................60

**New York Mets:** Did They Have the Best Defensive Infield of All Time?........................................................................................62

**Philadelphia Phillies:** How Unique Was Abreu's Season?..........65

**Pittsburgh Pirates:** How Good Was Giles' First Year As a Full-Timer? .....................................................................................67

**St. Louis Cardinals:** What If McGwire Had Stayed Healthy?.....69

**San Diego Padres:** How Long Can Gwynn Continue?..................71

**San Francisco Giants:** Will Pac Bell Provide a New-Park Boost? .............................................................................................73

## II. QUESTIONS ON OFFENSE                                        75

Can McGwire Beat Aaron?............................................................76

Is Guerrero on His Way to Immortality? ........................................79

Who Unloads the Bases?...............................................................81

Who Works the Most Hitters' Counts?............................................83

Can They Foul 'Em Off on Purpose?..............................................86

Who Bagged the Most Runs Created? ...........................................89

Who's Second to None?................................................................91

Who Puts 'Em Ahead?..................................................................93

Who Are the Real RBI Kings?........................................................96

Who Gets the Slidin' Billy Trophy? ................................................98

Who Are the Human Air Conditioners?........................................100

Will the Rockies' Heart Survive a Double-Bypass? ......................102

Who's the Best Bunter? ..............................................................104

Who Was the Real "Man on the Moon" in 1999? ........................107

## III. QUESTIONS ON PITCHING                                      109

Did Martinez Have the Most Spectacular Pitching Season Ever? ..................................................................................................110

How Long Can the Big Unit Dominate?........................................114

Who Threw the Most Pitches in a Single Season?........................116

Was Hampton the Best Combination Pitcher/Hitter of the DH Era? ..............................................................................................120

Who Are Baseball's Best-Hitting Pitchers? ..................................123

How Bad Were Bowie And Hawkins?...........................................125

How Many Records Did Orosco Set in 1999?...........................127

Which Pitchers Mop Up the Most?..............................................129

Who's Toughest to Pull?................................................................131

Which Pitchers Scored the Highest?.............................................133

Who Are the High-Quality Starters?.............................................135

Who's Heater Is Hottest?...............................................................137

Who Was 1999's Most Overpowering Pitcher?............................140

Who Gets the Easy Saves—And Who Toughs It Out?.................142

If You Hold the Fort, Will You Soon Be Closing the Gate? .......145

Who Knows How to Handle Their Inheritance? .........................148

Which Reliever Prevents the Most Runs?....................................150

Who Gets the Red Barrett Trophy?...............................................154

Which Pitchers Have Misleading ERAs?.....................................156

## IV. QUESTIONS ON DEFENSE                                    159

Does Pudge Intimidate the Best Basestealers?.............................160

Which Catchers Catch Thieves? ...................................................163

Can We Improve Zone Ratings?...................................................165

Who's Best in the Infield Zone? ...................................................174

Who Can Turn the Pivot?..............................................................178

Who's Best in the Outfield Zone?.................................................180

Which Outfielders Know How to Hold 'Em?...............................183

Which Fielders Have the Best Defensive Batting Average?........186

## V. GENERAL QUESTIONS — 191

Who Were the Winningest Players of the 1990s?..........192

Are the Late-1990s Yankees the Most Dominant Postseason Team Ever?...........................................................195

Which Teams Were 1999's Biggest Overachievers And Underachievers?..................................................198

What's the Real Truth About Wrigley Field's Dimensions?.......200

## VI. AWARDS & COMMENTS — 203

Which Players Cleaned Up at the Awards Banquet?...........204

What Do the Readers Have to Say?...........................212

## Appendix — 217

## Glossary — 300

## Index — 308

## About STATS, Inc. — 313

## About the Authors — 314

# Foreword

## by Gary Carter

More than any other game, baseball is dissected daily with the help of statistics. By way of statistics and that baseball institution called the box score, fans can "see" games they didn't attend.

For many of us, the box score was our first step to understanding and appreciating the game's many statistics. Although it appears simplistic and lists numbers without much explanation, the box score tells us so much about the game it covers.

In recent years, STATS has taken us beyond the traditional box score, providing an array of statistics that dig deeper into the game. This is STATS' forte. No one compiles, tracks and analyzes statistics like STATS does. That's their job, and they do it incredibly well. It is through their efforts that we all have access to a more in-depth, analytical look into the game of baseball.

To present this whole new world of statistics, STATS publishes the *Baseball Scoreboard*. This book goes beyond the basic story line. Its thorough coverage of the game appeals to any fan or professional who enjoys reading about baseball. That includes players too. If you don't think that players compare statistics, then you don't understand how competitive we tend to be.

Having played and broadcast baseball for so much of my life, I have come to truly appreciate the game. It is both beautiful and flawed, simple and deceptively difficult. Box scores are what helped me follow the hitters and call games during my career. Today *Baseball Scoreboard* gives me another opportunity to follow, enjoy and appreciate this great game.

The *Scoreboard* provides insight into the finer points of baseball. Yet, it wouldn't surprise me a bit to find out the gang at STATS fell in love with the game by tracking box scores as young fans.

*Former National League All-Star catcher Gary Carter now works as a broadcaster, most recently with the Expos.*

# Introduction

The 1999 season produced a whole new set of dramatic moments to remember. In April, Fernando Tatis became the first player in baseball history to stroke two grand slams in the same inning. Both Wade Boggs and Tony Gwynn reached the 3,000-hit plateau, Sammy Sosa and Mark McGwire surpassed the 60-homer mark for a second straight season, and 23-year-old Vladimir Guerrero put together another monster season for the Expos. Meanwhile, David Cone pitched a perfect game and Pedro Martinez turned in one of the best summers of pitching ever. Then the Yankees closed out the '99 campaign with a dominating postseason performance, winning 11 of 12 contests in defending their reign over baseball.

When looking at the memorable events of seasons passed, only sometimes do the numbers tell the whole story. As definitive as statistics can be, they frequently elicit as many questions as answers. Taking a look inside the numbers and answering the questions that they generate is what *STATS Baseball Scoreboard* is all about. As in previous editions, this Y2K version will study the offensive and defensive sides of the game, break down a question on each major league club, and undertake a statistical analysis of 1999's best, ranging from Ivan Rodriguez to Randy Johnson, from Bobby Abreu to Carlos Beltran, from Mike Hampton to Pedro Martinez.

Consider the numbers from Martinez' fine season. The Boston righthander averaged 13.2 strikeouts per nine innings, an all-time record for starters that was almost five whiffs better than any other American League starting pitcher. He produced a strikeout-walk ratio that was twice as good as any other American Leaguer, and he posted a 2.07 ERA that was more than a run better than the mark of David Cone, the AL runner-up. Here at STATS, these numbers begged the question whether Martinez had one of the game's best seasons ever on the hill.

The data of 1999 generated plenty of other questions as well. After hitting 65 homers in '99 to give him nearly 200 in the last three seasons, is McGwire now a strong candidate to catch Hank Aaron's career total? With a .338 average in '99, Gwynn keeps hitting as his 40th birthday approaches in May. How long can he keep it up? Guerrero, Montreal's young star, improved upon his breakout season of 1998, generating a .314 average, 42 homers and 131 RBI last year. Has anyone performed better at such a young age? Is immortality in the cards for him?

Of course, the raw numbers are the tools we use to *find* answers to these and other burning questions. They also provide a window into what we might see during the 2000 season. To speculate on the comeback of 38-year-old Andres Galarraga after a year-long battle with cancer, we look at how other aging veterans did after a layoff late in their careers. Tampa Bay begins the new campaign with four sluggers who hit 30 home runs last summer, and there are plenty of historical references that provide insight into the Y2K fortunes of the heavy-hitting Devil Rays. Or we can analyze the 1999 indexes for Safeco Field to see what might be in store this spring, the first full season in which the new-look Mariners will reside in their new home.

In addition to the projections and analysis, there are the usual standbys of the *Scoreboard*. You'll find out who were the best in '99 at bunting, setting the table, holding leads, stranding inherited runners, throwing out basestealers and turning the pivot at second base. Then there's always STATS' annual awards to wrap up the book. If your hunger for data remains upon finishing the essays, there's loads of appendices to digest at book's end.

We begin our second decade of bringing you this statistical look inside the game. In this newest edition, we've tried to answer the questions that the 1999 season stirred in us, and we encourage you to continue sharing your baseball questions and insights. Until the summer of 2000 has inspired the questions that will face us next offseason, we hope you find plenty of time between games to enjoy the 11th edition of *STATS Baseball Scoreboard*.

—Thom Henninger

# I. TEAM QUESTIONS

## Anaheim Angels: Can Percival Come Back?

**T**roy Percival has been one of the best closers in baseball in recent years. But even Percival probably will tell you that 1999 was not one of his better seasons. After saving a career-high 42 games in 1998, Percival saved only 31 in 1999. His eight blown saves were a career high. He also continued a disturbing trend of seeing his ERA increase. After posting a 1.95 ERA as a rookie in 1995, Percival has put up ERAs of 2.31, 3.46, 3.65 and 3.79.

Can Percival come back? One way of assessing his chances is to look at relievers who had a similar pattern of increasing ERAs. Were they able to turn things around? We found out pretty quickly that this sort of thing hasn't happened to many pitchers. Percival was one of only eight relievers with ERA increases in four or more straight seasons (minimum 30 relief games each season of the streak, with at least half of all appearances in each season in relief). Here's the list of pitchers and their yearly ERAs, including their ERA the year the streak ended—if it did:

**Relievers With ERA Increases in Four-Plus Straight Seasons**

| Pitcher | Base Year | Year1 | Year2 | Year3 | Year4 | Year5 | Year6 |
|---|---|---|---|---|---|---|---|
| Ernie Johnson | 1953 | 2.67 | 2.81 | 3.42 | 3.71 | 3.88 | 8.10 |
| Bob Lee | 1964 | 1.51 | 1.92 | 2.74 | 4.55 | 5.10 | — |
| Ramon Hernandez | 1972 | 1.67 | 2.41 | 2.75 | 2.95 | 3.43 | 6.64 |
| Tom Hall | 1972 | 2.61 | 3.47 | 4.08 | 4.60 | 4.63 | 3.52 |
| Tom Niedenfuer | 1983 | 1.90 | 2.47 | 2.71 | 3.71 | 4.46 | 3.51 |
| Juan Agosto | 1988 | 2.26 | 2.93 | 4.29 | 4.81 | 6.12 | 6.00 |
| Heathcliff Slocumb | 1994 | 2.86 | 2.89 | 3.02 | 5.16 | 5.32 | 3.77 |
| **Troy Percival** | **1995** | **1.95** | **2.31** | **3.46** | **3.65** | **3.79** | — |

(minimum 30 relief games each season and at least half of all appearances in relief in each season of streak)

There's not many pitchers here, so let's run them down:

**Ernie Johnson** was a reliever for the Boston and Milwaukee Braves before becoming one of the Braves' radio and TV announcers. In 1953, the Braves' first season in Milwaukee, Johnson posted a career-low 2.67 ERA. But his ERA steadily increased in each of the next four years. In 1958 it skyrocketed all the way up to 8.10 in 15 games, and after the season the Braves dealt him to the Orioles. Johnson, who was 35 years old at that point, had one so-so year with Baltimore (36 games, 4.11 ERA) before deciding to call it quits.

**Bob Lee**, the pitcher on the list most comparable to Percival, was a big, hard-throwing reliever in the early days of the Angels franchise. As a rookie in 1964, Lee posted a 1.51 ERA in 64 games along with 19 saves, a good total for that era. He had another good year in 1965 with 23 saves, though his ERA rose to 1.95. In 1966 he slipped to 16 saves with an ERA of 2.74. When he got off to a slow start in 1967, the Angels dealt him to the Reds, and he finished the year with a 4.55 ERA and only two saves in 31 appearances. He failed to bounce back in 1968, and after posting a 5.10 in 44 games, his career was over at age 30.

**Ramon Hernandez**, a lefty relief specialist who pitched from the late '60s to the late '70s, had his best year for the 1972 Pirates, going 5-0 with 14 saves and a 1.67 ERA. He continued to pitch good ball for the next few years, but his ERA went up a little each year, and when it rose to the mid-three range in 1976, the Pirates dealt him to the Cubs late in the year. His 1977 season was his worst yet—a 6.84 ERA for the Cubs and Red Sox—and Hernandez' career was history.

**Tom (The Blade) Hall**, a contemporary of Hernandez, was a slightly built but hard-throwing middle reliever who had some excellent years with Cincinnati's Big Red Machine of the 1970s. After posting a 2.61 ERA for the Reds in 1972, Hall saw his ERA rise steadily to 4.63 in 1976. By then he'd been dealt to the Mets and then the Royals. He did reverse the trend briefly in 1977, posting a 3.52 ERA in six games, but then his career abruptly ended at age 29.

**Tom Niedenfuer** was a middle reliever and occasional closer for the Dodgers in the 1980s. He's best known for giving up the home run to the Cardinals' Jack Clark that cost the Dodgers the 1985 National League Championship Series. At that point he was still a pretty effective pitcher, posting a 2.71 ERA and 19 saves that year, even though his ERA had risen two years in a row. Whether it was the effect of the home run or not, Niedenfuer's ERA rose by a run in 1986 and slid still further in 1987, a year in which he was traded to the Orioles. Niedenfuer played for three more seasons and two more teams after '87, bouncing back a bit in 1988, slipping badly in 1989 (6.69 ERA) and then finishing with a decent finale in 1990. He was only 31 when his career ended.

**Juan Agosto** was a lefty middle man who had an up-and-down 13-year career. He was already in his eighth season when he went 10-2 with a 2.26 ERA for the 1988 Astros. He regressed pretty steadily after that, and in 1992 his ERA was all the way up to 6.12. He got one more six-game chance with the Astros in '93, and when he showed little improvement (6.00 ERA), his career was over at age 35.

**Heathcliff Slocumb** has been around for nearly a decade, and he was a good pitcher in 1994-96, posting ERAs of 2.86, 2.89 and 3.02 while saving 32 and 31 games the latter two years. Then he bombed out in '97 and '98 before showing signs of a comeback after joining the Cardinals early in '99. He has yet to show he can handle an important relief role again, totaling only five saves and seven holds in 1998-99.

None of these pitchers really regained their form after several years of ERA slippage, even the guys who were still fairly young, as is the 30-year-old Percival. He has a couple of things in his favor. One is that despite several years of ERA increases, he still hasn't had a really bad year. His ERA was a respectable 3.79 last year, and he remained extremely tough to hit, allowing only 38 hits in 57 innings. The other is that he was pitching with shoulder soreness last year, and it took its toll late in the year: Percival had a 2.09 ERA through July 31, a 7.36 ERA afterward. He had surgery in October and is expected to be at full strength by Opening Day. If his shoulder is sound, there's no reason why he can't reverse his trend of rising ERAs. But if he does, he'll be the exception to the rule.

—Don Zminda

## Baltimore Orioles: Is Mussina on Track For the Hall of Fame?

The Orioles suffered through their second straight losing season in 1999, but don't blame Mike Mussina. The O's ace posted a splendid 18-7 record, and his .720 winning percentage marked the seventh time in the last eight years that Mussina had posted a winning percentage of .625 or higher. Mussina logged his 200th major league decision late in the year, and that enabled him to qualify for the all-time leaders list in career winning percentage. His .673 winning percentage (136-66) currently ranks as the fifth-best in major league history:

### Highest Winning Percentage—Career

| Pitcher | W-L | Pct |
| --- | --- | --- |
| Dave Foutz | 147-66 | .690 |
| Whitey Ford | 236-106 | .690 |
| Bob Caruthers | 217-98 | .688 |
| Lefty Grove | 300-141 | .680 |
| **Mike Mussina** | **136-66** | **.673** |
| Larry Corcoran | 177-89 | .665 |
| Christy Mathewson | 373-188 | .665 |
| Sam Leever | 195-100 | .661 |
| Sandy Koufax | 165-87 | .655 |
| Johnny Allen | 142-75 | .654 |

(minimum 200 decisions)

You might not recognize all the pitchers on this list. Dave Foutz, Bob Caruthers and Larry Corcoran were 19th-century stars. Sam Leever toiled for the Pirates in the first decade of the 20th century, and Johnny Allen had a brief but explosive career for several major league teams in the 1930s and '40s. We assume you've heard of Whitey Ford, Lefty Grove, Christy Mathewson and Sandy Koufax, however. "The Moose" is in some pretty good company.

Mussina turned 31 over the winter, and an obvious question is whether he can maintain that lofty winning percentage over the remainder of his career. The answer is almost certainly no, and not just because the Orioles no longer appear to be one of the American League's elite teams. Here's a list of the pitchers who were in Mussina's age group (29 to 32) and who had the highest career winning percentages through the season in which they recorded their 200th decision:

**Highest Winning Percentage,
Through Season Reaching 200 Decisions—Ages 29-32**

| Pitcher | Year | Age | Thru Season w/200th Dec W-L | Pct | Rest of Career W-L | Pct | Total W-L | Pct |
|---|---|---|---|---|---|---|---|---|
| Whitey Ford | 1961 | 32 | 158-63 | .715 | 78-43 | .645 | 236-106 | .690 |
| Old Hoss Radbourn | 1884 | 29 | 165-68 | .708 | 144-128 | .529 | 309-196 | .612 |
| Lefty Grove | 1931 | 31 | 146-61 | .705 | 154-80 | .658 | 300-141 | .680 |
| Three Finger Brown | 1909 | 32 | 144-65 | .689 | 95-64 | .597 | 239-129 | .649 |
| Pete Alexander | 1916 | 29 | 160-75 | .681 | 213-133 | .616 | 373-208 | .642 |
| Juan Marichal | 1967 | 29 | 144-68 | .679 | 99-74 | .572 | 243-142 | .631 |
| Roger Clemens | 1992 | 29 | 152-72 | .679 | 95-62 | .605 | 247-134 | .648 |
| **Mike Mussina** | **1999** | **30** | **136-66** | **.673** | 0-0 | — | **136-66** | **.673** |
| Ed Reulbach | 1913 | 30 | 143-71 | .668 | 39-35 | .527 | 182-106 | .632 |
| Jim Palmer | 1975 | 29 | 152-80 | .655 | 116-72 | .617 | 268-152 | .638 |

(age as of June 30)

As you can see, every pitcher on this list had a lower winning percentage in the years following the season in which they recorded their 200th decision. This is only natural; most pitchers lose velocity as they age, and it's hard to keep winning 65 percent or more of your decisions without the same stuff you had when you were younger. That's the bad news. The good news is that of the nine other pitchers on this list, seven have made the Hall of Fame, and an eighth, Roger Clemens, will be an automatic choice five years after he retires. The only exception is Ed Reulbach, a Cubs star of the Tinker-to-Evers-to-Chance days who flamed out early after being traded to the Dodgers at age 30 in 1913. While he didn't make the Hall of Fame, Reulbach finished his career with a .632 winning percentage and a lifetime ERA of 2.28. Had he won another 20 or 30 games, he would have been a strong candidate for Cooperstown.

Though he's yet to post a 20-win season, win an ERA title or capture a Cy Young Award, Mussina's brilliant record to date probably will make him a viable Hall of Fame candidate someday, presuming that he can stay healthy. His winning percentage is so high that he could be a .500 pitcher for the remainder of his career and still wind up with a very impressive record. For instance, if he went 90-90 over the remainder of his career, he'd wind up with a final mark of 226-156 (.592), a record that would be superior to such recent Hall of Fame candidates as Catfish Hunter (224-166) and Jim Bunning (224-184). Another couple of years at something approaching his current level—and maybe that 20-win season or Cy Young Award—and his credentials would look even more impressive.

Interestingly, Mussina's record through 200 decisions bears some resemblance to that of two Orioles aces of the past, Jim Palmer and Dave McNally:

**Comparison of Orioles Aces**

| Pitcher | Year | Age | Thru Season w/200th Dec W-L | Pct | Rest of Career W-L | Pct | Total W-L | Pct |
|---|---|---|---|---|---|---|---|---|
| Jim Palmer | 1975 | 29 | 152-80 | .655 | 116-72 | .617 | 268-152 | .638 |
| Dave McNally | 1971 | 28 | 135-69 | .662 | 49-50 | .495 | 184-119 | .607 |
| **Mike Mussina** | **1999** | **30** | 136-66 | **.673** | 0-0 | — | **136-66** | **.673** |

(age as of June 30)

Palmer, of course, stayed effective well past 1975, the year in which he recorded his 200th decision, and he went on to earn election to the Hall of Fame. McNally, whose career numbers through 1971 were very similar to Mussina's current record, faded pretty quickly after going 21-5 in '71 and is best known now as one of the two players (along with Andy Messersmith) who successfully challenged the reserve clause following the 1975 season. The verdict? Mussina has had a brilliant run thus far, but he's still a long way away from Cooperstown.

—Don Zminda

A more complete listing for this category can be found on page 218.

## Boston Red Sox: Did Martinez Deserve the MVP Award?

There was no element of surprise when Pedro Martinez overwhelmed the competition in the American League Cy Young Award voting at the close of the 1999 season. After all, the 5-foot-11, 170-pound fireballer dominated big league hitters all summer, en route to a 23-4 record and a 2.07 ERA that was 1.37 better than the next-best mark among AL qualifiers. He allowed a league-stingiest .205 batting average and fanned 313 batters in just 213.1 innings. That whiff total produced 13.2 strikeouts per nine innings, a record for big league starters. At 8.46, his strikeout-to-walk ratio was more than double that of any AL starter who pitched 162 innings.

Martinez' powerhouse numbers made him an automatic Most Valuable Player Award candidate, but the big surprise was that two baseball writers casting votes completely omitted Boston's ace from their MVP ballots. When the results were announced, Ivan Rodriguez of Texas became just the fourth player to win an MVP without getting the most first-place votes. While Martinez claimed eight first-place tallies to Rodriguez' seven, all 28 voters listed the Rangers backstop on their ballots—and Martinez finished a close second in the MVP race.

"I'm just not a pitcher-for-MVP kind of guy," said La Velle E. Neal III of the *Minneapolis Star Tribune*, one of the two writers who ignored Martinez when filling out his ballot. "I don't have anything against Pedro. He had a great season. I just don't think the award should go to a pitcher."

That kind of thinking usually begins with the argument that a pitcher who works every fifth day can't be as valuable as someone who's always in the lineup. Does the same reasoning come into play when two major league clubs are talking trade? Did you hear Cincinnati GM Jim Bowden rejecting a package that included Denny Neagle for a package built around Bret Boone because Neagle doesn't play every day? Of course not.

The truth is, while a major league hurler such as Martinez makes roughly 30 starts in the course of a 162-game season, he has a far greater impact on the game when he *is* on the field. It's clear that Martinez leaves a bigger imprint on his 30 appearances than a major league regular does in any 30 games in a season. For the top five finishers in the 1999 American League MVP vote, let's take a look at their teams' records, with and without their participation:

### Team Records With/Without MVP Candidate on the Field—1999

| Player, Team | MVP Voting Pts | W-L With | Pct | W-L Without | Pct | Diff |
|---|---|---|---|---|---|---|
| Ivan Rodriguez, Tex | 252 | 85-57 | .599 | 10-10 | .500 | .099 |
| Pedro Martinez, Bos | 239 | 24-5 | .828 | 70-63 | .526 | .302 |
| Roberto Alomar, Cle | 226 | 92-63 | .594 | 5-2 | .714 | -.120 |
| Manny Ramirez, Cle | 226 | 92-54 | .630 | 5-11 | .313 | .317 |
| Rafael Palmeiro, Tex | 193 | 90-66 | .577 | 5-1 | .833 | -.256 |

(records with MVP candidate include starts only)

Boston's winning percentage when Martinez didn't start was .302 less than when he did. Though the sample sizes were smaller for the hitters, the only other candidate with a similar impact was Manny Ramirez. Cleveland's winning percentage was .317 better with Ramirez in the starting lineup.

Another way to measure a player's impact is to analyze the number of runs he creates for his team or denies the opponent. Martinez had a profound impact on his 1999 opponents, and that's even more apparent when you compare him to other American League hurlers:

### ERA Comparisons—1999

|  | IP | ERA | Dif |
|---|---|---|---|
| Pedro Martinez | 213.1 | 2.07 | — |
| AL starters | 13,113.2 | 5.03 | -2.96 |
| All AL pitchers | 20,076.2 | 4.86 | -2.79 |

When you compare his performance to all American League pitching starts in 1999, Martinez allowed nearly three earned runs less per nine innings than his counterparts. The difference is nearly the same when simply comparing him to all AL pitchers. That's a remarkable gap. The runnerup in the American League ERA race last summer, David Cone, turned in a 3.44 ERA that was barely a run-and-a-half better than all AL starters. Over the course of his 213.1 innings, Martinez allowed 70 earned runs less than the average AL starter.

While three of the four hitters who placed in the top five in MVP voting generated a similar disparity in their runs created per 27 outs when compared to the league average, surprisingly the league MVP didn't:

### RC/27 Comparisons—1999

| Player | Pos | RC/27 | Lg RC/27 for Pos | Diff |
|---|---|---|---|---|
| Ivan Rodriguez | C | 5.95 | 4.36 | +1.59 |
| Roberto Alomar | 2B | 8.92 | 5.27 | +3.65 |
| Manny Ramirez | RF | 10.74 | 6.22 | +4.52 |
| Rafael Palmeiro | DH | 9.62 | 6.23 | +3.39 |

By finding the difference between each player's RC/27 and that of AL players at his position, then multiplying it by his playing time (outs made divided by the AL average of 26.7 per game), we can see how many runs better than average they were. Again, only Ramirez (76 runs) is in Martinez' class. Alomar (58) and Palmeiro (52) are close, while Rodriguez (22) lags far behind.

Obviously these position players are impacting their teams' run production every day. Plus, this approach isn't taking into account the fine defensive work of Rodriguez and Roberto Alomar. It's conceivable that Rodriguez, with his work behind the plate and his ability to control the opponent's running game, might be responsible for preventing at least a portion of a run per 27 outs. Still, Martinez had a staggering impact on the game in '99. The Boston righthander ranked far ahead of his best pitching peers, which we can't say as convincingly about Rodriguez when comparing him to the other finalists in the MVP race.

It's clear, at least to us, that Martinez was more valuable than Rodriguez in 1999. Ramirez and perhaps Alomar had a legitimate claim to the MVP Award, though as teammates they hurt the other's candidacy.

Besting his 1999 performance might seem improbable, but Martinez is just 28 years old. Still, it's unfortunate that a few baseball writers didn't view his remarkable achievement in a historical context that suggests his 1999 numbers were among the best of all time.

—Thom Henninger

## Chicago White Sox: Will the Youngest Soon Be the Best?

While the White Sox finished with a losing record (75-86) for the third straight season in 1999, they offered their fans some hope in terms of solid production by some of the team's younger players. The everyday lineup received important contributions from Paul Konerko (23 last year), Carlos Lee (23), Magglio Ordonez (25) and Chris Singleton (26). The pitching staff was spottier, but relievers Keith Foulke (26) and Bob Howry (25) pitched solidly and the starting rotation at the end of the year featured Jim Parque (23) and Kip Wells (22). There were other youthful contributors as well. Based on a weighted average using plate appearances for hitters (65 percent of the total weight) and batters faced for pitchers (35 percent), Chicago was the AL's youngest team with an average age of 26.5.

Do the youngest teams in the league tend to get better, moving into contention within two or three years? We went back to 1950 and identified the youngest team in each league, an even 100 teams overall. Here's how these teams fared in the season in which they were the league's youngest, and how they performed overall over the next five years, including the number of league pennants and World Championships won:

### Winning Percentage, Leagues' Youngest Teams—1950-99

|  | Year1 | Year2 | Year3 | Year4 | Year5 | Year6 |
|---|---|---|---|---|---|---|
| Winning Percentage | .451 | .479 | .502 | .514 | .515 | .516 |
| League Pennants | 3 | 5 | 11 | 9 | 8 | 12 |
| World Championships | 1 | 2 | 4 | 4 | 6 | 9 |

(weighted average age based on 65% PA for hitters, 35% BFP for pitchers)

As a group these teams played .451 ball in the year in which they were the youngest in their league, slightly worse than the .466 mark posted by the '99 White Sox. In year two they improved by 28 percentage points—a little less than five wins over a 162-game schedule—and the overall group made it over the .500 mark in year three. Further improvement took place over the next three seasons, but there was little change after year four.

Three teams—the '50 Phillies, the '70 Reds and the '86 Mets—won a pennant during a year in which they were the league's youngest team, and the Mets went on to win the World Series as well. Most of the championships came in years three through six, with the largest total (nine) of world titles coming in year six, or five years after the team was the league's youngest. Championships proved tough to come by: of the 570 team-seasons represented, there were only 48 pennants and 26 World Championships.

Probably the most successful team in the study, over the long haul, was the 1970 Reds. With a youthful lineup led by 22-year-old Johnny Bench and a pitching staff whose top four winners (Jim Merritt, Gary Nolan, Wayne Simpson and Jim McGlothlin) were all 26 years old or younger, the Reds won 102 games and the National League championship in 1970 while ranking as the youngest team in the National League. The Reds were the NL's youngest club again in 1971 while slipping to fourth place with a 79-83 record, but then they claimed four NL West titles, three National League pennants and two World Championships from 1972-76.

The Reds' chief rival for supremacy in the early-to-mid 1970s, the Oakland Athletics, also found success while building with youth. While still in Kansas City, the A's ranked as the AL's youngest team in 1964, 1966 and 1967, and they retained that distinction for two more years after moving to Oakland in 1968. It wasn't until '68 that the team finished over .500, and its first division title didn't arrive until 1971. A corps of players signed in the '60s, led by future Hall of Famers Reggie Jackson, Catfish Hunter and Rollie Fingers, paid off with three straight world titles in 1972-74.

A franchise which took even longer to find success after committing to youth was the 1950s Pirates, a team primarily built by Branch Rickey. Pittsburgh's commitment to youth was so extreme that the Bucs were the NL's youngest club for seven straight years from 1952-58. There was a difference between being young and being good, however, and it took the Pirates awhile to separate the Dick Groats and Roberto Clementes from the Art Swansons and Johnny O'Briens. The Pirates didn't get over .500 until 1958, then won the World Series two years later. The Pirates were hardly a dynasty, though, and didn't reach postseason play again until 1970.

The clear message for White Sox fans is that while a commitment to youth usually will get a team over the .500 mark within a few years, there's a big gap between that and a league championship, much less a dynasty. For inspiration, the Sox can look to two of the dominant teams of the 1990s, the Braves and Indians. The Braves ranked as the National League's youngest team in both 1989 and 1990 before reaching the World Series in '91. The Tribe was the AL's youngest team for three straight seasons, 1991-93, then made it the Series in '95. Will Konerko, Parque and Wells grow up to be the Thome, Glavine and Smoltz of the next decade? If they do, the American League's youngest team of 1999 has a chance to be one of its best.

—Don Zminda

A more complete listing for this category can be found on page 219.

## Cleveland Indians: Are Teams That Dominate Their Division at a Disadvantage in the Postseason?

Since 1995, the Indians have run roughshod over the American League Central. That year they won the division by a major league-record 30 games (in an abridged 144-game season, no less). They captured the next four AL Central crowns as well by, in order, 14.5, six, nine and 21.5 games.

But that regular-season dominance hasn't translated into postseason success, at least not on the ultimate scale. Cleveland still hasn't won a World Series since 1948. The Tribe has advanced to the Fall Classic twice in the last five years, and overall has won five of its 10 playoff series.

How does the Indians' postseason performance compare to other teams that have all but cakewalked into the playoffs since divisional play began in 1969? Here's the complete list of the 13 teams that have won titles by 15 or more games:

### Largest Margin of Victory, Division Winners—1969-99

| Year | Team | W-L | Margin | Postseason |
|---|---|---|---|---|
| **1995** | **Indians** | **100-44** | **30.0** | **Lost WS** |
| 1998 | Yankees | 114-48 | 22.0 | Won WS |
| 1984 | Tigers | 104-58 | 21.5 | Won WS |
| **1999** | **Indians** | **97-65** | **21.5** | **Lost ALDS** |
| 1975 | Reds | 108-54 | 20.0 | Won WS |
| 1983 | White Sox | 99-63 | 20.0 | Lost ALCS |
| 1969 | Orioles | 109-53 | 19.0 | Lost WS |
| 1998 | Braves | 106-56 | 18.0 | Lost NLCS |
| 1971 | Athletics | 101-60 | 16.0 | Lost ALCS |
| 1970 | Orioles | 108-54 | 15.0 | Won WS |
| 1986 | Mets | 108-54 | 15.0 | Won WS |
| 1988 | Mets | 100-60 | 15.0 | Lost NLCS |
| 1995 | Braves | 90-54 | 15.0 | Won WS |

Of the 13 teams that cruised easily into the postseason, six (46 percent) celebrated on the field when the last out of the World Series was made. They also combined to win 18 of 25 playoff series. By contrast, the clubs that won their divisions by fewer than 15 games or qualified via the wild card went just 24-for-131 (18 percent) in winning the World Series. The conclusion is obvious: teams that dominate during the regular season are at no disadvantage in the postseason. In fact, they were more successful in the playoffs than less-dominant regular-season teams.

Cleveland's lack of a World Series title to show for its 1995 and 1999 dominance is more bad luck than anything. In 1995, the Tribe ran into another powerful team, the Braves, and lost a hotly contested Fall Classic in six games. Last year, Cleveland's pitching imploded in September and collapsed in the final three games of the Division Series against the Red Sox, costing manager Mike Hargrove his job.

The Indians came closest to winning it all in 1997, when they finished atop the AL Central by a mere six games. Only a ninth-inning Florida run and an 11th-inning Cleveland error in Game 7 kept the Tribe from winning the World Series. But that defeat remains a thorn in the side of an organization that has dominated regular-season play while failing to win the ultimate prize.

—Thom Henninger

## Detroit Tigers: Will the Gonzalez Trade Pay Off?

Rangers GM Doug Melvin stunned many baseball observers on November 2 when he simultaneously traded Juan Gonzalez to the Tigers and created the concept of accelerated free agency. Though Gonzalez had hit 340 homers and won two American League MVP awards for Texas before turning 30, Melvin feared the salary Gonzalez might command as a free agent after the 2000 season. So he shipped him to Detroit for Frank Catalanotto, Francisco Cordero, Bill Haselman, Gabe Kapler, Justin Thompson and minor leaguer Alan Webb.

Juan Gonzalez

Never before had a player who had crushed that many longballs for his original team been traded before reaching a seasonal age of 30 (calculated as of June 30), though Ken Griffey Jr. and his 398 homers were traded by the Mariners to the Reds just as the *Scoreboard* went to press. In fact, just six previous players had been dealt after hitting 200 homers for their first team by that age. The first four transactions involved Hall of Famers:

### Most Home Runs For Original Team When Traded Before Age 30

| Player | Age | HR | First Team | Trade Year | New Team |
|---|---|---|---|---|---|
| Ken Griffey Jr. | 29 | 398 | Sea | 2000 | Cin |
| **Juan Gonzalez** | **29** | **340** | **Tex** | **1999** | **Det** |
| Frank Robinson | 29 | 324 | Cin | 1965 | Bal |
| Jimmie Foxx | 27 | 302 | PhiA | 1935 | BosA |
| Reggie Jackson | 29 | 254 | Oak | 1976 | Bal |
| Jose Canseco | 27 | 231 | Oak | 1992 | Tex |
| Orlando Cepeda | 28 | 226 | SF | 1966 | StL |
| Greg Luzinski | 29 | 223 | Phi | 1981 | CWS |

(age as of June 30)

**Jimmie Foxx**, the first of the sluggers to be traded, was sent by the Athletics to the Red Sox with Johnny Marcum after the 1935 season for Gordon Rhodes, George Savino and $150,000. The cash was the key component for Philadelphia owner Connie Mack, who took a beating in the stock-market crash and couldn't afford to keep the nucleus from his great 1929-31 clubs together during the Great Depression. The last of the great Athletics dumped by Mack, Foxx responded with six straight 100-RBI seasons in Boston. Advantage: Red Sox, though the trade was financially motivated.

It was another 30 years before the second trade occurred. **Frank Robinson** was the heart and soul of the Reds, who won 89 games in 1965 but were considered an underachieving ballclub. In his autobiography, *My Life In Baseball*, Robinson wrote that Cincinnati fans booed him that year and columnists suggested that trading him would solve the team's problems. GM Bill DeWitt apparently agreed with the writers, jettisoning Robinson to Baltimore for Jack Baldschun, Milt Pappas and Dick Simpson. In another autobiography, *Extra Innings*, Robinson wrote that he was considered a troublemaker by DeWitt, who defended the deal by calling Robinson "an old 30." Robinson immediately won the American League triple crown and MVP Award in 1966, leading Baltimore to a World Series sweep over the Dodgers. The Orioles would win four pennants and two championships in six years with Robinson, while the three players acquired by the Reds all had left Cincinnati by mid-1968. Advantage: Orioles, in one of the most lopsided trades in baseball history.

Another accomplished hitter debuted with a new team in 1966. **Orlando Cepeda** had played just 33 games the year before because of a knee injury, and was accused of not coming back as quickly as he could have. He hit .286 with three homers in his first 19 contests in 1966 with the Giants, who then traded him to the Cardinals for Ray Sadecki. The trade immediately backfired as San Francisco lost the pennant by 1.5 games to the Dodgers, missing Cepeda's bat while Sadecki went a disappointing 3-7, 5.40. Cepeda won the National League MVP Award as St. Louis captured the World Series in 1967, then helped the Cards grab another pennant in 1968. St. Louis traded him in March 1969 for Joe Torre, who would be named NL MVP two years later. Advantage: Cardinals, by a landslide.

The Athletics dealt another power hitter in his prime in 1976, again for financial reasons. The players successfully challenged the reserve clause during the 1975-76 offseason, paving the way for free agency. Oakland owner Charlie Finley realized that his team, which had won five consecutive AL West crowns, would dissolve at the end of the season. So shortly after an owners' lockout was aborted, Finley traded **Reggie Jackson**, Ken Holtzman and minor leaguer Bill Van Bommell, to the Orioles for Don Baylor, Paul Mitchell and Mike Torrez. Both teams fell disappointingly short of the postseason in '76 before Baylor, Holtzman, Jackson and Torrez signed with other clubs as free agents. Advantage: None.

Though the Phillies won the World Series in 1980, that didn't stop them from reshaping their outfield before the next season. They acquired Dick Davis and Gary Matthews in offseason deals, making **Greg Luzinski** expendable. Philadelphia sold Luzinski to the White Sox, for whom he served as a DH for four years, contributing 32 homers to their AL West title drive in 1983. Matthews was decent for the Phillies and certainly offered more defensively, while Luzinski was better offensively. Advantage: White Sox, though the Phillies had little use for Luzinski.

Before Gonzalez, the last slugger in his prime traded by his original team was **Jose Canseco** in 1992. While Canseco was helping the Athletics to their fourth AL West crown in five seasons, the club had grown tired of his constant injuries and off-field antics. On August 31, the day postseason rosters had to be finalized, he was discarded to the Rangers for Jeff Russell, Ruben Sierra, Bobby Witt and cash. Neither team got what it had hoped for. Oakland lost in the AL Championship Series to the Blue Jays, let Russell go as a free agent and got mediocre play out of Sierra and Witt until both departed by the end of 1995. In Texas, Canseco blew out his elbow pitching in 1993, then hit 31 homers in strike-shortened 1994 before being traded to Boston. Advantage: Rangers, though Canseco wasn't able to end their postseason drought.

Except for the Jackson deal, where all the principal players opted for free agency, in every case the team receiving the home-run hitter benefited the most from the trades. That almost certainly will be true in the deal involving Griffey, whose looming free agency and his rights to veto any trade allowed him to demand that he be sent to Cincinnati, an ultimatum that severely hindered Seattle's bargaining position.

Tigers GM Randy Smith certainly hopes that he got the better end of his trade by grabbing Gonzalez, whom he targeted as the perfect guy to revive a struggling franchise as it moves into brand-new Comerica Park in 2000. If Smith is wrong, he knows it probably will cost him his job, and he showed his commitment to Gonzalez by offering him an eight-year contract worth $140 million.

Most baseball cognoscenti, however, believe that Melvin got the better of Smith. If healthy, Thompson is one of the best lefthanded starters in baseball, while Cordero, Kapler and Webb are all young players with promise. Just as important, Texas won't have to tie up annual double-digit millions in one player. But if the Rangers do indeed wind up winning this trade, they'll be bucking history.

—Jim Callis

## Kansas City Royals: How Good Was Beltran's Rookie Season?

Considering that the Royals haven't made it to the postseason since 1985, it was hardly surprising that the team headed into the 1999 campaign with more questions than answers. This was a franchise that wasn't even sure who would be sitting in the owner's box by year's end. On the field, one of those question marks was 21-year-old prospect Carlos Beltran, whom Kansas City designated as its center fielder of the present despite the fact that he entered spring training with just 240 at-bats above Class-A. Was this tools player ready to bypass Triple-A and produce for an entire year in the bigs? The experts were divided. The Royals were crossing their fingers.

Beltran's answer came in the form of 22 home runs, 112 runs, 108 RBI and one American League Rookie of the Year Award. He certainly didn't leave much to the imagination. An August slump kept him from finishing with a .300 batting average, but the .293 mark that he actually posted was still well above realistic expectations. By season's end, he had firmly entrenched himself as Kansas City's No. 3 hitter. He also was just the 10th rookie in major league history to reach the 20-100-100 plateau.

### Rookies With 20 Home Runs, 100 Runs, 100 RBI

| Player, Team | Year | HR | Runs | RBI |
| --- | --- | --- | --- | --- |
| Buck Freeman, Was | 1899 | 25 | 107 | 122 |
| Dale Alexander, Det | 1929 | 25 | 110 | 137 |
| Hal Trosky, Cle | 1934 | 35 | 117 | 142 |
| Joe DiMaggio, NYY | 1936 | 29 | 132 | 125 |
| Jeff Heath, Cle | 1938 | 21 | 104 | 112 |
| Ted Williams, BosA | 1939 | 31 | 131 | 145 |
| Walt Dropo, BosA | 1950 | 34 | 101 | 144 |
| Al Rosen, Cle | 1950 | 37 | 100 | 116 |
| Fred Lynn, Bos | 1975 | 21 | 103 | 105 |
| **Carlos Beltran, KC** | **1999** | **22** | **112** | **108** |

(rookie status based on 130 or fewer previous AB)

Beltran joins Boston's Fred Lynn as the only two rookies to reach those levels during the second half of the 20th century. Lynn finished his career as a nine-time All-Star, while Ted Williams and Joe DiMaggio are, of course, Hall of Fame members. As for the other names on the list, most enjoyed serviceable if unspectacular major league careers.

**Carlos Beltran**

Before we go labeling Beltran a possible future tenant of Cooperstown, however, let's put his outstanding numbers into some context. You may notice that, with the exception of Lynn and Buck Freeman, everyone who made the 20-100-100 list played during eras dominated by offense. It might be more helpful to consider how Beltran and the others performed in relation to their given league.

We can do this by taking a look at a Bill James tool: runs created per 27 outs. Essentially, the stat measures how many runs a team made up of nine of the same player would score per game. An index then can be created by dividing a player's RC/27 by the average RC/27 of his league and multiplying by 100. Indices above 100 are progressively more impressive, with the opposite true for those below the 100 mark. Before this starts to sound *too* much like a college lecture, let's take a look at the highest rookie RC/27 indices of all time.

### Highest RC/27 Index—Rookies

| Player, Team | Year | RC/27 | LgRC/27 | Index |
|---|---|---|---|---|
| Joe Jackson, Cle | 1911 | 10.92 | 4.61 | 237.0 |
| Benny Kauff, Ind | 1914 | 9.55 | 4.11 | 232.7 |
| Dave Orr, NYG | 1884 | 11.25 | 5.23 | 215.3 |
| Stan Musial, StLN | 1942 | 7.97 | 3.90 | 204.2 |
| Carlton Fisk, Bos | 1972 | 6.98 | 3.47 | 201.3 |
| Bernie Carbo, Cin | 1970 | 9.07 | 4.52 | 200.9 |
| Ted Williams, BosA | 1939 | 10.44 | 5.21 | 200.5 |
| Johnny Mize, StLN | 1936 | 9.15 | 4.71 | 194.4 |
| Dick Allen, Phi | 1964 | 7.79 | 4.01 | 194.1 |
| Rico Carty, Mil | 1964 | 7.79 | 4.01 | 194.0 |

(minimum 400 PA, rookie status based on 130 or fewer previous AB)

Not surprisingly, many of these rookie performances came at times when

*Baseball Scoreboard*

the ball was a little less lively. In fact, Williams was our only 20-100-100 player to post a top 10 index, and that's simply because his rookie season was so phenomenal. For his part, Lynn's campaign was 11th on the index list, but remember his outstanding rookie effort came in the 1970s, hardly a golden era for batsmen. Though Lynn's stats were less impressive than Beltran's on the surface, they were much *more* impressive given the kind of numbers that his contemporaries were putting up.

So how did a team of nine Beltran's stack up against nine average American Leaguers in 1999? Well, Beltran finished the season with an RC/27 mark of 5.88, while a team of average American Leaguers posted an RC/27 of 5.18, meaning that a team of Beltrans scored .70 more runs per game than a team of average AL Joe's in 1999. Beltran's index of 113.6 was just the 396th-best mark among rookies with at least 450 plate appearances. Compare that to Joe Jackson, who had an index of 237.0. Jackson outscored a team of average 1911 American Leaguers by 6.31 runs per game! As for the highest rookie RC/27 index of the 1990s, that distinction went to David Justice, who hit 28 homers, drove in 78 runs and scored 76 times en route to a 178.3 mark in 1990. How quickly times have changed.

Still, hats off to Beltran, who more than justified his rapid promotion last season. He figures to be one-third of one of the best young outfields in baseball over the coming seasons, along with Johnny Damon and Jermaine Dye. As long as the team retains the services of Damon, who has been rumored to be on the trading block, the outfield *won't* be one of Kansas City's question marks heading into the 2000 season.

—Tony Nistler

A more complete listing for this category can be found on page 221.

## Minnesota Twins: Was Milton's No-Hitter a Sign of Things to Come?

On September 11, a crowd of 11,222 at the Metrodome was treated to a rare surprise. No, it wasn't free Dairy Queen Day or a postgame wrestling match featuring Jesse "The Governor" Ventura. Rather, loyal Minnesota fans witnessed a no-hitter. . . one that actually was thrown *by* the Twins instead of *against* them. Perhaps an even bigger surprise was that young up-and-comer Eric Milton—not established workhorse Brad Radke—turned the trick, holding the Angels without a hit. In doing so, Milton joined Jack Kralick (1962), Dean Chance (1967) and Scott Erickson (1994) as the only pitchers in Twins history to throw a nine-inning no-no.

But that wasn't the only exclusive group Milton joined with his performance. He was just five weeks removed from his 24th birthday on September 11. A grand total of 44 pitchers since 1900 have twirled no-hitters (or perfect games) at or before the age of 24. We wanted to look at what kind of careers those pitchers turned in, hoping for a glimpse of what we might look forward to from the young Minnesota hurler. Towards that end, we tallied the career victory totals for each pitcher in our group. Only three of those pitchers—Milton, Wilson Alvarez and Darryl Kile—are still active, so we didn't include their totals in the following breakdown:

**Career Wins For Pitchers With a No-Hitter Through Age 24—1900-99**

| W | No. |
|---|---|
| 0-49 | 10 |
| 50-99 | 10 |
| 100-149 | 10 |
| 150-199 | 6 |
| 200+ | 5 |

(pitchers who are no longer active only)

Unfortunately but perhaps not surprisingly, our crystal ball is pretty hazy. Working under the premise that 100 wins constitute at least a respectable stay in the majors, 20 pitchers in our group finished below that standard, while 21 managed to reach or exceed it. The "average" hurler among our sample of 41 posted 112 career wins and a winning percentage of .552, but those figures are bumped up considerably by the production of four Hall of Famers and one future Hall member who made the list. Dennis Eckersley, Bob Feller, Catfish Hunter, Christy Mathewson and Jim Palmer won an average of 266 games between them. Take away their contributions, and the average of the entire group falls from 112 career wins to 91. Still, just

13 of 41 pitchers left the majors with a winning percentage below .500, and the group ERA was a very sound 3.23.

With just 15 victories and 25 losses under his big league belt, Milton certainly has a long way to go before reaching either the century mark in wins or the .500 plateau. He does have age on his side, but his no-no is by no means a guarantee of even moderate success. Just ask the 10 pitchers who failed to crack even the 50-win barrier.

**Fewest Career Wins, Pitchers Who Threw a No-Hitter Through Age 24—1900-99**

| Pitcher | Year | Age | W |
|---|---|---|---|
| Iron Davis | 1914 | 24 | 7 |
| Mike Warren | 1983 | 22 | 9 |
| Ernie Koob | 1917 | 24 | 23 |
| Weldon Henley | 1905 | 24 | 32 |
| Juan Nieves | 1987 | 22 | 32 |
| Rex Barney | 1948 | 23 | 35 |
| Bobby Burke | 1931 | 24 | 38 |
| Tommy Greene | 1991 | 24 | 38 |
| Dave Morehead | 1965 | 23 | 40 |
| Nick Maddox | 1907 | 20 | 43 |

If Milton never pitches another inning, at least he would finish with more victories than Iron Davis and Mike Warren. As for the others on the above list, Nick Maddox was a 20-game winner and also posted a victory in the 1907 World Series for the Pirates. Perhaps the other two most promising talents were Juan Nieves and Tommy Greene, who finished with a combined 70-50 (.583) record. Shoulder injuries derailed both of them in their prime. Ironically, shoulder troubles are also a concern for Milton, who is double-jointed in his throwing shoulder and has had pain there in the past.

So what are the chances that Milton will add another no-hitter to his résumé? The possibility isn't out of the question, considering that seven players who threw a no-no at or before the age of 24 turned the trick again at some point in their careers. Four of those seven did it twice before turning 25. Still, the odds say that the Twins may want to have Dairy Queen or Jesse on standby just in case Milton can't come up with an encore.

—Tony Nistler

A more complete listing for this category can be found on page 222.

## New York Yankees: Were They the Sports Franchise of the Century?

The Yankees have performed so impressively over the last few years that one feels compelled to assess their place in history. Team of the decade? That one's pretty easy. Baseball team of the century? Another no-brainer, what with 25 World Championships during the 1900s. OK, how about sports franchise of the century? That one requires a little more analysis.

Let's restrict the study to the four major professional sports, baseball, football, basketball and hockey. The teams which have won the most titles in those sports are the Yankees (baseball), Montreal Canadiens (hockey), Boston Celtics (pro basketball) and Green Bay Packers (pro football). The most reasonable criteria, we think, are consistent dominance over time and the total number of titles won. Let's look at each team's championship totals by decade:

### Championships by Decade

| Decade | Yankees | Canadiens | Celtics | Packers |
|---|---|---|---|---|
| 1900-09 | 0 | — | — | — |
| 1910-19 | 0 | 1 | — | — |
| 1920-29 | 3 | 1 | — | 1 |
| 1930-39 | 5 | 2 | — | 4 |
| 1940-49 | 4 | 2 | 0 | 1 |
| 1950-59 | 6 | 5 | 2 | 0 |
| 1960-69 | 2 | 5 | 9 | 5 |
| 1970-79 | 2 | 6 | 2 | 0 |
| 1980-89 | 0 | 1 | 3 | 0 |
| 1990-99 | 3 | 1 | 0 | 1 |
| **Total** | **25** | **24** | **16** | **12** |

The NFL, NHL and NBA teams are at a bit of a disadvantage because the NHL didn't start until 1917, the NFL until 1920 and the NBA (originally the BAA) until 1946. Major league baseball, of course, was around for the entire century. Even after making an adjustment for that fact, you can quickly eliminate the Packers, who have only 12 titles overall and only one since the 1960s. No other NFL team has won more than nine championships. Ah, parity...

The Celtics, with 16 titles since the NBA began in 1946, have had an impressive history, but the Yankees have won 15 championships over the same time span, while the Canadiens have won 19. In addition, most of the

Celtics' titles came in a 13-year period from 1957-69, when Bill Russell led them to 11 championships. All in all, the Celtics seem to lack the consistent brilliance that the franchise of the century would need.

That leaves the Yankees and Canadiens. The Yankees have won one more title, 25 to 24, but the Canadiens started later and they've won at least one title in every decade of their existence. The Yankees, by contrast, didn't win any titles at all in the first two decades of the century, and they were blanked in the 1980s as well.

So are the Habs the North American sports franchise of the century? Not so fast. Throughout the 20th century, major league baseball had at least 16 teams in every season, and until 1969 the postseason was just one round, the World Series showdown between the two league champions. The NHL had far fewer teams than MLB up until the 1970s, including the six-team setup that existed from 1942-43 to 1966-67. When the Canadiens won their first title in 1919, the NHL had exactly *three* teams. In addition, hockey traditionally has invited also-ran teams into its postseason playoffs, and eight of Montreal's titles came in seasons in which they had failed to finish in first place during the regular season.

All in all, it seems pretty clear that the Yankees deserve the title of Sports Franchise of the Century. Will they continue to dominate the 21st century as well? Look us up in another hundred years, and we'll tell you the answer.

—Don Zminda

## Oakland Athletics: Were They the Ultimate Sabermetric Team?

Looking at some of the traditional methods for evaluating an offense, you'd think the 1999 Athletics would have had an anemic attack. Their batting average was just .259, second-worst in the American League. They stole only 70 bases, again next-to-last in the league. Meanwhile they lead the AL in strikeouts with 1,129 and in runners left on base with 1,246.

But the A's offense wasn't bad at all. It was one of the league's best, ranking fourth in runs scored. What were their secrets?

1. They hit 235 homers, second-most in the league.

2. They drew 770 walks, the top figure in baseball.

3. They also got on base via the hit-by-pitch, getting plunked 71 times, the third-highest total in the league.

4. They stayed out of the double play, grounding into 129 twin-killings, the third-lowest figure in the league (tied with Toronto).

With their combination of power and walks, you could say that the A's were a good sabermetric team, strong in areas that statistics like batting average don't measure. On page 91 we list the individual leaders in secondary average, a Bill James stat which measures offensive contributions in areas beyond hitting for average. Power and extra-base hits are two of the key components in secondary average, the complete formula for which is (TB - H + BB + SB - CS) / AB. Not surprisingly, the A's had the highest secondary average of any team in baseball:

**Highest Team Secondary Average—1999**

| Team | Sec |
|---|---|
| **Athletics** | **.332** |
| Indians | .327 |
| Mariners | .311 |
| Yankees | .309 |
| Rangers | .304 |
| Diamondbacks | .303 |
| Astros | .303 |
| Mets | .300 |
| Reds | .300 |
| Giants | .298 |
| **MLB Average** | **.281** |

Oakland's good secondary average is no accident. The A's front office values power, and the club stresses the importance of plate discipline throughout its farm system. "In our market, we can't afford the multisport athletes with great tools," A's GM Billy Beane told Peter Gammons last summer. "We have to get players who play the game with the most production, guys who get on base and hit the ball out of the ballpark. That's offense at its simplest: on-base percentage and power."

With that philosophy, the A's managed to average more than 5.5 runs per game last year despite their low batting average. In fact, Oakland had the highest scoring average of any team since 1900 with a team batting average of .260 or lower:

**Most Runs Per Game, .260 or Lower Team Batting Average—1900-99**

| Year | Team | R/G | Avg | Sec |
|---|---|---|---|---|
| **1999** | **Athletics** | **5.51** | **.259** | **.332** |
| 1940 | Yankees | 5.27 | .259 | .286 |
| 1991 | Tigers | 5.04 | .247 | .306 |
| 1948 | Giants | 5.03 | .256 | .275 |
| 1987 | Athletics | 4.98 | .260 | .290 |
| 1970 | Cubs | 4.98 | .259 | .270 |
| 1951 | Giants | 4.97 | .260 | .287 |
| 1998 | Cardinals | 4.97 | .258 | .320 |
| 1998 | Athletics | 4.96 | .257 | .270 |

Note the presence of three Oakland clubs in the top 10, including the 1998 and '99 teams. With its cool weather and large foul territory, Network Associates Coliseum traditionally has been a tough place to hit for average. But as long as they keep drawing walks and hitting home runs, the A's should be capable of mounting a very effective offense.

—Don Zminda

A more complete listing for this category can be found on page 223.

## Seattle Mariners: Does Safeco Field Really Cut Down on Homers?

The Mariners hadn't even opened Safeco Field last July 15 before *The Sporting News* noted that Ken Griffey Jr. could "bid adieu to any hopes of breaking Mark McGwire's single-season home run record or Hank Aaron's career mark." Seattle slugger Jay Buhner questioned whether the new park would be fair to home-run hitters, implying that it wouldn't. But is that really the case?

There are three main factors that affect how a ballpark plays: its altitude, its characteristics (dimensions, outfield walls, amount of foul territory, visibility) and the weather. The move from the Kingdome (16 feet above sea level) across the street to Safeco (2 feet below) resulted in a negligible change in altitude.

The characteristics of the two parks are essentially the same as well. Original plans called for Safeco to have a 422-foot corner in left-center, but that was moved in, as was the right-field power alley. Both the Kingdome and Safeco are 331 feet down the left-field line and 405 feet to dead center. There's also little differences in the alleys in left-center (389 feet in the Kingdome, 390 at Safeco) and right-center (up from 380 feet to 386).

The distance down the right-field line has increased from 312 to 326 feet. However, the right-field wall has shrunk from 23 feet at the Kingdome to 8 feet at Safeco. Another boon for hitters is a considerable reduction in foul territory at the new park.

The only major difference between the two ballparks is the weather. The elements weren't a factor at the totally enclosed Kingdome, but they come into play at Safeco, which does have a retractable roof to shut out the rain. The roof won't close fully, but it will be pressurized. Any precipitation or wind will be keep out when the roof is extended.

For the first two months of the season, winds are expected to enter Safeco from behind home plate and blow out toward left and left-center. This conceivably would help righthanded pull hitters, though those cold-weather winds could bring storms that would lead to the roof being closed, negating their effect.

From late June through September, warmer-weather winds are expected to come into Safeco from left field and swirl towards right. This would help lefthanded pull hitters, but their righthanded counterparts could have their long drives knocked down by the crosswind.

That's the theoretical discussion of what should happen at Safeco. We can take a look at what actually happened there in the final two-and-a-half months of the 1999 season by looking at park indexes. A park index compares how a team and its intraleague opponents performed both at home and on the road. We divide the home average by the road average, then multiply by 100. If the home and road averages are equal, then the index will be 100 and we can conclude that the park had no impact. An index above 100 indicates the park amplified that particular statistic, while one below 100 shows the park diminished it.

Below are the park indexes for Safeco and the Kingdome in 1999, as well as for the Kingdome over the past three years:

### Seattle Park Indexes

| Category | Safeco 1999 | Kingdome 1999 | Kingdome 1997-99 |
|---|---|---|---|
| Avg | 91 | 108 | 100 |
| R | 92 | 118 | 102 |
| 2B | 79 | 149 | 113 |
| 3B | 54 | 67 | 72 |
| HR | 107 | 126 | 108 |
| LHB-Avg | 84 | 107 | 99 |
| LHB-HR | 118 | 151 | 104 |
| RHB-Avg | 94 | 109 | 101 |
| RHB-HR | 100 | 114 | 111 |

(run indexes compiled per game, others per at-bat; excludes interleague games)

Granted, the Safeco sample size was small and didn't include any early-season games, when the climate will be colder. But thus far, it looks like a pitchers' park. The batting-average index of 91 is the lowest of any American League ballpark over the last three seasons combined, and the run index of 92 tops only Yankee Stadium's 89. The home-run index, however, was quite healthy at 107, the fourth-highest figure in the AL.

Though Kingdome was a hitters' haven in its final half-season, the longer trend was that it was a neutral park, as shown by its 100 batting-average index and 102 run index from 1997-99. It didn't promote offense nearly as much as its reputation suggested. It did boost homers significantly, with a 108 index, but that's hardly different from Safeco's 107.

Not only is the overall homer index virtually unchanged, but also the lefty homer index actually rose from 104 at the Kingdome in 1997-99 to 118 at

Safeco. If the new ballpark continues to play like that, Griffey's longball production in Seattle figured to improve by 14 percent annually, which would translate into an extra two homers per season. And a check of the raw data shows that he hit 13 homers in 34 AL games at Kingdome last year, compared to 13 in 36 AL contests at Safeco.

Of course, Safeco won't have any effect on Griffey in the future. The Mariners honored his request for a trade to Cincinnati in early February. If he had stayed put, however, it sure didn't look like Safeco was going to harm Griffey's chances of catching McGwire or Aaron.

—Jim Callis

## Tampa Bay Devil Rays: Is It Smart to Load Up on Old Sluggers?

After finishing the 1999 season with a 69-93 record, a mere six-game improvement over their inaugural campaign, the Devil Rays watched their expansion brethren in Arizona play postseason baseball after winning 100 regular-season games. Following the World Series, Tampa Bay quickly jumped into action trading and signing players, in search of the same success that quickly turned the Diamondbacks into pennant contenders.

While Arizona spent a good chunk of its change on pitchers Randy Johnson, Todd Stottlemyre and Armando Reynoso, the Devil Rays traded for Vinny Castilla and signed Greg Vaughn to a free-agent contract. Suddenly, the Rays had four hitters who connected on 30-plus homers in '99.

All four sluggers—Castilla, Vaughn, Jose Canseco and Fred McGriff—are 32 or older. Is this the ticket to success for the American League's latest entry? Let's check the five teams in baseball history that had a foursome that reached the 30 mark in homers the year before:

**Teams With Four-Plus Players Who Hit 30 Home Runs the Year Before**

| Year | Team | No. | HR | Players (HR) |
|------|------|-----|-----|--------------|
| 1997 | Rockies | 4 | 158 | Galarraga (47), Burks (40), Castilla (40), Bichette (31) |
| 1996 | Rockies | 4 | 139 | Bichette (40), Walker (36), Castilla (32), Galarraga (31) |
| 1998 | Dodgers | 4 | 132 | Piazza (40), Zeile (31), Karros (31), Mondesi (30) |
| 1951 | Dodgers | 4 | 130 | Pafko (36), Hodges (32), Campanella (31), Snider (31) |
| 1978 | Dodgers | 4 | 125 | Garvey (33), Smith (32), Baker (30), Cey (30) |

How did these five clubs do with their newfound power?

**1996 Rockies.** Not only did Colorado have four 30-homer hitters from 1995, but they had four in 1996 as well. Dante Bichette, Castilla and Andres Galarraga all repeated, and while Larry Walker was injured, Ellis Burks picked up the slack with 40 homers. But the Rockies fell from a wild-card berth to a third-place finish. Only Kevin Ritz posted double-digit victories on a pitching staff with the worst ERA in the National League.

**1997 Rockies.** Even with their slugging quartet back for another season of longball highlights, the '97 Rockies only could match their 83-79 mark of 1996. It didn't matter that a healthy Walker (49), Galarraga (41) and Castilla (40) each broke the 40 barrier in homers, or that Walker claimed the NL MVP Award. Ritz didn't repeat his magic and no Rockies pitcher won more than nine games. Roger Bailey was the staff ace with a 9-10, 4.29 record as the pitchers again had the worst ERA in the NL.

**1998 Dodgers.** Mike Piazza hit 40 homers for the first time and Todd Zeile collected a career-best 31 for the Los Angeles in 1997, but both were traded to Florida in May 1998. The '98 Dodgers retooled under new Fox ownership, making significant trades while the front office was in disarray. With an overhaul of the roster underway and the pitchers turning in a steady but unspectacular performance, LA dropped from 88 to 83 wins.

**1951 Dodgers.** Brooklyn finished in second place in 1950, just two games behind the Phillies with an 89-65 record as Roy Campanella, Gil Hodges and Duke Snider all broke the 30-homer barrier for the first time. Andy Pafko hit 36 dingers for the Cubs the same year, then came to Brooklyn via trade in the middle of the '51 season and hit 18 of his 30 longballs for the Dodgers. Brooklyn's three holdover sluggers all had fine seasons, and with a pitching staff sparked by Preacher Roe (22-3, 3.04) and Don Newcombe (20-9, 3.28), the '51 club improved to 97-60. But the Dodgers lost the NL flag to Bobby Thomson's Shot Heard 'Round the World.

**1978 Dodgers.** The 1977 Dodgers won the NL West behind their four sluggers and a pitching staff with the league's best ERA and five double-digit winners. Reggie Smith's 29 homers in '78 leads the club, but with the same five hurlers duplicating their double-digit wins and the staff repeating as the league's ERA leader, the Dodgers defended their NL West title (though they dropped from 98 to 95 wins) and lost a six-game World Series to the Yankees for a second straight year.

Only one of the five clubs, the 1951 Dodgers, won more games than the year before after assembling four 30-homer hitters. In fact, the key ingredient in determining the course of these teams was the pitching staffs. The Dodgers teams with solid staffs continued to win, while the Rockies couldn't overcome NL-worst ERAs.

What does this say about the Devil Rays' chances in 2000? Wilson Alvarez returns as the staff ace after going 9-9 in 1999, which makes him 28-34 with a 4.06 ERA over the last three seasons. Bobby Witt is gone and Rolando Arrojo departed in the Castilla trade. The Rays countered by signing Juan Guzman (11-12, 3.73) and Steve Trachsel (8-18, 5.56) as free agents, and they hope that promising Ryan Rupe (8-9, 4.55) quickly matures and that a fifth starter emerges among Chad Ogea, Dan Wheeler and a host of others.

It's probably not a rotation capable of taking Tampa Bay to the promised land. And history suggests you can't put that responsibility on the backs of four sluggers.

—Thom Henninger

## Texas Rangers: Will Palmeiro Post Cooperstown Numbers?

**R**afael Palmeiro, the Rangers' quiet superstar, may be 35 years old, but he's playing better than ever. Returning to Texas last year after five seasons with the Orioles, Palmeiro set career highs in home runs (47), RBI (148), batting average (.324), on-base percentage (.420) and slugging (.630).

Palmeiro's big season enabled him to reach a couple of career milestones: he hit his 350th home run (he finished the year with 361), and he also recorded his 2,000th career hit (he now has 2,158). Those milestones might not spell Hall of Fame just yet, but Palmeiro is beginning to look like a pretty serious candidate for Cooperstown. Here is a list of Hall of Fame-eligible players (those whose careers ended prior to 1995) who had attained at least 350 homers and 2,000 hits through age 34 (age as of June 30 of season in question):

### 350 Home Runs And 2,000 Hits Through Age 34—1876-1995

| Player | Year | H | HR | RBI | HOF? |
|---|---|---|---|---|---|
| Hank Aaron | 1968 | 2,792 | 510 | 1,627 | Y |
| Orlando Cepeda | 1972 | 2,169 | 358 | 1,261 | Y |
| Jimmie Foxx | 1942 | 2,585 | 527 | 1,882 | Y |
| Lou Gehrig | 1937 | 2,547 | 464 | 1,880 | Y |
| Mickey Mantle | 1966 | 2,204 | 496 | 1,400 | Y |
| Eddie Mathews | 1966 | 2,201 | 493 | 1,388 | Y |
| Willie Mays | 1965 | 2,381 | 505 | 1,402 | Y |
| Mel Ott | 1943 | 2,617 | 463 | 1,695 | Y |
| Jim Rice | 1987 | 2,275 | 364 | 1,351 | N |
| Frank Robinson | 1970 | 2,427 | 475 | 1,455 | Y |
| Babe Ruth | 1929 | 2,076 | 516 | 1,561 | Y |
| Billy Williams | 1972 | 2,231 | 356 | 1,199 | Y |

(age as of June 30)

There are 12 players on the list, and 11 have made the Hall of Fame. The only exception is Jim Rice, a strong candidate who finished third in this year's Hall of Fame balloting. The most marginal candidates on the list probably are Rice and Orlando Cepeda, who needed the Veterans Committee to make the Hall. Both players were outstanding in their 20s, but their careers were seriously winding down by the time they turned 35. That's hardly the case with Palmeiro, who has averaged 41 homers, 125 RBI and 175 hits a year since turning 30. Bill James' career projections system (see page 76) now gives him a 77 percent chance to hit 500 home runs and a 35 percent chance to reach 3,000 hits. He's gaining momentum, also. Three years ago, the same system gave him only a 32 percent chance at 500 homers and a 26 percent chance to get 3,000 hits. If Palmeiro reaches both milestones, he'll probably make the Hall of Fame with ease. Even if he only gets the 500 homers, he's going to be a very strong candidate.

If Palmeiro's impressive career numbers are a bit of a secret thus far, it's probably because he's been such a late bloomer. The Cubs traded him to Texas in 1989 because they were disappointed in his power numbers. Indeed, he played full-time in both 1988 and '89 but hit only eight homers each year. Palmeiro didn't hit more than 15 homers in a season until 1991, his fourth full year in the majors, and didn't reach the 100-RBI mark for the first time until 1993. Since then he's developed into one of the top power hitters in the majors, and he shows no signs of letting up. Whether he makes the Hall of Fame or not, Palmeiro figures to end his career with some very impressive numbers.

—Don Zminda

## Toronto Blue Jays: Is a Great Rookie Season a Good Sign For a Closer?

With a fastball that was clocked at more than 100 MPH, Billy Koch burst onto the major league scene last year. The former Clemson star didn't even join the Blue Jays until the season was more than a month old, but he still wound up ranking among the American League save leaders with 31. Though he struggled at times during the second half, Koch tunred in a remarkable performance for a pitcher only two years removed from Tommy John surgery on his right elbow.

How impressive was Koch's rookie performance? Only two other rookie pitchers have recorded 30 or more saves in a season, Todd Worrell and Kerry Ligtenberg. Had he been around for the entire season, Koch undoubtedly would have challenged Worrell's rookie record of 36. Here's a list of all the closers with the most saves in their rookie year, with a rookie defined as having no more than 30 games or 50 innings of experience:

### Most Saves—Rookies

| Pitcher, Team | Year | Sv |
| --- | --- | --- |
| Todd Worrell, StL | 1986 | 36 |
| **Billy Koch, Tor** | **1999** | **31** |
| Kerry Ligtenberg, Atl | 1998 | 30 |
| Rich Loiselle, Pit | 1997 | 29 |
| Gregg Olson, Bal | 1989 | 27 |
| Pete Ladd, Mil | 1983 | 25 |
| Dick Radatz, Bos | 1962 | 24 |
| Ernie Camacho, Cle | 1984 | 23 |
| Doug Corbett, Min | 1980 | 23 |
| Rawly Eastwick, Cin | 1975 | 22 |
| Ken Tatum, Cal | 1969 | 22 |

(maximum 30 G or 50 IP prior to rookie year)

Koch's record is worthy of praise, but a closer look at this list might give one pause. Of the 10 other pitchers on the list, only two went on to record more than 200 saves in the majors: Worrell (256) and Gregg Olson (217). There were some short-term sensations like Dick "The Monster" Radatz of the Red Sox and Rawly Eastwick of the Reds, who helped pitch his team to the World Championship as a rookie in 1975. Most of the others had one or two good years before fading out due to injuries or ineffectiveness. Along with Worrell and Olson, the only pitcher on the list who recorded even 100 major league saves was Radatz (122).

How did the pitchers who recorded the *most* saves in major league history fare as rookies? Here's the top 15:

### Saves in Rookie Season—All-Time Save Leaders

| Pitcher | Career | Rookie |
|---|---|---|
| Lee Smith | 478 | 1 |
| John Franco | 416 | 4 |
| Dennis Eckersley | 390 | 2 |
| Jeff Reardon | 367 | 6 |
| Randy Myers | 347 | 6 |
| Rollie Fingers | 341 | 12 |
| Tom Henke | 311 | 2 |
| Goose Gossage | 310 | 2 |
| Jeff Montgomery | 304 | 1 |
| Doug Jones | 301 | 8 |
| Bruce Sutter | 300 | 10 |
| John Wetteland | 296 | 1 |
| Rick Aguilera | 289 | 0 |
| Rod Beck | 260 | 1 |
| Todd Worrell | 256 | 36 |

Amazingly, the only pitcher on the above list to record more than a dozen saves as a rookie was Worrell, the No. 15 man in career saves. Most of the others had six or fewer saves as rookies, including a combined total of seven by the top three savemasters in history, Lee Smith, John Franco and Dennis Eckersley.

This isn't necessarily a bad sign for Koch. When the all-time save leaders were breaking in a decade or more ago, the role of closer was still evolving. Many of these pitchers broke in as starters and assumed a late-relief role only gradually. It's a far cry from the current game, when many pitchers are groomed as closers even before their professional careers begin. Still, it's a note of caution that long-term success for Koch is hardly guaranteed. He does, after all, have a history of elbow problems, and his ERA last year was 1.34 before the All-Star break, 5.70 afterward. When a guy throws as hard as Koch, it's hard not to get excited. But Lee Smith probably doesn't need to start worrying about his all-time save record just yet.

—Don Zminda

A more complete listing for this category can be found on page 224.

**Baseball Scoreboard**

## Arizona Diamondbacks: Why Can't Hitters Bank on Bank One?

When the Diamondbacks joined the National League in 1998, their home field, Bank One Ballpark, was expected to be one of the best hitters' parks in baseball. The club's home city, Phoenix, has the second-highest altitude of any city in the majors (1,090 feet), and while Arizona would be playing the majority of its games in an enclosed stadium, the BOB's retractable roof would mean a fair number of games in Arizona's warm, dry climate. Both the altitude and the weather figured to benefit hitters.

While two seasons aren't a lot to draw firm conclusions from, the BOB has yet to indicate that it's going to be a hitters' paradise. Using data from our *STATS Major League Handbook*, here are the park indexes for Bank One's first two seasons. Park indexes, in case you're unfamiliar with them, compare the averages for a team and its opponents in a club's home games with the same clubs' averages in the team's road games. A neutral park would have a park index of 100, while a park that favored the hitters in a particular category would have an index greater than 100:

### Bank One Ballpark Park Indexes—1998-99

| Category | Home | | | Road | | | Index |
|---|---|---|---|---|---|---|---|
| | Ari | Opp | Tot | Ari | Opp | Tot | |
| Avg | .268 | .257 | .262 | .254 | .257 | .255 | 103 |
| R | 708 | 655 | 1,363 | 701 | 686 | 1,387 | 98 |
| 2B | 228 | 249 | 477 | 247 | 227 | 474 | 100 |
| 3B | 54 | 41 | 95 | 33 | 21 | 54 | 174 |
| HR | 159 | 155 | 314 | 173 | 174 | 347 | 90 |
| LHB-Avg | .269 | .258 | .264 | .263 | .264 | .264 | 100 |
| LHB-HR | 70 | 45 | 115 | 75 | 50 | 125 | 92 |
| RHB-Avg | .267 | .256 | .261 | .244 | .253 | .249 | 105 |
| RHB-HR | 89 | 110 | 199 | 98 | 124 | 222 | 88 |

(run indexes compiled per game, others per at-bat; excludes interleague games)

Bank One has appeared to be a moderately good park for batting average, and its sharply angled walls and high center-field fence (25 feet) have helped make it a great park for triples. But in most other categories it either has shown neutral tendencies or been downright tough on the hitters. The biggest shock has been how tough it's been to hit a home run in Bank One. The park's home-run index of 90 for 1998-89 makes it one of the tougher home-run parks in the National League.

While Arizona had several hitters who posted great offensive numbers in 1999, only Jay Bell thrived at home, hitting .304 with 21 homers and .621 slugging vs. .274-17-.493 on the road. Matt Williams batted nearly 50 points higher on the road (.326 to .279) and hit 18 of his 35 homers in road parks. Luis Gonzalez also fared much better on the road, hitting .352 with 16 homers vs. .318 and 10 homers at the BOB.

What's going on? One thought is that the park might favor hitters more when the roof is open, while tending to favor pitchers in the cooler indoor games. In its first two seasons, BOB's roof was open 55 times and closed for 93 games. Here are Bank One's 1998-99 key park indexes in open-air contests vs. games with the roof closed:

**Bank One Ballpark Park Indexes by Roof Status—1998-99**

| Category | Open | Closed |
|---|---|---|
| Avg | 106 | 101 |
| R | 104 | 95 |
| 2B | 106 | 96 |
| 3B | 186 | 168 |
| HR | 90 | 90 |
| LHB-Avg | 105 | 97 |
| LHB-HR | 95 | 90 |
| RHB-Avg | 107 | 103 |
| RHB-HR | 87 | 89 |

(run indexes compiled per game, others per at-bat; excludes interleague games)

With the roof open, the park has been much more favorable for hitters in terms of batting average, runs scored, doubles and triples. However, it retains its toughness against the home run. Since the open-air games are played in the spring and fall when Arizona's weather is much cooler than it is in midsummer, one could speculate that the park would be a good hitters' park overall, if not for the roof, in every key category except home runs. It's possible that we simply overestimated the positive effects of a 1,000-foot altitude on home runs after years of watching home runs fly out of Fulton County Stadium in Atlanta, which has an altitude of 1,050 feet. Interestingly, the BOB's 1998-99 home-run indexes have been virtually identical to those of Atlanta's new park, Turner Field. Unlike Turner, the BOB may never be out-and-out favorable to pitchers, but it may prove to be just as resistant to home runs.

—Don Zminda

## Atlanta Braves: Can Galarraga Come Back?

The Braves' hopes of returning to the World Series this year depend in good part on a comeback by slugging first sacker Andres Galarraga. The Big Cat had an outstanding year in 1998, his first season in Atlanta, hitting 44 homers and driving in 121 runs. But then he missed the entire 1999 season after being diagnosed with lymphoma, a form of cancer. Galarraga expects to be fully recovered by the start of the season, and the Braves are counting on him to be their first baseman. But Galarraga will be 39 this June, and it's uncertain he'll be able to hold up for his usual 150 games. After missing an entire season, what are the chances that he'll be able to regain his prior form?

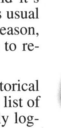

**Andres Galarraga**

In all honesty, there aren't a lot of historical precedents for this. Here's the complete list of players 36 or older who, after previously logging at least 300 plate appearances in the majors, missed at least one full year and then returned to bat 300 or more times in their comeback season:

### Hitters After Missing Previous Season, Age 36-Plus—1920-99

| Player, Team | Year | Age | AB | R | H | HR | RBI | Avg | RC | RC27 |
|---|---|---|---|---|---|---|---|---|---|---|
| Art Fletcher, PhN | 1922 | 37 | 396 | 46 | 111 | 7 | 53 | .280 | 50 | 4.43 |
| Al Nixon, PhN | 1926 | 40 | 311 | 38 | 91 | 4 | 41 | .293 | 39 | 4.49 |
| Earl Sheely, Pit | 1929 | 36 | 485 | 63 | 142 | 6 | 88 | .293 | 82 | 5.79 |
| Earl Sheely, BosN | 1931 | 38 | 538 | 30 | 147 | 1 | 77 | .273 | 51 | 3.26 |
| Edd Roush, Cin | 1931 | 38 | 376 | 46 | 102 | 1 | 41 | .271 | 38 | 3.52 |
| Phil Weintraub, NYG | 1944 | 36 | 361 | 55 | 114 | 13 | 77 | .316 | 79 | 8.32 |
| Myril Hoag, CWS-Cle | 1944 | 36 | 325 | 38 | 90 | 1 | 31 | .277 | 38 | 4.08 |
| Billy Herman, Bro-BosN | 1946 | 36 | 436 | 56 | 130 | 3 | 50 | .298 | 71 | 5.81 |
| Jim Pendleton, Hou | 1962 | 38 | 321 | 30 | 79 | 8 | 36 | .246 | 31 | 3.23 |
| Dave Winfield, NYY-Cal | 1990 | 38 | 475 | 70 | 127 | 21 | 78 | .267 | 65 | 4.67 |
| Ryne Sandberg, ChC | 1996 | 36 | 554 | 85 | 135 | 25 | 92 | .244 | 92 | 5.63 |

(minimum 300 PA in comeback year and in previous career; age as of June 30)

We can eliminate a few of these guys right away. Phil Weintraub and

Myril Hoag came back during World War II, when the majors were desperate for any players who were exempt from military service. Earl Sheely wasn't out of baseball in 1928 and 1930; he was playing in the Pacific Coast League in between stints in the majors. Veteran utilityman Jim Pendleton had drifted back to the minor leagues after playing in 65 games for the Reds in 1959, then got one last chance in the majors with the expansion Houston Colt .45s in 1962. I couldn't find any information on Al Nixon, who resurfaced with the 1926 Phillies after having last played in the majors with the 1923 Braves, but Nixon was a bit player who never batted more than 321 times in a season. That leaves these guys:

**Art Fletcher**. A star shortstop for John McGraw's Giants in the 1910s, Fletcher was traded to the Phillies early in the 1920 season. He batted .284, then missed the entire 1921 campaign after the death of his father and brother. Returning at age 37 in 1922, Fletcher was about as good as ever, hitting .280 in 110 games. He then retired to become manager of the Phils.

**Edd Roush**. A Hall of Famer who had his greatest seasons with the Reds, Roush was notorious for his long holdouts while battling for a higher salary. After hitting .324 for the 1929 Giants, Roush held out for the entire 1930 season. The Giants then released him and he re-signed with the Reds for the '31 campaign. The 38-year-old Roush had little left, and he retired after batting .271, 52 points below his career average.

**Billy Herman**. Another Hall of Famer, Herman batted .330 for the 1943 Dodgers, then went off to war for two years. Returning in 1946 at age 36, Herman had a fine season, hitting .298 with a .395 on-base percentage. He was named manager of the Pirates for the 1947 season and played only briefly before retiring.

**Dave Winfield**. After hitting .322 with 25 homers for the 1988 Yankees, Winfield underwent back surgery and missed the entire '89 season. His comeback at age 38 was so-so (.267-21-78), but he played for five more years and helped the Blue Jays win the World Championship in 1992 with a .290-26-108 season.

**Ryne Sandberg**. Sandberg was having a miserable 1994 season, hitting .238, when he announced his retirement in June, ostensibly to spend more time with his family. Sandberg sat out the rest of the '94 campaign and all of 1995 before attempting a comeback at age 36 in 1996. He batted only .244 but had 25 homers and 92 RBI. He retired after a mediocre 1997 campaign.

Looking at this list, it's surprising how many of the comebacks worked out. None of these guys were major stars again, but most of them, even

Sandberg, provided a decent level of productivity for at least one season after their return. Only Roush was a total flop. While most of the players were younger than Galarraga, he keeps himself in excellent shape and wouldn't seem to be too old to come back and be a productive player, given a clean bill of health. The closest parallel is Winfield, who was able to play well into his 40s and record his 3,000th major league hit. If the Braves can settle for something like what Winfield was after his return—no big star any more, but a useful power hitter—they should be satisfied. But if they're expecting something like 44 homers and 121 RBI again, they're likely to be disappointed.

—Don Zminda

## Chicago Cubs: Is Sosa the King of the Also-Rans?

It must be great to be Sammy Sosa, but it also has to be a little frustrating. Imagine hitting 66 homers in a season—five more than the old record—and yet finishing second, as Sosa did to Mark McGwire in 1998. Then a year later, imagine becoming the first player to hit 60 in back-to-back campaigns on the way to 63. . . only to finish second to McGwire *again*. What does a fellow have to do to win a home-run title?

Sosa's amazing performance while finishing second two years in a row made us wonder whether any other players had posted outstanding numbers in a major statistical category two years in a row, only to finish second each time. Let's take a look, beginning with home runs:

**Most Home Runs—No. 2 in League Two Straight Seasons**

| Player | Years | HR |
|---|---|---|
| **Sammy Sosa** | **1998-99** | **129** |
| Frank Thomas | 1994-95 | 78 |
| Lou Gehrig | 1929-30 | 76 |
| Babe Ruth | 1932-33 | 75 |
| Lou Gehrig | 1927-28 | 74 |

When it comes to frustration among home-run hitters, Sosa's got the category pretty much to himself. His former White Sox teammate, Frank Thomas, finished second in home runs in both 1994 and 1995, but his two-year total of 78 is miles behind Sosa. The presence of Babe Ruth and Lou Gehrig on this list shows that it's no disgrace to finish second. From 1927-30, Gehrig finished second to Ruth in home runs four straight times.

Here are the top RBI runners-up:

**Most RBI—No. 2 in League Two Straight Seasons**

| Player | Years | RBI |
|---|---|---|
| Lou Gehrig | 1932-33 | 290 |
| Lou Gehrig | 1935-36 | 271 |
| Jack Fournier | 1924-25 | 246 |
| Jimmy Collins | 1897-98 | 243 |
| Hack Wilson | 1926-27 | 238 |

Gehrig could have commiserated with Sosa. Along with those four straight years finishing second to Ruth in homers, Gehrig was second in the

American League in RBI four times. However, while his total of 290 ribbies in 1932-33 is very impressive, it can't compare with hitting 129 home runs.

Here's the list for batting average:

**Highest Batting Average—No. 2 in League Two Straight Seasons**

| Player | Years | Avg |
|---|---|---|
| Ed Delahanty | 1894-95 | .406 |
| Joe Jackson | 1911-12 | .402 |
| Ty Cobb | 1921-22 | .395 |
| Babe Herman | 1929-30 | .387 |
| Ed Delahanty | 1893-94 | .386 |

(minimum 3.1 PA per team G)

*Now* we're talking frustration. In 1894, Big Ed Delahanty batted .407 for the Phillies, but finished second in the National League to Boston's Hugh Duffy. A year later, Delahanty hit .404, but lost the batting title by five points to Cleveland's Jesse Burkett. Nearly two decades later, Shoeless Joe Jackson came close to duplicating Delahanty's feat of hitting .400 two years in a row while failing to win a batting title. Shoeless Joe hit .408 in 1911, his first full major league season, and .395 a year later. But Ty Cobb bested him each time.

How about great pitching runner-up performances? Because pitching rules and stats were totally different in the 19th century, we'll list the leaders since 1900. Here's the victory list:

**Most Wins—No. 2 in League Two Straight Seasons, 1900-99**

| Player | Years | W |
|---|---|---|
| Christy Mathewson | 1903-04 | 63 |
| Eddie Plank | 1904-05 | 50 |
| Eddie Plank | 1903-04 | 49 |
| Dick Rudolph | 1914-15 | 48 |
| Wes Ferrell | 1930-31 | 47 |

Christy Mathewson is another guy who would know what Sosa feels like. In 1903, Matty won 30 games but finished second in the NL to his Giant teammate, Joe McGinnity, who won 31. A year later, Mathewson won 33 games. . . but McGinnity won 35. Matty was so upset that he led the league in wins in four of the next six seasons.

Here are the top runners-up in earned run average:

**Lowest ERA—No. 2 in League Two Straight Seasons, 1900-99**

| Player | Years | ERA |
|---|---|---|
| Three Finger Brown | 1908-09 | 1.39 |
| Three Finger Brown | 1909-10 | 1.57 |
| Tiny Bonham | 1942-43 | 2.27 |
| Babe Adams | 1920-21 | 2.34 |
| Greg Maddux | 1996-97 | 2.47 |

(minimum 1 IP per team G)

From 1908-10, Mordecai (Three Finger) Brown of the Cubs posted ERAs of 1.47, 1.31 and 1.86, respectively. Great, but second each time, to Mathewson in 1908-09 and to Cubs teammate King Cole in 1910.

Finally, pitching strikeouts:

**Most Strikeouts—No. 2 in League Two Straight Seasons, 1900-99**

| Player | Years | SO |
|---|---|---|
| Pedro Martinez | 1997-98 | 556 |
| Bob Gibson | 1969-70 | 543 |
| Fergie Jenkins | 1970-71 | 537 |
| Mario Soto | 1982-83 | 516 |
| Bert Blyleven | 1973-74 | 507 |

Some great totals here, but nothing comparable to what Sosa accomplished. All in all, we'd rank the also-rans like this:

1. Sammy Sosa — 129 home runs in 1998-99
2. Ed Delahanty — .406 average in 1894-95
3. Joe Jackson — .402 average in 1911-12
4. Christy Mathewson — 63 wins in 1903-04
5. Three Finger Brown — 1.39 ERA in 1908-09

If it's any comfort to Sosa, three of the other four are in the Hall of Fame, and the fourth, Jackson, would have made it easily if not for his participation in the Black Sox scandal. Home-run title or not, Sosa is beginning to put up the sort of numbers that could put him in Cooperstown someday.

—Don Zminda

A more complete listing for this category can be found on page 225.

## Cincinnati Reds: Did They Overwork Their Bullpen?

Last season, the majority of Cincinnati's starting pitchers either were hit with injuries or failed to meet expectations. The run of bad luck started when Denny Neagle came down with shoulder weakness in spring training, a problem that lasted well into the season. Pete Harnisch pitched most of the season with a partially torn rotator cuff, while Steve Avery went down with a rotator-cuff injury during July. Though Brett Tomko remained healthy all season, he was inconsistent and a major disappointment.

These problems put a heavy burden on the Reds bullpen, which worked a National League-high 530.1 innings. Scott Sullivan led all major league relievers with 113.2 innings, posting 13 holds, five wins and three saves. Danny Graves ranked second in relief innings with 111 while topping Cincinnati with 27 saves and earning eight victories. National League Rookie of the Year Scott Williamson won a job in spring training, then led the majors with 12 relief wins, saved 19 games and tied for fifth in the NL with 93.1 relief innings.

Their efforts were a major reason the Reds surprisingly remained in contention all season long, reaching a wild-card playoff game against the Mets. But will Graves, Sullivan and Williamson pay a price in the future?

Ninety innings is now a fairly uncommon workload for a reliever. In the 10 seasons preceding 1999, 115 relievers reached that plateau, an average of roughly one for every two teams per year. Of that group, 57 percent experienced a significant increase in their ERA the following year:

**Relievers Working 90-Plus Innings—1989-98**

| ERA in Following Season | No. | Pct |
| --- | --- | --- |
| Increased more than 0.50 | 66 | 57 |
| Increased or decreased no more than 0.50 | 33 | 29 |
| Decreased more than 0.50 | 16 | 14 |

The relievers were four times more likely to see their ERA rise than shrink after being exposed to a heavy workload. This trend already affected Sullivan. He worked 97.1 innings for the Reds in 1997 (plus another 27.2 in the minors) and posted a 3.24 ERA. He nosedived the following year, recording a 5.21 ERA in 102 innings, though he did bounce back in 1999.

Not only do the Reds have to worry that their relievers could lose effectiveness, but they also must watch out for injuries. Sullivan could be especially vulnerable after posting three straight 90-plus inning seasons, and he also topped that mark in the minors in 1994 and '96.

During the 1989-98 period, only seven relievers had three or more 90-inning seasons. Joe Boever and Duane Ward had four each, while Todd Frohwirth, Greg Harris, Xavier Hernandez, Dennis Lamp and Jeff Montgomery had three apiece.

Of those five, only Montgomery had long-term success after his third 90-inning season. Ward had five consecutive 100-inning years starting in 1988, posted 45 saves upon becoming a closer in 1993, then hurt his arm and pitched in just four more major league games. Boever and Frohwirth faded quickly. Hernandez got hurt after his second 90-inning year in 1993 and had only one season with a sub-4.00 ERA before his career ended in 1998.

While Sullivan rebounded in 1999, there's plenty of evidence to suggest that his run of success might end shortly. Williamson also could be an injury risk considering his heavy workload at the relatively young age of 24. And it's unlikely that any of the three will be as effective in 2000 as they were in 1999.

—Rick Wilton

A more complete listing for this category can be found on page 227.

## Colorado Rockies: Can Cirillo Replace Castilla?

With new general manager Dan O'Dowd moving aggressively, the Rockies completely revamped their team over the winter. One of their most interesting moves involves a change in third basemen. Gone is Vinny Castilla, who was traded to Tampa Bay after averaging 40 homers and 118 RBI over the last four years. Taking his place will be ex-Brewer Jeff Cirillo, who averaged only 14 homers and 80 RBI over the same period.

Jeff Cirillo

The Rockies don't expect Cirillo to hit 40 homers a year, even with the boost that most hitters get from moving to Colorado's high altitude. They do expect him to hit for a higher average than Castilla, and they also look forward to more patience at the plate, greater mobility on the bases and excellent glovework from the slick-fielding Cirillo. O'Dowd has projected these figures for Cirillo's first season in Coors Field: a .353 average, .425 on-base percentage, .517 slugging percentage, 25 homers and 115 runs scored.

Is that a realistic projection? Will he make up for the loss of Castilla's power? Let's first break down Castilla's 1997-99 performance at home and on the road:

### Vinny Castilla, Home vs. Road—1997-99

|      | AB  | R   | H   | HR | RBI | BB | Avg  | OBP  | Slg  |
|------|-----|-----|-----|----|-----|----|------|------|------|
| Home | 949 | 168 | 307 | 67 | 209 | 71 | .323 | .371 | .588 |
| Road | 923 | 117 | 254 | 52 | 150 | 66 | .275 | .328 | .489 |

Away from Coors, Castilla performed respectably, averaging 17 homers and 50 RBI per year. But at home he averaged 22 homers and 70 RBI. He also batted nearly 50 points higher and slugged nearly 100 points better at Coors than he has on the road.

Here are Cirillo's home-road splits for the same period:

**Jeff Cirillo, Home vs. Road—1997-99**

|      | AB  | R   | H   | HR | RBI | BB  | Avg  | OBP  | Slg  |
|------|-----|-----|-----|----|-----|-----|------|------|------|
| Home | 891 | 119 | 283 | 18 | 128 | 111 | .318 | .395 | .435 |
| Road | 900 | 150 | 276 | 21 | 110 | 103 | .307 | .385 | .453 |

Cirillo has had fairly even splits over the last three years. To project how Cirillo figures to do at Coors, we use the 1997-99 park indexes for his old park, Milwaukee County Stadium, and adjust them for the 1997-99 park indexes at Coors Field. Here's what we came up with:

**Jeff Cirillo Home Games, Adjusted For Coors Field—1997-99**

|          | AB  | R   | H   | HR | RBI | BB  | Avg  | OBP  | Slg  |
|----------|-----|-----|-----|----|-----|-----|------|------|------|
| At Coors | 891 | 177 | 341 | 30 | 193 | 107 | .383 | .450 | .553 |

He gets a big boost across the board, with an eye-popping .383 adjusted batting average for his games at Coors. In case you think that's unrealistic, we'll note that in his career, Cirillo has batted .375 in 48 at-bats at Coors.

Now let's compare Castilla's actual overall numbers for 1997-99 with Cirillo's adjusted numbers:

**Vinny Castilla Actual vs. Jeff Cirillo Adjusted—1997-99**

|          | AB    | R   | H   | HR  | RBI | BB  | Avg  | OBP  | Slg  |
|----------|-------|-----|-----|-----|-----|-----|------|------|------|
| Castilla | 1,872 | 285 | 561 | 119 | 359 | 137 | .300 | .350 | .539 |
| Cirillo  | 1,791 | 327 | 617 | 51  | 303 | 210 | .345 | .417 | .504 |

Our projected figures for Cirillo are slightly lower than O'Dowd's, but remember they're based on three-year averages. Cirillo had his best overall season in 1999, so it's quite possible he'll surpass our three-year adjusted averages this season. All in all, it's not unrealistic at all to expect him to hit in the .340-.350 range this year, while driving in around 100 runs and scoring well over 100.

Even with the Coors boost, Cirillo isn't likely to approach Castilla's power numbers. But on-base-plus-slugging is one of the most useful measures of a player's overall offensive production, and our Coors-adjusted OPS for Cirillo's 1997-99 seasons is .921. Castilla's actual OPS for the same period was .889. When you throw in Cirillo's greater speed and his excellent defense, you have to think this is one exchange that's going to leave Rockies fans smiling.

—Don Zminda

## Florida Marlins: Has Anyone Had a Ground Game Like Castillo's?

In a wildly successful breakout season in 1999, Luis Castillo produced just 27 extra-base hits and slugged a mere .366 in 487 at-bats. But Florida's 24-year-old second baseman did the two things that speedsters at the top of the order must do: Castillo drew walks at an impressive rate for the first time in his career, and he put the ball in play on the ground.

Did he ever pound the ball into the ground. Of the 306 pitches that Castillo hit into the air or the dirt last season, 254 (83 percent) traveled by land for the largest percentage of groundballs hit in all of baseball. No one in the game topped him in groundball-flyball ratio, either:

### Highest Groundball-Flyball Ratio—1999

| Player, Team | PA | Grd | Fly | Ratio |
|---|---|---|---|---|
| **Luis Castillo, Fla** | **563** | **254** | **52** | **4.88** |
| Willie McGee, StL | 290 | 126 | 34 | 3.71 |
| Cristian Guzman, Min | 456 | 205 | 65 | 3.15 |
| Adrian Brown, Pit | 267 | 112 | 36 | 3.11 |
| Abraham Nunez, Pit | 301 | 120 | 39 | 3.08 |
| Wilton Guerrero, Mon | 340 | 159 | 52 | 3.06 |
| Ricky Gutierrez, Hou | 311 | 134 | 46 | 2.91 |
| Lance Johnson, ChC | 377 | 191 | 71 | 2.69 |
| Jose Vizcaino, LA | 298 | 137 | 51 | 2.69 |
| Randy Winn, TB | 324 | 138 | 52 | 2.65 |

(minimum 250 PA)

It's remarkable enough that Castillo outdistanced all flyball-challenged hitters by a large margin in 1999, but it's nearly unbelievable that his 254 grounders produced just three double plays. Speed is a major asset for a hitter who keeps the ball on the ground. While his groundball tendencies and speed are a dynamic combination, Castillo's recent success is more than just hitting the ball into the dirt. He produced an incredible 11.79 groundball-flyball ratio in 1997, but still batted .240 in 263 at-bats. Two numbers provide insight into the progress that Castillo has made since '97.

First of all, Castillo, who slugged an anemic .270 in '97, pushed his slugging percentage nearly 100 points higher in '99. His career-high .366 mark last summer demonstrated his newfound ability to drive a few balls from the left side of the plate. While Castillo isn't going to mature into a slugger, his development as a hitter should bolster his average and his pop.

Second, his notable spike in on-base percentage—from .307 in 1998 to .384 in '99— demonstrates his improved patience. Castillo was better at working hitters' counts and fouling off pitches last season, leading to 67 walks and 50 stolen bases, both easily career highs. His strike-zone judgment also aided his 99-point climb in batting average, as Castillo batted .300 from both sides of the plate in '99 after hitting .203 overall in 1998.

Hitting the ball on the ground so successfully is another example of Castillo understanding what he needs to do to excel in the majors. It's a lesson that Castillo has learned well. Since we've been tracking this stat, no position player has been more adept than Castillo:

**Highest Career Groundball-Flyball Ratio—1987-99**

| Player | PA | Grd | Fly | Ratio |
|---|---|---|---|---|
| Tom Glavine | 1,014 | 436 | 60 | 7.27 |
| **Luis Castillo** | **1,211** | **579** | **97** | **5.97** |
| Willie McGee | 5,323 | 2,533 | 734 | 3.45 |
| Milt Thompson | 3,519 | 1,598 | 507 | 3.15 |
| David Hulse | 1,370 | 592 | 202 | 2.93 |
| Greg Maddux | 1,109 | 427 | 146 | 2.92 |
| Felix Fermin | 3,072 | 1,520 | 538 | 2.83 |
| Curtis Goodwin | 1,138 | 442 | 157 | 2.82 |
| Wally Backman | 1,686 | 676 | 249 | 2.71 |
| Steve Sax | 4,237 | 2,073 | 766 | 2.71 |

(minimum 1,000 PA)

Only Braves pitcher Tom Glavine, who barely met the 1,000 plate appearance minimum, had a higher groundball-flyball ratio as a hitter than Castillo. (Since Greg Maddux also made the list, perhaps the theme of that famous Glavine-Maddux commercial should have been "Chicks love the groundball.") Apart from the two pitchers, the leaders list consists of singles hitters like Castillo who depend on their speed.

Surgery in September may put an end to a chronic shoulder ailment that has plagued Castillo. That may mean a bit more pop for the switch-hitting infielder. A little more pop and a little more patience went a long way in 1999. A little more progress in 2000, coupled with a ton of groundballs, may mean even better things for Castillo in the upcoming season.

—Thom Henninger

A more complete listing for this category can be found on page 229.

## Houston Astros: How Underrated Is Biggio?

There's little argument that Craig Biggio is one of baseball's best players. But do you think of Biggio when discussing the game's greats?

The baseball writers didn't take Biggio too seriously when they cast their MVP ballots after his career year in 1998. In an impressive display of his power and speed, he joined Hall of Famer Tris Speaker as the only players in the 20th century to collect 50 doubles and 50 steals in the same season. After hitting .325 and amassing 210 hits, 123 runs scored, 51 doubles, 20 homers and 50 steals, he placed just fifth in the National League MVP vote.

While he isn't one of the great home-run threats of the day, Biggio is a complete player who excels at nearly everything he does. The former catcher has won four Gold Gloves at second base, and while he didn't win one in '99, Biggio ranked second among second baseman in turning double plays.

It's remarkable enough how well Biggio has handled the positional change, but even more so how he has blossomed as a potent offensive force. Over the last five summers (1995-99), Biggio has averaged 19 homers a season, batted .304 with a .399 on-base percentage, and has become a doubles machine.

After leading the major leagues with 51 doubles in 1998, Biggio broke his own Houston record in '99 with 56 two-baggers. He became just the sixth major leaguer ever to produce back-to-back 50-double seasons, an accomplishment that puts Biggio in some serious Hall of Fame company:

**Most Doubles, Two-Year Span—1876-1999**

| Player | Years | 2B |
| --- | --- | --- |
| Joe Medwick | 1936-37 | 120 |
| George Burns | 1926-27 | 115 |
| Billy Herman | 1935-36 | 114 |
| Joe Medwick | 1935-36 | 110 |
| Hank Greenberg | 1934-35 | 109 |
| Tris Speaker | 1922-23 | 107 |
| **Craig Biggio** | **1998-99** | **107** |
| George Burns | 1925-26 | 105 |
| Chuck Klein | 1929-30 | 104 |
| Edgar Martinez | 1995-96 | 104 |

Yet scoring runs has been Biggio's forte. Few have done it better. The 34-year-old veteran has surpassed 100 runs scored in each of the last five seasons, and he has averaged 126 runs a campaign over that span. Twice in the last five years, Biggio has led the National League in runs scored, and only Barry Bonds scored more runs than him in the 1990s, 1,091 to 1,042.

To further examine Biggio's productivity, let's take a look at runs created, a Bill James statistic that factors in a player's total offensive contribution. It's a better indicator of a player's run production than runs or RBI, which are strongly affected by the other batters in the lineup.

In four of the last seven NL campaigns, Biggio has ranked in the top 10 in runs created, a stat that generates a leader board largely populated by sluggers. A list of the leaders for the last five seasons shows Biggio among the beefiest and most feared hitters in the game:

**Most Runs Created—1995-99**

| Player | RC |
| --- | --- |
| Mark McGwire | 659 |
| Jeff Bagwell | 658 |
| Barry Bonds | 641 |
| Edgar Martinez | 638 |
| Albert Belle | 634 |
| **Craig Biggio** | **633** |
| Frank Thomas | 621 |
| Rafael Palmeiro | 608 |
| Mo Vaughn | 607 |
| Ken Griffey Jr. | 600 |

Combine that kind of run production with Biggio's solid defense at a key position, and you have one of the game's great players. If a seven-time All-Star or a four-time Gold Glove winner can be considered underrated, Biggio just might be the man.

—Thom Henninger

A more complete listing for this category can be found on page 230.

## Los Angeles Dodgers: Is Brown the Best Travelin' Pitcher Ever?

Kevin Brown sure gets around. In 1994, he pitched for the Rangers. In 1995, he was an Oriole. Then he spent two years with the Marlins. In 1998 he worked for the Padres, and in '99 he joined the Dodgers. Most of these moves were Brown's choice—he only has been traded once, from the Marlins to the Padres following the 1997 season—and after signing a seven-year, $105 million contract with the Dodgers prior to the '99 campaign, he figures to remain in LA for awhile. But the way things have gone for him, who can really say?

Brown not only has been a travelin' pitcher, he also has been very successful while continuing to move around. His 18 wins for the Dodgers last year meant that he now has won at least 15 games (actually, 16-plus) for four different franchises: the Rangers, Marlins, Padres and Dodgers. This is a very rare feat. Since 1920, only five other pitchers have posted at least 15 wins for four different teams. Here's the list:

### 15-Plus Wins For Most Teams—1920-99

| Pitcher | No. | Teams |
|---|---|---|
| **Kevin Brown** | 4 | **Tex, Fla, SD, LA** |
| Burleigh Grimes | 4 | Bro, NYG, Pit, StL |
| Gaylord Perry | 4 | SF, Cle, Tex, SD |
| Rick Sutcliffe | 4 | LA, Cle, ChC, Bal |
| Mike Torrez | 4 | Mon, Bal, Oak, Bos |
| Rick Wise | 4 | Phi, StL, Bos, Cle |

Over the last 30 years, Gaylord Perry, Rick Sutcliffe, Rick Wise and Mike Torrez all went through stretches where they seemed to be with a new team every year. Usually they did so without losing effectiveness. The same goes for Burleigh Grimes, a Hall of Famer and the last pitcher to legally throw a spitball in the major leagues. In one seven-year span from 1926-32, Grimes pitched for six of the eight National League clubs (all except Cincinnati and Philadelphia), averaging 16 wins a season over the span.

Brown hasn't moved around quite *that* much, but over the last five years he has totaled 79 wins while pitching for four different teams. Is that a record for pitchers who have worked for at least four teams over a five-year period? No, not even close. The record is 94 victories, shared by Grimes (1927-31, Giants-Pirates-Braves-Cardinals) and the legendary vagabond Bobo Newsom (1936-40, Senators-Red Sox-Browns-Tigers). Brown does hold one impressive record for travelin' pitchers, however. Over the last five years, he has posted a 2.66 ERA while working for four different teams. No one has had a lower ERA while working for four or more clubs in a five-year stretch:

**Lowest ERA, Four-Plus Teams Over Five-Year Span—1920-99**

| Pitcher | ERA | IP | Years | No. | Teams |
|---|---|---|---|---|---|
| **Kevin Brown** | **2.66** | **1,152.0** | **1995-99** | **4** | **Bal-Fla-SD-LA** |
| Hoyt Wilhelm | 2.87 | 652.0 | 1956-60 | 4 | NYG-StL-Cle-Bal |
| Kevin Brown | 2.93 | 1,069.2 | 1994-98 | 4 | Tex-Bal-Fla-SD |
| Hoyt Wilhelm | 2.95 | 608.0 | 1955-59 | 4 | NYG-StL-Cle-Bal |
| Al Downing | 2.99 | 791.1 | 1967-71 | 4 | NYY-Oak-Mil-LA |
| Dean Chance | 3.01 | 1,080.2 | 1966-70 | 4 | Cal-Min-Cle-NYM |
| Mike Marshall | 3.03 | 637.2 | 1973-77 | 4 | Mon-LA-Atl-Tex |
| Dean Chance | 3.04 | 910.2 | 1967-71 | 4 | Min-Cle-NYM-Det |
| Dick Selma | 3.07 | 600.2 | 1967-71 | 4 | NYM-SD-ChC-Phi |
| Al Downing | 3.08 | 792.1 | 1968-72 | 4 | NYY-Oak-Mil-LA |

(minimum 600 IP)

All in all, Brown must be ranked among the very best pitchers who have modeled a lot of uniforms. *The* best? That might be a bit of a stretch. Right now the best would probably be Grimes, who totaled 270 wins while toiling for seven different major league clubs, and Hall of Fame reliever Hoyt Wilhelm, whose 2.52 career ERA was divided up among eight clubs. Brown even has a rival among active pitchers: over the last five seasons, David Wells has compiled 78 wins, one fewer than Brown, while toiling for five different teams—one more than him. One kind of wishes the two would get traded for each other someday.

—Don Zminda

A more complete listing for this category can be found on page 231.

## Milwaukee Brewers: Can Burnitz Become Their Biggest Basher Ever?

**J**eromy Burnitz' professional career started with a bang in 1990. After leading Oklahoma State to the College World Series title game that June, Burnitz signed with the Mets as a first-round pick and claimed MVP honors in the short-season New York-Penn League. In 1991, Burnitz jumped to Double-A and became the first Eastern League player ever to hit 30 homers and steal 30 bases in the same season.

While Burnitz surfaced in New York for the first time in 1993, he endured a string of trips to Triple-A locales, a 1994 trade to Cleveland and a subsequent move to Milwaukee in August 1996. He didn't play his first full season as a major league regular until 1997 at age 28.

Burnitz quickly made up for lost time, breaking out with 27 homers and 85 RBI in 1997. In '98, Burnitz stroked 38 longballs, the most for a Brewer since Gorman Thomas connected for 39 in 1982, and he posted 125 RBI, one shy of Cecil Cooper's franchise record set in '83. In '99, despite missing five weeks with a broken hand that also compromised his power after his return, Burnitz still homered 33 times and knocked in 103 runs.

In his first three-plus seasons as a Brewer, Burnitz delivered 100 homers, good for 13th all-time on the Milwaukee leader board. Still, for a guy who was 30 in 1999, his 100 homers weren't overly impressive when compared to other Brewers with at least that many through the season in which they played as a 30-year-old:

**Most Home Runs by Brewers Hitters—Through Age 30**

| Player | Age as First-Year Regular | HR |
|---|---|---|
| Greg Vaughn | 25 | 169 |
| Gorman Thomas | 27 | 158 |
| Robin Yount | 19 | 153 |
| Rob Deer | 25 | 137 |
| Dave Nilsson | 23 | 105 |
| Sixto Lezcano | 21 | 102 |
| **Jeromy Burnitz** | **28** | **100** |
| Paul Molitor | 21 | 95 |
| Jose Valentin | 25 | 90 |
| John Jaha | 27 | 87 |

(age as of June 30)

Clearly Burnitz got a late start by playing his first full season as a major league regular at age 28. But he has come on quickly with 98 homers in the last three years, the most ever for a Brewer in his first three exclusive seasons with the club.

Robin Yount currently holds the franchise record with 251 longballs. How good are Burnitz' chances of passing him? Pretty good, according to Bill James' Career Assessments system. We'll spare you all the math (the formula is in the Glossary), but the system pegs Burnitz' chances as 83 percent and projects him to hit another 202 homers before his career ends. Of course, there's always the possibility that he might not finish his career in Milwaukee.

Even if he can't catch Yount, Burnitz is firmly established in the franchise record book. He already is the Brewers' career slugging percentage leader, by a wide margin:

### Highest Slugging Percentage by Brewers Hitters—Career

| Player | Slg |
|---|---|
| **Jeromy Burnitz** | .527 |
| Cecil Cooper | .470 |
| John Jaha | .463 |
| Gorman Thomas | .461 |
| Ben Oglivie | .461 |
| Dave Nilsson | .461 |
| Greg Vaughn | .459 |
| George Scott | .456 |
| Jeff Cirillo | .453 |
| Sixto Lezcano | .452 |

(minimum 1,500 PA)

It would take a long-term slump for Burnitz to lose the slugging percentage mark. And barring a trade or injury, his odds are good of surpassing Yount's homer record. If that happens, there will be no question that Burnitz is the most dangerous Brewers basher ever. Better late than never.

—Thom Henninger

## Montreal Expos: Can You Win Without Walking?

Things are starting to look up in Montreal. While the Expos finished fourth in the National League's five-team Eastern Division last year with a 68-94 record, they boasted one of the league's best young players in Vladimir Guerrero (see page 79); one of baseball's top relievers in Ugueth Urbina; other promising young players such as Michael Barrett, Dustin Hermanson and Jose Vidro; some top prospects down on the farm; and one of baseball's most highly regarded managers in Felipe Alou. Even better news arrived after the season, when New York art dealer Jeffrey Loria purchased the Expos. Along with vowing to keep the Expos in Montreal while fighting for a new stadium, Loria promised to keep his good players rather than let them leave for financial reasons, as was the case all too often in the recent past. He showed his commitment to add to a sparse payroll by signing free-agent reliever Graeme Lloyd and trading for pitcher Hideki Irabu during the offseason.

But if the Expos want to move up in the standings, they may need to change one of the club's dominant characteristics: this team hates to take a walk. Last year the Expos finished last in the majors with only 438 walks, the third time in the last five years they've led the majors in this dubious category. For all of Alou's skills as a manager, he doesn't seem to regard the base on balls as much of a weapon, at least not lately:

**Expos' Walks Rank Under Felipe Alou**

| Year | Walks | NL Rank | Team W-L |
|------|-------|---------|----------|
| 1993 | 542 | 4th | 94-68 |
| 1994 | 379 | 5th | 74-40 |
| 1995 | 400 | *14th | 66-78 |
| 1996 | 492 | 13th | 88-74 |
| 1997 | 420 | *14th | 78-84 |
| 1998 | 439 | 15th | 65-97 |
| 1999 | 438 | *16th | 68-94 |

(* last in majors)

Alou's early Expos teams (he took over during the 1992 season) boasted at least a few patient hitters, such as Larry Walker and Delino DeShields. Since then it's been hack hack hack, probably not too surprising given that, as a player, Alou drew more than 40 walks only once in a 17-year career. Last year's Montreal team had only two players who drew more than 32 walks: Guerrero, who led the team with 55, and Shane Andrews, who drew 43 before being released by the Expos late in the year.

Can you win without walking? It sure ain't easy. Going back to 1901, the average winning percentage for teams which finished last in their league in walks was a dismal .445. That percentage has been only slightly better in recent years, .461 since World War II and .468 since the first major league expansion in 1961. More to the point, no team—not a single one—has won a World Championship since 1900 while finishing last in its league in walks:

| | Teams Ranking Last in Walks—1900-99 | | |
|---|---|---|---|
| W-L Pct | World Titles | League Titles | Division Titles |
| .445 | 0 | 4 | 4 |

Only a handful of these teams have finished in first place in their league or division. The best was almost certainly the 1943 St. Louis Cardinals, who went 105-49 in the regular season but lost the World Series to the Yankees in five games. Other "last in walks, first in the standings" clubs since 1900 were the 1961 Reds, 1963 Yankees and 1968 Cardinals (league champions), along with the 1970 and '72 Pirates, 1984 Royals and 1989 Cubs (division champions).

Perhaps those Pirates teams, which contended throughout the 1970s despite very low walk totals, left an impression on Alou. If anything, however, winning without walking has become even more difficult in recent years. In the 1990s, only one team managed to finish over .500 while ranking last in its league in walks: the 1993 Royals, who eked out an 84-78 record. We're not saying that Alou needs to turn his club into a team of Rickey Hendersons. But the Expos probably never will be serious contenders unless they show at least a little patience.

—Don Zminda

A more complete listing for this category can be found on page 232.

## New York Mets: Did They Have the Best Defensive Infield of All Time?

Heading into the 1999 season, 14 players had manned third base for the Mets since 1992. New York ended the revolving door at the hot corner by signing Robin Ventura to a four-year, $32 million contract in December 1998. Certainly the Mets were pleased with Ventura's offensive output. He batted a career-high .301 with 32 homers, and his 120 RBI were a career-best mark as well.

Perhaps the biggest payoff in signing Ventura came in the field. Budding star Edgardo Alfonzo moved from third to second base, allowing the Mets to put one of the best set of infielders on the diamond in the history of the game.

No major league team has seen its infielders produce fewer errors. Here's a rundown of the least error-prone infields in major league history:

**Fewest Infield Errors—1876-1999**

| Year | Team | G | E |
|------|------|-----|----|
| **1999** | **Mets** | **163** | **33** |
| 1964 | Orioles | 163 | 45 |
| 1998 | Orioles | 162 | 46 |
| 1988 | Twins | 162 | 46 |
| 1963 | Orioles | 162 | 49 |
| 1999 | Indians | 162 | 51 |
| 1997 | Tigers | 162 | 51 |
| 1993 | Pirates | 162 | 51 |
| 1990 | Athletics | 162 | 51 |
| 3 tied with | | | 52 |

(minimum 150 G)

Not only did the '99 Mets infield commit the fewest errors ever, it also generated the best fielding percentage in baseball history by a comfortable margin:

**Highest Infield Fielding Percentage—1876-1999**

| Year | Team | G | E | FPct |
|------|------|-----|----|------|
| **1999** | **Mets** | **163** | **33** | **.991** |
| 1964 | Orioles | 163 | 45 | .988 |
| 1998 | Orioles | 162 | 46 | .9873 |
| 1995 | Orioles | 144 | 40 | .9869 |

| Year | Team | G | E | FPct |
|------|---------|-----|----|-------|
| 1994 | Orioles | 112 | 32 | .9868 |
| 1963 | Orioles | 162 | 49 | .9867 |
| 1993 | Pirates | 162 | 51 | .9866 |
| 1988 | Twins   | 162 | 46 | .9862 |
| 1994 | Angels  | 115 | 34 | .9861 |
| 1997 | Tigers  | 162 | 51 | .9859 |

(minimum 100 G)

You can't say enough about this Mets infield. The two fixtures on the left side of the diamond, Ventura and Rey Ordonez, ranked first in the majors last year in zone rating at their positions. That is, they converted the largest percentage of groundballs hit into their designated zones into outs. Alfonzo enjoyed a breakout season offensively and had no problems making a permanent move to second base to allow Ventura to come aboard. Alfonzo not only committed just five errors in 158 games, but he also was the most successful of all second basemen at turning the pivot in 1999 (see page 178) while ranking second in zone rating. John Olerud placed fourth in zone rating at first base.

Let's take a statistical look at the starters in the three infields that ranked the best in both errors committed and fielding percentage over a full season:

### 1999 Mets Infield

|                  | Age | Pos | G   | E | FPct | MLB FPct | Zone | MLB Zone |
|------------------|-----|-----|-----|---|------|----------|------|----------|
| John Olerud      | 30  | 1B  | 160 | 9 | .994 | .993     | .879 | .846     |
| Edgardo Alfonzo  | 25  | 2B  | 158 | 5 | .993 | .981     | .855 | .827     |
| Robin Ventura    | 31  | 3B  | 160 | 9 | .980 | .951     | .815 | .745     |
| Rey Ordonez      | 26  | SS  | 154 | 4 | .994 | .969     | .894 | .837     |

### 1964 Orioles Infield

|                 | Age | Pos | G   | E  | FPct | MLB FPct | Zone | MLB Zone |
|-----------------|-----|-----|-----|----|------|----------|------|----------|
| Norm Siebern    | 30  | 1B  | 150 | 6  | .995 | .991     | —    | —        |
| Jerry Adair     | 27  | 2B  | 155 | 5  | .994 | .980     | —    | —        |
| Brooks Robinson | 27  | 3B  | 163 | 14 | .972 | .954     | —    | —        |
| Luis Aparicio   | 30  | SS  | 146 | 15 | .979 | .968     | —    | —        |

**1998 Orioles Infield**

|               | Age | Pos | G   | E  | FPct | MLB FPct | Zone | MLB Zone |
|---------------|-----|-----|-----|----|------|----------|------|----------|
| Rafael Palmeiro | 33 | 1B  | 162 | 9  | .994 | .993     | .862 | .843     |
| Roberto Alomar  | 30 | 2B  | 147 | 11 | .985 | .980     | .839 | .821     |
| Cal Ripken Jr.  | 37 | 3B  | 161 | 8  | .979 | .953     | .755 | .747     |
| Mike Bordick    | 32 | SS  | 151 | 7  | .990 | .970     | .873 | .841     |

The 1999 Mets clearly had more range than the 1998 Orioles, according to zone rating. In fact, each of New York's infielders outdid the major league average at his position by a far greater margin than each of Baltimore's. Zone ratings aren't available for the 1964 Orioles, of course. Comparing range factors wouldn't do justice to the 1999 Mets because their pitchers induced the second-smallest amount of groundballs in the major leagues last season.

New York's infield will change in 2000. Olerud chose to sign a long-term contract with his hometown team in Seattle, which prompted New York to sign catcher/third baseman Todd Zeile to take over at first base. Zeile brings a so-so .983 fielding percentage in 76 career games at first, and that begs the question whether he'll save his infield mates many errors with his glove.

Regardless of the makeup and fate of their new infield, clearly the Mets' 1999 version was the most surehanded of all time. Ventura owns six career Gold Gloves, Ordonez has won three straight and both Olerud and Alfonzo made strong cases for winning the award last year. Combine their relatively error-free play with their ability to dazzle, and it's hard to imagine a foursome having a better season.

—Thom Henninger

A more complete listing for this category can be found on page 234.

## Philadelphia Phillies: How Unique Was Abreu's Season?

Both the Astros and Devil Rays have had plenty of cause to shake their heads while watching Bobby Abreu develop into one of the brightest young stars in the game during the last two seasons. Houston signed Abreu out of Venezuela in 1990, then nurtured him all the way to the majors before leaving him unprotected in the 1997 expansion draft. Tampa Bay took Abreu with the sixth overall pick in the expansion proceedings, but swapped him with Philadelphia in a prearranged deal for Kevin Stocker.

Given his first chance to play full-time, Abreu responded with a .312-17-74 season in 1998. He was even better last year, hitting .335-20-93 with 27 stolen bases. His .549 slugging percentage ranked second on the Phillies to Mike Lieberthal's .551, the highest marks for the club since Hall of Famer Mike Schmidt slugged .644 in 1981. Abreu's .446 on-base percentage, which like his batting average ranked third in the National League, was the best seen in Philadelphia since another Cooperstown immortal, Richie Ashburn, posted a .449 mark in 1955.

It was quite a season for any player, especially a 25-year-old. Abreu became just the fifth player that age or younger to put up a .300 batting average, .400 on-base percentage, .500 slugging percentage and 25 steals in the same year since the advent of the lively ball in 1920:

### .300 Avg, .400 OBP, .500 Slg And 25 SB at Age 25 or Younger—1920-99

| Player, Team | Year | Age | Avg | OBP | Slg | SB |
| --- | --- | --- | --- | --- | --- | --- |
| Kiki Cuyler, Pit | 1924 | 25 | .354 | .402 | .539 | 32 |
| Mitchell Page, Oak | 1977 | 25 | .307 | .405 | .521 | 42 |
| Kal Daniels, Cin | 1987 | 23 | .334 | .429 | .617 | 26 |
| Barry Bonds, Pit | 1990 | 25 | .301 | .406 | .565 | 52 |
| **Bobby Abreu, Phi** | **1999** | **25** | **.335** | **.446** | **.549** | **27** |

(minimum 400 PA, age as of June 30)

That's certainly an eclectic group. Kiki Cuyler is a Hall of Famer, and he'll be joined in Cooperstown one day by Barry Bonds. Conversely, Mitchell Page and Kal Daniels took advantage of expansion and a one-year surge in offense, respectively, to post years they never would duplicate.

This feat was much more common in the early years of baseball. It happened three times in the 1880s, 17 times in the hitter-friendly 1890s, four times in 1900s and 12 in 1910s. But after Benny Kauff pulled it off in the

Federal League in 1914 and 1915, Cuyler was the only man to do so in the next 61 years.

The main reason the .300-.400-.500-25 combo has become so uncommon is that the game has changed dramatically. Before home runs came into vogue, players couldn't rely on just brute power to compile a high slugging percentage. They had to be able to hit for average and have the speed to produce extra-base hits. That quickness often translated into stolen bases as well. Ty Cobb, Joe Jackson and Tris Speaker had those attributes, and they combined for 10 such seasons (four by Cobb) from 1909-13.

It takes special ability indeed to be able to generate a high batting average, on-base percentage and slugging percentage while also stealing a significant number of bases. And as the Astros and Devil Rays have learned, on the rare occasions when a team finds such a player, it pays to hold onto him.

—Jim Callis

A more complete listing for this category can be found on page 235.

## Pittsburgh Pirates: How Good Was Giles' First Year As a Full-Timer?

Maybe if Brian Giles had been a first-round draft pick, things would have been different. But he was a 17th-round choice by the Indians in 1989, mainly because he was short and stocky rather than athletic. Giles quickly realized that Cleveland wasn't going to put him on the fast track. After hitting .310 or better for three straight seasons in the high minors and improving his power each year, he finally reached the majors in September 1995 and went 5-for-9.

**Brian Giles**

All that earned him was another half-season in Triple-A to start 1996. Recalled for good that July, he hit .355 in 51 games for the Tribe. Despite his consistent success and burgeoning power at the plate, Giles still couldn't win a full-time job. He held down a platoon role in 1997 and 1998, and even fared decently against lefthanders in limited exposure against them.

Cleveland had plenty of outfield depth and wanted to bolster its bullpen, so it traded Giles to Pittsburgh for lefty reliever Ricky Rincon in November 1998. While Rincon was somewhat disappointing in '99, Giles was a revelation, hitting .315 and ranking in the National League top 10 in homers (39), extra-base hits (75), RBI (115), walks (95), on-base percentage (.418) and slugging percentage (.614).

Not only was Giles' one of the best seasons among Senior Circuit hitters, he also had one of the best in the 118-year history of the Pittsburgh franchise. He became just the 11th Pirates hitter to have a combined on-base plus slugging percentage of 1.000 or greater:

### Pirates Hitters With 1.000 OPS—1882-1999

| Player | Year | OBP | Slg | OPS |
|---|---|---|---|---|
| Arky Vaughan | 1935 | .491 | .607 | 1.098 |
| Ralph Kiner | 1949 | .432 | .658 | 1.089 |
| Barry Bonds | 1992 | .456 | .624 | 1.080 |
| Ralph Kiner | 1951 | .452 | .627 | 1.079 |
| Ralph Kiner | 1947 | .417 | .639 | 1.055 |
| Willie Stargell | 1973 | .392 | .646 | 1.038 |

| Player | Year | OBP | Slg | OPS |
|---|---|---|---|---|
| **Brian Giles** | **1999** | **.418** | **.614** | **1.032** |
| Willie Stargell | 1971 | .398 | .628 | 1.026 |
| Jake Stenzel | 1894 | .441 | .580 | 1.022 |
| Kiki Cuyler | 1925 | .423 | .598 | 1.021 |
| Honus Wagner | 1900 | .434 | .573 | 1.007 |

(minimum 502 PA)

Kiki Cuyler, Ralph Kiner, Willie Stargell, Arky Vaughan and Honus Wagner are Hall of Famers, and Barry Bonds is destined for Cooperstown five years after he retires. Jake Stenzel, the only other player on the list besides Giles, had a career .339 average while playing in the hitter-friendly 1890s.

While Giles has a way to go to match the glittering careers of those seven sluggers, none of them posted a 1.000 OPS in his first season as a batting qualifier (defined by the modern standard of 3.1 plate appearances per team game). Giles became just the fifth player to accomplish that feat:

### 35 HR, 100 RBI and 1.000 OPS in First Season as Batting Qualifier

| Player, Team | Year | Age | HR | RBI | OPS |
|---|---|---|---|---|---|
| Chuck Klein, PhiN | 1929 | 24 | 43 | 145 | 1.065 |
| Jim Gentile, Bal | 1961 | 27 | 46 | 141 | 1.069 |
| Norm Cash, Det | 1961 | 26 | 41 | 132 | 1.148 |
| Alex Rodriguez, Sea | 1996 | 20 | 36 | 123 | 1.045 |
| **Brian Giles, Pit** | **1999** | **28** | **39** | **115** | **1.032** |

(first season with 3.1 PA per team G, age as of June 30)

Chuck Klein is enshrined in Cooperstown and Alex Rodriguez certainly seems headed there. Norm Cash and Jim Gentile made the most of expansion in 1961, then never approached those numbers again. The other four players got the chance to play full-time at an earlier age than Giles did.

The Braves may want to take note. Atlanta drafted Marcus Giles, Brian's younger brother, in the 53rd round in 1996. Like Brian, he lacks a sexy draft pedigree and an athletic build. But also like Brian, he can flat-out hit. A second baseman, Marcus has a career .331 average in three years in the lower minors and has been named MVP of Class-A leagues in each of the last two seasons. He's 22 this season, and the Braves may not want to take too much longer before finding out if he's ready for the majors.

—Jim Callis

## St. Louis Cardinals: What If McGwire Had Stayed Healthy?

A few years ago, when Mark McGwire was still a member of the A's, we did a *Scoreboard* article entitled, "What If McGwire Could Stay Healthy?" McGwire *has* stayed healthy the last three years, and the result has been staggering, with home-run totals of 58, 70 and 65. As we point out in the article on page 76 of this year's book, McGwire's epic home-run output over the last few years has given him a fighting chance to break Hank Aaron's career record of 755 homers.

Even so, McGwire's chances would be a whole lot better had he not missed so many games due to injury, especially from 1992-96. So let's revise the chart we presented in 1997, and re-create McGwire's career as it might have unfolded given better health. We used his actual at-bat and home-run totals for all seasons except 1989 and 1992-96; for those years we projected him to a get 625 plate appearances in all years except strike-shortened 1994 and 1995, for which we gave him 450 and 550 PA, respectively. The 625 plate appearances are actually a pretty conservative projection, as McGwire has had more than 650 PA in each of the last three years. We based his home-run totals for the projected seasons on his actual homer rates for the years in question. Anyway, here's what we came up with:

**Mark McGwire—Actual And Projected Home-Run Totals**

| Year | Actual AB | Actual HR | Projected AB | Projected HR |
|---|---|---|---|---|
| 1986 | 53 | 3 | 53 | 3 |
| 1987 | 557 | 49 | 557 | 49 |
| 1988 | 550 | 32 | 550 | 32 |
| 1989 | 490 | 33 | **522** | **35** |
| 1990 | 523 | 39 | 523 | 39 |
| 1991 | 483 | 22 | 483 | 22 |
| 1992 | 467 | 42 | **511** | **46** |
| 1993 | 84 | 9 | **491** | **53** |
| 1994 | 135 | 9 | **353** | **24** |
| 1995 | 317 | 39 | **413** | **51** |
| 1996 | 423 | 52 | **482** | **59** |
| 1997 | 540 | 58 | 540 | 58 |
| 1998 | 509 | 70 | 509 | 70 |
| 1999 | 521 | 65 | 521 | 65 |
| Total | 5,652 | 522 | **6,508** | **606** |

Our projection is that McGwire would have hit 84 more home runs given good health, with the bulk of them (59) coming in 1993-94, seasons in which he was only able to play a total of 74 games. He would now be on a streak of five straight 50-homer seasons, and six of the last seven. Given the way he's performed the last three years, does anyone doubt he could have done that?

Eighty-four more homers would give McGwire a career total of 606 through the age of 35. At the same age Ruth had 565 homers, Aaron 554, Willie Mays 542. McGwire would be way ahead of all of them, and we wouldn't be talking about him breaking Aaron's record—Bill James' career assessments system would boost McGwire's chances from his current 48 percent to 76 percent—we'd be speculating on whether he could hit 800 or more.

The amazing thing about McGwire is that he still has a chance at Aaron's record even with all the time he's missed. It might have been so much easier for him. . . but then, he's probably grateful that he's finally had three straight healthy seasons. If he can continue to remain relatively injury-free, there's no telling what he might accomplish over the next few years.

—Don Zminda

## San Diego Padres: How Long Can Gwynn Continue?

Tony Gwynn continues to amaze. Last year at age 39, the Padres right fielder collected his 3,000th major league hit, and he shows no signs of slowing down. By hitting .338 last year, Gwynn recorded his 17th straight .300 season, the 16th straight in which he has had at least 400 plate appearances. Only Ty Cobb, with 19 from 1907-25, has had a longer streak of consecutive .300 seasons with at least 400 PA each year.

In addition, Gwynn's .338 average last year marked the seventh straight season he'd batted .320 or better. Among players who were age 33 or older at the start of the streak (as of June 30 of the season in question), only Eddie Collins has had as long a streak:

### Most Consecutive .320-Plus Seasons, Age 33 or Older

| Player | Years | Span |
|---|---|---|
| Eddie Collins | 7 | 1920-26 |
| **Tony Gwynn** | **7** | **1993-99** |
| Ty Cobb | 6 | 1920-25 |
| Bill Terry | 6 | 1930-35 |
| Honus Wagner | 6 | 1907-12 |
| Babe Ruth | 5 | 1928-32 |
| Tris Speaker | 5 | 1921-25 |
| Ted Williams | 5 | 1954-58 |
| Edgar Martinez | 4 | 1996-99 |
| Paul Molitor | 4 | 1991-94 |

(minimum 400 PA each season)

How high can Gwynn, who turns 40 on May 9, move up on the all-time hit list? Here's how the 16 players who rank ahead of him in career hits fared from seasonal age 40 (age as of June 30) onward:

### Hits After Age 39—All-Time Hit Leaders

| Player | Thru 39 | Age 40+ | Total |
|---|---|---|---|
| Pete Rose | 3,557 | 699 | 4,256 |
| Ty Cobb | 3,901 | 289 | 4,190 |
| Hank Aaron | 3,509 | 262 | 3,771 |
| Stan Musial | 3,294 | 336 | 3,630 |
| Tris Speaker | 3,463 | 51 | 3,514 |
| Carl Yastrzemski | 3,009 | 410 | 3,419 |

| Player | Thru 39 | Age 40+ | Total |
|---|---|---|---|
| Honus Wagner | 2,936 | 479 | 3,415 |
| Paul Molitor | 3,014 | 305 | 3,319 |
| Eddie Collins | 3,225 | 87 | 3,312 |
| Willie Mays | 3,065 | 218 | 3,283 |
| Eddie Murray | 3,071 | 184 | 3,255 |
| Nap Lajoie | 3,000 | 242 | 3,242 |
| George Brett | 3,005 | 149 | 3,154 |
| Paul Waner | 3,042 | 110 | 3,152 |
| Robin Yount | 3,142 | 0 | 3,142 |
| Dave Winfield | 2,697 | 413 | 3,110 |
| **Tony Gwynn** | **3,067** | — | **3,067** |

(age as of June 30)

While he continues to hit for a high average, Gwynn also continues to miss considerable time due to injuries, and over the last two years he has averaged only 144 hits per season. Only four players on this list amassed more than 400 hits from age 40 onward. Gwynn needs 352 hits to tie Carl Yastrzemski for sixth place on the all-time list, 447 to tie Tris Speaker for fifth. Passing Yaz seems like a reachable goal. Making the top five will be a lot more difficult, but if Gwynn can stay reasonably healthy and keep cranking out those .320 seasons, it's a possibility.

—Don Zminda

A more complete listing for this category can be found on page 236.

## San Francisco Giants: Will Pac Bell Provide a New-Park Boost?

After 30 seasons in Candlestick Park (renamed 3Com Park in 1997), the Giants are moving into a new downtown stadium, Pacific Bell Park, this year. At this point we can only speculate about whether the park will favor pitchers or hitters and about which Giants will benefit or suffer from the change. We can, however, address one question: does moving to a new park give a first-year boost to a team's won-lost percentage?

Since 1950, there have been 24 cases of a team moving into a new stadium in the same metropolitan area. In a few cases, teams moved to a new park in midseason. For simplicity's sake, our new-park record for those years included the club's record for the entire season. Overall, here's how teams have fared in their first season in the new park, compared with the last full season in their old park:

**First-Year Winning Percentages in New Parks—1950-99**

| Old Park | | New Park | | |
|---|---|---|---|---|
| W-L | Pct | W-L | Pct | Diff |
| 1,795-1,964 | .478 | 1,915-1,849 | .509 | .031 |

(parks in same metropolitan area only)

Interestingly, the first team since 1950 to move to a new park in the same metropolitan area was the Giants, who moved from Seals Stadium to Candlestick Park in 1960. The move didn't help San Francisco on the field, as they went from 83-71 (.539) in 1959 to 79-75 (.513) in '60. The Giants' experience was the exception to the rule, however. Overall, clubs have improved their winning percentage by 31 points in their first season in a new park, a boost of about five victories in a 162-game schedule.

Seventeen of the 24 teams saw their winning percentage improve, sometimes dramatically. The biggest boost was enjoyed by the Orioles, who improved from .414 (67-95) in 1991, their last year in Memorial Stadium, to .549 (89-73) in 1992, their first season at Oriole Park at Camden Yards. The Expos improved by 123 percentage points, from .340 to .463, when they moved from Jarry Park to Olympic Stadium in 1977. The Indians, a .469 team in 1993, their final season in Cleveland Stadium, played .584 ball when they moved into Jacobs Field a year later. Of the 17 teams which bettered their won-lost record, nine improved by at least 50 percentage points, the equivalent of eight extra victories over 162 games.

By contrast, only one team saw its winning percentage decline by more than 50 percentage points. The Rangers, a .531 team in 1993, their final season in Arlington Stadium, played .456 ball in their first year in The Ballpark at Arlington, 1994. Even then, the year wasn't a disaster, as the Rangers were leading the American League West when the strike ended the season in August.

All in all, there seems little reason to doubt that most teams get a first-year boost from moving to a new park. This makes perfect sense: a new ballpark generally means higher attendance, enthusiastic fans and new excitement in the home city. It also can coincide with a stronger commitment to winning. The best example in recent years has been the Indians, who carefully nurtured a group of talented young players with the intention of cashing in when they moved to Jacobs Field. The strategy worked brilliantly, and the Tribe has been a success both on the field and at the box office.

The Giants, who have to make do on a limited budget, may not be capable of emulating the success enjoyed by the Orioles and Indians in their first year in their new stadium. But even an average boost of five victories would put them at 91 wins, enough to make them serious wild-card contenders at the very least. Playoffs or not, it should be a very interesting year in San Francisco. It also could be an interesting year in Houston and Detroit, the other two cities which are unveiling new parks in 2000.

—Don Zminda

A more complete listing for this category can be found on page 237.

# II. QUESTIONS ON OFFENSE

## Can McGwire Beat Aaron?

A decade ago, there seemed to be only a remote chance that anyone would top Hank Aaron's record total of 756 home runs. But then came the offensive explosion of the mid- and late 1990s. Instead of leading a league with 35 or 36 home runs for a full season, as Fred McGriff did in 1989 and 1992, players were hitting that many by the end of July. Both Mark McGwire and Sammy Sosa shattered Roger Maris' single-season record of 61 in 1998, and in '99 they topped Maris' total again. Over the last four seasons, McGwire has *averaged* 61 homers a year, Ken Griffey Jr. 52, Sosa 51. Is Aaron's record in serious jeopardy? You bet it is.

Originally know as The Favorite Toy, the Career Assessments system is a tool designed by Bill James to estimate the chances players have of reaching a milestone. The formula is in the Glossary, but basically the system uses a player's performance over the last three seasons to estimate his chances of reaching a particular goal. Age is factored in as well. While it's done mostly for fun, the projection system gives us a good feel for which milestones are in jeopardy, and which players have the best chance at a record-shattering performance.

Let's start with Aaron's record. According to the projection system, five players have at least a 10 percent chance of hitting 756 homers, and two more have established at least a 1 percent chance:

**Players With a 1% Chance For 756 Home Runs**

| Player, Team | Age | Current | Projected | Chance |
|---|---|---|---|---|
| Mark McGwire | 35 | 522 | 751 | 48% |
| Ken Griffey Jr. | 29 | 398 | 736 | 44% |
| Sammy Sosa | 30 | 336 | 693 | 35% |
| Juan Gonzalez | 29 | 340 | 610 | 15% |
| Alex Rodriguez | 23 | 148 | 517 | 11% |
| Manny Ramirez | 27 | 198 | 508 | 6% |
| Vladimir Guerrero | 23 | 92 | 429 | 1% |

(age as of June 30, 1999)

No player has yet established a 50 percent chance of breaking Aaron's home-run mark. But McGwire and Griffey are creeping up. It might surprise you that we currently estimate McGwire as having a better chance to top Aaron's record than Griffey does. There are two reasons for this: one, he's a lot closer to actually reaching the goal, and two, he has established more momentum with his recent performance. McGwire's age—he'll be

36 this year—is against him, but when you're averaging 60-plus homers a year, you can advance on the record pretty quickly. The home-run pace of the last few seasons has been so dizzying that we give three players (Griffey 34 percent, McGwire 32, Sosa 27) a better than 25 percent chance to hit 800 home runs and the same trio a better than 10 percent chance (Griffey 17 percent, Sosa 13, McGwire 11) to hit 900. Those are real longshots, of course, but if the current home-run climate stays the way it is, once-impossible feats may soon become possible.

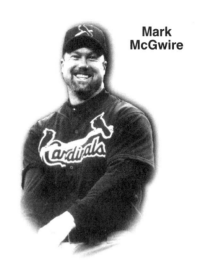

Mark McGwire

Aaron is as proud of his record for most career RBI—2,297—as he is of his home-run mark. The RBI record currently seems in a lot less danger, as no one has established more than a 30 percent chance of breaking it. Only Griffey (57 percent) currently is given more than a 50 percent chance of reaching 2,000 ribbies, a milestone reached thus far only by Aaron and Babe Ruth. It will take more seasons like Manny Ramirez' 165-RBI performance in 1999 to put Aaron's RBI record in true jeopardy:

**Players With a 1% Chance For 2,298 Runs Batted In**

| Player, Team | Age | Current | Projected | Chance |
|---|---|---|---|---|
| Ken Griffey Jr. | 29 | 1,152 | 2,063 | 30% |
| Juan Gonzalez | 29 | 1,075 | 1,973 | 23% |
| Manny Ramirez | 27 | 682 | 1,773 | 18% |
| Sammy Sosa | 30 | 941 | 1,799 | 13% |
| Alex Rodriguez | 23 | 463 | 1,516 | 7% |
| Albert Belle | 32 | 1,136 | 1,779 | 5% |
| Vladimir Guerrero | 23 | 281 | 1,312 | 1% |

(age as of June 30, 1999)

The safest of the glamour batting marks, currently, is Pete Rose's record total of 4,256 hits. Only one player, Derek Jeter, has established even a 1 percent chance of breaking Rose's record. Jeter has established a 6 percent chance to reach 4,000 hits, and he and Griffey currently have a 16 percent chance to reach 3,500. Given those long odds, we're presenting the players with the best chance at reaching 3,000 hits, still considered a milestone that earns automatic entry into the Hall of Fame:

**Players With a 20% Chance For 3,000 Hits**

| Player, Team | Age | Current | Projected | Chance |
|---|---|---|---|---|
| Cal Ripken Jr. | 38 | 2,991 | 3,268 | 100% |
| Rickey Henderson | 40 | 2,816 | 3,009 | 55% |
| Roberto Alomar | 31 | 2,007 | 2,937 | 44% |
| Ken Griffey Jr. | 29 | 1,742 | 2,895 | 42% |
| Rafael Palmeiro | 34 | 2,158 | 2,872 | 35% |
| Harold Baines | 40 | 2,783 | 2,962 | 32% |
| Derek Jeter | 25 | 807 | 2,582 | 31% |
| Craig Biggio | 33 | 1,868 | 2,749 | 28% |
| Juan Gonzalez | 29 | 1,421 | 2,605 | 25% |
| Alex Rodriguez | 23 | 791 | 2,423 | 24% |
| Chuck Knoblauch | 30 | 1,533 | 2,559 | 20% |

(age as of June 30, 1999)

Only Cal Ripken Jr., who's nine hits away, and Rickey Henderson, who needs 184, are currently better than 50/50 to make it. But watch Roberto Alomar, Griffey, Rafael Palmeiro and even Harold Baines over the next couple of years. All of them have to be considered very serious 3,000-hit candidates.

—Don Zminda

A more complete listing for this category can be found on page 238.

## Is Guerrero on His Way to Immortality?

Last March, Bret Boone sat in the Braves' spring-training clubhouse in Orlando and offered his opinion as to the best young player in baseball. While he might have been expected to choose then-teammate Andruw Jones, Boone went in another direction.

"There's other guys, and then there's Vladimir Guerrero," Boone said. "I think in another year or two years, hands down he'll be the best player in baseball."

Guerrero made major strides toward fulfilling that prediction in 1999. He had an Expos-record 31-game hitting streak, joining Rogers Hornsby (1922), Joe DiMaggio (1941) and Nomar Garciaparra (1997) as the only players to have a 30-game hitting streak and 30 homers in the same year. Guerrero also set Montreal marks for home runs (42), RBI (131), extra-base hits (84) and slugging percentage (.600).

Perhaps most impressively, Guerrero did all that at age 23. He became just the ninth player ever to have a .300-40-120 season at that age or younger:

### .300 Avg, 40 HR And 120 RBI at Age 23 or Younger

| Player | Year | Age | Avg | HR | RBI |
|---|---|---|---|---|---|
| Mel Ott | 1929 | 20 | .328 | 42 | 151 |
| Hal Trosky | 1936 | 23 | .343 | 42 | 162 |
| Joe DiMaggio | 1937 | 22 | .346 | 46 | 167 |
| Eddie Mathews | 1953 | 21 | .302 | 47 | 135 |
| Hank Aaron | 1957 | 23 | .322 | 44 | 132 |
| Orlando Cepeda | 1961 | 23 | .311 | 46 | 142 |
| Jose Canseco | 1988 | 23 | .307 | 42 | 124 |
| Alex Rodriguez | 1998 | 22 | .310 | 42 | 124 |
| **Vladimir Guerrero** | **1999** | **23** | **.316** | **42** | **131** |

(age as of June 30)

That's certainly some distinguished company. Hank Aaron, Orlando Cepeda, DiMaggio, Eddie Mathews and Mel Ott all are Hall of Famers. Hal Trosky seemed destined for Cooperstown before migraine headaches curtailed his career, and Jose Canseco already would be a lock for the Hall of Fame had injuries not cut down on his production. Unless he gets hurt, it's difficult to imagine Alex Rodriguez not being remembered as one of the best shortstops in the game's history.

And now for the kicker. While nine men have had a .300-40-120 year by 23, no one had averaged those numbers over a two-year period by that age until Guerrero did so in 1998-99. He hit .324-38-109 in 1998, and if his post-All-Star break numbers last year (.341-24-66 in 76 games) are any indication, he's still getting better.

Another way to measure how impressive Guerrero's young career has been is to use similarity scores. Bill James developed this method, which compares players' statistics in several categories. The resultant score can range from 1 to 1,000, with the latter indicating a perfect match. Anything above 900 is considered very similar, and scores from 850-899 are rated as substantially similar, according to Bill.

Here are the best matches to Guerrero through age 23:

### Most Similar Players to Vladimir Guerrero Through Age 23

| Player | Pos | AB | R | H | 2B | 3B | HR | RBI | BB | K | SB | Avg | Slg | Score |
|---|---|---|---|---|---|---|---|---|---|---|---|---|---|---|
| **Vladimir Guerrero** | **OF** | **1585** | **256** | **498** | **96** | **14** | **92** | **281** | **116** | **199** | **28** | **.314** | **.567** | — |
| Willie Mays | OF | 1156 | 195 | 352 | 57 | 22 | 65 | 201 | 139 | 134 | 19 | .304 | .561 | 924 |
| Hal Trosky | 1B | 1930 | 331 | 606 | 124 | 27 | 104 | 425 | 142 | 179 | 9 | .314 | .568 | 909 |
| Hank Aaron | OF | 2294 | 387 | 718 | 125 | 35 | 110 | 399 | 171 | 212 | 8 | .313 | .542 | 894 |
| Juan Gonzalez | OF | 1815 | 277 | 497 | 101 | 5 | 121 | 348 | 122 | 395 | 8 | .274 | .535 | 892 |
| Joe Medwick | OF | 1955 | 347 | 641 | 138 | 42 | 61 | 342 | 79 | 208 | 15 | .328 | .535 | 889 |
| Tony Conigliaro | OF | 1832 | 287 | 505 | 79 | 19 | 104 | 294 | 165 | 364 | 10 | .276 | .510 | 878 |
| Duke Snider | OF | 1415 | 237 | 419 | 68 | 24 | 59 | 225 | 129 | 222 | 34 | .296 | .503 | 877 |
| Stan Musial | OF | 1699 | 315 | 584 | 135 | 44 | 36 | 254 | 226 | 72 | 23 | .344 | .539 | 876 |
| Joe DiMaggio | OF | 1857 | 412 | 615 | 111 | 43 | 107 | 432 | 147 | 97 | 13 | .331 | .610 | 876 |
| Frank Robinson | OF | 2277 | 415 | 680 | 112 | 21 | 134 | 366 | 239 | 360 | 46 | .299 | .543 | 873 |

(age as of June 30)

The best match for Guerrero is Willie Mays, unquestionably one of baseball's all-time greats. Aaron, DiMaggio, Stan Musial and Frank Robinson also fit into the category, while Joe Medwick and Duke Snider are Hall of Famers. The only retired players on this list not enshrined in Cooperstown are the star-crossed Tony Conigliaro and Trosky. Juan Gonzalez is building an impressive career that may land him there when he's finished.

The Expos have a reputation for developing All-Star talent, including players such as Gary Carter, Andre Dawson and Tim Raines. If his career continues on the same path it has taken thus far, Guerrero not only will become the best player in baseball but also the best in franchise history. Boone was right on target, though he might have set the bar a bit too low.

—Jim Callis

## Who Unloads the Bases?

Most players would be happy with hitting two grand slams over the course of an entire career. Then there's Fernando Tatis, who on April 23 against the Dodgers hit two grand slams in the same *inning*. Tatis' history-making frame, which came at the expense of Chan Ho Park, was the first of its kind in the annals of baseball. The Cardinals slugger also finished the inning with eight ribbies, and both feats may never be duplicated.

Tatis didn't stop there, either. He notched his third granny of the year on August 9 against the Phillies. Just how effective has Tatis been throughout his career with the bases loaded? He finished the 1999 campaign with a .424 career batting average with the bags full, which puts him within a few plate appearances of joining our list of players with the highest career bases-loaded batting averages (minimum 50 bases-loaded PA) since 1987.

### Highest Batting Average, Bases Loaded—1987-99

| Player | AB | H | Avg |
| --- | --- | --- | --- |
| Felix Jose | 48 | 24 | .500 |
| Pat Tabler | 42 | 19 | .452 |
| Joe Orsulak | 68 | 30 | .441 |
| Tony Gwynn | 94 | 41 | .436 |
| Rusty Greer | 66 | 28 | .424 |
| Mike Blowers | 81 | 34 | .420 |
| Johnny Damon | 48 | 20 | .417 |
| Mike LaValliere | 53 | 22 | .415 |
| Carl Everett | 63 | 26 | .413 |
| Mark Grace | 85 | 35 | .412 |
| **MLB Average** | | | **.281** |

(minimum 50 PA)

Tatis has come to the plate just 41 times with a teammate at every base, so he figures to crack our top 10 sometime in 2000. As for our current group, you'll find a few surprises mixed in with the Tony Gwynns, Rusty Greers and Mark Graces of the world. Though guys like Pat Tabler and Mike Blowers built well-established reputations for coming through with the sacks full, who knew that Felix Jose and "Spanky" LaValliere were so effective in those situations? For his part, LaValliere finished with an overall career batting average of .268, 147 points lower than his average with the bases loaded.

As for Jose, whose fall from the big leagues was even more meteoric than his rise, he hit just .271 in his career with the bases empty, but nearly doubled that figure when the sacks were juiced. He suddenly stopped hitting in 1995 and quickly got lost in the minor leagues, but not before he also topped our list of players with the most career RBI per plate appearance with the bases loaded, again since '87 with a minimum of 50 such PA.

### Most RBI Per Plate Appearance, Bases Loaded—1987-99

| Player | PA | RBI | RBI/PA |
|---|---|---|---|
| Felix Jose | 51 | 56 | 1.10 |
| Matt Stairs | 63 | 68 | 1.08 |
| Ryan Klesko | 65 | 69 | 1.06 |
| Manny Ramirez | 113 | 117 | 1.04 |
| Carl Everett | 70 | 72 | 1.03 |
| Rusty Greer | 82 | 83 | 1.01 |
| Mike Blowers | 92 | 92 | 1.00 |
| Mike Piazza | 81 | 81 | 1.00 |
| Alvin Davis | 67 | 67 | 1.00 |
| Ken Griffey Jr. | 116 | 114 | 0.98 |
| **MLB Average** | | | **0.70** |

(minimum 50 PA)

It's amazing that Jose didn't stick in the majors longer, if for no other reason than to serve as a pinch-hitter in bases-loaded situations. Carl Everett, Greer and Blowers are the only other players to make both lists. As for the other six hitters to crack the top 10, all are capable of clearing the bases in a hurry, combining for 52 career grand slams. Ken Griffey Jr. has hit at "just" a .330 clip with the bases loaded, but his 12 career grand slams do wonders for his ratio.

If you're wondering where Tatis fits into the ratio picture, his 43 RBI in 41 bases-loaded plate appearances would put him just behind Ryan Klesko if he qualified. If he keeps going at his 1999 pace, Tatis not only will qualify for this category next season, but jump straight to the top.

—Tony Nistler

A more complete listing for this category can be found on page 240.

## Who Works the Most Hitters' Counts?

In the cat-and-mouse game of successfully hitting against major league pitching, batters constantly are encouraged to get ahead in the count. Don't give away an at-bat. In fact, it's counterproductive to give away even one pitch. The difference in getting ahead in the count and behind in it has a dramatic impact on the success of major league hitters.

So, let's take a look at the big leaguers who faced the largest percentage of pitches in hitters' counts (counts of 1-0, 2-0, 2-1, 3-0 and 3-1) during 1999:

### Highest Percentage of Pitches Seen in Hitters' Counts—1999

| Player, Team | PA | Total | Ahead | Pct |
|---|---|---|---|---|
| Eric Young, LA | 534 | 1,916 | 641 | 33.5 |
| Gary Sheffield, LA | 663 | 2,623 | 868 | 33.1 |
| Mark Grace, ChC | 688 | 2,607 | 861 | 33.0 |
| Bill Spiers, Hou | 444 | 1,706 | 548 | 32.1 |
| Matt Lawton, Min | 476 | 1,682 | 535 | 31.8 |
| Frank Thomas, CWS | 590 | 2,305 | 732 | 31.8 |
| John Olerud, NYM | 723 | 2,824 | 892 | 31.6 |
| Rusty Greer, Tex | 662 | 2,742 | 859 | 31.3 |
| Mark McLemore, Tex | 664 | 2,576 | 803 | 31.2 |
| Barry Larkin, Cin | 687 | 2,658 | 818 | 30.8 |
| **MLB Average** | | | | **25.7** |

(minimum 400 PA)

Most of these guys are among the most patient hitters in the game. Only Bill Spiers and Mark McLemore have career on-base percentages below .365.

Getting into hitters' counts isn't the end of the story. It's simply the means to get a good pitch to hit, and not surprisingly, most of these guys do their best hitting when they're ahead in the count:

### Production Ahead in the Count—1999

| | Season Totals | | | Ahead in the Count | | |
|---|---|---|---|---|---|---|
| | Avg | OBP | Slg | Avg | OBP | Slg |
| Eric Young | .281 | .371 | .355 | .346 | .509 | .462 |
| Gary Sheffield | .301 | .407 | .523 | .338 | .561 | .612 |
| Mark Grace | .309 | .390 | .481 | .390 | .516 | .626 |

*Baseball Scoreboard*

|  | Season Totals | | | Ahead in the Count | | |
| --- | --- | --- | --- | --- | --- | --- |
|  | Avg | OBP | Slg | Avg | OBP | Slg |
| Bill Spiers | .288 | .363 | .389 | .273 | .403 | .400 |
| Matt Lawton | .259 | .353 | .355 | .295 | .453 | .388 |
| Frank Thomas | .305 | .414 | .471 | .374 | .516 | .532 |
| John Olerud | .298 | .427 | .463 | .310 | .540 | .452 |
| Rusty Greer | .300 | .405 | .493 | .360 | .526 | .567 |
| Mark McLemore | .274 | .363 | .366 | .279 | .443 | .364 |
| Barry Larkin | .293 | .390 | .420 | .333 | .513 | .512 |
| **MLB Average** | **.271** | **.345** | **.434** | **.346** | **.479** | **.588** |

The spike in hitting performance is clear. Every player got on base at least 40 percent of the time when they completed a plate appearance while ahead in the count, and seven of these 10 hitters reached base more than half the time. Gary Sheffield posted a .561 OBP in hitters' counts.

Most pitchers know this already, but it's begging for trouble to fall behind in the count when Mark Grace is at the plate. In 1999, he enjoyed a power surge when he was in a favorable count and swung at a pitch to his liking. Grace hit half of his 16 homers in those 195 at-bats when the count was in his favor.

How about the guys who worked the lowest percentage of hitters' counts during the 1999 season? Half of these 10 players have a career on-base percentage under .300, but the man who had the lowest percentage of hitters' counts in '99 is the American League's Most Valuable Player:

**Lowest Percentage of Pitches Seen in Hitters' Counts—1999**

| Player, Team | PA | Total | Ahead | Pct |
| --- | --- | --- | --- | --- |
| Ivan Rodriguez, Tex | 630 | 2,072 | 379 | 18.3 |
| Cristian Guzman, Min | 456 | 1,546 | 300 | 19.4 |
| Mike Benjamin, Pit | 404 | 1,483 | 288 | 19.4 |
| Richie Sexson, Cle | 525 | 1,960 | 404 | 20.6 |
| Alex Gonzalez, Fla | 591 | 2,073 | 433 | 20.9 |
| Geoff Jenkins, Mil | 493 | 1,755 | 371 | 21.1 |
| Homer Bush, Tor | 523 | 1,869 | 396 | 21.2 |
| Marty Cordova, Min | 488 | 1,868 | 397 | 21.3 |
| Deivi Cruz, Det | 553 | 1,738 | 371 | 21.3 |
| John Flaherty, TB | 482 | 1,554 | 333 | 21.4 |

(minimum 400 PA)

Seeing Pudge Rodriguez here is a bit of a surprise, but otherwise there's nothing unusual about having two rookies and two second-year players on the list. Patience at the plate takes time to learn. Just ask John Flaherty and Mike Benjamin, two veterans with poor OBPs who still haven't developed a knack for getting ahead in the count.

Let's see how these guys do when they get ahead in the count:

### Production Ahead in the Count—1999

| | Season Totals | | | Ahead in the Count | | |
|---|---|---|---|---|---|---|
| | Avg | OBP | Slg | AVG | OBP | SLG |
| Ivan Rodriguez | .332 | .356 | .558 | .360 | .398 | .523 |
| Cristian Guzman | .226 | .267 | .276 | .286 | .386 | .386 |
| Mike Benjamin | .247 | .288 | .364 | .443 | .521 | .705 |
| Richie Sexson | .255 | .305 | .514 | .421 | .467 | .832 |
| Alex Gonzalez | .277 | .308 | .430 | .415 | .462 | .723 |
| Geoff Jenkins | .313 | .371 | .564 | .398 | .495 | .771 |
| Homer Bush | .320 | .353 | .421 | .402 | .474 | .537 |
| Marty Cordova | .285 | .365 | .464 | .319 | .490 | .556 |
| Deivi Cruz | .284 | .302 | .427 | .333 | .371 | .491 |
| John Flaherty | .278 | .310 | .415 | .274 | .355 | .453 |

The numbers this group produced when ahead of pitchers could make these guys the poster children for the benefits of working the count. Especially the young quartet of Homer Bush, Richie Sexson, Alex Gonzalez and Geoff Jenkins, who performed extremely well in hitters' counts and have the most to gain by learning that lesson well.

Unfortunately for those four, the at-bats they recorded when ahead in the count are about half of what the leaders in hitters' counts posted in '99. Maybe that's a good thing for the American League's MVP. While Rodriguez' average and OBP rose a bit in those 111 at-bats in hitters' counts, his slugging percentage of .523 was *lower* than his .558 mark for the entire season.

—Thom Henninger

A more complete listing for this category can be found on page 241.

## Can They Foul 'Em Off on Purpose?

This question comes from reader Tim Mauro, who originally asked it of our old colleague, ESPN.com columnist Rob Neyer. Rob passed the question along to us as perfect material for the *Scoreboard*:

*Rob,*

*Here's a quote from Joe Morgan from last night's Game 5 of the NLCS (quoted from the Oct 19, 1999 NY Times):*

*"Guys like Tony Gwynn keep fouling off pitches until you make a mistake. Carew and Brett could do it. Normal hitters don't do it."*

*Morgan is not alone, of course; I hear this said all the time by other announcers. Any opinion?*

This is indeed an intriguing question, and you do hear announcers rave about the ability of Gwynn, Wade Boggs, etc., to do it. So let's look at some data from the 1999 season. Here are the players with the greatest percentage of fouls on swings with two strikes (minimum 400 total plate appearances):

### Highest Percentage of Fouls on Swings With Two Strikes—1999

| Player, Team | Swung | Fouled | Pct |
|---|---|---|---|
| Jeromy Burnitz, Mil | 423 | 198 | 46.8 |
| Derek Jeter, NYY | 414 | 192 | 46.4 |
| Jorge Posada, NYY | 257 | 118 | 45.9 |
| Brian Daubach, Bos | 303 | 139 | 45.9 |
| Tino Martinez, NYY | 399 | 181 | 45.4 |
| Scott Rolen, Phi | 347 | 155 | 44.7 |
| Tony Fernandez, Tor | 309 | 137 | 44.3 |
| Dave Nilsson, Mil | 250 | 108 | 43.2 |
| Dave Martinez, TB | 359 | 155 | 43.2 |
| Kevin Young, Pit | 502 | 216 | 43.0 |
| **MLB Average** | | | **37.4** |

(minimum 400 PA)

An interesting list, to be sure, but not what we'd expect to see. Derek Jeter does seem like the sort of batsman who would be adept at fouling off pitches he didn't like until he gets a fat one to cream. Ditto for Scott Rolen and that smart old veteran, Tony Fernandez. But Jeromy Burnitz, the most skilled fouler-offer in baseball? He struck out 124 times in only 467 at-bats last year, and had 158 Ks in 1998. That doesn't seem like a skilled batsman to us. Apart from the presence of three Yankees in the top five (Jorge Posada, master batsman?), nothing jumps out at you.

Now here are the hitters with the *lowest* percentage of two-strike fouls in 1999:

**Lowest Percentage of Fouls on Swings With Two Strikes—1999**

| Player, Team | Swung | Fouled | Pct |
|---|---|---|---|
| Tony Gwynn, SD | 154 | 40 | 26.0 |
| Eric Young, LA | 227 | 65 | 28.6 |
| Damion Easley, Det | 340 | 101 | 29.7 |
| Magglio Ordonez, CWS | 333 | 99 | 29.7 |
| Shane Andrews, Mon-ChC | 205 | 61 | 29.8 |
| Raul Mondesi, LA | 320 | 96 | 30.0 |
| Richie Sexson, Cle | 308 | 93 | 30.2 |
| Einar Diaz, Cle | 198 | 60 | 30.3 |
| Roger Cedeno, NYM | 287 | 87 | 30.3 |
| Matt Lawton, Min | 179 | 55 | 30.7 |

Look at the name at the top of the list: Tony Gwynn! Instead of being the kind of hitter who fouls off a lot of two-strike pitches, which is what we've been led to believe, Gwynn fouled off fewer two-strike pitches in 1999 than anyone in baseball, on a per-swing basis. It's no fluke, either. We ranked all the hitters who had a minimum of 1,500 plate appearances in the 1990s, and Gwynn ranked 14th from the bottom with a two-strike foul percentage of 31.8. Who would think we'd find Gwynn among such wild swingers as Raul Mondesi, Richie Sexson and Shane Andrews?

The team data is not easy to explain, either. The Yankees had the highest percentage of two-strike fouls last year (40.3 percent), which fits their reputation as a disciplined team which makes pitchers work. At the other end of the spectrum, the teams with the lowest percentages of two-strike fouls were two clubs generally known for their lack of plate discipline, the Cubs (35.0) and Angels (35.5). But ranking just behind New York at the top of the list were the Brewers (39.8), Blue Jays (39.2) and Orioles (39.0), none of whom have anything like the Yankees' reputation for disciplined hitting and working long counts. A developing team which *has* that reputation, the Athletics, had one of the lowest percentages of two-strike fouls (36.0) in 1999, as did the Astros (35.6), who led the National League in walks.

*Baseball Scoreboard*

All in all, there's little evidence that the great hitters possess some sort of supernatural ability to foul off two-strike pitches until they get one they like. There may be some truth to the idea that in an individual at-bat against a tough pitcher, a hitter with good bat control will be able to foul off a few pitches he has trouble with until he gets one he can handle. Those are the at-bats Joe Morgan was talking about. But as a regular part of a hitter's arsenal, a calculated weapon to wear pitchers out, a skill which explains why the great hitters are great and the lousy ones are lousy. . . there's no evidence that such a skill really exists. Putting it another way, it's not Tony Gwynn's ability to hit the ball foul that makes him a great hitter. It's his ability to hit the ball fair.

—Don Zminda

A more complete listing for this category can be found on page 242.

## Who Bagged the Most Runs Created?

He didn't bat .379 like Larry Walker. He didn't slam 65 homers like Mark McGwire. He didn't drive in 165 runs like Manny Ramirez. But no one in baseball created more runs last year than Jeff Bagwell.

Runs created has been a popular statistic since Bill James introduced it in his *Baseball Abstracts* in the 1980s. Revised several times, the formula expresses how many runs a player contributed to his team.

The two biggest components of runs created are a player's ability to get on base and produce for power. Bagwell ranked second in the majors in on-base percentage (.454) and 11th in slugging percentage (.591). Runs created also rewards a player who can steal bases at an efficient rate, and Bagwell swiped 30 bases while getting caught just 11 times. He also gets a boost for being especially dangerous with runners in scoring position (batting .331) and for hitting homers at a higher rate with men on base (22 in 271 at-bats, compared to 20 in 291 at-bats with no one on). And he was in the lineup for all 162 of Houston's games, so he didn't lose any opportunities while he was sitting on the bench.

All told, Bagwell created 157 runs. That was seven more than Ramirez, his closest pursuer:

THE RUN MAKERS 1999 — Runs created

| Player | Runs created |
|---|---|
| Jeff Bagwell | 157 |
| Manny Ramirez | 150 |
| Rafael Palmeiro | 147 |
| Derek Jeter | 146 |
| Mark McGwire | 145 |
| Chipper Jones | 144 |
| Roberto Alomar | 142 |
| Ken Griffey Jr. | 140 |
| Jason Giambi | 136 |
| Vladimir Guerrero | 134 |

Sammy Sosa, who had 63 home runs, finished 11th with 131 runs created. Though he hit 10 points higher and had 34 more total bases while playing nine more games than his home-run rival, Mark McGwire, Sosa created 14 fewer runs. The reason was that McGwire's .424 on-base percentage and .697 slugging percentage dwarfed Sosa's marks of .367 and .635, respectively.

While he ranked first in runs created, Bagwell didn't fare quite as well in terms of offensive winning percentage, an offshoot of runs created. OWP represents the winning percentage a team of nine of the same hitter would compile against a club of nine average hitters, assuming pitching and defense to be equal. Bagwell slipped to fourth on the list, with Larry Walker taking top honors for the second time in three seasons:

**Highest Offensive Winning Percentage—1999**

| Player, Team | OWP |
|---|---|
| Larry Walker, Col | .848 |
| Manny Ramirez, Cle | .812 |
| Mark McGwire, StL | .797 |
| Jeff Bagwell, Hou | .796 |
| Chipper Jones, Atl | .777 |
| Rafael Palmeiro, Tex | .776 |
| Brian Giles, Pit | .768 |
| Bobby Abreu, Phi | .755 |
| Nomar Garciaparra, Bos | .754 |
| Carl Everett, Hou | .750 |
| **MLB Average** | **.500** |

(minimum 502 PA)

This list also highlights three outfielders who had breakthrough seasons in 1999: Brian Giles, Bobby Abreu and Carl Everett. A team of nine Gileses would have gone 124-38. That's certainly impressive, though that club would have finished 13 games behind the Walkers, who would have gone 137-25.

—Jim Callis

A more complete listing for this category can be found on page 244.

## Who's Second to None?

At the beginning of the 1900s, batting average was considered the ultimate statistic for a hitter. Fans followed the batting races with great interest, and at one point the Chalmers automobile company gave new cars to the winners.

At the beginning of the 2000s, it's known that batting average provides far from a complete picture of a player's worth. While there's still interest in the batting races, the fervor has died down. With power a much bigger part of the game than it was during the dead-ball era, we have learned to look at what a player contributes to the offense besides reaching base via a hit.

Bill James did exactly that when he introduced the concept of secondary average. The formula:

Secondary Average = (TB - H + BB + SB - CS) / AB

The secondary average for the entire majors was .281 last year, the highest in major league history in seasons where all of the needed data is available. As home-run rates have risen to unprecedented levels, so too has secondary average. It also hasn't hurt that walk rates are at their highest since the 1950s.

The 1999 leader in secondary average should come as no surprise. Mark McGwire combines unmatched power with exceptional patience at the plate:

### Highest Secondary Average—1999

| Player, Team | Sec |
|---|---|
| Mark McGwire, StL | .674 |
| Jeff Bagwell, Hou | .585 |
| Chipper Jones, Atl | .575 |
| Jim Thome, Cle | .520 |
| Manny Ramirez, Cle | .510 |
| John Jaha, Oak | .505 |
| Jeromy Burnitz, Mil | .495 |
| Brian Giles, Pit | .489 |
| Larry Walker, Col | .477 |
| Rafael Palmeiro, Tex | .474 |
| **MLB Average** | **.281** |

(minimum 502 PA)

McGwire topped all players in secondary average for the third time in four seasons. His .674 mark is the second-highest mark in National League history, trailing only his .774 from a year ago. The all-time record is held by Babe Ruth, who celebrated the advent of the lively ball with an .825 secondary average in 1920.

"Lively" is definitely not a word associated with Mike Caruso's bat. His .306 batting average as a rookie in 1998 was exposed by his .141 secondary average, the worst among American League qualifiers. Last season he was even worse, plummeting 60 points to post the poorest secondary average in the majors:

**Lowest Secondary Average—1999**

| Player, Team | Sec |
| --- | --- |
| Mike Caruso, CWS | .081 |
| Rey Sanchez, KC | .134 |
| Miguel Cairo, TB | .157 |
| Deivi Cruz, Det | .160 |
| Rey Ordonez, NYM | .162 |
| Mark Grudzielanek, LA | .174 |
| Neifi Perez, Col | .175 |
| Alex Gonzalez, Fla | .177 |
| Darren Lewis, Bos | .177 |
| Mark Kotsay, Fla | .192 |

(minimum 502 PA)

It's difficult to put up an .081 secondary average. That was the lowest for a batting qualifier in 10 years, since Alvaro Espinoza had an .078 mark in 1989. How did Caruso do it? By eschewing the walk (20 in 136 games) and the extra-base hit (17) while being a disaster as a basestealer (an AL-high 14 caught stealings in just 26 attempts).

No wonder the White Sox traded for Jose Valentin during the offseason. Valentin batted just .227 last year, 23 points worse than Caruso, but his secondary average was a sterling .383.

—Jim Callis

A more complete listing for this category can be found on page 246.

## Who Puts 'Em Ahead?

In a way, the go-ahead RBI is an offshoot of the game-winning RBI, a much-criticized stat of the 1970s and '80s which credited hitters for driving in the run that gave their team the lead for good. People knocked the game-winning RBI because a player could earn one for giving his team the lead in the first inning, and first-inning RBI usually aren't thought of as crucial or clutch. In actuality, that argument is rather short-sighted, as taking the lead *any time* puts a team well on the road to victory. In 1999, for example, major league teams won more than 64 percent of the games in which they took the lead in the first inning, with the percentage going up from there as you'd expect. Clearly, giving your team the lead any time is important, even in the first:

### Winning Game After Taking Lead in Inning—1999

| Inning | Won Game | Took Lead | Pct |
|---|---|---|---|
| 1 | 917 | 1,421 | .645 |
| 2 | 420 | 645 | .651 |
| 3 | 323 | 496 | .651 |
| 4 | 263 | 387 | .680 |
| 5 | 213 | 294 | .724 |
| 6 | 197 | 272 | .724 |
| 7 | 176 | 231 | .762 |
| 8 | 177 | 204 | .868 |
| 9 | 172 | 178 | .966 |
| 10+ | 174 | 181 | .961 |

A more fundamental criticism of the game-winning RBI was that it depended in part not on the hitter driving in the run, but also on the effectiveness of his team's pitching staff. In essence, two players could perform exactly the same action—putting their team ahead with an RBI in the first inning, eighth inning or whenever—but if one player's pitching staff blew the lead, he'd get no credit for a game-winner. That doesn't make sense. So for the past few years we've been compiling go-ahead RBI, a stat which simply measures the number of times a player drove in a run that gave his team the lead at any point during the game. Here are the 1999 leaders in go-ahead RBI:

**Most Go-Ahead RBI—1999**

| Player, Team | GARBI |
|---|---|
| Manny Ramirez, Cle | 41 |
| Matt Williams, Ari | 39 |
| Dante Bichette, Col | 37 |
| Vladimir Guerrero, Mon | 37 |
| Mark McGwire, StL | 34 |
| Mo Vaughn, Ana | 33 |
| Shawn Green, Tor | 32 |
| Ken Griffey Jr., Sea | 32 |
| Luis Gonzalez, Ari | 31 |
| Brian Jordan, Atl | 31 |
| Rafael Palmeiro, Tex | 31 |
| Sammy Sosa, ChC | 31 |

No real surprises here, as all these guys are big-time run-producers. But you can be a top RBI man without driving in a lot of those crucial runs which put the team ahead. Just ask Manny Ramirez. In 1998 Ramirez, drove in 145 runs, one of the highest totals in the majors, but only 25 of them were go-ahead RBI. Ramirez came back big in 1999, not only driving in 165 runs—the highest total for a major leaguer in 61 years—but also leading both leagues in go-ahead RBI as well with 41.

The critics of the game-winning RBI did have a point when they affirmed that a go-ahead RBI in the first inning doesn't carry the same pressure, or have quite the same effect on winning or losing, as one driven in during the seventh or eighth. All right, then—here are the 1999 leaders in go-ahead RBI from the seventh inning on:

**Most Go-Ahead RBI in 7th Inning or Later—1999**

| Player, Team | GARBI |
|---|---|
| Matt Williams, Ari | 11 |
| Chipper Jones, Atl | 8 |
| Rafael Palmeiro, Tex | 8 |
| Todd Helton, Col | 7 |
| Andruw Jones, Atl | 7 |
| Phil Nevin, SD | 7 |
| Henry Rodriguez, ChC | 7 |
| Sammy Sosa, ChC | 7 |
| 14 tied with | 6 |

Matt Williams, Chipper Jones and Rafael Palmeiro all had reputations for driving in a lot of big, late-inning runs last year, and those reputations were obviously well-deserved. But were they one-year wonders? Here are the players with the most late-inning go-ahead RBI over the last five seasons:

**Most Go-Ahead RBI in 7th Inning or Later—1995-99**

| Player | GARBI |
|---|---|
| Dante Bichette | 33 |
| Rafael Palmeiro | 29 |
| Chipper Jones | 29 |
| Sammy Sosa | 27 |
| Tino Martinez | 26 |
| Barry Bonds | 25 |
| Mo Vaughn | 24 |
| Eric Karros | 24 |
| 7 tied with | 23 |

Palmeiro, Jones and Williams (one of the seven players tied with 23) all rank high on the five-year list as well, but the overall leader is a player who was traded over the winter. Dante Bichette, Mr. Clutch? The Reds certainly hope so.

—Don Zminda

A more complete listing for this category can be found on page 248.

## Who Are the Real RBI Kings?

**M**anny Ramirez was Mr. RBI last year, plating an astonishing 165 runners. That not only was 17 more ribbies than any other major league player produced in 1999, but also the highest total for any big leaguer since 1938. As outstanding as Ramirez' performance was, however, he benefited by being part of a potent Indians offense that constantly was putting runners on base for him. Before we can say that Ramirez was the most effective run producer of 1999, we need to know how many runs he drove in *per opportunity*, compared with other players.

**Manny Ramirez**

There are various ways of measuring RBI productivity, but we continue to prefer the method suggested a few years ago by reader Bill Penn. In this system, RBI available are the number of RBI a hitter would accumulate if he homered every time he came to bat. Thus an at-bat with the bases loaded counts as four RBI available, while an AB with the bases empty counts as one. There's one exception: if a batter comes to the plate and reaches base via a walk, hit by pitch or catcher's interference, we don't charge him with any RBI opportunities unless a run scores as a result of the play. The reason is simple: reaching base is a positive act which increases a team's run potential, and it doesn't make sense to penalize the hitter for doing something which benefits his team.

So is Ramirez the real RBI king or not? Here are the 1999 leaders in RBI per opportunity:

### Most RBI Per Opportunity—1999

| Player, Team | RBI Available | RBI | Pct |
|---|---|---|---|
| Mark McGwire, StL | 853 | 147 | 17.2 |
| Manny Ramirez, Cle | 965 | 165 | 17.1 |
| Larry Walker, Col | 731 | 115 | 15.7 |
| Rafael Palmeiro, Tex | 985 | 148 | 15.0 |
| Ellis Burks, SF | 651 | 96 | 14.7 |
| Barry Bonds, SF | 598 | 83 | 13.9 |
| Harold Baines, Bal-Cle | 745 | 103 | 13.8 |
| Sammy Sosa, ChC | 1,036 | 141 | 13.6 |
| John Jaha, Oak | 820 | 111 | 13.5 |
| Brian Giles, Pit | 854 | 115 | 13.5 |
| **MLB Average** | | | **8.4** |

(minimum 80 RBI)

Ramirez came close, but he was edged for the title by Mark McGwire, who managed to drive in 147 runs despite drawing 133 walks and playing for a Cardinals team that finished ninth in the National League in runs scored. What kind of handicap was McGwire laboring under? Let's compare the tablesetters of the Indians, who usually batted Ramirez in the cleanup spot, with those of the Cardinals, who had McGwire hitting third:

### Indians And Cardinals OBP by Lineup Spot—1999

| Spot | Indians | Cardinals |
|---|---|---|
| 1st | .378 | .349 |
| 2nd | .379 | .311 |
| 3rd | .406 | N/A |

Had he been batting fourth for the Indians last year, McGwire probably would have driven in 165 runs, if not more. That's not to denigrate the performance of Ramirez, whose RBI percentage was virtually the same as McGwire's. Ramirez had a remarkable year as a run producer. But so did Big Mac, who has led the majors in RBI percentage in four of the last five years. With all the hoopla over his home runs, we sometimes forget how great an RBI man McGwire is.

—Don Zminda

A more complete listing for this category can be found on page 249.

## Who Gets the Slidin' Billy Trophy?

At some point, legs slow down, vision blurs, reflexes deteriorate. It's inevitable. It's unavoidable. It's part of being human... unless perhaps your name is Rickey Henderson. At the ripe old age of 40, Henderson returned to the Big Apple and continued his assault on one of baseball's most unassailable records. On his way to helping lead the Mets to the playoffs, Henderson raised his career runs scored to 2,103, moving him into fifth place on the all-time list, just 142 runs behind Ty Cobb's record. His performance was further proof that he's one of the best leadoff hitters the game has ever seen. But here we are more concerned with whether Henderson was one of the best leadoff hitters of 1999.

Towards that end, we once again count the ballots and hand out the Slidin' Billy Trophy. The annual award, named for the legendary Slidin' Billy Hamilton, is given to the best leadoff man in the game. Hamilton perfected the art of hitting leadoff back in the 19th century. Not only did he cross the plate at least 100 times in 10 consecutive seasons, but he also scored a mind-boggling 192 runs in 1894. He finished with a *career* on-base percentage of .455, a mark that most of today's leadoff men only dream about. How did last year's crop stack up? Here are the '99 leaders in on-base percentage while batting from the No. 1 spot:

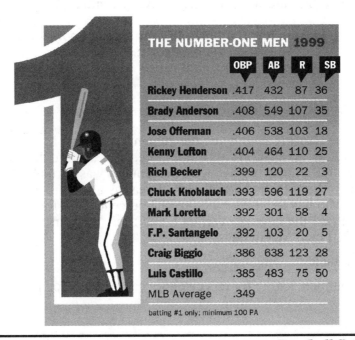

**THE NUMBER-ONE MEN 1999**

| | OBP | AB | R | SB |
|---|---|---|---|---|
| Rickey Henderson | .417 | 432 | 87 | 36 |
| Brady Anderson | .408 | 549 | 107 | 35 |
| Jose Offerman | .406 | 538 | 103 | 18 |
| Kenny Lofton | .404 | 464 | 110 | 25 |
| Rich Becker | .399 | 120 | 22 | 3 |
| Chuck Knoblauch | .393 | 596 | 119 | 27 |
| Mark Loretta | .392 | 301 | 58 | 4 |
| F.P. Santangelo | .392 | 103 | 20 | 5 |
| Craig Biggio | .386 | 638 | 123 | 28 |
| Luis Castillo | .385 | 483 | 75 | 50 |
| MLB Average | .349 | | | |

batting #1 only; minimum 100 PA

Henderson's overall .423 on-base percentage was his best mark since 1993, and he raised his overall career OBP to a lofty .405. Injuries made it tough to place him among our Slidin' Billy finalists, as he suited up for only 121 games, but he still deserves consideration. Here, then, are our other five '99 finalists:

**Brady Anderson.** The Orioles didn't rebound from a disappointing 1998 campaign, but Anderson did. After hitting just .206 with an on-base percentage of .317 from the No. 1 spot two seasons ago, Anderson came back with a much more respectable .286-.408 split last year. He also posted the second highest stolen-base total of his 12-year career.

**Craig Biggio.** The two-time defending Slidin' Billy champ made a strong case for a three-peat with 123 runs and 28 stolen bases while batting at the top of the Houston lineup. Though he failed to reach the 200-hit mark, he did top 50 doubles (56) for the second straight year. He now has scored more than 100 runs in five consecutive seasons.

**Chuck Knoblauch.** His throwing problems at second base aside, Knoblauch turned in another outstanding effort from the top of the order. He, too, topped the 100-run mark for the fifth year in a row. He also converted 28 of his 37 stolen-base attempts, and struck out just 57 times in 596 at-bats while hitting leadoff.

**Kenny Lofton.** A second-half slump that was exacerbated by a hamstring injury kept Lofton's numbers from possibly topping the charts. Considering he played in just 120 games, his total of 110 runs was very impressive. Still, like Henderson, his injuries make him a Slidin' Billy longshot at best.

**Jose Offerman.** Perhaps Offerman's most important contribution to the Red Sox last season was that he helped take the sting out of losing Mo Vaughn. Offerman set career highs in doubles (37), runs (107), RBI (69) and walks (96). He also led the AL in triples for the second straight season.

So now it's time for the envelope. The 1999 Slidin' Billy winner is. . . Craig Biggio by a nose over Chuck Knoblauch. Though Knoblauch won a World Series ring, Biggio edged him in batting average, slugging percentage, runs, doubles, RBI, walks and stolen bases while batting leadoff. The Houston second baseman becomes the first three-time winner of the award, and considering the fact that he's only 34 years old, a few more trophies aren't out of the question. Just ask Rickey Henderson, who still may be making this list when he's 44.

—Tony Nistler

A more complete listing for this category can be found on page 252.

## Who Are the Human Air Conditioners?

**B**asketball has "Air" Jordan, football has "Air" McNair, and baseball has "Air" Sosa? OK, maybe Sammy Sosa is better known by other monikers, but once again no one in the majors grabbed more air in 1999 than the Cubs slugger, who swung and missed a hefty 479 times:

Sosa has paced the bigs in this category in five of the past seven seasons, coming up empty on 2,743 swings over that span. But those misses are not what fans will remember. What they will tell their grandkids about are the 66 homers he hit in 1998 or the 63 he connected on last season. We can be pretty forgiving of hitters who miss a lot, as long as they also produce a steady stream of longballs. Such was the case for every player among the top five in swings-and-misses in '99, as they each earned their "air time" by connecting for at least 30 homers.

Of course, not every power hitter has to be so dramatic. Take 1999 MVP candidate Rafael Palmeiro, who cranked 47 homers while swinging and missing just 157 times. Barry Bonds also posted a fine ratio of 34 homers to 114 misses. The same could not be said of guys like Jay Buhner, Shane Andrews, Ruben Rivera and Todd Greene, each of whom finished among the top 10 last season in highest percentage of swings that missed:

| Highest Percentage of Swings That Missed—1999 | | | |
|---|---|---|---|
| Player, Team | Swung | Missed | Pct |
| Jay Buhner, Sea | 541 | 210 | 38.8 |
| Sammy Sosa, ChC | 1,363 | 479 | 35.1 |
| Shane Andrews, Mon-ChC | 689 | 239 | 34.7 |
| Ruben Rivera, SD | 925 | 315 | 34.1 |
| Paul Sorrento, TB | 585 | 197 | 33.7 |

| Player, Team | Swung | Missed | Pct |
|---|---|---|---|
| Dean Palmer, Det | 1,222 | 399 | 32.7 |
| Jim Thome, Cle | 1,029 | 331 | 32.2 |
| Todd Greene, Ana | 654 | 209 | 32.0 |
| Preston Wilson, Fla | 1,030 | 328 | 31.8 |
| Greg Vaughn, Cin | 1,180 | 368 | 31.2 |
| **MLB Average** | | | **20.1** |

(minimum 500 swings)

Buhner, Andrews and Greene each tallied more than 200 misses, but none hit as many as 20 homers. Rivera found himself below the Mendoza line by season's end. They all could take a lesson from the group at the other end of the spectrum, a group that always includes the king of contact himself, Tony Gwynn:

**Lowest Percentage of Swings That Missed—1999**

| Player, Team | Swung | Missed | Pct |
|---|---|---|---|
| Alex Arias, Phi | 574 | 40 | 7.0 |
| Omar Vizquel, Cle | 1,058 | 74 | 7.0 |
| Chuck Knoblauch, NYY | 1,108 | 80 | 7.2 |
| Orlando Palmeiro, Ana | 608 | 44 | 7.2 |
| Tony Gwynn, SD | 641 | 48 | 7.5 |

(minimum 500 swings)

Omar Vizquel, Chuck Knoblauch and Mark Loretta (1,047 swings, 92 misses) were the only members of the 1,000-swing club who came up empty fewer than 100 times last season. As for Gwynn, his legs won't be confused with Jordan's, his arm won't be confused with McNair's and his batting eye certainly won't be confused with Sosa's. Perhaps that's just as well, as "Air" Gwynn doesn't have much of a ring to it anyway.

—Tony Nistler

A more complete listing for this category can be found on page 253.

## Will the Rockies' Heart Survive a Double-Bypass?

Following a disappointing 72-90 campaign that saw them finish dead last in the National League West, the Rockies fired their GM, hired a new manager and headed to the ER for open-heart surgery. The heart of the order, of course, consists of the Nos. 3, 4 and 5 slots in the lineup, and the Rockies wasted no time retooling theirs once the season ended. They traded away both Dante Bichette and Vinny Castilla—two-thirds of a heart that was one of the strongest in the league in 1999:

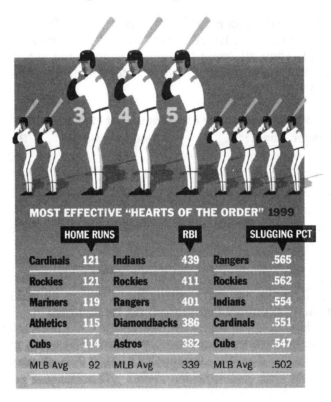

**MOST EFFECTIVE "HEARTS OF THE ORDER" 1999**

| HOME RUNS | | RBI | | SLUGGING PCT | |
|---|---|---|---|---|---|
| Cardinals | 121 | Indians | 439 | Rangers | .565 |
| Rockies | 121 | Rockies | 411 | Rockies | .562 |
| Mariners | 119 | Rangers | 401 | Indians | .554 |
| Athletics | 115 | Diamondbacks | 386 | Cardinals | .551 |
| Cubs | 114 | Astros | 382 | Cubs | .547 |
| MLB Avg | 92 | MLB Avg | 339 | MLB Avg | .502 |

The heart of the order for Colorado finished among the top two in home runs, RBI and slugging percentage, but Coors Field kept them from being our choice for the top ticker in the league last season. The distinction went to the Rangers, a team that also has undergone heart surgery.

**1. Rangers.** If not for a sixth-place finish in homers, Texas would have joined the Rockies as the only other heart to place among the top five in all three categories. The trio of Rusty Greer, Juan Gonzalez and Rafael Palmeiro was amazingly consistent, with both Gonzalez and Palmeiro slugging better than .600 while hitting from the Nos. 4 and 5 holes, respectively. With Gonzalez moving on to Detroit in the offseason, the question is: Who will keep the hearts of Rangers fans racing in 2000?

**2. Indians.** Had the heart of the order in Cleveland cranked out a few more homers, the Indians would have been in line for top honors—the race with Texas was *that* close. The addition of Roberto Alomar to an already healthy heart paid huge dividends, as Manny Ramirez and Jim Thome spent most of the year driving home their new teammate. Alomar led the league with 138 runs, while Ramirez tallied a gaudy 165 ribbies.

**3. Rockies.** The Rockies were our top choice in 1997, but that season Colorado's 3, 4 and 5 hitters actually enjoyed some success on the road. In '99, neither Larry Walker, Dante Bichette, Vinny Castilla nor Todd Helton were able to inflict much damage outside of Coors Field. To wit, Walker hit .461 at home last season but just .286 on the road, while Castilla pounded out seven fewer homers on the road than he did at home. Castilla and Bichette now will have to show some heart outside of Coors, while Jeff Cirillo figures to supply the fresh blood in Colorado in 2000.

**4. Cardinals.** The heart of the order in St. Louis continues to beat in the chest of one man. Mark McGwire accounted for more than half of the home runs hit by the Cardinals' Nos. 3, 4 and 5 hitters, and he fell just short of a .700 slugging percentage from his No. 3 perch. Without him, Nos. 4 and 5 hitters Ray Lankford and Fernando Tatis would have been little more than blips on an EKG.

**5. Athletics.** The A's surprising run in the American League West was fueled by a healthy heart that consisted primarily of Jason Giambi, Ben Grieve, John Jaha and Matt Stairs. Considering that all four sluggers produced career highs in home runs, one must wonder if Oakland's heart won't give out next year.

On the other end of the spectrum were the league's weakest hearts in '99. Though both the White Sox and Marlins received little in the way of production from the middle of their respective lineups, the heart of the order in Minnesota barely registered a pulse. With just 39 homers from their 3, 4 and 5 hitters, the Twins recorded just 105 longballs as a team—the lowest total in a non-strike year since 1993, when the expansion Marlins hit just 94. Forget the bypass... the Twins should be thinking about a transplant.

—Tony Nistler

A more complete listing for this category can be found on page 255.

## Who's the Best Bunter?

In an era in which sluggers rule, bunting has become a specialist's art. It's definitely not a *lost* art, however. There are plenty of great bunters around, and as usual, STATS can provide the proof.

Let's first look at the players who had the best success rates when attempting to sacrifice last year:

### Top Sacrifice Bunters—1999

| Bunter, Team | SH | Att | Pct |
| --- | --- | --- | --- |
| Omar Vizquel, Cle | 17 | 17 | 1.000 |
| Deivi Cruz, Det | 14 | 14 | 1.000 |
| Al Leiter, NYM | 11 | 11 | 1.000 |
| Rey Ordonez, NYM | 11 | 11 | 1.000 |
| Andy Benes, Ari | 10 | 10 | 1.000 |
| Greg Maddux, Atl | 13 | 14 | .929 |
| Dave Martinez, TB | 10 | 11 | .909 |
| Royce Clayton, Tex | 9 | 10 | .900 |
| A.J. Hinch, Oak | 9 | 10 | .900 |
| Mark Loretta, Mil | 9 | 10 | .900 |
| Miguel Tejada, Oak | 9 | 10 | .900 |
| Jose Vizcaino, LA | 9 | 10 | .900 |
| Tony Womack, Ari | 9 | 10 | .900 |
| **MLB Average** | | | **.755** |

(minimum 10 Att)

We awarded Cleveland's Omar Vizquel the coveted STATS FlatBat as baseball's best bunter in both 1997 and 1998, and Omar the Buntmaker was up to his old tricks in '99. On sacrifice-bunt attempts, our records report that the last time Vizquel failed to move a runner over when he laid down a bunt was way back in 1996. He was 16-for-16 in 1997, 12-for-12 in 1998 and 17-for-17 in '99. Pretty awesome stuff.

Vizquel wasn't the only player to post a perfect record when he attempted to lay down a sacrifice last year. Four other players were perfect on at least 10 attempts, including National League pitchers Al Leiter (11-for-11) and Andy Benes (10-for-10). Greg Maddux also ranked among the leaders in sacrifice bunt percentage, proving once again that he can beat you with his arm, his glove or his bat.

Bunting for a hit takes slightly different skills than bunting for a sacrifice: the bunter needs not only the ability to lay down a bunt while in motion out of the batter's box, but also the speed to beat the throw. Vizquel has this part down, also. He had more bunt hits than any other major league player last year:

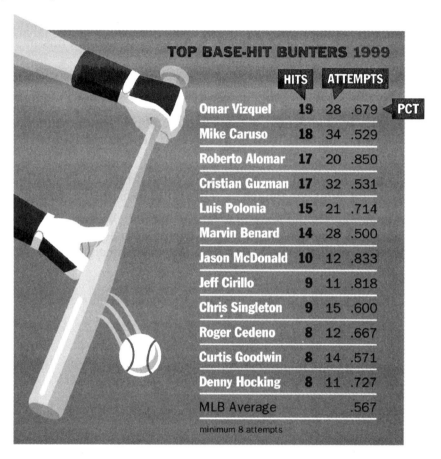

### TOP BASE-HIT BUNTERS 1999

| | HITS | ATTEMPTS | PCT |
|---|---|---|---|
| Omar Vizquel | 19 | 28 | .679 |
| Mike Caruso | 18 | 34 | .529 |
| Roberto Alomar | 17 | 20 | .850 |
| Cristian Guzman | 17 | 32 | .531 |
| Luis Polonia | 15 | 21 | .714 |
| Marvin Benard | 14 | 28 | .500 |
| Jason McDonald | 10 | 12 | .833 |
| Jeff Cirillo | 9 | 11 | .818 |
| Chris Singleton | 9 | 15 | .600 |
| Roger Cedeno | 8 | 12 | .667 |
| Curtis Goodwin | 8 | 14 | .571 |
| Denny Hocking | 8 | 11 | .727 |
| MLB Average | | | .567 |

minimum 8 attempts

Vizquel may have had the most bunt hits last year, but the true bunt-for-a-hit king in 1999 was the man who batted behind him in the Indians' lineup, Roberto Alomar. Alomar had 17 bunt hits in only 20 attempts for an astonishing percentage of .850. Since we began tracking this stat in 1990, the only player with a better success rate in a season (minimum 15 attempts) was—you guessed it—Vizquel, who went 19-for-20 (.950) in 1993 and 13-for-15 (.867) in '96.

*Baseball Scoreboard*

And now, the candidates for the 1999 STATS FlatBat Award, which goes to the best bunter of the year:

**Roberto Alomar.** Along with the 17 bunt hits in 20 attempts, Alomar had 12 sac hits. Problem is, he needed 17 attempts to do it for a subpar .706 sacrifice success rate.

**Mike Caruso.** Caruso's overall performance was a disappointment to the White Sox last year, but not his bunting. Along with 18 bunt hits in 34 attempts, Caruso had 11 sacrifice bunts in 13 tries.

**Cristian Guzman.** The Twins' rookie shortstop was one of the bunt-hit leaders with 17, and he also laid down seven sacrifices in nine attempts.

**Jason McDonald.** McDonald was a part-time player for the Athletics last year, but he was a fabulous bunter when given the chance: 10-for-12 in hit attempts, 4-for-4 on sacrifice tries.

**Omar Vizquel.** 17-for-17 on the sacrifice, tops in bunt hits with 19 and a superior bunt-for-a-hit percentage as well (.679). What more can a guy do?

And the winner of the STATS FlatBat for 1999 is Vizquel for the third straight year and the fourth time in his career. If there's ever a bunter's wing in the Hall of Fame, Omar will be a charter member.

—Don Zminda

A more complete listing for this category can be found on page 256.

## Who Was the Real "Man on the Moon" in 1999?

Forget Jim *Carrey* as Andy Kaufman—the real "man on the moon" in 1999 was the Indians' Jim *Thome*, whose 511-foot moonshot on July 3 was the longest homer in the major leagues last season. Thome also launched a 480-foot rocket on July 27, giving him a pair of entries on the list of longest home runs of '99:

Thome's 511-foot blast off Kansas City's Don Wengert at Jacobs Field made Thome the 10th player to join the 500-foot club since 1987. Of course, the two other sluggers to crack the barrier last season already are card-carrying members, with Mark McGwire picking up his 11th and 12th 500-foot homers of his career while Sammy Sosa notched his third. Big Mac has had at least two such bombs in each of the past three seasons.

As for the other names on the list, there are no real surprises. Besides the aforementioned big three, Glenallen Hill, Paul Sorrento and Brian Giles all carry big sticks as well. The one out-of-place entry from last season was Brant Brown, who tagged Willie Blair for 480 feet on June 9 at Tiger Stadium. The shot cleared the roof on the fly—the second-to-last roof shot ever at the now-defunct ballpark. Brown, whose next-longest homer is 440 feet, hit just 16 dingers all year.

Brown's 16 home runs were 112 fewer than McGwire and Sosa combined to hit in 1999. It's not surprising, then, that the two topped the list of players with the most homers of 450 feet or more last season. This time, however, Sosa finished on top:

**450-Plus-Foot Home Runs—1999**

| Player, Team | 450+ |
|---|---|
| Sammy Sosa, ChC | 11 |
| Mark McGwire, StL | 10 |
| Ken Griffey Jr., Sea | 5 |
| Jim Thome, Cle | 5 |
| Larry Walker, Col | 5 |

Last season, 95 home runs traveled at least 450 feet in the majors, up from 77 in 1998. Part of the reason for the increase was Sosa, who continued to wow his minions at Wrigley Field with his powerful cut—five of his 450-plus foot homers found a final resting place on Waveland Avenue. He also put on quite a show for the folks in Florida, hitting a pair of 460-footers and a 450-footer in one three-game stretch against the Marlins in mid-May.

McGwire was not far behind Sosa, thanks in no small part to Padres pitcher Andy Ashby. Ashby was the victim of three 450-plus foot McGwire shots in '99. But Ashby shouldn't feel too bad about serving up so much distance to one individual, as even the game's best aren't immune from McGwire's mighty swing (just ask Randy Johnson). When it comes time to make a movie about the life and times of Big Mac, you can bet that the working title of the film will be "Man on the Moon, Part II."

—Tony Nistler

A more complete listing for this category can be found on page 257.

# III. QUESTIONS ON PITCHING

## Did Martinez Have the Most Spectacular Pitching Season Ever?

Was Pedro Martinez the best pitcher in the big leagues last season? No question. He led the majors in several categories, including wins (23), ERA (2.07) and strikeouts per nine innings (13.2). Was he the most valuable player in the American League? A case certainly can be made for him, which we get into on page 12.

But in this section of the *Scoreboard*, we want to pursue a larger question: Was Martinez' 1999 performance the most brilliant by a pitcher in major league history? To answer that, we'll examine his season in a number of ways.

A pitcher's primary job is to prevent opponents from scoring. Martinez did exactly that last year, with an ERA that was 1.37 runs better than AL runner-up David Cone and 2.79 runs less than the Junior Circuit as a whole. Martinez' ERA index (league ERA divided by pitcher ERA) was 235.0, the eight-best figure in the 20th century:

Pedro Martinez

**Highest ERA Index—1900-99**

| Pitcher, Team | Year | IP | ERA | LgERA | Index |
|---|---|---|---|---|---|
| Dutch Leonard, BosA | 1914 | 224.2 | 0.96 | 2.73 | 284.4 |
| Greg Maddux, Atl | 1994 | 202.0 | 1.56 | 4.21 | 270.0 |
| Bob Gibson, StL | 1968 | 304.2 | 1.12 | 2.99 | 266.0 |
| Greg Maddux, Atl | 1995 | 209.2 | 1.63 | 4.18 | 256.3 |
| Walter Johnson, Was | 1913 | 346.0 | 1.14 | 2.93 | 256.0 |
| Three Finger Brown, ChC | 1906 | 277.1 | 1.04 | 2.62 | 252.7 |
| Walter Johnson, Was | 1912 | 369.0 | 1.39 | 3.34 | 240.1 |
| **Pedro Martinez, Bos** | **1999** | **213.1** | **2.07** | **4.86** | **235.0** |
| Dwight Gooden, NYM | 1985 | 276.2 | 1.53 | 3.59 | 234.9 |
| Christy Mathewson, NYG | 1905 | 338.2 | 1.28 | 2.99 | 234.5 |

(minimum 1 IP per team G)

Not all ERAs are created equal, however. ERAs can be distorted by the quality of relief pitching as it affects a pitcher's inherited runners, or by unusually good or bad luck. To remove those possible biases, Bill James created a statistic called component ERA that uses a pitcher's innings, hits, walks, homers and hit batsmen to show what his ERA should have been. Martinez' ERC of 1.79 was even better than his ERA, and his ERC index of 271.2 was the second-best since 1900:

### Highest Component ERA Index—1900-99

| Pitcher, Team | Year | IP | ERC | LgERA | Index |
|---|---|---|---|---|---|
| Greg Maddux, Atl | 1995 | 209.2 | 1.41 | 4.18 | 297.1 |
| **Pedro Martinez, Bos** | **1999** | **213.1** | **1.79** | **4.86** | **271.2** |
| Greg Maddux, Atl | 1994 | 202.0 | 1.59 | 4.21 | 265.6 |
| Pedro Martinez, Mon | 1997 | 241.1 | 1.79 | 4.20 | 234.3 |
| Walter Johnson, Was | 1913 | 346.0 | 1.27 | 2.93 | 231.5 |
| Sandy Koufax, LA | 1965 | 335.2 | 1.56 | 3.54 | 226.5 |
| Mike Scott, Hou | 1986 | 275.1 | 1.67 | 3.72 | 222.9 |
| Ron Guidry, NYY | 1978 | 273.2 | 1.71 | 3.76 | 219.7 |
| Walter Johnson, Was | 1912 | 369.0 | 1.52 | 3.34 | 219.4 |
| Randy Johnson, Sea | 1995 | 214.1 | 2.18 | 4.71 | 215.7 |

(minimum 1 IP per team G)

Greg Maddux' 1994 and 1995 seasons also have shown up on both lists, as have Walter Johnson's 1912 and 1913 performances. Martinez also posted the fourth-best ERC index while with the Expos in 1997. His ERA index of 220.8 (1.90 vs. 4.20) that year ranks 16th all-time.

Because we're interested in the most brilliant pitching season ever, we're going to look beyond mere efficiency and also look at dominance. One way to do that is to check out strikeout-walk ratios, which measure a pitcher's power and precision. Martinez struck out 313 batters while walking just 37 last year, giving him an 8.5 ratio. That's easily a record for a 200-whiff season and ranks third among ERA qualifiers in the 1900s:

### Highest Strikeout-Walk Ratio—1900-99

| Pitcher, Team | Year | IP | SO | BB | SO/BB |
|---|---|---|---|---|---|
| Bret Saberhagen, NYM | 1994 | 177.1 | 143 | 13 | 11.0 |
| Greg Maddux, Atl | 1997 | 232.2 | 177 | 20 | 8.9 |
| **Pedro Martinez, Bos** | **1999** | **213.1** | **313** | **37** | **8.5** |
| Greg Maddux, Atl | 1995 | 209.2 | 181 | 23 | 7.9 |

Baseball Scoreboard

| Pitcher, Team | Year | IP | SO | BB | SO/BB |
|---|---|---|---|---|---|
| Fergie Jenkins, ChC | 1971 | 325.0 | 263 | 37 | 7.1 |
| Cy Young, BosA | 1905 | 320.2 | 210 | 30 | 7.0 |
| Cy Young, BosA | 1904 | 380.0 | 200 | 29 | 6.9 |
| Walter Johnson, Was | 1913 | 346.0 | 243 | 38 | 6.4 |
| Christy Mathewson, NYG | 1908 | 390.2 | 259 | 42 | 6.2 |
| Juan Marichal, SF | 1966 | 307.1 | 222 | 36 | 6.2 |

(minimum 1 IP per team G)

Thus far, Johnson's 1913, Maddux' 1995, Martinez' 1999 are the only three seasons to make the top 10 on each list. In terms of sheer name recognition, this last chart may be the most impressive yet. Every retired pitcher included is a member of the Hall of Fame, including three of the four biggest winners ever in Cy Young, Johnson and Christy Mathewson.

The best way to measure how overpowering a hurler is may be strikeout-baserunner ratio. Finesse pitchers need not apply, because while they may be able to keep opponents off the bases, they're not going to send them back to the dugout shaking their heads. Martinez' strikeout-baserunner ratio last year was 1.52, easily the best in the century:

### Highest Strikeout-Baserunner Ratio—1900-99

| Pitcher, Team | Year | IP | SO | BR | SO/BR |
|---|---|---|---|---|---|
| **Pedro Martinez, Bos** | **1999** | **213.1** | **313** | **206** | **1.52** |
| Sandy Koufax, LA | 1965 | 335.2 | 382 | 292 | 1.31 |
| Pedro Martinez, Mon | 1997 | 241.1 | 305 | 234 | 1.30 |
| Randy Johnson, Sea | 1995 | 214.1 | 294 | 230 | 1.28 |
| Randy Johnson, Ari | 1999 | 271.2 | 364 | 286 | 1.27 |
| Randy Johnson, Sea | 1997 | 213.0 | 291 | 234 | 1.24 |
| Mike Scott, Hou | 1986 | 275.1 | 306 | 256 | 1.20 |
| Curt Schilling, Phi | 1997 | 254.1 | 319 | 271 | 1.18 |
| Dwight Gooden, NYM | 1984 | 218.0 | 276 | 236 | 1.17 |
| Luis Tiant, Cle | 1968 | 258.1 | 264 | 229 | 1.15 |

(minimum 1 IP per team G)

It must be noted that strikeout-baserunner ratio favors more recent pitchers because whiff rates continue to rise. Batters during Walter Johnson's era put a greater premium on making contact at the expense of power.

Martinez is the only man to rank in the top 10 on each list, though it's important to remember that each statistic was a percentage rather than a total. In a close call, we have to give Johnson's 1913 season the nod as the best ever.

Walter Johnson rates an edge because he worked in 346.0 innings, 132.2 more than Martinez threw last year. The only category in which the Big Train rated significantly behind Martinez was strikeout-baserunner ratio, and as we mentioned that was mainly because of the era he pitched in. Johnson's 1913 SO/BR was 0.87, which ranked 74th, but it was also 2.64 times the AL average of 0.33. By comparison, Martinez' 1.52 SO/BR last year was 3.30 times the league average of 0.46.

Of course, it's no disgrace to finish second to Johnson, considered by many to be the greatest pitcher of all time. On a per-game or per-inning basis, Martinez' 1999 performance was the best in baseball history. For the season as a whole, Johnson's 1913 was a bit better.

—Jim Callis

A more complete listing for this category can be found on page 258.

## How Long Can the Big Unit Dominate?

**R**andy Johnson's 1999 season was a tremendous accomplishment for a man of any age. He won the National League Cy Young Award after going 17-9 with a league-best 2.48 ERA and a career-high 364 strikeouts. Since 1900, only Nolan Ryan and Sandy Koufax have fanned more batters in a season.

Perhaps the most incredible thing about Johnson's '99 campaign was that he was 35. No player that age or older ever has come close to fanning 364 batters.

Randy Johnson

So how long can the Big Unit amass those kinds of strikeout numbers? If it's any inspiration, Ryan registered 301 strikeouts at the age of 42 in 1989.

Let's view the best single-season strikeout rates among pitchers at least 35 years old:

### Most Strikeouts Per Nine Innings, Season—Age 35 or Older

| Pitcher, Team | Year | Age | SO | IP | SO/9 |
| --- | --- | --- | --- | --- | --- |
| **Randy Johnson, Ari** | **1999** | **35** | **364** | **271.2** | **12.06** |
| Nolan Ryan, Hou | 1987 | 40 | 270 | 211.2 | 11.48 |
| Nolan Ryan, Tex | 1989 | 42 | 301 | 239.1 | 11.32 |
| Nolan Ryan, Tex | 1991 | 44 | 203 | 173.0 | 10.56 |
| Roger Clemens, Tor | 1998 | 35 | 271 | 234.2 | 10.39 |
| Nolan Ryan, Tex | 1990 | 43 | 232 | 204.0 | 10.24 |
| Nolan Ryan, Hou | 1986 | 39 | 194 | 178.0 | 9.81 |
| Nolan Ryan, Hou | 1984 | 37 | 197 | 183.2 | 9.65 |
| Nolan Ryan, Hou | 1988 | 41 | 228 | 220.0 | 9.33 |
| David Cone, NYY | 1998 | 35 | 209 | 207.2 | 9.06 |

(minimum 150 IP, age as of June 30)

While no one can top the Big Unit's strikeout rate, seven of the top 10 seasons come courtesy of Ryan, the ageless wonder. A list of the best two dozen seasons produces three active players who are at least 35—Roger Clemens, David Cone and Chuck Finley—and four retired hurlers—Ryan, Steve Carlton, Jim Bunning and Dazzy Vance. It's too hard to speculate on the fate of the active guys, but maybe the retirees can shed some light on Johnson's future.

**Nolan Ryan.** It's hard to use Ryan as a gauge because he defied the aging process. If it wasn't so lucrative to represent the painkiller Advil, he still might be pitching. He played seven seasons into his 40s, and in all but two he averaged a strikeout an inning. He averaged a mere 8.98 whiffs per nine innings in 1992—at the tender age of 45. His 2,465 strikeouts after the age of 35 ranks first all-time.

**Steve Carlton.** At age 37, Lefty won 23 games for the 1982 Phillies, and he collected 561 strikeouts in '82 and '83 combined. Despite a 13-7 record in 1984, his strikeout rate began to fade as he approached his 40th birthday that December. A strained shoulder in 1985 put Carlton on the disabled list for the first time ever at age 41, and he dropped off while playing for five major league clubs in the twilight of his career.

**Jim Bunning.** As a 35-year-old in 1967, Bunning posted his last solid season, going 17-15 with a 2.29 ERA and 253 strikeouts as the ace of a so-so Phillies club. That December he was traded to Pittsburgh for four players, but ankle, groin and hip injuries led to a disappointing 4-14 record in 1968. At age 37, Bunning rebounded to go 13-10 with a respectable 3.69 ERA in '69, but his strikeout rate started to sag. He wasn't the same pitcher in two final seasons after returning to the Phils.

**Dazzy Vance.** After not winning his first major league game until 1922 at the age of 31, Vance went 28-6 and won the NL Most Valuable Player Award in 1924 and led the league in wins again in '25. The Dodgers righthander had an off year in 1926, but he bounced back to post double-digit wins in the next six seasons. At the age of 37, he went 22-10 for the '28 Dodgers, and he fanned more than 1,200 batters between the time he turned 35 in 1926 and his retirement in 1935.

All but Bunning showed remarkable durability after their 35th birthday. Only occasional back troubles seem to put Johnson's longevity at risk. Otherwise, his arm suggests he can pitch for many years to come. After all, this is a 35-year-old pitcher who has accumulated 693 strikeouts over the last two seasons. Only Ryan has posted two-year totals better than that as a senior citizen of the game. Johnson may not have Ryan's longevity, but he figures to remain a good pitcher for at least several more years.

—Thom Henninger

A more complete listing for this category can be found on page 260.

## Who Threw the Most Pitches in a Single Season?

Until relatively recently, innings pitched were just about the only tool we could use to measure a hurler's workload. But in the last decade or so, pitch counts have become increasingly available.

The advantage of pitch counts is obvious when we consider that Kerry Wood needed 2,838 pitches to record 166.2 innings in 1998. Brian Anderson, on the other hand, needed only 2,819 pitches to throw over 40 more innings (208.0). Clearly, Wood expended much more energy per inning than Anderson did. While there were obviously many other factors involved, the strain that Wood put on his arm in '98 was probably a contributing factor to the torn elbow ligament he suffered in the spring of 1999.

STATS has been tracking game-by-game pitch counts for a while now. Unfortunately, similar information isn't readily accessible before the mid-1980s. But that doesn't mean we can't do something to try to estimate those pitch counts. Given more than a decade's worth of information, we should be able to come up with a formula that would provide a certain degree of accuracy.

We looked at the average number of pitches that were required to generate three simple events in the 12 seasons from 1988-99—strikeouts, walks and hits. Here are the results:

**Pitches Per Event—1988-99**

| Event | Pitches |
|---|---|
| Strikeouts | 4.815 |
| Walks | 5.147 |
| Hits | 3.277 |

Keeping these rates in mind, it's possible to then compute the average number of pitches required to record all other non-strikeout outs. In other words, subtract all the pitches thrown while recording strikeouts, walks and hits from total pitches thrown, and then divide by the result of innings pitched minus strikeouts. By such a convention, we arrive at 3.160 pitches per recorded non-strikeout out.

Thus, to estimate the number of pitches thrown by David Wells last year, we really need only four of his stats:

**David Wells, Estimated Pitches Thrown—1999**

| Stat | No. | Rate | Pit |
|---|---|---|---|
| Strikeouts | 169 | 4.815 | 814 |
| Walks | 62 | 5.147 | 319 |
| Hits | 246 | 3.277 | 806 |
| Other outs | 526 | 3.160 | 1,662 |
| Total | | | 3,601 |

In actuality, Wells threw 3,499 pitches in 1999, a difference of 2.9 percent from our estimate of 3,601. Not all estimates are that close to reality. Greg Maddux, for instance, would have been expected to throw 3,340 pitches in order to compile his statistical line. However, he required only 3,044, a difference of 9.7 percent. Maddux is a rather unique case, though. He's such an efficient hurler that the pitch-count formula consistently overestimates his workload. In fact, since 1995, four of the six largest formula discrepancies involved Maddux.

The total combined pitch count difference, at least for pitchers throwing a minimum of 2,000 estimated pitches in a season since 1995, was 0.7 percent. The average individual difference for this group was 3.1 percent. Not perfect, but seemingly reasonable.

We believe the formula can provide some insights on usage patterns in the past. We want to be clear about that, and caution you about the uncertainty of what we've just measured. We really don't know if these rates have remained constant throughout the various eras of baseball history.

Do we really think these rates were the same in the days before the DH? How about during the power-pitching-dominated mid-1960s? The offensive explosion of the '30s? The dead-ball era? We don't have an answer. We have no evidence to support the contention that the rates have remained constant. On the other hand, we have no evidence to indicate they definitely haven't.

For the sake of argument and for the pure fascination of it, let's assume to begin with that these rates *are* relatively accurate at least back to the end of World War II. Using estimated pitch counts, here are the top 10 in pitches thrown in a season since 1946:

### Most Estimated Pitches, Season—1946-99

| Pitcher, Team | Year | Est |
|---|---|---|
| Bob Feller, Cle | 1946 | 5,791 |
| Mickey Lolich, Det | 1971 | 5,649 |
| Nolan Ryan, Cal | 1974 | 5,525 |
| Wilbur Wood, CWS | 1973 | 5,453 |
| Phil Niekro, Atl | 1977 | 5,442 |
| Nolan Ryan, Cal | 1973 | 5,338 |
| Wilbur Wood, CWS | 1972 | 5,336 |
| Gaylord Perry, Cle | 1973 | 5,279 |
| Phil Niekro, Atl | 1979 | 5,187 |
| Nolan Ryan, Cal | 1977 | 5,098 |

Nine of the 10 highest estimated pitch counts since 1946 occurred during the 1970s, when pitchers like Mickey Lolich, Nolan Ryan and Gaylord Perry—not to mention knuckleballers Wilbur Wood and Phil Niekro—were in their heyday. Clearly, that kind of heavy workload has gotten rarer in recent years. But if we apply the estimated-pitch formula farther, to 1890 (the rules setting three strikes for a strikeout and four balls for a walk came in with the 1889 season), the burden carried by pitchers in the 1970s would seem light compared to the workload borne by hurlers at the turn of the century:

### Most Estimated Pitches, by Decade—1890-1999

| Decade | Entire Decade | Single Season | |
|---|---|---|---|
| 1890-99 | Kid Nichols (58,182) | 1892 | Bill Hutchison (9,262) |
| 1900-09 | Cy Young (45,996) | 1904 | Jack Chesbro (6,266) |
| 1910-19 | Walter Johnson (48,101) | 1912 | Ed Walsh (5,718) |
| 1920-29 | Burleigh Grimes (42,331) | 1923 | George Uhle (5,335) |
| 1930-39 | Red Ruffing (37,247) | 1938 | Bobo Newsom (5,582) |
| 1940-49 | Hal Newhouser (38,340) | 1946 | Bob Feller (5,791) |
| 1950-59 | Robin Roberts (43,179) | 1953 | Robin Roberts (4,990) |
| 1960-69 | Don Drysdale (38,840) | 1965 | Sandy Koufax (4,888) |
| | | 1969 | Gaylord Perry (4,888) |
| 1970-79 | Phil Niekro (43,794) | 1971 | Mickey Lolich (5,649) |
| 1980-89 | Jack Morris (37,525) | 1980 | Steve Carlton (4,615) |
| 1990-99 | Greg Maddux (34,730) | 1999 | Randy Johnson (4,216) |

To give you an idea about the grain of salt you may want to take with these figures, Roger Clemens actually has thrown the most pitches since 1990, with 35,400. Johnson really threw 4,206 pitches in 1999, not the 4,216 estimated here. Yes, that's a lot, but Clemens actually threw a decade-high 4,260 pitches in 1996.

Irregardless, Johnson's and Clemens' figures both are dwarfed by the season Bill Hutchison compiled in 1892. "Wild Bill" chucked an estimated 9,262 pitches while toiling a whopping 622 innings that year. No, his arm didn't fall off, but his effectiveness sure did. The next season, his ERA jumped by two runs, while his strikeout-walk ratio deteriorated from 312-190 to a pathetic 80-156. He never really recovered, apparently becoming one of the very first victims of pitcher burnout.

—Jim Henzler

A more complete listing for this category can be found on page 261.

## Was Hampton the Best Combination Pitcher/Hitter of the DH Era?

Mike Hampton's 1999 batting exploits already have been covered in the essay, "Who Are Baseball's Best-Hitting Pitchers?" (see page 123). But Hampton, a member of the Astros before being traded to the Mets in the offseason, did more than swing some solid lumber last year. He was also one of the best pitchers in the game, going 22-4 and finishing in second place in the National League Cy Young Award voting. His combined pitching and hitting exploits made us wonder whether his '99 campaign was the best combination of pitching and hitting since the DH era began in 1973.

A simple way to produce a list of viable candidates is to list the pitchers with the largest combined total of pitching victories and batting hits in an individual season. Hampton had 22 victories and 23 hits for a total of 45. Is that the best combined total since '73? No, but it's close:

### Most Combined Pitching Wins Plus Batting Hits—1973-99

| Pitcher, Team | Year | W | H | Tot | W-L | ERA | Avg | Slg |
|---|---|---|---|---|---|---|---|---|
| Steve Carlton, Phi | 1977 | 23 | 26 | 49 | 23-10 | 2.64 | .268 | .402 |
| Phil Niekro, Atl | 1978 | 19 | 27 | 46 | 19-18 | 2.88 | .225 | .258 |
| Steve Carlton, Phi | 1982 | 23 | 22 | 45 | 23-11 | 3.10 | .218 | .317 |
| Dwight Gooden, NYM | 1985 | 24 | 21 | 45 | 24-4 | 1.53 | .226 | .280 |
| **Mike Hampton, Hou** | **1999** | **22** | **23** | **45** | **22-4** | **2.90** | **.311** | **.432** |
| Phil Niekro, Atl | 1979 | 21 | 24 | 45 | 21-20 | 3.39 | .195 | .244 |
| Fernando Valenzuela, LA | 1986 | 21 | 24 | 45 | 21-11 | 3.14 | .220 | .257 |
| Jim Rooker, Pit | 1974 | 15 | 29 | 44 | 15-11 | 2.78 | .305 | .400 |
| Steve Carlton, Phi | 1980 | 24 | 19 | 43 | 24-9 | 2.34 | .188 | .198 |
| Andy Messersmith, LA | 1974 | 20 | 23 | 43 | 20-6 | 2.59 | .240 | .354 |

(minimum 12 W)

Hampton's total of 45 wins-plus-hits puts him in a tie for third place behind Steve Carlton (23 wins and 26 hits in 1977) and Phil Niekro (19 wins and 27 hits in 1978). Niekro (1979) and Carlton (1982) had other seasons in which they matched Hampton's wins-plus-hits total, and Dwight Gooden (1985) and Fernando Valenzuela (1986) also had years with a combined total of 45.

But a deeper look into the numbers indicates that overall, no one could match Hampton. Jim Rooker of the 1974 Pirates was the only other member of the top 10 who batted .300, and Rooker had only 15 pitching victories compared to Hampton's 22. There were other pitchers farther down the list who could top either Hampton's batting average or slugging percentage, and other hurlers could top his win total or better his 2.90 ERA, but no one else pitched *and* hit so well in the same season. Since the DH era began, no one has pitched and hit as well in the same campaign as Hampton did in 1999.

How about if we went back farther? Here are the pitchers with the most combined wins-plus-hits since the lively ball era began in 1920:

**Most Combined Pitching Wins Plus Batting Hits—1920-99**

| Pitcher, Team | Year | W | H | Tot | W-L | ERA | Avg | Slg |
|---|---|---|---|---|---|---|---|---|
| George Uhle, Cle | 1923 | 26 | 52 | 78 | 26-16 | 3.77 | .361 | .472 |
| Wes Ferrell, BosA | 1935 | 25 | 52 | 77 | 25-14 | 3.52 | .347 | .533 |
| Carl Mays, NYY | 1921 | 27 | 49 | 76 | 27-9 | 3.05 | .343 | .434 |
| Burleigh Grimes, Pit | 1928 | 25 | 42 | 67 | 25-14 | 2.99 | .321 | .397 |
| Bucky Walters, Cin | 1939 | 27 | 39 | 66 | 27-11 | 2.29 | .325 | .433 |
| Red Lucas, Cin | 1927 | 18 | 47 | 65 | 18-11 | 3.38 | .313 | .373 |
| Jim Bagby, Cle | 1920 | 31 | 33 | 64 | 31-12 | 2.89 | .252 | .374 |
| Dizzy Trout, Det | 1944 | 27 | 36 | 63 | 27-14 | 2.12 | .271 | .429 |
| Curt Davis, StLN | 1939 | 22 | 40 | 62 | 22-16 | 3.63 | .381 | .457 |
| Don Drysdale, LA | 1965 | 23 | 39 | 62 | 23-12 | 2.77 | .300 | .508 |
| Walter Johnson, Was | 1925 | 20 | 42 | 62 | 20-7 | 3.07 | .433 | .577 |
| Don Newcombe, Bro | 1955 | 20 | 42 | 62 | 20-5 | 3.20 | .359 | .632 |

(minimum 12 W)

Hampton's total of 45 wins-plus-hits pales in comparison to guys like George Uhle, who had 26 wins and 52 hits for the 1923 Indians, or Wes Ferrell of the 1935 Red Sox, who had 25 wins and 52 hits. In fact, Hampton's total of 45 didn't even crack the top 100 since 1920. His batting and slugging averages, while impressive for the DH era, can't compare with the batting exploits of the pitchers of earlier eras. A few who stood out:

**Walter Johnson, 1925 Senators.** Everyone knows that Johnson was one of the greatest pitchers of all time, with more than 400 major league victories. But in 1925 Johnson not only went 20-7 with a 3.07 ERA, he also batted .433 with 42 hits and a .577 slugging percentage.

**George Uhle, 1923 Indians.** One of the best-hitting pitchers ever (.289 lifetime average), Uhle was extraordinary as both a pitcher and a hitter in several seasons. His best overall year was 1923, when he went 26-16 and batted .361 with 52 hits.

**Wes Ferrell, 1931 Indians and 1935 Red Sox.** A .280 lifetime hitter, Ferrell still holds the record for most career homers by a pitcher with 37. He also was an outstanding pitcher with six 20-win seasons. His best years for combining pitching with hitting were probably 1931 (22-12 on the mound along with a .319 average, .621 slugging percentage and nine homers, the last stat still the single-season record for pitchers) and 1935 (25-14 on the hill, .347 average with 52 hits and .533 slugging).

**Don Newcombe, 1955 Dodgers.** Since World War II, no one has combined pitching and hitting the way Newcombe did in 1955. On the mound he went 20-5, 3.20; at the plate he hit .359, slugged .632 and blasted seven homers.

**Don Drysdale, 1965 Dodgers.** A decade after Newcombe's big year, Drysdale had a season which rivaled it for pitching-hitting brilliance. Big D was 23-12, 2.77 on the mound, and he also batted .300 with a .508 slugging percentage and seven homers. When you factor in that Drysdale was playing in Dodger Stadium, one of the toughest hitters' parks ever, his batting exploits become even more remarkable.

**Carl Mays, 1921 Yankees.** One year after throwing the tragic pitch that killed the Indians' Ray Chapman, Mays went 27-9, 3.05 and batted .343 with 49 hits while helping lead the Yankees to their first pennant.

**Babe Ruth, 1915 Red Sox.** Though it took place before 1920, we should also mention the Babe's exploits in 1915, his first full year in the majors. Then a full-time pitcher, he went 18-8 with a 2.44 ERA while batting .315 with 29 hits and a .576 slugging average. He also hit his first four major league homers that year.

—Don Zminda

A more complete listing for this category can be found on page 262.

## Who Are Baseball's Best-Hitting Pitchers?

Contrary to popular opinion, some pitchers *can* hit. The pity is that a lot of the best hitters seldom get to swing a bat because they play in the American League. Take a look at the chart below, for instance. The pitcher with the top lifetime average, Allen Watson, began the 1999 season with the Mets but then spent the rest of the year with the Mariners and Yankees. Omar Olivares, the No. 2 man, worked for the Angels and Athletics in 1999 and hasn't played in the National League since 1995. That's a shame, because neither man has lost his hitting stroke. Watson batted 10 times during his stint with the Mets last year and had three hits, including a double. Interleague play gave Olivares a chance to hit six times in '99, and he had two hits, including a double, for a .333 average.

**ACTIVE PITCHERS WHO CAN HIT** — CAREER

| | AVG | SLG |
|---|---|---|
| Allen Watson | .257 | .343 |
| Omar Olivares | .238 | .341 |
| Livan Hernandez | .223 | .297 |
| Mike Hampton | .221 | .278 |
| Brian Bohanon | .218 | .279 |
| MLB Average | .147 | .184 |

minimum 150 career PA

Watson and Olivares ranked one-two when we ran this study a year ago, but Livan Hernandez, Mike Hampton and Brian Bohanon are new to the top five. Bohanon, whose .197 average last year included two doubles, a homer and seven RBI, actually saw his lifetime average go *down* in '99. He would have ranked among the top five earlier, but he didn't have enough plate appearances to qualify. Hampton and Hernandez, though, pounded their way onto the leaders list. The two ranked among the pitchers with the top 1999 batting averages:

### Best-Hitting Pitchers in Baseball—1999

| Pitcher, Team | Avg | OBP | Slg | AB | H | 2B | HR | RBI | BB |
|---|---|---|---|---|---|---|---|---|---|
| Mike Hampton, Hou | .311 | .373 | .432 | 74 | 23 | 3 | 0 | 10 | 7 |
| Carlos Perez, LA | .296 | .345 | .481 | 27 | 8 | 2 | 1 | 2 | 2 |
| Javier Vazquez, Mon | .286 | .333 | .333 | 42 | 12 | 2 | 0 | 5 | 3 |
| John Smoltz, Atl | .274 | .338 | .387 | 62 | 17 | 4 | 1 | 7 | 5 |
| Darren Oliver, StL | .274 | .303 | .329 | 73 | 20 | 4 | 0 | 6 | 3 |
| Livan Hernandez, SF | .270 | .288 | .397 | 63 | 17 | 2 | 2 | 8 | 1 |
| Rick Reed, NYM | .244 | .261 | .289 | 45 | 11 | 2 | 0 | 5 | 1 |
| Randy Wolf, Phi | .233 | .281 | .267 | 30 | 7 | 1 | 0 | 0 | 2 |
| Alex Fernandez, Fla | .233 | .233 | .465 | 43 | 10 | 1 | 3 | 7 | 0 |
| Pedro Astacio, Col | .233 | .241 | .279 | 86 | 20 | 2 | 0 | 7 | 1 |

(minimum 30 PA)

Critics of the DH will duly note that a few of these guys—Hampton, Darren Oliver and Alex Fernandez—began their careers as American Leaguers—and another one, John Smoltz, served his minor league apprenticeship in the Tigers system. Not that many guys could do this, but Hampton's major league hitting record shows a pitcher who's made fairly steady progress in learning how to hit:

### Mike Hampton's Major League Batting Record

| Year | Team | Lg | G | AB | R | H | 2B | 3B | HR | RBI | BB | SO | Avg | OBP | Slg |
|---|---|---|---|---|---|---|---|---|---|---|---|---|---|---|---|
| 1993 | Sea | AL | 13 | 0 | 0 | 0 | 0 | 0 | 0 | 0 | 0 | 0 | .000 | .000 | .000 |
| 1994 | Hou | NL | 44 | 1 | 0 | 0 | 0 | 0 | 0 | 0 | 0 | 1 | .000 | .000 | .000 |
| 1995 | Hou | NL | 24 | 48 | 7 | 7 | 0 | 0 | 0 | 0 | 4 | 14 | .146 | .226 | .146 |
| 1996 | Hou | NL | 29 | 42 | 9 | 10 | 1 | 0 | 0 | 3 | 4 | 11 | .238 | .319 | .262 |
| 1997 | Hou | NL | 34 | 73 | 6 | 10 | 1 | 1 | 0 | 8 | 5 | 21 | .137 | .190 | .178 |
| 1998 | Hou | NL | 32 | 61 | 3 | 16 | 4 | 0 | 0 | 2 | 7 | 12 | .262 | .348 | .328 |
| 1999 | Hou | NL | 34 | 74 | 10 | 23 | 3 | 3 | 0 | 10 | 7 | 18 | .311 | .373 | .432 |
| TOTALS | | | 210 | 299 | 35 | 66 | 9 | 4 | 0 | 23 | 27 | 77 | .221 | .292 | .278 |

Hampton must be excited to join a Mets staff that already includes Dennis Cook (.266 lifetime in 109 at-bats) and Rick Reed (.244 in '99). As Greg Maddux and Tom Glavine pointed out to pitchers everywhere last year, chicks love the longball. . . and they're in the right league to show their stuff. If only the Mets still had Allan Watson!

—Don Zminda

A more complete listing for this category can be found on page 263.

## How Bad Were Bowie And Hawkins?

It's a good time to be a major league hitter. Last year, there were more home runs hit per game than ever before, and scoring was at its highest level since 1936. Mark McGwire and Sammy Sosa eclipsed Roger Maris yet again, and Manny Ramirez' 165 RBI were the most in 61 seasons. Larry Walker became the first player in 68 years to hit .360 or better for three consecutive seasons.

It isn't a good time, however, to be a major league pitcher. The combined ERA for the American and National leagues in 1999 was 4.70, the second-highest mark in the 1900s. The only season that was more pitcher-unfriendly was 1930, when the big league ERA was 4.81.

That 4.70 ERA must have looked awfully good to LaTroy Hawkins. He got shelled for a 9.95 ERA in April, lowered that mark to 7.84 by the All-Star break and only could reduce it to 6.66 by season's end. Among ERA qualifiers in the 1900s, that was the fourth-worst performance ever:

### Highest ERA—1900-99

| Pitcher, Team | Year | IP | ER | ERA |
| --- | --- | --- | --- | --- |
| Leo Sweetland, PhiN | 1930 | 167.0 | 143 | 7.71 |
| Jim Deshaies, Min | 1994 | 130.1 | 107 | 7.39 |
| Jack Knott, StLA | 1936 | 192.2 | 156 | 7.29 |
| **LaTroy Hawkins, Min** | **1999** | **174.1** | **129** | **6.66** |
| Greg W. Harris, Col | 1994 | 130.0 | 96 | 6.65 |
| Chubby Dean, PhiA | 1940 | 159.1 | 117 | 6.61 |
| Darryl Kile, Col | 1999 | 190.2 | 140 | 6.61 |
| Nels Potter, PhiA | 1939 | 196.1 | 144 | 6.60 |
| Ernie Wingard, StLA | 1927 | 156.1 | 114 | 6.56 |
| George Caster, PhiA | 1940 | 178.1 | 130 | 6.56 |

(minimum 1 IP per team G)

Darryl Kile also struggled mightily last year. It's interesting to note that as bad as Hawkins and Kile were, Twins and Rockies fans saw worse efforts in 1994, when Jim Deshaies and Greg Harris got battered. Athletics pitchers had a rough time of it in 1939-40. Nels Potter had a 6.60 ERA in 1939, then Chubby Dean (6.61) and George Caster (6.56) turned in a tag-team effort the following season.

The worst-ever ERA belongs to Leo Sweetland, who had the misfortune of spending the bulk of his career pitching his home games in Baker Bowl, the Phillies' bandbox ballpark. Sweetland also held the distinction of having the highest career ERA (6.10) of pitchers who worked at least 500 innings. Now he's off the hook, as Todd Van Poppel (6.24) and Hawkins (6.16) have passed him in the last two years.

As tough a time as Hawkins must have had stomaching his bloated ERA, just imagine how Micah Bowie felt. He broke into the majors in late July with the Braves, then was shipped to the Cubs as part of a deadline trade for Jose Hernandez and Terry Mulholland. Bowie managed just two quality starts in 11 outings with Chicago, and was torched for a total of 12 runs in 2.2 innings in starts against the Giants and Padres at the end of August.

By season's end, Bowie's ERA had swelled to 10.24, the highest in big league history among pitchers with at least 50 innings:

### Highest ERA—1900-99

| Pitcher, Team | Year | IP | ER | ERA |
|---|---|---|---|---|
| **Micah Bowie, Atl-ChC** | **1999** | **51.0** | **58** | **10.24** |
| Steve Blass, Pit | 1973 | 88.2 | 97 | 9.85 |
| Andy Larkin, Fla | 1998 | 74.2 | 80 | 9.64 |
| Frank Gabler, BosN-CWS | 1938 | 69.2 | 73 | 9.43 |
| Reggie Grabowski, PhiN | 1934 | 65.1 | 67 | 9.23 |
| Todd Van Poppel, Oak-Det | 1996 | 99.1 | 100 | 9.06 |
| Willis Hudlin, Cle | 1936 | 64.0 | 64 | 9.00 |
| Bryan Rekar, Col | 1996 | 58.1 | 58 | 8.95 |
| Herman Besse, PhiA | 1940 | 53.0 | 52 | 8.83 |
| Glenn Liebhardt, StLA | 1936 | 55.1 | 54 | 8.78 |

(minimum 50 IP)

Since Steve Blass' control mysteriously deserted him in 1973, his 9.85 ERA had been challenged seriously just once, by Andy Larkin in 1998, before Bowie fared so poorly. Bowie can take some solace in that while he was the worst 50-inning pitcher of the 1900s, he's not quite the worst ever.

Charlie Stecher started 10 games for the American Association's Philadelphia Athletics in 1890, and the best that can be said about Stecher is that he was consistent. He lost all 10 of his outings, surrendering 78 earned runs in 68 innings for a 10.32 ERA. That was Stecher's first season in the majors and, not surprisingly, it was his last.

—Jim Callis

A more complete listing for this category can be found on page 265.

## How Many Records Did Orosco Set in 1999?

Jesse Orosco entered 1999 needing 47 appearances to pass Dennis Eckersley for first place on the all-time games-pitched list. Considering that Orosco had worked at least that many games in every non-strike season since 1982, it was inevitable that the record would become his. Orosco reached the milestone on August 17 against the Twins, when he retired the only batter he faced, Todd Walker, on a deep fly to center in the seventh inning of an 8-3 Orioles victory.

That workload was typical for Orosco in 1999. He pitched in 65 games for the Orioles, getting only one out 37 times and retiring no one on five occasions. All told, he worked just 32 innings, averaging .492 per game. While his appearance record gained some attention, this one didn't:

**Fewest Innings Per Game—Season**

| Pitcher, Team | Year | G | IP | IP/G |
|---|---|---|---|---|
| **Jesse Orosco, Bal** | **1999** | **65** | **32.0** | **.492** |
| Tony Fossas, Bos | 1992 | 60 | 29.2 | .494 |
| John Candelaria, LA | 1992 | 50 | 25.1 | .507 |
| Larry Thomas, CWS | 1996 | 57 | 30.2 | .538 |
| Tony Fossas, Sea-ChC-Tex | 1998 | 41 | 22.2 | .553 |
| Larry Casian, ChC | 1995 | 42 | 23.1 | .556 |
| Tony Fossas, Bos | 1993 | 71 | 40.0 | .563 |
| John Candelaria, LA | 1991 | 59 | 33.2 | .571 |
| Sean Runyan, Det | 1998 | 88 | 50.1 | .572 |
| Mike Holtz, Ana | 1998 | 53 | 30.1 | .572 |

(minimum 40 G)

Orosco barely edged out Tony Fossas, who claimed three of the seven lightest per-game workloads. All 10 of the pitchers on the above list were lefthanders who worked during the 1990s, which isn't surprising. Not until the last decade did lefthanded specialists come into vogue.

Southpaws from the 1990s dominate the list so much that the first pitcher from a previous decade to appear is Joe Hoerner, who ranked 61st with 32 innings in 42 games (.762) for the Braves and Royals in 1973. The first righthander to make it is Eckersley, who placed 76th with 39.2 innings in 50 outings (.793) in 1998, his final season.

We're still not done with Orosco, who established a third record last year. No pitcher ever has made more middle-relief appearances (games minus games started minus games finished):

### Most Middle-Relief Appearances—Career

| Pitcher | Relief G | GF | Middle Relief |
|---|---|---|---|
| Jesse Orosco | 1,086 | 473 | 613 |
| Paul Assenmacher | 883 | 275 | 608 |
| Mike Jackson | 828 | 377 | 451 |
| Eric Plunk | 673 | 234 | 439 |
| Larry Andersen | 698 | 267 | 431 |
| Dan Plesac | 808 | 386 | 422 |
| Tony Fossas | 567 | 149 | 418 |
| Rob Murphy | 597 | 181 | 416 |
| Kent Tekulve | 1,050 | 638 | 412 |
| Rick Honeycutt | 529 | 118 | 411 |

This mark didn't come without a fight. Paul Assenmacher opened the year with a 561-560 edge over Orosco, who tied him at 564 on April 16. The battle went back and forth, with Assenmacher taking the lead five different times and Orosco on two occasions, not to mention the seven other times they tied each other. Orosco finally took the lead for good on August 11, when he retired Wade Boggs in a one-batter appearance in a 4-2 win over the Devil Rays.

Orosco will add to his records with the Mets, who acquired him in a December trade for Chuck McElroy. Orosco posted a 2.08 ERA and didn't allow a homer after the All-Star break last year, so there's no telling how long he can last. He may not have to worry about Assenmacher, whose 8.18 ERA in 1999 was easily the worst of his career. After becoming a free agent in November, he didn't sign with the Braves until mid-February and is no lock to make the team.

—Jim Callis

A more complete listing for this category can be found on page 266.

## Which Pitchers Mop Up the Most?

Some fans bring their brooms to the game. Some pitchers bring their mops. But while the broom is generally a good thing, signifying a sweep of the opposition, the mop isn't so positive. Why are we talking about mops? We're referring to the relievers who are called upon to clean up the mess— to "mop up" in those situations when their team is losing by four or more runs. It's not a pretty job, but someone's gotta do it. Here are the pitchers who got stuck with mop-up duty the most in 1999:

**Most Appearances With Team Trailing by Four-Plus Runs—1999**

| Pitcher, Team | Mop |
|---|---|
| Dan Serafini, ChC | 21 |
| Sean Lowe, CWS | 20 |
| Rodney Myers, ChC | 19 |
| Onan Masaoka, LA | 18 |
| Mike Myers, Mil | 18 |
| Carlos Reyes, SD | 18 |
| Benj Sampson, Min | 18 |
| Rick White, TB | 18 |
| 8 tied with | 17 |

Clearly, the first requirement for making this list is that a player must pitch for a team that isn't afraid to lose. . . and lose big. In 1999, each of the seven clubs represented above finished the season below .500, with the Devil Rays, Twins and Cubs laying claim to the basements of their respective divisions. The Cubs lost 35 games by five or more runs last season, while the Twins (33), White Sox (32) and Devil Rays (32) weren't far behind. It's hardly surprising then that a trio of Windy City hurlers topped our mop-up group.

The next requirement seems to be either that a player must be young and unproven, or a journeyman who can eat some innings. A starter for much of his minor league career, the Dodgers' Onan Masaoka will be just 22 years old when the 2000 season opens. The Twins' Benj Sampson will be 24. But Rodney Myers, Mike Myers, Carlos Reyes and Rick White all will be older than 30. Unlike the yearly leaders in holds, who often move on to closing games, the hurlers who comprise this list probably never will make a living racking up saves.

We can track this category back to 1987, so we thought it would be fun to look at the pitchers who could be classified as mop-toting "experts."

**Most Relief Appearances With Team Trailing by Four-Plus Runs—1987-99**

| Pitcher | Mop |
|---|---|
| Tony Fossas | 109 |
| Rich Rodriguez | 104 |
| Mike Munoz | 103 |
| Chuck McElroy | 99 |
| Eric Plunk | 99 |
| Joe Boever | 98 |
| Paul Assenmacher | 94 |
| Jesse Orosco | 93 |
| Mark Eichhorn | 91 |
| Mike Maddux | 91 |
| Dan Plesac | 91 |

As is the case with all counting categories, longevity makes a big difference. Each of the above relievers has logged at least 11 seasons in the majors, with the one exception being Rich Rodriguez (nine). One thing to remember here is that we track mop-ups back to 1987, so we only have complete career totals for the top four players on the list. As for the others, we generally are missing one or two years of data, again with a single exception: Jesse Orosco. Orosco began his 20-seasons-and-counting stint in the big leagues in 1979, and he probably would top Tony Fossas in mop-up appearances if we could look at Orosco's entire career.

Still, let's give Fossas some credit, and perhaps some sympathy, for taking one for the team so many times. Considering that he's made it to the postseason just once in 12 years, it's probably a safe bet that Fossas is a lot more familiar with mops than he is with brooms.

—Tony Nistler

A more complete listing for this category can be found on page 267.

## Who's Toughest to Pull?

When we looked at the question of which pitchers were toughest to pull in the *Scoreboard* a year ago, our expectation was that the leaders list would be dominated by hard throwers. To our surprise, there were several pitchers on the list not noted for throwing hard, including Tom Glavine, Scott Eyre and Shayne Bennett. And *all* the Braves' pitchers proved tough to pull, whether they threw hard or not. Our conclusion was that while the ability to throw hard is an important factor in whether or not a pitcher is tough to pull, an equally crucial factor is location. If a pitcher consistently spots his pitches on the outside corner, as Atlanta's starters do, the hitters likely will tend to go the other way rather than make an effort to pull the ball. Does another year of data do anything to make us change our conclusions? The chart shows the results:

**TOUGHEST PITCHERS TO PULL 1999**

| | IN PLAY | PULLED | PCT |
|---|---|---|---|
| Tom Glavine | 763 | 177 | 23.2 |
| Dave Weathers | 286 | 76 | 26.6 |
| Anthony Telford | 311 | 88 | 28.3 |
| Roy Halladay | 499 | 147 | 29.5 |
| LaTroy Hawkins | 627 | 189 | 30.1 |
| Alex Fernandez | 442 | 137 | 31.0 |
| Chris Carpenter | 491 | 153 | 31.2 |
| Kevin Millwood | 606 | 194 | 32.0 |
| Justin Thompson | 470 | 152 | 32.3 |
| Jimmy Haynes | 462 | 150 | 32.5 |
| MLB Average | | | 37.7 |

minimum 400 batters faced; bunts and popups less than 70 feet excluded

This time Glavine advances to first place, but there are still a lot of power pitchers on the list. Hard throwers include Roy Halladay, LaTroy Hawkins (the only pitcher to make the top 10 both years, along with Glavine), Chris Carpenter, Kevin Millwood and Jimmy Haynes. As for the rest, there's nobody who was breaking any radar guns last year. Justin Thompson and Alex Fernandez threw hard on occasion in 1999, but arm and shoulder problems put them more in the finesse camp. Dave Weathers' fastball probably would be considered average at best, and Anthony Telford is definitely a junkballer.

As in 1998, guys you'd think *would be* at the top of this list are much farther down: Randy Johnson is 37th, for example, Bartolo Colon 38th and Roger Clemens 82nd out of 168. Meanwhile finesse guys like Mike Mussina (14th) and Greg Maddux (16th) rank near the top for the same reason Glavine does: they throw a steady stream of strikes on the outside corner. Here are the pitchers who were easiest to pull in 1999:

### Easiest Pitchers to Pull—1999

| Pitcher, Team | T | Hit | Pull | Pct |
|---|---|---|---|---|
| Al Leiter, NYM | L | 629 | 311 | 49.4 |
| Tim Wakefield, Bos | R | 433 | 211 | 48.7 |
| Jose Jimenez, StL | R | 517 | 248 | 48.0 |
| Jose Lima, Hou | R | 769 | 358 | 46.6 |
| Matt Clement, SD | R | 553 | 255 | 46.1 |
| Steve Avery, Cin | L | 285 | 131 | 46.0 |
| Steve Woodard, Mil | R | 621 | 285 | 45.9 |
| Charles Nagy, Cle | R | 679 | 310 | 45.7 |
| Chad Ogea, Phi | R | 576 | 259 | 45.0 |
| John Burkett, Tex | R | 489 | 219 | 44.8 |

(minimum 400 batters faced; bunt and popups less than 70 feet excluded)

As in 1998, the most surprising name on the list, at least at first glance, is the Mets' Al Leiter. Though decidedly a power pitcher, Leiter is known for working the *inside* corner, exactly the opposite style of pitchers like Glavine, Maddux and Mussina. To be sure, there are a number of soft tossers on this list—Steve Avery, John Burkett, Steve Woodard, Chad Ogea, knuckleballer Tim Wakefield—just as there are a number of fireballers on the hardest-to-pull list. Velocity or lack of same *is* an important factor in whether or not a pitcher is easy to pull. But where he puts the ball in the strike zone seems to be just as important.

—Don Zminda

A more complete listing for this category can be found on page 268.

## Which Pitchers Scored the Highest?

The game score, a Bill James invention, is a fun way of measuring how dominant a pitcher was in a particular start. It is compiled as follows:

1. Start with 50.
2. Add one point for each out recorded.
3. Add two points for each inning completed after the fourth.
4. Add one point for each strikeout.
5. Subtract one point for each walk.
6. Subtract two points for each hit.
7. Subtract four points for each earned run.
8. Subtract two points for each unearned run.

The key here is dominance: you get credit for allowing a low number of hits, runs and walks, but there's a big bonus for strikeouts. The top nine-inning game score of all time occurred in 1998, when Kerry Wood of the Cubs earned a score of 105 for his 20-strikeout, no-walk, one-hit shutout of the Astros. Wood missed the entire '99 season with arm trouble, and no one could come close to matching his legendary performance. Here are the top game scores of 1999:

### Highest Game Scores—1999

| Pitcher, Team | Date | Opp | W/L | IP | H | R | ER | BB | K | Score |
|---|---|---|---|---|---|---|---|---|---|---|
| Pedro Martinez, Bos | 9/10 | @NYY | W | 9.0 | 1 | 1 | 1 | 0 | 17 | 98 |
| Eric Milton, Min | 9/11 | Ana | W | 9.0 | 0 | 0 | 0 | 2 | 13 | 98 |
| David Cone, NYY | 7/18 | Mon | W | 9.0 | 0 | 0 | 0 | 0 | 10 | 97 |
| Kevin Millwood, Atl | 8/28 | @StL | ND | 10.0 | 2 | 0 | 0 | 1 | 9 | 96 |
| Javier Vazquez, Mon | 9/14 | @LA | W | 9.0 | 1 | 0 | 0 | 1 | 10 | 94 |
| Ryan Rupe, TB | 5/23 | Ana | ND | 9.0 | 1 | 0 | 0 | 0 | 8 | 93 |
| Jose Jimenez, StL | 6/25 | @Ari | W | 9.0 | 0 | 0 | 0 | 2 | 8 | 93 |
| Rick Reed, NYM | 10/2 | Pit | W | 9.0 | 3 | 0 | 0 | 0 | 12 | 93 |
| Pedro Martinez, Bos | 6/4 | Atl | W | 9.0 | 3 | 1 | 1 | 2 | 16 | 91 |
| Jose Jimenez, StL | 7/5 | Ari | W | 9.0 | 2 | 0 | 0 | 1 | 9 | 91 |
| Pedro Martinez, Bos | 9/21 | Tor | W | 9.0 | 3 | 0 | 0 | 2 | 12 | 91 |

Fittingly, the pitcher of the year, Pedro Martinez, turned in one of the season's two top game scores with his one-hit, 17-strikeout performance against the Yankees on September 10. The only hit allowed by Martinez was a second-inning homer by Chili Davis. Had Martinez pitched a shutout rather than giving up a run, his game score would have been 102.

Matching Martinez for the top game score was Minnesota's Eric Milton, who earned a 98 for his 13-strikeout, two-walk no-hitter against the Angels. The 13 strikeouts helped him edge the Yankees' David Cone, who scored "only" a 97 for his perfect game against the Expos on July 18.

I was fortunate enough to witness the season's only other no-hitter, a 1-0 gem by Jose Jimenez, then of the Cardinals, against the Diamondbacks at Bank One Ballpark on June 25. Jimenez needed to record a big game score the night he tossed his no-hitter, because the Diamondbacks' Randy Johnson was nearly as good. The Big Unit fanned 14 and allowed only five hits that night, with the only run of the game coming in the ninth inning on a single by St. Louis' Thomas Howard. The Jimenez/Johnson duel produced a combined game score of 178, but it wasn't the top pitchers' duel of the year, at least according to game scores:

**Best Pitchers' Duels—1999**

| Pitcher, Team | Date | W/L | IP | H | R | ER | BB | K | Score | Total |
|---|---|---|---|---|---|---|---|---|---|---|
| Darren Oliver, StL | 8/28 | ND | 9.0 | 4 | 0 | 0 | 1 | 6 | 84 | 180 |
| Kevin Millwood, Atl | | ND | 10.0 | 2 | 0 | 0 | 1 | 9 | 96 | |
| Randy Johnson, Ari | 6/25 | L | 9.0 | 5 | 1 | 1 | 2 | 14 | 85 | 178 |
| Jose Jimenez, StL | | W | 9.0 | 0 | 0 | 0 | 2 | 8 | 93 | |
| Ryan Rupe, TB | 5/23 | ND | 9.0 | 1 | 0 | 0 | 0 | 8 | 93 | 177 |
| Chuck Finley, Ana | | W | 9.0 | 3 | 0 | 0 | 4 | 7 | 84 | |
| Willie Blair, Det | 4/12 | ND | 8.0 | 3 | 0 | 0 | 0 | 4 | 80 | 162 |
| Eric Milton, Min | | ND | 7.1 | 1 | 0 | 0 | 1 | 7 | 82 | |
| Jarrod Washburn, Ana | 10/3 | W | 8.2 | 5 | 0 | 0 | 0 | 7 | 81 | 161 |
| Matt Perisho, Tex | | ND | 6.0 | 2 | 0 | 0 | 0 | 12 | 80 | |

(minimum 80 game score for each starter)

On August 28 at Busch Stadium, Darren Oliver of the Cardinals and Kevin Millwood of the Braves battled through nine scoreless innings, with each hurler pitching magnificently. Oliver allowed only four hits for the night, while Millwood permitted just two. Oliver was lifted for a pinch-hitter in the 10th, but Millwood added another shutout frame before leaving the game himself. The clubs battled scorelessly through 12 before the Braves broke through with three in the top of the 13th to win it. Some duel, especially in the slugging season of 1999.

—Don Zminda

A more complete listing for this category can be found on page 270.

## Who Are the High-Quality Starters?

The quality start—any start in which a pitcher works six or more innings while giving up three or fewer earned runs—still gets criticized in some circles, but it's a trusted stat among people who know the game. The reason? It correlates very highly with winning. In 1999, major league teams had a winning percentage of .689 (1,549-699) in games in which their starting pitcher recorded a quality start. . . and that included games where *both* pitchers had a QS. In games where one team's starting pitcher had a quality start but his opponent didn't, the team with the quality starter had a winning percentage of .879 (985-135).

The chart, which lists the 1999 pitchers with the highest percentage of quality starts (minimum 25 games started), is practically a Who's Who of the best starters in baseball, beginning with Cy Young Award winners Randy Johnson and Pedro Martinez. Mike Hampton, Kevin Millwood, Kevin Brown, Jose Lima, Orlando Hernandez. . . that's quality.

Probably the only real surprise is Masato Yoshii, a Met in 1999 and a Rockie in 2000. Yoshii is going to have trouble making this list two years in a row, however. With Coors Field giving pitchers the usual nightmares, Colorado starters had only 57 quality starts last year, the fewest in baseball. Led by Hampton and Lima, the Astros had the most quality starts, 104. Ranking behind the Astros in most quality starts were four other playoff teams, the Diamondbacks (98), Braves (96), Yankees (90) and Mets (87).

**THE QUALITY STARTERS 1999**

| | GAMES STARTED | QUALITY STARTS | PCT |
|---|---|---|---|
| Randy Johnson | 35 | 29 | 82.9 |
| Pedro Martinez | 29 | 24 | 82.8 |
| Mike Hampton | 34 | 27 | 79.4 |
| Kevin Millwood | 33 | 25 | 75.8 |
| Kevin Brown | 35 | 25 | 71.4 |
| Jose Lima | 35 | 25 | 71.4 |
| Orlando Hernandez | 33 | 23 | 69.7 |
| Masato Yoshii | 29 | 20 | 69.0 |
| Omar Daal | 32 | 21 | 65.6 |
| Al Leiter | 32 | 21 | 65.6 |
| Jamie Moyer | 32 | 21 | 65.6 |
| MLB Average | | | 46.3 |

minimum 25 GS

*Baseball Scoreboard*

The most notable name missing from the individual leaders list is Greg Maddux, who had 19 quality starts in 33 attempts for a 57.6 percent rate. That was well above average (the major league average last year was 46.3 percent), but far below Maddux' usual standards. From 1994-98, Maddux had worked a quality start in 80 percent of his outings, the top mark in baseball. His subpar '99 performance pushed him to second place behind Kevin Brown in our new five-year leaders list:

**Highest Quality Start Percentage—1995-99**

| Pitcher | GS | QS | Pct |
|---|---|---|---|
| Kevin Brown | 161 | 120 | 74.5 |
| Greg Maddux | 163 | 119 | 73.0 |
| Randy Johnson | 136 | 99 | 72.8 |
| Pedro Martinez | 156 | 109 | 69.9 |
| Tom Glavine | 166 | 114 | 68.7 |
| Denny Neagle | 148 | 101 | 68.2 |
| Curt Schilling | 137 | 93 | 67.9 |
| Ismael Valdes | 149 | 98 | 65.8 |
| John Smoltz | 154 | 101 | 65.6 |
| Mike Hampton | 151 | 97 | 64.2 |
| **MLB Average** | | | **47.4** |

(minimum 100 GS)

With Maddux, Tom Glavine and John Smoltz in the top 10, it's no mystery why the Braves keep winning.

—Don Zminda

A more complete listing for this category can be found on page 271.

## Whose Heater Is Hottest?

Ever since the first *Baseball Scoreboard* in 1990, we've presented an article listing the pitchers who averaged the most strikeouts per nine innings over the previous season. The title, as we note annually, is a bit of a misnomer, because some pitchers can produce a lot of strikeouts without possessing a high-velocity fastball. But the relationship between heat and strikeouts is pretty strong, and anyway, it's a catchy title.

This year we're presenting the data in a somewhat different form, splitting it into separate leaders lists for starters and relievers. That makes perfect sense, because relief pitchers work in short stints and don't have to worry about pacing themselves the way starters do. The graphic below shows the strikeouts-per-nine leaders among starting pitchers:

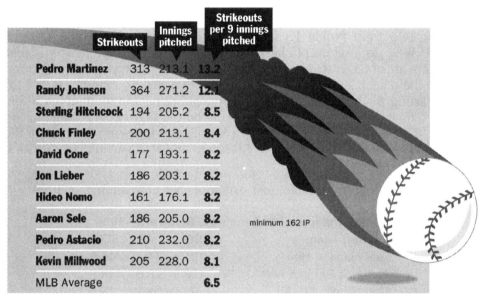

| | Strikeouts | Innings pitched | Strikeouts per 9 innings pitched |
|---|---|---|---|
| Pedro Martinez | 313 | 213.1 | 13.2 |
| Randy Johnson | 364 | 271.2 | 12.1 |
| Sterling Hitchcock | 194 | 205.2 | 8.5 |
| Chuck Finley | 200 | 213.1 | 8.4 |
| David Cone | 177 | 193.1 | 8.2 |
| Jon Lieber | 186 | 203.1 | 8.2 |
| Hideo Nomo | 161 | 176.1 | 8.2 |
| Aaron Sele | 186 | 205.0 | 8.2 |
| Pedro Astacio | 210 | 232.0 | 8.2 |
| Kevin Millwood | 205 | 228.0 | 8.1 |
| MLB Average | | | 6.5 |

minimum 162 IP

There was some history made in 1999, as American League Cy Young Award winner Pedro Martinez set a new record for most strikeouts per nine innings by an ERA qualifier. Martinez' feat didn't earn many headlines, because the previous record had been set just one year earlier by Kerry Wood of the Cubs. And it wouldn't surprise us if the record gets broken again in 2000. Of the 10 best seasons in strikeouts per nine innings by a pitcher with at least 162 innings, all of them have occurred since 1984:

### Most Strikeouts Per 9 Innings, Starters—1876-1999

| Pitcher, Team | Year | SO | IP | SO/9 |
|---|---|---|---|---|
| Pedro Martinez, Bos | 1999 | 313 | 213.1 | 13.2 |
| Kerry Wood, ChC | 1998 | 233 | 166.2 | 12.6 |
| Randy Johnson, Sea | 1995 | 294 | 214.1 | 12.4 |
| Randy Johnson, Sea | 1997 | 291 | 213.0 | 12.3 |
| Randy Johnson, Sea-Hou | 1998 | 329 | 244.1 | 12.1 |
| Randy Johnson, Ari | 1999 | 364 | 271.2 | 12.1 |
| Nolan Ryan, Hou | 1987 | 270 | 211.2 | 11.5 |
| Dwight Gooden, NYM | 1984 | 276 | 218.0 | 11.4 |
| Pedro Martinez, Mon | 1997 | 305 | 241.1 | 11.4 |
| Nolan Ryan, Tex | 1989 | 301 | 239.1 | 11.3 |

(minimum 162 IP)

Martinez appears twice on the list, along with four seasons from Randy Johnson, two from Nolan Ryan and one each from Wood and Dwight Gooden. Why do modern pitchers monopolize the list? One reason is that the stigma attached to striking out has pretty much disappeared for hitters. Most of them keep swinging hard even with two strikes. Another is that today's starting pitchers don't have to worry about pacing themselves in order to go nine innings, so they're throwing hard a bigger percentage of the time. A third is that there are simply a lot of hard-throwing pitchers in the modern game. Guys like Johnson, Martinez and Ryan would have struck out a lot of hitters in *any* era.

Here are the relievers with the most strikeouts per nine innings in 1999:

### Most Strikeouts Per 9 Innings, Relievers—1999

| Pitcher, Team | SO | IP | SO/9 |
|---|---|---|---|
| Billy Wagner, Hou | 124 | 74.2 | 15.0 |
| Armando Benitez, NYM | 128 | 78.0 | 14.8 |
| Matt Mantei, Fla-Ari | 99 | 65.1 | 13.6 |
| John Rocker, Atl | 104 | 72.1 | 12.9 |
| Ugueth Urbina, Mon | 100 | 75.2 | 11.9 |
| Mike Williams, Pit | 76 | 58.1 | 11.7 |
| Paul Shuey, Cle | 103 | 81.2 | 11.4 |
| Rich Croushore, StL | 88 | 71.2 | 11.1 |
| Bob Howry, CWS | 80 | 67.2 | 10.6 |
| Keith Foulke, CWS | 123 | 105.1 | 10.5 |

(minimum 40 G and 50 IP)

Maybe we should call the relief portion of the Hottest Heater Award the Billy Wagner Trophy, because the Astros' fireballing lefty has averaged the most strikeouts per nine innings in each of the last three seasons. In fact, he set a major league record each year for most strikeouts per nine by a pitcher with 50 or more innings, averaging 14.4 in 1997, 14.6 in 1998 and an incredible 15.0 in 1999. Wagner can't rest on his laurels, however: Armando Benitez' 1999 average of 14.8 Ks per nine was second all-time to Wagner, and four of the all-time top 10 strikeout rates were recorded in '99, with Matt Mantei and John Rocker joining Wagner and Benitez. Will the record be broken again in 2000, and could a relief pitcher soon be averaging 16 or more Ks per nine innings? It wouldn't surprise us a bit.

While Wagner, Benitez et al. deserve kudos for their efforts, the true answer to the question "Whose Heater Is Hottest?" for 1999 would have to be Pedro Martinez. Consider this: despite the fact that he was expected to go seven innings or more every time out, Martinez fanned hitters at a rate that would have placed him in fourth place on the relievers' list! It's yet another indication of what an awesome season Martinez had in 1999.

—Don Zminda

A more complete listing for this category can be found on page 272.

## Who Were 1999's Most Overpowering Pitchers?

Last year we introduced a new statistic, the strikeout-hit ratio, to express the dominance of a pitcher. There are a number of hurlers who are effective at either fanning hitters or holding their average down, but only a select few excel at doing both.

For example, Omar Daal ranked fourth in the National League last year with a .236 opponent batting average, but his lackluster whiff total of 148 in 214.2 innings led to a strikeout-hit ratio of 0.69, which equaled the major league average. By contrast, Aaron Sele placed fourth in the American League with 8.17 strikeouts per nine innings. But opponents hit him very well when they made contact, batting .293 overall. That gave Sele a 0.76 ratio, not much better than average.

Daal and Sele combined for 34 victories in 1999, so they obviously were getting the job done. They just weren't getting it done as spectacularly as the pitchers who had the game's best strikeout-hit ratios:

### Highest Strikeout-Hit Ratio—1999

| Pitcher, Team | SO | H | SO/H |
|---|---|---|---|
| Pedro Martinez, Bos | 313 | 160 | 1.96 |
| Randy Johnson, Ari | 364 | 207 | 1.76 |
| Kevin Millwood, Atl | 205 | 168 | 1.22 |
| David Cone, NYY | 177 | 164 | 1.08 |
| Kevin Brown, LA | 221 | 210 | 1.05 |
| Chuck Finley, Ana | 200 | 197 | 1.02 |
| Sterling Hitchcock, SD | 194 | 202 | 0.96 |
| Curt Schilling, Phi | 152 | 159 | 0.96 |
| Hideo Nomo, Mil | 161 | 173 | 0.93 |
| John Smoltz, Atl | 156 | 168 | 0.93 |
| **MLB Average** | | | **0.69** |

(minimum 162 IP)

It should be no surprise that AL Cy Young Award winner Pedro Martinez, who had one of the best seasons ever by a pitcher, tops the chart. He's followed by NL Cy Young Award winner Randy Johnson, who made a run at Nolan Ryan's single-season strikeout record, then by Kevin Millwood and David Cone, the ERA runners-up in each league.

Martinez' 1.96 ratio was the fifth-highest in major league history, just ahead of his 1.93 figure from his NL Cy Young Award season in 1997.

Kerry Wood set the single-season record in 1998 with a 1.991 ratio, just ahead of Nolan Ryan's 1.990 in 1991. Johnson's performance last year raised his career mark to 1.56, extending his lead over Ryan (1.46) for the best ratio ever among pitchers with 1,500 innings.

At the other end of the spectrum are the pitchers who don't overpower anyone. Of the five pitchers with the lowest strikeout-hit ratios last year, only Omar Olivares managed a winning record or an ERA better than the major league average:

**Lowest Strikeout-Hit Ratio—1999**

| Pitcher, Team | SO | H | SO/H |
|---|---|---|---|
| Scott Karl, Mil | 74 | 246 | 0.30 |
| Brian Meadows, Fla | 72 | 214 | 0.34 |
| Dennis Springer, Fla | 83 | 231 | 0.36 |
| Omar Olivares, Ana-Oak | 85 | 217 | 0.39 |
| Chad Ogea, Phi | 77 | 192 | 0.40 |

Karl's uninspiring effort was the worst in the majors since Ricky Bones' 0.28 mark in 1993. Bones (0.37) and Karl (0.46) also have the lowest ratios among active big league pitchers with 750 innings. Of the 10 active hurlers with the worst career marks, only Kirk Rueter (0.49, 70-39) and Armando Reynoso (0.47, 56-44) have winning records.

When it comes to strikeout-hit ratio, style clearly equals substance.

—Jim Callis

A more complete listing for this category can be found on page 275.

## Who Gets the Easy Saves—And Who Toughs It Out?

Today's relievers are judged primarily on their save percentages (saves divided by the number of opportunities). But as we point out every year, not all save opportunities are alike. That's why we classify save opportunities as Easy, Regular and Tough. The definitions are as follows:

**Easy Save Opportunity:** First batter faced is not the tying run *and* the relief pitcher pitches one inning or less. Example: Mariano Rivera comes in to start the bottom of the ninth with the Yankees holding a 4-2 lead.

**Tough Save Opportunity:** The reliever comes in with the tying run anywhere on base. Example: with the Devil Rays holding a 3-2 lead, Roberto Hernandez enters with a man on first and one out in the ninth.

**Regular Save Opportunity:** All save opportunities which do not fall into either the Easy or Tough categories.

In 1999, relievers converted 90 percent of their Easy opportunities last year but only 25 percent of their Tough opportunities. The conversion rate for Regular opportunities was exactly the same as the overall save conversion rate, 67 percent.

Here are the Easy, Regular and Tough breakdowns for all 1999 closers who had 30 or more saves:

### Save Conversion Rates—1999

| Pitcher, Team | Easy Sv/Opp | Pct | Regular Sv/Opp | Pct | Tough Sv/Opp | Pct | Overall Sv/Opp | Pct |
|---|---|---|---|---|---|---|---|---|
| Mariano Rivera, NYY | 26/26 | 100 | 16/19 | 84 | 3/4 | 75 | 45/49 | 92 |
| Roberto Hernandez, TB | 22/23 | 96 | 19/21 | 90 | 2/3 | 67 | 43/47 | 91 |
| John Wetteland, Tex | 25/25 | 100 | 13/20 | 65 | 5/5 | 100 | 43/50 | 86 |
| Ugueth Urbina, Mon | 27/29 | 93 | 8/12 | 67 | 6/9 | 67 | 41/50 | 82 |
| Trevor Hoffman, SD | 23/24 | 96 | 14/16 | 88 | 3/3 | 100 | 40/43 | 93 |
| Billy Wagner, Hou | 19/19 | 100 | 15/16 | 94 | 5/7 | 71 | 39/42 | 93 |
| Mike Jackson, Cle | 25/25 | 100 | 14/18 | 78 | 0/0 | — | 39/43 | 91 |
| John Rocker, Atl | 24/25 | 96 | 13/16 | 81 | 1/4 | 25 | 38/45 | 84 |
| Bob Wickman, Mil | 21/21 | 100 | 14/19 | 74 | 2/5 | 40 | 37/45 | 82 |
| Robb Nen, SF | 26/28 | 93 | 11/14 | 79 | 0/4 | 0 | 37/46 | 80 |
| Jeff Shaw, LA | 21/22 | 95 | 11/14 | 79 | 2/3 | 67 | 34/39 | 87 |
| Jose Mesa, Sea | 19/19 | 100 | 12/16 | 75 | 2/3 | 67 | 33/38 | 87 |
| Matt Mantei, Fla-Ari | 21/25 | 84 | 10/11 | 91 | 1/1 | 100 | 32/37 | 86 |

| Pitcher, Team | Easy Sv/Opp | Pct | Regular Sv/Opp | Pct | Tough Sv/Opp | Pct | Overall Sv/Opp | Pct |
|---|---|---|---|---|---|---|---|---|
| Billy Koch, Tor | 12/12 | 100 | 19/22 | 86 | 0/1 | 0 | 31/35 | 89 |
| Troy Percival, Ana | 17/19 | 89 | 14/18 | 78 | 0/2 | 0 | 31/39 | 79 |
| Dave Veres, Col | 17/20 | 85 | 12/17 | 71 | 2/2 | 100 | 31/39 | 79 |
| Todd Jones, Det | 21/22 | 95 | 8/11 | 73 | 1/2 | 50 | 30/35 | 86 |
| **MLB Average** | | 90 | | 67 | | 25 | | 67 |

(minimum 30 Sv, ranked by Sv)

As always, this chart reveals some real differences in what kind of burden different closers are being asked to shoulder. Let's compare Billy Wagner and Mike Jackson. Overall they had virtually the same conversion rate: 39 of 42 for Wagner, 39 of 43 for Jackson. But while Wagner was a splendid 5-for-7 in Tough save chances, Jackson didn't have a single Tough save opportunity all year. His impressive save record was largely a function of being given 25 Easy opportunities. Jackson converted all 25 of them, but virtually all the good closers are perfect or nearly so when given Easy save opportunities.

Closers who excelled in their Tough save opportunities, along with Wagner, were John Wetteland (5-for-5), Ugueth Urbina (6-for-9), and Mike Trombley (4-for-6). Among those who struggled were Mike Timlin (1-for-6), Robb Nen (0-for-4) and John Rocker (1-for-4). But let's face it, today's closers just aren't given very many difficult save opportunities. We've been tracking saves like this since 1987, just before Dennis Eckersley and Lee Smith began revolutionizing the role of closer. Back then 30.4 percent of all save opportunities were of the Tough variety. That figure has been steadily slipping, and in 1999 only 19.4 percent of all save opportunities were Tough. The success rate for converting Tough opportunities also has been dropping, to about half of what it was in 1988:

### Save Conversion Percentages—1987-99

| Year | Easy | Regular | Tough | Overall |
|---|---|---|---|---|
| 1987 | 85 | 76 | 41 | 66 |
| 1988 | 92 | 78 | 50 | 72 |
| 1989 | 91 | 78 | 48 | 71 |
| 1990 | 91 | 74 | 49 | 72 |
| 1991 | 91 | 74 | 42 | 71 |
| 1992 | 93 | 74 | 41 | 70 |
| 1993 | 93 | 70 | 38 | 69 |

| Year | Easy | Regular | Tough | Overall |
|------|------|---------|-------|---------|
| 1994 | 88 | 67 | 37 | 67 |
| 1995 | 90 | 66 | 36 | 68 |
| 1996 | 91 | 65 | 33 | 67 |
| 1997 | 90 | 63 | 35 | 67 |
| 1998 | 89 | 66 | 33 | 68 |
| 1999 | 90 | 67 | 25 | 67 |

A lot of the drop in Tough save conversion percentage is due, no doubt, to the offensive explosion in recent years. Another factor might be that many of today's closers are neither familiar nor comfortable with the idea of coming in with runners on base. That wasn't the case back in 1989. Check out this comparison:

| | Easy | | Regular | | Tough | | Overall | |
|---|---|---|---|---|---|---|---|---|
| Pitcher, Year | Sv/Opp | Pct | Sv/Opp | Pct | Sv/Opp | Pct | Sv/Opp | Pct |
| Mark Davis, 1989 | 7/7 | 100 | 15/17 | 88 | 22/24 | 92 | 44/48 | 92 |
| Mariano Rivera, 1999 | 26/26 | 100 | 16/19 | 84 | 3/4 | 75 | 45/49 | 92 |

One guy was 44-for-48, the other 45-for-49, two great pitching performances. But Mark Davis, the 1989 National League Cy Young Award winner, was asked to handle the sort of load that would be unimaginable today. Along with having to deal with many more pressure situations, Davis worked 92.2 innings in 1989, over a third more than the 69 innings worked by Mariano Rivera a decade later. That's not to insinuate that Rivera is some sort of wimp. Davis was fantastic in 1989, but he crashed in 1990 and never was the same pitcher again. Meanwhile closers who were being given less demanding workloads, like Eckersley and Smith, remained effective year after year. Not coincidentally, the Tough save opportunity began to fade out as a regular part of a closer's diet.

—Don Zminda

A more complete listing for this category can be found on page 276.

## *If You Hold the Fort, Will You Soon Be Closing the Gate?*

Relief pitchers earn a hold when they enter a game in a save situation, retire at least one batter and then pass the save situation to the next reliever. It's an important job, and the setup men who rank among the league leaders in holds are now among the most highly valued relievers in the game.

Often they end up as their team's closer before very long. That tradition continued last season: John Rocker (Braves), Mike Trombley (Twins) and Bob Howry (White Sox), all of whom had posted at least 15 holds in '98, were promoted to closer during the '99 season. The chart below shows the leaders from last year:

**HOLDING THE FORT 1999** — HOLDS

| Player | Holds |
|---|---|
| John Johnstone | 28 |
| Buddy Groom | 27 |
| Jeff Zimmerman | 24 |
| Doug Brocail | 23 |
| Alan Embree | 22 |
| Keith Foulke | 22 |
| Graeme Lloyd | 22 |
| Derek Lowe | 22 |
| Mike Remlinger | 21 |
| Mike Stanton | 21 |
| Turk Wendell | 21 |

As usual, there are some potential closers in the group. John Johnstone of the Giants, the '99 hold leader, was so solid in his role that the Giants may turn to him if their closer, Robb Nen, continues to struggle as he did last season. Keith Foulke of the White Sox showed he was capable of closing games last season, nailing down nine saves, and he'll be the first to get the call if Howry falters this year. Derek Lowe of the Red Sox, who had 15 saves to go along with his 22 holds last season, is the odds-on favorite to be Boston's fulltime closer this year with Tom Gordon out for the year.

A growing trend in baseball these days is to have both a lefty and righty setup man who can be used as the situation demands. The Giants not only had Johnstone, but lefthander Alan Embree (22 holds). The Mets' righty/lefty duo of Turk Wendell (21 holds) and Dennis Cook (19) was one of the keys to the team's success. The Rangers got effective work out of righty Jeff Zimmerman (24 holds) and lefty Mike Venafro (19), both rookies.

With Johnstone and Embree leading the way, the Giants had more holds than any major league team last season. Here are the team totals:

### Holds by Team—1999

| AL Team | Holds | NL Team | Holds |
| --- | --- | --- | --- |
| Rangers | 72 | Giants | 82 |
| Red Sox | 66 | Cardinals | 75 |
| Athletics | 66 | Brewers | 68 |
| Blue Jays | 58 | Mets | 66 |
| Indians | 57 | Braves | 58 |
| Tigers | 57 | Diamondbacks | 58 |
| Twins | 53 | Dodgers | 54 |
| Devil Rays | 48 | Pirates | 54 |
| White Sox | 48 | Cubs | 52 |
| Orioles | 47 | Padres | 51 |
| Yankees | 45 | Marlins | 50 |
| Royals | 44 | Phillies | 49 |
| Angels | 36 | Expos | 47 |
| Mariners | 33 | Rockies | 43 |
|  |  | Reds | 38 |
|  |  | Astros | 36 |

As we noted last year, there isn't always a correlation between team holds and success on the field. The Yankees, baseball's mightiest team, had one of the lowest hold totals in the American League in both 1998 and '99. The Reds and Astros, who battled for the National League Central title down to the last day of the regular season, had the two lowest hold totals in the NL. This is more a reflection of managerial philosophy than it is of a weak bullpen. The Reds, for instance, had one of the National League's *best* bullpens last year, but manager Jack McKeon's habit of using his closers for more than an inning on occasion took away a lot of hold opportunities. Larry Dierker's Astros, meanwhile, ranked low in holds because he let his solid starting corps work deeper into games than most managers could.

On the other hand, the low hold totals of the Mariners, Angels and Royals were a definite reflection of clubs with struggling bullpens. Sometimes you just need to look deeper into the numbers.

—Don Zminda

A more complete listing for this category can be found on page 277.

## Who Knows How to Handle Their Inheritance?

In the pre-Eckersley days, closers routinely came in prior to the ninth inning, and there were runners on base as often as not. These days, it's the setup and middle men who usually enter a game with ducks on the pond, and their ability to keep those runners from scoring often makes the difference between a win and a loss. As has been the case for several years, the 1999 leaders list in best inherited runners scoring percentage (minimum 30 inherited runners) is full of middle men, with only a couple of closers making the list:

**Best Inherited Runners Scoring Percentages—1999**

| Pitcher, Team | IR | Scored | Pct |
|---|---|---|---|
| Ricky Rincon, Cle | 42 | 5 | 11.9 |
| Jerry Dipoto, Col | 32 | 4 | 12.5 |
| Mike Myers, Mil | 78 | 12 | 15.4 |
| Wayne Gomes, Phi | 30 | 5 | 16.7 |
| Steve Kline, Mon | 65 | 11 | 16.9 |
| Travis Miller, Min | 40 | 7 | 17.5 |
| Lance Painter, StL | 40 | 7 | 17.5 |
| Masao Kida, Det | 37 | 7 | 18.9 |
| Shigetoshi Hasegawa, Ana | 52 | 10 | 19.2 |
| Armando Benitez, NYM | 30 | 6 | 20.0 |
| Rich Rodriguez, SF | 55 | 11 | 20.0 |
| **MLB Average** | | | **33.2** |

(minimum 30 IR)

As we've noted for the last couple of years, the inherited runners leaders list tends to be dominated by lefty specialists who often come in to face a lefthanded hitter, then exit the game. The 1999 list was no exception; it includes southpaw situational aces Ricky Rincon, Mike Myers, Steve Kline, Travis Miller, Lance Painter and Rich Rodriguez. The best last year was Rincon, who permitted only five of the 42 runners he inherited to cross the plate. There were also a couple of righty middle men on the list, Shigetoshi Hasegawa and Masao Kida. Even the two pitchers who did a fair amount of closing, Wayne Gomes and Armando Benitez, worked in middle relief for at least part of the year.

Modern closers *do* come in with men on base at least on occasion, however. Here are the 1999 closers who did the best job of stranding their inherited runners (minimum 20 saves and 15 inherited runners):

**Best Inherited Runners Scoring Percentages—1999 Closers**

| Pitcher, Team | IR | Scored | Pct |
|---|---|---|---|
| Trevor Hoffman, SD | 22 | 3 | 13.6 |
| Mariano Rivera, NYY | 27 | 5 | 18.5 |
| Armando Benitez, NYM | 30 | 6 | 20.0 |
| Danny Graves, Cin | 44 | 9 | 20.5 |
| Antonio Alfonseca, Fla | 25 | 6 | 24.0 |
| Dave Veres, Col | 16 | 4 | 25.0 |
| Billy Wagner, Hou | 18 | 5 | 27.8 |
| Ugueth Urbina, Mon | 37 | 11 | 29.7 |
| Jose Mesa, Sea | 32 | 10 | 31.3 |
| Roberto Hernandez, TB | 19 | 6 | 31.6 |
| **MLB Average** | | | **31.2** |

(minimum 20 SV and 15 IR)

A couple of the guys on this list, Danny Graves and Antonio Alfonseca, worked in middle relief at times last season, as did Benitez, but this is mostly a list of bona fide closers. The top two were Trevor Hoffman of the Padres and Mariano Rivera of the Yankees. When you consider that *their* inherited runners were almost certainly the tying or winning runs in either the eighth or ninth innings, their performance is all the more impressive. It's another reason why many regard Hoffman and Rivera as the two top closers in the game.

As would be expected, the closers were better than relievers as a whole in preventing inherited runners from scoring. The advantage was fairly slight, however, as the 2 percent differential translates into one extra run per 50 inherited runners.

On the team front, the top clubs at preventing inherited runners from scoring were last year's World Series opponents, the Yankees (22.6 percent) and Braves (23.2). Not too much of a surprise, is it?

—Don Zminda

A more complete listing for this category can be found on page 278.

*Baseball Scoreboard*

## Which Relievers Prevent the Most Runs?

**R**elief pitchers, pulled into and yanked out of games with the wave of the manager's arm, always have had it rough—and so have statisticians who have tried to measure a reliever's performance. We agree that ERA falls short and that wins are pretty meaningless. Saves are better, but really only for one guy in the bullpen. Holds are good, but don't always help evaluate pitchers on bad teams. In 1997, we introduced runs prevented, a statistic that levels the playing field a bit by measuring what it is that relievers are supposed to do: prevent runners from scoring.

Runs prevented measures a reliever's performance using run expectation, which is the number of runs we expect to score in a given base/out situation. Take, for instance, bases loaded and nobody out. Using data from 1995-99, we expect approximately 2.33 runs to score the rest of that half-inning. So if a reliever allows more than 2.33 runs to score, he's doing a bad job; if he allows fewer, he's doing a good job. Simple, right? Here's the run expectation data for the last five years:

**MLB Run Expectation—1995-99**

| Runners | Number of Outs | | |
|---|---|---|---|
| | 0 | 1 | 2 |
| None | .55 | .29 | .11 |
| 1st | .94 | .56 | .24 |
| 2nd | 1.19 | .71 | .34 |
| 3rd | 1.43 | .99 | .37 |
| 1st & 2nd | 1.55 | .96 | .47 |
| 1st & 3rd | 1.86 | 1.20 | .52 |
| 2nd & 3rd | 2.05 | 1.42 | .59 |
| Bases Loaded | 2.33 | 1.63 | .79 |

Runs prevented measures the run expectation when a reliever enters the game, accounts for runs that score when he's on the mound and any errors made behind him, and then subtracts the run expectation when he trudges back to the dugout. (For a more complete definition, see the Glossary.) We calculate runs prevented inning by inning, and tabulate it for each pitcher for the entire season. An average pitcher scores around zero (meaning that he prevented exactly as many runs as we expected). On the following page we list the top 10 for 1999:

### Most Total Runs Prevented—1999

| Pitcher, Team | Relief IP | RP |
|---|---|---|
| Keith Foulke, CWS | 105.1 | 38.2 |
| Danny Graves, Cin | 111.0 | 33.3 |
| Derek Lowe, Bos | 109.1 | 32.2 |
| Mike Remlinger, Atl | 83.2 | 31.7 |
| Jeff Zimmerman, Tex | 87.2 | 29.3 |
| Armando Benitez, NYM | 78.0 | 29.3 |
| Billy Wagner, Hou | 74.2 | 29.1 |
| Scott Sullivan, Cin | 113.2 | 26.8 |
| Doug Brocail, Det | 82.0 | 26.5 |
| Mariano Rivera, NYY | 69.0 | 25.6 |

As I sit here in Washington, D.C., I can hear the screams coming down the East Coast. How can any valid relief pitching statistic rank Mariano Rivera *10th*, cry the Yankees fans? Indeed, in the four years that we've been measuring runs prevented, Rivera *has* been the most valuable relief pitcher in the majors. He's the only pitcher to finish in the top 10 every year, and has by far the highest cumulative runs prevented. Any sane GM would take Mariano Rivera for the 2000 season over any of the guys listed above him. *But he wasn't the most valuable relief pitcher in 1999!*

That honor goes to Keith Foulke, who labored in relative obscurity on the South Side of Chicago. Foulke outpaced the field by a long shot. What made him so good? Well, for starters he gave Chisox manager Jerry Manuel more than 105 relief innings. But it wasn't merely the innings that propelled Foulke to the top: piling on innings doesn't automatically translate into a higher runs-prevented total, as an average inning is worth *zero* runs prevented. Foulke faced tough situations when he entered games (therefore giving him a higher initial run expectation), didn't allow many of his teammates' runners to score (only three of his 23 inherited runners crossed the plate), and stopped his own batters from getting on base and scoring (he allowed less than one baserunner per inning).

Likewise, Danny Graves, Derek Lowe and Scott Sullivan each gave their managers both quality *and* quantity, which is precisely what runs prevented measures. Any manager will tell you that a guy who can pitch nearly every day, for one or two innings at a time, is a lifesaver for the bullpen. As an example, to meet Foulke's productivity, the Yankees needed Rivera *plus* another 36 relief innings of nearly identical quality. That's because even on an inning-by-inning basis, Foulke prevented nearly as many runs as Rivera:

**Most Runs Prevented Per Relief Inning Pitched—1999**

| Player, Team | RP | Relief IP | RP/IP |
|---|---|---|---|
| Billy Wagner, Hou | 29.1 | 74.2 | 0.392 |
| Mike Remlinger, Atl | 31.7 | 83.2 | 0.381 |
| Armando Benitez, NYM | 29.3 | 78.0 | 0.376 |
| Trevor Hoffman, SD | 25.1 | 67.1 | 0.374 |
| Rich Garces, Bos | 15.0 | 40.2 | 0.373 |
| Mariano Rivera, NYY | 25.6 | 69.0 | 0.371 |
| Keith Foulke, CWS | 38.2 | 105.1 | 0.363 |
| Scott Elarton, Hou | 13.7 | 39.1 | 0.350 |
| Jeff Zimmerman, Tex | 29.3 | 87.2 | 0.336 |
| Jose Silva, Pit | 10.6 | 32.1 | 0.330 |

(minimum 30 relief IP)

Not surprisingly, Billy Wagner was the most productive run preventer per relief inning. This list also includes the other dominant closers of 1999: Rivera, Armando Benitez and Trevor Hoffman. Also noteworthy is that Mike Remlinger, not John Rocker, picked up the Atlanta bullpen the most after the injury to Kerry Ligtenberg in 1999. So what do these lists mean for the 2000 season? Here's a runs-prevented analysis of a few bullpens:

**Cincinnati.** In 1999, the Cincinnati bullpen relied heavily on three pitchers, Danny Graves (second in total runs prevented), Scott Sullivan (eighth) and Scott Williamson (12th) to take them to the brink of the playoffs. These three relievers combined to pitch 312 relief innings (nearly two innings for every Reds game), racking up an impressive total of 84.5 runs prevented (a total higher than any single bullpen in 1999). Because linear-weights systems like runs prevented indicate that, historically, every 10 runs equal a win, these three relievers accounted for approximately 8.5 Cincinnati victories in 1999. Recent history is full of relievers who pitch triple-digit innings one season, only to break down the next. So, unless Graves, Sullivan and Williamson are Face, Marshall and Radatz, expect fewer innings, fewer runs prevented and fewer wins for the 2000 Reds.

**Houston.** The Astros might do well to emulate the 1999 Reds. Last season Wagner continued to dominate hitters, but the Houston bullpen also was boosted by the performances of Scott Elarton (13.7 runs prevented in 39.1 relief innings) and Jose Cabrera (10.7 in 29.1 relief innings). The runs-prevented rankings of both Elarton and Cabrera suffered from a relatively light bullpen workload. Houston's bullpen could be dominant if these two relievers are able to increase their contributions in 2000. Of course, Elarton already was headed to the rotation before the Mike Hampton trade and is coming off arm surgery.

**Chicago (NL).** In 1999 Chicago was a *Tale of Two Cities*—it was the best of times with Keith Foulke on the South Side, but the worst of times on the North Side, where no reliever finished in the top 100 in runs prevented. The Cubs' top three relievers (Rodney Myers, Matt Karchner and Terry Adams) combined for 10.3 runs prevented, less than 30 percent of Foulke's total. Chicago's most significant offseason bullpen additions were Greg McMichael and Brian Williams, and it lost the marginal Adams. The 2000 season looks no better for the relievers who finished 1999 with the lowest runs prevented total (-26.1) for a National League team that plays less than a mile above sea level.

**Seattle.** In last year's *Scoreboard*, we predicted that the additions of Jose Mesa and Mark Leiter weren't likely to help the Mariners' bullpen. In a way, we were right: the pair combined for just 0.1 runs prevented in 1999. But Mesa and Leiter were a relative treat for Lou Piniella, who watched his other relievers finish with a major league-worst -69.3 runs prevented. During the offseason, Seattle added both Arthur Rhodes and Kazuhiro Sasaki, Japan's career saves leader, leading to some high expectations. But Rhodes was subpar in 1999 (-2.1 runs prevented) and Sasaki never has pitched in the United States, so expect to see plenty more of Piniella trudging to the mound this year at Safeco Field.

**Anaheim.** The Angels may have had the most underrated bullpen in the majors. Anaheim had some tough times in 1999, including some brutal blown saves by Troy Percival (1.0 runs prevented in 1999, 184th in the majors). But the Halos bullpen was blessed by some other, less renowned arms, such as Al Levine (14.8 runs prevented), Lou Pote (11.5 in just 29.1 relief innings), Mike Magnante (10.2) and Shigetoshi Hasegawa (8.4), who helped the relief corps rank second in the AL in runs prevented. Percival should bounce back, and these other guys are capable of approaching their 1999 performances. The 2000 season could be heavenly in Anaheim.

—Steven Schulman

*Steven Schulman, the creator of runs prevented, is a SABR member and an attorney practicing in Washington, D.C.*

A more complete listing for this category can be found on page 279.

## Who Gets the Red Barrett Trophy?

Pitcher Charles Henry "Red" Barrett toiled 11 rather nondescript seasons in the major leagues, finishing his career in 1949 with exactly 69 wins and 69 losses—hardly the sort of numbers that are remembered in perpetuity. Legend has it, however, that Barrett threw all of 58 pitches in a complete game back in 1944. Now *that's* a memorable feat! So in his honor, STATS annually recognizes the hurlers who needed the fewest pitches to navigate a nine-inning complete game. Without further ado, here are the 1999 honorees:

### Fewest Pitches in a Nine-Inning Complete Game—1999

| Pitcher, Team | Date | Score | Opp | W/L | IP | H | ER | BB | SO | Pit |
|---|---|---|---|---|---|---|---|---|---|---|
| David Cone, NYY | 7/18 | 6-0 | Mon | W | 9 | 0 | 0 | 0 | 10 | 88 |
| David Wells, Tor | 7/17 | 6-1 | Fla | W | 9 | 6 | 1 | 0 | 6 | 92 |
| James Baldwin, CWS | 5/29 | 7-1 | @Det | W | 9 | 5 | 1 | 0 | 7 | 95 |
| Jose Lima, Hou | 6/2 | 9-1 | @Mil | W | 9 | 4 | 1 | 0 | 8 | 98 |
| David Wells, Tor | 6/20 | 2-1 | KC | W | 9 | 4 | 1 | 0 | 7 | 98 |
| Alex Fernandez, Fla | 8/6 | 9-1 | Col | W | 9 | 3 | 1 | 0 | 2 | 98 |
| Steve Woodard, Mil | 5/15 | 7-2 | Fla | W | 9 | 4 | 2 | 1 | 6 | 99 |
| Dave Mlicki, Det | 6/26 | 0-1 | Min | L | 9 | 6 | 1 | 1 | 4 | 99 |
| Brian Anderson, Ari | 8/17 | 4-0 | ChC | W | 9 | 3 | 0 | 0 | 5 | 99 |
| Jeff Suppan, KC | 9/16 | 7-1 | Ana | W | 9 | 6 | 1 | 1 | 5 | 99 |
| **MLB Average** | | | | | | | | | | **116** |

Congratulations to David Cone, who got a perfect game after years of flirting with no-hitters. Cone needed just 88 pitches to set down the Expos in order on July 18, and he may have used even fewer tosses if he hadn't insisted on taking care of 10 batters himself. You might think that perfect games and no-hitters would top this list every year, but that's rarely the case. In fact, Cone and Darryl Kile (1993) are the only two hurlers in the last 12 seasons to use 90 or fewer pitches in a perfect game or no-no.

Cone's masterpiece was also his only complete game of the season. On the other end of the spectrum was his former Yankees teammate David Wells. Wells went the distance an American League-leading seven times, with two of those efforts placing among the top five most-efficient outings of '99. Not surprisingly, the Toronto ace averaged just 3.55 pitches per batter last year, the fourth-best figure in the AL among ERA qualifiers. Wells, by the way, used 120 pitches in his perfect game against the Twins in 1998.

Our condolences go out to Dave Mlicki, who is the first pitcher to finish among the top 10 in this category and come away with a loss since Milwaukee's Bill Wegman threw 90 pitches in a 1-0 complete-game loss to the Red Sox in 1993. For his part, Mlicki was outdone by the Minnesota trio of Joe Mays, Bob Wells and Mike Trombley. At least Mlicki didn't have to work too hard in a losing effort. The same can't be said for some of the guys who cracked the list of *most* pitches thrown in a single game last year.

**Most Pitches in a Game—1999**

| Pitcher, Team | Date | Score | Opp | W/L | IP | H | ER | BB | SO | Pit |
|---|---|---|---|---|---|---|---|---|---|---|
| Pedro Astacio, Col | 6/6 | 10-5 | Mil | W | 7.2 | 9 | 5 | 4 | 10 | 153 |
| Robert Person, Phi | 8/20 | 5-8 | LA | ND | 8.2 | 3 | 4 | 5 | 11 | 144 |
| Wilson Alvarez, TB | 8/29 | 6-4 | @Cle | W | 8.0 | 8 | 3 | 2 | 6 | 144 |
| Randy Johnson, Ari | 7/25 | 1-2 | LA | L | 7.0 | 8 | 2 | 1 | 11 | 143 |
| Jamie Moyer, Sea | 9/19 | 1-2 | Min | L | 9.0 | 6 | 2 | 2 | 6 | 143 |
| Ken Bottenfield, StL | 8/24 | 4-8 | @Mon | L | 7.2 | 11 | 8 | 5 | 1 | 142 |
| Randy Johnson, Ari | 4/25 | 5-3 | @SD | ND | 8.0 | 5 | 3 | 3 | 11 | 141 |
| Livan Hernandez, Fla | 6/12 | 4-5 | NYY | L | 7.2 | 6 | 5 | 5 | 5 | 141 |
| Russ Ortiz, SF | 7/10 | 4-2 | StL | W | 8.2 | 2 | 2 | 2 | 10 | 141 |
| Livan Hernandez, SF | 8/9 | 4-5 | @Fla | ND | 7.2 | 8 | 3 | 2 | 4 | 141 |
| Jamey Wright, Col | 9/3 | 5-2 | @NYM | ND | 8.0 | 10 | 2 | 3 | 4 | 141 |

In 1998, Jim Leyland's Marlins earned five of the top 10 spots in this category. Last season, Leyland's Rockies nailed down the first and 10th positions, with Pedro Astacio throwing an arm-numbing 153 pitches in a June win over the Brewers. Leyland certainly won't be remembered as a pitch-count man, will he? Then there's the case of Livan Hernandez, whose arm is either bionic or about to fall off. The former Marlin and current Giant has logged *seven* 140-plus pitch efforts in the last two seasons, all before he turned 25, under the direction of three different managers. Unless San Francisco skipper Dusty Baker puts Hernandez on a shorter leash, his career may never reach the heights he seemed destined for after dominating the 1997 postseason. One thing is certain, however: a Livan Hernandez-Red Barrett matchup would be quite a contrast in styles.

—Tony Nistler

A more complete listing for this category can be found on page 280.

## Which Pitchers Have Misleading ERAs?

Time for a quick question. Who pitched better last year, Steve Parris or Carl Pavano?

Parris went 11-4, 3.50 for the Reds, while Pavano went 6-8, 5.63 for the Expos. And while the answer may seem obvious, it's not. Pavano actually pitched better than Parris.

A pitcher's main job is to prevent runs. And generally, his success in getting hitters out determines how many runs he allows. Former STATS employee Mat Olkin devised a stat called predicted ERA, which measures the runs created by opposing hitters and expresses it in the same form as an ERA. Here's the formula:

**Predicted ERA = Opponent OBP x Opponent SLG x 31**

Last year, for instance, the major league on-base and slugging percentages were .345 and .434, respectively, which yielded a predicted ERA of 4.64. The major league ERA, by comparison, was 4.70.

Opponents reached base at a .338 clip and slugged .426 against Parris, leading to a predicted ERA of 4.46. Meanwhile, hitters had a .345 on-base percentage and .401 slugging percentage against Pavano, whose predicted ERA was 4.30.

So why was Parris' ERA so much lower than his predicted ERA, and why did Pavano's go even further in the opposite direction? When that happens, it's usually just a fluke. Parris may have gotten much better bullpen support than Pavano, or he might just have been luckier. Parris certainly had good fortune when it came to run support, getting 2.04 more runs per game to work with than Pavano.

More often than not, when a pitcher's ERA diverges from his predicted ERA one season, it swings back in line with his performance the following year. Each year, we list the five pitchers whose ERAs are most likely to improve (those with predicted ERAs the furthest below their actual marks) and those whose are most likely to decline (those with predicted ERAs the furthest above their actual ERAs).

In the 1999 edition of this book, we targeted Paul Quantrill, Mike Morgan, John Hudek, Scott Radinsky and Jim Bruske as the pitchers whose ERAs should rise compared to 1998. Only Morgan made our cutoff (100 innings for starters, 50 for relievers), and indeed his ERA jumped from 4.18 to 6.24. Quantrill, Hudek and Radinsky saw their ERAs worsen as well, while Bruske didn't pitch in the majors.

We also identified Bobby Ayala, Doug Drabek, Mike Stanton, Rich Croushore and Blake Stein as the five pitchers whose ERAs should improve. Ayala, Stanton and Croushore all came through, while Stein did so without reaching the 100-inning cutoff for starters. Drabek didn't catch on with a big league team in 1999.

That's an impressive track record. So let's take a look at the pitchers who overachieved in 1999 and should come back to earth in 2000:

**Predicted ERA Furthest Above Actual ERA—1999**

| Pitcher, Team | Predicted | Actual | Diff |
|---|---|---|---|
| Scott Sauerbeck, Pit | 3.54 | 2.00 | 1.55 |
| Alan Mills, LA | 5.18 | 3.73 | 1.44 |
| Alvin Morman, KC | 5.40 | 4.05 | 1.35 |
| Guillermo Mota, Mon | 4.14 | 2.93 | 1.21 |
| John Frascatore, Ari-Tor | 4.86 | 3.73 | 1.13 |

(minimum 100 IP for starters, 50 IP for relievers)

Though major league Rule 5 draft selection Scott Sauerbeck was a welcome addition to the Pirates bullpen, he wasn't nearly as successful as his ERA would indicate. The flip side is the pitchers who performed better than their ERAs looked and should be due for a turnaround in 2000:

**Predicted ERA Furthest Below Actual ERA—1999**

| Pitcher, Team | Predicted | Actual | Diff |
|---|---|---|---|
| Mark Gardner, SF | 4.99 | 6.47 | -1.49 |
| Jose Jimenez, StL | 4.49 | 5.85 | -1.37 |
| Matt Whisenant, KC-SD | 4.27 | 5.63 | -1.36 |
| Carl Pavano, Mon | 4.30 | 5.63 | -1.33 |
| Mike DeJean, Col | 7.13 | 8.41 | -1.28 |

(minimum 100 IP for starters, 50 IP for relievers)

Mark Gardner's 1999 season wasn't as dreadful as it seemed, though it may have been enough to cost him a regular turn in the San Francisco rotation. At least Jose Jimenez could take some solace in the fact that he threw a no-hitter. He may have a difficult time lowering his ERA in 2000, however, as he changes addresses from Busch Stadium to Coors Field.

—Jim Callis

A more complete listing for this category can be found on page 281.

# IV. QUESTIONS ON DEFENSE

## *Does Pudge Intimidate the Best Basestealers?*

Ivan Rodriguez may have batted .332 with 35 homers and 25 stolen bases last year, but most voters will tell you that they chose him as the American League's Most Valuable Player as much for his defense as for his offense—if not more so. It's often said that Rodriguez' cannon arm shuts down the opposition's running game, and the numbers support that notion. We've already catalogued Rodriguez' overall record against opposing baserunners in the essay on page 163. But does Pudge have the same sort of intimidation factor against the *best* basestealers?

Let's look at the numbers. Our group of top basestealers consisted of all players who had stolen 30 bases in one season over the last five years (25 in strike-shortened 1995) and who also had started at least one game with Rodriguez behind the plate in that season. Here's how the elite basestealers fared against Pudge:

### SB Success vs. Ivan Rodriguez by Top Basestealers—1995-99

| Year | vs. Rodriguez | | | | | vs. Other Catchers | | | | |
|---|---|---|---|---|---|---|---|---|---|---|
| | GS | Att | SB | Att/GS | Pct | GS | Att | SB | Att/GS | Pct |
| 1995-99 | 424 | 101 | 59 | .24 | 58.4 | 7,542 | 2,981 | 2,357 | .40 | 79.1 |
| 1999 only | 99 | 22 | 13 | .22 | 59.1 | 2,021 | 764 | 603 | .38 | 78.9 |

(minimum 25 SB in 1995 or 30 SB in all other seasons;
minimum one game started vs. Rodriguez during that year)

The top basestealers were as reluctant as anyone else to attempt to steal against Rodriguez, and it usually was a losing proposition when they did. Overall the group attempted only .24 steals per game when playing against Pudge, versus .40 steals per game against other catchers. When not playing against Rodriguez, they stole at a 79 percent success rate; with Pudge behind the plate, their success rate dropped to a very poor 58 percent. The numbers for 1999 alone showed no significant differences.

How about on an individual level? Here's how all the 30-steal players who started at least five games against Rodriguez in 1999 fared against him, and then against everyone else:

### SB Success vs. Ivan Rodriguez by Top Basestealers—1999

| Player, Team | vs. Rodriguez | | | | | vs. Other Catchers | | | | |
|---|---|---|---|---|---|---|---|---|---|---|
| | GS | Att | SB | Att/GS | Pct | GS | Att | SB | Att/GS | Pct |
| Roberto Alomar, Cle | 9 | 2 | 2 | .22 | 100.0 | 146 | 41 | 35 | .28 | 85.4 |
| Brady Anderson, Bal | 11 | 1 | 0 | .09 | 0.0 | 132 | 42 | 36 | .32 | 85.7 |

| Player, Team | vs. Rodriguez | | | | | vs. Other Catchers | | | | |
|---|---|---|---|---|---|---|---|---|---|---|
| | GS | Att | SB | Att/GS | Pct | GS | Att | SB | Att/GS | Pct |
| Homer Bush, Tor | 7 | 1 | 0 | .14 | 0.0 | 118 | 39 | 32 | .33 | 82.1 |
| Johnny Damon, KC | 8 | 3 | 3 | .38 | 100.0 | 136 | 39 | 33 | .29 | 84.6 |
| Ray Durham, CWS | 6 | 1 | 0 | .17 | 0.0 | 145 | 44 | 34 | .30 | 77.3 |
| J. Encarnacion, Det | 7 | 2 | 1 | .29 | 50.0 | 120 | 43 | 32 | .36 | 74.4 |
| B. Hunter, Det-Sea | 9 | 1 | 1 | .11 | 100.0 | 120 | 51 | 43 | .43 | 84.3 |
| S. Stewart, Tor | 10 | 3 | 0 | .30 | 0.0 | 134 | 48 | 37 | .36 | 77.1 |
| Omar Vizquel, Cle | 9 | 3 | 3 | .33 | 100.0 | 131 | 48 | 39 | .37 | 81.3 |
| Tony Womack, Ari | 6 | 1 | 1 | .17 | 100.0 | 136 | 84 | 71 | .62 | 84.5 |

(minimum 30 SB and five games started vs. Rodriguez)

Some of these guys seemed as intimidated by Rodriguez as boxers used to be going up against the young Mike Tyson. Brady Anderson of the Orioles had a splendid basestealing year overall, going 36-for-43, but in 11 games against Rodriguez, he attempted one steal. . . and got thrown out. Brian Hunter, 44-for-52 on the year, attempted one steal in nine games against Pudge. Homer Bush, 32-for-40 overall, got tossed out in his only attempt against Rodriguez in seven games. There were, at least, a few fearless runners. Johnny Damon was 3-for-3 against Pudge in eight games, Omar Vizquel 3-for-3 in nine contests. Shannon Stewart also attempted three steals in his 10 games against Pudge, but got gunned down all three times.

How about the top basestealing teams? We looked at all teams which swiped at least 125 bases in a season over the last five years (110 SB in 1995). Here's how they fared against Pudge:

**SB vs. Ivan Rodriguez by Top Basestealing Teams—1995-99**

| Year | vs. Rodriguez | | | | | vs. Other Catchers | | | | |
|---|---|---|---|---|---|---|---|---|---|---|
| | GS | Att | SB | Att/GS | Pct | GS | Att | SB | Att/GS | Pct |
| 1995-99 | 246 | 194 | 103 | .79 | 53.1 | 4361 | 5519 | 3981 | 1.27 | 72.1 |
| 1999 only | 41 | 27 | 21 | .66 | 77.8 | 930 | 1163 | 861 | 1.25 | 74.0 |

(minimum 110 SB in 1995 or 125 SB in all other seasons; minimum one game vs. Rodriguez start in the season)

It's pretty much the same story. Over the last five years, the top basestealing clubs have attempted 1.27 steals per game in their non-Rodriguez starts; against Pudge, their attempt rate drops 38 percent. Against other catchers these clubs have stolen at a 72 percent success rate; against Rodriguez, they've succeeded only 53 percent of the time. In 1999, the best basestealing teams attempted fewer steals against Rodriguez, but their success rate was a surprisingly high 78 percent. This was mostly the work of the Indians, who were an amazing 6-for-6 in nine games against Pudge, and the Royals, who went 6-for-7 in eight contests. Kansas City has been especially fearless against Rodriguez in recent years, attempting 25 steals in 26 games against Pudge over the last three years and succeeding 17 times. But the Royals are the exception to the rule, to say the least.

In a way, the low attempt rates against Rodriguez aren't intimidation as much as they are simple common sense. Study after study has shown that if you can't succeed on two-thirds of your steal attempts, you're costing your team runs. Even the best basestealers have a tough time succeeding at that high a rate when Rodriguez is behind the plate, so most of them wisely don't even try. One could argue about how important it really is to shut down the running game in a high-scoring era where the stolen base is already on the decline, and about how many extra wins Rodriguez' arm is really worth to a team. But if the question is whether the best basestealers and the top basestealing teams change their strategy because Rodriguez is behind the plate, the answer is a resounding yes, with very few exceptions.

—Don Zminda

A more complete listing for this category can be found on page 282.

## Which Catchers Catch Thieves?

Clearly 1999 was a year to remember for Ivan Rodriguez, who stroked a career-high 35 homers while batting .332, broke the 100-RBI plateau for the first time and won the American League MVP Award for the West Division champs. And for a fifth straight season, he took top honors among major league catchers for throwing out baserunners.

Some things simply don't change. Rodriguez' caught-stealing percentage has been inching upward in each of the five seasons he has led his big league colleagues. He boosted his league-best mark from 52.5 percent in 1998 to 52.8 in '99, and that was his third straight season with a caught-stealing percentage better than 50 percent:

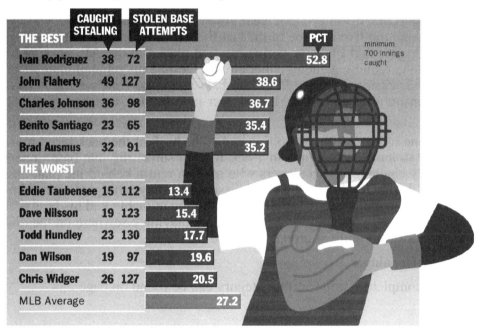

| THE BEST | CAUGHT STEALING | STOLEN BASE ATTEMPTS | PCT |
|---|---|---|---|
| Ivan Rodriguez | 38 | 72 | 52.8 |
| John Flaherty | 49 | 127 | 38.6 |
| Charles Johnson | 36 | 98 | 36.7 |
| Benito Santiago | 23 | 65 | 35.4 |
| Brad Ausmus | 32 | 91 | 35.2 |
| THE WORST | | | |
| Eddie Taubensee | 15 | 112 | 13.4 |
| Dave Nilsson | 19 | 123 | 15.4 |
| Todd Hundley | 23 | 130 | 17.7 |
| Dan Wilson | 19 | 97 | 19.6 |
| Chris Widger | 26 | 127 | 20.5 |
| MLB Average | | | 27.2 |

minimum 700 innings caught

Once again he outdistanced his AL competition by a significant margin, as he finished more than 14 percentage points ahead of runner-up John Flaherty of Tampa Bay. And as Rodriguez has been known to do in recent seasons, he easily led the majors in picking off baserunners as well. In 1999 he nailed 10 wayward runners, twice the combined total of pickoffs recorded by the AL's next four finishers in caught-stealing percentage.

Another statistic that demonstrates Rodriguez' dominance in throwing out runners is the number of stolen bases he allows per nine innings. He gave up just 0.25 stolen bases per nine frames in 1999. The next-best figures were generated by Benito Santiago (0.45) and part-time catcher Tony Eusebio (0.46).

While Flaherty allowed 0.71 stolen bases per nine innings—the major league average, but a high figure among caught-stealing leaders—he still was successful at thwarting 38.6 percent of all basestealing attempts. The fact is, men on base ran on Tampa Bay pitching and didn't give Flaherty the respect he deserved. No catcher retired as many baserunners as the 33-year-old veteran, who has ranked in the top five in caught-stealing percentage two years in a row.

Returning to this list after a one-year absence is Charles Johnson, who has ranked in the top five in three of the last five seasons. Johnson finished behind Rodriguez and Flaherty during his first season in the AL, proving he can stunt the running game in either circuit. Despite his reputation as a fine defensive backstop, he faced 98 stolen-base attempts. That's a high figure. Still, Johnson allowed just 0.51 steals per nine frames, a very respectable number.

All but one of the catchers who finished at the back of the pack faced more than 100 stolen-base attempts in 1999. It's not surprising that baserunners frequently challenged two players who made a return behind the plate last summer, Todd Hundley and Dave Nilsson. Hundley struggled after coming back from major elbow surgery, and Nilsson arguably had his best year at the plate after spending the last few years playing elsewhere on the diamond. He wasn't quite as effective behind it.

—Thom Henninger

A more complete listing for this category can be found on page 284.

## Can We Improve Zone Ratings?

Since 1988, we have rated infielders and outfielders based on their ability to make plays on balls hit into zones that we define for each position on the field. Take the number of outs that a player makes, divide that number by the total number of balls hit into his zone and the result is the player's zone rating.

This year, we have taken a closer look at this system, analyzing more than 10 years' worth of data on every batted ball in order to further refine the zone rating. By analyzing this wealth of data, we wanted to ensure that all of the factors that we use in calculating the zone rating were accurate indicators of a player's fielding talents.

### The Results

We found a few areas where we believed it was appropriate to make adjustments. Here are the revisions that we have incorporated:

Infielders:
1. Count double plays as one converted opportunity, rather than two outs for one opportunity.

Outfielders:
1. Include popups in the ratings.
2. Increase the zone of responsibility for left and right fielders on flyballs.
3. Decrease the zone of responsibility for center fielders on flyballs.
4. Decrease the zone of responsibility for all outfielders on line drives.

### Infielder Analysis

As we mentioned, the original zone ratings for infielders were simply the number of outs initiated by a fielder divided by the number of balls hit into the player's zone. Under that system, a player received twice as much credit for starting a double play than for making any other play on the ball.

We wanted to determine if this was an appropriate way to handle these plays. We had concerns because clearly the number of double plays that a player initiates is affected by how well a teammate turns the pivot (see page 178) or how often his pitching staff induces double-play balls. Also, the effort made to start a double play often can be less impressive than a play on a ball made elsewhere on the field. We were concerned that by putting too much emphasis on starting double plays, we weren't giving enough credit for making other plays on the ball.

We wanted to look at how the ratings would be affected if we reduced the extra credit for double plays by some fraction and how they would be affected if we eliminated the extra credit entirely. We reran the ratings using no extra credit, 1/4 credit, 1/2 credit, and 3/4 credit for double plays. For example, Omar Vizquel, who started 44 double plays in 1999, was credited with 425 outs in 442 chances under the original system. In the variations outlined above, he was credited with 381, 392, 403 and 414 outs, respectively.

In order to test these variations, we looked specifically at how Gold Glove winners were affected by the various changes. For each year since 1988, we determined how many Gold Glovers were positively affected (their rank within their position went up) in each variation and how many were negatively affected (their rank went down). The net effect gave us a rating for each adjustment. Here's what we found:

### Net Effects on Gold Glove Infielders Compared to Existing Zone Rating—1988-99

| Year | Double Play Credit | | | |
|---|---|---|---|---|
| | 3/4 credit | 1/2 credit | 1/4 credit | no credit |
| 1988 | +1 | +2 | +1 | +2 |
| 1989 | -1 | -2 | 0 | 0 |
| 1990 | +1 | 0 | +2 | +3 |
| 1991 | +3 | +3 | +2 | +4 |
| 1992 | 0 | +3 | +1 | +3 |
| 1993 | 0 | +1 | +2 | +2 |
| 1994 | -2 | -2 | -4 | -4 |
| 1995 | 0 | -1 | +2 | +3 |
| 1996 | 0 | -2 | +1 | +2 |
| 1997 | -1 | -1 | +1 | +2 |
| 1998 | -1 | 0 | 0 | 0 |
| 1999 | +2 | +2 | +1 | +1 |
| Net effect | +2 | +3 | +9 | +18 |

By eliminating the extra credit on double plays, 18 more Gold Glovers improved in their ranking than decreased in their ranking. It's very difficult to say exactly how much starting double plays should be weighted in the zone rating. Clearly, this is an ability that carries some value, but based on this study, and in order to keep the rating as simple as possible, we've decided to eliminate the extra credit entirely. Note that a fielder still gets credit with both a zone opportunity and a conversion when he makes a play on a ball that is outside of his zone.

**Outfielder Analysis**

Now let's take a look at the changes that we made to the outfield ratings. The existing rating system discounted popups for all players because these plays are so routinely converted into outs that they seemed to be a poor indicator of range. However, for outfielders, we felt that it made sense to begin to include popups in the rating since charging in to grab a pop fly is often more difficult than getting to a flyball hit deeper.

Additionally, we looked at where line drives and flyballs are hit in the outfield and how often these plays are converted into outs. What we found is that flyballs hit down the foul lines are usually caught for outs. So we added the area down the lines as zones of responsibility for the left and right fielders. Similarly, we looked at the area in left-center and right-center fields and found that there were two sets of zones where no one fielder consistently made the catch. These areas of the field had been assigned to the center fielder, but we believe it's more accurate to designate these as unassigned areas.

Finally for outfielders, we significantly reduced the area of responsibility on line drives. Again, we analyzed all of the available data to determine exactly where line drives usually fall in for hits, and eliminated these areas from the zones of responsibility. The net effect is that the zone area has been reduced by about two-thirds on line drives to the outfield.

The charts on the next two pages show how zone areas have been reassigned. The shaded areas on the charts indicate the locations on the field where at least half the balls hit to that area were converted into outs by a particular position in the past 13 years.

## Old Flyball Zones

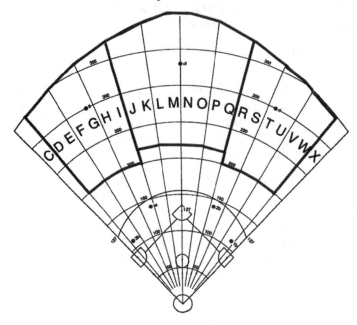

## New Flyball Zones

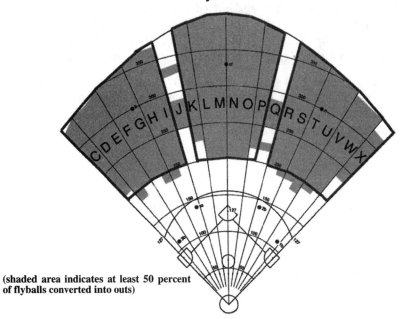

(shaded area indicates at least 50 percent of flyballs converted into outs)

## Old Line-Drive Zones

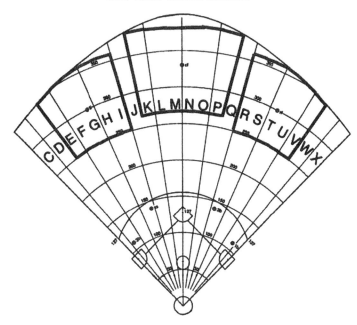

## New Line-Drive Zones

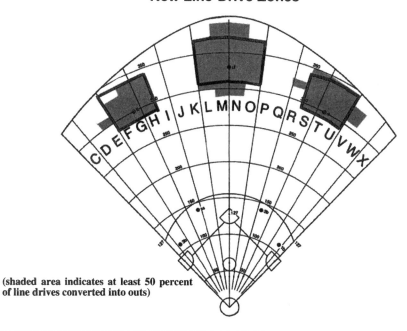

(shaded area indicates at least 50 percent of line drives converted into outs)

*Baseball Scoreboard*

Just as we did with infielders, we looked at the effect these adjustments had on Gold Glove winners. Here are the results:

**Net Effect on Gold Glove Outfielders Compared to Existing Zone Ratings—1988-99**

| Year | Effect |
|---|---|
| 1988 | +3 |
| 1989 | +1 |
| 1990 | +1 |
| 1991 | +2 |
| 1992 | 0 |
| 1993 | -1 |
| 1994 | +2 |
| 1995 | +2 |
| 1996 | -5 |
| 1997 | 0 |
| 1998 | 0 |
| 1999 | +1 |
| Net effect | +6 |

By instituting these changes, six more Gold Glovers improved in their ranking than decreased. Similar to infielders, outfielders who make a play on a ball outside their zone get a zone opportunity as well as credit for converting that opportunity.

### Ultimate Zone Ratings

As long as we were going through this process, we thought that it would be interesting to take an even more detailed look at the range of fielders in comparison to the average. We developed a system that gave more credit for plays made that are less often converted and less credit for routine plays. The result is ultimate zone rating. Here are the leaders for 1999:

**Highest Ultimate Zone Rating—1999**

| First Basemen | UZR |
|---|---|
| Kevin Young, Pit | 26.15 |
| John Olerud, NYM | 25.35 |
| Rico Brogna, Phi | 20.13 |
| Tino Martinez, NYY | 16.15 |
| Mark Grace, ChC | 15.62 |

| Second Basemen | UZR |
|---|---|
| Pokey Reese, Cin | 56.28 |
| Homer Bush, Tor | 24.93 |
| Craig Biggio, Hou | 20.27 |
| Randy Velarde, Ana-Oak | 17.81 |
| Jay Bell, Ari | 16.10 |

| Third Basemen | UZR |
|---|---|
| Robin Ventura, NYM | 45.66 |
| Adrian Beltre, LA | 33.57 |
| Scott Rolen, Phi | 22.51 |
| Aaron Boone, Cin | 16.71 |
| John Valentin, Bos | 16.63 |

| Shortstops | UZR |
|---|---|
| Rey Sanchez, KC | 56.75 |
| Rey Ordonez, NYM | 46.40 |
| Omar Vizquel, Cle | 25.19 |
| Royce Clayton, Tex | 17.56 |
| Tony Batista, Ari-Tor | 16.66 |

| Left Fielders | UZR |
|---|---|
| Geoff Jenkins, Mil | 32.35 |
| Ray Lankford, StL | 24.89 |
| Johnny Damon, KC | 21.33 |
| Luis Gonzalez, Ari | 16.47 |
| B.J. Surhoff, Bal | 15.14 |

| Center Fielders | UZR |
|---|---|
| Andruw Jones, Atl | 44.72 |
| Mike Cameron, Cin | 35.82 |
| Gabe Kapler, Det | 32.23 |
| Ruben Rivera, SD | 28.65 |
| Chris Singleton, CWS | 22.84 |

| Right Fielders | UZR |
|---|---|
| Shawn Green, Tor | 28.78 |
| Mark Kotsay, Fla | 26.54 |
| Jermaine Dye, KC | 19.36 |
| Tony Womack, Ari | 15.59 |
| Sammy Sosa, ChC | 14.67 |

So how did we come up with those numbers? First we computed (for each position) the percentage of time that an out was recorded for every type of batted ball, for every segment of the field. A segment of the field consists of lengths, from home plate toward the outfield stands in 10-foot increments, and widths, consisting of a single letter based on our A-Z demarcation of the field. Then we used these percentages to rank every fielder on every batted ball where they were on the field. For instance, if a flyball is hit 340 feet to direction Q in right-center field, 40 percent of the time that play is converted to an out by the right fielder. So, if the right fielder makes an out on this particular play, we would give him .6 points based on the fact that 60 percent of the time that the play is not made. If the right fielder failed to make the play, we would subtract .4 from his rating. An average fielder winds up with an ultimate zone rating of 0. In essence, the ultimate zone rating represents the number of outs recorded by the fielder that are above or below the average fielder with the same number of chances. A more complete list can be found in the Appendix.

## Future Refinements

Quantifying fielding ability is a difficult task and we constantly are looking to improve our methodology. While these zone ratings go a long way toward examining fielding ability, there still are further refinements that we would like to research in the future. The questions we would like to answer include:

*What effect does the ballpark in which a player plays have on his zone rating?*

For instance, J.T. Snow, who won the Gold Glove at first base last year, ranks very low in the ultimate zone rating with a -9.12 rating. However, his ranking on the road is 8.69, which is best in the major leagues.

*Are STATS' official scorers consistent in their reporting of where balls land?*

Just as Major League Baseball's official scorers vary from city to city, so do STATS reporters. And just as one official scorer may be less likely to charge an error to a fielder, our reporters may have certain tendencies as well. For instance, one reporter may tend to track base hits into section Q more often than another reporter.

*Can we more precisely determine how to weight double plays?*

In the future, we would like to look into the specific value of being able to start a double play by looking at several factors including the ability of an average fielder vs. an above-average one, and what the overall benefit that ability brings to a team. We then could compare that difference in ability to the same difference in other fielding areas.

*What other methods can we use to evaluate our zone ratings?*

We've often looked at Gold Glove Award winners to compare with zone ratings. Sometimes there's a correlation, while others there's not. Part of the reason they may not correlate is that the Gold Glove is an award given for a player's total defensive ability, rather than just range. Also, the Gold Glove is often given to a player who has earned a reputation, not just for one particular season but over an entire career. It's possible that the Gold Glove isn't always given to the appropriate fielder in a given season, which makes it difficult to learn much from any comparisons in these cases. We'd like to look into other methods of evaluating our zone rating effectiveness.

We're looking forward to analyzing these and other issues as we continue to publish statistics that provide you with the greatest insight into the game of baseball.

—John Dewan, Jim Osborne

A more complete listing for this category can be found on page 285.

## Who's Best in the Infield Zone?

Would you trade Pokey Reese in order to acquire Ken Griffey Jr.? The Reds balked at doing that and eventually got Griffey without surrendering Reese. Here's what Ken Griffey Sr. had to say about Reese in the midst of negotiations:

"There's no way I'd give up Pokey Reese," the Reds' coach told *The Cincinnati Post*. "There's just no way. You've got to be strong up the middle, and you can't weaken yourself that way. Pokey is an amazing second baseman, and anyone who has watched him knows it."

If you haven't seen Reese play, the numbers paint a remarkable picture. In our annual look at infield zone rating, Reese proved capable of fielding nearly everything within his designated zone during the 1999 season:

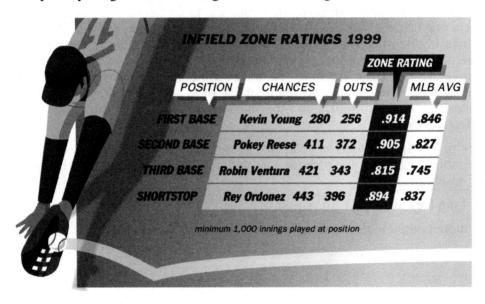

**INFIELD ZONE RATINGS 1999**

| POSITION | CHANCES | OUTS | ZONE RATING | MLB AVG |
|---|---|---|---|---|
| FIRST BASE | Kevin Young 280 | 256 | .914 | .846 |
| SECOND BASE | Pokey Reese 411 | 372 | .905 | .827 |
| THIRD BASE | Robin Ventura 421 | 343 | .815 | .745 |
| SHORTSTOP | Rey Ordonez 443 | 396 | .894 | .837 |

minimum 1,000 innings played at position

By charting the distance and direction of every batted ball, STATS reporters covering major league games document how many groundballs are hit into the designated zone of each defensive player on the field. Each infielder gets a zone rating based on the number of grounders he converts into outs. Popups and flyballs are ignored for infielders. STATS' John Dewan and Jim Osborne revamped zone-rating calculations in February 2000 (see page 165), and infielders no longer get credit for two outs when they start a groundball double play. As a result, our new zone ratings are lower than our old ones.

Let's take a look at the 1999 leaders at each infield position:

**Highest Zone Rating, First Basemen—1999**

| Player, Team | Rtg |
|---|---|
| Kevin Young, Pit | .914 |
| Mark Grace, ChC | .893 |
| Tony Clark, Det | .889 |
| John Olerud, NYM | .879 |
| Tino Martinez, NYY | .876 |
| **Lowest** | |
| Fred McGriff, TB | .806 |
| **MLB Average** | **.846** |

(minimum 1,000 innings)

It has been a well-kept secret that Kevin Young, drafted as a third baseman, is one of the best defensive first basemen around. Surprisingly, he made 23 errors in 1999, the major league high among first sackers. But he managed an impressive zone rating despite playing with bad knees.

**Highest Zone Rating, Second Basemen—1999**

| Player, Team | Rtg |
|---|---|
| Pokey Reese, Cin | .905 |
| Edgardo Alfonzo, NYM | .855 |
| Craig Biggio, Hou | .854 |
| Randy Velarde, Ana-Oak | .853 |
| Roberto Alomar, Cle | .852 |
| **Lowest** | |
| Chuck Knoblauch, NYY | .778 |
| **MLB Average** | **.827** |

(minimum 1,000 innings)

Reese and Edgardo Alfonzo moved to second base full-time in 1999, and the change didn't hurt either a bit. Not only did they post the best zone ratings at second, they also committed just 12 errors between them all season.

**Highest Zone Rating, Third Basemen—1999**

| Player, Team | Rtg |
|---|---|
| Robin Ventura, NYM | .815 |
| Adrian Beltre, LA | .792 |

*Baseball Scoreboard*

| Player, Team | Rtg |
|---|---|
| Aaron Boone, Cin | .772 |
| Scott Brosius, NYY | .769 |
| Jeff Cirillo, Mil | .765 |
| **Lowest** | |
| Tony Fernandez, Tor | .685 |
| **MLB Average** | **.745** |

(minimum 1,000 innings)

After breaking his leg in 1997, Robin Ventura has bounced back to win Gold Gloves and finish first in zone rating in both 1998 and '99.

**Highest Zone Rating, Shortstops—1999**

| Player, Team | Rtg |
|---|---|
| Rey Ordonez, NYM | .894 |
| Rey Sanchez, KC | .889 |
| Barry Larkin, Cin | .878 |
| Mike Bordick, Bal | .867 |
| Omar Vizquel, Cle | .862 |
| **Lowest** | |
| Christian Guzman, Min | .782 |
| **MLB Average** | **.837** |

(minimum 1,000 innings)

It shouldn't be any shock that dazzling Rey Ordonez came out on top. However, Rey Sanchez' No. 2 ranking was somewhat of a surprise.

And here's a look at the leaders over the last three seasons:

**Highest Infield Zone Rating—1997-99**

| First Basemen | Rtg |
|---|---|
| Jeff King | .886 |
| Kevin Young | .880 |
| John Olerud | .872 |
| Mark Grace | .872 |
| Tony Clark | .870 |
| **Lowest** | |
| Mo Vaughn | .779 |
| **MLB Average** | **.841** |

| Second Basemen | Rtg |
|---|---|
| Craig Biggio | .853 |
| Eric Young | .843 |
| Jeff Kent | .841 |
| Luis Castillo | .841 |
| Mike Lansing | .837 |
| **Lowest** | |
| Todd Walker | .761 |
| **MLB Average** | **.824** |

| Third Basemen | Rtg |
|---|---|
| Robin Ventura | .803 |
| Scott Rolen | .799 |
| Scott Brosius | .794 |
| Jeff Cirillo | .791 |
| Kevin Orie | .787 |
| **Lowest** | |
| Russ Davis | .686 |
| **MLB Average** | **.746** |

| Shortstops | Rtg |
|---|---|
| Barry Larkin | .875 |
| Omar Vizquel | .873 |
| Mike Bordick | .870 |
| Rey Ordonez | .868 |
| Royce Clayton | .863 |
| **Lowest** | |
| Miguel Tejada | .814 |
| **MLB Average** | **.842** |

(minimum 2,000 innings)

Young and Ventura are the active leaders for 1999 *and* 1997-99 at first and third base, respectively. Reese's .905 rating at second over the last three years would lead the majors if he qualified. Barry Larkin's excellence at shortstop is one of the reasons that the Reds shifted Reese to second.

—Thom Henninger

A more complete listing for this category can be found on page 287.

## Who Can Turn the Pivot?

After a solid 1998 in which he was one of the National League's best defensive third basemen, Edgardo Alfonzo abandoned the hot corner to accommodate the Mets' signing of free agent Robin Ventura. Alfonzo responded by committing just five errors in 158 games for a major league-best fielding percentage of .993. On top of that, he didn't let the move compromise his offense. Alfonzo batted .304 with a career-high 27 homers, and he topped the century mark in RBI for the first time in five major league seasons.

If that wasn't enough, among all major league second basemen, no second sacker completed a larger percentage of his double-play opportunities than Alfonzo.

STATS defines a double-play opportunity as any situation with a runner on first and less than two outs in which the second baseman records a put-out at second base. With a double play on the line, the better pivot men at second will execute the throw for the twin killing better than 60 percent of the time.

Here are the keystone kings who completed the highest percentage of their double-play opportunities in 1999:

### Best Pivot Men—1999

| Player, Team | Opp | DP | Pct |
| --- | --- | --- | --- |
| Edgardo Alfonzo, NYM | 84 | 62 | .738 |
| Mark McLemore, Tex | 83 | 59 | .711 |
| Randy Velarde, Ana-Oak | 80 | 55 | .688 |
| Miguel Cairo, TB | 89 | 60 | .674 |
| Damion Easley, Det | 99 | 65 | .657 |
| Quilvio Veras, SD | 79 | 50 | .633 |
| Ron Belliard, Mil | 70 | 44 | .629 |
| Mickey Morandini, ChC | 75 | 47 | .627 |
| David Bell, Sea | 99 | 61 | .616 |
| Pokey Reese, Cin | 78 | 48 | .615 |
| **MLB Average** | | | **.584** |

(minimum 50 Opp)

While Alfonzo accepted a positional move that made the Mets' infield the best in baseball, it's amazing that so many other pivot kings are changing teams these days. The second-place finisher in double-play conversion,

Mark McLemore, has inked a deal with Seattle this offseason, putting himself in competition for playing time with rookie Carlos Guillen and David Bell, who ranked ninth in pivot success in 1999. In July, Randy Velarde was traded to Oakland in the midst of his best major league season at age 36, and the Athletics re-signed him for two more years in October. Quilvio Veras was dealt to Atlanta in December, in exchange for another second baseman who has appeared on this list, Bret Boone. Mickey Morandini signed a minor league deal with Montreal.

Over the last five seasons, no one has produced a success rate on double-play pivots like Fernando Vina. Injuries kept the smooth and always quick Vina from qualifying for the 1999 leader board, but he clearly has been the best at finishing the double play in the latter half of the 1990s, by a wide margin:

**Best Pivot Men—1995-99**

| Player | Opp | DP | Pct |
|---|---|---|---|
| Fernando Vina | 324 | 239 | .738 |
| Damion Easley | 317 | 212 | .669 |
| Bret Boone | 383 | 238 | .621 |
| Miguel Cairo | 188 | 116 | .617 |
| Luis Alicea | 272 | 166 | .610 |
| Ray Durham | 457 | 277 | .606 |
| Jeff Kent | 314 | 190 | .605 |
| Mark Lemke | 182 | 110 | .604 |
| Randy Velarde | 222 | 133 | .599 |
| Mark McLemore | 354 | 211 | .596 |
| **MLB Average** | | | **.586** |

(minimum 180 Opp)

Of course, Vina is on the move, too. The Brewers traded Vina to the Cardinals in December, opening up a permanent spot for Ron Belliard, who ranked in the top 10 in pivot success for '99. Despite missing 264 games over the last five seasons, Vina has turned more double plays on the pivot than anyone, with the exception of Chuck Knoblauch, Craig Biggio and Ray Durham. If Vina stays healthy, he'll make a noteworthy impact on the ERA of the St. Louis staff.

—Thom Henninger

A more complete listing for this category can be found on page 289.

## Who's Best in the Outfield Zone?

Blinding speed is a great asset in the outfield, but so are soft hands, accurate reads and quick jumps. None of these skills is that valuable by itself.

Likewise, fielding percentage alone isn't a good indicator of an outfielder's defensive prowess. It only tells you what he does when he tries to put a glove on the ball. It takes another stat to evaluate how efficient an outfielder is at getting to the ball in the first place.

As we do with infielders, STATS measures an outfielder's zone rating by comparing the number of outs recorded by a player to the number of balls that are hit into his defensive area. Dividing the outs recorded by the balls hit into an outfielder's zone gives us his zone rating, and zone rating gives us an idea which outfielders cover the most ground. STATS' John Dewan and Jim Osborne have revamped our zone ratings (see page 165), adding popups to an outfielder's responsibility, while also increasing their zone for flyballs and decreasing their zone for liners. The new, improved outfield zone ratings are considerably higher than those we ran in the past.

For those outfielders who played 1,000 innings in 1999, here are the leaders in zone rating, starting with left field:

**Highest Zone Rating, Left Fielders—1999**

| Player, Team | Rtg |
|---|---|
| Ron Gant, Phi | .942 |
| Geoff Jenkins, Mil | .926 |
| Johnny Damon, KC | .926 |
| Luis Gonzalez, Ari | .910 |
| Greg Vaughn, Cin | .892 |
| **Lowest** | |
| Dante Bichette, Col | .765 |
| **MLB Average** | **.873** |

(minimum 1,000 innings)

The leaders here are proof that raw speed isn't mandatory to getting to the most balls in the outfield. Ron Gant isn't nearly as fast as he was before breaking his right leg in a 1994 minibike accident, but he topped our left-field list for the second time in three years. Johnny Damon is the only left fielder in the top five with truly impressive wheels.

**Highest Zone Rating, Center Fielders—1999**

| Player, Team | Rtg |
|---|---|
| Ruben Rivera, SD | .910 |
| Mike Cameron, Cin | .908 |
| Carlos Beltran, KC | .908 |
| Andruw Jones, Atl | .901 |
| Chris Singleton, CWS | .892 |
| **Lowest** | |
| Bernie Williams, NYY | .846 |
| **MLB Average** | **.878** |

(minimum 1,000 innings)

Ruben Rivera has struggled with the bat, but he sure does cover a lot of ground in center field. The White Sox traded away Mike Cameron to get Paul Konerko, but quickly found another stellar center fielder in Chris Singleton. American League Rookie of the Year Carlos Beltran showed he could play a little defense, too. But how Bernie Williams won a Gold Glove he clearly didn't deserve is beyond us.

**Highest Zone Rating, Right Fielders—1999**

| Player, Team | Rtg |
|---|---|
| Brian Jordan, Atl | .917 |
| Magglio Ordonez, CWS | .917 |
| Bobby Abreu, Phi | .900 |
| Trot Nixon, Bos | .897 |
| Jeromy Burnitz, Mil | .895 |
| **Lowest** | |
| Matt Stairs, Oak | .796 |
| **MLB Average** | **.874** |

(minimum 1,000 innings)

Brian Jordan brought both a solid glove and bat to the Braves when he signed as a free agent. Magglio Ordonez, one of the most underrated young players in the game, proved his defensive game is coming along as well as his offense. He placed fifth on this list last year and now springs to second on the leader board. As with the left-field list, there's not a lot of blazing speed on this chart.

Here's what the leaders over the past three seasons look like:

*Baseball Scoreboard*

**Highest Outfield Zone Rating—1997-99**

| Left Fielders | Rtg |
|---|---|
| Ron Gant | .926 |
| Greg Vaughn | .894 |
| Rickey Henderson | .892 |
| Shannon Stewart | .890 |
| Bernard Gilkey | .886 |
| **Lowest** | |
| Dante Bichette | .803 |
| **MLB Average** | **.874** |

| Center Fielders | Rtg |
|---|---|
| Brian Hunter | .918 |
| Mike Cameron | .914 |
| Andruw Jones | .911 |
| Damon Buford | .910 |
| Lance Johnson | .904 |
| **Lowest** | |
| Darryl Hamilton | .857 |
| **MLB Average** | **.886** |

| Right Fielders | Rtg |
|---|---|
| Brian Jordan | .915 |
| Raul Mondesi | .913 |
| Magglio Ordonez | .912 |
| Jeromy Burnitz | .909 |
| Jermaine Dye | .908 |
| **Lowest** | |
| Larry Walker | .824 |
| **MLB Average** | **.878** |

(minimum 2,000 innings)

Gant and Jordan repeat as both the one-year and three-year leaders in left and right field. The Mariners may have been forced to trade Ken Griffey Jr., but at least they have the top two zone-rating performers in center field in Brian Hunter and Cameron. It's no coincidence that the trailers at each position all have played for the Rockies. Zone ratings don't make adjustments for the fact that balls are hit harder in Colorado's thin air.

—Thom Henninger

A more complete listing for this category can be found on page 290.

## Which Outfielders Know How to Hold 'Em?

If the names Jermaine Dye, Chris Singleton and Juan Encarnacion are mentioned, what probably first comes to mind are the breakout seasons offensively these three young players enjoyed in 1999. While they still have plenty of adjustments to make as major league hitters, all three surpassed most of their previous single-season highs. Dye, the elder statesman of this trio with four years of big league experience, batted .294 with 27 homers and 119 RBI.

What may not be common knowledge is that baserunners are less likely to take an extra base on them when they are in the outfield. Using a statistic called outfield advance percentage, the chart below shows the outfielders who command the most respect when it comes to taking an extra base:

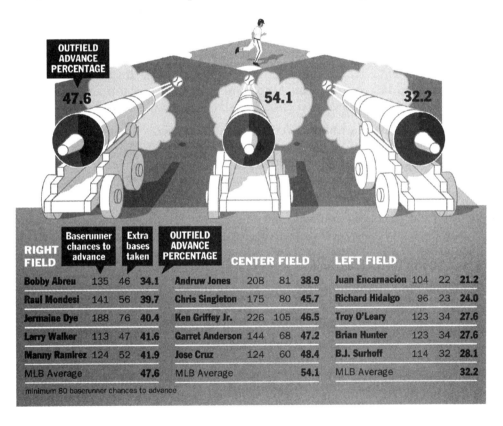

| RIGHT FIELD | Baserunner chances to advance | Extra bases taken | OUTFIELD ADVANCE PERCENTAGE | CENTER FIELD | | | | LEFT FIELD | | | |
|---|---|---|---|---|---|---|---|---|---|---|---|
| Bobby Abreu | 135 | 46 | 34.1 | Andruw Jones | 208 | 81 | 38.9 | Juan Encarnacion | 104 | 22 | 21.2 |
| Raul Mondesi | 141 | 56 | 39.7 | Chris Singleton | 175 | 80 | 45.7 | Richard Hidalgo | 96 | 23 | 24.0 |
| Jermaine Dye | 188 | 76 | 40.4 | Ken Griffey Jr. | 226 | 105 | 46.5 | Troy O'Leary | 123 | 34 | 27.6 |
| Larry Walker | 113 | 47 | 41.6 | Garret Anderson | 144 | 68 | 47.2 | Brian Hunter | 123 | 34 | 27.6 |
| Manny Ramirez | 124 | 52 | 41.9 | Jose Cruz | 124 | 60 | 48.4 | B.J. Surhoff | 114 | 32 | 28.1 |
| MLB Average | | | 47.6 | MLB Average | | | 54.1 | MLB Average | | | 32.2 |

minimum 80 baserunner chances to advance

Dye, Singleton and Encarnacion are new to this annual STATS leader board, which gives us a numerical glimpse at some of the outfielders with the most respected arms in the business. An advance is charged whenever a runner takes an extra base on a hit to that particular fielder. As an example, if a batter singles to center with a runner on first base, the center fielder is tagged with an advance if the baserunner moves to third.

It's common for center fielders to have the poorest outfield advance percentages; left fielders often have the best ones. Center fielders often throw the longest distances, and they're more likely to have their arms tested.

It's widely believed that outfielders with reputations for strong arms are challenged less often, so they sometimes record lower assist totals. The outfield advance percentage may be more revealing in documenting an outfielder's success against baserunners. It records the real effects as well as the perceived threat of his arm.

In a fraternity that includes strong-armed veterans Raul Mondesi and Manny Ramirez, Bobby Abreu has emerged as one of the new shining lights. For a second straight season he ranks first among right fielders in outfield advance percentage. As a regular for the first time in 1998, Abreu also led all major league right fielders in assists. The respect factor must have surfaced last summer, as Abreu didn't rank in the top five in assists. Still, his outfield advance percentage easily was the best at his position.

Another of baseball's impressive young guns, Andruw Jones, also repeated as a leader in outfield advance percentage in just his third full season in the majors. Like Abreu in right field, Jones led big league center fielders in both assists and outfield advance percentage in 1998, but his arm now garners enough respect that he didn't repeat as the assist leader in '99.

In left field, Encarnacion was the leader in outfield advance percentage during his first full season in Detroit. While Encarnacion may have the furthest to go of all of these young players in terms of hitting, he's exceptionally quick in the outfield and has a strong, accurate arm.

Let's also take a look at the leaders in outfield assists in 1999:

### Most Outfield Assists—1999

| Right Field | | Center Field | | Left Field | |
| --- | --- | --- | --- | --- | --- |
| Mark Kotsay, Fla | 19 | Carlos Beltran, KC | 16 | Dante Bichette, Col | 17 |
| Albert Belle, Bal | 17 | Doug Glanville, Phi | 13 | B.J. Surhoff, Bal | 16 |
| Jermaine Dye, KC | 17 | Andruw Jones, Atl | 13 | Brian Hunter, Det-Sea | 14 |
| Vladimir Guerrero, Mon | 15 | Kenny Lofton, Cle | 11 | Geoff Jenkins, Mil | 14 |
| 2 tied with | 13 | 2 tied with | 10 | Richard Hidalgo, Hou | 13 |

Dante Bichette has led all left fielders in outfield assists for two straight years now. While Bichette still has a decent arm, his high assist total simply has had more to do with the far-greater number of advancement opportunities he faced playing half of his home games at hitting-happy Coors Field. Baserunners had 151 advancement chances against Bichette in 1999—nearly 50 percent more than Encarnacion—and Bichette recorded a 39.1 outfield advance percentage that was below the league average.

In Philadelphia, however, runners have to contend with *two* intimidating arms. Abreu works alongside Doug Glanville, who has ranked among assist leaders in center the last two seasons. In Kansas City, another young twosome strikes fear into the hearts of baserunners. Dye and 1999 American League Rookie of the Year Carlos Beltran have impressive arms, with Beltran ranking first in assists among all center fielders and Dye placing third in both assists and outfield advance percentage.

Leading all right fielders in assists was Mark Kotsay, who produced a league-high 20 assists. Now that Kotsay and Beltran have established their credentials as threats to retire baserunners, it may be that both will join the leader board for outfield advance percentage during the 2000 season.

You've met the young studs. Now let's look at the guys who have produced the best outfield advance percentages over the last three seasons:

### Highest Outfield Advance Percentage—1997-99

| Right Field | | Center Field | | Left Field | |
|---|---|---|---|---|---|
| Bobby Abreu | 34.4 | Andruw Jones | 41.5 | B.J. Surhoff | 28.1 |
| Raul Mondesi | 41.4 | Ken Griffey Jr. | 46.3 | Bernard Gilkey | 29.5 |
| Dave Martinez | 42.5 | Doug Glanville | 48.1 | Greg Vaughn | 30.1 |
| Manny Ramirez | 42.7 | Jim Edmonds | 48.7 | Shannon Stewart | 30.4 |
| Brian Jordan | 44.1 | Brian Hunter | 49.7 | Luis Gonzalez | 31.5 |
| **Worst** | | **Worst** | | **Worst** | |
| Jeromy Burnitz | 56.8 | Otis Nixon | 61.0 | Henry Rodriguez | 39.5 |
| **MLB Average** | 47.7 | **MLB Average** | 54.5 | **MLB Average** | 32.3 |

(minimum 200 baserunner chances to advance)

While B.J. Surhoff emerges as the three-year leader in left field, the new guard, led by Abreu and Jones, has taken over in this category. They hold leads over two guys who established themselves as power-armed youngsters early in the 1990s, Raul Mondesi and Ken Griffey Jr.

—Thom Henninger

A more complete listing for this category can be found on page 291.

## Which Fielders Have the Best Defensive Batting Average?

There are any number of statistics that can provide an instant evaluation of a hitter's or pitcher's ability, but the same isn't true for defenders. There's no single stat that can tell the complete picture of a player's glovework. For instance, zone rating (range), pivot percentage (ability to turn the double play) and fielding percentage (reliability) all have relevance when discussing second basemen.

In an attempt to develop a single number that evaluates all key aspects of a player's defense, John Dewan created defensive batting average, an annual *Scoreboard* feature. Using standard deviations of a variety of stats, the defensive batting average produces a number similar to a regular batting average. Last year's overall DBA was .280, while major league hitters batted .271. Here are the statistics and weighting used for each position:

### DBA Statistics and Weighting

| Pos | Statistics (Weighting) |
| --- | --- |
| 1B | Zone Rating (75%), Fielding Percentage (25%) |
| 2B | Zone Rating (60%), Pivot Pct. (25%), Fielding Pct. (15%) |
| 3B | Zone Rating (60%), Fielding Percentage (40%) |
| SS | Zone Rating (80%), Fielding Percentage (20%) |
| LF | Zone Rating (65%), OF Advance Pct. (20%), Fielding Pct. (15%) |
| CF | Zone Rating (55%), OF Advance Pct. (30%), Fielding Pct. (15%) |
| RF | Zone Rating (50%), OF Advance Pct. (35%), Fielding Pct. (15%) |

Let's take a look at the five best and single worst player at each position last year:

### Highest Defensive Batting Average, First Basemen—1999

| Player, Team | Zone | FPct | DBA |
| --- | --- | --- | --- |
| Mark Grace, ChC | .318 | .292 | .311 |
| Kevin Young, Pit | .337 | .213 | .306 |
| Tony Clark, Det | .314 | .270 | .303 |
| Tino Martinez, NYY | .303 | .297 | .302 |
| John Olerud, NYM | .306 | .287 | .301 |
| **Lowest** | | | |
| Fred McGriff, TB | .241 | .243 | .241 |

(minimum 1,000 innings)

First base is a fine example of how defensive batting average demands all-around play. Kevin Young had easily the best zone rating in the majors at .914, but he also made 23 errors, nine more than any other first sacker. Meanwhile, Mark Grace both covered a lot of ground and was surehanded, so he earned the top spot. Interestingly, last-place finisher Fred McGriff had a better DBA than Grace just a year ago.

**Highest Defensive Batting Average, Second Basemen—1999**

| Player, Team | Zone | Pivot | FPct | DBA |
|---|---|---|---|---|
| Pokey Reese, Cin | .369 | .295 | .322 | .343 |
| Edgardo Alfonzo, NYM | .312 | .342 | .333 | .323 |
| Randy Velarde, Ana-Oak | .309 | .322 | .286 | .309 |
| Roberto Alomar, Cle | .308 | .280 | .328 | .304 |
| Mark McLemore, Tex | .297 | .331 | .287 | .304 |
| **Lowest** | | | | |
| Chuck Knoblauch, NYY | .225 | .248 | .197 | .226 |

(minimum 1,000 innings)

Converted shortstop Pokey Reese's first season as a full-time second baseman was nothing short of spectacular. His overall .343 average and his .369 mark in zone rating were both records for any position since we started tracking DBA after the 1993 season. And while Chuck Knoblauch's throwing woes received a lot of attention, his defensive play was atrocious across the board.

**Highest Defensive Batting Average, Third Basemen—1999**

| Player, Team | Zone | FPct | DBA |
|---|---|---|---|
| Robin Ventura, NYM | .329 | .332 | .330 |
| Matt Williams, Ari | .289 | .325 | .303 |
| Jeff Cirillo, Mil | .292 | .305 | .297 |
| Scott Brosius, NYY | .296 | .296 | .296 |
| Aaron Boone, Cin | .299 | .288 | .294 |
| **Lowest** | | | |
| Ed Sprague, Pit | .243 | .215 | .232 |

(minimum 1,000 innings)

Robin Ventura finishing a close second to Jeff Cirillo in 1998, but claimed the top spot in 1999 thanks to major league bests in both zone rating and fielding percentage at the hot corner. At the other extreme, Ed Sprague ranked third-worst in zone rating and dead last in fielding percentage, contributing to his last-place finish in DBA.

**Highest Defensive Batting Average, Shortstops—1999**

| Player, Team | Zone | FPct | DBA |
|---|---|---|---|
| Rey Ordonez, NYM | .342 | .336 | .341 |
| Rey Sanchez, KC | .337 | .308 | .331 |
| Barry Larkin, Cin | .325 | .300 | .320 |
| Mike Bordick, Bal | .314 | .324 | .316 |
| Omar Vizquel, Cle | .308 | .296 | .305 |
| **Lowest** | | | |
| Cristian Guzman, Min | .220 | .256 | .227 |

(minimum 1,000 innings)

As we've remarked elsewhere in this book, Rey Ordonez earned a lot of "SportsCenter" time with his fielding wizardry while Rey Sanchez excelled in anonymity. All four Mets infielders ranked in the top five at their positions. Cristian Guzman arrived in the majors last year with a reputation for strong glovework, but he didn't live up to it.

**Highest Defensive Batting Average, Left Fielders—1999**

| Player, Team | Zone | Adv | FPct | DBA |
|---|---|---|---|---|
| Ron Gant, Phi | .324 | .290 | .310 | .315 |
| Geoff Jenkins, Mil | .313 | .279 | .272 | .300 |
| Johnny Damon, KC | .313 | .247 | .297 | .297 |
| Luis Gonzalez, Ari | .302 | .288 | .289 | .297 |
| B.J. Surhoff, Bal | .283 | .302 | .325 | .293 |
| **Lowest** | | | | |
| Dante Bichette, Col | .198 | .243 | .225 | .211 |

(minimum 1,000 innings)

Though he doesn't jump to mind when talk turns to the game's top defensive left fielders, Ron Gant had a strong year with the glove in 1999. He ranked well above average in zone rating, outfield advance percentage and fielding percentage. Dante Bichette was horrible across the board, especially in terms of covering ground. It's not entirely his fault, however, as Coors Field causes all Colorado outfielders to look bad due to the fact that there are many more hard-hit balls than at other parks.

### Highest Defensive Batting Average, Center Fielders—1999

| Player, Team | Zone | Adv | FPct | DBA |
|---|---|---|---|---|
| Andruw Jones, Atl | .305 | .358 | .266 | .315 |
| Chris Singleton, CWS | .293 | .327 | .296 | .304 |
| Ruben Rivera, SD | .316 | .287 | .248 | .297 |
| Mike Cameron, Cin | .313 | .283 | .262 | .296 |
| Carlos Beltran, KC | .313 | .277 | .234 | .290 |
| **Lowest** | | | | |
| Marvin Benard, SF | .241 | .233 | .288 | .246 |

(minimum 1,000 innings)

After just three full seasons in the majors, Andruw Jones already is starting to earn recognition as one of the game's best center fielders—ever. He has won two Gold Gloves and led major league center fielders in DBA and outfield advance percentage for two years running since moving to the position on an everyday basis in 1998. Marvin Benard's shortcomings are a concern for the Giants as they move into Pacific Bell Park, which has a vast right-center field.

### Highest Defensive Batting Average, Right Fielders—1999

| Player, Team | Zone | Adv | FPct | DBA |
|---|---|---|---|---|
| Bobby Abreu, Phi | .305 | .354 | .301 | .321 |
| Magglio Ordonez, CWS | .319 | .294 | .308 | .309 |
| Brian Jordan, Atl | .319 | .291 | .305 | .307 |
| Jermaine Dye, KC | .298 | .323 | .287 | .305 |
| Raul Mondesi, LA | .300 | .322 | .279 | .304 |
| **Lowest** | | | | |
| Matt Stairs, Oak | .215 | .254 | .276 | .238 |

(minimum 1,000 innings)

Bobby Abreu not only enjoyed a breakthrough year with the bat, but he also had the best defensive season of any big league right fielder. Though he registered just eight assists, he was the toughest right fielder to take an extra base on. In fairness to Matt Stairs, he's a born DH who played right field only to accommodate the slower and more fragile John Jaha.

—Jim Callis

A more complete listing for this category can be found on page 292.

# V. GENERAL QUESTIONS

## Who Were the Winningest Players of the 1990s?

**P**ete Rose used to boast that he had played in more winning games than any player in major league history. Our day-by-day database doesn't go back quite far enough to verify that claim, but we *can* tell you who the winningest players of the 1990s were. You'd probably expect a Brave or Yankee to top the list, but you'd be wrong:

**Most Starts in Team Wins—1990-99**

| Player | W |
|---|---|
| Rafael Palmeiro | 793 |
| Fred McGriff | 782 |
| Paul O'Neill | 777 |
| Craig Biggio | 772 |
| Barry Bonds | 771 |
| Cal Ripken Jr. | 762 |
| Roberto Alomar | 737 |
| Robin Ventura | 732 |
| Marquis Grissom | 730 |
| Jay Bell | 723 |

Rafael Palmeiro has never played for a World Series champion, but he spent the 1990s with teams (the Rangers and Orioles) that usually stayed in contention. It helped even more that Palmeiro was a regular throughout the decade, and still more that he hardly ever missed a game. The same things could have been said about Fred McGriff until he joined the expansion Devil Rays in 1998, but two years with a loser have cost the Crime Dog the top spot. Paul O'Neill of the Yankees hasn't been quite as durable as Palmeiro or McGriff, but he got close to the top thanks to his clubs' .583 winning percentage for the decade.

Speaking of good winning percentages, here are the players whose teams had the best winning percentages in their games started during the '90s (minimum 500 decisions):

**Highest Team Winning Percentage in Starts—1990-99**

| Player | W-L | Pct |
|---|---|---|
| Chipper Jones | 478-285 | .626 |
| Javy Lopez | 362-218 | .624 |
| Ryan Klesko | 426-264 | .617 |

| Player | W-L | Pct |
|---|---|---|
| Derek Jeter | 386-249 | .608 |
| Mark Lemke | 514-338 | .603 |
| Manny Ramirez | 491-333 | .596 |
| Jim Thome | 517-359 | .590 |
| Jeff Blauser | 596-424 | .584 |
| Paul O'Neill | 777-555 | .583 |
| David Justice | 677-492 | .579 |

(minimum 500 decisions)

Here's where you find your Braves and Yankees. Six of the top 10 players spent most of the decade with the Braves, with the Indians and Yankees dividing up the other four spots. We'll buy the notion of Chipper Jones and Derek Jeter as winning ballplayers, but we're a little less sure about Mark Lemke and Jeff Blauser.

Enough of this positive stuff. Who played in the most *losing* games during the 1990s? Durable guy, plays on the North Side of Chicago.

**Most Starts in Team Losses—1990-99**

| Player | L |
|---|---|
| Mark Grace | 758 |
| Jay Bell | 721 |
| Todd Zeile | 714 |
| Cal Ripken Jr. | 711 |
| Rafael Palmeiro | 708 |
| Ken Griffey Jr. | 705 |
| Craig Biggio | 699 |
| Fred McGriff | 676 |
| Travis Fryman | 675 |
| Sammy Sosa | 653 |

Poor Mark Grace, toiling for all those bad Cubs teams throughout the '90s. At least he kept a smile on his face most of the time. In a way, making this list is a tribute to Grace's durability. You'll also note that Jay Bell, Cal Ripken Jr., Palmeiro, Craig Biggio and McGriff made the top 10 in both most wins and most losses. It might be more useful to look at the players with the worst winning percentages in their games started during the decade. Here's the list:

*Baseball Scoreboard*

**Lowest Team Winning Percentage in Starts—1990-99**

| Player | W-L | Pct |
|---|---|---|
| Marty Cordova | 257-349 | .424 |
| Joe Randa | 214-287 | .427 |
| Tony Clark | 248-332 | .428 |
| Bob Higginson | 269-359 | .428 |
| John Flaherty | 247-325 | .432 |
| Kevin Stocker | 313-397 | .441 |
| Alan Trammell | 239-303 | .441 |
| Pat Meares | 320-404 | .442 |
| Mark Lewis | 290-366 | .442 |
| Joe Orsulak | 270-340 | .443 |

(minimum 500 decisions)

The Red Sox don't seem to think that former Twin Marty Cordova is a loser, because they signed him to a minor league contract over the winter. But if they play .424 ball this year, we'll know something.

—Don Zminda

A more complete listing for this category can be found on page 294.

## Are the Late-1990s Yankees the Most Dominant Postseason Team Ever?

Over the last four years, the Yankees have been the most dominant team in baseball, claiming nine of 10 postseason series while winning at a .778 clip. Fans riding the No. 4 train to the Bronx have witnessed three World Series championships in four seasons, which brings to mind old Yankees dynasties.

Could the late-'90s version be the most dominant postseason team *ever* in any four-year reign over baseball? The following chart gives us a glimpse of the top four-year runs in postseason play since the World Series began in 1903. The teams are ranked by their postseason winning percentage during that span:

**Best Postseason Overall Record, Four-Year Span—1903-99**

| Span | Team | Years | Total W-L | Pct | Series W-L | Pct |
|---|---|---|---|---|---|---|
| 1937-40 | Yankees | 3 | 12-1 | .923 | 3-0 | 1.000 |
| 1938-41 | Yankees | 3 | 12-1 | .923 | 3-0 | 1.000 |
| 1936-39 | Yankees | 4 | 16-3 | .842 | 4-0 | 1.000 |
| 1935-38 | Yankees | 3 | 12-3 | .800 | 3-0 | 1.000 |
| 1948-51 | Yankees | 3 | 12-3 | .800 | 3-0 | 1.000 |
| **1996-99** | **Yankees** | **4** | **35-10** | **.778** | **9-1** | **.900** |
| 1910-13 | Athletics | 3 | 12-4 | .750 | 3-0 | 1.000 |
| 1915-18 | Red Sox | 3 | 12-4 | .750 | 3-0 | 1.000 |
| 1947-50 | Yankees | 3 | 12-4 | .750 | 3-0 | 1.000 |
| 1925-28 | Yankees | 3 | 11-4 | .733 | 2-1 | .667 |
| 1926-29 | Yankees | 3 | 11-4 | .733 | 2-1 | .667 |
| 1949-52 | Yankees | 4 | 16-6 | .727 | 4-0 | 1.000 |
| 1973-76 | Reds | 3 | 16-6 | .727 | 4-1 | .800 |

(minimum 3 years in postseason during span)

Among these 13 four-year runs, four of them cover a Yankees dynasty that spans 1936-43. New York claimed the American League pennant in every year except 1940 during that period, winning 799 games in eight years for a regular-season winning percentage of .630. And those clubs tended to turn it up a notch when the World Series got underway.

The Yanks won six world titles in this dynasty's eight seasons, including four in a row beginning in 1936. With four consecutive World Series championships and only three losses along the way, the 1936-39 Yanks and their .842 postseason winning percentage are the measure by which to look at the 1996-99 Yanks.

It's easy to make a case for the 1936-39 Yankees. The 1936 club won 102 games and captured the AL flag by 19.5 games. Lou Gehrig led the AL with 49 homers, Red Ruffing enjoyed the first of four straight 20-win seasons and Monte Pearson went 19-7.

Ruffing absorbed a 6-1 loss to the Giants in Game 1 of the '36 Series, the first time ever that New York played the Fall Classic without Babe Ruth. With Gehrig hitting safely in the next five games, homering twice and driving in seven runs, the Yanks won four of the next five for the world title. The dynasty was on.

The Yankees won 102 games again in 1937, with Lefty Gomez going 21-11 and Ruffing 20-7. This time the Yanks needed just five games to dispose of the Giants, who scored a mere five runs in their four postseason losses. The starting trio of Ruffing, Gomez and Pearson dominated the World Series—with Gomez winning twice—and this threesome would lead the way in Series sweeps over the Cubs and Reds in '38 and '39. The Yanks of 1936-39 won their final nine postseason games.

The 1996-99 Yankees didn't look anything like a dominating force when their four-year run began in 1996, barely surviving a thrilling Division Series with Texas. David Cone wasn't sharp in a Game 1 loss at Yankee Stadium, and the Yankees needed single tallies in the seventh and eighth frames of Game 2 to force extra innings. They pulled out a 5-4 victory on a Dean Palmer throwing error in the 12th. When the series resumed in Texas, the Yankees stole Game 3 with two ninth-inning runs that secured a 3-2 victory. New York closed out the Division Series with a tight 6-4 win in Game 4.

The '96 Yankees grabbed the American League Championship Series from Baltimore in five games before winning a six-game World Series from Atlanta. Still, it was hard to forecast greatness for a New York club that fell behind two games to one in the 1998 ALCS—to the same Indians who banished the Yankees early in the '97 playoffs.

With New York's playoff hopes on the line, Orlando Hernandez made his postseason debut against Cleveland in Game 4, and his seven shutout innings allowed New York to knot the ALCS at two games apiece. That 4-0 win also started one of the most impressive postseason runs of all time. With El Duque contributing five victories, the Yankees won 18 of their next 19 postseason contests to claim consecutive world titles.

New York finished off the Tribe with three straight wins for the '98 AL flag, then swept the Padres for its second World Series crown in three years. To open the playoffs in 1999, the Yanks swept Texas in Division Series play for a second straight year. Then they absorbed their only loss in 19 postseason games in a five-game ALCS with Boston. Finally, for a second year in a row, New York swept the Fall Classic—this time over an equally impressive Braves team that won 103 regular-season games and had the pitching to match the Yankees.

Winning 18 of 19 postseason games is an incredible feat, and the current-day Yankees had to win nine postseason series to claim three titles. Still, for consistently dominating over a four-year period, it's hard to argue against the 1936-39 Yanks. It wouldn't even be close if it was the late-'30s Yankees who had the modern team's closer. Mariano Rivera has been the epitome of domination in postseason play, securing 13 saves while allowing just two earned runs in 42 innings from 1996-99.

Only the New York teams of 1949-52 can match the four titles in four years of the 1936-39 Yanks. In fact, Casey Stengel set a major league record by leading the Yanks to a fifth-straight world title in 1953, surpassing the managerial mark of Joe McCarthy's teams of 1936-39. Yet, the postseason winning percentage of the 1949-52 Yankees ranked last among those 13 teams with marks better than .700. These Yankees were more dominant early in their four-year run, and Brooklyn took them to seven games in 1952.

While the 1936-39 Yankees reign supreme in four-year postseason dominance, upcoming versions of the Bronx Bombers have a chance to change that. If the Yankees can build on their dynastic tendencies and maintain their playoff magic in the fall, today's team soon may approach the postseason winning percentage of the late-'30s club that captured World Series crowns with ease.

—Thom Henninger

A more complete listing for this category can be found on page 297.

## Which Teams Were 1999's Biggest Overachievers And Underachievers?

When Bill James developed his Pythagorean theorem—that a team's winning percentage closely parallels the square of its runs scored, divided by sum of the square of its runs and the square of its opponent runs—he also made another discovery. Bill learned that teams that diverged significantly from their expected winning percentage one year mostly did so by chance. They didn't have a special ability or inability to win close games, which was shown by the fact that they didn't continue to overachieve or underachieve in future seasons.

In other words, what goes up must come down, or vice versa. And a perfect example is the Royals.

In 1998, Kansas City scored 714 runs and surrendered 899. That should have translated into a .387 winning percentage and 62.3 wins in 161 games. Instead, the Royals managed 72 victories and a .447 percentage. Their positive differential of 9.7 wins made them the luckiest team in baseball.

Last year, the Royals plated 856 runs and permitted 921, both figures the highest in franchise history. Obviously, with their run differential improving by 120, they figured to do better than they had the season before. But while their expected winning percentage was .463, which would have meant 74.6 wins, they went just 64-97 (.398), underperforming by 10.6 games. That made them the unluckiest club in the game:

### Unluckiest Teams—1999

| Team | W-L | Pct | Pythag W | Pythag Pct | +/- |
|---|---|---|---|---|---|
| Royals | 64-97 | .398 | 74.6 | .463 | -10.6 |
| Orioles | 78-84 | .481 | 84.5 | .522 | -6.5 |
| Dodgers | 77-85 | .475 | 81.6 | .504 | -4.6 |
| Diamondbacks | 100-62 | .617 | 104.2 | .643 | -4.2 |
| Phillies | 77-85 | .475 | 80.5 | .497 | -3.5 |

Like the Royals, the Phillies had been one of the baseball's more fortunate teams in 1998, when they won 4.1 more games than the Pythagorean theorem predicted. And if everything had gone according to plan, the Diamondbacks and not the Braves would have had the best regular-season record in the major leagues.

As it was, Atlanta won three games more than expected, making them one of the luckier teams in the game. No team had better fortune than the

Rangers, who came out 6.3 victories better than the Pythagorean theorem thought they should have:

**Luckiest Teams—1999**

| Team | W-L | Pct | Pythag W | Pythag Pct | +/- |
|---|---|---|---|---|---|
| Rangers | 95-67 | .586 | 88.7 | .548 | 6.3 |
| White Sox | 75-86 | .466 | 71.4 | .444 | 3.6 |
| Indians | 97-65 | .599 | 93.8 | .579 | 3.2 |
| Braves | 103-59 | .636 | 100.0 | .618 | 3.0 |
| Cubs | 67-95 | .414 | 64.4 | .397 | 2.6 |

As bad as the Royals' luck was in 1999, the Reds may have more reason to be bitter. Their expected winning percentage was .597, compared to .590 for the Mets. If both teams' records would have paralleled the Pythagorean results, then Cincinnati would have won the National League wild-card race by a game over New York. But exactly the opposite occurred, leaving the Reds at home for the playoffs.

—Jim Callis

A more complete listing for this category can be found on page 299.

## What's the Real Truth About Wrigley Field's Dimensions?

For many years, I was just like you. I assumed it was 400 feet to center field at Wrigley Field, and 368 feet to both power alleys. But I, like you, was wrong!

It was sometime during the 1980 season when I noticed a few things while sitting in the lower boxes behind home plate. First, the center-field scoreboard isn't in dead center. Second, the 400 sign painted in bright yellow on the old red bricks in center wasn't in line with the plate, the pitcher's mound and second base. Third, the 368 in left-center and right-center weren't exactly where they belonged either.

As luck would have it, in 1981 my best buddy Nick got a job on the Wrigley Field grounds crew. I was able to convince him to let me into the ballpark late one summer afternoon while the Cubs were on the road, so I finally could solve the mystery of Wrigley.

We entered the ballpark and made our way to home plate. A tape wheel that I had picked up at a rental store was our companion. The first order of business was to determine the true distances of the five yellow signs that have marked Wrigley Field since the bleachers were built in 1938 under the direction of young Cubs executive Bill Veeck.

I walked the wheel down the left-field line, and as I arrived at the left-field foul pole, it read 355 feet. So far, so good. The distance exactly corresponded with the sign on the wall. Next was a check of the 353 sign down the right-field line, and it too was correct. The 368 and the 400 signs also checked out.

Then came the moment of truth. I took the tape wheel directly from home plate, over the pitcher's mound, through the middle of second base and all the way to true center field. When I arrived at the ivy-covered wall, the wheel read 395 feet. So while it's 400 feet to the deepest part of Wrigley, it's actually five feet shorter to dead-center.

Next up was a trip to true right-center. To do this, a little high school geometry was called for. We ran the tape well halfway between first and second base, stopping at the 45-foot mark. Nick stood on that spot while I returned to home plate. With the wheel I rolled a path straight through the bisection where Nick was standing and continued to the brick wall where many a homer by Billy Williams sailed into the hands of the Bleacher Bums.

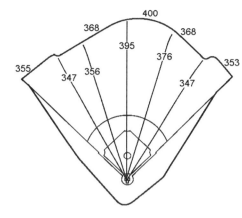

As I approached the wall, I could see the 368 sign a good 15 feet to my right toward the right-field corner. The wheel measured 368, 369, 370, 371, 372, 373, 374, 375 and, finally, 376 feet before it touched the wall.

Then it was time to repeat the journey of the many homers launched by righthanded sluggers such as Ernie Banks, Ron Santo and Sammy Sosa. Again, Nick stood halfway between second and third base. I guided the wheel from home plate, though Nick's footprints and onward to the bleacher wall.

As I neared the barrier, I was beginning to realize why Mr. Cub, Ernie Banks, named his home field the Friendly Confines. I could see the 368 sign which we had measured a half-hour ago, a full 15 feet to my right, more toward center field than toward the left-field line.

My tape wheel kissed the Wrigley wall at a friendly distance of only 356 feet! It was true! The unknown secret of Wrigley Field had been uncovered. The home-run alley for Ernie Banks was a full 20 feet shorter than the home-run distance for Billy Williams!

Sammy Sosa's blasts 10 rows deep into the left-center bleachers last year would have been nothing more than long outs to right field by teammate Henry Rodriguez. As the sun set and dusk set in, we had time for just two more measurements to solve Wrigley's final mystery.

I had to check out the wells in left and right field, where the walls curve in toward the infield, approximately 50 feet from the foul poles. Both wells are an equally inviting 347 feet from the plate.

This information has remained with Nick and me for almost 20 years, and was laid to rest with Bill Veeck and the architect's blueprints many years ago. Now the info is public for the fans of STATS, Inc. If a certain general manager or field manager would like to use this knowledge, it's now in the public domain.

—Mike Murphy

*Mike Murphy hosts a daily sports talk show on Chicago's WSCR 1160-AM.*

# VI. AWARDS & COMMENTS

## Which Players Cleaned Up at the Awards Banquet?

You won't find Joan Rivers at this awards show. You won't find Billy Crystal or Dan Patrick, either. Heck, we can't even book Whoopi Goldberg! What you *will* find are the recipients of our unique set of annual honors, including the esteemed STATS FlatBat (best bunter), the GARBI (go-ahead RBI), the coveted Slidin' Billy Trophy (best leadoff man), the Hottest Heater Award (most strikeouts per nine innings) and the control artist's prize, the Red Barrett Trophy (fewest pitches in a nine-inning complete game). We'll also hand out another set of STATS Gold Gloves.

Black tie not required. Enjoy.

### STATS FlatBat

The STATS FlatBat goes to the game's best all-around bunter. We give credit to those who can either bunt over a runner or beat one out for a base hit. Here are the annual winners:

| Year | Player | Year | Player |
|------|--------|------|--------|
| 1989 | Brett Butler | 1995 | Otis Nixon |
| 1990 | Brett Butler | 1996 | Kenny Lofton |
| 1991 | Steve Finley | 1997 | Omar Vizquel |
| 1992 | Brett Butler | 1998 | Omar Vizquel |
| 1993 | Omar Vizquel | 1999 | Omar Vizquel |
| 1994 | Kenny Lofton | | |

No, this isn't a broken record you are listening to. Omar Vizquel took the honors for the third year in a row and the fourth time in his career. The best sacrifice bunter in the game, Vizquel is a perfect 45-for-45 in sacrifice attempts over the past three years. He also paced the majors with 19 bunt hits in 1999. He has to be every corner infielder's worst nightmare when he steps to the plate... with or without runners on base.

### Slidin' Billy Trophy

Forget Mark McGwire's 70 home runs or Hack Wilson's 191 ribbies. Slidin' Billy Hamilton's record of 192 runs scored in a single season will stand for eternity. In his honor, the Slidin' Billy Trophy goes to the top leadoff hitter each season:

| Year | Player | Year | Player |
|---|---|---|---|
| 1989 | Rickey Henderson | 1995 | Chuck Knoblauch |
| 1990 | Rickey Henderson | 1996 | Chuck Knoblauch |
| 1991 | Paul Molitor | 1997 | Craig Biggio |
| 1992 | Brady Anderson | 1998 | Craig Biggio |
| 1993 | Lenny Dykstra | 1999 | Craig Biggio |
| 1994 | Kenny Lofton | | |

We have another three-peat winner. Craig Biggio scored 123 runs while batting No. 1 in the Houston lineup, and also added 56 doubles—the second year in a row he topped the 50 mark in two-baggers. Biggio edged out Chuck Knoblauch, who refused to let his throwing woes affect him at the plate. Also worth a mention is Rickey Henderson and his major league-best .417 on-base percentage while hitting out of the No. 1 spot.

## Go-Ahead RBI Leaders

The 1970s and '80s had disco, bell bottoms, Reaganomics, the Rubik's Cube and the the game-winning RBI. While we don't advocate an updated version of pants that have a life of their own or a puzzle that can take a lifetime to solve, we do want to continue to measure "important" RBI. So in the '90s we've tracked the go-ahead RBI. Here are the players who have led the majors in RBI that put their team ahead at any point in a game, even if their team failed to hold the lead:

| Year | Player | GARBI | Year | Player | GARBI |
|---|---|---|---|---|---|
| 1989 | Pedro Guerrero | 40 | 1995 | Barry Bonds | 38 |
| 1990 | Joe Carter | 36 | 1996 | Dante Bichette | 35 |
| 1991 | Fred McGriff | 37 | 1997 | Jeff Bagwell | 46 |
| 1992 | Carlos Baerga | 42 | 1998 | Sammy Sosa | 43 |
| 1993 | Albert Belle | 36 | 1999 | Manny Ramirez | 41 |
| 1994 | Jeff Bagwell | 36 | | | |

Manny Ramirez broke a five-year National League stranglehold on this award, as 41 of his 165 ribbies in 1999 gave the Indians the lead. Matt Williams finished second with 36 go-ahead RBI and led the majors with 11 GARBI in the seventh inning or later.

## RBI Percentage Leaders

The leaders in RBI percentage are the players who drive in the highest percentage of their available RBI (i.e., if they homered in every at-bat). And for the fourth time in five years, the winner is...

| Year | Player | Pct |
|------|--------|-----|
| 1994 | Jeff Bagwell | 17.2 |
| 1995 | Mark McGwire | 16.4 |
| 1996 | Mark McGwire | 16.1 |
| 1997 | Ken Griffey Jr. | 14.7 |
| 1998 | Mark McGwire | 18.0 |
| 1999 | Mark McGwire | 17.2 |

McGwire's encore in this category is all the more impressive when you consider that he hit just .278 on the season. His batting average jumped to .312 with runners on base, however, and it skyrocketed to .356 with teammates in scoring position. McGwire edged out Ramirez, who posted an RBI percentage of 17.1.

## Hottest Heater

Chicks may dig the longball, but we'd be willing to bet that the fastball is next on the "digability" list. The winner of each year's Hottest Heater Award is the pitcher with the highest strikeout rate per nine innings:

| Year | Pitcher | SO/9 | Year | Pitcher | SO/9 |
|------|---------|------|------|---------|------|
| 1989 | Rob Dibble | 12.8 | 1995 | Roberto Hernandez | 12.7 |
| 1990 | Rob Dibble | 12.5 | 1996 | Randy Johnson | 12.5 |
| 1991 | Rob Dibble | 13.6 | 1997 | Billy Wagner | 14.4 |
| 1992 | Rob Dibble | 14.1 | 1998 | Billy Wagner | 14.6 |
| 1993 | Duane Ward | 12.2 | 1999 | Billy Wagner | 15.0 |
| 1994 | Bobby Ayala | 12.1 | | | |

Billy Wagner just keeps upping the ante. The flame-throwing Houston reliever has increased his SO/9 mark in each of his first five seasons in the bigs and has established a new major league record in each of the last three years. As for the Hottest Heater among starters last season, Pedro Martinez sewed up that honor with an impressive 13.2 strikeouts per nine innings—a new all-time record for starting hurlers.

## Red Barrett Trophy

In 1944, Red Barrett threw a complete game using only 58 pitches, or so the legend goes. Amazing, especially when you consider that 58 pitches may buy you only a complete *inning* at Coors Field. In honor of Barrett's achievement, we dole out the award for the pitcher who throws the fewest pitches in a nine-inning complete game each season:

| Year | Pitcher | Pitches | Year | Pitcher | Pitches |
|---|---|---|---|---|---|
| 1989 | Frank Viola | 85 | 1995 | Greg Maddux | 88 |
| 1990 | Bob Tewksbury | 76 | 1996 | Bob Wolcott | 79 |
| 1991 | Chris Bosio | 82 | 1997 | Greg Maddux | 78 |
| 1992 | John Smiley | 80 | 1998 | Andy Ashby | 75 |
| 1993 | Tom Glavine | 79 | 1999 | David Cone | 88 |
| 1994 | Bobby Munoz | 80 | | | |

David Cone treated the Yankee Stadium faithful to their second perfect game in as many seasons, needing just 88 pitches to set down 27 Expos on July 18. Ironically enough, he finished just ahead of 1998 perfectionist David Wells, who threw 92 pitches in a complete-game victory over Florida the day before Cone's masterpiece.

## Hold Leaders

Like offensive linemen in football and defensemen in hockey, middle relievers don't have a lot of stats to point to when trying to establish their effectiveness. Hence, the hold was invented to measure how well each middle man succeeds at his most important function—protecting the leads he's given.

| Year | Pitcher | Holds | Year | Pitcher | Holds |
|---|---|---|---|---|---|
| 1989 | Rick Honeycutt | 24 | 1995 | Troy Percival | 29 |
| 1990 | Barry Jones | 30 | 1996 | Mariano Rivera | 27 |
| 1991 | Mark Eichhorn | 25 | 1997 | Stan Belinda | 28 |
| 1992 | Duane Ward | 25 | | Bob Wickman | 28 |
| | Todd Worrell | 25 | 1998 | Dan Plesac | 27 |
| 1993 | Mike Jackson | 34 | | Paul Quantrill | 27 |
| 1994 | Mel Rojas | 19 | 1999 | John Johnstone | 28 |

As we note in the essay on holds, the leaders in this category often move into a closer's role within a season or two. The Giants' John Johnstone could follow that path as early as 2000 if Robb Nen struggles, while the White Sox' Keith Foulke (22 holds in '99) and the Red Sox' Derek Lowe (22 holds) also could have the opportunity to rack up a few saves this season.

## Best-Throwing Catchers

When it comes to handing out this honor, there's Ivan Rodriguez... and there is everyone else. Upon his retirement, this award will be renamed in his honor.

| Year | Catcher | CS% | Year | Catcher | CS% |
|---|---|---|---|---|---|
| 1989 | Damon Berryhill | 44.6 | 1995 | Ivan Rodriguez | 43.7 |
| 1990 | Ron Karkovice | 50.0 | 1996 | Ivan Rodriguez | 48.9 |
| 1991 | Gil Reyes | 50.6 | 1997 | Ivan Rodriguez | 51.9 |
| 1992 | Ivan Rodriguez | 49.0 | 1998 | Ivan Rodriguez | 52.5 |
| 1993 | Steve Lake | 54.5 | 1999 | Ivan Rodriguez | 52.8 |
| 1994 | Tom Pagnozzi | 46.8 | | | |

Rodriguez simply can't get much better in this category, so instead he decided to go out and boost his offensive game last season en route to an American League MVP Award. As for his arm, even the league's best basestealers run at their own risk, a topic we explore on page 160.

## STATS Gold Gloves

Sure, there are those "other" Gold Gloves, but we believe that when it comes to picking the game's best defensive players, there's enough room for differences of opinion. We like jaw-dropping stops as much as the next guy, but we try to keep in mind that range, reliability and a host of other factors merit consideration too.

### Catcher

| Year | American | National | Year | American | National |
|---|---|---|---|---|---|
| 1997 | Ivan Rodriguez | Charles Johnson | 1999 | Ivan Rodriguez | Mike Lieberthal |
| 1998 | Ivan Rodriguez | Charles Johnson | | | |

Charles Johnson moved from the NL to the AL, but he couldn't really challenge Rodriguez for Junior Circuit supremacy. Mike Lieberthal led the majors with 143 games caught and topped NL regulars by throwing out 29 percent of the basestealers who challenged him.

## First Base

| Year | American | National | Year | American | National |
|------|----------|----------|------|----------|----------|
| 1989 | Don Mattingly | Will Clark | 1995 | Wally Joyner | Jeff Bagwell |
| 1990 | Mark McGwire | Sid Bream | 1996 | Rafael Palmeiro | Mark Grace |
| 1991 | Don Mattingly | Mark Grace | 1997 | Jeff King | Wally Joyner |
| 1992 | Wally Joyner | Mark Grace | 1998 | David Segui | John Olerud |
| 1993 | Don Mattingly | Mark Grace | 1999 | Tino Martinez | Mark Grace |
| 1994 | Don Mattingly | Jeff Bagwell | | | |

Neither Mark Grace nor Tino Martinez won a real Gold Glove last season, but they should have. Grace had the highest defensive batting average in baseball in 1999. He ranked second in zone rating while Martinez ranked fifth, and both posted above-average fielding percentages. Tony Clark had a slightly higher defensive batting average than Martinez, but made too many errors for our taste.

## Second Base

| Year | American | National | Year | American | National |
|------|----------|----------|------|----------|----------|
| 1989 | Harold Reynolds | Ryne Sandberg | 1995 | Carlos Baerga | Jody Reed |
| 1990 | Billy Ripken | Ryne Sandberg | 1996 | Fernando Vina | Bret Boone |
| 1991 | Mike Gallego | Ryne Sandberg | 1997 | Chuck Knoblauch | Bret Boone |
| 1992 | Carlos Baerga | Ryne Sandberg | 1998 | Roberto Alomar | Fernando Vina |
| 1993 | Harold Reynolds | Robby Thompson | 1999 | Roberto Alomar | Pokey Reese |
| 1994 | Jody Reed | Mickey Morandini | | | |

Just as we did at catcher, we'll endorse the major league selections at second base. Roberto Alomar and Pokey Reese are two of the most dazzling second basemen in recent memory, plus they're surehanded. Reese posted the highest defensive batting average in all of baseball last year at .343.

## Third Base

| Year | American | National | Year | American | National |
|------|----------|----------|------|----------|----------|
| 1989 | Gary Gaetti | Tim Wallach | 1995 | Travis Fryman | Charlie Hayes |
| 1990 | Gary Gaetti | Charlie Hayes | 1996 | Robin Ventura | Ken Caminiti |
| 1991 | Wade Boggs | Steve Buechele | 1997 | Jeff Cirillo | Edgardo Alfonzo |
| 1992 | Robin Ventura | Terry Pendleton | 1998 | Robin Ventura | Jeff Cirillo |
| 1993 | Robin Ventura | Matt Williams | 1999 | Scott Brosius | Robin Ventura |
| 1994 | Wade Boggs | Matt Williams | | | |

Again, not much controversy at third base, where we again rubber-stamp the official selections. Scott Brosius and Robin Ventura both led their leagues in zone rating and posted above-average fielding percentages. As a result, they had the highest defensive batting average in their leagues.

## Shortstop

| Year | American | National | Year | American | National |
|------|----------|----------|------|----------|----------|
| 1989 | Ozzie Guillen | Ozzie Smith | 1995 | Gary DiSarcina | Kevin Stocker |
| 1990 | Ozzie Guillen | Ozzie Smith | 1996 | Omar Vizquel | Greg Gagne |
| 1991 | Cal Ripken | Ozzie Smith | 1997 | Omar Vizquel | Rey Ordonez |
| 1992 | Cal Ripken | Ozzie Smith | 1998 | Omar Vizquel | Barry Larkin |
| 1993 | Ozzie Guillen | Ozzie Smith | 1999 | Rey Sanchez | Rey Ordonez |
| 1994 | Gary DiSarcina | Barry Larkin | | | |

Rey Ordonez was an obvious choice, while Rey Sanchez may be a surprise to many readers. He outdid Omar Vizquel in zone rating (.889 to .862), fielding percentage (.982 to .976) and double plays (111 to 88), so Sanchez gets the edge. Ordonez and Sanchez had easily the highest defensive batting averages at shortstop.

## Left Field

| Year | American | National | Year | American | National |
|------|----------|----------|------|----------|----------|
| 1989 | Rickey Henderson | Barry Bonds | 1995 | Garret Anderson | Luis Gonzalez |
| 1990 | Rickey Henderson | Barry Bonds | 1996 | Tony Phillips | Bernard Gilkey |
| 1991 | Dan Gladden | Bernard Gilkey | 1997 | B.J. Surhoff | Barry Bonds |
| 1992 | Greg Vaughn | Barry Bonds | 1998 | B.J. Surhoff | Barry Bonds |
| 1993 | Greg Vaughn | Barry Bonds | 1999 | B.J. Surhoff | Ron Gant |
| 1994 | Tony Phillips | Moises Alou | | | |

B.J. Surhoff earns a third straight STATS Gold Glove after covering plenty of ground while totaling 16 assists and no errors. Ron Gant, who topped major league left fielders in zone rating, edges Geoff Jenkins and Luis Gonzalez in the NL.

## Center Field

| Year | American | National | Year | American | National |
|------|----------|----------|------|----------|----------|
| 1989 | Devon White | Eric Davis | 1995 | Jim Edmonds | Marquis Grissom |
| 1990 | Gary Pettis | Lenny Dykstra | 1996 | Kenny Lofton | Steve Finley |
| 1991 | Devon White | Brett Butler | 1997 | Jim Edmonds | Steve Finley |
| 1992 | Devon White | Darrin Jackson | 1998 | Brian Hunter | Andruw Jones |
| 1993 | Kenny Lofton | Darren Lewis | 1999 | Chris Singleton | Andruw Jones |
| 1994 | Devon White | Marquis Grissom | | | |

Andruw Jones and Chris Singleton have excellent range and also keep runners from taking extra bases. They also finished 1-2 in defensive batting average. Underappreciated Mike Cameron deserves an honorable mention, but he's not better than Jones.

## Right Field

| Year | American | National | Year | American | National |
|------|----------|----------|------|----------|----------|
| 1989 | Jesse Barfield | Andre Dawson | 1995 | Tim Salmon | Reggie Sanders |
| 1990 | Jesse Barfield | Tony Gwynn | 1996 | Paul O'Neill | Sammy Sosa |
| 1991 | Joe Carter | Larry Walker | 1997 | Tim Salmon | Sammy Sosa |
| 1992 | Mark Whiten | Larry Walker | 1998 | Paul O'Neill | Derek Bell |
| 1993 | Paul O'Neill | Tony Gwynn | 1999 | Magglio Ordonez | Bobby Abreu |
| 1994 | Paul O'Neill | Reggie Sanders | | | |

Magglio Ordonez gives the White Sox two-thirds of our AL outfield. Bobby Abreu's outstanding arm gives him a slight edge over Brian Jordan in the NL. Abreu's defensive batting average also was the highest among outfielders.

—Tony Nistler, Jim Callis

## What Do the Readers Have to Say?

The *Scoreboard* annually provokes many comments, questions and great thoughts from our readers. As usual, the final essay is devoted to the some of the letters and e-mails we've received over the past year.

Sanjay Singh of Redwood City, CA, writes:

*You have discussed the importance of scoring early in your book. My question is this: are teams more likely to score in any particular inning or is scoring independent of previous innings? Basically, if the Yankees score a run in the third, are they more or less likely to score in the fourth, fifth, etc.? Is there an effect? I would say there is no effect. That would also explain why the team that scores first typically wins. On average both teams should score the same amount after that inning.*

We haven't run any data on this lately, but past studies indicate that teams are more likely to score in particular innings, based partly on who is up in the batting order and partly on who is pitching for the opposition. For instance, a team is more likely to score in the first than in any other inning, for an obvious reason: the first inning is the only one in which a club's batting order is guaranteed to be set the way the manager designed it for maximum efficiency, with the leadoff man (typically a high on-base guy) coming up first and the No. 3 hitter (generally the best or second-best overall hitter on the club) guaranteed to bat in the inning. Conversely, the second inning is apt to be not as good an inning for scoring because it will usually feature less dangerous hitters, say the Nos. 5 through 8 hitters. After that, teams are likely to score not based on whether they've scored earlier, but on who's coming to the plate in that inning. For the Cardinals, any inning in which Mark McGwire is batting will be a higher-scoring inning overall than any inning in which he doesn't. The caliber of the opposing pitcher is another factor. In the modern game, the fifth through seventh innings tend to be good innings for scoring, because those innings are so often worked by the opponent's lesser relievers. Conversely it's tougher to score in the ninth because the opposing pitcher is apt to be the team's closer, the pitcher who is usually the most effective moundsman on the staff for a single inning of work.

Keith Scherer of Chicago e-mails:

*Has STATS normalized McGwire and Sosa's numbers from 1998-99? Arguments with non-numbers fans pop up regularly. Two observations: in one year, Ruth (or was it Ruth-plus-Gehrig?) outhomered the major leagues, which is to my mind the most impressive home-run feat we'll ever see. This is baseball's live-ball era, and if we normalize the S/M numbers we're likely to see them fall back to the Foxx, Greenberg, Mays, Mantle pack. Have you done the numbers to back up this argument?*

This is a little tricky. Let's do what Keith seems to be suggesting, which is to normalize home-run rates by comparing a hitter's home-run percentage to the league average and then computing an index based on the ratio. For instance, McGwire in 1998 had a home-run percentage of .1375 (70 HR in 509 AB). The National League average for the year was .0289 (2,565 HR in 88,700 AB). Thus McGwire homered at 4.76 times the league average. Let's compare that to Mickey Mantle, 1956. The Mick homered 52 times in 533 at-bats, a rate of .0976 homers per at-bat. The overall AL homer rate in '56 was .0256 HR/AB, putting Mantle at 3.81 times the league average. If you use that figure to put Mantle's '56 homer rate into the context of the 1998 National League, also adjusting for the eight extra games on the schedule, you wind up with him hitting 62 homers (.0289 x 3.81 x 533 x 1.052). McGwire's total still looks pretty impressive.

Fine so far, but watch what happens when you try to use this system for eras in which the home run was much less of a weapon overall. Let's take Babe Ruth's first huge home-run season, 1920. With 54 homers in 458 at-bats, Ruth's homer rate was .1179. The entire American League hit only 369 homers in 1920, with a homer rate of .0088. Ruth's home-run rate was a staggering 13.40 times the league average. Putting that into the context of 1998, again with the adjustment for eight extra games, you have .0289 x 13.4 x 458 x 1.052, which computes to 187 homers! That's ridiculous, of course. Ruth would have been a great slugger in any era, but comparing him to his league averages is deceiving because it took other players and teams awhile to follow the Babe's lead and start swinging for home runs. There's probably another way to try to normalize home-run totals, but comparing someone with the league average simply doesn't work.

John Rickert of Terre Haute, IN, a long-time *Scoreboard* contributor, e-mails:

*I was a little disappointed in you article "Will Shane Spencer Be a Star?" Why did you concentrate only on his 75 major league at-bats and ignore his hundreds of minor league at-bats? A look at your* Major League Handbook *shows a projection of mediocrity."*

Good point. Our projection for Spencer in the 1999 *STATS Major League Handbook* wound up on the high side, but it was correct in computing that Shane would *not* be a star:

|                       | Avg  | OBP  | Slg  |
|-----------------------|------|------|------|
| Spencer 1999 projected | .253 | .330 | .474 |
| Spencer 1999 actual    | .234 | .301 | .390 |
| Spencer 1998-99 actual | .268 | .328 | .518 |

We're not predicting much for Spencer in 2000, either: our *Handbook* projection was for a .256 average, a .329 on-base percentage and .463 slugging.

Bill Robens of Santa Fe, NM, takes issue with a 1999 *Scoreboard* essay which describes Kerry Wood's 1998 season as the most dominant pitching season of all time, based on strikeout-hit ratio:

*Dominance and strikeouts for you are synonymous.... Back in the '70s, I saw a very dominant pitcher who couldn't strike out anyone—Randy Jones. He was flat-out the best pitcher in the National League in 1975, and the best in 1976 until he was in an automobile accident in late August.*

Bill adds that "the goal in pitching is to minimize runs, and that is done by keeping people off base. A strikeout is simply one way of doing that." He feels that we should quit equating strikeouts to dominance, and that we should remove strikeouts from the game-score calculation. He'd also like us to conduct a study on the relative merit of strikeouts.

It is certainly true that the strikeout is only one way of keeping people off base, but it's also the most effective one, because any time the batter hits the ball, it can dribble through for a hit even if the batter is badly fooled. And while Jones may have been a dominant pitcher for a couple of years, there have been very few pitchers in major league history who have had long-term success without a good strikeout rate. We'll concede that there's a danger in overrating pitchers with high strikeout rates, with Nolan Ryan probably the No. 1 example. While Ryan had an outstanding career, to even rank him among the top 20 pitchers of all time simply isn't justified based on his complete pitching record. Bill points this out in his letter, and he's absolutely right.

David Smyth of Riverwoods, IL, also talks about the same article in his annual commentary on various *Scoreboard* articles:

*The strikeout-to-hit ratio seems to have an almost perfect correlation (negative) with the number of balls in play per inning. So I'd rather characterize the stat as indicating the pitcher's reliance on his defense instead of his "dominance." A pitcher who walks a lot of batters—like Randy*

*Johnson in his earlier years—isn't really showing dominance, no matter what his K/H ratio is.*

Absolutely correct, and of course the same applies to Ryan for much of his career. Thanks to both Bill and David for their comments. We'll try to be a little more careful in how we use the word "dominant."

Finally, Ron Replogle of Hopkins, MN, writes:

*You guys are so good in your field of expertise that I have read all 10 of your yearly productions with interest and, I hope, enlightenment. However, when you stray out of your field of expertise in a tidy little typhoon of drunken enthusiasm, you display such gratuitous stupidity (at least, in the eyes of an old Latin teacher) that the mind truly boggles. My reference is the article in the 1999 edition called "Should We Just Call Them 'M-Shots'?" by Don Zminda, who tries to foist off on us the idea that M in Latin stands for 500. That is patently absurd. M is the abbreviation for mille, which means 1,000. The abbreviation for 500 is D, which probably stands for dimidium mille, half a thousand, which, unfortunately, does not lend itself to DZ's purposes.*

Ouch. Ron wasn't the only person to point out the gaffe in my article on the longest home runs of 1998. Since McGwire hit so many of them, I suggested we just call 500-foot homers "M Shots," not only for McGwire but "because in Roman numerals, M equals 500." What really galls me is that, when I was in high school, I took four years of Latin! If my old Latin instructor, Father Seidel, had seen this article, he probably would have said, "Maybe we should call them 'D Shots'—D for Dummy!"

—Don Zminda

# Appendix

Each Appendix has two pieces of information to help reference it to its corresponding essay: the title which matches the title in the Table of Contents, and the page number of the corresponding essay.

In some appendices, we couldn't include every team for players who played with more than one club in 1999. In those cases, the player is listed with the number of teams he played for. The team abbreviations for current franchises:

| **American League Teams** | | **National League Teams** | |
|---|---|---|---|
| Ana | Anaheim Angels | Ari | Arizona Diamondbacks |
| Bal | Baltimore Orioles | Atl | Atlanta Braves |
| Bos | Boston Red Sox | ChC | Chicago Cubs |
| CWS | Chicago White Sox | Cin | Cincinnati Reds |
| Cle | Cleveland Indians | Col | Colorado Rockies |
| Det | Detroit Tigers | Fla | Florida Marlins |
| KC | Kansas City Royals | Hou | Houston Astros |
| Min | Minnesota Twins | LA | Los Angeles Dodgers |
| NYY | New York Yankees | Mil | Milwaukee Brewers |
| Oak | Oakland Athletics | Mon | Montreal Expos |
| Sea | Seattle Mariners | NYM | New York Mets |
| TB | Tampa Bay Devil Rays | Phi | Philadelphia Phillies |
| Tex | Texas Rangers | Pit | Pittsburgh Pirates |
| Tor | Toronto Blue Jays | StL | St. Louis Cardinals |
| | | SD | San Diego Padres |
| | | SF | San Francisco Giants |

## Baltimore Orioles: Is Mussina on Track For the Hall of Fame? (p. 9)

### Highest Winning Percentage Through Season Reaching 200 Decisions—Ages 29-32
(age as of June 30)

| Pitcher | Year | Age | Thru Season w/200th Dec W-L | Pct | Rest of Career W-L | Pct | Total W-L | Pct |
|---|---|---|---|---|---|---|---|---|
| Whitey Ford | 1961 | 32 | 158-63 | .715 | 78-43 | .645 | 236-106 | .690 |
| Old Hoss Radbourn | 1884 | 29 | 165-68 | .708 | 144-128 | .529 | 309-196 | .612 |
| Lefty Grove | 1931 | 31 | 146-61 | .705 | 154-80 | .658 | 300-141 | .680 |
| Three Finger Brown | 1909 | 32 | 144-65 | .689 | 95-64 | .597 | 239-129 | .649 |
| Pete Alexander | 1916 | 29 | 160-75 | .681 | 213-133 | .616 | 373-208 | .642 |
| Juan Marichal | 1967 | 29 | 144-68 | .679 | 99-74 | .572 | 243-142 | .631 |
| Roger Clemens | 1992 | 29 | 152-72 | .679 | 95-62 | .605 | 247-134 | .648 |
| Mike Mussina | 1999 | 30 | 136-66 | .673 | — | — | 136-66 | .673 |
| Ed Reulbach | 1913 | 30 | 143-71 | .668 | 39-35 | .527 | 182-106 | .632 |
| Jim Palmer | 1975 | 29 | 152-80 | .655 | 116-72 | .617 | 268-152 | .638 |
| Jack Chesbro | 1905 | 31 | 151-80 | .654 | 47-52 | .475 | 198-132 | .600 |
| Carl Mays | 1921 | 29 | 134-74 | .644 | 73-52 | .584 | 207-126 | .622 |
| Don Newcombe | 1958 | 32 | 130-73 | .640 | 19-17 | .528 | 149-90 | .623 |
| Sandy Koufax | 1965 | 29 | 138-78 | .639 | 27-9 | .750 | 165-87 | .655 |
| Jack Coombs | 1915 | 32 | 130-77 | .628 | 28-33 | .459 | 158-110 | .590 |
| Lon Warneke | 1938 | 29 | 131-78 | .627 | 61-43 | .587 | 192-121 | .613 |
| Jim Maloney | 1969 | 29 | 134-80 | .626 | 0-4 | .000 | 134-84 | .615 |
| Joe McGinnity | 1903 | 32 | 134-81 | .623 | 112-60 | .651 | 246-141 | .636 |
| David Cone | 1995 | 32 | 129-78 | .623 | 51-24 | .680 | 180-102 | .638 |
| Bob Lemon | 1953 | 32 | 140-85 | .622 | 67-43 | .609 | 207-128 | .618 |
| Freddie Fitzsimmons | 1933 | 31 | 136-83 | .621 | 81-63 | .563 | 217-146 | .598 |
| Carl Hubbell | 1935 | 32 | 144-88 | .621 | 109-66 | .623 | 253-154 | .622 |
| Eddie Plank | 1906 | 30 | 129-79 | .620 | 197-115 | .631 | 326-194 | .627 |
| Hooks Wiltse | 1911 | 30 | 126-78 | .618 | 13-12 | .520 | 139-90 | .607 |
| Stan Coveleski | 1921 | 31 | 129-80 | .617 | 86-62 | .581 | 215-142 | .602 |
| Ramon Martinez | 1998 | 30 | 123-77 | .615 | 2-1 | .667 | 125-78 | .616 |
| Red Faber | 1921 | 32 | 130-83 | .610 | 124-130 | .488 | 254-213 | .544 |
| Carl Erskine | 1959 | 32 | 122-78 | .610 | 0-0 | — | 122-78 | .610 |
| Ed Walsh | 1910 | 29 | 128-83 | .607 | 67-43 | .609 | 195-126 | .607 |
| Jimmy Key | 1993 | 32 | 134-87 | .606 | 52-30 | .634 | 186-117 | .614 |
| Lew Burdette | 1959 | 32 | 126-82 | .606 | 77-62 | .554 | 203-144 | .585 |
| Mike Garcia | 1956 | 32 | 126-82 | .606 | 16-15 | .516 | 142-97 | .594 |
| John Candelaria | 1984 | 30 | 122-80 | .604 | 55-42 | .567 | 177-122 | .592 |
| Jack McDowell | 1997 | 31 | 122-80 | .604 | 5-7 | .417 | 127-87 | .593 |
| Art Nehf | 1923 | 30 | 134-88 | .604 | 50-32 | .610 | 184-120 | .605 |
| Tom Glavine | 1995 | 29 | 124-82 | .602 | 63-34 | .649 | 187-116 | .617 |
| Scott McGregor | 1985 | 31 | 125-83 | .601 | 13-25 | .342 | 138-108 | .561 |
| Jim Bagby | 1921 | 31 | 120-80 | .600 | 7-7 | .500 | 127-87 | .593 |
| Guy Hecker | 1886 | 30 | 140-95 | .596 | 33-53 | .384 | 173-148 | .539 |
| Guy Bush | 1933 | 31 | 134-91 | .596 | 42-45 | .483 | 176-136 | .564 |
| Fred Toney | 1921 | 32 | 121-84 | .590 | 16-18 | .471 | 137-102 | .573 |
| Mike Flanagan | 1984 | 32 | 125-87 | .590 | 42-56 | .429 | 167-143 | .539 |
| Jack Morris | 1985 | 30 | 123-86 | .589 | 131-100 | .567 | 254-186 | .577 |
| Dennis Leonard | 1981 | 30 | 120-84 | .588 | 24-22 | .522 | 144-106 | .576 |
| Bill Hutchison | 1892 | 32 | 137-96 | .588 | 44-62 | .415 | 181-158 | .534 |
| Bob Gibson | 1967 | 31 | 125-88 | .587 | 126-86 | .594 | 251-174 | .591 |
| Charles Nagy | 1999 | 32 | 121-86 | .585 | — | — | 121-86 | .585 |
| Hippo Vaughn | 1918 | 30 | 135-96 | .584 | 43-41 | .512 | 178-137 | .565 |
| Larry Jansen | 1953 | 32 | 118-84 | .584 | 4-5 | .444 | 122-89 | .578 |
| Pat Malone | 1935 | 32 | 118-84 | .584 | 16-8 | .667 | 134-92 | .593 |
| Rube Marquard | 1916 | 29 | 118-84 | .584 | 83-93 | .472 | 201-177 | .532 |
| Andy Messersmith | 1976 | 30 | 123-88 | .583 | 7-11 | .389 | 130-99 | .568 |
| Tommy Bridges | 1937 | 30 | 120-86 | .583 | 74-52 | .587 | 194-138 | .584 |
| Dutch Ruether | 1926 | 32 | 124-89 | .582 | 13-6 | .684 | 137-95 | .591 |
| Bob Shawkey | 1921 | 30 | 128-92 | .582 | 68-58 | .540 | 196-150 | .566 |
| Hal Schumacher | 1940 | 29 | 130-94 | .580 | 28-27 | .509 | 158-121 | .566 |

## Chicago White Sox: Will the Youngest Soon Be the Best? (p. 15)

### Winning Percentage, League's Youngest Teams—1950-99
### (average age based on 65% PA for hitters, 35% BFP for pitchers)

| Lg | Year | Team | Avg Age | Year1 | Year2 | Year3 | Year4 | Year5 | Year6 |
|---|---|---|---|---|---|---|---|---|---|
| AL | 1950 | Browns | 26.5 | .377 | .338 | .416 | .351 | .351 | .370 |
| NL | 1950 | Phillies | 26.6 | .591 | .474 | .565 | .539 | .487 | .500 |
| AL | 1951 | Browns | 27.7 | .338 | .416 | .351 | .351 | .370 | .448 |
| NL | 1951 | Phillies | 28.2 | .474 | .565 | .539 | .487 | .500 | .461 |
| AL | 1952 | Red Sox | 28.8 | .494 | .549 | .448 | .545 | .545 | .532 |
| NL | 1952 | Pirates | 27.2 | .273 | .325 | .344 | .390 | .429 | .403 |
| AL | 1953 | Red Sox | 27.9 | .549 | .448 | .545 | .545 | .532 | .513 |
| NL | 1953 | Pirates | 28.0 | .325 | .344 | .390 | .429 | .403 | .545 |
| AL | 1954 | Tigers | 26.8 | .442 | .513 | .532 | .506 | .500 | .494 |
| NL | 1954 | Pirates | 27.0 | .344 | .390 | .429 | .403 | .545 | .506 |
| AL | 1955 | Tigers | 27.4 | .513 | .532 | .506 | .500 | .494 | .461 |
| NL | 1955 | Pirates | 26.4 | .390 | .429 | .403 | .545 | .506 | .617 |
| AL | 1956 | Nationals | 26.7 | .383 | .357 | .396 | .409 | .474 | .438 |
| NL | 1956 | Pirates | 26.1 | .429 | .403 | .545 | .506 | .617 | .487 |
| AL | 1957 | Tigers | 27.4 | .506 | .500 | .494 | .461 | .623 | .528 |
| NL | 1957 | Pirates | 26.7 | .403 | .545 | .506 | .617 | .487 | .578 |
| AL | 1958 | Tigers | 27.8 | .500 | .494 | .461 | .623 | .528 | .488 |
| NL | 1958 | Pirates | 27.1 | .545 | .506 | .617 | .487 | .578 | .457 |
| AL | 1959 | Senators | 27.4 | .409 | .474 | .438 | .562 | .565 | .488 |
| NL | 1959 | Giants | 27.3 | .539 | .513 | .552 | .624 | .543 | .556 |
| AL | 1960 | Orioles | 27.1 | .578 | .586 | .475 | .531 | .599 | .580 |
| NL | 1960 | Phillies | 26.9 | .383 | .305 | .503 | .537 | .568 | .528 |
| AL | 1961 | Orioles | 27.3 | .586 | .475 | .531 | .599 | .580 | .606 |
| NL | 1961 | Phillies | 26.6 | .305 | .503 | .537 | .568 | .528 | .537 |
| AL | 1962 | Twins | 27.0 | .562 | .565 | .488 | .630 | .549 | .562 |
| NL | 1962 | Cubs | 26.4 | .364 | .506 | .469 | .444 | .364 | .540 |
| AL | 1963 | Twins | 27.4 | .565 | .488 | .630 | .549 | .562 | .488 |
| NL | 1963 | Cubs | 27.0 | .506 | .469 | .444 | .364 | .540 | .519 |
| AL | 1964 | Athletics | 27.1 | .352 | .364 | .463 | .385 | .506 | .543 |
| NL | 1964 | Dodgers | 27.1 | .494 | .599 | .586 | .451 | .469 | .525 |
| AL | 1965 | Angels | 26.3 | .463 | .494 | .522 | .414 | .438 | .531 |
| NL | 1965 | Reds | 27.1 | .549 | .475 | .537 | .512 | .549 | .630 |
| AL | 1966 | Athletics | 25.4 | .463 | .385 | .506 | .543 | .549 | .627 |
| NL | 1966 | Astros | 26.8 | .444 | .426 | .444 | .500 | .488 | .488 |
| AL | 1967 | Athletics | 24.8 | .385 | .506 | .543 | .549 | .627 | .600 |
| NL | 1967 | Mets | 26.4 | .377 | .451 | .617 | .512 | .512 | .532 |
| AL | 1968 | Athletics | 24.9 | .506 | .543 | .549 | .627 | .600 | .580 |
| NL | 1968 | Astros | 26.2 | .444 | .500 | .488 | .488 | .549 | .506 |
| AL | 1969 | Athletics | 25.9 | .543 | .549 | .627 | .600 | .580 | .556 |
| NL | 1969 | Padres | 26.1 | .321 | .389 | .379 | .379 | .370 | .370 |
| AL | 1970 | Royals | 26.6 | .401 | .528 | .494 | .543 | .475 | .562 |
| NL | 1970 | Reds | 26.0 | .630 | .488 | .617 | .611 | .605 | .667 |
| AL | 1971 | White Sox | 26.4 | .488 | .565 | .475 | .500 | .466 | .398 |
| NL | 1971 | Reds | 26.4 | .488 | .617 | .611 | .605 | .667 | .630 |
| AL | 1972 | Rangers | 26.4 | .351 | .352 | .525 | .488 | .469 | .580 |
| NL | 1972 | Padres | 25.5 | .379 | .370 | .370 | .438 | .451 | .426 |
| AL | 1973 | Brewers | 26.2 | .457 | .469 | .420 | .410 | .414 | .574 |
| NL | 1973 | Padres | 25.6 | .370 | .370 | .438 | .451 | .426 | .519 |

Baseball Scoreboard

| Lg | Year | Team | Avg Age | Year1 | Year2 | Year3 | Year4 | Year5 | Year6 |
|---|---|---|---|---|---|---|---|---|---|
| AL | 1974 | Brewers | 26.8 | .469 | .420 | .410 | .414 | .574 | .590 |
| NL | 1974 | Giants | 25.7 | .444 | .497 | .457 | .463 | .549 | .438 |
| AL | 1975 | Angels | 26.4 | .447 | .469 | .457 | .537 | .543 | .406 |
| NL | 1975 | Giants | 25.8 | .497 | .457 | .463 | .549 | .438 | .466 |
| AL | 1976 | White Sox | 26.7 | .398 | .556 | .441 | .456 | .438 | .509 |
| NL | 1976 | Expos | 26.4 | .340 | .463 | .469 | .594 | .556 | .556 |
| AL | 1977 | Brewers | 26.5 | .414 | .574 | .590 | .531 | .569 | .586 |
| NL | 1977 | Padres | 26.2 | .426 | .519 | .422 | .451 | .373 | .500 |
| AL | 1978 | Athletics | 26.6 | .426 | .333 | .512 | .587 | .420 | .457 |
| NL | 1978 | Cardinals | 26.9 | .426 | .531 | .457 | .578 | .568 | .488 |
| AL | 1979 | Athletics | 26.4 | .333 | .512 | .587 | .420 | .457 | .475 |
| NL | 1979 | Cardinals | 27.4 | .531 | .457 | .578 | .568 | .488 | .519 |
| AL | 1980 | Blue Jays | 26.4 | .414 | .349 | .481 | .549 | .549 | .615 |
| NL | 1980 | Mets | 27.7 | .414 | .398 | .401 | .420 | .556 | .605 |
| AL | 1981 | Blue Jays | 26.4 | .349 | .481 | .549 | .549 | .615 | .531 |
| NL | 1981 | Padres | 26.9 | .373 | .500 | .500 | .568 | .512 | .457 |
| AL | 1982 | Twins | 25.7 | .370 | .432 | .500 | .475 | .438 | .525 |
| NL | 1982 | Padres | 27.3 | .500 | .500 | .568 | .512 | .457 | .401 |
| AL | 1983 | Twins | 26.5 | .432 | .500 | .475 | .438 | .525 | .562 |
| NL | 1983 | Padres | 27.8 | .500 | .568 | .512 | .457 | .401 | .516 |
| AL | 1984 | Twins | 26.6 | .500 | .475 | .438 | .525 | .562 | .494 |
| NL | 1984 | Mets | 27.0 | .556 | .605 | .667 | .568 | .625 | .537 |
| AL | 1985 | Twins | 27.3 | .475 | .438 | .525 | .562 | .494 | .457 |
| NL | 1985 | Mets | 27.4 | .605 | .667 | .568 | .625 | .537 | .562 |
| AL | 1986 | Mariners | 27.3 | .414 | .481 | .422 | .451 | .475 | .512 |
| NL | 1986 | Mets | 27.6 | .667 | .568 | .625 | .537 | .562 | .478 |
| AL | 1987 | Mariners | 27.2 | .481 | .422 | .451 | .475 | .512 | .395 |
| NL | 1987 | Pirates | 27.1 | .494 | .531 | .457 | .586 | .605 | .593 |
| AL | 1988 | Mariners | 27.4 | .422 | .451 | .475 | .512 | .395 | .506 |
| NL | 1988 | Pirates | 26.6 | .531 | .457 | .586 | .605 | .593 | .463 |
| AL | 1989 | Mariners | 27.0 | .451 | .475 | .512 | .395 | .506 | .438 |
| NL | 1989 | Braves | 27.7 | .394 | .401 | .580 | .605 | .642 | .596 |
| AL | 1990 | White Sox | 27.3 | .580 | .537 | .531 | .580 | .593 | .472 |
| NL | 1990 | Braves | 27.4 | .401 | .580 | .605 | .642 | .596 | .625 |
| AL | 1991 | Indians | 26.5 | .352 | .469 | .469 | .584 | .694 | .615 |
| NL | 1991 | Astros | 26.6 | .401 | .500 | .525 | .574 | .528 | .506 |
| AL | 1992 | Indians | 26.7 | .469 | .469 | .584 | .694 | .615 | .534 |
| NL | 1992 | Astros | 26.8 | .500 | .525 | .574 | .528 | .506 | .519 |
| AL | 1993 | Indians | 27.7 | .469 | .584 | .694 | .615 | .534 | .549 |
| NL | 1993 | Expos | 27.0 | .580 | .649 | .458 | .543 | .481 | .401 |
| AL | 1994 | Mariners | 27.9 | .438 | .545 | .528 | .556 | .472 | .488 |
| NL | 1994 | Expos | 26.7 | .649 | .458 | .543 | .481 | .401 | .420 |
| AL | 1995 | Twins | 27.3 | .389 | .481 | .420 | .432 | .394 | — |
| NL | 1995 | Expos | 27.1 | .458 | .543 | .481 | .401 | .420 | — |
| AL | 1996 | Tigers | 27.4 | .327 | .488 | .401 | .429 | — | — |
| NL | 1996 | Mets | 27.5 | .438 | .543 | .543 | .595 | — | — |
| AL | 1997 | Tigers | 27.1 | .488 | .401 | .429 | — | — | — |
| NL | 1997 | Pirates | 26.7 | .488 | .426 | .484 | — | — | — |
| AL | 1998 | Tigers | 27.4 | .401 | .429 | — | — | — | — |
| NL | 1998 | Marlins | 25.6 | .333 | .395 | — | — | — | — |
| AL | 1999 | White Sox | 26.5 | .466 | — | — | — | — | — |
| NL | 1999 | Marlins | 26.0 | .395 | — | — | — | — | — |
| **MLB Average** | | | **26.8** | **.451** | **.479** | **.502** | **.514** | **.515** | **.516** |

# Kansas City Royals: How Good Was Beltran's Rookie Season? (p. 22)

## Highest RC/27 Index—Rookies
### (minimum 400 PA; maximum 130 AB prior to rookie year)

| Player, Team | Year | RC27 | Lg RC27 | Index | Player, Team | Year | RC27 | Lg RC27 | Index |
|---|---|---|---|---|---|---|---|---|---|
| Joe Jackson, Cle | 1911 | 10.92 | 4.61 | 237.0 | Chick Stahl, Bos | 1897 | 9.39 | 5.87 | 160.0 |
| Benny Kauff, Ind | 1914 | 9.55 | 4.11 | 232.7 | Rudy York, Det | 1937 | 8.35 | 5.23 | 159.7 |
| Dave Orr, NYAA | 1884 | 11.25 | 5.23 | 215.3 | Vada Pinson, Cin | 1959 | 7.02 | 4.40 | 159.3 |
| F Fennelly, WaD-CinAA | 1884 | 10.92 | 5.23 | 209.0 | Alvin Davis, Sea | 1984 | 7.00 | 4.42 | 158.4 |
| Stan Musial, StLN | 1942 | 7.97 | 3.90 | 204.2 | Jeff Heath, Cle | 1938 | 8.48 | 5.37 | 158.0 |
| Carlton Fisk, Bos | 1972 | 6.98 | 3.47 | 201.3 | Mike Hargrove, Tex | 1974 | 6.47 | 4.10 | 157.8 |
| Bernie Carbo, Cin | 1970 | 9.07 | 4.52 | 200.9 | Del Bissonette, Bro | 1928 | 7.41 | 4.70 | 157.7 |
| Ted Williams, BosA | 1939 | 10.44 | 5.21 | 200.5 | Ginger Beaumont, Pit | 1899 | 8.22 | 5.23 | 157.3 |
| Johnny Mize, StLN | 1936 | 9.15 | 4.71 | 194.4 | Monte Irvin, NYG | 1950 | 7.30 | 4.66 | 156.7 |
| Dick Allen, Phi | 1964 | 7.79 | 4.01 | 194.1 | Les Fleming, Cle | 1942 | 6.66 | 4.26 | 156.3 |
| Rico Carty, Mil | 1964 | 7.79 | 4.01 | 194.0 | Todd Helton, Col | 1998 | 7.18 | 4.60 | 156.2 |
| Fred Lynn, Bos | 1975 | 8.32 | 4.30 | 193.5 | Braggo Roth, CWS-Cle | 1915 | 6.17 | 3.96 | 155.6 |
| Mitchell Page, Oak | 1977 | 8.47 | 4.53 | 187.1 | Roy Thomas, Phi | 1899 | 8.13 | 5.23 | 155.6 |
| Harry Rice, StLA | 1925 | 9.66 | 5.20 | 185.9 | Gil McDougald, NYY | 1951 | 7.21 | 4.63 | 155.6 |
| Fred Snodgrass, NYG | 1910 | 7.44 | 4.03 | 184.4 | Joe Ferguson, LA | 1973 | 6.45 | 4.15 | 155.4 |
| Paul Waner, Pit | 1926 | 8.24 | 4.54 | 181.4 | Mike Piazza, LA | 1993 | 6.94 | 4.49 | 154.6 |
| David Justice, Atl | 1990 | 7.49 | 4.20 | 178.3 | Ross Youngs, NYG | 1918 | 5.59 | 3.62 | 154.3 |
| Harry Moore, Was | 1884 | 10.00 | 5.64 | 177.4 | Bobby Grich, Bal | 1972 | 5.35 | 3.47 | 154.2 |
| Charlie Keller, NYY | 1939 | 9.21 | 5.21 | 176.9 | Dick Wakefield, Det | 1943 | 5.99 | 3.89 | 154.2 |
| Jimmy Williams, Pit | 1899 | 9.19 | 5.23 | 175.9 | Ferris Fain, PhiA | 1947 | 6.39 | 4.14 | 154.2 |
| Jim Gentile, Bal | 1960 | 7.70 | 4.39 | 175.5 | Jeff Bagwell, Hou | 1991 | 6.32 | 4.10 | 154.1 |
| Elmer Flick, Phi | 1898 | 8.67 | 4.96 | 175.0 | Tim Jordan, Bro | 1906 | 5.50 | 3.57 | 154.1 |
| Norm Cash, Det | 1960 | 7.67 | 4.39 | 174.7 | Al Scheer, Ind | 1914 | 6.33 | 4.11 | 154.1 |
| George Watkins, StLN | 1930 | 9.86 | 5.68 | 173.6 | Pete Ward, CWS | 1963 | 6.29 | 4.08 | 154.0 |
| Kiki Cuyler, Pit | 1924 | 7.85 | 4.54 | 172.8 | Buzz Arlett, PhiN | 1931 | 6.89 | 4.48 | 153.8 |
| Cupid Childs, Syr | 1890 | 9.59 | 5.59 | 171.5 | Buck Freeman, Was | 1899 | 8.04 | 5.23 | 153.8 |
| Curt Blefary, Bal | 1965 | 6.74 | 3.94 | 171.0 | Sam Barkley, Tol | 1884 | 8.03 | 5.23 | 153.6 |
| Emmett Seery, BalU-KC | 1884 | 9.62 | 5.64 | 170.6 | Billy Grabarkewitz, LA | 1970 | 6.93 | 4.52 | 153.5 |
| Al Bumbry, Bal | 1973 | 7.25 | 4.28 | 169.6 | Floyd Robinson, CWS | 1961 | 6.94 | 4.53 | 153.3 |
| Billy Hamilton, KC | 1889 | 10.27 | 6.07 | 169.3 | Del Ennis, PhiN | 1946 | 6.05 | 3.96 | 152.9 |
| Rogers Hornsby, StLN | 1916 | 5.83 | 3.45 | 169.2 | Doc Hoblitzell, Cin | 1909 | 5.59 | 3.66 | 152.8 |
| Duke Kenworthy, KC | 1914 | 6.92 | 4.11 | 168.6 | Ed Bouchee, Phi | 1957 | 6.70 | 4.38 | 152.8 |
| Tony Oliva, Min | 1964 | 6.83 | 4.06 | 168.4 | Home Run Baker, PhiA | 1909 | 5.25 | 3.44 | 152.7 |
| Mike Fiore, KC | 1969 | 6.85 | 4.09 | 167.5 | Carlos May, CWS | 1969 | 6.25 | 4.09 | 152.7 |
| Minnie Minoso, Cle-CWS | 1951 | 7.75 | 4.63 | 167.3 | Tom McCreery, Lou | 1896 | 9.21 | 6.03 | 152.7 |
| Mark McGwire, Oak | 1987 | 8.17 | 4.90 | 166.8 | Earl Torgeson, BosN | 1947 | 6.97 | 4.57 | 152.5 |
| Dan Gladden, SF | 1984 | 6.78 | 4.06 | 166.7 | Joe Medwick, StLN | 1933 | 6.05 | 3.97 | 152.4 |
| Joe Harris, Cle | 1917 | 6.08 | 3.65 | 166.6 | Darryl Strawberry, NYM | 1983 | 6.24 | 4.10 | 152.1 |
| Dusty Baker, Atl | 1972 | 6.50 | 3.91 | 166.5 | Ike Boone, BosA | 1924 | 7.54 | 4.98 | 151.5 |
| Socks Seybold, PhiA | 1901 | 8.90 | 5.35 | 166.4 | Scott Rolen, Phi | 1997 | 6.97 | 4.60 | 151.4 |
| Dummy Hoy, WaN | 1888 | 7.54 | 4.54 | 166.1 | Lefty Davis, Bro-Pit | 1901 | 6.99 | 4.63 | 151.1 |
| Jim Viox, Pit | 1913 | 6.85 | 4.15 | 165.2 | Randy Milligan, Bal | 1989 | 6.49 | 4.29 | 151.0 |
| Frank Robinson, Cin | 1956 | 7.01 | 4.25 | 165.0 | Zeke Bonura, CWS | 1934 | 7.70 | 5.13 | 150.2 |
| Hal Trosky, Cle | 1934 | 8.43 | 5.13 | 164.4 | Art Devlin, NYG | 1904 | 5.87 | 3.91 | 150.2 |
| Dale Alexander, Det | 1929 | 8.13 | 5.01 | 162.4 | Ralph Garr, Atl | 1971 | 5.86 | 3.91 | 149.9 |
| Ed Crane, BosU | 1884 | 9.12 | 5.64 | 161.9 | Sandy Griffin, Roc | 1890 | 8.35 | 5.59 | 149.3 |
| Charlie Hollocher, ChC | 1918 | 5.83 | 3.62 | 160.9 | Orlando Merced, Pit | 1991 | 6.11 | 4.10 | 148.9 |
| Walt Dropo, BosA | 1950 | 8.09 | 5.04 | 160.5 | Reggie Jackson, Oak | 1968 | 5.06 | 3.41 | 148.6 |
| Mike Greenwell, Bos | 1987 | 7.85 | 4.90 | 160.2 | Hack Miller, ChC | 1922 | 7.41 | 5.00 | 148.4 |
| George Stone, StLA | 1905 | 5.90 | 3.69 | 160.2 | Johnny Rizzo, Pit | 1938 | 6.55 | 4.42 | 148.4 |

## Minnesota Twins: Was Milton's No-Hitter a Sign of Things To Come? (p. 25)

### Career Records For Pitchers With a No-Hitter Through Age 24—1900-99

| Pitcher, Team | Date | Age | W-L | Pct | IP | H | BB | SO | ERA |
|---|---|---|---|---|---|---|---|---|---|
| Wilson Alvarez, CWS | 8/11/91 | 21 | 86-77 | .528 | 1,433.0 | 1,324 | 708 | 1,074 | 3.96 |
| Rex Barney, Bro | 9/9/48 | 23 | 35-31 | .530 | 597.2 | 474 | 410 | 336 | 4.34 |
| Ewell Blackwell, Cin | 6/18/47 | 24 | 82-78 | .513 | 1,321.0 | 1,150 | 562 | 839 | 3.30 |
| Vida Blue, Oak | 9/21/70 | 21 | 209-161 | .565 | 3,343.1 | 2,939 | 1,185 | 2,175 | 3.26 |
| Bobby Burke, Was | 8/8/31 | 24 | 38-46 | .452 | 918.2 | 926 | 360 | 299 | 4.29 |
| Steve Busby, KC | 4/27/73 | 23 | 70-54 | .565 | 1,060.2 | 1,003 | 433 | 659 | 3.72 |
| Steve Busby, KC | 6/19/74 | 24 | 70-54 | .565 | 1,060.2 | 1,003 | 433 | 659 | 3.72 |
| Joe Bush, PhiA | 8/26/16 | 23 | 195-183 | .516 | 3,087.1 | 2,992 | 1,263 | 1,319 | 3.51 |
| John Candelaria, Pit | 8/9/76 | 22 | 177-122 | .592 | 2,525.2 | 2,399 | 592 | 1,673 | 3.33 |
| Don Cardwell, ChC | 5/15/60 | 24 | 102-138 | .425 | 2,122.2 | 2,009 | 671 | 1,211 | 3.92 |
| Iron Davis, BosN | 9/9/14 | 24 | 7-10 | .412 | 191.0 | 195 | 78 | 77 | 4.48 |
| Paul Dean, StLN | 9/21/34 | 21 | 50-34 | .595 | 787.1 | 825 | 179 | 387 | 3.75 |
| Dennis Eckersley, Cle | 5/20/77 | 22 | 197-171 | .535 | 3,285.2 | 3,076 | 738 | 2,401 | 3.50 |
| Hod Eller, Cin | 5/11/19 | 24 | 61-40 | .604 | 863.0 | 806 | 213 | 381 | 2.62 |
| Bob Feller, Cle | 4/16/40 | 21 | 266-162 | .621 | 3,827.0 | 3,271 | 1,764 | 2,581 | 3.25 |
| Wes Ferrell, Cle | 4/29/31 | 23 | 193-128 | .601 | 2,623.0 | 2,845 | 1,040 | 985 | 4.04 |
| Dick Fowler, PhiA | 9/9/45 | 24 | 66-79 | .455 | 1,303.0 | 1,367 | 578 | 382 | 4.11 |
| Tommy Greene, Phi | 5/23/91 | 24 | 38-25 | .603 | 628.0 | 591 | 241 | 461 | 4.14 |
| Noodles Hahn, Cin | 7/12/00 | 21 | 130-93 | .583 | 2,029.1 | 1,916 | 381 | 917 | 2.55 |
| Ed Halicki, SF | 8/24/75 | 24 | 55-66 | .455 | 1,063.0 | 1,007 | 334 | 707 | 3.62 |
| Earl Hamilton, StLA | 8/30/12 | 21 | 116-147 | .441 | 2,342.2 | 2,319 | 773 | 790 | 3.16 |
| Weldon Henley, PhiA | 7/22/05 | 24 | 32-43 | .427 | 721.2 | 640 | 231 | 309 | 2.94 |
| Ken Holtzman, ChC | 8/19/69 | 23 | 174-150 | .537 | 2,867.1 | 2,787 | 910 | 1,601 | 3.49 |
| Burt Hooton, ChC | 4/16/72 | 22 | 151-136 | .526 | 2,652.0 | 2,497 | 799 | 1,491 | 3.38 |
| Catfish Hunter, Oak | 5/8/68 | 22 | 224-166 | .574 | 3,449.1 | 2,958 | 954 | 2,012 | 3.26 |
| Darryl Kile, Hou | 9/8/93 | 24 | 92-95 | .492 | 1,621.0 | 1,610 | 767 | 1,247 | 4.32 |
| Ernie Koob, StLA | 5/5/17 | 24 | 23-30 | .434 | 500.0 | 488 | 186 | 121 | 3.13 |
| Charlie Lea, Mon | 5/10/81 | 24 | 62-48 | .564 | 923.1 | 864 | 341 | 535 | 3.54 |
| Dutch Leonard, BosA | 8/30/16 | 24 | 139-112 | .554 | 2,192.0 | 2,022 | 664 | 1,160 | 2.76 |
| Johnny Lush, PhiN | 5/1/06 | 20 | 66-85 | .437 | 1,239.1 | 1,169 | 413 | 490 | 2.68 |
| Nick Maddox, Pit | 9/20/07 | 20 | 43-20 | .683 | 605.1 | 487 | 170 | 193 | 2.29 |
| Christy Mathewson, NYG | 7/15/01 | 20 | 373-188 | .665 | 4,780.2 | 4,218 | 844 | 2,502 | 2.13 |
| Christy Mathewson, NYG | 6/13/05 | 24 | 373-188 | .665 | 4,780.2 | 4,218 | 844 | 2,502 | 2.13 |
| Eric Milton, Min | 9/11/99 | 24 | 15-25 | .375 | 378.2 | 385 | 133 | 270 | 5.01 |
| Bob Moose, Pit | 9/20/69 | 21 | 76-71 | .517 | 1,304.1 | 1,308 | 387 | 827 | 3.50 |
| Dave Morehead, BosA | 9/16/65 | 23 | 40-64 | .385 | 819.1 | 730 | 463 | 627 | 4.15 |
| Juan Nieves, Mil | 4/15/87 | 22 | 32-25 | .561 | 490.2 | 507 | 227 | 352 | 4.71 |
| Jim Palmer, Bal | 8/13/69 | 23 | 268-152 | .638 | 3,948.0 | 3,349 | 1,311 | 2,212 | 2.86 |
| Dave Righetti, NYY | 7/4/83 | 24 | 82-79 | .509 | 1,403.2 | 1,287 | 591 | 1,112 | 3.46 |
| Nap Rucker, Bro | 9/5/08 | 23 | 134-134 | .500 | 2,375.1 | 2,089 | 701 | 1,217 | 2.42 |
| Jeff Tesreau, NYG | 9/6/12 | 23 | 115-72 | .615 | 1,679.0 | 1,350 | 572 | 880 | 2.43 |
| Johnny Vander Meer, Cin | 6/11/38 | 23 | 119-121 | .496 | 2,104.2 | 1,799 | 1,132 | 1,294 | 3.44 |
| Johnny Vander Meer, Cin | 6/15/38 | 23 | 119-121 | .496 | 2,104.2 | 1,799 | 1,132 | 1,294 | 3.44 |
| Mike Warren, Oak | 9/29/83 | 22 | 9-13 | .409 | 204.2 | 207 | 100 | 139 | 5.06 |
| Don Wilson, Hou | 6/18/67 | 22 | 104-92 | .531 | 1,748.1 | 1,479 | 640 | 1,283 | 3.15 |
| Don Wilson, Hou | 5/1/69 | 24 | 104-92 | .531 | 1,748.1 | 1,479 | 640 | 1,283 | 3.15 |
| Mike Witt, Cal | 9/30/84 | 24 | 117-116 | .502 | 2,108.1 | 2,066 | 713 | 1,373 | 3.83 |
| Joe Wood, BosA | 7/29/11 | 21 | 116-57 | .671 | 1,436.1 | 1,138 | 421 | 989 | 2.03 |

## Oakland Athletics: Were They the Ultimate Sabermetric Team? (p. 29)

### Most Runs Per Game, .260 or Lower Team Batting Average—1900-99

| Year | Team | R/G | Avg | Sec | Year | Team | R/G | Avg | Sec |
|---|---|---|---|---|---|---|---|---|---|
| 1999 | Athletics | 5.51 | .259 | .332 | 1970 | Astros | 4.59 | .259 | .252 |
| 1940 | Yankees | 5.27 | .259 | .286 | 1972 | Reds | 4.59 | .251 | .259 |
| 1991 | Tigers | 5.04 | .247 | .306 | 1986 | Phillies | 4.59 | .253 | .272 |
| 1948 | Giants | 5.03 | .256 | .275 | 1953 | White Sox | 4.59 | .258 | .225 |
| 1987 | Athletics | 4.98 | .260 | .290 | 1969 | Red Sox | 4.59 | .251 | .282 |
| 1970 | Cubs | 4.98 | .259 | .270 | 1956 | Braves | 4.57 | .259 | .258 |
| 1951 | Giants | 4.97 | .260 | .287 | 1973 | Reds | 4.57 | .254 | .262 |
| 1998 | Cardinals | 4.97 | .258 | .320 | 1997 | Marlins | 4.57 | .259 | .272 |
| 1998 | Athletics | 4.96 | .257 | .270 | 1969 | Athletics | 4.57 | .249 | .247 |
| 1955 | Yankees | 4.95 | .260 | .282 | 1905 | Phillies | 4.57 | .260 | .188 |
| 1962 | Twins | 4.90 | .260 | .272 | 1982 | Braves | 4.56 | .256 | .241 |
| 1970 | Orioles | 4.89 | .257 | .282 | 1957 | White Sox | 4.56 | .260 | .247 |
| 1992 | Tigers | 4.88 | .256 | .277 | 1955 | Giants | 4.56 | .260 | .238 |
| 1986 | Angels | 4.85 | .255 | .285 | 1984 | Athletics | 4.56 | .259 | .264 |
| 1997 | Giants | 4.84 | .258 | .286 | 1946 | Tigers | 4.54 | .258 | .238 |
| 1997 | Tigers | 4.84 | .258 | .279 | 1995 | Tigers | 4.54 | .247 | .278 |
| 1942 | Browns | 4.83 | .259 | .242 | 1912 | Nationals | 4.54 | .256 | .233 |
| 1996 | Tigers | 4.83 | .256 | .270 | 1909 | Pirates | 4.54 | .260 | .222 |
| 1987 | Giants | 4.83 | .260 | .266 | 1958 | Indians | 4.54 | .258 | .240 |
| 1911 | Cubs | 4.82 | .260 | .269 | 1955 | Indians | 4.53 | .257 | .277 |
| 1994 | Athletics | 4.82 | .260 | .260 | 1993 | Mariners | 4.53 | .260 | .264 |
| 1999 | Pirates | 4.81 | .259 | .277 | 1950 | Cardinals | 4.53 | .259 | .247 |
| 1960 | Yankees | 4.81 | .260 | .269 | 1985 | Tigers | 4.53 | .253 | .271 |
| 1996 | Reds | 4.80 | .256 | .296 | 1995 | Giants | 4.53 | .253 | .265 |
| 1997 | Astros | 4.80 | .259 | .277 | 1990 | Athletics | 4.52 | .254 | .273 |
| 1990 | Mets | 4.78 | .256 | .263 | 1990 | Pirates | 4.52 | .259 | .270 |
| 1965 | Twins | 4.78 | .254 | .256 | 1993 | Brewers | 4.52 | .258 | .229 |
| 1950 | Giants | 4.77 | .258 | .262 | 1981 | Brewers | 4.52 | .257 | .215 |
| 1996 | Cubs | 4.77 | .251 | .255 | 1964 | Twins | 4.52 | .252 | .278 |
| 1963 | Twins | 4.76 | .255 | .277 | 1959 | Dodgers | 4.52 | .257 | .257 |
| 1974 | Reds | 4.76 | .260 | .278 | 1947 | Tigers | 4.52 | .258 | .262 |
| 1987 | Angels | 4.75 | .252 | .269 | 1985 | Angels | 4.52 | .251 | .264 |
| 1948 | Athletics | 4.73 | .260 | .244 | 1986 | Reds | 4.52 | .254 | .262 |
| 1984 | Cubs | 4.73 | .260 | .257 | 1990 | Brewers | 4.52 | .256 | .239 |
| 1996 | Blue Jays | 4.73 | .259 | .270 | 1985 | White Sox | 4.52 | .253 | .234 |
| 1979 | Indians | 4.72 | .258 | .258 | 1958 | Redlegs | 4.51 | .258 | .244 |
| 1966 | Orioles | 4.72 | .258 | .247 | 1931 | White Sox | 4.51 | .260 | .182 |
| 1997 | Athletics | 4.72 | .260 | .284 | 1986 | Athletics | 4.51 | .252 | .254 |
| 1949 | Athletics | 4.71 | .260 | .264 | 1989 | Blue Jays | 4.51 | .260 | .247 |
| 1959 | Red Sox | 4.71 | .256 | .258 | 1962 | Braves | 4.51 | .252 | .263 |
| 1962 | Tigers | 4.71 | .248 | .291 | 1987 | Orioles | 4.50 | .258 | .258 |
| 1991 | Athletics | 4.69 | .248 | .275 | 1949 | Braves | 4.50 | .258 | .250 |
| 1952 | Giants | 4.69 | .256 | .246 | 1958 | Red Sox | 4.50 | .256 | .268 |
| 1975 | Athletics | 4.68 | .254 | .268 | 1993 | Expos | 4.49 | .257 | .259 |
| 1973 | Athletics | 4.68 | .260 | .250 | 1951 | Indians | 4.49 | .256 | .252 |
| 1956 | Dodgers | 4.68 | .258 | .294 | 1957 | Dodgers | 4.48 | .253 | .244 |
| 1938 | Dodgers | 4.66 | .257 | .242 | 1995 | Braves | 4.48 | .250 | .274 |
| 1913 | Cubs | 4.65 | .257 | .259 | 1994 | Mets | 4.48 | .250 | .231 |
| 1996 | Giants | 4.64 | .253 | .257 | 1963 | Giants | 4.48 | .258 | .236 |
| 1987 | Braves | 4.64 | .258 | .276 | 1961 | Red Sox | 4.47 | .254 | .241 |
| 1959 | Tigers | 4.63 | .258 | .256 | 1940 | Dodgers | 4.47 | .260 | .229 |
| 1990 | Tigers | 4.63 | .259 | .270 | 1946 | Dodgers | 4.46 | .260 | .242 |
| 1972 | Astros | 4.63 | .258 | .245 | 1995 | Blue Jays | 4.46 | .260 | .258 |
| 1915 | White Sox | 4.63 | .258 | .219 | 1957 | Indians | 4.46 | .252 | .243 |
| 1998 | Padres | 4.62 | .253 | .273 | 1967 | Red Sox | 4.46 | .255 | .237 |
| 1991 | Braves | 4.62 | .258 | .255 | 1983 | Angels | 4.46 | .260 | .223 |
| 1987 | White Sox | 4.62 | .258 | .261 | 1950 | Nationals | 4.45 | .260 | .231 |
| 1999 | Cubs | 4.61 | .257 | .270 | 1964 | Yankees | 4.45 | .253 | .231 |
| 1992 | Athletics | 4.60 | .258 | .275 | 1945 | Yankees | 4.45 | .259 | .237 |
| 1956 | Indians | 4.59 | .244 | .271 | 1951 | Pirates | 4.45 | .258 | .244 |
| 1961 | Braves | 4.59 | .258 | .263 | 1946 | Yankees | 4.44 | .248 | .264 |
| 1961 | Angels | 4.59 | .245 | .280 | 1950 | Browns | 4.44 | .246 | .257 |

*Baseball Scoreboard*

## Toronto Blue Jays: Is a Great Rookie Season a Good Sign For a Closer? (p. 38)

### Most Saves—Rookies
### (maximum 30 G or 50 IP prior to rookie year)

| Pitcher, Team | Year | SV | Pitcher, Team | Year | SV |
|---|---|---|---|---|---|
| Todd Worrell, StL | 1986 | 36 | Chuck Seelbach, Det | 1972 | 14 |
| Billy Koch, Tor | 1999 | 31 | Dave Campbell, Atl | 1977 | 13 |
| Kerry Ligtenberg, Atl | 1998 | 30 | Joe Hoerner, StL | 1966 | 13 |
| Rich Loiselle, Pit | 1997 | 29 | Darold Knowles, Phi | 1966 | 13 |
| Gregg Olson, Bal | 1989 | 27 | Wilcy Moore, NYY | 1927 | 13 |
| Pete Ladd, Mil | 1983 | 25 | Ray Narleski, Cle | 1954 | 13 |
| Dick Radatz, Bos | 1962 | 24 | Dave Baldwin, Was | 1967 | 12 |
| Ernie Camacho, Cle | 1984 | 23 | Joe Berry, Phi | 1944 | 12 |
| Doug Corbett, Min | 1980 | 23 | Francisco Cordova, Pit | 1996 | 12 |
| Rawly Eastwick, Cin | 1975 | 22 | Chuck Crim, Mil | 1987 | 12 |
| Ken Tatum, Cal | 1969 | 22 | Rollie Fingers, Oak | 1969 | 12 |
| Salome Barojas, CWS | 1982 | 21 | Terry Fox, Det | 1961 | 12 |
| Frank Linzy, SF | 1965 | 21 | Roberto Hernandez, CWS | 1992 | 12 |
| Doug Bird, KC | 1973 | 20 | Pete Mikkelsen, NYY | 1964 | 12 |
| Frank DiPino, Hou | 1983 | 20 | Julio Navarro, LAA | 1963 | 12 |
| Ryne Duren, NYY | 1958 | 20 | Al Osuna, Hou | 1991 | 12 |
| Bob Lee, LAA | 1964 | 19 | Ed Roebuck, Bro | 1955 | 12 |
| Greg McMichael, Atl | 1993 | 19 | Vicente Romo, LA-Cle | 1968 | 12 |
| Scott Williamson, Cin | 1999 | 19 | Dave Beard, Oak | 1982 | 11 |
| Cy Acosta, CWS | 1973 | 18 | Steve Bedrosian, Atl | 1982 | 11 |
| Tom Buskey, NYY-Cle | 1974 | 18 | Jerry Dipoto, Cle | 1993 | 11 |
| Hal Reniff, NYY | 1963 | 18 | Frank Funk, Cle | 1961 | 11 |
| Elias Sosa, SF | 1973 | 18 | Gene Garber, KC | 1973 | 11 |
| DeWayne Buice, Cal | 1987 | 17 | Bill Kelso, Cal | 1967 | 11 |
| Darren Hall, Tor | 1994 | 17 | Sparky Lyle, Bos | 1968 | 11 |
| Bryan Harvey, Cal | 1988 | 17 | Doug Sisk, NYM | 1983 | 11 |
| Steve Howe, LA | 1980 | 17 | Ron Taylor, StL | 1963 | 11 |
| Roger McDowell, NYM | 1985 | 17 | Hoyt Wilhelm, NYG | 1952 | 11 |
| John Hudek, Hou | 1994 | 16 | John Wyatt, KCA | 1962 | 11 |
| Butch Metzger, SD | 1976 | 16 | Rick Camp, Atl | 1977 | 10 |
| Jack Meyer, Phi | 1955 | 16 | Mark Eichhorn, Tor | 1986 | 10 |
| Enrique Romo, Sea | 1977 | 16 | Turk Farrell, Phi | 1957 | 10 |
| Bobby Thigpen, CWS | 1987 | 16 | Chuck Hartenstein, ChC | 1967 | 10 |
| Lloyd Allen, Cal | 1971 | 15 | Dave Jolly, Mil | 1954 | 10 |
| Joe Black, Bro | 1952 | 15 | Jimmy Key, Tor | 1984 | 10 |
| Luis DeLeon, SD | 1982 | 15 | Mike Marshall, Det | 1967 | 10 |
| Doug Henry, Mil | 1991 | 15 | Dale Murray, Mon | 1974 | 10 |
| Firpo Marberry, Was | 1924 | 15 | Claude Raymond, Mil | 1962 | 10 |
| Will McEnaney, Cin | 1975 | 15 | Minnie Rojas, Cal | 1966 | 10 |
| Mike Schooler, Sea | 1988 | 15 | Bill Scherrer, Cin | 1983 | 10 |
| Duane Ward, Tor | 1988 | 15 | Dave Sells, Cal | 1973 | 10 |
| Anthony Young, NYM | 1992 | 15 | Dave Smith, Hou | 1980 | 10 |
| Mark Clear, Cal | 1979 | 14 | Dave Stevens, Min | 1995 | 10 |
| Bill Dawley, Hou | 1983 | 14 | Bruce Sutter, ChC | 1976 | 10 |
| Sammy Ellis, Cin | 1964 | 14 | Murray Wall, Bos | 1958 | 10 |
| Kelvim Escobar, Tor | 1997 | 14 | Bill Wilkinson, Sea | 1987 | 10 |
| Brian Fisher, NYY | 1985 | 14 | Ron Willis, StL | 1967 | 10 |
| Gordon Maltzberger, CWS | 1943 | 14 | Oscar Zamora, ChC | 1974 | 10 |
| Dan Plesac, Mil | 1986 | 14 | | | |

## Chicago Cubs: Is Sosa the King of the Also-Rans? (p. 45)

### Most Home Runs—No. 2 in League Two Straight Seasons

| Player | Years | HR | Player | Years | HR |
|---|---|---|---|---|---|
| Sammy Sosa | 1998-99 | 129 | Mel Ott | 1943-44 | 44 |
| Frank Thomas | 1994-95 | 78 | Bill Joyce | 1894-95 | 34 |
| Lou Gehrig | 1929-30 | 76 | Roger Connor | 1887-88 | 31 |
| Babe Ruth | 1932-33 | 75 | George Sisler | 1919-20 | 29 |
| Lou Gehrig | 1927-28 | 74 | Charlie Hickman | 1902-03 | 23 |
| Dave Kingman | 1975-76 | 73 | Buck Freeman | 1901-02 | 23 |
| Dale Murphy | 1982-83 | 72 | Harry Lumley | 1906-07 | 18 |
| Dave Parker | 1985-86 | 65 | Sam Crawford | 1913-14 | 17 |
| Lou Gehrig | 1928-29 | 62 | Ty Cobb | 1910-11 | 16 |
| Joe Gordon | 1947-48 | 61 | | | |

### Most RBI—No. 2 in League Two Straight Seasons

| Player | Years | RBI | Player | Years | RBI |
|---|---|---|---|---|---|
| Lou Gehrig | 1932-33 | 290 | Ron Santo | 1968-69 | 221 |
| Lou Gehrig | 1935-36 | 271 | Ed Delahanty | 1900-01 | 217 |
| Jack Fournier | 1924-25 | 246 | Bob Elliott | 1943-44 | 209 |
| Jimmy Collins | 1897-98 | 243 | Charlie Hickman | 1902-03 | 207 |
| Hack Wilson | 1926-27 | 238 | Duffy Lewis | 1912-13 | 199 |
| Roberto Clemente | 1966-67 | 229 | Sam Mertes | 1904-05 | 186 |
| Ralph Kiner | 1950-51 | 227 | Stuffy McInnis | 1913-14 | 185 |
| Rocky Colavito | 1958-59 | 224 | Sam Crawford | 1908-09 | 177 |
| Sam Crawford | 1911-12 | 224 | Hal Chase | 1916-17 | 168 |
| Harmon Killebrew | 1966-67 | 223 | | | |

### Highest Batting Average—No. 2 in League Two Straight Seasons
### (minimum 3.1 PA per team G)

| Player | Years | Avg | Player | Years | Avg |
|---|---|---|---|---|---|
| Ed Delahanty | 1894-95 | .406 | Bill Terry | 1931-32 | .349 |
| Joe Jackson | 1911-12 | .402 | Willie Mays | 1957-58 | .340 |
| Ty Cobb | 1921-22 | .395 | Dave Orr | 1885-86 | .340 |
| Babe Herman | 1929-30 | .387 | Eddie Collins | 1914-15 | .338 |
| Ed Delahanty | 1893-94 | .386 | Ralph Garr | 1971-72 | .334 |
| Joe Jackson | 1912-13 | .385 | Sam Crawford | 1902-03 | .334 |
| Cap Anson | 1886-87 | .360 | Willie Keeler | 1904-05 | .322 |
| Johnny Mize | 1937-38 | .351 | Sam Crawford | 1907-08 | .317 |

## Most Wins—No. 2 in League Two Straight Seasons, 1900-99

| Pitcher | Years | W | Pitcher | Years | W |
|---|---|---|---|---|---|
| Tim Keefe | 1883-84 | 78 | Dave Stewart | 1989-90 | 43 |
| Will White | 1878-79 | 73 | Tommy John | 1979-80 | 43 |
| Cy Young | 1892-93 | 70 | Dave Stewart | 1988-89 | 42 |
| Silver King | 1889-90 | 64 | Vic Raschi | 1950-51 | 42 |
| Christy Mathewson | 1903-04 | 63 | Tom Seaver | 1971-72 | 41 |
| Eddie Plank | 1904-05 | 50 | Camilo Pascual | 1962-63 | 41 |
| Eddie Plank | 1903-04 | 49 | Johnny Sain | 1946-47 | 41 |
| Dick Rudolph | 1914-15 | 48 | Tom Seaver | 1972-73 | 40 |
| Wes Ferrell | 1930-31 | 47 | Steve Rogers | 1982-83 | 36 |
| Paul Derringer | 1938-39 | 46 | Mario Soto | 1983-84 | 35 |
| Wes Ferrell | 1929-30 | 46 | David Cone | 1994-95 | 34 |
| Stan Coveleski | 1918-19 | 46 | Fernando Valenzuela | 1981-82 | 32 |
| Paul Derringer | 1939-40 | 45 | | | |

## Lowest ERA—No. 2 in League Two Straight Seasons, 1900-99
### (minimum 1 IP per team G)

| Pitcher | Years | ERA | Pitcher | Years | ERA |
|---|---|---|---|---|---|
| Three Finger Brown | 1908-09 | 1.39 | Chuck Finley | 1989-90 | 2.48 |
| Three Finger Brown | 1909-10 | 1.57 | Carl Hubbell | 1931-32 | 2.57 |
| Old Hoss Radbourn | 1882-83 | 2.07 | Jim Palmer | 1969-70 | 2.57 |
| Tiny Bonham | 1942-43 | 2.27 | Kid Nichols | 1896-97 | 2.74 |
| Kid Nichols | 1890-91 | 2.31 | Mel Harder | 1933-34 | 2.78 |
| Babe Adams | 1920-21 | 2.34 | Sal Maglie | 1950-51 | 2.84 |
| Greg Maddux | 1996-97 | 2.47 | Carl Hubbell | 1930-31 | 3.25 |

## Most Strikeouts—No. 2 in League Two Straight Seasons, 1900-99

| Pitcher | Years | SO | Pitcher | Years | SO |
|---|---|---|---|---|---|
| Pedro Martinez | 1997-98 | 556 | Bobo Newsom | 1937-38 | 392 |
| Bill Hutchison | 1890-91 | 550 | Jim Bunning | 1962-63 | 380 |
| Bob Gibson | 1969-70 | 543 | Jim McCormick | 1881-82 | 378 |
| Fergie Jenkins | 1970-71 | 537 | Jeff Tesreau | 1914-15 | 365 |
| Mario Soto | 1982-83 | 516 | Jim Bunning | 1957-58 | 359 |
| Bert Blyleven | 1973-74 | 507 | Bobo Newsom | 1939-40 | 356 |
| Mickey Lolich | 1969-70 | 501 | Jeff Tesreau | 1913-14 | 356 |
| Fergie Jenkins | 1967-68 | 496 | George Earnshaw | 1930-31 | 345 |
| Roger Clemens | 1986-87 | 494 | George Earnshaw | 1929-30 | 342 |
| Joe Wood | 1911-12 | 489 | Bobo Newsom | 1940-41 | 339 |
| Bert Blyleven | 1974-75 | 482 | Whit Wyatt | 1940-41 | 300 |
| Kevin Brown | 1998-99 | 478 | Mort Cooper | 1942-43 | 293 |
| Hal Newhouser | 1946-47 | 451 | Carl Hubbell | 1932-33 | 293 |
| Ron Guidry | 1978-79 | 449 | Carl Hubbell | 1931-32 | 292 |
| Jim McCormick | 1880-81 | 438 | Early Wynn | 1951-52 | 286 |
| J.R. Richard | 1976-77 | 428 | Pink Hawley | 1895-96 | 279 |
| Bobo Newsom | 1938-39 | 418 | Charlie Root | 1926-27 | 272 |
| Will White | 1878-79 | 401 | Wilbur Cooper | 1921-22 | 263 |
| Nap Rucker | 1908-09 | 400 | Jim Shaw | 1918-19 | 257 |

## Cincinnati Reds: Did They Overwork Their Bullpen? (p. 48)

### Relievers Working 90-Plus Innings—1989-98, Listed Alphabetically
### (combined starting and relieving statistics listed)

| Pitcher | Year1 | IP | ERA | Year2 | IP | ERA |
|---|---|---|---|---|---|---|
| Jim Acker | 1989 | 126.0 | 2.43 | 1990 | 91.2 | 3.83 |
| Jim Acker | 1990 | 91.2 | 3.83 | 1991 | 88.1 | 5.20 |
| Terry Adams | 1996 | 101.0 | 2.94 | 1997 | 74.0 | 4.62 |
| Juan Agosto | 1990 | 92.1 | 4.29 | 1991 | 86.0 | 4.81 |
| Darrel Akerfelds | 1990 | 93.0 | 3.77 | 1991 | 49.2 | 5.26 |
| Larry Andersen | 1990 | 95.2 | 1.79 | 1991 | 47.0 | 2.30 |
| Paul Assenmacher | 1990 | 103.0 | 2.80 | 1991 | 102.2 | 3.24 |
| Paul Assenmacher | 1991 | 102.2 | 3.24 | 1992 | 68.0 | 4.10 |
| Bobby Ayala | 1997 | 96.2 | 3.82 | 1998 | 75.1 | 7.29 |
| Rod Beck | 1992 | 92.0 | 1.76 | 1993 | 79.1 | 2.16 |
| Stan Belinda | 1997 | 99.1 | 3.71 | 1998 | 61.1 | 3.23 |
| Shayne Bennett | 1998 | 91.2 | 5.50 | 1999 | 11.1 | 14.29 |
| Juan Berenguer | 1989 | 106.0 | 3.48 | 1990 | 100.1 | 3.41 |
| Juan Berenguer | 1990 | 100.1 | 3.41 | 1991 | 64.1 | 2.24 |
| Joe Boever | 1991 | 98.1 | 3.84 | 1992 | 111.1 | 2.51 |
| Joe Boever | 1992 | 111.1 | 2.51 | 1993 | 102.1 | 3.61 |
| Joe Boever | 1993 | 102.1 | 3.61 | 1994 | 81.1 | 3.98 |
| Joe Boever | 1995 | 98.2 | 6.39 | 1996 | 15.0 | 5.40 |
| Toby Borland | 1996 | 90.2 | 4.07 | 1997 | 16.2 | 7.56 |
| Jeff Brantley | 1989 | 97.1 | 4.07 | 1990 | 86.2 | 1.56 |
| Jeff Brantley | 1991 | 95.1 | 2.45 | 1992 | 91.2 | 2.95 |
| Tim Burke | 1991 | 101.2 | 3.36 | 1992 | 43.1 | 4.15 |
| Greg Cadaret | 1990 | 121.1 | 4.15 | 1991 | 121.2 | 3.62 |
| Greg Cadaret | 1991 | 121.2 | 3.62 | 1992 | 103.2 | 4.25 |
| Carlos Castillo | 1998 | 100.1 | 5.11 | 1999 | 41.0 | 5.71 |
| Tony Castillo | 1996 | 95.0 | 3.60 | 1997 | 62.1 | 4.91 |
| Norm Charlton | 1989 | 95.1 | 2.93 | 1990 | 154.1 | 2.74 |
| Tim Crews | 1990 | 107.1 | 2.77 | 1991 | 76.0 | 3.43 |
| Chuck Crim | 1989 | 117.2 | 2.83 | 1990 | 85.2 | 3.47 |
| Chuck Crim | 1991 | 91.1 | 4.63 | 1992 | 87.0 | 5.17 |
| Danny Darwin | 1989 | 122.0 | 2.36 | 1990 | 162.2 | 2.21 |
| Mark Davis | 1989 | 92.2 | 1.85 | 1990 | 68.2 | 5.11 |
| Rob Dibble | 1989 | 99.0 | 2.09 | 1990 | 98.0 | 1.74 |
| Rob Dibble | 1990 | 98.0 | 1.74 | 1991 | 82.1 | 3.17 |
| Jerry Dipoto | 1997 | 95.2 | 4.70 | 1998 | 71.1 | 3.53 |
| John Doherty | 1995 | 113.0 | 5.10 | 1996 | 6.1 | 5.68 |
| Steve Farr | 1990 | 127.0 | 1.98 | 1991 | 70.0 | 2.19 |
| Mike Flanagan | 1991 | 98.1 | 2.38 | 1992 | 34.2 | 8.05 |
| John Frascatore | 1998 | 95.2 | 4.14 | 1999 | 70.0 | 3.73 |
| Willie Fraser | 1989 | 91.2 | 3.24 | 1990 | 76.0 | 3.08 |
| Todd Frohwirth | 1991 | 96.1 | 1.87 | 1992 | 106.0 | 2.46 |
| Todd Frohwirth | 1992 | 106.0 | 2.46 | 1993 | 96.1 | 3.83 |
| Todd Frohwirth | 1993 | 96.1 | 3.83 | 1994 | 26.2 | 10.80 |
| Paul Gibson | 1990 | 97.1 | 3.05 | 1991 | 96.0 | 4.59 |
| Paul Gibson | 1991 | 96.0 | 4.59 | 1992 | 62.0 | 5.23 |
| Wayne Gomes | 1998 | 93.1 | 4.24 | 1999 | 74.0 | 4.26 |
| Mark Grant | 1989 | 116.1 | 3.33 | 1990 | 91.1 | 4.73 |
| Lee Guetterman | 1989 | 103.0 | 2.45 | 1990 | 93.0 | 3.39 |
| Lee Guetterman | 1990 | 93.0 | 3.39 | 1991 | 88.0 | 3.68 |
| John Habyan | 1991 | 90.0 | 2.30 | 1992 | 72.2 | 3.84 |
| Greg Harris | 1989 | 103.1 | 3.31 | 1990 | 184.1 | 4.00 |
| Greg Harris | 1992 | 107.2 | 2.51 | 1993 | 112.1 | 3.77 |
| Greg Harris | 1993 | 112.1 | 3.77 | 1994 | 50.2 | 7.99 |
| Greg W. Harris | 1990 | 117.1 | 2.30 | 1991 | 133.0 | 2.23 |
| Shigetoshi Hasegawa | 1998 | 97.1 | 3.14 | 1999 | 77.0 | 4.91 |
| Mike Henneman | 1989 | 90.0 | 3.70 | 1990 | 94.1 | 3.05 |
| Mike Henneman | 1990 | 94.1 | 3.05 | 1991 | 84.1 | 2.88 |
| Jeremy Hernandez | 1993 | 111.2 | 3.63 | 1994 | 23.1 | 2.70 |

| Pitcher | Year1 | IP | ERA | Year2 | IP | ERA |
|---|---|---|---|---|---|---|
| Xavier Hernandez | 1992 | 111.0 | 2.11 | 1993 | 96.2 | 2.61 |
| Xavier Hernandez | 1993 | 96.2 | 2.61 | 1994 | 40.0 | 5.85 |
| Xavier Hernandez | 1995 | 90.0 | 4.60 | 1996 | 78.0 | 4.62 |
| Trevor Hoffman | 1993 | 90.0 | 3.90 | 1994 | 56.0 | 2.57 |
| Mike Jackson | 1989 | 99.1 | 3.17 | 1990 | 77.1 | 4.54 |
| Doug Jones | 1992 | 111.2 | 1.85 | 1993 | 85.1 | 4.54 |
| Todd Jones | 1995 | 99.2 | 3.07 | 1996 | 57.1 | 4.40 |
| Dennis Lamp | 1989 | 112.1 | 2.32 | 1990 | 105.2 | 4.68 |
| Dennis Lamp | 1990 | 105.2 | 4.68 | 1991 | 92.0 | 4.70 |
| Dennis Lamp | 1991 | 92.0 | 4.70 | 1992 | 28.0 | 5.14 |
| Craig Lefferts | 1989 | 107.0 | 2.69 | 1990 | 78.2 | 2.52 |
| Curtis Leskanic | 1995 | 98.0 | 3.40 | 1996 | 73.2 | 6.23 |
| Richie Lewis | 1996 | 90.1 | 4.18 | 1997 | 24.1 | 8.88 |
| Mike Maddux | 1991 | 98.2 | 2.46 | 1992 | 79.2 | 2.37 |
| Pedro Martinez | 1993 | 107.0 | 2.61 | 1994 | 144.2 | 3.42 |
| Roger Mason | 1993 | 99.2 | 4.06 | 1994 | 60.0 | 3.75 |
| Roger McDowell | 1989 | 92.0 | 1.96 | 1990 | 86.1 | 3.86 |
| Roger McDowell | 1991 | 101.1 | 2.93 | 1992 | 83.2 | 4.09 |
| Chuck McElroy | 1991 | 101.1 | 1.95 | 1992 | 83.2 | 3.55 |
| Greg McMichael | 1993 | 91.2 | 2.06 | 1994 | 58.2 | 3.84 |
| Rusty Meacham | 1992 | 101.2 | 2.74 | 1993 | 21.0 | 5.57 |
| Alan Mills | 1992 | 103.1 | 2.61 | 1993 | 100.1 | 3.23 |
| Alan Mills | 1993 | 100.1 | 3.23 | 1994 | 45.1 | 5.16 |
| Blas Minor | 1993 | 94.1 | 4.10 | 1994 | 19.0 | 8.05 |
| Greg Minton | 1989 | 90.0 | 2.20 | 1990 | 15.1 | 2.35 |
| Rich Monteleone | 1992 | 92.2 | 3.30 | 1993 | 85.2 | 4.94 |
| Jeff Montgomery | 1989 | 92.0 | 1.37 | 1990 | 94.1 | 2.39 |
| Jeff Montgomery | 1990 | 94.1 | 2.39 | 1991 | 90.0 | 2.90 |
| Jeff Montgomery | 1991 | 90.0 | 2.90 | 1992 | 82.2 | 2.18 |
| Rob Murphy | 1989 | 105.0 | 2.74 | 1990 | 57.0 | 6.32 |
| Jeff Parrett | 1989 | 105.2 | 2.98 | 1990 | 108.2 | 4.64 |
| Jeff Parrett | 1992 | 98.1 | 3.02 | 1993 | 73.2 | 5.38 |
| Mike Perez | 1992 | 93.0 | 1.84 | 1993 | 72.2 | 2.48 |
| Ted Power | 1992 | 99.1 | 2.54 | 1993 | 45.1 | 5.36 |
| Jerry Reed | 1989 | 101.2 | 3.19 | 1990 | 52.1 | 4.82 |
| Arthur Rhodes | 1997 | 95.1 | 3.02 | 1998 | 77.0 | 3.51 |
| Mariano Rivera | 1996 | 107.2 | 2.09 | 1997 | 71.2 | 1.88 |
| Mel Rojas | 1992 | 100.2 | 1.43 | 1993 | 88.1 | 2.95 |
| Jeff Shaw | 1996 | 104.2 | 2.49 | 1997 | 94.2 | 2.38 |
| Jeff Shaw | 1997 | 94.2 | 2.38 | 1998 | 85.0 | 2.12 |
| Aaron Small | 1997 | 96.2 | 4.28 | 1998 | 67.2 | 5.59 |
| Scott Sullivan | 1997 | 97.1 | 3.24 | 1998 | 102.0 | 5.21 |
| Scott Sullivan | 1998 | 102.0 | 5.21 | 1999 | 113.2 | 3.01 |
| Bill Swift | 1991 | 90.1 | 1.99 | 1992 | 164.2 | 2.08 |
| Greg Swindell | 1997 | 115.2 | 3.58 | 1998 | 90.1 | 3.59 |
| Greg Swindell | 1998 | 90.1 | 3.59 | 1999 | 64.2 | 2.51 |
| Anthony Telford | 1998 | 91.0 | 3.86 | 1999 | 96.0 | 3.94 |
| Mike Timlin | 1991 | 108.1 | 3.16 | 1992 | 43.2 | 4.12 |
| Mike Trombley | 1998 | 96.2 | 3.63 | 1999 | 87.1 | 4.33 |
| Dave Veres | 1995 | 103.1 | 2.26 | 1996 | 77.2 | 4.17 |
| Duane Ward | 1989 | 114.2 | 3.77 | 1990 | 127.2 | 3.45 |
| Duane Ward | 1990 | 127.2 | 3.45 | 1991 | 107.1 | 2.77 |
| Duane Ward | 1991 | 107.1 | 2.77 | 1992 | 101.1 | 1.95 |
| Duane Ward | 1992 | 101.1 | 1.95 | 1993 | 71.2 | 2.13 |
| Bob Wickman | 1996 | 95.2 | 4.42 | 1997 | 95.2 | 2.73 |
| Bob Wickman | 1997 | 95.2 | 2.73 | 1998 | 82.1 | 3.72 |
| Mark Williamson | 1989 | 107.1 | 2.93 | 1990 | 85.1 | 2.21 |

## *Florida Marlins: Has Anyone Had a Ground Game Like Castillo's? (p. 52)*

### Highest Groundball-Flyball Ratio

| 1999 (minimum 250 PA) | | | | | 1987-99 (minimum 1,000 PA) | | | | |
|---|---|---|---|---|---|---|---|---|---|
| Player, Team | PA | Grd | Fly | Ratio | Player | PA | Grd | Fly | Ratio |
| Luis Castillo, Fla | 563 | 254 | 52 | 4.88 | Tom Glavine | 1,014 | 436 | 60 | 7.27 |
| Willie McGee, StL | 290 | 126 | 34 | 3.71 | Luis Castillo | 1,211 | 579 | 97 | 5.97 |
| Cristian Guzman, Min | 456 | 205 | 65 | 3.15 | Willie McGee | 5,323 | 2,533 | 734 | 3.45 |
| Adrian Brown, Pit | 267 | 112 | 36 | 3.11 | Milt Thompson | 3,519 | 1,598 | 507 | 3.15 |
| Abraham Nunez, Pit | 301 | 120 | 39 | 3.08 | David Hulse | 1,370 | 592 | 202 | 2.93 |
| Wilton Guerrero, Mon | 340 | 159 | 52 | 3.06 | Greg Maddux | 1,109 | 427 | 146 | 2.92 |
| Ricky Gutierrez, Hou | 311 | 134 | 46 | 2.91 | Felix Fermin | 3,072 | 1,520 | 538 | 2.83 |
| Lance Johnson, ChC | 377 | 191 | 71 | 2.69 | Curtis Goodwin | 1,138 | 442 | 157 | 2.82 |
| Jose Vizcaino, LA | 298 | 137 | 51 | 2.69 | Wally Backman | 1,686 | 676 | 249 | 2.71 |
| Randy Winn, TB | 324 | 138 | 52 | 2.65 | Steve Sax | 4,237 | 2,073 | 766 | 2.71 |
| Carlos Febles, KC | 524 | 201 | 79 | 2.54 | Ricky Gutierrez | 2,426 | 996 | 372 | 2.68 |
| Brent Gates, Min | 346 | 151 | 63 | 2.40 | Joel Skinner | 1,066 | 419 | 159 | 2.64 |
| Rey Sanchez, KC | 518 | 225 | 96 | 2.34 | Steve Jeltz | 1,216 | 497 | 190 | 2.62 |
| Roger Cedeno, NYM | 525 | 183 | 82 | 2.23 | Carlos Quintana | 1,557 | 673 | 260 | 2.59 |
| Homer Bush, Tor | 523 | 217 | 99 | 2.19 | Rafael Belliard | 2,129 | 932 | 367 | 2.54 |
| Mike Caruso, CWS | 564 | 261 | 123 | 2.12 | Otis Nixon | 5,398 | 2,125 | 847 | 2.51 |
| Quilvio Veras, SD | 545 | 193 | 94 | 2.05 | Tony Eusebio | 1,532 | 644 | 265 | 2.43 |
| Eric Owens, SD | 485 | 216 | 106 | 2.04 | Junior Ortiz | 1,559 | 716 | 307 | 2.33 |
| Royce Clayton, Tex | 520 | 183 | 90 | 2.03 | Bip Roberts | 4,373 | 1,766 | 771 | 2.29 |
| Ivan Rodriguez, Tex | 630 | 275 | 140 | 1.96 | Derek Jeter | 2,886 | 1,104 | 491 | 2.25 |
| Stan Javier, SF-Hou | 75 | 175 | 91 | 1.92 | Julio Franco | 5,426 | 2,099 | 940 | 2.23 |
| Craig Wilson, CWS | 282 | 126 | 66 | 1.91 | Manuel Lee | 2,832 | 1,098 | 496 | 2.21 |
| Tom Goodwin, Tex | 455 | 174 | 92 | 1.89 | Tom Goodwin | 2,928 | 1,116 | 505 | 2.21 |
| Brian Hunter, Det-Sea | 527 | 238 | 128 | 1.86 | Lance Johnson | 5,770 | 2,608 | 1,190 | 2.19 |
| Alberto Castillo, StL | 290 | 108 | 59 | 1.83 | Brett Butler | 6,461 | 2,387 | 1,104 | 2.16 |
| Derek Bell, Hou | 568 | 205 | 112 | 1.83 | Phil Bradley | 2,476 | 919 | 427 | 2.15 |
| Wade Boggs, TB | 334 | 137 | 76 | 1.80 | Jose Vizcaino | 3,947 | 1,583 | 743 | 2.13 |
| Darren Lewis, Bos | 538 | 209 | 116 | 1.80 | Wilton Guerrero | 1,148 | 483 | 227 | 2.13 |
| Dmitri Young, Cin | 409 | 162 | 90 | 1.80 | Mookie Wilson | 2,231 | 905 | 429 | 2.11 |
| Chad Allen, Min | 523 | 204 | 114 | 1.79 | Lenny Harris | 3,343 | 1,535 | 731 | 2.10 |
| Bernie Williams, NYY | 697 | 257 | 144 | 1.78 | Rey Ordonez | 2,057 | 902 | 431 | 2.09 |
| Rey Ordonez, NYM | 588 | 232 | 130 | 1.78 | Darren Lewis | 4,080 | 1,625 | 777 | 2.09 |
| Javy Lopez, Atl | 269 | 103 | 58 | 1.78 | Warren Newson | 1,193 | 366 | 176 | 2.08 |
| Joe McEwing, StL | 575 | 197 | 111 | 1.77 | Mike Aldrete | 2,242 | 844 | 406 | 2.08 |
| Shannon Stewart, Tor | 682 | 266 | 150 | 1.77 | Luis Polonia | 4,913 | 1,987 | 966 | 2.06 |
| Matt Lawton, Min | 476 | 195 | 110 | 1.77 | Dave Clark | 2,143 | 792 | 386 | 2.05 |
| Sean Casey, Cin | 669 | 236 | 134 | 1.76 | Reggie Jefferson | 2,306 | 849 | 419 | 2.03 |
| Ray Durham, CWS | 694 | 241 | 137 | 1.76 | Gary Pettis | 2,529 | 796 | 393 | 2.03 |
| Todd Walker, Min | 586 | 224 | 128 | 1.75 | Alex Ochoa | 1,194 | 512 | 253 | 2.02 |
| Aaron Ledesma, TB | 312 | 133 | 77 | 1.73 | Joe Girardi | 3,593 | 1,491 | 739 | 2.02 |
| Tony Eusebio, Hou | 363 | 129 | 75 | 1.72 | Al Newman | 2,165 | 905 | 453 | 2.00 |
| Ben Davis, SD | 293 | 97 | 57 | 1.70 | Hal Morris | 4,239 | 1,674 | 843 | 1.99 |
| Chris Gomez, SD | 265 | 90 | 53 | 1.70 | Tony Gwynn | 7,390 | 3,095 | 1,564 | 1.98 |
| Alex Arias, Phi | 390 | 145 | 86 | 1.69 | Pat Listach | 1,991 | 694 | 351 | 1.98 |
| Todd Hollandsworth, LA | 287 | 94 | 56 | 1.68 | Tony Pena | 3,982 | 1,657 | 848 | 1.95 |
| Mark Grudzielanek, LA | 534 | 203 | 122 | 1.66 | Quilvio Veras | 2,634 | 941 | 482 | 1.95 |
| **MLB Average** | | | | **1.23** | **MLB Average** | | | | **1.29** |

## Houston Astros: How Underrated Is Biggio? (p. 54)

### Most Doubles, Two-Year Span—1876-1999

| Player | Years | 2B | Player | Years | 2B | Player | Years | 2B |
|---|---|---|---|---|---|---|---|---|
| Joe Medwick | 1936-37 | 120 | Wade Boggs | 1988-89 | 96 | George Kell | 1950-51 | 92 |
| George Burns | 1926-27 | 115 | Tris Speaker | 1923-24 | 95 | Pete Rose | 1974-75 | 92 |
| Billy Herman | 1935-36 | 114 | Tris Speaker | 1926-27 | 95 | Don Mattingly | 1984-85 | 92 |
| Joe Medwick | 1935-36 | 110 | Earl Webb | 1931-32 | 95 | Jeff Cirillo | 1996-97 | 92 |
| Hank Greenberg | 1934-35 | 109 | Joe Medwick | 1938-39 | 95 | Larry Walker | 1997-98 | 92 |
| Tris Speaker | 1922-23 | 107 | Stan Musial | 1952-53 | 95 | Ed Delahanty | 1898-99 | 91 |
| Craig Biggio | 1998-99 | 107 | Wade Boggs | 1989-90 | 95 | Harry Heilmann | 1926-27 | 91 |
| George Burns | 1925-26 | 105 | Heinie Manush | 1929-30 | 94 | Babe Herman | 1930-31 | 91 |
| Chuck Klein | 1929-30 | 104 | Chuck Klein | 1932-33 | 94 | Dick Bartell | 1931-32 | 91 |
| Edgar Martinez | 1995-96 | 104 | George Kell | 1949-50 | 94 | Beau Bell | 1936-37 | 91 |
| Joe Medwick | 1937-38 | 103 | Stan Musial | 1953-54 | 94 | Joe Cronin | 1937-38 | 91 |
| Tris Speaker | 1920-21 | 102 | Alex Rodriguez | 1996-97 | 94 | Lou Boudreau | 1940-41 | 91 |
| Don Mattingly | 1985-86 | 101 | Ed Delahanty | 1895-96 | 93 | Pete Rose | 1978-79 | 91 |
| Tris Speaker | 1921-22 | 100 | Chick Hafey | 1928-29 | 93 | Don Mattingly | 1986-87 | 91 |
| Paul Waner | 1932-33 | 100 | Paul Waner | 1928-29 | 93 | John Valentin | 1997-98 | 91 |
| Charlie Gehringer | 1936-37 | 100 | Chuck Klein | 1930-31 | 93 | Nap Lajoie | 1903-04 | 90 |
| Lou Gehrig | 1926-27 | 99 | Hal McRae | 1977-78 | 93 | Rogers Hornsby | 1921-22 | 90 |
| Lou Gehrig | 1927-28 | 99 | Albert Belle | 1997-98 | 93 | Paul Waner | 1927-28 | 90 |
| Stan Musial | 1943-44 | 99 | Bob Meusel | 1927-28 | 92 | Babe Herman | 1929-30 | 90 |
| Earl Webb | 1930-31 | 97 | Heinie Manush | 1928-29 | 92 | Heinie Manush | 1930-31 | 90 |
| Paul Waner | 1931-32 | 97 | Charlie Gehringer | 1929-30 | 92 | Moose Solters | 1935-36 | 90 |
| Gee Walker | 1936-37 | 97 | Charlie Gehringer | 1933-34 | 92 | Albert Belle | 1995-96 | 90 |
| Al Simmons | 1925-26 | 96 | Charlie Gehringer | 1935-36 | 92 | Mark Grace | 1995-96 | 90 |
| Johnny Frederick | 1929-30 | 96 | Billy Herman | 1936-37 | 92 | | | |
| Hank Greenberg | 1933-34 | 96 | Hank Greenberg | 1939-40 | 92 | | | |

### Most Runs Created—1995-99

| Player | RC | Player | RC | Player | RC |
|---|---|---|---|---|---|
| Mark McGwire | 659 | Paul O'Neill | 516 | Jose Offerman | 422 |
| Jeff Bagwell | 658 | Gary Sheffield | 512 | Bob Higginson | 422 |
| Barry Bonds | 641 | Roberto Alomar | 511 | Robin Ventura | 419 |
| Edgar Martinez | 638 | John Olerud | 492 | Greg Vaughn | 415 |
| Albert Belle | 634 | Alex Rodriguez | 489 | Rickey Henderson | 410 |
| Craig Biggio | 633 | Ray Lankford | 485 | Matt Williams | 410 |
| Frank Thomas | 621 | Raul Mondesi | 482 | Omar Vizquel | 409 |
| Rafael Palmeiro | 608 | Fred McGriff | 481 | J.T. Snow | 409 |
| Mo Vaughn | 607 | Andres Galarraga | 480 | Carlos Delgado | 408 |
| Ken Griffey Jr. | 600 | Tony Gwynn | 478 | Shawn Green | 407 |
| Manny Ramirez | 593 | Eric Karros | 474 | Tony Phillips | 404 |
| Chipper Jones | 580 | Kenny Lofton | 471 | Brian Jordan | 398 |
| Chuck Knoblauch | 578 | Barry Larkin | 470 | Jeff Kent | 398 |
| Bernie Williams | 566 | Steve Finley | 458 | Jay Buhner | 396 |
| Dante Bichette | 563 | Jason Giambi | 458 | Ryan Klesko | 395 |
| Sammy Sosa | 562 | Jeff Cirillo | 457 | Troy O'Leary | 395 |
| Jim Thome | 560 | Ellis Burks | 454 | Cal Ripken Jr. | 393 |
| Mike Piazza | 554 | Ken Caminiti | 454 | David Justice | 393 |
| Tim Salmon | 542 | Ivan Rodriguez | 450 | Brian McRae | 391 |
| Mark Grace | 534 | Jay Bell | 445 | Jim Edmonds | 391 |
| Juan Gonzalez | 532 | John Valentin | 441 | Edgardo Alfonzo | 391 |
| Larry Walker | 531 | B.J. Surhoff | 440 | Travis Fryman | 390 |
| Brady Anderson | 528 | Luis Gonzalez | 438 | Marquis Grissom | 386 |
| Tino Martinez | 522 | Derek Jeter | 434 | Eric Young | 386 |
| Vinny Castilla | 521 | Ray Durham | 424 | Jose Canseco | 384 |
| Rusty Greer | 521 | Todd Zeile | 422 | Mike Stanley | 384 |

## Los Angeles Dodgers: Is Brown the Best Travelin' Pitcher Ever? (p. 56)

### Lowest ERA, Four-Plus Teams Over Five-Year Span—1920-99 (minimum 600 IP)

| Pitcher | ERA | IP | Years | No. | Teams |
|---|---|---|---|---|---|
| Kevin Brown | 2.66 | 1,152.0 | 1995-99 | 4 | Bal-Fla-SD-LA |
| Hoyt Wilhelm | 2.87 | 652.0 | 1956-60 | 4 | NYG-StL-Cle-Bal |
| Kevin Brown | 2.93 | 1,069.2 | 1994-98 | 4 | Tex-Bal-Fla-SD |
| Hoyt Wilhelm | 2.95 | 608.0 | 1955-59 | 4 | NYG-StL-Cle-Bal |
| Al Downing | 2.99 | 791.1 | 1967-71 | 4 | NYY-Oak-Mil-LA |
| Dean Chance | 3.01 | 1,080.2 | 1966-70 | 4 | Cal-Min-Cle-NYM |
| Mike Marshall | 3.03 | 637.2 | 1973-77 | 4 | Mon-LA-Atl-Tex |
| Dean Chance | 3.04 | 910.2 | 1967-71 | 4 | Min-Cle-NYM-Det |
| Dick Selma | 3.07 | 600.2 | 1967-71 | 4 | NYM-SD-ChC-Phi |
| Al Downing | 3.08 | 792.1 | 1968-72 | 4 | NYY-Oak-Mil-LA |
| Al Downing | 3.10 | 924.0 | 1969-73 | 4 | NYY-Oak-Mil-LA |
| Bobo Newsom | 3.11 | 984.0 | 1944-48 | 4 | PhiA-Was-NYY-NYG |
| Bob Shaw | 3.15 | 934.0 | 1961-65 | 4 | CWS-KC-Mil-SF |
| David Cone | 3.15 | 976.2 | 1992-96 | 4 | NYM-Tor-KC-NYY |
| David Cone | 3.20 | 1,137.1 | 1991-95 | 4 | NYM-Tor-KC-NYY |
| Dick Selma | 3.21 | 656.2 | 1966-70 | 4 | NYM-SD-ChC-Phi |
| Virgil Trucks | 3.21 | 940.0 | 1953-57 | 4 | StLA-CWS-Det-KCA |
| Mudcat Grant | 3.22 | 688.1 | 1966-70 | 6 | Min-LA-Mon-StL-Oak-Pit |
| Bobo Newsom | 3.22 | 719.0 | 1945-49 | 4 | PhiA-Was-NYY-NYG |
| Denny McLain | 3.25 | 1,045.1 | 1968-72 | 4 | Det-Was-Oak-Atl |
| Ken Johnson | 3.26 | 641.0 | 1966-70 | 4 | Atl-NYY-ChC-Mon |
| Ken Johnson | 3.27 | 866.1 | 1965-69 | 4 | Hou-Mil-NYY-ChC |
| Gaylord Perry | 3.29 | 1,087.2 | 1977-81 | 4 | Tex-SD-NYY-Atl |
| Pat Dobson | 3.29 | 1,282.2 | 1970-74 | 4 | SD-Bal-Atl-NYY |
| Bobo Newsom | 3.29 | 1,175.2 | 1943-47 | 5 | Bro-StLA-Was-PhiA-NYY |
| Sal Maglie | 3.32 | 773.1 | 1954-58 | 5 | NYG-Cle-Bro-NYY-StL |
| Sal Maglie | 3.33 | 842.1 | 1953-57 | 4 | NYG-Cle-Bro-NYY |
| Virgil Trucks | 3.34 | 737.1 | 1954-58 | 4 | CWS-Det-KC-NYY |
| Dock Ellis | 3.35 | 933.1 | 1973-77 | 4 | Pit-NYY-Oak-Tex |
| Mike Torrez | 3.37 | 1,216.2 | 1974-78 | 5 | Mon-Bal-Oak-NYY-Bos |
| Pat Dobson | 3.38 | 1,106.2 | 1969-73 | 5 | Det-SD-Bal-Atl-NYY |
| Burleigh Grimes | 3.42 | 1,236.2 | 1927-31 | 4 | NYG-Pit-Bos-StL |
| John Candelaria | 3.43 | 688.1 | 1984-88 | 4 | Pit-Cal-NYM-NYY |
| Ken Johnson | 3.43 | 962.2 | 1961-65 | 4 | KC-Cin-Hou-Mil |
| Mike Torrez | 3.43 | 1,174.2 | 1973-77 | 4 | Mon-Bal-Oak-NYY |
| Gary Bell | 3.43 | 883.1 | 1965-69 | 4 | Cle-Bos-Sea-CWS |
| Roger Wolff | 3.43 | 794.0 | 1943-47 | 4 | PhiA-Was-Cle-Pit |
| Burleigh Grimes | 3.44 | 1,249.2 | 1926-30 | 5 | Bro-NYG-Pit-BosN-StLN |
| Tom Murphy | 3.44 | 607.2 | 1971-75 | 4 | Cal-KC-StL-Mil |
| Pat Dobson | 3.46 | 1,174.1 | 1972-76 | 4 | Bal-Atl-NYY-Cle |
| Mudcat Grant | 3.47 | 823.1 | 1965-69 | 4 | Min-LA-Mon-StL |
| Claude Osteen | 3.47 | 1,113.0 | 1971-75 | 4 | LA-Hou-StL-CWS |
| Bob Shaw | 3.48 | 807.2 | 1963-67 | 4 | Mil-SF-NYM-ChC |
| Bob Shaw | 3.48 | 891.2 | 1960-64 | 4 | CWS-KC-Mil-SF |
| Ken Hill | 3.48 | 992.0 | 1992-96 | 4 | Mon-StL-Cle-Tex |
| Rudy May | 3.49 | 969.1 | 1974-78 | 4 | Cal-NYY-Bal-Mon |
| Gaylord Perry | 3.49 | 1,066.1 | 1978-82 | 5 | SD-Tex-NYY-Atl-Sea |
| George Brunet | 3.51 | 1,006.1 | 1966-70 | 4 | Cal-Sea-Was-Pit |
| Jack Harshman | 3.51 | 931.2 | 1955-59 | 4 | CWS-Bal-Bos-Cle |
| Dick Selma | 3.51 | 618.0 | 1968-72 | 4 | NYM-SD-ChC-Phi |
| Don Sutton | 3.52 | 1,067.1 | 1981-85 | 4 | Hou-Mil-Oak-Cal |
| Bob Shaw | 3.52 | 960.2 | 1958-62 | 4 | Det-CWS-KC-Mil |
| Nelson Briles | 3.52 | 756.0 | 1973-77 | 4 | Pit-KC-Tex-Bal |
| Ken Brett | 3.53 | 856.2 | 1972-76 | 5 | Mil-Phi-Pit-NYY-CWS |
| Ralph Terry | 3.54 | 936.0 | 1962-66 | 4 | NYY-Cle-KC-NYM |

## Montreal Expos: Can You Win Without Walking? (p. 60)

### Teams Ranking Last in Walks—1900-99

| Year | Lg | Team | BB | W-L | Pct | Year | Lg | Team | BB | W-L | Pct |
|---|---|---|---|---|---|---|---|---|---|---|---|
| 1900 | NL | Pirates | 327 | 79-60 | .568 | 1924 | AL | Athletics | 374 | 71-81 | .467 |
| 1901 | AL | Blues | 243 | 54-82 | .397 | 1924 | NL | Reds | 349 | 83-70 | .542 |
| 1901 | NL | Beaneaters | 303 | 69-69 | .500 | 1925 | AL | Athletics | 453 | 88-64 | .579 |
| 1901 | NL | Giants | 303 | 52-85 | .380 | 1925 | NL | Cubs | 397 | 68-86 | .442 |
| 1902 | AL | Somersets | 275 | 77-60 | .562 | 1926 | AL | Browns | 437 | 62-92 | .403 |
| 1902 | NL | Giants | 252 | 48-88 | .353 | 1926 | NL | Giants | 339 | 74-77 | .490 |
| 1903 | AL | Nationals | 257 | 43-94 | .314 | 1927 | AL | Indians | 381 | 66-87 | .431 |
| 1903 | NL | Cardinals | 277 | 43-94 | .314 | 1927 | NL | Braves | 346 | 60-94 | .390 |
| 1904 | AL | Nationals | 283 | 38-113 | .252 | 1928 | AL | Indians | 377 | 62-92 | .403 |
| 1904 | NL | Cubs | 298 | 93-60 | .608 | 1928 | NL | Reds | 386 | 78-74 | .513 |
| 1905 | AL | Naps | 286 | 76-78 | .494 | 1929 | AL | Red Sox | 413 | 58-96 | .377 |
| 1905 | NL | Beaneaters | 302 | 51-103 | .331 | 1929 | NL | Braves | 408 | 56-98 | .364 |
| 1906 | AL | Pilgrims | 298 | 49-105 | .318 | 1930 | AL | Red Sox | 358 | 52-102 | .338 |
| 1906 | NL | Beaneaters | 356 | 49-102 | .325 | 1930 | NL | Braves | 332 | 70-84 | .455 |
| 1907 | AL | Highlanders | 304 | 70-78 | .473 | 1931 | AL | Red Sox | 405 | 62-90 | .408 |
| 1907 | NL | Cardinals | 312 | 52-101 | .340 | 1931 | NL | Braves | 368 | 64-90 | .416 |
| 1908 | AL | Highlanders | 288 | 51-103 | .331 | 1932 | AL | White Sox | 459 | 49-102 | .325 |
| 1908 | NL | Cardinals | 282 | 49-105 | .318 | 1932 | NL | Braves | 347 | 77-77 | .500 |
| 1909 | AL | Naps | 283 | 71-82 | .464 | 1933 | AL | Indians | 448 | 75-76 | .497 |
| 1909 | NL | Superbas | 330 | 55-98 | .359 | 1933 | NL | Braves | 326 | 83-71 | .539 |
| 1910 | AL | Naps | 366 | 71-81 | .467 | 1934 | AL | Athletics | 491 | 68-82 | .453 |
| 1910 | NL | Doves | 359 | 53-100 | .346 | 1934 | NL | Reds | 313 | 52-99 | .344 |
| 1911 | AL | Naps | 354 | 80-73 | .523 | 1935 | AL | Indians | 460 | 82-71 | .536 |
| 1911 | NL | Dodgers | 425 | 64-86 | .427 | 1935 | NL | Braves | 353 | 38-115 | .248 |
| 1912 | AL | Naps | 407 | 75-78 | .490 | 1936 | AL | Indians | 514 | 80-74 | .519 |
| 1912 | NL | Pirates | 420 | 93-58 | .616 | 1936 | NL | Dodgers | 390 | 67-87 | .435 |
| 1913 | AL | White Sox | 398 | 78-74 | .513 | 1937 | AL | Browns | 514 | 46-108 | .299 |
| 1913 | NL | Dodgers | 361 | 65-84 | .436 | 1937 | NL | Cardinals | 385 | 81-73 | .526 |
| 1914 | AL | White Sox | 408 | 70-84 | .455 | 1938 | AL | White Sox | 514 | 65-83 | .439 |
| 1914 | NL | Robins | 376 | 75-79 | .487 | 1938 | NL | Reds | 366 | 82-68 | .547 |
| 1914 | FL | Packers | 399 | 67-84 | .444 | 1939 | AL | Athletics | 503 | 55-97 | .362 |
| 1915 | AL | Athletics | 436 | 43-109 | .283 | 1939 | NL | Bees | 366 | 63-88 | .417 |
| 1915 | NL | Robins | 313 | 80-72 | .526 | 1940 | AL | Nationals | 468 | 64-90 | .416 |
| 1915 | FL | Packers | 368 | 81-72 | .529 | 1940 | NL | Bees | 402 | 65-87 | .428 |
| 1916 | AL | Athletics | 406 | 36-117 | .235 | 1941 | AL | Nationals | 470 | 70-84 | .455 |
| 1916 | NL | Cardinals | 335 | 60-93 | .392 | 1941 | NL | Phillies | 451 | 43-111 | .279 |
| 1917 | AL | Browns | 405 | 57-97 | .370 | 1942 | AL | Athletics | 440 | 55-99 | .357 |
| 1917 | NL | Reds | 312 | 78-76 | .506 | 1942 | NL | Phillies | 392 | 42-109 | .278 |
| 1918 | AL | Athletics | 343 | 52-76 | .406 | 1943 | AL | Athletics | 430 | 49-105 | .318 |
| 1918 | NL | Robins | 212 | 57-69 | .452 | 1943 | NL | Cardinals | 428 | 105-49 | .682 |
| 1919 | AL | Athletics | 349 | 36-104 | .257 | 1944 | AL | Athletics | 422 | 72-82 | .468 |
| 1919 | NL | Robins | 258 | 69-71 | .493 | 1944 | NL | Reds | 423 | 89-65 | .578 |
| 1920 | AL | Athletics | 353 | 48-106 | .312 | 1945 | AL | Athletics | 449 | 52-98 | .347 |
| 1920 | NL | Phillies | 283 | 62-91 | .405 | 1945 | NL | Reds | 392 | 61-93 | .396 |
| 1921 | AL | Browns | 413 | 81-73 | .526 | 1946 | AL | Browns | 465 | 66-88 | .429 |
| 1921 | NL | Phillies | 294 | 51-103 | .331 | 1946 | NL | Phillies | 417 | 69-85 | .448 |
| 1922 | AL | Red Sox | 366 | 61-93 | .396 | 1947 | AL | White Sox | 492 | 70-84 | .455 |
| 1922 | NL | Robins | 339 | 76-78 | .494 | 1947 | NL | Phillies | 464 | 62-92 | .403 |
| 1923 | AL | Red Sox | 391 | 61-91 | .401 | 1948 | AL | Nationals | 568 | 56-97 | .366 |
| 1923 | NL | Pirates | 407 | 87-67 | .565 | 1948 | NL | Phillies | 440 | 66-88 | .429 |

| Year | Lg | Team | BB | W-L | Pct | Year | Lg | Team | BB | W-L | Pct |
|---|---|---|---|---|---|---|---|---|---|---|---|
| 1949 | AL | Nationals | 593 | 50-104 | .325 | 1975 | AL | Tigers | 383 | 57-102 | .358 |
| 1949 | NL | Cubs | 396 | 61-93 | .396 | 1975 | NL | Cardinals | 444 | 82-80 | .506 |
| 1950 | AL | White Sox | 551 | 60-94 | .390 | 1976 | AL | Tigers | 450 | 74-87 | .460 |
| 1950 | NL | Cubs | 479 | 64-89 | .418 | 1976 | NL | Expos | 433 | 55-107 | .340 |
| 1951 | AL | Browns | 521 | 52-102 | .338 | 1976 | NL | Pirates | 433 | 92-70 | .568 |
| 1951 | NL | Reds | 415 | 68-86 | .442 | 1977 | AL | Mariners | 426 | 64-98 | .395 |
| 1952 | AL | Browns | 540 | 64-90 | .416 | 1977 | NL | Pirates | 474 | 96-66 | .593 |
| 1952 | NL | Cubs | 422 | 77-77 | .500 | 1978 | AL | White Sox | 409 | 71-90 | .441 |
| 1953 | AL | Red Sox | 496 | 84-69 | .549 | 1978 | NL | Expos | 396 | 76-86 | .469 |
| 1953 | NL | Braves | 439 | 92-62 | .597 | 1979 | AL | Blue Jays | 448 | 53-109 | .327 |
| 1954 | AL | Orioles | 468 | 54-100 | .351 | 1979 | NL | Expos | 432 | 95-65 | .594 |
| 1954 | NL | Braves | 471 | 89-65 | .578 | 1980 | AL | White Sox | 399 | 70-90 | .438 |
| 1955 | AL | Athletics | 463 | 63-91 | .409 | 1980 | NL | Braves | 434 | 81-80 | .503 |
| 1955 | NL | Cubs | 428 | 72-81 | .471 | 1981 | AL | Twins | 275 | 41-68 | .376 |
| 1956 | AL | Athletics | 480 | 52-102 | .338 | 1981 | NL | Pirates | 278 | 46-56 | .451 |
| 1956 | NL | Pirates | 383 | 66-88 | .429 | 1982 | AL | Blue Jays | 415 | 78-84 | .481 |
| 1957 | AL | Athletics | 364 | 59-94 | .386 | 1982 | NL | Padres | 429 | 81-81 | .500 |
| 1957 | NL | Pirates | 374 | 62-92 | .403 | 1983 | AL | Royals | 397 | 79-83 | .488 |
| 1958 | AL | Athletics | 452 | 73-81 | .474 | 1983 | NL | Mets | 436 | 68-94 | .420 |
| 1958 | NL | Pirates | 396 | 84-70 | .545 | 1984 | AL | Royals | 400 | 84-78 | .519 |
| 1959 | AL | Indians | 433 | 89-65 | .578 | 1984 | NL | Pirates | 438 | 75-87 | .463 |
| 1959 | NL | Pirates | 442 | 78-76 | .506 | 1985 | AL | Brewers | 462 | 71-90 | .441 |
| 1960 | AL | Indians | 444 | 76-78 | .494 | 1985 | NL | Astros | 477 | 83-79 | .512 |
| 1960 | NL | Phillies | 448 | 59-95 | .383 | 1986 | AL | Indians | 456 | 84-78 | .519 |
| 1961 | AL | Indians | 492 | 78-83 | .484 | 1986 | NL | Dodgers | 478 | 73-89 | .451 |
| 1961 | NL | Reds | 423 | 93-61 | .604 | 1987 | AL | White Sox | 487 | 77-85 | .475 |
| 1962 | AL | Senators | 466 | 60-101 | .373 | 1987 | NL | Dodgers | 445 | 73-89 | .451 |
| 1962 | NL | Pirates | 432 | 93-68 | .578 | 1988 | AL | Indians | 416 | 78-84 | .481 |
| 1963 | AL | Yankees | 434 | 104-57 | .646 | 1988 | NL | Cubs | 403 | 77-85 | .475 |
| 1963 | NL | Phillies | 403 | 87-75 | .537 | 1989 | AL | Angels | 429 | 91-71 | .562 |
| 1964 | AL | Angels | 472 | 82-80 | .506 | 1989 | NL | Cubs | 472 | 93-69 | .574 |
| 1964 | NL | Mets | 353 | 53-109 | .327 | 1990 | AL | Yankees | 427 | 67-95 | .414 |
| 1965 | AL | Angels | 443 | 75-87 | .463 | 1990 | NL | Cubs | 406 | 77-85 | .475 |
| 1965 | NL | Mets | 392 | 50-112 | .309 | 1991 | AL | Angels | 448 | 81-81 | .500 |
| 1966 | AL | Athletics | 421 | 74-86 | .463 | 1991 | NL | Cubs | 442 | 77-83 | .481 |
| 1966 | NL | Cardinals | 345 | 83-79 | .512 | 1992 | AL | Angels | 416 | 72-90 | .444 |
| 1967 | AL | Indians | 413 | 75-87 | .463 | 1992 | NL | Cubs | 417 | 78-84 | .481 |
| 1967 | NL | Mets | 362 | 61-101 | .377 | 1993 | AL | Royals | 428 | 84-78 | .519 |
| 1968 | AL | White Sox | 397 | 67-95 | .414 | 1993 | NL | Rockies | 388 | 67-95 | .414 |
| 1968 | NL | Cardinals | 378 | 97-65 | .599 | 1994 | AL | Twins | 359 | 53-60 | .469 |
| 1969 | AL | Angels | 516 | 71-91 | .438 | 1994 | NL | Padres | 319 | 47-70 | .402 |
| 1969 | NL | Padres | 423 | 52-110 | .321 | 1995 | AL | Twins | 471 | 56-88 | .389 |
| 1970 | AL | Angels | 447 | 86-76 | .531 | 1995 | NL | Expos | 400 | 66-78 | .458 |
| 1970 | NL | Pirates | 444 | 89-73 | .549 | 1996 | AL | Angels | 527 | 70-91 | .435 |
| 1971 | AL | Angels | 441 | 76-86 | .469 | 1996 | NL | Mets | 445 | 71-91 | .438 |
| 1971 | NL | Braves | 434 | 82-80 | .506 | 1997 | AL | Blue Jays | 487 | 76-86 | .469 |
| 1972 | AL | Angels | 358 | 75-80 | .484 | 1997 | NL | Expos | 420 | 78-84 | .481 |
| 1972 | NL | Pirates | 404 | 96-59 | .619 | 1998 | AL | Tigers | 455 | 65-97 | .401 |
| 1973 | AL | Indians | 471 | 71-91 | .438 | 1998 | NL | Pirates | 393 | 69-93 | .426 |
| 1973 | NL | Padres | 401 | 60-102 | .370 | 1999 | AL | Tigers | 458 | 69-92 | .429 |
| 1974 | AL | Indians | 432 | 77-85 | .475 | 1999 | NL | Expos | 438 | 68-94 | .420 |
| 1974 | NL | Phillies | 469 | 80-82 | .494 | **MLB Average** | | | | | **.445** |

## New York Mets: Did They Have the Best Defensive Infield of All Time? (p. 62)

### Best Defensive Infields—1876-1999

| Fewest Infield Errors (minimum 150 G) | | | | | Highest Infield Fielding Percentage (minimum 100 G) | | | | |
|---|---|---|---|---|---|---|---|---|---|
| Year | Team | G | E | | Year | Team | G | E | Pct |
| 1999 | Mets | 163 | 33 | | 1999 | Mets | 163 | 33 | .991 |
| 1964 | Orioles | 163 | 45 | | 1964 | Orioles | 163 | 45 | .988 |
| 1998 | Orioles | 162 | 46 | | 1998 | Orioles | 162 | 46 | .987 |
| 1988 | Twins | 162 | 46 | | 1995 | Orioles | 144 | 40 | .987 |
| 1963 | Orioles | 162 | 49 | | 1994 | Orioles | 112 | 32 | .987 |
| 1999 | Indians | 162 | 51 | | 1963 | Orioles | 162 | 49 | .987 |
| 1997 | Tigers | 162 | 51 | | 1993 | Pirates | 162 | 51 | .987 |
| 1993 | Pirates | 162 | 51 | | 1988 | Twins | 162 | 46 | .986 |
| 1990 | Athletics | 162 | 51 | | 1994 | Angels | 115 | 34 | .986 |
| 1998 | Mets | 162 | 52 | | 1997 | Tigers | 162 | 51 | .986 |
| 1992 | Reds | 162 | 52 | | 1989 | Orioles | 162 | 54 | .986 |
| 1990 | Blue Jays | 162 | 52 | | 1995 | Reds | 144 | 45 | .986 |
| 1998 | Diamondbacks | 162 | 53 | | 1990 | Blue Jays | 162 | 52 | .986 |
| 1988 | Athletics | 162 | 53 | | 1990 | Athletics | 162 | 51 | .986 |
| 1972 | Phillies | 156 | 53 | | 1989 | Angels | 162 | 55 | .986 |
| 1998 | Rockies | 162 | 54 | | 1999 | Indians | 162 | 51 | .986 |
| 1989 | Orioles | 162 | 54 | | 1995 | Yankees | 145 | 44 | .986 |
| 1977 | Reds | 162 | 54 | | 1998 | Rockies | 162 | 54 | .986 |
| 1999 | Twins | 161 | 54 | | 1993 | Cubs | 163 | 57 | .985 |
| 1990 | Orioles | 161 | 54 | | 1972 | Phillies | 156 | 53 | .985 |
| 1999 | Reds | 163 | 55 | | 1982 | Cardinals | 162 | 63 | .985 |
| 1980 | Reds | 163 | 55 | | 1998 | Diamondbacks | 162 | 53 | .985 |
| 1999 | Orioles | 162 | 55 | | 1998 | Mets | 162 | 52 | .985 |
| 1989 | Angels | 162 | 55 | | 1999 | Orioles | 162 | 55 | .985 |
| 1988 | Red Sox | 162 | 55 | | 1978 | Orioles | 161 | 58 | .985 |
| 1997 | Indians | 161 | 55 | | 1988 | Athletics | 162 | 53 | .985 |
| 1997 | Royals | 161 | 55 | | 1983 | Cubs | 162 | 60 | .985 |
| 1998 | Cubs | 163 | 56 | | 1980 | Reds | 163 | 55 | .985 |
| 1993 | Royals | 162 | 56 | | 1992 | Reds | 162 | 52 | .985 |
| 1991 | Athletics | 162 | 56 | | 1994 | Royals | 115 | 40 | .985 |
| 1993 | Cubs | 163 | 57 | | 1977 | Reds | 162 | 54 | .985 |
| 1996 | Cubs | 162 | 57 | | 1990 | Orioles | 161 | 54 | .985 |
| 1993 | Mariners | 162 | 57 | | 1997 | Indians | 161 | 55 | .985 |
| 1992 | Blue Jays | 162 | 57 | | 1984 | Cardinals | 162 | 63 | .985 |
| 1978 | Yankees | 163 | 58 | | 1999 | Twins | 161 | 54 | .985 |
| 1998 | Indians | 162 | 58 | | 1992 | Cubs | 162 | 61 | .985 |
| 1992 | Orioles | 162 | 58 | | 1996 | Cubs | 162 | 57 | .985 |
| 1990 | Expos | 162 | 58 | | 1977 | Orioles | 161 | 62 | .984 |
| 1999 | Tigers | 161 | 58 | | 1993 | Royals | 162 | 56 | .984 |
| 1978 | Orioles | 161 | 58 | | 1981 | Brewers | 109 | 44 | .984 |
| 1972 | Tigers | 156 | 58 | | 1978 | Yankees | 163 | 58 | .984 |
| 1996 | Orioles | 163 | 59 | | 1992 | Pirates | 162 | 62 | .984 |
| 1996 | Rangers | 163 | 59 | | 1971 | Reds | 162 | 62 | .984 |
| 1996 | Twins | 162 | 59 | | 1993 | Mariners | 162 | 57 | .984 |
| 1991 | Orioles | 162 | 59 | | 1991 | Tigers | 162 | 59 | .984 |
| 1991 | Tigers | 162 | 59 | | 1979 | Phillies | 163 | 60 | .984 |
| 1970 | Phillies | 161 | 59 | | 1976 | Orioles | 162 | 62 | .984 |
| 1989 | Dodgers | 160 | 59 | | 1991 | Cubs | 160 | 60 | .984 |
| 1979 | Phillies | 163 | 60 | | 1997 | Royals | 161 | 55 | .984 |
| 1997 | Phillies | 162 | 60 | | 1981 | Tigers | 109 | 42 | .984 |
| 1993 | Twins | 162 | 60 | | 1991 | Orioles | 162 | 59 | .984 |
| 1992 | Brewers | 162 | 60 | | 1984 | Cubs | 161 | 60 | .984 |
| 1992 | Twins | 162 | 60 | | 1991 | Twins | 162 | 60 | .984 |

## Philadelphia Phillies: How Unique Was Abreu's Season? (p. 65)

### .300 Avg, .400 OBP, .500 Slg And 25 SB at Age 25 or Younger—1876-1999
### (minimum 400 PA; age as of June 30)

| Player, Team | Year | Age | Avg | OBP | Slg | SB |
|---|---|---|---|---|---|---|
| Oyster Burns, Bal | 1887 | 22 | .341 | .414 | .519 | 58 |
| Bob Caruthers, StL | 1887 | 23 | .357 | .463 | .547 | 49 |
| Denny Lyons, PhiAA | 1887 | 21 | .367 | .421 | .523 | 73 |
| George Davis, NYG | 1893 | 22 | .355 | .410 | .554 | 37 |
| Ed Delahanty, Phi | 1893 | 25 | .368 | .423 | .583 | 37 |
| Elmer Smith, Pit | 1893 | 25 | .346 | .435 | .525 | 26 |
| Jimmy Bannon, Bos | 1894 | 23 | .336 | .414 | .514 | 47 |
| Jesse Burkett, Cle | 1894 | 25 | .358 | .447 | .509 | 28 |
| Bill Dahlen, ChC | 1894 | 24 | .357 | .444 | .566 | 42 |
| George Davis, NYG | 1894 | 23 | .352 | .435 | .537 | 40 |
| Willie Keeler, Bal | 1894 | 22 | .371 | .427 | .517 | 32 |
| Joe Kelley, Bal | 1894 | 22 | .393 | .502 | .602 | 46 |
| George Davis, NYG | 1895 | 24 | .340 | .417 | .500 | 48 |
| Joe Kelley, Bal | 1895 | 23 | .365 | .456 | .546 | 54 |
| Bill Lange, ChC | 1895 | 24 | .389 | .456 | .575 | 67 |
| Joe Kelley, Bal | 1896 | 24 | .364 | .469 | .543 | 87 |
| Tom McCreery, Lou | 1896 | 21 | .351 | .409 | .546 | 26 |
| Fred Clarke, Lou | 1897 | 24 | .390 | .462 | .533 | 57 |
| Willie Keeler, Bal | 1897 | 25 | .424 | .464 | .539 | 64 |
| Jimmy Williams, Pit | 1899 | 22 | .355 | .417 | .532 | 26 |
| Elmer Flick, Phi | 1900 | 24 | .367 | .441 | .545 | 35 |
| Jimmy Sheckard, Bro | 1901 | 22 | .354 | .407 | .534 | 35 |
| Mike Donlin, Cin | 1903 | 25 | .351 | .420 | .516 | 26 |
| Ty Cobb, Det | 1909 | 22 | .377 | .431 | .517 | 76 |
| Ty Cobb, Det | 1910 | 23 | .383 | .456 | .551 | 65 |
| Sherry Magee, PhiN | 1910 | 25 | .331 | .445 | .507 | 49 |
| Ty Cobb, Det | 1911 | 24 | .420 | .467 | .621 | 83 |
| Joe Jackson, Cle | 1911 | 21 | .408 | .468 | .590 | 41 |
| Tris Speaker, BosA | 1911 | 23 | .334 | .418 | .502 | 25 |
| Ty Cobb, Det | 1912 | 25 | .410 | .458 | .586 | 61 |
| Joe Jackson, Cle | 1912 | 22 | .395 | .458 | .579 | 35 |
| Tris Speaker, BosA | 1912 | 24 | .383 | .464 | .567 | 52 |
| Joe Jackson, Cle | 1913 | 23 | .373 | .460 | .551 | 26 |
| Tris Speaker, BosA | 1913 | 25 | .363 | .441 | .533 | 46 |
| Benny Kauff, Ind | 1914 | 24 | .370 | .447 | .534 | 75 |
| Benny Kauff, BroF | 1915 | 25 | .342 | .446 | .509 | 55 |
| Kiki Cuyler, Pit | 1924 | 25 | .354 | .402 | .539 | 32 |
| Mitchell Page, Oak | 1977 | 25 | .307 | .405 | .521 | 42 |
| Kal Daniels, Cin | 1987 | 23 | .334 | .429 | .617 | 26 |
| Barry Bonds, Pit | 1990 | 25 | .301 | .406 | .565 | 52 |
| Bobby Abreu, Phi | 1999 | 25 | .335 | .446 | .549 | 27 |

## San Diego Padres: How Long Can Gwynn Continue? (p. 71)

### Most Consecutive .320-Plus Seasons, Age 33 or Older
### (minimum 400 PA each season; age as of June 30)

| Player | Years | Span | Player | Years | Span |
|---|---|---|---|---|---|
| Eddie Collins | 7 | 1920-26 | Roberto Clemente | 3 | 1969-71 |
| Tony Gwynn | 7 | 1993-99 | Jim O'Rourke | 2 | 1889-90 |
| Honus Wagner | 6 | 1907-12 | Dan Brouthers | 2 | 1891-92 |
| Ty Cobb | 6 | 1920-25 | Cap Anson | 2 | 1895-96 |
| Bill Terry | 6 | 1930-35 | Ed Delahanty | 2 | 1901-02 |
| Tris Speaker | 5 | 1921-25 | Lave Cross | 2 | 1901-02 |
| Babe Ruth | 5 | 1928-32 | Nap Lajoie | 2 | 1909-10 |
| Ted Williams | 5 | 1954-58 | Nap Lajoie | 2 | 1912-13 |
| Paul Molitor | 4 | 1991-94 | Bobby Veach | 2 | 1921-22 |
| Edgar Martinez | 4 | 1996-99 | Zack Wheat | 2 | 1921-22 |
| Cap Anson | 3 | 1886-88 | Zack Wheat | 2 | 1924-25 |
| Sam Thompson | 3 | 1893-95 | Bing Miller | 2 | 1928-29 |
| Jake Beckley | 3 | 1902-04 | Johnny Moore | 2 | 1935-36 |
| Ken Williams | 3 | 1923-25 | Paul Waner | 2 | 1936-37 |
| Jack Fournier | 3 | 1923-25 | Charlie Gehringer | 2 | 1936-37 |
| Sam Rice | 3 | 1924-26 | Lou Gehrig | 2 | 1936-37 |
| George Sisler | 3 | 1927-29 | Stan Musial | 2 | 1957-58 |
| Sam Rice | 3 | 1928-30 | Wade Boggs | 2 | 1994-95 |
| Harry Heilmann | 3 | 1928-30 | Tony Fernandez | 2 | 1998-99 |
| Lefty O'Doul | 3 | 1930-32 | | | |

### Hits After Age 39—All-Time Hit Leaders
### (age as of June 30)

| Player | Thru 39 | Age 40+ | Total | Player | Thru 39 | Age 40+ | Total |
|---|---|---|---|---|---|---|---|
| Pete Rose | 3,557 | 699 | 4,256 | Al Simmons | 2,897 | 30 | 2,927 |
| Ty Cobb | 3,901 | 289 | 4,190 | Zack Wheat | 2,884 | 0 | 2,884 |
| Hank Aaron | 3,509 | 262 | 3,771 | Frankie Frisch | 2,880 | 0 | 2,880 |
| Stan Musial | 3,294 | 336 | 3,630 | Mel Ott | 2,876 | 0 | 2,876 |
| Tris Speaker | 3,463 | 51 | 3,514 | Babe Ruth | 2,860 | 13 | 2,873 |
| Carl Yastrzemski | 3,009 | 410 | 3,419 | Jesse Burkett | 2,850 | 0 | 2,850 |
| Honus Wagner | 2,936 | 479 | 3,415 | Brooks Robinson | 2,841 | 7 | 2,848 |
| Paul Molitor | 3,014 | 305 | 3,319 | Charlie Gehringer | 2,839 | 0 | 2,839 |
| Eddie Collins | 3,225 | 87 | 3,312 | Rickey Henderson | 2,678 | 138 | 2,816 |
| Willie Mays | 3,065 | 218 | 3,283 | George Sisler | 2,812 | 0 | 2,812 |
| Eddie Murray | 3,071 | 184 | 3,255 | Harold Baines | 2,649 | 134 | 2,783 |
| Nap Lajoie | 3,000 | 242 | 3,242 | Andre Dawson | 2,700 | 74 | 2,774 |
| George Brett | 3,005 | 149 | 3,154 | Vada Pinson | 2,757 | 0 | 2,757 |
| Paul Waner | 3,042 | 110 | 3,152 | Luke Appling | 2,261 | 488 | 2,749 |
| Robin Yount | 3,142 | 0 | 3,142 | Al Oliver | 2,743 | 0 | 2,743 |
| Dave Winfield | 2,697 | 413 | 3,110 | Goose Goslin | 2,735 | 0 | 2,735 |
| Tony Gwynn | 3,067 | 0 | 3,067 | Tony Perez | 2,476 | 256 | 2,732 |
| Rod Carew | 3,053 | 0 | 3,053 | Lou Gehrig | 2,721 | 0 | 2,721 |
| Lou Brock | 2,900 | 123 | 3,023 | Rusty Staub | 2,685 | 31 | 2,716 |
| Wade Boggs | 2,800 | 210 | 3,010 | Bill Buckner | 2,707 | 8 | 2,715 |
| Al Kaline | 3,007 | 0 | 3,007 | Dave Parker | 2,592 | 120 | 2,712 |
| Roberto Clemente | 3,000 | 0 | 3,000 | Billy Williams | 2,711 | 0 | 2,711 |
| Cap Anson | 2,173 | 822 | 2,995 | Doc Cramer | 2,603 | 102 | 2,705 |
| Cal Ripken Jr. | 2,991 | 0 | 2,991 | Luis Aparicio | 2,677 | 0 | 2,677 |
| Sam Rice | 2,436 | 551 | 2,987 | Fred Clarke | 2,670 | 2 | 2,672 |
| Sam Crawford | 2,961 | 0 | 2,961 | Max Carey | 2,665 | 0 | 2,665 |
| Frank Robinson | 2,928 | 15 | 2,943 | Nellie Fox | 2,663 | 0 | 2,663 |
| Willie Keeler | 2,932 | 0 | 2,932 | George Davis | 2,660 | 0 | 2,660 |
| Jake Beckley | 2,930 | 0 | 2,930 | Harry Heilmann | 2,660 | 0 | 2,660 |
| Rogers Hornsby | 2,910 | 20 | 2,930 | Ted Williams | 2,487 | 167 | 2,654 |

## San Francisco Giants: Will Pac Bell Provide a New-Park Boost? (p. 73)

### First-Year Winning Percentages in New Parks—1950-99
### (parks in same metropolitan area only)

| Team | Years | Old Park | W-L | Pct | New Park | W-L | Pct | Diff |
|---|---|---|---|---|---|---|---|---|
| Giants | 1959-60 | Seals Stadium | 83-71 | .539 | Candlestick Park | 79-75 | .513 | -.026 |
| Angels | 1961-62 | Wrigley Field (LA) | 70-91 | .435 | Dodger Stadium | 86-76 | .531 | .096 |
| Dodgers | 1961-62 | Los Angeles Memorial Coliseum | 89-65 | .578 | Dodger Stadium | 102-63 | .618 | .040 |
| Senators | 1961-62 | Griffith Stadium | 61-100 | .379 | RFK Stadium | 60-101 | .373 | -.006 |
| Mets | 1963-64 | Polo Grounds V | 51-111 | .315 | Shea Stadium | 53-109 | .327 | .012 |
| Colt .45s | 1964-65 | Colt Stadium | 66-96 | .407 | Astrodome | 65-97 | .401 | -.006 |
| Angels | 1965-66 | Dodger Stadium | 75-87 | .463 | Anaheim Stadium | 80-82 | .494 | .031 |
| Cardinals | 1965-66 | Busch Stadium I | 80-81 | .497 | Busch Stadium I & Busch Stadium II (shared) | 83-79 | .512 | .015 |
| Pirates | 1969-70 | Forbes Field | 88-74 | .543 | Forbes Field & Three Rivers Stadium (shared) | 89-73 | .549 | .006 |
| Reds | 1969-70 | Crosley Field | 89-73 | .549 | Crosley Field & Riverfront Stadium (shared) | 102-60 | .630 | .080 |
| Phillies | 1970-71 | Connie Mack Stadium | 73-88 | .453 | Veterans Stadium | 67-95 | .414 | -.040 |
| Royals | 1972-73 | Municipal Stadium | 76-78 | .494 | Royals Stadium | 88-74 | .543 | .050 |
| Yankees | 1973-74 | Yankee Stadium I | 80-82 | .494 | Shea Stadium | 89-73 | .549 | .056 |
| Yankees | 1975-76 | Shea Stadium | 83-77 | .519 | Yankee Stadium II | 97-62 | .610 | .091 |
| Expos | 1976-77 | Parc Jarry | 55-107 | .340 | Stade Olympique | 75-87 | .463 | .123 |
| Twins | 1981-82 | Metropolitan Stadium | 41-68 | .376 | Hubert H. Humphrey Metrodome | 60-102 | .370 | -.006 |
| Blue Jays | 1988-89 | Exhibition Stadium | 87-75 | .537 | Exhibition Stadium & SkyDome (shared) | 89-73 | .549 | .012 |
| White Sox | 1990-91 | Comiskey Park I | 94-68 | .580 | Comiskey Park II | 87-75 | .537 | -.043 |
| Orioles | 1991-92 | Memorial Stadium | 67-95 | .414 | Oriole Park at Camden Yards | 89-73 | .549 | .136 |
| Indians | 1993-94 | Cleveland Stadium | 76-86 | .469 | Jacobs Field | 66-47 | .584 | .115 |
| Rangers | 1993-94 | Arlington Stadium | 86-76 | .531 | The Ballpark at Arlington | 52-62 | .456 | -.075 |
| Rockies | 1994-95 | Mile High Stadium | 53-64 | .453 | Coors Field | 77-67 | .535 | .082 |
| Braves | 1996-97 | Atlanta-Fulton County Stadium | 96-66 | .593 | Ted Turner Field | 101-61 | .623 | .031 |
| Mariners | 1998-99 | Kingdome | 76-85 | .472 | Kingdome & Safeco Field (shared) | 79-83 | .488 | .016 |

## Can McGwire Beat Aaron? (p. 76)

### Chances of Reaching Milestones

| Player | Age | Current H | HR | RBI | Home Runs 500 | 600 | 700 | 756 | 800 | Hits 3000 | 4000 | 4257 | RBI 2000 | 2298 |
|---|---|---|---|---|---|---|---|---|---|---|---|---|---|---|
| Mark McGwire | 35 | 1498 | 522 | 1277 | NA | 96% | 79% | 48% | 32% | — | — | — | 19% | — |
| Barry Bonds | 34 | 2010 | 445 | 1299 | 95% | 43% | 6% | — | — | 2% | — | — | 6% | — |
| Ken Griffey Jr. | 29 | 1742 | 398 | 1152 | 94% | 89% | 62% | 44% | 34% | 42% | 1% | — | 57% | 30% |
| Jose Canseco | 34 | 1728 | 431 | 1309 | 94% | 36% | 4% | — | — | — | — | — | 5% | — |
| Sammy Sosa | 30 | 1413 | 336 | 941 | 92% | 85% | 48% | 35% | 27% | 19% | — | — | 31% | 13% |
| Albert Belle | 32 | 1569 | 358 | 1136 | 90% | 32% | 8% | — | — | 15% | — | — | 24% | 5% |
| Juan Gonzalez | 29 | 1421 | 340 | 1075 | 89% | 54% | 25% | 15% | 9% | 25% | — | — | 47% | 23% |
| Rafael Palmeiro | 34 | 2158 | 361 | 1227 | 77% | 24% | 2% | — | — | 35% | — | — | 19% | — |
| Alex Rodriguez | 23 | 791 | 148 | 463 | 55% | 32% | 17% | 11% | 7% | 24% | 1% | — | 19% | 7% |
| Manny Ramirez | 27 | 932 | 198 | 682 | 53% | 27% | 12% | 6% | 1% | 13% | — | — | 33% | 18% |
| Jeff Bagwell | 31 | 1447 | 263 | 961 | 42% | 14% | — | — | — | 9% | — | — | 15% | — |
| Greg Vaughn | 33 | 1197 | 292 | 882 | 41% | 12% | — | — | — | — | — | — | — | — |
| Carlos Delgado | 27 | 622 | 149 | 467 | 35% | 16% | 4% | — | — | — | — | — | 9% | — |
| Vladimir Guerrero | 23 | 498 | 92 | 281 | 33% | 16% | 5% | 1% | — | 18% | — | — | 10% | 1% |
| Mo Vaughn | 31 | 1312 | 263 | 860 | 33% | 8% | — | — | — | 5% | — | — | 2% | — |
| Fred McGriff | 35 | 1946 | 390 | 1192 | 33% | — | — | — | — | 4% | — | — | — | — |
| Chipper Jones | 27 | 871 | 153 | 524 | 31% | 13% | 1% | — | — | 14% | — | — | 5% | — |
| Matt Williams | 33 | 1575 | 334 | 1050 | 30% | — | — | — | — | 3% | — | — | 3% | — |
| Dean Palmer | 30 | 1035 | 235 | 701 | 27% | 6% | — | — | — | — | — | — | — | — |
| Jim Thome | 28 | 883 | 196 | 579 | 26% | 7% | — | — | — | — | — | — | — | — |
| Shawn Green | 26 | 718 | 119 | 376 | 24% | 9% | — | — | — | 11% | — | — | 1% | — |
| Larry Walker | 32 | 1431 | 262 | 855 | 22% | 1% | — | — | — | 5% | — | — | — | — |
| Vinny Castilla | 31 | 1049 | 203 | 611 | 21% | 3% | — | — | — | 2% | — | — | — | — |
| Tony Clark | 27 | 603 | 127 | 402 | 15% | 1% | — | — | — | — | — | — | — | — |
| Raul Mondesi | 28 | 1004 | 163 | 518 | 15% | — | — | — | — | 7% | — | — | — | — |
| Frank Thomas | 31 | 1564 | 301 | 1040 | 14% | — | — | — | — | 10% | — | — | 5% | — |
| Nomar Garciaparra | 25 | 615 | 96 | 340 | 13% | 1% | — | — | — | 19% | — | — | 6% | — |
| Andruw Jones | 22 | 436 | 80 | 257 | 13% | 1% | — | — | — | 8% | — | — | — | — |
| Gary Sheffield | 30 | 1345 | 236 | 807 | 13% | — | — | — | — | 3% | — | — | — | — |
| Mike Piazza | 30 | 1200 | 240 | 768 | 10% | — | — | — | — | — | — | — | — | — |
| Tino Martinez | 31 | 1156 | 213 | 798 | 9% | — | — | — | — | — | — | — | 4% | — |
| Scott Rolen | 24 | 479 | 82 | 297 | 8% | — | — | — | — | — | — | — | — | — |
| Eric Karros | 31 | 1217 | 211 | 734 | 7% | — | — | — | — | 1% | — | — | — | — |
| Jeromy Burnitz | 30 | 580 | 123 | 406 | 4% | — | — | — | — | — | — | — | — | — |
| Todd Helton | 25 | 378 | 65 | 221 | 2% | — | — | — | — | — | — | — | — | — |
| Jason Giambi | 28 | 700 | 106 | 418 | 1% | — | — | — | — | 2% | — | — | — | — |
| Fernando Tatis | 24 | 364 | 53 | 194 | 1% | — | — | — | — | — | — | — | — | — |
| Cal Ripken Jr. | 38 | 2991 | 402 | 1571 | — | — | — | — | — | 100% | — | — | — | — |
| Rickey Henderson | 40 | 2816 | 278 | 1020 | — | — | — | — | — | 55% | — | — | — | — |
| Roberto Alomar | 31 | 2007 | 151 | 829 | — | — | — | — | — | 44% | — | — | — | — |
| Harold Baines | 40 | 2783 | 373 | 1583 | — | — | — | — | — | 32% | — | — | — | — |
| Derek Jeter | 25 | 807 | 63 | 341 | — | — | — | — | — | 31% | 6% | 1% | — | — |

| | | | | | | | | | | | | | |
|---|---|---|---|---|---|---|---|---|---|---|---|---|---|
| Craig Biggio | 33 | 1868 | 152 | 706 | — | — | — | — | — | 28% | — | — | — | — |
| Chuck Knoblauch | 30 | 1533 | 78 | 523 | — | — | — | — | — | 20% | — | — | — | — |
| Mark Grace | 35 | 2058 | 137 | 922 | — | — | — | — | — | 18% | — | — | — | — |
| John Olerud | 30 | 1434 | 172 | 762 | — | — | — | — | — | 18% | — | — | — | — |
| Bernie Williams | 30 | 1298 | 151 | 681 | — | — | — | — | — | 15% | — | — | — | — |
| Garret Anderson | 27 | 858 | 72 | 393 | — | — | — | — | — | 15% | — | — | — | — |
| Edgardo Alfonzo | 25 | 698 | 62 | 339 | — | — | — | — | — | 14% | — | — | — | — |
| Edgar Renteria | 23 | 611 | 23 | 177 | — | — | — | — | — | 13% | — | — | — | — |
| Johnny Damon | 25 | 680 | 49 | 264 | — | — | — | — | — | 12% | — | — | — | — |
| Ivan Rodriguez | 27 | 1333 | 144 | 621 | — | — | — | — | — | 11% | — | — | — | — |
| Ray Durham | 27 | 808 | 60 | 296 | — | — | — | — | — | 11% | — | — | — | — |
| Neifi Perez | 24 | 468 | 26 | 163 | — | — | — | — | — | 11% | — | — | — | — |
| B.J. Surhoff | 34 | 1738 | 146 | 893 | — | — | — | — | — | 8% | — | — | — | — |
| Jeff Cirillo | 29 | 864 | 66 | 372 | — | — | — | — | — | 8% | — | — | — | — |
| Omar Vizquel | 32 | 1429 | 34 | 449 | — | — | — | — | — | 6% | — | — | — | — |
| Jose Offerman | 30 | 1162 | 30 | 381 | — | — | — | — | — | 6% | — | — | — | — |
| Luis Gonzalez | 31 | 1242 | 133 | 661 | — | — | — | — | — | 5% | — | — | — | — |
| Jay Bell | 33 | 1677 | 162 | 732 | — | — | — | — | — | 4% | — | — | — | — |
| Doug Glanville | 28 | 555 | 24 | 167 | — | — | — | — | — | 4% | — | — | — | — |
| Marquis Grissom | 32 | 1550 | 131 | 601 | — | — | — | — | — | 3% | — | — | — | — |
| Darin Erstad | 25 | 527 | 52 | 232 | — | — | — | — | — | 3% | — | — | — | — |
| Robin Ventura | 31 | 1421 | 203 | 861 | — | — | — | — | — | 2% | — | — | — | — |
| Carlos Beltran | 22 | 210 | 22 | 115 | — | — | — | — | — | 2% | — | — | — | — |
| Rusty Greer | 30 | 923 | 103 | 503 | — | — | — | — | — | 1% | — | — | — | — |

*Baseball Scoreboard*

## Who Unloads the Bases? (p. 81)

### Best Performances, Bases Loaded—1987-99

| Highest Batting Average (minimum 50 PA) | | | | Most RBI Per Plate Appearance (minimum 50 PA) | | | |
|---|---|---|---|---|---|---|---|
| Player | AB | H | Avg | Player | PA | RBI | RBI/PA |
| Felix Jose | 48 | 24 | .500 | Felix Jose | 51 | 56 | 1.10 |
| Pat Tabler | 42 | 19 | .452 | Matt Stairs | 63 | 68 | 1.08 |
| Joe Orsulak | 68 | 30 | .441 | Ryan Klesko | 65 | 69 | 1.06 |
| Tony Gwynn | 94 | 41 | .436 | Manny Ramirez | 113 | 117 | 1.04 |
| Rusty Greer | 66 | 28 | .424 | Carl Everett | 70 | 72 | 1.03 |
| Mike Blowers | 81 | 34 | .420 | Rusty Greer | 82 | 83 | 1.01 |
| Johnny Damon | 48 | 20 | .417 | Mike Blowers | 92 | 92 | 1.00 |
| Mike LaValliere | 53 | 22 | .415 | Mike Piazza | 81 | 81 | 1.00 |
| Carl Everett | 63 | 26 | .413 | Alvin Davis | 67 | 67 | 1.00 |
| Mark Grace | 85 | 35 | .412 | Ken Griffey Jr. | 116 | 114 | 0.98 |
| B.J. Surhoff | 146 | 60 | .411 | Tim Salmon | 94 | 92 | 0.98 |
| Matt Stairs | 54 | 22 | .407 | Chris Hoiles | 77 | 75 | 0.97 |
| Tim Salmon | 69 | 28 | .406 | Albert Belle | 135 | 131 | 0.97 |
| Sandy Alomar Jr. | 84 | 34 | .405 | John Olerud | 129 | 125 | 0.97 |
| Jason Kendall | 47 | 19 | .404 | B.J. Surhoff | 175 | 169 | 0.97 |
| Nomar Garciaparra | 50 | 20 | .400 | Tony Gwynn | 114 | 110 | 0.96 |
| Kevin Seitzer | 93 | 37 | .398 | Alex Rodriguez | 60 | 57 | 0.95 |
| Manny Ramirez | 88 | 35 | .398 | John Jaha | 78 | 74 | 0.95 |
| Ryan Klesko | 58 | 23 | .397 | Kevin Seitzer | 116 | 110 | 0.95 |
| John Olerud | 98 | 38 | .388 | J.T. Snow | 122 | 115 | 0.94 |
| Chris Hoiles | 57 | 22 | .386 | Brian Hunter | 55 | 51 | 0.93 |
| Todd Zeile | 140 | 54 | .386 | Joe Oliver | 95 | 88 | 0.93 |
| David Segui | 83 | 32 | .386 | Mark Grace | 116 | 107 | 0.92 |
| Kevin McReynolds | 66 | 25 | .379 | Kevin McReynolds | 85 | 78 | 0.92 |
| Mike Piazza | 74 | 28 | .378 | Kirby Puckett | 116 | 106 | 0.91 |
| Pedro Guerrero | 45 | 17 | .378 | Johnny Damon | 58 | 53 | 0.91 |
| Lenny Harris | 61 | 23 | .377 | Frank Thomas | 122 | 111 | 0.91 |
| Frank Thomas | 93 | 35 | .376 | Pat Tabler | 55 | 50 | 0.91 |
| Roberto Alomar | 125 | 47 | .376 | Robin Ventura | 161 | 146 | 0.91 |
| J.T. Snow | 96 | 36 | .375 | Mike LaValliere | 64 | 58 | 0.91 |
| Jeff Cirillo | 48 | 18 | .375 | Butch Huskey | 52 | 47 | 0.90 |
| Butch Huskey | 40 | 15 | .375 | Joe Orsulak | 82 | 74 | 0.90 |
| Andres Galarraga | 105 | 39 | .371 | Mo Vaughn | 112 | 101 | 0.90 |
| Alvin Davis | 54 | 20 | .370 | David Segui | 99 | 89 | 0.90 |
| Darren Lewis | 68 | 25 | .368 | Nomar Garciaparra | 57 | 51 | 0.89 |
| Pat Meares | 63 | 23 | .365 | Dante Bichette | 142 | 127 | 0.89 |
| Julio Franco | 105 | 38 | .362 | Sandy Alomar Jr. | 93 | 83 | 0.89 |
| David Justice | 94 | 34 | .362 | Leo Gomez | 52 | 46 | 0.88 |
| Barry Bonds | 133 | 48 | .361 | Dave Magadan | 94 | 83 | 0.88 |
| Alan Trammell | 86 | 31 | .360 | Jose Canseco | 152 | 134 | 0.88 |
| Fred McGriff | 111 | 40 | .360 | Dave Nilsson | 92 | 81 | 0.88 |
| Tim Naehring | 64 | 23 | .359 | Todd Zeile | 166 | 146 | 0.88 |
| Joe Oliver | 78 | 28 | .359 | Jeff King | 115 | 101 | 0.88 |
| Ellis Burks | 154 | 55 | .357 | Andres Galarraga | 128 | 112 | 0.88 |
| Robin Ventura | 126 | 45 | .357 | Chipper Jones | 64 | 56 | 0.88 |
| Ozzie Smith | 84 | 30 | .357 | George Bell | 94 | 82 | 0.87 |
| Dave Magadan | 70 | 25 | .357 | Shane Mack | 85 | 74 | 0.87 |
| Dante Bichette | 129 | 46 | .357 | Wally Joyner | 145 | 126 | 0.87 |
| Hal Morris | 87 | 31 | .356 | Paul Sorrento | 121 | 105 | 0.87 |
| Jerry Browne | 59 | 21 | .356 | Andre Dawson | 98 | 85 | 0.87 |
| Brian Hunter | 45 | 16 | .356 | Alfredo Griffin | 66 | 57 | 0.86 |
| Rich Aurilia | 45 | 16 | .356 | Julio Franco | 123 | 106 | 0.86 |
| Garret Anderson | 76 | 27 | .355 | Matt Williams | 160 | 137 | 0.86 |
| **MLB Totals** | | | .281 | **MLB Totals** | | | 0.70 |

## Who Works the Most Hitters' Counts? (p. 83)

### Highest Percentage of Pitches Seen in Hitters' Counts—1999
### (minimum 400 PA)

| Player, Team | PA | Total | Ahead | Pct |
|---|---|---|---|---|
| Eric Young, LA | 534 | 1,916 | 641 | 33.5 |
| Gary Sheffield, LA | 663 | 2,623 | 868 | 33.1 |
| Mark Grace, ChC | 688 | 2,607 | 861 | 33.0 |
| Bill Spiers, Hou | 444 | 1,706 | 548 | 32.1 |
| Matt Lawton, Min | 476 | 1,682 | 535 | 31.8 |
| Frank Thomas, CWS | 590 | 2,305 | 732 | 31.8 |
| John Olerud, NYM | 723 | 2,824 | 892 | 31.6 |
| Rusty Greer, Tex | 662 | 2,742 | 859 | 31.3 |
| Mark McLemore, Tex | 664 | 2,576 | 803 | 31.2 |
| Barry Larkin, Cin | 687 | 2,658 | 818 | 30.8 |
| Todd Hundley, LA | 428 | 1,809 | 554 | 30.6 |
| Edgar Martinez, Sea | 608 | 2,619 | 802 | 30.6 |
| Jeromy Burnitz, Mil | 580 | 2,480 | 757 | 30.5 |
| Mark McGwire, StL | 661 | 2,454 | 745 | 30.4 |
| Chipper Jones, Atl | 701 | 2,559 | 773 | 30.2 |
| Bobby Abreu, Phi | 662 | 2,857 | 860 | 30.1 |
| Bernie Williams, NYY | 697 | 2,631 | 791 | 30.1 |
| Bob Higginson, Det | 445 | 1,720 | 517 | 30.1 |
| Jeff Bagwell, Hou | 729 | 2,968 | 890 | 30.0 |
| Rickey Henderson, NYM | 526 | 2,247 | 668 | 29.7 |
| Bill Mueller, SF | 492 | 1,853 | 548 | 29.6 |
| Gabe Kapler, Det | 468 | 1,786 | 526 | 29.5 |
| Jason Giambi, Oak | 695 | 2,824 | 831 | 29.4 |
| Ellis Burks, SF | 469 | 1,768 | 519 | 29.4 |
| Nomar Garciaparra, Bos | 595 | 1,922 | 564 | 29.3 |
| Brady Anderson, Bal | 692 | 2,665 | 782 | 29.3 |
| Tony Gwynn, SD | 446 | 1,405 | 412 | 29.3 |
| Jeff Cirillo, Mil | 697 | 2,661 | 780 | 29.3 |
| Brian S. Giles, Pit | 627 | 2,388 | 698 | 29.2 |
| Ken Griffey Jr., Sea | 706 | 2,679 | 783 | 29.2 |
| Luis Gonzalez, Ari | 693 | 2,413 | 702 | 29.1 |
| Jim Thome, Cle | 629 | 2,703 | 784 | 29.0 |
| Rafael Palmeiro, Tex | 674 | 2,482 | 719 | 29.0 |
| Matt Stairs, Oak | 623 | 2,643 | 765 | 28.9 |
| Jay Bell, Ari | 688 | 3,039 | 879 | 28.9 |
| Carlos Delgado, Tor | 681 | 2,726 | 787 | 28.9 |
| Troy O'Leary, Bos | 661 | 2,363 | 682 | 28.9 |
| Ben Grieve, Oak | 558 | 2,206 | 636 | 28.8 |
| Travis Lee, Ari | 436 | 1,561 | 448 | 28.7 |
| Roberto Alomar, Cle | 694 | 2,956 | 847 | 28.7 |
| Greg Vaughn, Cin | 643 | 2,555 | 730 | 28.6 |
| John Jaha, Oak | 570 | 2,502 | 714 | 28.5 |
| Todd Helton, Col | 657 | 2,493 | 706 | 28.3 |
| Ryan Klesko, Atl | 466 | 1,625 | 460 | 28.3 |
| David Justice, Cle | 530 | 2,124 | 601 | 28.3 |
| Darryl Hamilton, Col-NYM | 568 | 2,256 | 637 | 28.2 |
| Mike Stanley, Bos | 512 | 1,968 | 555 | 28.2 |
| Barry Bonds, SF | 434 | 1,678 | 471 | 28.1 |
| John Valentin, Bos | 503 | 1,906 | 534 | 28.0 |
| Fred McGriff, TB | 620 | 2,361 | 661 | 28.0 |
| Ron Belliard, Mil | 531 | 2,094 | 586 | 28.0 |
| Ray Durham, CWS | 694 | 2,837 | 792 | 27.9 |
| Randy Velarde, Ana-Oak | 711 | 2,771 | 772 | 27.9 |
| Mike Cameron, Cin | 636 | 2,577 | 717 | 27.8 |
| **MLB Average** | | | | **25.7** |

*Baseball Scoreboard*

## Can They Foul 'Em Off on Purpose? (p. 86)

### Highest Percentage of Fouls on Swings With Two Strikes—1999
### (minimum 400 PA)

| Player, Team | Swing | Fouled | Pct | Player, Team | Swing | Fouled | Pct |
|---|---|---|---|---|---|---|---|
| Jeromy Burnitz, Mil | 423 | 198 | 46.8 | Todd Hundley, LA | 294 | 117 | 39.8 |
| Derek Jeter, NYY | 414 | 192 | 46.4 | Joe McEwing, StL | 405 | 161 | 39.8 |
| Jorge Posada, NYY | 257 | 118 | 45.9 | Bobby Abreu, Phi | 436 | 173 | 39.7 |
| Brian Daubach, Bos | 303 | 139 | 45.9 | Mark Grace, ChC | 336 | 133 | 39.6 |
| Tino Martinez, NYY | 399 | 181 | 45.4 | Jason Giambi, Oak | 412 | 163 | 39.6 |
| Scott Rolen, Phi | 347 | 155 | 44.7 | Paul Konerko, CWS | 367 | 145 | 39.5 |
| Tony Fernandez, Tor | 309 | 137 | 44.3 | Richard Hidalgo, Hou | 271 | 107 | 39.5 |
| Dave Nilsson, Mil | 250 | 108 | 43.2 | Robin Ventura, NYM | 441 | 174 | 39.5 |
| Dave Martinez, TB | 359 | 155 | 43.2 | Roberto Alomar, Cle | 502 | 198 | 39.4 |
| Kevin Young, Pit | 502 | 216 | 43.0 | Brad Ausmus, Det | 322 | 127 | 39.4 |
| Shannon Stewart, Tor | 372 | 160 | 43.0 | Pokey Reese, Cin | 401 | 158 | 39.4 |
| Edgardo Alfonzo, NYM | 479 | 206 | 43.0 | Jeff Conine, Bal | 201 | 79 | 39.3 |
| Luis Castillo, Fla | 361 | 155 | 42.9 | Jim Thome, Cle | 364 | 143 | 39.3 |
| Chuck Knoblauch, NYY | 428 | 183 | 42.8 | Dante Bichette, Col | 449 | 176 | 39.2 |
| Mickey Morandini, ChC | 334 | 142 | 42.5 | Todd Walker, Min | 401 | 157 | 39.2 |
| Ivan Rodriguez, Tex | 394 | 167 | 42.4 | Tony Batista, Ari-Tor | 394 | 154 | 39.1 |
| Rusty Greer, Tex | 390 | 165 | 42.3 | Jose Vidro, Mon | 297 | 116 | 39.1 |
| David Justice, Cle | 306 | 129 | 42.2 | Mike Caruso, CWS | 269 | 105 | 39.0 |
| Mark Loretta, Mil | 407 | 171 | 42.0 | Darren Lewis, Bos | 287 | 112 | 39.0 |
| David Segui, Sea-Tor | 301 | 126 | 41.9 | John Valentin, Bos | 287 | 112 | 39.0 |
| Marvin Benard, SF | 392 | 164 | 41.8 | Carlos Febles, KC | 287 | 112 | 39.0 |
| David Bell, Sea | 447 | 187 | 41.8 | Jeff Cirillo, Mil | 377 | 147 | 39.0 |
| Brian McRae, 3Tm | 269 | 112 | 41.6 | Todd Zeile, Tex | 408 | 159 | 39.0 |
| Bill Mueller, SF | 257 | 107 | 41.6 | Rich Aurilia, SF | 326 | 127 | 39.0 |
| Edgar Martinez, Sea | 395 | 164 | 41.5 | Jeff Bagwell, Hou | 398 | 155 | 38.9 |
| Russ Davis, Sea | 319 | 132 | 41.4 | Carlos Delgado, Tor | 416 | 162 | 38.9 |
| Kenny Lofton, Cle | 324 | 134 | 41.4 | Quilvio Veras, SD | 283 | 110 | 38.9 |
| Jose Offerman, Bos | 374 | 154 | 41.2 | Rey Sanchez, KC | 263 | 102 | 38.8 |
| Shawn Green, Tor | 406 | 167 | 41.1 | John Flaherty, TB | 266 | 103 | 38.7 |
| B.J. Surhoff, Bal | 428 | 176 | 41.1 | Mike Bordick, Bal | 399 | 154 | 38.6 |
| Rafael Palmeiro, Tex | 326 | 134 | 41.1 | Larry Walker, Col | 262 | 101 | 38.5 |
| Ruben Rivera, SD | 346 | 142 | 41.0 | Al Martin, Pit | 327 | 126 | 38.5 |
| Bruce Aven, Fla | 251 | 103 | 41.0 | Royce Clayton, Tex | 333 | 128 | 38.4 |
| Todd Helton, Col | 410 | 168 | 41.0 | Warren Morris, Pit | 279 | 107 | 38.4 |
| Ken Griffey Jr., Sea | 415 | 170 | 41.0 | Luis Gonzalez, Ari | 321 | 123 | 38.3 |
| Brian S. Giles, Pit | 315 | 129 | 41.0 | Tony Womack, Ari | 439 | 168 | 38.3 |
| Mark Grudzielanek, LA | 333 | 136 | 40.8 | Chili Davis, NYY | 285 | 109 | 38.2 |
| Ray Lankford, StL | 378 | 154 | 40.7 | Darryl Hamilton, 2Tm | 340 | 130 | 38.2 |
| Omar Vizquel, Cle | 416 | 169 | 40.6 | Darrin Fletcher, Tor | 246 | 94 | 38.2 |
| Cristian Guzman, Min | 281 | 114 | 40.6 | Travis Lee, Ari | 194 | 74 | 38.1 |
| Carlos Lee, CWS | 380 | 154 | 40.5 | Marquis Grissom, Mil | 365 | 139 | 38.1 |
| Manny Ramirez, Cle | 420 | 170 | 40.5 | Chad Allen, Min | 316 | 120 | 38.0 |
| Albert Belle, Bal | 336 | 136 | 40.5 | Mike Benjamin, Pit | 295 | 112 | 38.0 |
| Marty Cordova, Min | 314 | 127 | 40.4 | Mike Lieberthal, Phi | 369 | 140 | 37.9 |
| J.T. Snow, SF | 391 | 158 | 40.4 | Mike Stanley, Bos | 277 | 105 | 37.9 |
| Geoff Jenkins, Mil | 325 | 131 | 40.3 | Brady Anderson, Bal | 367 | 139 | 37.9 |
| Jay Bell, Ari | 536 | 216 | 40.3 | Tony Clark, Det | 407 | 154 | 37.8 |
| Greg Norton, CWS | 296 | 119 | 40.2 | Frank Thomas, CWS | 305 | 115 | 37.7 |
| Eric Owens, SD | 264 | 106 | 40.2 | John Olerud, NYM | 345 | 130 | 37.7 |
| Sean Casey, Cin | 362 | 145 | 40.1 | Miguel Tejada, Oak | 449 | 169 | 37.6 |
| Paul O'Neill, NYY | 395 | 158 | 40.0 | Barry Larkin, Cin | 363 | 136 | 37.5 |
| Bob Higginson, Det | 225 | 90 | 40.0 | Gary Sheffield, LA | 363 | 136 | 37.5 |

| Player, Team | Swing | Fouled | Pct | Player, Team | Swing | Fouled | Pct |
|---|---|---|---|---|---|---|---|
| Ron Belliard, Mil | 342 | 128 | 37.4 | Deivi Cruz, Det | 283 | 98 | 34.6 |
| Marlon Anderson, Phi | 313 | 117 | 37.4 | Steve Finley, Ari | 355 | 122 | 34.4 |
| Harold Baines, Bal-Cle | 217 | 81 | 37.3 | Brian L. Hunter, Det-Sea | 364 | 125 | 34.3 |
| Fernando Tatis, StL | 389 | 145 | 37.3 | Matt Stairs, Oak | 379 | 130 | 34.3 |
| Bill Spiers, Hou | 234 | 87 | 37.2 | Sammy Sosa, ChC | 429 | 147 | 34.3 |
| Dan Wilson, Sea | 318 | 118 | 37.1 | Phil Nevin, SD | 286 | 98 | 34.3 |
| Rickey Henderson, NYM | 324 | 120 | 37.0 | Rico Brogna, Phi | 409 | 140 | 34.2 |
| Tom Goodwin, Tex | 230 | 85 | 37.0 | Ed Sprague, Pit | 269 | 92 | 34.2 |
| Jose Canseco, TB | 317 | 117 | 36.9 | Mike Piazza, NYM | 316 | 108 | 34.2 |
| Stan Javier, SF-Hou | 252 | 93 | 36.9 | Gabe Kapler, Det | 249 | 85 | 34.1 |
| Brian Jordan, Atl | 361 | 133 | 36.8 | Mo Vaughn, Ana | 349 | 119 | 34.1 |
| Michael Barrett, Mon | 239 | 88 | 36.8 | Orlando Cabrera, Mon | 220 | 75 | 34.1 |
| Barry Bonds, SF | 204 | 75 | 36.8 | Butch Huskey, Sea-Bos | 276 | 94 | 34.1 |
| Gerald Williams, Atl | 324 | 119 | 36.7 | Denny Hocking, Min | 235 | 80 | 34.0 |
| Alex Rodriguez, Sea | 444 | 163 | 36.7 | Joe Randa, KC | 332 | 113 | 34.0 |
| J.D. Drew, StL | 237 | 87 | 36.7 | Darin Erstad, Ana | 377 | 128 | 34.0 |
| Preston Wilson, Fla | 393 | 144 | 36.6 | Craig Biggio, Hou | 413 | 140 | 33.9 |
| Tim Salmon, Ana | 243 | 89 | 36.6 | Mike Cameron, Cin | 325 | 110 | 33.8 |
| Fred McGriff, TB | 317 | 116 | 36.6 | Rondell White, Mon | 314 | 106 | 33.8 |
| Ron Gant, Phi | 372 | 136 | 36.6 | Derek Bell, Hou | 341 | 115 | 33.7 |
| Jose Cruz, Tor | 214 | 78 | 36.4 | Matt Williams, Ari | 279 | 94 | 33.7 |
| Devon White, LA | 343 | 125 | 36.4 | Ron Coomer, Min | 235 | 79 | 33.6 |
| Mark Kotsay, Fla | 269 | 98 | 36.4 | Troy O'Leary, Bos | 322 | 108 | 33.5 |
| Tony Phillips, Oak | 313 | 114 | 36.4 | Andruw Jones, Atl | 358 | 120 | 33.5 |
| Bernie Williams, NYY | 335 | 122 | 36.4 | Vladimir Guerrero, Mon | 305 | 102 | 33.4 |
| Vinny Castilla, Col | 316 | 115 | 36.4 | Juan Gonzalez, Tex | 348 | 116 | 33.3 |
| Charles Johnson, Bal | 308 | 112 | 36.4 | Nomar Garciaparra, Bos | 244 | 81 | 33.2 |
| Alex Gonzalez, Fla | 427 | 155 | 36.3 | Torii Hunter, Min | 244 | 81 | 33.2 |
| Dmitri Young, Cin | 237 | 86 | 36.3 | Dean Palmer, Det | 419 | 139 | 33.2 |
| Ben Grieve, Oak | 295 | 107 | 36.3 | Trot Nixon, Bos | 234 | 77 | 32.9 |
| Ray Durham, CWS | 466 | 169 | 36.3 | Lee Stevens, Tex | 338 | 111 | 32.8 |
| Kevin Millar, Fla | 251 | 91 | 36.3 | Greg Vaughn, Cin | 357 | 117 | 32.8 |
| Adrian Beltre, LA | 411 | 149 | 36.3 | Ryan Klesko, Atl | 200 | 65 | 32.5 |
| Miguel Cairo, TB | 334 | 121 | 36.2 | Chris Widger, Mon | 264 | 85 | 32.2 |
| Edgar Renteria, StL | 379 | 137 | 36.1 | Neifi Perez, Col | 345 | 111 | 32.2 |
| Troy Glaus, Ana | 402 | 144 | 35.8 | Ellis Burks, SF | 232 | 74 | 31.9 |
| Carl Everett, Hou | 335 | 120 | 35.8 | John Jaha, Oak | 343 | 109 | 31.8 |
| Jose Hernandez, 2Tm | 390 | 139 | 35.6 | Mark McGwire, StL | 271 | 86 | 31.7 |
| Henry Rodriguez, ChC | 323 | 115 | 35.6 | Chris Singleton, CWS | 265 | 84 | 31.7 |
| Eric Chavez, Oak | 231 | 82 | 35.5 | Randy Velarde, Ana-Oak | 387 | 122 | 31.5 |
| Chipper Jones, Atl | 279 | 99 | 35.5 | Mark McLemore, Tex | 299 | 94 | 31.4 |
| Doug Glanville, Phi | 413 | 146 | 35.4 | Juan Encarnacion, Det | 322 | 101 | 31.4 |
| Jeff Kent, SF | 300 | 106 | 35.3 | Garret Anderson, Ana | 350 | 109 | 31.1 |
| Jermaine Dye, KC | 371 | 131 | 35.3 | Bret Boone, Atl | 390 | 121 | 31.0 |
| Jason Varitek, Bos | 272 | 96 | 35.3 | Matt Lawton, Min | 179 | 55 | 30.7 |
| Rey Ordonez, NYM | 267 | 94 | 35.2 | Roger Cedeno, NYM | 287 | 87 | 30.3 |
| Damian Jackson, SD | 267 | 94 | 35.2 | Einar Diaz, Cle | 198 | 60 | 30.3 |
| Carlos Beltran, KC | 347 | 122 | 35.2 | Richie Sexson, Cle | 308 | 93 | 30.2 |
| Reggie Sanders, SD | 299 | 105 | 35.1 | Raul Mondesi, LA | 320 | 96 | 30.0 |
| Aaron Boone, Cin | 282 | 99 | 35.1 | Shane Andrews, 2Tm | 205 | 61 | 29.8 |
| Eric Karros, LA | 365 | 128 | 35.1 | Magglio Ordonez, CWS | 333 | 99 | 29.7 |
| Scott Brosius, NYY | 300 | 105 | 35.0 | Damion Easley, Det | 340 | 101 | 29.7 |
| Johnny Damon, KC | 349 | 122 | 35.0 | Eric Young, LA | 227 | 65 | 28.6 |
| Homer Bush, Tor | 367 | 128 | 34.9 | Tony Gwynn, SD | 154 | 40 | 26.0 |
| Mike Sweeney, KC | 336 | 117 | 34.8 | **MLB Average** | | | **37.4** |
| Eddie Taubensee, Cin | 219 | 76 | 34.7 | | | | |

*Baseball Scoreboard*

## Who Bagged the Most Runs Created? (p. 89)

### Runs Created—Listed Alphabetically
### (minimum 350 PA in 1999)

| Player, Team | RC | OWP | Player, Team | RC | OWP | Player, Team | RC | OWP |
|---|---|---|---|---|---|---|---|---|
| Abreu, Phi | 127 | .755 | Casey, Cin | 116 | .689 | Goodwin T, Tex | 46 | .344 |
| Alfonzo, NYM | 117 | .649 | Castilla, Col | 87 | .499 | Grace, ChC | 111 | .650 |
| Allen, Min | 58 | .398 | Castillo L, Fla | 72 | .524 | Green S, Tor | 121 | .659 |
| Alomar, Cle | 142 | .748 | Cedeno R, NYM | 77 | .595 | Greer, Tex | 117 | .681 |
| Anderson B, Bal | 113 | .652 | Chavez, Oak | 51 | .476 | Grieve, Oak | 84 | .572 |
| Anderson G, Ana | 86 | .485 | Cirillo, Mil | 100 | .601 | Griffey Jr., Sea | 140 | .720 |
| Anderson M, Phi | 54 | .405 | Clark T, Det | 101 | .625 | Grissom, Mil | 78 | .444 |
| Aurilia, SF | 79 | .496 | Clayton, Tex | 69 | .501 | Grudzielanek, LA | 67 | .510 |
| Ausmus, Det | 70 | .507 | Conine, Bal | 67 | .511 | Guerrero V, Mon | 134 | .725 |
| Aven, Fla | 70 | .639 | Coomer, Min | 56 | .387 | Guzman C, Min | 27 | .138 |
| Bagwell, Hou | 157 | .796 | Cordova, Min | 70 | .536 | Gwynn, SD | 82 | .694 |
| Baines, Bal-Cle | 89 | .679 | Cruz D, Det | 60 | .370 | Hamilton, Col-NYM | 74 | .540 |
| Barrett, Mon | 59 | .485 | Damon, KC | 110 | .635 | Helton, Col | 121 | .709 |
| Batista, Ari-Tor | 87 | .567 | Daubach, Bos | 77 | .676 | Henderson, NYM | 80 | .641 |
| Bell D, Sea | 84 | .472 | Davis C, NYY | 78 | .550 | Hernandez, ChC-Atl | 74 | .511 |
| Bell D, Hou | 48 | .274 | Davis R, Sea | 52 | .369 | Hidalgo, Hou | 52 | .447 |
| Bell J, Ari | 121 | .681 | Delgado C, Tor | 112 | .637 | Higginson, Det | 58 | .504 |
| Belle, Bal | 125 | .668 | Diaz E, Cle | 48 | .401 | Hocking, Min | 50 | .409 |
| Belliard, Mil | 73 | .553 | Drew, StL | 60 | .550 | Hundley, LA | 42 | .351 |
| Beltran, KC | 111 | .564 | Durham, CWS | 96 | .541 | Hunter B, Det-Sea | 49 | .247 |
| Beltre, LA | 79 | .518 | Dye, KC | 101 | .567 | Hunter T, Min | 40 | .311 |
| Benard, SF | 92 | .581 | Easley, Det | 69 | .408 | Huskey, Sea-Bos | 64 | .565 |
| Benjamin, Pit | 42 | .370 | Encarnacion, Det | 66 | .409 | Jackson D, SD | 48 | .400 |
| Bichette, Col | 110 | .637 | Erstad, Ana | 63 | .328 | Jaha, Oak | 108 | .719 |
| Biggio, Hou | 119 | .639 | Everett, Hou | 108 | .750 | Javier, SF-Hou | 49 | .424 |
| Bonds, SF | 82 | .723 | Febles, KC | 67 | .463 | Jenkins, Mil | 87 | .679 |
| Boone A, Cin | 70 | .520 | Fernandez T, Tor | 99 | .684 | Jeter, NYY | 146 | .748 |
| Boone B, Atl | 77 | .421 | Finley, Ari | 102 | .599 | Johnson C, Bal | 58 | .438 |
| Bordick, Bal | 76 | .378 | Flaherty, TB | 53 | .380 | Jones A, Atl | 101 | .588 |
| Brogna, Phi | 84 | .475 | Fletcher, Tor | 66 | .544 | Jones C, Atl | 144 | .777 |
| Brosius, NYY | 62 | .411 | Gant, Phi | 88 | .591 | Jordan B, Atl | 99 | .595 |
| Burks, SF | 97 | .752 | Garciaparra, Bos | 122 | .754 | Justice, Cle | 85 | .641 |
| Burnitz, Mil | 95 | .667 | Giambi J, Oak | 136 | .742 | Kapler, Det | 56 | .428 |
| Bush, Tor | 72 | .519 | Giles, Pit | 129 | .768 | Karros, LA | 103 | .623 |
| Cabrera O, Mon | 42 | .362 | Glanville, Phi | 109 | .634 | Kent, SF | 95 | .633 |
| Cairo, TB | 54 | .375 | Glaus, Ana | 88 | .525 | Klesko, Atl | 82 | .685 |
| Cameron, Cin | 87 | .546 | Gonzalez A, Fla | 69 | .430 | Knoblauch, NYY | 113 | .626 |
| Canseco, TB | 77 | .590 | Gonzalez J, Tex | 119 | .698 | Konerko, CWS | 83 | .553 |
| Caruso, CWS | 36 | .158 | Gonzalez L, Ari | 126 | .711 | Kotsay, Fla | 49 | .315 |

| Player, Team | RC | OWP | Player, Team | RC | OWP | Player, Team | RC | OWP |
|---|---|---|---|---|---|---|---|---|
| Lankford, StL | 72 | .617 | Owens, SD | 62 | .482 | Surhoff, Bal | 100 | .525 |
| Larkin, Cin | 100 | .598 | Palmeiro R, Tex | 147 | .776 | Sweeney M, KC | 109 | .646 |
| Lawton, Min | 57 | .453 | Palmer, Det | 91 | .542 | Tatis, StL | 112 | .693 |
| Lee C, CWS | 67 | .467 | Perez N, Col | 84 | .431 | Taubensee, Cin | 70 | .593 |
| Lee T, Ari | 47 | .412 | Phillips T, Oak | 68 | .547 | Tejada, Oak | 88 | .476 |
| Lewis D, Bos | 41 | .227 | Piazza, NYM | 95 | .611 | Thomas, CWS | 87 | .603 |
| Lieberthal, Phi | 89 | .612 | Posada, NYY | 51 | .440 | Thome, Cle | 123 | .749 |
| Lofton, Cle | 77 | .567 | Ramirez M, Cle | 150 | .812 | Valentin J, Bos | 60 | .429 |
| Loretta, Mil | 80 | .481 | Randa, KC | 101 | .564 | Varitek, Bos | 66 | .444 |
| Martin A, Pit | 90 | .589 | Reese, Cin | 76 | .459 | Vaughn G, Cin | 113 | .665 |
| Martinez D, TB | 81 | .528 | Renteria, StL | 77 | .447 | Vaughn M, Ana | 105 | .658 |
| Martinez E, Sea | 113 | .735 | Rivera, SD | 40 | .273 | Velarde, Ana-Oak | 112 | .610 |
| Martinez T, NYY | 91 | .515 | Rodriguez A, Sea | 97 | .626 | Ventura, NYM | 116 | .676 |
| McEwing, StL | 64 | .434 | Rodriguez H, ChC | 88 | .680 | Veras Q, SD | 66 | .481 |
| McGriff, TB | 118 | .719 | Rodriguez I, Tex | 100 | .569 | Vidro, Mon | 71 | .524 |
| McGwire, StL | 145 | .797 | Rolen, Phi | 72 | .588 | Vizquel, Cle | 107 | .629 |
| McLemore, Tex | 77 | .447 | Salmon, Ana | 72 | .649 | Walker L, Col | 129 | .848 |
| McRae, 3Tm | 44 | .332 | Sanchez, KC | 59 | .404 | Walker T, Min | 63 | .386 |
| Millar, Fla | 63 | .617 | Sanders R, SD | 91 | .641 | White D, LA | 63 | .464 |
| Mondesi, LA | 105 | .595 | Santiago, ChC | 40 | .375 | White R, Mon | 83 | .555 |
| Morandini, ChC | 49 | .333 | Segui, Sea-Tor | 62 | .491 | Widger, Mon | 44 | .396 |
| Morris W, Pit | 77 | .527 | Sexson, Cle | 67 | .444 | Williams B, NYY | 129 | .720 |
| Mueller, SF | 60 | .509 | Sheffield, LA | 113 | .689 | Williams G, Atl | 66 | .535 |
| Nevin, SD | 79 | .678 | Singleton, CWS | 81 | .558 | Williams M, Ari | 118 | .654 |
| Nixon T, Bos | 56 | .488 | Snow, SF | 86 | .524 | Wilson D, Sea | 47 | .356 |
| Norton, CWS | 57 | .424 | Sosa S, ChC | 131 | .687 | Wilson P, Fla | 71 | .513 |
| O'Leary, Bos | 95 | .535 | Spiers, Hou | 54 | .485 | Womack, Ari | 80 | .449 |
| O'Neill, NYY | 86 | .471 | Sprague, Pit | 86 | .592 | Young D, Cin | 55 | .533 |
| Offerman, Bos | 99 | .567 | Stairs, Oak | 101 | .618 | Young E, LA | 66 | .477 |
| Olerud, NYM | 118 | .679 | Stanley, Bos | 77 | .608 | Young K, Pit | 117 | .675 |
| Ordonez M, CWS | 102 | .555 | Stevens, Tex | 74 | .477 | Zeile, Tex | 96 | .552 |
| Ordonez R, NYM | 52 | .303 | Stewart, Tor | 100 | .562 | **MLB Average** | | .500 |

*Baseball Scoreboard*

## Who's Second to None? (p. 91)

### Secondary Average—Listed Alphabetically
### (minimum 400 PA in 1999)

| Player, Team | Sec | Player, Team | Sec | Player, Team | Sec | Player, Team | Sec |
|---|---|---|---|---|---|---|---|
| Abreu, Phi | .447 | Caruso, CWS | .081 | Gonzalez J, Tex | .367 | Konerko, CWS | .306 |
| Alfonzo, NYM | .344 | Casey, Cin | .306 | Gonzalez L, Ari | .327 | Kotsay, Fla | .192 |
| Allen, Min | .210 | Castilla, Col | .288 | Goodwin T, Tex | .249 | Lankford, StL | .327 |
| Alomar, Cle | .440 | Castillo L, Fla | .269 | Grace, ChC | .310 | Larkin, Cin | .324 |
| Anderson B, Bal | .417 | Cedeno R, NYM | .336 | Green S, Tor | .407 | Lawton, Min | .291 |
| Anderson G, Ana | .219 | Chavez, Oak | .309 | Greer, Tex | .365 | Lee C, CWS | .201 |
| Anderson M, Phi | .186 | Cirillo, Mil | .264 | Grieve, Oak | .354 | Lee T, Ari | .317 |
| Andrews, 2Tm | .316 | Clark T, Det | .349 | Griffey Jr., Sea | .469 | Lewis D, Bos | .177 |
| Aurilia, SF | .238 | Clayton, Tex | .245 | Grissom, Mil | .259 | Lieberthal, Phi | .337 |
| Ausmus, Det | .258 | Conine, Bal | .223 | Grudzielanek, LA | .174 | Lofton, Cle | .342 |
| Aven, Fla | .278 | Coomer, Min | .227 | Guerrero V, Mon | .385 | Loretta, Mil | .194 |
| Bagwell, Hou | .585 | Cordova, Min | .313 | Guzman C, Min | .107 | Martin A, Pit | .351 |
| Baines, Bal-Cle | .344 | Cruz D, Det | .160 | Gwynn, SD | .221 | Martinez D, TB | .233 |
| Barrett, Mon | .212 | Cruz J, Tor | .404 | Hamilton, 2Tm | .216 | Martinez E, Sea | .420 |
| Batista, Ari-Tor | .322 | Damon, KC | .336 | Helton, Col | .386 | Martinez T, NYY | .311 |
| Bell D, Sea | .266 | Daubach, Bos | .360 | Henderson, NYM | .390 | McEwing, StL | .209 |
| Bell D, Hou | .236 | Davis C, NYY | .336 | Hernandez, 2Tm | .278 | McGriff, TB | .406 |
| Bell J, Ari | .413 | Davis R, Sea | .264 | Hidalgo, Hou | .347 | McGwire, StL | .674 |
| Belle, Bal | .433 | Delgado C, Tor | .449 | Higginson, Det | .308 | McLemore, Tex | .253 |
| Belliard, Mil | .271 | Diaz E, Cle | .158 | Hocking, Min | .179 | McRae, 3Tm | .270 |
| Beltran, KC | .259 | Drew, StL | .361 | Hundley, LA | .354 | Millar, Fla | .265 |
| Beltre, LA | .286 | Durham, CWS | .296 | Hunter B, 2Tm | .204 | Mondesi, LA | .393 |
| Benard, SF | .288 | Dye, KC | .326 | Hunter T, Min | .203 | Morandini, ChC | .193 |
| Benjamin, Pit | .196 | Easley, Det | .275 | Huskey, Sea-Bos | .303 | Morris W, Pit | .247 |
| Bichette, Col | .334 | Encarnacion, Det | .263 | Jackson D, SD | .330 | Mueller, SF | .234 |
| Biggio, Hou | .322 | Erstad, Ana | .212 | Jaha, Oak | .505 | Nevin, SD | .394 |
| Bonds, SF | .597 | Everett, Hou | .397 | Javier, SF-Hou | .199 | Nilsson, Mil | .397 |
| Boone A, Cin | .252 | Febles, KC | .294 | Jenkins, Mil | .338 | Nixon T, Bos | .346 |
| Boone B, Atl | .250 | Fernandez T, Tor | .278 | Jeter, NYY | .365 | Norton, CWS | .328 |
| Bordick, Bal | .227 | Finley, Ari | .375 | Johnson C, Bal | .291 | O'Leary, Bos | .307 |
| Brogna, Phi | .268 | Flaherty, TB | .175 | Jones A, Atl | .356 | O'Neill, NYY | .288 |
| Brosius, NYY | .262 | Fletcher, Tor | .257 | Jones C, Atl | .575 | Offerman, Bos | .316 |
| Burks, SF | .469 | Gant, Phi | .355 | Jordan B, Atl | .280 | Olerud, NYM | .386 |
| Burnitz, Mil | .495 | Garciaparra, Bos | .363 | Justice, Cle | .403 | Ordonez M, CWS | .295 |
| Bush, Tor | .194 | Giambi J, Oak | .421 | Kapler, Det | .317 | Ordonez R, NYM | .162 |
| Cabrera O, Mon | .196 | Giles, Pit | .489 | Karros, LA | .343 | Owens, SD | .270 |
| Cairo, TB | .157 | Glanville, Phi | .260 | Kent, SF | .354 | Palmeiro R, Tex | .474 |
| Cameron, Cin | .408 | Glaus, Ana | .347 | Klesko, Atl | .374 | Palmer, Det | .357 |
| Canseco, TB | .426 | Gonzalez A, Fla | .177 | Knoblauch, NYY | .332 | Perez N, Col | .175 |

| Player, Team | Sec | Player, Team | Sec | Player, Team | Sec | Player, Team | Sec |
|---|---|---|---|---|---|---|---|
| Phillips T, Oak | .384 | Segui, Sea-Tor | .259 | Taubensee, Cin | .276 | White D, LA | .251 |
| Piazza, NYM | .367 | Sexson, Cle | .330 | Tejada, Oak | .273 | White R, Mon | .260 |
| Posada, NYY | .298 | Sheffield, LA | .417 | Thomas, CWS | .346 | Widger, Mon | .243 |
| Ramirez M, Cle | .510 | Singleton, CWS | .264 | Thome, Cle | .520 | Williams B, NYY | .362 |
| Randa, KC | .240 | Snow, SF | .321 | Valentin J, Bos | .231 | Williams G, Atl | .280 |
| Reese, Cin | .244 | Sosa S, ChC | .470 | Varitek, Bos | .306 | Williams M, Ari | .301 |
| Renteria, StL | .265 | Spiers, Hou | .234 | Vaughn G, Cin | .467 | Wilson D, Sea | .198 |
| Rivera, SD | .372 | Sprague, Pit | .294 | Vaughn M, Ana | .330 | Wilson P, Fla | .332 |
| Rodriguez A, Sea | .440 | Stairs, Oak | .433 | Velarde, Ana-Oak | .274 | Womack, Ari | .274 |
| Rodriguez, ChC | .360 | Stanley, Bos | .349 | Ventura, NYM | .354 | Young D, Cin | .290 |
| Rodriguez I, Tex | .288 | Stevens, Tex | .302 | Veras Q, SD | .263 | Young E, LA | .276 |
| Rolen, Phi | .439 | Stewart, Tor | .242 | Vidro, Mon | .223 | Young K, Pit | .373 |
| Salmon, Ana | .411 | Surhoff, Bal | .254 | Vizquel, Cle | .274 | Zeile, Tex | .289 |
| Sanchez, KC | .134 | Sweeney M, KC | .301 | Walker L, Col | .477 | **MLB Average** | **.281** |
| Sanders R, SD | .427 | Tatis, StL | .430 | Walker T, Min | .232 | | |

*Baseball Scoreboard*

## Who Puts 'Em Ahead? (p. 93)

### Go-Ahead RBI Percentage—Listed Alphabetically
### (minimum 75 total RBI in 1999)

| Player, Team | Tot RBI | GA RBI | GA Opp | Pct | Player, Team | Tot RBI | GA RBI | GA Opp | Pct |
|---|---|---|---|---|---|---|---|---|---|
| Abreu, Phi | 93 | 16 | 38 | .421 | Jordan B, Atl | 115 | 31 | 68 | .456 |
| Alfonzo, NYM | 108 | 28 | 46 | .609 | Justice, Cle | 88 | 15 | 36 | .417 |
| Alomar, Cle | 120 | 26 | 54 | .481 | Karros, LA | 112 | 20 | 55 | .364 |
| Anderson B, Bal | 81 | 14 | 23 | .609 | Kent, SF | 101 | 27 | 49 | .551 |
| Anderson G, Ana | 80 | 14 | 48 | .292 | Klesko, Atl | 80 | 13 | 31 | .419 |
| Aurilia, SF | 80 | 10 | 24 | .417 | Konerko, CWS | 81 | 16 | 34 | .471 |
| Bagwell, Hou | 126 | 28 | 50 | .560 | Larkin, Cin | 75 | 24 | 45 | .533 |
| Baines, Bal-Cle | 103 | 15 | 29 | .517 | Lee C, CWS | 84 | 20 | 41 | .488 |
| Batista, Ari-Tor | 100 | 16 | 40 | .400 | Lieberthal, Phi | 96 | 24 | 46 | .522 |
| Bell D, Sea | 78 | 15 | 30 | .500 | Martinez E, Sea | 86 | 14 | 40 | .350 |
| Bell J, Ari | 112 | 26 | 50 | .520 | Martinez T, NYY | 105 | 26 | 63 | .413 |
| Belle, Bal | 117 | 29 | 62 | .468 | McGriff, TB | 104 | 21 | 56 | .375 |
| Beltran, KC | 108 | 23 | 39 | .590 | McGwire, StL | 147 | 34 | 59 | .576 |
| Bichette, Col | 133 | 37 | 79 | .468 | Mondesi, LA | 99 | 13 | 52 | .250 |
| Bonds, SF | 83 | 26 | 42 | .619 | Nevin, SD | 85 | 26 | 52 | .500 |
| Bordick, Bal | 77 | 12 | 39 | .308 | O'Leary, Bos | 103 | 26 | 58 | .448 |
| Brogna, Phi | 102 | 15 | 49 | .306 | O'Neill, NYY | 110 | 24 | 62 | .387 |
| Burks, SF | 96 | 19 | 31 | .613 | Olerud, NYM | 96 | 19 | 46 | .413 |
| Burnitz, Mil | 103 | 20 | 45 | .444 | Ordonez M, CWS | 117 | 26 | 63 | .413 |
| Canseco, TB | 95 | 19 | 47 | .404 | Palmeiro R, Tex | 148 | 31 | 54 | .574 |
| Casey, Cin | 99 | 26 | 54 | .481 | Palmer, Det | 100 | 28 | 57 | .491 |
| Castilla, Col | 102 | 21 | 55 | .382 | Piazza, NYM | 124 | 26 | 55 | .473 |
| Cirillo, Mil | 88 | 18 | 52 | .346 | Ramirez M, Cle | 165 | 41 | 77 | .532 |
| Clark T, Det | 99 | 18 | 38 | .474 | Randa, KC | 84 | 13 | 38 | .342 |
| Conine, Bal | 75 | 14 | 32 | .438 | Rodriguez A, Sea | 111 | 24 | 51 | .471 |
| Damon, KC | 77 | 16 | 37 | .432 | Rodriguez H, ChC | 87 | 17 | 37 | .459 |
| Davis C, NYY | 78 | 16 | 33 | .485 | Rodriguez I, Tex | 113 | 19 | 38 | .500 |
| Delgado C, Tor | 134 | 30 | 72 | .417 | Rolen, Phi | 77 | 20 | 47 | .426 |
| Dye, KC | 119 | 19 | 55 | .345 | Sexson, Cle | 116 | 19 | 39 | .487 |
| Everett, Hou | 108 | 18 | 46 | .391 | Sheffield, LA | 101 | 26 | 49 | .531 |
| Fernandez T, Tor | 75 | 9 | 34 | .265 | Snow, SF | 98 | 15 | 29 | .517 |
| Finley, Ari | 103 | 10 | 40 | .250 | Sosa S, ChC | 141 | 31 | 61 | .508 |
| Fletcher, Tor | 80 | 17 | 31 | .548 | Sprague, Pit | 81 | 16 | 35 | .457 |
| Gant, Phi | 77 | 11 | 37 | .297 | Stairs, Oak | 102 | 22 | 54 | .407 |
| Garciaparra, Bos | 104 | 19 | 47 | .404 | Stevens, Tex | 81 | 20 | 29 | .690 |
| Giambi J, Oak | 123 | 21 | 52 | .404 | Surhoff, Bal | 107 | 23 | 63 | .365 |
| Giles, Pit | 115 | 26 | 49 | .531 | Sweeney M, KC | 102 | 20 | 56 | .357 |
| Glaus, Ana | 79 | 11 | 36 | .306 | Tatis, StL | 107 | 17 | 39 | .436 |
| Gonzalez J, Tex | 128 | 27 | 62 | .435 | Taubensee, Cin | 87 | 11 | 26 | .423 |
| Gonzalez L, Ari | 111 | 31 | 63 | .492 | Tejada, Oak | 84 | 21 | 42 | .500 |
| Grace, ChC | 91 | 18 | 44 | .409 | Thomas, CWS | 77 | 20 | 41 | .488 |
| Green S, Tor | 123 | 32 | 63 | .508 | Thome, Cle | 108 | 8 | 24 | .333 |
| Greer, Tex | 101 | 22 | 50 | .440 | Varitek, Bos | 76 | 9 | 26 | .346 |
| Grieve, Oak | 86 | 18 | 37 | .486 | Vaughn G, Cin | 118 | 22 | 53 | .415 |
| Griffey Jr., Sea | 134 | 32 | 63 | .508 | Vaughn M, Ana | 108 | 33 | 63 | .524 |
| Grissom, Mil | 83 | 16 | 43 | .372 | Velarde, Ana-Oak | 76 | 18 | 30 | .600 |
| Guerrero V, Mon | 131 | 37 | 64 | .578 | Ventura, NYM | 120 | 24 | 49 | .490 |
| Helton, Col | 113 | 18 | 37 | .486 | Walker L, Col | 115 | 28 | 45 | .622 |
| Huskey, Sea-Bos | 77 | 13 | 23 | .565 | Williams B, NYY | 115 | 24 | 68 | .353 |
| Jaha, Oak | 111 | 19 | 46 | .413 | Williams M, Ari | 142 | 39 | 77 | .506 |
| Jenkins, Mil | 82 | 17 | 34 | .500 | Young K, Pit | 106 | 24 | 60 | .400 |
| Jeter, NYY | 102 | 24 | 41 | .585 | Zeile, Tex | 98 | 15 | 33 | .455 |
| Jones A, Atl | 84 | 21 | 46 | .457 | **MLB Average** | | | | **.398** |
| Jones C, Atl | 110 | 30 | 60 | .500 | | | | | |

## Who Are the Real RBI Kings? (p. 96)

### RBI Percentage—1999
### (minimum 500 RBI opportunities in 1999)

| Player, Team | Avail | RBI | Pct | Player, Team | Avail | RBI | Pct |
|---|---|---|---|---|---|---|---|
| Abreu, Phi | 903 | 93 | 10.3 | Cabrera O, Mon | 603 | 39 | 6.5 |
| Alfonzo, NYM | 1,037 | 108 | 10.4 | Cairo, TB | 735 | 36 | 4.9 |
| Allen, Min | 783 | 46 | 5.9 | Cameron, Cin | 861 | 66 | 7.7 |
| Alomar, Cle | 1,011 | 120 | 11.9 | Caminiti, Hou | 506 | 56 | 11.1 |
| Anderson B, Bal | 874 | 81 | 9.3 | Canseco, TB | 751 | 95 | 12.6 |
| Anderson G, Ana | 1,017 | 80 | 7.9 | Caruso, CWS | 883 | 35 | 4.0 |
| Anderson M, Phi | 755 | 54 | 7.2 | Casey, Cin | 958 | 99 | 10.3 |
| Andrews, Mon-ChC | 599 | 51 | 8.5 | Castilla, Col | 1,014 | 102 | 10.1 |
| Arias A, Phi | 584 | 48 | 8.2 | Castillo L, Fla | 710 | 28 | 3.9 |
| Aurilia, SF | 949 | 80 | 8.4 | Cedeno R, NYM | 724 | 36 | 5.0 |
| Ausmus, Det | 691 | 54 | 7.8 | Chavez, Oak | 577 | 50 | 8.7 |
| Aven, Fla | 649 | 70 | 10.8 | Cirillo, Mil | 1,075 | 88 | 8.2 |
| Bagwell, Hou | 938 | 126 | 13.4 | Clark T, Det | 871 | 99 | 11.4 |
| Baines, Bal-Cle | 745 | 103 | 13.8 | Clayton, Tex | 747 | 52 | 7.0 |
| Barrett, Mon | 678 | 52 | 7.7 | Conine, Bal | 787 | 75 | 9.5 |
| Batista, Ari-Tor | 893 | 100 | 11.2 | Coomer, Min | 768 | 65 | 8.5 |
| Bell D, Sea | 927 | 78 | 8.4 | Cordova, Min | 718 | 70 | 9.7 |
| Bell D, Hou | 888 | 66 | 7.4 | Cruz D, Det | 859 | 58 | 6.8 |
| Bell J, Ari | 924 | 112 | 12.1 | Cruz J, Tor | 578 | 45 | 7.8 |
| Belle, Bal | 1,044 | 117 | 11.2 | Damon, KC | 947 | 77 | 8.1 |
| Belliard, Mil | 755 | 58 | 7.7 | Daubach, Bos | 629 | 73 | 11.6 |
| Beltran, KC | 1,071 | 108 | 10.1 | Davis C, NYY | 832 | 78 | 9.4 |
| Beltre, LA | 895 | 67 | 7.5 | Davis R, Sea | 712 | 59 | 8.3 |
| Benard, SF | 866 | 64 | 7.4 | Delgado C, Tor | 1,013 | 134 | 13.2 |
| Benjamin, Pit | 612 | 37 | 6.0 | DeShields, Bal | 540 | 34 | 6.3 |
| Bichette, Col | 1,057 | 133 | 12.6 | Diaz E, Cle | 663 | 32 | 4.8 |
| Biggio, Hou | 963 | 73 | 7.6 | Drew, StL | 557 | 39 | 7.0 |
| Bogar, Hou | 524 | 31 | 5.9 | Durham, CWS | 931 | 60 | 6.4 |
| Bonds, SF | 598 | 83 | 13.9 | Dye, KC | 1,058 | 119 | 11.2 |
| Boone A, Cin | 807 | 72 | 8.9 | Easley, Det | 891 | 65 | 7.3 |
| Boone B, Atl | 937 | 63 | 6.7 | Encarnacion, Det | 802 | 74 | 9.2 |
| Bordick, Bal | 1,108 | 77 | 6.9 | Erstad, Ana | 905 | 53 | 5.9 |
| Brogna, Phi | 1,052 | 102 | 9.7 | Eusebio, Hou | 550 | 33 | 6.0 |
| Brosius, NYY | 821 | 71 | 8.6 | Everett, Hou | 826 | 108 | 13.1 |
| Brown B, Pit | 589 | 58 | 9.8 | Febles, KC | 784 | 53 | 6.8 |
| Buford, Bos | 512 | 38 | 7.4 | Fernandez T, Tor | 834 | 75 | 9.0 |
| Burks, SF | 651 | 96 | 14.7 | Finley, Ari | 971 | 103 | 10.6 |
| Burnitz, Mil | 839 | 103 | 12.3 | Flaherty, TB | 798 | 71 | 8.9 |
| Bush, Tor | 804 | 55 | 6.8 | Fletcher, Tor | 736 | 80 | 10.9 |

| Player, Team | Avail | RBI | Pct | Player, Team | Avail | RBI | Pct |
|---|---|---|---|---|---|---|---|
| Fordyce, CWS | 546 | 49 | 9.0 | Jeter, NYY | 1,040 | 102 | 9.8 |
| Fryman, Cle | 567 | 48 | 8.5 | Johnson C, Bal | 725 | 54 | 7.4 |
| Fullmer, Mon | 574 | 47 | 8.2 | Jones A, Atl | 993 | 84 | 8.5 |
| Gant, Phi | 816 | 77 | 9.4 | Jones C, Atl | 887 | 110 | 12.4 |
| Garciaparra, Bos | 887 | 104 | 11.7 | Jones J, Min | 500 | 44 | 8.8 |
| Gates, Min | 508 | 38 | 7.5 | Jordan B, Atl | 1,027 | 115 | 11.2 |
| Giambi J, Oak | 990 | 123 | 12.4 | Jordan K, Phi | 610 | 51 | 8.4 |
| Giles, Pit | 854 | 115 | 13.5 | Joyner, SD | 538 | 43 | 8.0 |
| Glanville, Phi | 940 | 73 | 7.8 | Justice, Cle | 769 | 88 | 11.4 |
| Glaus, Ana | 889 | 79 | 8.9 | Kapler, Det | 677 | 49 | 7.2 |
| Gonzalez A, Fla | 891 | 59 | 6.6 | Karros, LA | 995 | 112 | 11.3 |
| Gonzalez J, Tex | 1,004 | 128 | 12.7 | Kent, SF | 895 | 101 | 11.3 |
| Gonzalez L, Ari | 1,014 | 111 | 10.9 | Klesko, Atl | 677 | 80 | 11.8 |
| Goodwin T, Tex | 649 | 33 | 5.1 | Knoblauch, NYY | 893 | 68 | 7.6 |
| Grace, ChC | 979 | 91 | 9.3 | Konerko, CWS | 843 | 81 | 9.6 |
| Green S, Tor | 1,043 | 123 | 11.8 | Koskie, Min | 587 | 58 | 9.9 |
| Greene T, Ana | 526 | 42 | 8.0 | Kotsay, Fla | 830 | 50 | 6.0 |
| Greer, Tex | 922 | 101 | 11.0 | Kreuter, KC | 566 | 35 | 6.2 |
| Grieve, Oak | 822 | 86 | 10.5 | Lankford, StL | 696 | 63 | 9.1 |
| Griffey Jr., Sea | 1,000 | 134 | 13.4 | Larkin, Cin | 954 | 75 | 7.9 |
| Grissom, Mil | 985 | 83 | 8.4 | Lawton, Min | 685 | 54 | 7.9 |
| Grudzielanek, LA | 796 | 46 | 5.8 | Lee C, CWS | 835 | 84 | 10.1 |
| Guerrero V, Mon | 1,001 | 131 | 13.1 | Lee T, Ari | 638 | 50 | 7.8 |
| Guerrero W, Mon | 504 | 31 | 6.2 | Lewis D, Bos | 827 | 40 | 4.8 |
| Guillen J, Pit-TB | 505 | 31 | 6.1 | Lieberthal, Phi | 869 | 96 | 11.0 |
| Guzman C, Min | 705 | 26 | 3.7 | Lofton, Cle | 728 | 39 | 5.4 |
| Gwynn, SD | 666 | 62 | 9.3 | Loretta, Mil | 933 | 67 | 7.2 |
| Hamilton, Col-NYM | 796 | 45 | 5.7 | Lowell, Fla | 508 | 47 | 9.3 |
| Hayes, SF | 505 | 48 | 9.5 | Marrero, StL | 567 | 34 | 6.0 |
| Helton, Col | 945 | 113 | 12.0 | Martin A, Pit | 800 | 63 | 7.9 |
| Henderson, NYM | 636 | 42 | 6.6 | Martinez D, TB | 855 | 66 | 7.7 |
| Hernandez J, ChC-Atl | 823 | 62 | 7.5 | Martinez E, Sea | 816 | 86 | 10.5 |
| Hidalgo, Hou | 664 | 56 | 8.4 | Martinez M, Mon | 508 | 26 | 5.1 |
| Higginson, Det | 606 | 46 | 7.6 | Martinez T, NYY | 1,053 | 105 | 10.0 |
| Hocking, Min | 613 | 41 | 6.7 | Mayne, SF | 554 | 39 | 7.0 |
| Hundley, LA | 630 | 55 | 8.7 | McEwing, StL | 809 | 44 | 5.4 |
| Hunter B, Det-Sea | 822 | 34 | 4.1 | McGriff, TB | 903 | 104 | 11.5 |
| Hunter T, Min | 621 | 35 | 5.6 | McGwire, StL | 853 | 147 | 17.2 |
| Huskey, Sea-Bos | 673 | 77 | 11.4 | McLemore, Tex | 880 | 45 | 5.1 |
| Jackson D, SD | 619 | 39 | 6.3 | McRae, NYM-Col-Tor | 674 | 48 | 7.1 |
| Jaha, Oak | 820 | 111 | 13.5 | Mientkiewicz, Min | 544 | 32 | 5.9 |
| Javier, SF-Hou | 646 | 34 | 5.3 | Millar, Fla | 633 | 67 | 10.6 |
| Jenkins, Mil | 758 | 82 | 10.8 | Miller, Ari | 519 | 47 | 9.1 |

| Player, Team | Avail | RBI | Pct | Player, Team | Avail | RBI | Pct |
|---|---|---|---|---|---|---|---|
| Mondesi, LA | 1,007 | 99 | 9.8 | Sosa S, ChC | 1,036 | 141 | 13.6 |
| Morandini, ChC | 690 | 37 | 5.4 | Spiers, Hou | 645 | 39 | 6.0 |
| Morris W, Pit | 860 | 73 | 8.5 | Sprague, Pit | 798 | 81 | 10.2 |
| Mueller, SF | 691 | 36 | 5.2 | Stairs, Oak | 905 | 102 | 11.3 |
| Nevin, SD | 646 | 85 | 13.2 | Stanley, Bos | 739 | 72 | 9.7 |
| Nilsson, Mil | 599 | 62 | 10.4 | Steinbach, Min | 563 | 42 | 7.5 |
| Nixon T, Bos | 645 | 52 | 8.1 | Stevens, Tex | 872 | 81 | 9.3 |
| Norton, CWS | 692 | 50 | 7.2 | Stewart, Tor | 905 | 67 | 7.4 |
| O'Leary, Bos | 1,038 | 103 | 9.9 | Surhoff, Bal | 1,152 | 107 | 9.3 |
| O'Neill, NYY | 1,084 | 110 | 10.1 | Sweeney M, KC | 985 | 102 | 10.4 |
| Offerman, Bos | 928 | 69 | 7.4 | Tatis, StL | 904 | 107 | 11.8 |
| Olerud, NYM | 979 | 96 | 9.8 | Taubensee, Cin | 753 | 87 | 11.6 |
| Ordonez M, CWS | 1,082 | 117 | 10.8 | Tejada, Oak | 992 | 84 | 8.5 |
| Ordonez R, NYM | 927 | 60 | 6.5 | Thomas, CWS | 807 | 77 | 9.5 |
| Owens, SD | 725 | 61 | 8.4 | Thome, Cle | 852 | 108 | 12.7 |
| Palmeiro R, Tex | 985 | 148 | 15.0 | Valentin J, Bos | 764 | 70 | 9.2 |
| Palmer, Det | 907 | 100 | 11.0 | Varitek, Bos | 845 | 76 | 9.0 |
| Perez E, Atl | 510 | 30 | 5.9 | Vaughn G, Cin | 908 | 118 | 13.0 |
| Perez N, Col | 1,077 | 70 | 6.5 | Vaughn M, Ana | 864 | 108 | 12.5 |
| Phillips T, Oak | 600 | 49 | 8.2 | Velarde, Ana-Oak | 1,006 | 76 | 7.6 |
| Piazza, NYM | 988 | 124 | 12.6 | Ventura, NYM | 1,019 | 120 | 11.8 |
| Posada, NYY | 675 | 57 | 8.4 | Veras Q, SD | 687 | 41 | 6.0 |
| Ramirez M, Cle | 965 | 165 | 17.1 | Vidro, Mon | 771 | 59 | 7.7 |
| Randa, KC | 1,034 | 84 | 8.1 | Vizquel, Cle | 979 | 66 | 6.7 |
| Reese, Cin | 887 | 52 | 5.9 | Walker L, Col | 731 | 115 | 15.7 |
| Renteria, StL | 938 | 63 | 6.7 | Walker T, Min | 849 | 46 | 5.4 |
| Ripken Jr., Bal | 575 | 57 | 9.9 | White D, LA | 792 | 68 | 8.6 |
| Rivera, SD | 698 | 48 | 6.9 | White R, Mon | 805 | 64 | 8.0 |
| Rodriguez A, Sea | 828 | 111 | 13.4 | Widger, Mon | 644 | 56 | 8.7 |
| Rodriguez H, ChC | 756 | 87 | 11.5 | Williams B, NYY | 1,023 | 115 | 11.2 |
| Rodriguez I, Tex | 1,026 | 113 | 11.0 | Williams G, Atl | 682 | 68 | 10.0 |
| Rolen, Phi | 737 | 77 | 10.4 | Williams M, Ari | 1,090 | 142 | 13.0 |
| Salmon, Ana | 604 | 69 | 11.4 | Wilson D, Sea | 704 | 38 | 5.4 |
| Sanchez, KC | 837 | 56 | 6.7 | Wilson E, Cle | 589 | 24 | 4.1 |
| Sanders R, SD | 758 | 72 | 9.5 | Wilson P, Fla | 794 | 71 | 8.9 |
| Santiago, ChC | 587 | 36 | 6.1 | Womack, Ari | 921 | 41 | 4.5 |
| Segui, Sea-Tor | 732 | 52 | 7.1 | Young D, Cin | 624 | 56 | 9.0 |
| Sexson, Cle | 909 | 116 | 12.8 | Young E, LA | 690 | 41 | 5.9 |
| Sheffield, LA | 889 | 101 | 11.4 | Young K, Pit | 988 | 106 | 10.7 |
| Singleton, CWS | 788 | 72 | 9.1 | Zeile, Tex | 1,015 | 98 | 9.7 |
| Snow, SF | 953 | 98 | 10.3 | **MLB Average** | | | 8.4 |
| Sorrento, TB | 511 | 42 | 8.2 | | | | |

*Baseball Scoreboard*

## Who Gets the Slidin' Billy Trophy? (p. 98)

### Leadoff Men—Listed Alphabetically
### (minimum 125 leadoff PA in 1999)

| Player, Team | OBP | AB | R | H | BB | HBP | SB |
|---|---|---|---|---|---|---|---|
| Anderson B, Bal | .408 | 549 | 107 | 157 | 95 | 23 | 35 |
| Becker, Mil-Oak | .399 | 120 | 22 | 31 | 26 | 2 | 3 |
| Bell D, Sea | .310 | 174 | 32 | 46 | 12 | 0 | 3 |
| Beltran, KC | .336 | 298 | 48 | 90 | 16 | 1 | 11 |
| Benard, SF | .362 | 537 | 98 | 157 | 55 | 4 | 23 |
| Berg, Fla | .288 | 125 | 16 | 31 | 7 | 0 | 0 |
| Biggio, Hou | .386 | 638 | 123 | 188 | 88 | 11 | 28 |
| Bragg, StL | .383 | 113 | 16 | 31 | 19 | 1 | 1 |
| Cairo, TB | .333 | 277 | 38 | 81 | 15 | 3 | 14 |
| Cameron, Cin | .366 | 333 | 59 | 91 | 45 | 4 | 22 |
| Castillo L, Fla | .385 | 483 | 75 | 146 | 67 | 0 | 50 |
| Cedeno R, NYM | .371 | 191 | 43 | 57 | 19 | 3 | 30 |
| Damon, KC | .371 | 243 | 39 | 75 | 25 | 1 | 21 |
| Durham, CWS | .377 | 537 | 99 | 160 | 65 | 4 | 27 |
| Encarnacion, Det | .308 | 123 | 21 | 34 | 5 | 1 | 9 |
| Erstad, Ana | .321 | 408 | 62 | 110 | 31 | 1 | 9 |
| Glanville, Phi | .376 | 626 | 100 | 204 | 47 | 6 | 34 |
| Goodwin T, Tex | .307 | 240 | 40 | 57 | 25 | 0 | 25 |
| Grissom, Mil | .316 | 162 | 32 | 43 | 12 | 0 | 10 |
| Guillen O, Atl | .301 | 121 | 10 | 30 | 10 | 0 | 4 |
| Hamilton, Col-NYM | .367 | 261 | 47 | 81 | 24 | 0 | 3 |
| Henderson, NYM | .417 | 432 | 87 | 134 | 79 | 2 | 36 |
| Hocking, Min | .309 | 151 | 19 | 41 | 8 | 1 | 8 |
| Hunter B, Det-Sea | .285 | 466 | 71 | 112 | 31 | 1 | 38 |
| Johnson L, ChC | .327 | 316 | 41 | 82 | 32 | 0 | 12 |
| Jones J, Min | .314 | 279 | 41 | 77 | 14 | 3 | 3 |
| Knoblauch, NYY | .393 | 596 | 119 | 174 | 81 | 21 | 27 |
| Lofton, Cle | .404 | 464 | 110 | 139 | 79 | 6 | 25 |
| Loretta, Mil | .392 | 301 | 58 | 97 | 31 | 6 | 4 |
| Martin A, Pit | .327 | 492 | 94 | 136 | 37 | 1 | 19 |
| Martinez M, Mon | .306 | 139 | 17 | 37 | 8 | 0 | 6 |
| McEwing, StL | .309 | 194 | 23 | 54 | 9 | 0 | 1 |
| McLemore, Tex | .363 | 360 | 66 | 98 | 55 | 0 | 13 |
| Nixon O, Atl | .323 | 114 | 18 | 25 | 18 | 0 | 11 |
| Offerman, Bos | .406 | 538 | 103 | 163 | 95 | 2 | 18 |
| Palmeiro O, Ana | .367 | 151 | 24 | 41 | 19 | 5 | 4 |
| Perez N, Col | .297 | 423 | 67 | 115 | 16 | 1 | 8 |
| Phillips T, Oak | .365 | 402 | 76 | 99 | 71 | 5 | 11 |
| Polonia, Det | .356 | 328 | 45 | 106 | 16 | 2 | 17 |
| Reese, Cin | .316 | 327 | 49 | 89 | 20 | 2 | 20 |
| Renteria, StL | .352 | 198 | 37 | 57 | 20 | 0 | 15 |
| Roberts, Cle | .293 | 137 | 25 | 34 | 9 | 0 | 10 |
| Santangelo, SF | .392 | 103 | 20 | 27 | 17 | 5 | 5 |
| Stewart, Tor | .377 | 589 | 101 | 182 | 58 | 8 | 36 |
| Veras Q, SD | .377 | 462 | 95 | 133 | 65 | 2 | 30 |
| Vina, Mil | .339 | 154 | 17 | 41 | 14 | 4 | 5 |
| Walker T, Min | .368 | 155 | 22 | 47 | 15 | 1 | 5 |
| Weiss, Atl | .287 | 114 | 13 | 22 | 14 | 1 | 4 |
| White R, Mon | .371 | 206 | 34 | 67 | 14 | 2 | 5 |
| Williams G, Atl | .342 | 319 | 63 | 90 | 24 | 6 | 12 |
| Winn, TB | .333 | 255 | 41 | 75 | 15 | 1 | 7 |
| Womack, Ari | .333 | 611 | 111 | 170 | 52 | 2 | 72 |
| Young E, LA | .382 | 422 | 68 | 123 | 59 | 5 | 50 |
| **MLB Average Team** | **.349** | **686** | **115** | **190** | **72** | **7** | **34** |

## Who Are the Human Air Conditioners? (p. 100)

### Percentage of Swings That Missed—Listed Alphabetically
### (minimum 500 swings in 1999)

| Player, Team | Sw | Miss | Pct | Player, Team | Sw | Miss | Pct | Player, Team | Sw | Miss | Pct |
|---|---|---|---|---|---|---|---|---|---|---|---|
| Abbott K, Col | 581 | 147 | 25 | Cairo, TB | 841 | 80 | 10 | Fullmer, Mon | 602 | 82 | 14 |
| Abreu, Phi | 1061 | 216 | 20 | Cameron, Cin | 997 | 231 | 23 | Gaetti, ChC | 590 | 140 | 24 |
| Agbayani, NYM | 545 | 134 | 25 | Caminiti, Hou | 554 | 129 | 23 | Gant, Phi | 1018 | 242 | 24 |
| Alfonzo, NYM | 1234 | 194 | 16 | Canseco, TB | 921 | 286 | 31 | Garcia K, Det | 586 | 160 | 27 |
| Allen, Min | 872 | 150 | 17 | Caruso, CWS | 893 | 85 | 10 | Garciaparra, Bos | 986 | 159 | 16 |
| Alomar, Cle | 1164 | 173 | 15 | Casey, Cin | 1165 | 200 | 17 | Gates, Min | 525 | 71 | 14 |
| Anderson B, Bal | 1067 | 184 | 17 | Castilla, Col | 1188 | 274 | 23 | Giambi J, KC | 606 | 115 | 19 |
| Anderson G, Ana | 1094 | 188 | 17 | Castillo A, StL | 506 | 107 | 21 | Giambi J, Oak | 1100 | 198 | 18 |
| Anderson M, Phi | 881 | 154 | 17 | Castillo L, Fla | 894 | 95 | 11 | Giles, Pit | 924 | 118 | 13 |
| Andrews, 2Tm | 689 | 239 | 35 | Catalanotto, Det | 581 | 96 | 17 | Glanville, Phi | 1083 | 158 | 15 |
| Arias A, Phi | 574 | 40 | 7 | Cedeno R, NYM | 801 | 149 | 19 | Glaus, Ana | 1036 | 253 | 24 |
| Aurilia, SF | 1016 | 167 | 16 | Chavez, Oak | 667 | 133 | 20 | Gonzalez A, Fla | 1167 | 270 | 23 |
| Ausmus, Det | 821 | 113 | 14 | Christenson, Oak | 525 | 102 | 19 | Gonzalez J, Tex | 1132 | 285 | 25 |
| Aven, Fla | 804 | 201 | 25 | Cirillo, Mil | 1096 | 149 | 14 | Gonzalez L, Ari | 1097 | 150 | 14 |
| Bagwell, Hou | 1187 | 286 | 24 | Clark T, Det | 1173 | 339 | 29 | Goodwin T, Tex | 653 | 89 | 14 |
| Baines, Bal-Cle | 749 | 125 | 17 | Clayton, Tex | 959 | 207 | 22 | Grace, ChC | 1031 | 104 | 10 |
| Barrett, Mon | 757 | 101 | 13 | Conine, Bal | 786 | 87 | 11 | Green S, Tor | 1256 | 276 | 22 |
| Batista, Ari-Tor | 1095 | 215 | 20 | Coomer, Min | 852 | 168 | 20 | Greene T, Ana | 654 | 209 | 32 |
| Bell D, Hou | 1005 | 270 | 27 | Cordova, Min | 910 | 212 | 23 | Greer, Tex | 1068 | 148 | 14 |
| Bell D, Sea | 1071 | 149 | 14 | Cruz D, Det | 938 | 148 | 16 | Grieve, Oak | 840 | 175 | 21 |
| Bell J, Ari | 1205 | 269 | 22 | Cruz J, Tor | 711 | 202 | 28 | Griffey Jr., Sea | 1244 | 265 | 21 |
| Belle, Bal | 1119 | 183 | 16 | Damon, KC | 1059 | 126 | 12 | Grissom, Mil | 1155 | 219 | 19 |
| Belliard, Mil | 860 | 140 | 16 | Daubach, Bos | 828 | 196 | 24 | Grudzielanek, LA | 907 | 136 | 15 |
| Beltran, KC | 1253 | 273 | 22 | Davis B, SD | 557 | 152 | 27 | Guerrero V, Mon | 1198 | 230 | 19 |
| Beltre, LA | 1107 | 247 | 22 | Davis C, NYY | 933 | 205 | 22 | Guerrero W, Mon | 616 | 91 | 15 |
| Benard, SF | 1097 | 190 | 17 | Davis R, Sea | 883 | 210 | 24 | Guillen J, Pit-TB | 590 | 121 | 21 |
| Benjamin, Pit | 834 | 211 | 25 | Delgado C, Tor | 1146 | 299 | 26 | Guzman C, Min | 825 | 166 | 20 |
| Berg, Fla | 596 | 93 | 16 | DeShields, Bal | 565 | 87 | 15 | Gwynn, SD | 641 | 48 | 7 |
| Berry, Mil | 505 | 111 | 22 | Diaz E, Cle | 641 | 95 | 15 | Hamilton, 2Tm | 902 | 77 | 9 |
| Bichette, Col | 1187 | 216 | 18 | Drew, StL | 738 | 162 | 22 | Hammonds, Cin | 528 | 144 | 27 |
| Biggio, Hou | 1244 | 274 | 22 | Durham, CWS | 1118 | 186 | 17 | Hayes, SF | 511 | 99 | 19 |
| Bogar, Hou | 609 | 108 | 18 | Dye, KC | 1117 | 222 | 20 | Helton, Col | 1080 | 150 | 14 |
| Bonds, SF | 694 | 114 | 16 | Easley, Det | 1028 | 252 | 25 | Henderson, NYM | 787 | 114 | 14 |
| Boone A, Cin | 909 | 225 | 25 | Encarnacion, Det | 1006 | 270 | 27 | Hernandez, 2Tm | 1010 | 279 | 28 |
| Boone B, Atl | 1059 | 198 | 19 | Erstad, Ana | 1016 | 193 | 19 | Hidalgo, Hou | 736 | 137 | 19 |
| Bordick, Bal | 1145 | 166 | 14 | Eusebio, Hou | 601 | 121 | 20 | Higginson, Det | 657 | 95 | 14 |
| Bragg, StL | 542 | 110 | 20 | Everett, Hou | 1033 | 292 | 28 | Hill, ChC | 515 | 157 | 30 |
| Brogna, Phi | 1250 | 326 | 26 | Febles, KC | 823 | 121 | 15 | Hocking, Min | 681 | 99 | 15 |
| Brosius, NYY | 904 | 160 | 18 | Fernandez T, Tor | 974 | 155 | 16 | Hollandsw'th, LA | 537 | 142 | 26 |
| Brown B, Pit | 801 | 240 | 30 | Finley, Ari | 1087 | 200 | 18 | Houston, 2Tm | 594 | 167 | 28 |
| Buford, Bos | 567 | 131 | 23 | Flaherty, TB | 852 | 153 | 18 | Hundley, LA | 732 | 209 | 29 |
| Buhner, Sea | 541 | 210 | 39 | Fletcher, Tor | 756 | 107 | 14 | Hunter B, 2Tm | 943 | 162 | 17 |
| Burks, SF | 735 | 194 | 26 | Floyd, Fla | 508 | 136 | 27 | Hunter T, Min | 805 | 197 | 24 |
| Burnitz, Mil | 1055 | 276 | 26 | Fordyce, CWS | 620 | 100 | 16 | Huskey, Sea-Bos | 794 | 201 | 25 |
| Bush, Tor | 950 | 185 | 19 | Fox, Ari | 562 | 112 | 20 | Jackson D, SD | 731 | 157 | 21 |
| Cabrera O, Mon | 703 | 114 | 16 | Fryman, Cle | 585 | 113 | 19 | Jaha, Oak | 823 | 226 | 27 |

*Baseball Scoreboard*

| Player, Team | Sw | Miss | Pct | Player, Team | Sw | Miss | Pct | Player, Team | Sw | Miss | Pct |
|---|---|---|---|---|---|---|---|---|---|---|---|
| Javier, SF-Hou | 734 | 117 | 16 | Millar, Fla | 669 | 127 | 19 | Sosa S, ChC | 1363 | 479 | 35 |
| Jenkins, Mil | 979 | 229 | 23 | Miller, Ari | 619 | 172 | 28 | Spiers, Hou | 681 | 86 | 13 |
| Jeter, NYY | 1361 | 259 | 19 | Mondesi, LA | 1147 | 327 | 29 | Sprague, Pit | 885 | 189 | 21 |
| Johnson C, Bal | 922 | 270 | 29 | Morandini, ChC | 889 | 117 | 13 | Stairs, Oak | 940 | 217 | 23 |
| Johnson L, ChC | 531 | 44 | 8 | Morris W, Pit | 949 | 181 | 19 | Stanley, Bos | 817 | 172 | 21 |
| Jones A, Atl | 1168 | 263 | 23 | Mueller, SF | 753 | 72 | 10 | Steinbach, Min | 648 | 133 | 21 |
| Jones C, Atl | 1060 | 219 | 21 | Nevin, SD | 794 | 193 | 24 | Stevens, Tex | 1057 | 301 | 28 |
| Jones J, Min | 705 | 201 | 29 | Nilsson, Mil | 682 | 107 | 16 | Stewart, Tor | 1140 | 174 | 15 |
| Jordan B, Atl | 1132 | 213 | 19 | Nixon T, Bos | 702 | 138 | 20 | Stinnett, Ari | 651 | 187 | 29 |
| Jordan K, Phi | 666 | 75 | 11 | Norton, CWS | 843 | 172 | 20 | Surhoff, Bal | 1256 | 150 | 12 |
| Joyner, SD | 598 | 105 | 18 | O'Leary, Bos | 1084 | 190 | 18 | Sweeney M, KC | 1043 | 123 | 12 |
| Justice, Cle | 844 | 184 | 22 | O'Neill, NYY | 1183 | 206 | 17 | Tatis, StL | 1092 | 271 | 25 |
| Kapler, Det | 712 | 140 | 20 | Ochoa, Mil | 507 | 89 | 18 | Taubensee, Cin | 776 | 154 | 20 |
| Karros, LA | 1098 | 254 | 23 | Offerman, Bos | 1043 | 112 | 11 | Tejada, Oak | 1145 | 208 | 18 |
| Kelly R, Tex | 584 | 139 | 24 | Olerud, NYM | 997 | 120 | 12 | Thomas, CWS | 875 | 107 | 12 |
| Kendall, Pit | 565 | 85 | 15 | Ordonez, CWS | 1131 | 222 | 20 | Thome, Cle | 1029 | 331 | 32 |
| Kent, SF | 988 | 242 | 24 | Ordonez R, NYM | 866 | 107 | 12 | Trammell, TB | 532 | 104 | 20 |
| Klesko, Atl | 781 | 151 | 19 | Owens, SD | 816 | 102 | 13 | Tucker, Cin | 609 | 176 | 29 |
| Knoblauch, NYY | 1108 | 80 | 7 | Palmeiro O, Ana | 608 | 44 | 7 | Valentin J, Mil | 559 | 111 | 20 |
| Konerko, CWS | 954 | 151 | 16 | Palmeiro R, Tex | 1101 | 157 | 14 | Valentin J, Bos | 782 | 117 | 15 |
| Koskie, Min | 714 | 147 | 21 | Palmer, Det | 1222 | 399 | 33 | Vander Wal, SD | 502 | 140 | 28 |
| Kotsay, Fla | 862 | 105 | 12 | Perez E, Atl | 619 | 105 | 17 | Varitek, Bos | 887 | 175 | 20 |
| Kreuter, KC | 590 | 111 | 19 | Perez N, Col | 1219 | 141 | 12 | Vaughn G, Cin | 1180 | 368 | 31 |
| Lankford, StL | 997 | 275 | 28 | Phillips T, Oak | 769 | 162 | 21 | Vaughn M, Ana | 1101 | 328 | 30 |
| Larkin, Cin | 1024 | 114 | 11 | Piazza, NYM | 1026 | 202 | 20 | Velarde, 2Tm | 1095 | 181 | 17 |
| Lawton, Min | 671 | 68 | 10 | Polonia, Det | 602 | 75 | 12 | Ventura, NYM | 1208 | 276 | 23 |
| Ledesma, TB | 525 | 68 | 13 | Posada, NYY | 695 | 138 | 20 | Veras Q, SD | 826 | 114 | 14 |
| Lee C, CWS | 970 | 161 | 17 | Ramirez M, Cle | 1139 | 283 | 25 | Vidro, Mon | 913 | 136 | 15 |
| Lee T, Ari | 680 | 110 | 16 | Randa, KC | 1064 | 139 | 13 | Vizquel, Cle | 1058 | 74 | 7 |
| Lewis D, Bos | 771 | 74 | 10 | Reed, Col-ChC | 524 | 111 | 21 | Walbeck, Ana | 531 | 82 | 15 |
| Lieberthal, Phi | 1091 | 210 | 19 | Reese, Cin | 1084 | 155 | 14 | Walker L, Col | 888 | 168 | 19 |
| Lofton, Cle | 873 | 99 | 11 | Renteria, StL | 1127 | 200 | 18 | Walker T, Min | 1053 | 194 | 18 |
| Loretta, Mil | 1047 | 92 | 9 | Ripken Jr., Bal | 609 | 75 | 12 | Weiss, Atl | 501 | 67 | 13 |
| Lowell, Fla | 575 | 118 | 21 | Rivera, SD | 925 | 315 | 34 | White D, LA | 951 | 231 | 24 |
| Mabry, Sea | 549 | 133 | 24 | Rodriguez A, Sea | 1059 | 274 | 26 | White R, Mon | 1033 | 233 | 23 |
| Marrero, StL | 635 | 143 | 23 | Rodriguez, ChC | 983 | 277 | 28 | Widger, Mon | 766 | 190 | 25 |
| Martin A, Pit | 1096 | 290 | 26 | Rodriguez I, Tex | 1224 | 204 | 17 | Williams B, NYY | 1058 | 172 | 16 |
| Martinez D, TB | 925 | 91 | 10 | Rolen, Phi | 949 | 231 | 24 | Williams G, Atl | 881 | 172 | 20 |
| Martinez E, Sea | 922 | 136 | 15 | Salmon, Ana | 723 | 188 | 26 | Williams M, Ari | 1174 | 253 | 22 |
| Martinez M, Mon | 730 | 140 | 19 | Sanchez, KC | 874 | 87 | 10 | Wilson D, Sea | 833 | 175 | 21 |
| Martinez T, NYY | 1080 | 154 | 14 | Sanders R, SD | 947 | 247 | 26 | Wilson E, Cle | 661 | 79 | 12 |
| Mayne, SF | 601 | 121 | 20 | Santiago, ChC | 745 | 201 | 27 | Wilson P, Fla | 1030 | 328 | 32 |
| McEwing, StL | 1018 | 180 | 18 | Segui, Sea-Tor | 916 | 164 | 18 | Winn, TB | 576 | 115 | 20 |
| McGee, StL | 581 | 127 | 22 | Sexson, Cle | 960 | 274 | 29 | Womack, Ari | 1162 | 146 | 13 |
| McGriff, TB | 1048 | 251 | 24 | Sheffield, LA | 1020 | 173 | 17 | Young D, Cin | 765 | 182 | 24 |
| McGwire, StL | 1052 | 321 | 31 | Shumpert, Col | 550 | 104 | 19 | Young E, LA | 700 | 66 | 9 |
| McLemore, Tex | 903 | 111 | 12 | Singleton, CWS | 913 | 138 | 15 | Young K, Pit | 1342 | 288 | 21 |
| McRae, 3Tm | 770 | 137 | 18 | Snow, SF | 1120 | 200 | 18 | Zeile, Tex | 1022 | 141 | 14 |
| Mientkiewicz, Min | 584 | 70 | 12 | Sorrento, TB | 585 | 197 | 34 | **MLB Average** | | | **20** |

## *Will the Rockies' Heart Survive a Double-Bypass? (p. 142)*

### American League—Sorted by Most RBI in 1999

| Team | Avg | HR | RBI | Slg | Main 3-4-5 Hitters |
|---|---|---|---|---|---|
| Cleveland | .302 | 109 | 439 | .554 | Alomar, Ramirez M, Thome |
| Texas | .318 | 113 | 401 | .565 | Greer, Gonzalez J, Palmeiro R |
| Oakland | .278 | 115 | 370 | .525 | Giambi J, Jaha, Stairs |
| Toronto | .290 | 98 | 360 | .516 | Green S, Delgado C, Fernandez T |
| Baltimore | .303 | 98 | 352 | .515 | Surhoff, Belle, Baines |
| Seattle | .293 | 119 | 352 | .540 | Griffey Jr., Martinez E, Segui |
| Boston | .300 | 95 | 351 | .527 | Daubach, Garciaparra, O'Leary |
| New York | .288 | 69 | 344 | .462 | O'Neill, Williams B, Martinez T |
| Kansas City | .293 | 69 | 327 | .481 | Damon, Sweeney M, Dye |
| Tampa Bay | .276 | 91 | 314 | .477 | Canseco, McGriff, Flaherty |
| Chicago | .287 | 64 | 289 | .454 | Thomas, Ordonez M, Lee C |
| Anaheim | .264 | 85 | 289 | .459 | Vaughn M, Salmon, Anderson G |
| Detroit | .255 | 90 | 284 | .453 | Higginson, Palmer, Clark T |
| Minnesota | .273 | 39 | 226 | .400 | Walker T, Cordova, Coomer |

### National League—Sorted by Most RBI in 1999

| Team | Avg | HR | RBI | Slg | Main 3-4-5 Hitters |
|---|---|---|---|---|---|
| Colorado | .309 | 121 | 411 | .562 | Walker L, Bichette, Castilla |
| Arizona | .301 | 95 | 386 | .523 | Gonzalez L, Williams M, Finley |
| Houston | .285 | 102 | 382 | .508 | Bagwell, Everett, Hidalgo |
| San Francisco | .279 | 105 | 372 | .514 | Bonds, Kent, Snow |
| St. Louis | .291 | 121 | 370 | .551 | McGwire, Lankford, Tatis |
| New York | .290 | 96 | 357 | .496 | Olerud, Piazza, Ventura |
| Atlanta | .300 | 104 | 355 | .543 | Jones C, Jordan B, Klesko |
| Chicago | .297 | 114 | 351 | .547 | Sosa S, Grace, Rodriguez H |
| Pittsburgh | .289 | 90 | 336 | .512 | Giles, Young K, Kendall |
| Milwaukee | .298 | 85 | 327 | .503 | Cirillo, Burnitz, Nilsson |
| Los Angeles | .291 | 103 | 327 | .510 | Sheffield, Karros, Mondesi |
| Cincinnati | .290 | 91 | 324 | .498 | Casey, Vaughn G, Larkin |
| Philadelphia | .286 | 74 | 317 | .478 | Abreu, Brogna, Gant |
| San Diego | .280 | 74 | 307 | .472 | Sanders R, Nevin, Joyner |
| Montreal | .296 | 76 | 276 | .499 | White R, Guerrero V, Fullmer |
| Florida | .264 | 46 | 275 | .408 | Aven, Millar, Kotsay |
| **MLB Average** | **.289** | **92** | **339** | **.502** | |

## Who's the Best Bunter? (p. 104)

### Sacrifice Hits and Bunt Hits—Listed Alphabetically
### (minimum 12 bunts in play in 1999)

| Player, Team | SH Fail | Pct | H Fail | Pct | Player, Team | SH Fail | Pct | H Fail | Pct |
|---|---|---|---|---|---|---|---|---|---|
| Alomar, Cle | 12 5 | .706 | 17 3 | .850 | Lima, Hou | 13 5 | .722 | 0 0 | — |
| Anderson M, Phi | 4 1 | .800 | 4 4 | .500 | Lofton, Cle | 5 2 | .714 | 6 7 | .462 |
| Astacio, Col | 7 5 | .583 | 0 0 | — | Loretta, Mil | 9 1 | .900 | 5 1 | .833 |
| Benard, SF | 1 1 | .500 | 14 14 | .500 | Maddux G, Atl | 13 1 | .929 | 0 0 | — |
| Benjamin, Pit | 11 2 | .846 | 1 0 | 1.000 | Martinez D, TB | 10 1 | .909 | 7 3 | .700 |
| Biggio, Hou | 5 0 | 1.000 | 5 4 | .556 | McDonald J, Oak | 4 0 | 1.000 | 10 2 | .833 |
| Brown, LA | 13 7 | .650 | 0 0 | — | McEwing, StL | 9 2 | .818 | 5 1 | .833 |
| Bush, Tor | 8 1 | .889 | 3 2 | .600 | McLemore, Tex | 9 3 | .750 | 3 2 | .600 |
| Byrd, Phi | 11 3 | .786 | 0 1 | .000 | Meadows, Fla | 7 5 | .583 | 0 0 | — |
| Cairo, TB | 7 1 | .875 | 5 3 | .625 | Nixon O, Atl | 1 0 | 1.000 | 4 8 | .333 |
| Cameron, Cin | 5 1 | .833 | 4 6 | .400 | Nunez, Pit | 13 2 | .867 | 3 6 | .333 |
| Caruso, CWS | 11 2 | .846 | 18 16 | .529 | Ordonez R, NYM | 11 0 | 1.000 | 1 1 | .500 |
| Castillo L, Fla | 6 1 | .857 | 7 17 | .292 | Perez N, Col | 9 5 | .643 | 4 9 | .308 |
| Cedeno R, NYM | 7 2 | .778 | 8 4 | .667 | Polonia, Det | 2 3 | .400 | 15 6 | .714 |
| Christenson, Oak | 8 1 | .889 | 4 5 | .444 | Pulsipher, Mil | 8 4 | .667 | 0 0 | — |
| Cirillo, Mil | 3 2 | .600 | 9 2 | .818 | Reese, Cin | 5 4 | .556 | 1 2 | .333 |
| Cruz D, Det | 14 0 | 1.000 | 2 1 | .667 | Reynolds, Hou | 17 2 | .895 | 1 0 | 1.000 |
| Daal, Ari | 6 5 | .545 | 5 1 | .833 | Roberts, Cle | 3 0 | 1.000 | 4 8 | .333 |
| Damon, KC | 3 2 | .600 | 5 3 | .625 | Sanchez, KC | 10 3 | .769 | 6 4 | .600 |
| Drew, StL | 3 1 | .750 | 6 4 | .600 | Santangelo, SF | 5 1 | .833 | 3 3 | .500 |
| Durham, CWS | 3 2 | .600 | 6 7 | .462 | Schilling, Phi | 9 3 | .750 | 0 0 | — |
| Encarnacion, Det | 4 1 | .800 | 3 6 | .333 | Schmidt, Pit | 12 7 | .632 | 0 0 | — |
| Estes, SF | 10 4 | .714 | 0 1 | .000 | Sheets, Ana | 6 1 | .857 | 2 3 | .400 |
| Febles, KC | 12 4 | .750 | 6 5 | .545 | Singleton, CWS | 4 4 | .500 | 9 6 | .600 |
| Girardi, NYY | 8 2 | .800 | 1 2 | .333 | Stocker, TB | 4 1 | .800 | 6 5 | .545 |
| Glanville, Phi | 5 1 | .833 | 5 1 | .833 | Tejada, Oak | 9 1 | .900 | 7 3 | .700 |
| Goodwin C, 2Tm | 4 1 | .800 | 8 6 | .571 | Valdes, LA | 10 5 | .667 | 0 1 | .000 |
| Goodwin T, Tex | 7 1 | .875 | 4 3 | .571 | Vina, Mil | 3 0 | 1.000 | 4 6 | .400 |
| Guerrero W, Mon | 10 3 | .769 | 3 3 | .500 | Vizcaino, LA | 9 1 | .900 | 3 0 | 1.000 |
| Guzman C, Min | 7 2 | .778 | 17 15 | .531 | Vizquel, Cle | 17 0 | 1.000 | 19 9 | .679 |
| Hocking, Min | 4 0 | 1.000 | 8 3 | .727 | Williams G, Atl | 4 2 | .667 | 3 4 | .429 |
| Holbert, KC | 6 1 | .857 | 3 2 | .600 | Wilson D, Sea | 10 3 | .769 | 1 1 | .500 |
| Hunter B, 2Tm | 4 3 | .571 | 7 9 | .438 | Winn, TB | 1 2 | .333 | 5 6 | .455 |
| Javier, SF-Hou | 8 0 | 1.000 | 3 3 | .500 | Womack, Ari | 9 1 | .900 | 6 6 | .500 |
| Johnson R, Ari | 7 6 | .538 | 0 0 | — | Woodard, Mil | 10 2 | .833 | 1 2 | .333 |
| Karl, Mil | 12 2 | .857 | 0 0 | — | **MLB Average** | | .755 | | .567 |
| Lewis D, Bos | 14 3 | .824 | 2 11 | .154 | | | | | |

## Who Was the Real "Man on the Moon" in 1999? (p. 107)

### Longest Home Runs—1999

| Dis | Player, Team | Pitcher, Team | Date | Site |
|---|---|---|---|---|
| 511 | Thome, Cle | Wengert, KC | 7/3 | Cle |
| 502 | McGwire, StL | Dotel, NYM | 8/22 | NYM |
| 500 | McGwire, StL | Arnold, LA | 5/22 | LA |
| 500 | Sosa S, ChC | Nomo, Mil | 9/19 | ChC |
| 495 | Hill, ChC | Rodriguez F, SF | 8/25 | ChC |
| 491 | Sorrento, TB | Clark, Tex | 5/19 | Tex |
| 480 | Brown B, Pit | Blair, Det | 6/9 | Det |
| 480 | Giles, Pit | Ogea, Phi | 6/30 | Pit |
| 480 | Thome, Cle | Borkowski, Det | 7/27 | Cle |
| 480 | Sosa S, ChC | Rueter, SF | 8/25 | ChC |
| 480 | Hill, ChC | Benson, Pit | 9/26 | ChC |
| 479 | McGwire, StL | Ashby, SD | 8/5 | StL |
| 478 | Griffey Jr., Sea | Bohanon, Col | 6/9 | Col |
| 474 | Drew, StL | Harnisch, Cin | 7/8 | StL |
| 473 | McGwire, StL | Bergman, Hou | 6/21 | StL |
| 471 | Ramirez M, Cle | Cone, NYY | 9/19 | Cle |
| 470 | Canseco, TB | Portugal, Bos | 4/17 | Bos |
| 470 | Rolen, Phi | Daal, Ari | 4/19 | Ari |
| 470 | McGriff, TB | Witasick, KC | 5/5 | TB |
| 470 | Lieberthal, Phi | Bohanon, Col | 5/8 | Col |
| 470 | Walker L, Col | Sanders, ChC | 6/22 | Col |
| 467 | McGwire, StL | Ashby, SD | 9/29 | StL |
| 465 | Sosa S, ChC | Person, Phi | 6/26 | ChC |
| 465 | Walker L, Col | Hitchcock, SD | 7/2 | Col |
| 465 | Sosa S, ChC | Yoshii, NYM | 7/30 | ChC |
| 463 | Palmer, Det | Guthrie, Bos | 7/25 | Det |
| 462 | Thome, Cle | Mulholland, ChC | 6/4 | Cle |
| 462 | McGwire, StL | Clement, SD | 9/29 | StL |
| 461 | Williams M, Ari | Hackman, Col | 9/22 | Col |
| 461 | McGwire, StL | Trachsel, ChC | 10/3 | StL |
| 460 | Thome, Cle | Perkins, Min | 4/9 | Min |
| 460 | Andrews, Mon | Wright J, Col | 4/19 | Col |
| 460 | Gant, Phi | Stottlemyre, Ari | 4/21 | Ari |
| 460 | Vaughn M, Ana | Hentgen, Tor | 4/22 | Tor |
| 460 | Sosa S, ChC | Looper, Fla | 5/17 | Fla |
| 460 | Sosa S, ChC | Sanchez, Fla | 5/19 | Fla |
| 460 | Garcia K, Det | Navarro, CWS | 5/28 | Det |
| 460 | Griffey Jr., Sea | Rincon, Cle | 6/18 | Cle |
| 460 | Sosa S, ChC | Leskanic, Col | 6/24 | Col |
| 460 | Rivera, SD | Ramirez R, Col | 7/3 | Col |
| 460 | Walker L, Col | Murray H, SD | 7/3 | Col |
| 460 | Walker L, Col | Lima, Hou | 7/27 | Col |
| 460 | Anderson G, Ana | Thompson J, Det | 8/15 | Det |
| 460 | Bonds, SF | Rain, ChC | 8/25 | ChC |
| 460 | Wilson P, Fla | Valdes, LA | 9/6 | Fla |
| 460 | Vaughn M, Ana | Mays, Min | 9/12 | Min |
| 460 | Giambi J, Oak | Wheeler, TB | 9/12 | TB |
| 460 | Tatis, StL | Lima, Hou | 9/17 | StL |
| 459 | Canseco, TB | Lloyd, Tor | 4/12 | Tor |
| 459 | Everett, Hou | Yoshii, NYM | 8/24 | NYM |
| 458 | Thome, Cle | Irabu, NYY | 9/16 | Cle |
| 456 | Justice, Cle | Lieber, ChC | 6/5 | Cle |
| 455 | Helton, Col | Jones B, NYM | 5/11 | Col |
| 455 | Rodriguez I, Tex | Cho, Bos | 6/19 | Bos |
| 455 | McGriff, TB | Escobar, Tor | 6/27 | TB |
| **390** | **MLB Average** | | | |

## Did Martinez Have the Most Spectacular Pitching Season Ever? (p. 110)

### Highest ERA, Component ERA Indexes—1900-99

| Highest ERA Index (minimum 1 IP per team G) | | | | | Highest Component ERA Index (minimum 1 IP per team G) | | | |
|---|---|---|---|---|---|---|---|---|
| Pitcher, Team | Year | ERA | Lg ERA | Index | Pitcher, Team | Year | ERC | Lg ERA Index |
| Dutch Leonard, Bos | 1914 | 0.96 | 2.73 | 284.4 | Greg Maddux, Atl | 1995 | 1.41 | 4.18 297.1 |
| Greg Maddux, Atl | 1994 | 1.56 | 4.21 | 270.0 | Pedro Martinez, Bos | 1999 | 1.79 | 4.86 271.2 |
| Bob Gibson, StL | 1968 | 1.12 | 2.99 | 266.0 | Greg Maddux, Atl | 1994 | 1.59 | 4.21 265.6 |
| Greg Maddux, Atl | 1995 | 1.63 | 4.18 | 256.3 | Pedro Martinez, Mon | 1997 | 1.79 | 4.20 234.3 |
| Walter Johnson, Was | 1913 | 1.14 | 2.93 | 256.0 | Walter Johnson, Was | 1913 | 1.27 | 2.93 231.5 |
| TF Brown, ChC | 1906 | 1.04 | 2.62 | 252.7 | Sandy Koufax, LA | 1965 | 1.56 | 3.54 226.5 |
| Walter Johnson, Was | 1912 | 1.39 | 3.34 | 240.1 | Mike Scott, Hou | 1986 | 1.67 | 3.72 222.9 |
| Pedro Martinez, Bos | 1999 | 2.07 | 4.86 | 235.0 | Ron Guidry, NYY | 1978 | 1.71 | 3.76 219.7 |
| Dwight Gooden, NYM | 1985 | 1.53 | 3.59 | 234.9 | Walter Johnson, Was | 1912 | 1.52 | 3.34 219.4 |
| Christy Mathewson, NYG | 1905 | 1.28 | 2.99 | 234.5 | Randy Johnson, Sea | 1995 | 2.18 | 4.71 215.7 |
| Christy Mathewson, NYG | 1909 | 1.14 | 2.59 | 226.4 | Greg Maddux, Atl | 1997 | 1.95 | 4.20 215.2 |
| Cy Young, BosA | 1901 | 1.62 | 3.66 | 225.5 | Sandy Koufax, LA | 1964 | 1.66 | 3.54 212.8 |
| Pete Alexander, PhiN | 1915 | 1.22 | 2.75 | 225.1 | Sandy Koufax, LA | 1963 | 1.55 | 3.29 212.8 |
| Roger Clemens, Tor | 1997 | 2.05 | 4.56 | 223.1 | Don Sutton, LA | 1972 | 1.63 | 3.45 211.6 |
| Kevin Brown, Fla | 1996 | 1.89 | 4.21 | 222.7 | Bill Bernhard, PhiA-Cle | 1902 | 1.69 | 3.57 211.2 |
| Pedro Martinez, Mon | 1997 | 1.90 | 4.20 | 220.8 | Joe Horlen, CWS | 1964 | 1.72 | 3.63 210.9 |
| Dean Chance, LAA | 1964 | 1.65 | 3.63 | 219.8 | Garland Braxton, Was | 1928 | 1.92 | 4.04 210.8 |
| Walter Johnson, Was | 1918 | 1.27 | 2.77 | 218.3 | Roger Clemens, Tor | 1997 | 2.17 | 4.56 210.6 |
| Walter Johnson, Was | 1919 | 1.49 | 3.22 | 216.7 | Kevin Brown, Fla | 1996 | 2.00 | 4.21 210.4 |
| Ron Guidry, NYY | 1978 | 1.74 | 3.76 | 215.9 | Greg Maddux, Atl | 1998 | 2.01 | 4.23 210.3 |
| Jack Pfiester, ChC | 1907 | 1.15 | 2.46 | 213.6 | Bob Gibson, StL | 1968 | 1.44 | 2.99 206.8 |
| Lefty Grove, PhiA | 1931 | 2.06 | 4.38 | 212.8 | Nolan Ryan, Tex | 1991 | 1.98 | 4.09 206.7 |
| Ed Reulbach, ChC | 1905 | 1.42 | 2.99 | 210.8 | Pete Alexander, PhiN | 1915 | 1.33 | 2.75 206.6 |
| Carl Lundgren, ChC | 1907 | 1.17 | 2.46 | 209.9 | Roger Clemens, Bos | 1986 | 2.03 | 4.18 206.2 |
| Jack Taylor, ChC | 1902 | 1.33 | 2.78 | 208.8 | Dean Chance, LAA | 1964 | 1.76 | 3.63 206.0 |
| Sandy Koufax, LA | 1966 | 1.73 | 3.61 | 208.8 | Bret Saberhagen, KC | 1989 | 1.89 | 3.88 205.5 |
| Dolf Luque, Cin | 1923 | 1.93 | 3.99 | 207.1 | Roger Clemens, Tor | 1998 | 2.27 | 4.65 204.5 |
| Nolan Ryan, Hou | 1981 | 1.69 | 3.49 | 206.4 | Steve Ontiveros, Oak | 1994 | 2.35 | 4.80 203.8 |
| Addie Joss, Cle | 1908 | 1.16 | 2.39 | 205.2 | Kevin Millwood, Atl | 1999 | 2.26 | 4.56 201.6 |
| Warren Spahn, Mil | 1953 | 2.10 | 4.29 | 204.1 | Claude Hendrix, ChiF | 1914 | 1.59 | 3.20 201.2 |
| Sandy Koufax, LA | 1964 | 1.74 | 3.54 | 203.7 | Christy Mathewson, NYG | 1909 | 1.29 | 2.59 200.1 |
| Roger Clemens, Bos | 1990 | 1.93 | 3.91 | 202.2 | Juan Marichal, SF | 1966 | 1.80 | 3.61 199.9 |
| Spud Chandler, NYY | 1943 | 1.64 | 3.30 | 201.4 | Ed Walsh, CWS | 1910 | 1.27 | 2.52 198.5 |
| Billy Pierce, CWS | 1955 | 1.97 | 3.96 | 201.1 | Luis Tiant, Cle | 1968 | 1.51 | 2.98 196.8 |
| Carl Hubbell, NYG | 1933 | 1.66 | 3.34 | 200.7 | Dwight Gooden, NYM | 1985 | 1.83 | 3.59 196.6 |
| Randy Johnson, Sea | 1997 | 2.28 | 4.56 | 200.0 | Lefty Grove, PhiA | 1931 | 2.23 | 4.38 196.5 |
| Ed Walsh, CWS | 1910 | 1.27 | 2.52 | 198.7 | Harry Brecheen, StLN | 1948 | 2.01 | 3.95 196.5 |
| Lefty Gomez, NYY | 1937 | 2.33 | 4.62 | 198.6 | Cy Young, BosA | 1901 | 1.87 | 3.66 196.1 |
| TF Brown, ChC | 1909 | 1.31 | 2.59 | 197.2 | Monty Stratton, CWS | 1937 | 2.36 | 4.62 196.0 |
| Joe Wood, BosA | 1915 | 1.49 | 2.93 | 197.1 | Warren Spahn, Mil | 1953 | 2.19 | 4.29 195.8 |
| Tom Seaver, NYM | 1971 | 1.76 | 3.47 | 197.0 | John Tudor, StL | 1985 | 1.84 | 3.59 195.6 |
| Jack Coombs, PhiA | 1910 | 1.30 | 2.52 | 193.5 | John Smoltz, Atl | 1996 | 2.17 | 4.21 194.3 |
| Joe Horlen, CWS | 1964 | 1.88 | 3.63 | 192.9 | Addie Joss, Cle | 1908 | 1.23 | 2.39 193.9 |
| Lefty Gomez, NYY | 1934 | 2.33 | 4.50 | 192.8 | Christy Mathewson, NYG | 1905 | 1.54 | 2.99 193.9 |
| Monty Stratton, CWS | 1937 | 2.40 | 4.62 | 192.3 | Dutch Leonard, BosA | 1914 | 1.41 | 2.73 193.8 |
| Dazzy Vance, Bro | 1928 | 2.09 | 3.99 | 191.0 | Cy Blanton, Pit | 1935 | 2.08 | 4.02 193.4 |
| Greg Maddux, Atl | 1997 | 2.20 | 4.20 | 190.5 | Hideo Nomo, LA | 1995 | 2.16 | 4.18 193.3 |
| Vida Blue, Oak | 1971 | 1.82 | 3.46 | 190.5 | Lefty Gomez, NYY | 1934 | 2.33 | 4.50 192.9 |
| Dazzy Vance, Bro | 1930 | 2.61 | 4.97 | 190.4 | Ted Lyons, CWS | 1939 | 2.40 | 4.62 192.5 |
| Greg Maddux, Atl | 1998 | 2.22 | 4.23 | 190.3 | Kevin Appier, KC | 1993 | 2.25 | 4.32 191.8 |
| Randy Johnson, Sea | 1995 | 2.48 | 4.71 | 190.2 | Babe Adams, Pit | 1919 | 1.52 | 2.91 191.1 |
| Claude Hendrix, ChiF | 1914 | 1.69 | 3.20 | 189.6 | Dazzy Vance, Bro | 1924 | 2.02 | 3.87 191.1 |
| Walter Johnson, Was | 1915 | 1.55 | 2.93 | 189.1 | Vida Blue, Oak | 1971 | 1.81 | 3.46 191.0 |

## Highest Strikeout Ratios—1900-99

### Highest Strikeout-Walk Ratio (minimum 1 IP per team G)

| Pitcher, Team | Year | SO | BB | SO/BB |
|---|---|---|---|---|
| Bret Saberhagen, NYM | 1994 | 143 | 13 | 11.0 |
| Greg Maddux, Atl | 1997 | 177 | 20 | 8.9 |
| Pedro Martinez, Bos | 1999 | 313 | 37 | 8.5 |
| Greg Maddux, Atl | 1995 | 181 | 23 | 7.9 |
| Fergie Jenkins, ChC | 1971 | 263 | 37 | 7.1 |
| Cy Young, BosA | 1905 | 210 | 30 | 7.0 |
| Cy Young, BosA | 1904 | 200 | 29 | 6.9 |
| Walter Johnson, Was | 1913 | 243 | 38 | 6.4 |
| Christy Mathewson, NYG | 1908 | 259 | 42 | 6.2 |
| Juan Marichal, SF | 1966 | 222 | 36 | 6.2 |
| Dennis Eckersley, ChC | 1985 | 117 | 19 | 6.2 |
| Greg Maddux, Atl | 1996 | 172 | 28 | 6.1 |
| David Wells, NYY | 1998 | 163 | 29 | 5.6 |
| Cy Young, BosA | 1906 | 140 | 25 | 5.6 |
| Curt Schilling, Phi | 1997 | 319 | 58 | 5.5 |
| Greg Swindell, Cle | 1991 | 169 | 31 | 5.5 |
| Sandy Koufax, LA | 1965 | 382 | 71 | 5.4 |
| Jim Merritt, Min | 1967 | 161 | 30 | 5.4 |
| Shane Reynolds, Hou | 1999 | 197 | 37 | 5.3 |
| Jose Lima, Hou | 1998 | 169 | 32 | 5.3 |
| Sandy Koufax, LA | 1963 | 306 | 58 | 5.3 |
| Rick Reed, NYM | 1998 | 153 | 29 | 5.3 |
| Kevin Brown, SD | 1998 | 257 | 49 | 5.2 |
| Shane Reynolds, Hou | 1994 | 110 | 21 | 5.2 |
| Juan Marichal, SF | 1965 | 240 | 46 | 5.2 |
| Randy Johnson, Ari | 1999 | 364 | 70 | 5.2 |
| Greg Maddux, Atl | 1994 | 156 | 31 | 5.0 |
| Gaylord Perry, SF | 1966 | 201 | 40 | 5.0 |
| Jim Kaat, Min | 1967 | 211 | 42 | 5.0 |
| John Smoltz, Atl | 1996 | 276 | 55 | 5.0 |
| Fergie Jenkins, Tex | 1974 | 225 | 45 | 5.0 |
| Curt Schilling, Phi | 1998 | 300 | 61 | 4.9 |
| Bob Tewksbury, StL | 1993 | 97 | 20 | 4.9 |
| Kevin Brown, Fla | 1996 | 159 | 33 | 4.8 |
| Ed Walsh, CWS | 1908 | 269 | 56 | 4.8 |
| LaMarr Hoyt, CWS | 1983 | 148 | 31 | 4.8 |
| Jim Bunning, Phi | 1964 | 219 | 46 | 4.8 |
| Cy Young, BosA | 1903 | 176 | 37 | 4.8 |
| Juan Marichal, SF | 1968 | 218 | 46 | 4.7 |
| Tom Seaver, NYM | 1971 | 289 | 61 | 4.7 |
| Shane Reynolds, Hou | 1995 | 175 | 37 | 4.7 |
| Roger Clemens, Bos | 1988 | 291 | 62 | 4.7 |
| Deacon Phillippe, Pit | 1902 | 122 | 26 | 4.7 |
| Babe Adams, Pit | 1920 | 84 | 18 | 4.7 |
| Shane Reynolds, Hou | 1996 | 204 | 44 | 4.6 |
| John Burkett, Tex | 1997 | 139 | 30 | 4.6 |
| Jim Bunning, Phi | 1966 | 252 | 55 | 4.6 |
| Fergie Jenkins, ChC | 1970 | 274 | 60 | 4.6 |
| Pedro Martinez, Mon | 1997 | 305 | 67 | 4.6 |
| Bob Tewksbury, StL | 1992 | 91 | 20 | 4.6 |
| Greg Maddux, Atl | 1998 | 204 | 45 | 4.5 |
| Randy Johnson, Sea | 1995 | 294 | 65 | 4.5 |
| Bret Saberhagen, KC | 1989 | 193 | 43 | 4.5 |
| Scott Sanderson, NYY | 1991 | 130 | 29 | 4.5 |
| Denny McLain, Det | 1968 | 280 | 63 | 4.4 |
| Christy Mathewson, NYG | 1913 | 93 | 21 | 4.4 |
| Don Drysdale, LA | 1963 | 251 | 57 | 4.4 |

### Highest Strikeout-Baserunner Ratio (minimum 1 IP per team G)

| Pitcher, Team | Year | SO | BR | SO/BR |
|---|---|---|---|---|
| Pedro Martinez, Bos | 1999 | 313 | 206 | 1.52 |
| Sandy Koufax, LA | 1965 | 382 | 292 | 1.31 |
| Pedro Martinez, Mon | 1997 | 305 | 234 | 1.30 |
| Randy Johnson, Sea | 1995 | 294 | 230 | 1.28 |
| Randy Johnson, Ari | 1999 | 364 | 286 | 1.27 |
| Randy Johnson, Sea | 1997 | 291 | 234 | 1.24 |
| Mike Scott, Hou | 1986 | 306 | 256 | 1.20 |
| Curt Schilling, Phi | 1997 | 319 | 271 | 1.18 |
| Dwight Gooden, NYM | 1984 | 276 | 236 | 1.17 |
| Luis Tiant, Cle | 1968 | 264 | 229 | 1.15 |
| Hideo Nomo, LA | 1995 | 236 | 207 | 1.14 |
| Nolan Ryan, Tex | 1991 | 203 | 179 | 1.13 |
| Sandy Koufax, LA | 1962 | 216 | 193 | 1.12 |
| Nolan Ryan, Tex | 1989 | 301 | 269 | 1.12 |
| Sandy Koufax, LA | 1963 | 306 | 275 | 1.11 |
| Nolan Ryan, Hou | 1987 | 270 | 245 | 1.10 |
| Kerry Wood, ChC | 1998 | 233 | 213 | 1.09 |
| Randy Johnson, 2Tm | 1998 | 329 | 303 | 1.09 |
| John Smoltz, Atl | 1996 | 276 | 256 | 1.08 |
| Sandy Koufax, LA | 1964 | 223 | 207 | 1.08 |
| Nolan Ryan, Tex | 1990 | 232 | 218 | 1.06 |
| Tom Seaver, NYM | 1971 | 289 | 275 | 1.05 |
| Greg Maddux, Atl | 1995 | 181 | 174 | 1.04 |
| Sam McDowell, Cle | 1965 | 325 | 316 | 1.03 |
| Roger Clemens, Tor | 1997 | 292 | 284 | 1.03 |
| Randy Johnson, Sea | 1993 | 308 | 300 | 1.03 |
| Roger Clemens, Tor | 1998 | 271 | 264 | 1.03 |
| Roger Clemens, Bos | 1988 | 291 | 285 | 1.02 |
| Sonny Siebert, Cle | 1965 | 191 | 190 | 1.01 |
| Bob Gibson, StL | 1968 | 268 | 267 | 1.00 |
| Vida Blue, Oak | 1971 | 301 | 301 | 1.00 |
| Sandy Koufax, LA | 1966 | 317 | 318 | 1.00 |
| Dwight Gooden, NYM | 1985 | 268 | 269 | 1.00 |
| Curt Schilling, Phi | 1998 | 300 | 303 | 0.99 |
| Mario Soto, Cin | 1982 | 274 | 277 | 0.99 |
| Nolan Ryan, Cal | 1972 | 329 | 333 | 0.99 |
| J.R. Richard, Hou | 1979 | 313 | 321 | 0.98 |
| Randy Johnson, Sea | 1994 | 204 | 210 | 0.97 |
| David Cone, NYM | 1990 | 233 | 243 | 0.96 |
| Jim Maloney, Cin | 1963 | 265 | 277 | 0.96 |
| Pedro Martinez, Bos | 1998 | 251 | 263 | 0.95 |
| Ron Guidry, NYY | 1978 | 248 | 260 | 0.95 |
| Roger Clemens, Bos | 1986 | 238 | 250 | 0.95 |
| Sid Fernandez, NYM | 1985 | 180 | 190 | 0.95 |
| Nolan Ryan, Hou | 1986 | 194 | 205 | 0.95 |
| Sam McDowell, Cle | 1966 | 225 | 238 | 0.95 |
| Nolan Ryan, Cal | 1973 | 383 | 407 | 0.94 |
| Sam McDowell, Cle | 1968 | 283 | 301 | 0.94 |
| Sid Fernandez, NYM | 1988 | 189 | 203 | 0.93 |
| Frank Tanana, Cal | 1975 | 269 | 291 | 0.92 |
| Andy Benes, SD | 1994 | 189 | 207 | 0.91 |
| Nolan Ryan, Hou | 1984 | 197 | 216 | 0.91 |
| Dave Boswell, Min | 1966 | 173 | 190 | 0.91 |
| David Cone, NYY | 1997 | 222 | 245 | 0.91 |
| Kevin Brown, SD | 1998 | 257 | 284 | 0.90 |
| J.R. Richard, Hou | 1978 | 303 | 335 | 0.90 |
| Denny McLain, Det | 1968 | 280 | 310 | 0.90 |

*Baseball Scoreboard*

## How Long Can the Big Unit Dominate? (p. 114)

### Most Strikeouts Per Nine Innings, Season—Age 35 or Older
### (minimum 150 IP; age as of June 30)

| Pitcher, Team | Year | SO | IP | SO/9 | Pitcher, Team | Year | SO | IP | SO/9 |
|---|---|---|---|---|---|---|---|---|---|
| Randy Johnson, Ari | 1999 | 364 | 271.2 | 12.06 | Gaylord Perry, Tex | 1977 | 177 | 238.0 | 6.69 |
| Nolan Ryan, Hou | 1987 | 270 | 211.2 | 11.48 | Phil Niekro, Atl | 1978 | 248 | 334.1 | 6.68 |
| Nolan Ryan, Tex | 1989 | 301 | 239.1 | 11.32 | Tom Candiotti, LA | 1995 | 141 | 190.1 | 6.67 |
| Nolan Ryan, Tex | 1991 | 203 | 173.0 | 10.56 | Jim Bunning, Pit-LA | 1969 | 157 | 212.1 | 6.65 |
| Roger Clemens, Tor | 1998 | 271 | 234.2 | 10.39 | Greg Harris, Bos | 1991 | 127 | 173.0 | 6.61 |
| Nolan Ryan, Tex | 1990 | 232 | 204.0 | 10.24 | Bert Blyleven, Min | 1987 | 196 | 267.0 | 6.61 |
| Nolan Ryan, Hou | 1986 | 194 | 178.0 | 9.81 | David Wells, Tor | 1999 | 169 | 231.2 | 6.57 |
| Nolan Ryan, Hou | 1984 | 197 | 183.2 | 9.65 | Jeff Fassero, Sea-Tex | 1999 | 114 | 156.1 | 6.56 |
| Nolan Ryan, Hou | 1988 | 228 | 220.0 | 9.33 | Bob Gibson, StL | 1973 | 142 | 195.0 | 6.55 |
| David Cone, NYY | 1998 | 209 | 207.2 | 9.06 | Ron Guidry, NYY | 1986 | 140 | 192.1 | 6.55 |
| Nolan Ryan, Tex | 1992 | 157 | 157.1 | 8.98 | Tom Candiotti, LA | 1993 | 155 | 213.2 | 6.53 |
| Nolan Ryan, Hou | 1982 | 245 | 250.1 | 8.81 | Joe Nuxhall, Cin | 1964 | 111 | 154.2 | 6.46 |
| Steve Carlton, Phi | 1983 | 275 | 283.2 | 8.73 | Dazzy Vance, Bro | 1928 | 200 | 280.1 | 6.42 |
| Steve Carlton, Phi | 1982 | 286 | 295.2 | 8.71 | Mark Gardner, SF | 1998 | 151 | 212.0 | 6.41 |
| Chuck Finley, Ana | 1998 | 212 | 223.1 | 8.54 | Steve Carlton, Phi | 1984 | 163 | 229.0 | 6.41 |
| Steve Carlton, Phi | 1981 | 179 | 190.0 | 8.48 | Rick Reuschel, Pit | 1985 | 138 | 194.0 | 6.40 |
| Steve Carlton, Phi | 1980 | 286 | 304.0 | 8.47 | Whitey Ford, NYY | 1964 | 172 | 244.2 | 6.33 |
| Chuck Finley, Ana | 1999 | 200 | 213.1 | 8.44 | Don Sutton, Hou-Mil | 1982 | 175 | 249.2 | 6.31 |
| Nolan Ryan, Hou | 1983 | 183 | 196.1 | 8.39 | Early Wynn, CWS | 1959 | 179 | 255.2 | 6.30 |
| David Cone, NYY | 1999 | 177 | 193.1 | 8.24 | Early Wynn, Cle | 1957 | 184 | 263.0 | 6.30 |
| Nolan Ryan, Hou | 1985 | 209 | 232.0 | 8.11 | Bert Blyleven, Min | 1988 | 145 | 207.1 | 6.29 |
| Roger Clemens, NYY | 1999 | 163 | 187.2 | 7.82 | Charlie Hough, Tex | 1988 | 174 | 252.0 | 6.21 |
| Jim Bunning, Phi | 1967 | 253 | 302.1 | 7.53 | Dennis Martinez, Mon | 1990 | 156 | 226.0 | 6.21 |
| Dazzy Vance, Bro | 1926 | 140 | 169.0 | 7.46 | Dazzy Vance, Bro | 1931 | 150 | 218.2 | 6.17 |
| Phil Niekro, Atl | 1977 | 262 | 330.1 | 7.14 | Jimmy Key, NYY | 1996 | 116 | 169.1 | 6.17 |
| Bert Blyleven, Min | 1986 | 215 | 271.2 | 7.12 | Bobby Witt, TB | 1999 | 123 | 180.1 | 6.14 |
| Jeff Fassero, Sea | 1998 | 176 | 224.2 | 7.05 | Steve Carlton, 3TM | 1986 | 120 | 176.1 | 6.12 |
| Charlie Hough, Tex | 1987 | 223 | 285.1 | 7.03 | Jerry Koosman, NYM | 1978 | 160 | 235.1 | 6.12 |
| Danny Darwin, Bos | 1992 | 124 | 161.1 | 6.92 | Phil Niekro, NYY | 1985 | 149 | 220.0 | 6.10 |
| Gaylord Perry, 2Tm | 1975 | 233 | 305.2 | 6.86 | Jack Morris, Tor | 1993 | 103 | 152.2 | 6.07 |
| David Wells, NYY | 1998 | 163 | 214.1 | 6.84 | Jamie Moyer, Sea | 1998 | 158 | 234.1 | 6.07 |
| Rudy May, NYY | 1980 | 133 | 175.1 | 6.83 | Dazzy Vance, Bro | 1927 | 184 | 273.1 | 6.06 |
| Mark Gardner, SF | 1997 | 136 | 180.1 | 6.79 | Don Sutton, Mil | 1984 | 143 | 212.2 | 6.05 |
| Bob Gibson, StL | 1971 | 185 | 245.2 | 6.78 | Jim Bunning, Phi | 1970 | 147 | 219.0 | 6.04 |
| Woodie Fryman, Mon | 1975 | 118 | 157.0 | 6.76 | Gaylord Perry, Cle | 1974 | 216 | 322.1 | 6.03 |
| Bob Gibson, StL | 1972 | 208 | 278.0 | 6.73 | Dazzy Vance, Bro | 1930 | 173 | 258.2 | 6.02 |
| Early Wynn, CWS | 1958 | 179 | 239.2 | 6.72 | Tom Candiotti, LA | 1994 | 102 | 153.0 | 6.00 |

## Who Threw the Most Pitches in a Single Season? (p. 116)

### Most Estimated Pitches, Season—1946-99

| Pitcher, Team | Year | Est | Pitcher, Team | Year | Est |
|---|---|---|---|---|---|
| Bob Feller, Cle | 1946 | 5,791 | Jim Colborn, Mil | 1973 | 4,624 |
| Mickey Lolich, Det | 1971 | 5,649 | Jim Palmer, Bal | 1975 | 4,622 |
| Nolan Ryan, Cal | 1974 | 5,525 | Juan Marichal, SF | 1963 | 4,619 |
| Wilbur Wood, CWS | 1973 | 5,453 | Steve Carlton, Phi | 1980 | 4,615 |
| Phil Niekro, Atl | 1977 | 5,442 | J.R. Richard, Hou | 1976 | 4,614 |
| Nolan Ryan, Cal | 1973 | 5,338 | Johnny Sain, BosN | 1948 | 4,610 |
| Wilbur Wood, CWS | 1972 | 5,336 | Bob Gibson, StL | 1965 | 4,608 |
| Gaylord Perry, Cle | 1973 | 5,279 | Frank Lary, Det | 1956 | 4,604 |
| Phil Niekro, Atl | 1979 | 5,187 | Fergie Jenkins, ChC | 1970 | 4,598 |
| Nolan Ryan, Cal | 1977 | 5,098 | Jim Palmer, Bal | 1970 | 4,597 |
| Steve Carlton, Phi | 1972 | 5,086 | Vida Blue, Oak | 1971 | 4,594 |
| Phil Niekro, Atl | 1978 | 5,072 | Nolan Ryan, Cal | 1972 | 4,589 |
| Robin Roberts, PhiN | 1953 | 4,990 | Luis Tiant, Bos | 1974 | 4,586 |
| Bill Singer, Cal | 1973 | 4,978 | Bill Singer, LA | 1969 | 4,582 |
| Gaylord Perry, SF | 1969 | 4,888 | Don Drysdale, LA | 1964 | 4,582 |
| Sandy Koufax, LA | 1965 | 4,888 | Dave Goltz, Min | 1977 | 4,579 |
| Gaylord Perry, Cle | 1972 | 4,887 | Bob Feller, Cle | 1947 | 4,566 |
| Gaylord Perry, SF | 1970 | 4,859 | Jim Kaat, CWS | 1975 | 4,562 |
| Sam McDowell, Cle | 1970 | 4,842 | Robin Roberts, PhiN | 1952 | 4,562 |
| Bert Blyleven, Min | 1973 | 4,823 | Bob Gibson, StL | 1970 | 4,552 |
| Mickey Lolich, Det | 1972 | 4,822 | Gaylord Perry, Cle-Tex | 1975 | 4,551 |
| Nolan Ryan, Cal | 1976 | 4,811 | Steve Carlton, Phi | 1982 | 4,548 |
| Sandy Koufax, LA | 1966 | 4,773 | Mel Parnell, BosA | 1949 | 4,537 |
| Denny McLain, Det | 1968 | 4,763 | Bert Blyleven, Min-Tex | 1976 | 4,529 |
| Bill Stoneman, Mon | 1971 | 4,757 | Jim Bunning, Phi | 1966 | 4,529 |
| Vern Bickford, BosN | 1950 | 4,751 | Chris Short, Phi | 1965 | 4,521 |
| Bob Gibson, StL | 1969 | 4,733 | Fergie Jenkins, ChC | 1968 | 4,520 |
| Robin Roberts, PhiN | 1954 | 4,733 | Carl Morton, Mon | 1970 | 4,518 |
| Wilbur Wood, CWS | 1974 | 4,728 | Jim Palmer, Bal | 1976 | 4,517 |
| Wilbur Wood, CWS | 1971 | 4,724 | J.R. Richard, Hou | 1979 | 4,515 |
| Mickey Lolich, Det | 1973 | 4,719 | Steve Rogers, Mon | 1977 | 4,509 |
| Jim Palmer, Bal | 1977 | 4,715 | Steve Busby, KC | 1974 | 4,503 |
| Bob Friend, Pit | 1956 | 4,708 | Don Drysdale, LA | 1965 | 4,495 |
| Joe Coleman, Det | 1974 | 4,706 | Charlie Hough, Tex | 1987 | 4,492 |
| Fergie Jenkins, ChC | 1971 | 4,703 | Don Sutton, LA | 1969 | 4,490 |
| Fergie Jenkins, ChC | 1969 | 4,699 | Warren Spahn, BosN | 1949 | 4,486 |
| Andy Messersmith, LA | 1975 | 4,696 | Hal Newhouser, Det | 1949 | 4,486 |
| Steve Carlton, Phi | 1973 | 4,692 | Steve Carlton, Phi | 1983 | 4,484 |
| Warren Spahn, BosN | 1951 | 4,689 | Wilbur Wood, CWS | 1975 | 4,480 |
| Claude Osteen, LA | 1969 | 4,687 | Warren Spahn, BosN | 1950 | 4,478 |
| Bob Lemon, Cle | 1950 | 4,684 | Joe Coleman, Det | 1973 | 4,474 |
| Gaylord Perry, Cle | 1974 | 4,676 | J.R. Richard, Hou | 1978 | 4,467 |
| Steve Carlton, Phi | 1974 | 4,672 | Bob Lemon, Cle | 1952 | 4,466 |
| Mickey Lolich, Det | 1974 | 4,671 | Phil Niekro, Atl | 1974 | 4,458 |
| Denny McLain, Det | 1969 | 4,669 | Robin Roberts, PhiN | 1951 | 4,456 |
| Don Drysdale, LA | 1962 | 4,657 | Sandy Koufax, LA | 1963 | 4,455 |
| Juan Marichal, SF | 1968 | 4,655 | Jim Bunning, Phi | 1967 | 4,450 |
| Fergie Jenkins, Tex | 1974 | 4,654 | Bob Lemon, Cle | 1948 | 4,448 |
| Catfish Hunter, NYY | 1975 | 4,642 | Robin Roberts, PhiN | 1950 | 4,447 |
| Don Drysdale, LA | 1963 | 4,639 | Hal Newhouser, Det | 1946 | 4,439 |

## *Was Hampton the Best Combination Pitcher/Hitter of the DH Era? (p. 120)*

### Most Combined Pitching Wins Plus Batting Hits—1920-99
### (minimum 12 W)

| Pitcher, Team | Year | W | H | Tot | W-L | ERA | Avg | Slg |
|---|---|---|---|---|---|---|---|---|
| George Uhle, Cle | 1923 | 26 | 52 | 78 | 26-16 | 3.77 | .361 | .472 |
| Wes Ferrell, BosA | 1935 | 25 | 52 | 77 | 25-14 | 3.52 | .347 | .533 |
| Carl Mays, NYY | 1921 | 27 | 49 | 76 | 27-9 | 3.05 | .343 | .434 |
| Burleigh Grimes, Pit | 1928 | 25 | 42 | 67 | 25-14 | 2.99 | .321 | .397 |
| Bucky Walters, Cin | 1939 | 27 | 39 | 66 | 27-11 | 2.29 | .325 | .433 |
| Red Lucas, Cin | 1927 | 18 | 47 | 65 | 18-11 | 3.38 | .313 | .373 |
| Jim Bagby, Cle | 1920 | 31 | 33 | 64 | 31-12 | 2.89 | .252 | .374 |
| Dizzy Trout, Det | 1944 | 27 | 36 | 63 | 27-14 | 2.12 | .271 | .429 |
| Curt Davis, StLN | 1939 | 22 | 40 | 62 | 22-16 | 3.63 | .381 | .457 |
| Don Drysdale, LA | 1965 | 23 | 39 | 62 | 23-12 | 2.77 | .300 | .508 |
| Walter Johnson, Was | 1925 | 20 | 42 | 62 | 20-7 | 3.07 | .433 | .577 |
| Don Newcombe, Bro | 1955 | 20 | 42 | 62 | 20-5 | 3.20 | .359 | .632 |
| Wes Ferrell, Cle | 1930 | 25 | 35 | 60 | 25-13 | 3.31 | .297 | .415 |
| Bob Lemon, Cle | 1950 | 23 | 37 | 60 | 23-11 | 3.84 | .272 | .485 |
| Red Lucas, Cin | 1929 | 19 | 41 | 60 | 19-12 | 3.60 | .293 | .336 |
| Ted Lyons, CWS | 1930 | 22 | 38 | 60 | 22-15 | 3.78 | .311 | .434 |
| Joe Bush, NYY | 1924 | 17 | 42 | 59 | 17-16 | 3.57 | .339 | .484 |
| Dizzy Dean, StLN | 1934 | 30 | 29 | 59 | 30-7 | 2.66 | .246 | .339 |
| Wes Ferrell, Cle | 1931 | 22 | 37 | 59 | 22-12 | 3.75 | .319 | .621 |
| Burleigh Grimes, Bro | 1924 | 22 | 37 | 59 | 22-13 | 3.82 | .298 | .323 |
| Erv Brame, Pit | 1930 | 17 | 41 | 58 | 17-8 | 4.70 | .353 | .474 |
| Dizzy Dean, StLN | 1935 | 28 | 30 | 58 | 28-12 | 3.04 | .234 | .313 |
| Hal Newhouser, Det | 1944 | 29 | 29 | 58 | 29-9 | 2.22 | .242 | .275 |
| Johnny Sain, BosN | 1947 | 21 | 37 | 58 | 21-12 | 3.52 | .346 | .411 |
| Warren Spahn, Mil | 1958 | 22 | 36 | 58 | 22-11 | 3.07 | .333 | .463 |
| Joe Bush, NYY | 1922 | 26 | 31 | 57 | 26-7 | 3.31 | .326 | .432 |
| Burleigh Grimes, Bro | 1920 | 23 | 34 | 57 | 23-11 | 2.22 | .306 | .432 |
| Catfish Hunter, Oak | 1971 | 21 | 36 | 57 | 21-11 | 2.96 | .350 | .408 |
| Red Lucas, Cin | 1931 | 14 | 43 | 57 | 14-13 | 3.59 | .281 | .307 |
| Schoolboy Rowe, Det | 1934 | 24 | 33 | 57 | 24-8 | 3.45 | .303 | .450 |
| Red Ruffing, NYY | 1936 | 20 | 37 | 57 | 20-12 | 3.85 | .291 | .449 |
| George Uhle, Cle | 1926 | 27 | 30 | 57 | 27-11 | 2.83 | .227 | .273 |
| Wilbur Cooper, Pit | 1924 | 20 | 36 | 56 | 20-14 | 3.28 | .346 | .433 |
| Wes Ferrell, BosA | 1936 | 20 | 36 | 56 | 20-15 | 4.19 | .267 | .437 |
| Bob Gibson, StL | 1970 | 23 | 33 | 56 | 23-7 | 3.12 | .303 | .404 |
| Red Lucas, Cin | 1932 | 13 | 43 | 56 | 13-17 | 2.94 | .287 | .387 |
| Red Ruffing, NYY | 1932 | 18 | 38 | 56 | 18-7 | 3.09 | .306 | .444 |
| Red Ruffing, NYY | 1939 | 21 | 35 | 56 | 21-7 | 2.93 | .307 | .342 |
| Joe Bush, BosA | 1921 | 16 | 39 | 55 | 16-9 | 3.50 | .325 | .433 |
| Walter Johnson, Was | 1924 | 23 | 32 | 55 | 23-7 | 2.72 | .283 | .389 |
| Red Ruffing, BosA-NYY | 1930 | 15 | 40 | 55 | 15-8 | 4.38 | .364 | .582 |
| Pete Alexander, ChC | 1920 | 27 | 27 | 54 | 27-14 | 1.91 | .229 | .305 |
| Wes Ferrell, Cle | 1932 | 23 | 31 | 54 | 23-13 | 3.66 | .242 | .359 |
| Lefty Grove, PhiA | 1931 | 31 | 23 | 54 | 31-4 | 2.06 | .200 | .226 |
| Bob Lemon, Cle | 1948 | 20 | 34 | 54 | 20-14 | 2.82 | .286 | .487 |
| Johnny Marcum, PhiA | 1935 | 17 | 37 | 54 | 17-12 | 4.08 | .311 | .395 |
| Mel Parnell, BosA | 1949 | 25 | 29 | 54 | 25-7 | 2.77 | .254 | .281 |
| Dutch Ruether, Was | 1925 | 18 | 36 | 54 | 18-7 | 3.87 | .333 | .426 |
| Joe Shaute, Cle | 1924 | 20 | 34 | 54 | 20-17 | 3.75 | .318 | .430 |
| Urban Shocker, StLA | 1921 | 27 | 27 | 54 | 27-12 | 3.55 | .260 | .317 |

## Who Are Baseball's Best-Hitting Pitchers? (p. 123)

### Career Hitting Statistics—Active Pitchers, Listed Alphabetically
### (minimum 50 lifetime PA)

| Pitcher | Avg | AB | H | HR | RBI | Pitcher | Avg | AB | H | HR | RBI |
|---|---|---|---|---|---|---|---|---|---|---|---|
| Acevedo | .082 | 61 | 5 | 0 | 0 | Glavine | .200 | 831 | 166 | 1 | 62 |
| Aguilera | .201 | 139 | 28 | 3 | 11 | Gooden | .196 | 738 | 145 | 8 | 67 |
| Anderson B | .115 | 104 | 12 | 1 | 2 | Grace | .096 | 73 | 7 | 0 | 1 |
| Ashby | .136 | 396 | 54 | 0 | 15 | Hamilton | .117 | 300 | 35 | 4 | 20 |
| Astacio | .141 | 427 | 60 | 0 | 17 | Hampton | .221 | 299 | 66 | 0 | 23 |
| Avery | .172 | 436 | 75 | 4 | 32 | Harnisch | .120 | 459 | 55 | 1 | 21 |
| Aybar | .167 | 60 | 10 | 1 | 5 | Heredia G | .202 | 84 | 17 | 0 | 3 |
| Batista | .093 | 75 | 7 | 1 | 3 | Hermanson | .085 | 164 | 14 | 2 | 5 |
| Belcher | .124 | 388 | 48 | 2 | 25 | Hernandez L | .223 | 175 | 39 | 2 | 16 |
| Benes Al | .151 | 119 | 18 | 0 | 8 | Hershiser | .203 | 803 | 163 | 0 | 50 |
| Benes An | .144 | 625 | 90 | 6 | 43 | Hill | .148 | 330 | 49 | 1 | 21 |
| Benson | .154 | 65 | 10 | 0 | 7 | Hitchcock | .106 | 161 | 17 | 0 | 3 |
| Bergman | .107 | 131 | 14 | 3 | 11 | Holt | .080 | 113 | 9 | 0 | 3 |
| Blair | .070 | 143 | 10 | 0 | 5 | Isringhausen | .196 | 97 | 19 | 2 | 11 |
| Bohanon | .218 | 147 | 32 | 1 | 16 | Jimenez | .085 | 59 | 5 | 0 | 3 |
| Bottenfield | .169 | 160 | 27 | 0 | 10 | Johnson R | .112 | 152 | 17 | 0 | 8 |
| Brantley | .118 | 68 | 8 | 0 | 5 | Jones B | .143 | 308 | 44 | 1 | 14 |
| Brocail | .164 | 67 | 11 | 0 | 1 | Jones BM | .169 | 77 | 13 | 0 | 8 |
| Brock | .184 | 49 | 9 | 0 | 5 | Karl | .125 | 120 | 15 | 2 | 7 |
| Brown | .130 | 308 | 40 | 0 | 20 | Kile | .136 | 491 | 67 | 1 | 33 |
| Burba | .145 | 172 | 25 | 3 | 12 | Langston | .152 | 92 | 14 | 0 | 5 |
| Burkett | .089 | 429 | 38 | 0 | 14 | Leiter A | .103 | 232 | 24 | 0 | 11 |
| Byrd | .145 | 83 | 12 | 0 | 6 | Lieber | .131 | 260 | 34 | 0 | 14 |
| Candiotti | .117 | 299 | 35 | 0 | 12 | Lima | .108 | 157 | 17 | 0 | 6 |
| Charlton | .092 | 87 | 8 | 0 | 1 | Loaiza | .184 | 158 | 29 | 0 | 11 |
| Clark | .058 | 242 | 14 | 1 | 9 | Loewer | .140 | 57 | 8 | 0 | 2 |
| Clement | .074 | 54 | 4 | 0 | 1 | Maddux G | .178 | 990 | 176 | 4 | 52 |
| Cone | .153 | 404 | 62 | 0 | 22 | Maddux M | .067 | 90 | 6 | 0 | 4 |
| Cook | .266 | 109 | 29 | 2 | 9 | Martinez P | .098 | 255 | 25 | 0 | 11 |
| Cordova | .122 | 196 | 24 | 0 | 5 | Meadows | .135 | 104 | 14 | 0 | 4 |
| Cormier | .185 | 184 | 34 | 0 | 12 | Mercker | .115 | 244 | 28 | 1 | 18 |
| Daal | .168 | 131 | 22 | 0 | 6 | Millwood | .114 | 140 | 16 | 1 | 7 |
| Dempster | .081 | 62 | 5 | 0 | 2 | Mlicki | .118 | 152 | 18 | 0 | 5 |
| Dreifort | .213 | 122 | 26 | 2 | 12 | Morgan | .098 | 481 | 47 | 0 | 14 |
| Eldred | .102 | 59 | 6 | 0 | 4 | Moyer | .146 | 158 | 23 | 0 | 4 |
| Estes | .159 | 195 | 31 | 1 | 9 | Mulholland | .105 | 570 | 60 | 2 | 19 |
| Fassero | .077 | 222 | 17 | 0 | 5 | Navarro | .150 | 147 | 22 | 0 | 10 |
| Fernandez | .183 | 109 | 20 | 3 | 11 | Neagle | .149 | 382 | 57 | 3 | 31 |
| Gardner | .129 | 442 | 57 | 1 | 21 | Nomo | .152 | 316 | 48 | 1 | 19 |

*Baseball Scoreboard*

| Pitcher | Avg | AB | H | HR | RBI | Pitcher | Avg | AB | H | HR | RBI |
|---|---|---|---|---|---|---|---|---|---|---|---|
| Ogea | .087 | 46 | 4 | 0 | 0 | Silva | .074 | 54 | 4 | 0 | 3 |
| Olivares | .238 | 214 | 51 | 4 | 23 | Smoltz | .175 | 727 | 127 | 5 | 51 |
| Oliver | .231 | 104 | 24 | 0 | 9 | Springer D | .113 | 62 | 7 | 0 | 2 |
| Orosco | .169 | 59 | 10 | 0 | 4 | Stephenson | .092 | 65 | 6 | 0 | 1 |
| Ortiz R | .219 | 96 | 21 | 2 | 10 | Stottlemyre | .213 | 207 | 44 | 0 | 7 |
| Osborne | .164 | 256 | 42 | 1 | 19 | Swindell | .189 | 244 | 46 | 0 | 13 |
| Painter | .156 | 64 | 10 | 0 | 5 | Tapani | .116 | 155 | 18 | 1 | 16 |
| Park | .163 | 202 | 33 | 0 | 13 | Telemaco | .110 | 73 | 8 | 0 | 3 |
| Parris | .178 | 101 | 18 | 0 | 11 | Thompson M | .158 | 101 | 16 | 1 | 3 |
| Pavano | .113 | 71 | 8 | 0 | 5 | Thomson | .165 | 115 | 19 | 0 | 8 |
| Perez C | .174 | 207 | 36 | 4 | 12 | Thurman | .031 | 65 | 2 | 0 | 0 |
| Person | .116 | 69 | 8 | 0 | 1 | Tomko | .149 | 148 | 22 | 0 | 8 |
| Peters | .238 | 84 | 20 | 0 | 6 | Trachsel | .171 | 351 | 60 | 2 | 23 |
| Petkovsek | .163 | 86 | 14 | 0 | 3 | Urbina | .098 | 51 | 5 | 0 | 1 |
| Portugal | .198 | 450 | 89 | 2 | 36 | Valdes | .114 | 297 | 34 | 0 | 8 |
| Pulsipher | .127 | 79 | 10 | 0 | 4 | Vazquez | .223 | 94 | 21 | 0 | 10 |
| Quantrill | .098 | 61 | 6 | 0 | 0 | Villone | .067 | 45 | 3 | 0 | 0 |
| Rapp | .121 | 239 | 29 | 1 | 13 | Wakefield | .117 | 77 | 9 | 1 | 3 |
| Reed R | .172 | 204 | 35 | 2 | 18 | Wall | .179 | 67 | 12 | 0 | 1 |
| Rekar | .140 | 50 | 7 | 0 | 0 | Watson | .257 | 175 | 45 | 0 | 19 |
| Remlinger | .079 | 101 | 8 | 0 | 8 | Weathers | .109 | 129 | 14 | 2 | 4 |
| Reynolds | .153 | 379 | 58 | 3 | 31 | Wetteland | .167 | 42 | 7 | 1 | 8 |
| Reynoso | .158 | 279 | 44 | 3 | 11 | Williams B | .169 | 83 | 14 | 0 | 8 |
| Ritchie | .145 | 55 | 8 | 0 | 1 | Williams M | .160 | 106 | 17 | 0 | 7 |
| Rojas | .119 | 59 | 7 | 0 | 3 | Williams W | .198 | 81 | 16 | 0 | 6 |
| Rueter | .141 | 298 | 42 | 0 | 21 | Witt | .115 | 52 | 6 | 1 | 5 |
| Saberhagen | .121 | 190 | 23 | 0 | 1 | Woodall | .271 | 48 | 13 | 1 | 3 |
| Sanchez | .125 | 64 | 8 | 0 | 1 | Woodard | .136 | 103 | 14 | 0 | 4 |
| Sanders | .194 | 129 | 25 | 0 | 8 | Worrell | .116 | 69 | 8 | 0 | 4 |
| Schilling | .150 | 480 | 72 | 0 | 21 | Wright Jam | .135 | 163 | 22 | 1 | 9 |
| Schmidt | .089 | 214 | 19 | 0 | 8 | Yoshii | .117 | 103 | 12 | 0 | 5 |
| Schourek | .158 | 265 | 42 | 2 | 20 | **MLB Average** | **.147** | | | | |

## How Bad Were Bowie And Hawkins? (p. 125)

### Highest ERA—1900-99

| (minimum 1 IP per team G) | | | | | (minimum 50 IP) | | | | |
|---|---|---|---|---|---|---|---|---|---|
| Pitcher, Team | Year | IP | ER | ERA | Pitcher, Team | Year | IP | ER | ERA |
| Leo Sweetland, PhiN | 1930 | 167.0 | 143 | 7.71 | Micah Bowie, Atl-ChC | 1999 | 51.0 | 58 | 10.24 |
| Jim Deshaies, Min | 1994 | 130.1 | 107 | 7.39 | Steve Blass, Pit | 1973 | 88.2 | 97 | 9.85 |
| Jack Knott, StLA | 1936 | 192.2 | 156 | 7.29 | Andy Larkin, Fla | 1998 | 74.2 | 80 | 9.64 |
| LaTroy Hawkins, Min | 1999 | 174.1 | 129 | 6.66 | Frank Gabler, BosN-CWS | 1938 | 69.2 | 73 | 9.43 |
| Greg W. Harris, Col | 1994 | 130.0 | 96 | 6.65 | Reggie Grabowski, PhiN | 1934 | 65.1 | 67 | 9.23 |
| Chubby Dean, PhiA | 1940 | 159.1 | 117 | 6.61 | Todd Van Poppel, 2Tm | 1996 | 99.1 | 100 | 9.06 |
| Darryl Kile, Col | 1999 | 190.2 | 140 | 6.61 | Willis Hudlin, Cle | 1936 | 64.0 | 64 | 9.00 |
| Nels Potter, PhiA | 1939 | 196.1 | 144 | 6.60 | Bryan Rekar, Col | 1996 | 58.1 | 58 | 8.95 |
| Ernie Wingard, StLA | 1927 | 156.1 | 114 | 6.56 | Herman Besse, PhiA | 1940 | 53.0 | 52 | 8.83 |
| George Caster, PhiA | 1940 | 178.1 | 130 | 6.56 | Glenn Liebhardt, StLA | 1936 | 55.1 | 54 | 8.78 |
| Terry Mulholland, NYY | 1994 | 120.2 | 87 | 6.49 | Mark Clark, Tex | 1999 | 74.1 | 71 | 8.60 |
| Dave Fleming, Sea | 1994 | 117.0 | 84 | 6.46 | Ron Davis, Min-ChC | 1986 | 58.2 | 56 | 8.59 |
| Jimmy Ring, PhiN | 1928 | 173.0 | 123 | 6.40 | Jesse Jefferson, CWS | 1976 | 62.1 | 59 | 8.52 |
| Jaime Navarro, CWS | 1998 | 172.2 | 122 | 6.36 | Joe Coleman, PhiA | 1950 | 54.0 | 51 | 8.50 |
| Chief Hogsett, StLA | 1937 | 177.1 | 124 | 6.29 | Mike DeJean, Col | 1999 | 61.0 | 57 | 8.41 |
| Ray Benge, PhiN | 1929 | 199.0 | 139 | 6.29 | Bill Hubbell, PhiN | 1923 | 55.0 | 51 | 8.35 |
| Wes Ferrell, Was-NYY | 1938 | 179.0 | 125 | 6.28 | Jimmy Haynes, Bal | 1996 | 89.0 | 82 | 8.29 |
| Sam Gray, StLA | 1930 | 167.2 | 117 | 6.28 | Luther Roy, PhiN-Bro | 1929 | 92.1 | 85 | 8.29 |
| Jim Walkup, StLA | 1935 | 181.1 | 126 | 6.25 | Brad Havens, Min | 1983 | 80.1 | 73 | 8.18 |
| Pedro Astacio, Col | 1998 | 209.1 | 145 | 6.23 | Willie Adams, Oak | 1997 | 58.1 | 53 | 8.18 |
| Mike Oquist, Oak | 1998 | 175.0 | 121 | 6.22 | Ed Holley, PhiN-Pit | 1934 | 82.0 | 74 | 8.12 |
| Pat Caraway, CWS | 1931 | 220.0 | 152 | 6.22 | Benj Sampson, Min | 1999 | 71.0 | 64 | 8.11 |
| Scott Aldred, Det-Min | 1996 | 165.1 | 114 | 6.21 | Roy Mahaffey, StLA | 1936 | 60.0 | 54 | 8.10 |
| Brian Bohanon, Col | 1999 | 197.1 | 136 | 6.20 | John Thomson, Col | 1999 | 62.2 | 56 | 8.04 |
| Guy Bush, ChC | 1930 | 225.0 | 155 | 6.20 | Hank McDonald, 2Tm | 1933 | 70.2 | 63 | 8.02 |
| Todd Van Poppel, Oak | 1994 | 116.2 | 79 | 6.09 | Laurin Pepper, Pit | 1954 | 50.2 | 45 | 7.99 |
| Javier Vazquez, Mon | 1998 | 172.1 | 116 | 6.06 | Greg Harris, Bos-NYY | 1994 | 50.2 | 45 | 7.99 |
| Hub Pruett, PhiN | 1927 | 186.0 | 125 | 6.05 | Milt Shoffner, Cle | 1930 | 84.2 | 75 | 7.97 |
| Earl Caldwell, StLA | 1936 | 189.0 | 126 | 6.00 | Ken Cloude, Sea | 1999 | 72.1 | 64 | 7.96 |
| Buck Ross, PhiA | 1939 | 174.0 | 116 | 6.00 | Marsh Williams, PhiA | 1916 | 51.1 | 45 | 7.89 |
| Sloppy Thurston, CWS | 1925 | 183.0 | 121 | 5.95 | Cuddles Marshall, StLA | 1950 | 53.2 | 47 | 7.88 |
| Claude Willoughby, PhiN | 1926 | 168.0 | 111 | 5.95 | Garland Braxton, 2Tm | 1931 | 65.1 | 57 | 7.85 |
| Bill Sherdel, StLN | 1929 | 195.2 | 129 | 5.93 | Tony Kaufmann, 3Tm | 1927 | 72.1 | 63 | 7.84 |
| Bill Gullickson, Det | 1994 | 115.1 | 76 | 5.93 | Steve Trout, Sea | 1988 | 56.1 | 49 | 7.83 |
| Whitey Glazner, PhiN | 1924 | 156.2 | 103 | 5.92 | Connie Grob, Was | 1956 | 79.1 | 69 | 7.83 |
| Tim Belcher, Det | 1994 | 162.0 | 106 | 5.89 | Cal McLish, Bro | 1944 | 84.0 | 73 | 7.82 |
| Jack Lamabe, Bos | 1964 | 177.1 | 116 | 5.89 | Herm Holshouser, StLA | 1930 | 62.1 | 54 | 7.80 |
| Sid Hudson, Was | 1948 | 182.0 | 119 | 5.88 | Cal Eldred, Mil | 1999 | 82.0 | 71 | 7.79 |
| Dave Stewart, Tor | 1994 | 133.1 | 87 | 5.87 | Lefty Mills, StLA | 1940 | 59.0 | 51 | 7.78 |
| Camilo Pascual, Was | 1956 | 188.2 | 123 | 5.87 | Jay Hook, Cin | 1961 | 62.2 | 54 | 7.76 |
| Hank Wyse, PhiA | 1950 | 170.2 | 111 | 5.85 | Leo Sweetland, PhiN | 1930 | 167.0 | 143 | 7.71 |
| Jose Jimenez, StL | 1999 | 163.0 | 106 | 5.85 | Al Benton, PhiA | 1935 | 78.1 | 67 | 7.70 |
| Milt Gaston, CWS | 1934 | 194.0 | 126 | 5.85 | Mike Grace, Phi | 1999 | 55.0 | 47 | 7.69 |
| Bobby Witt, TB | 1999 | 180.1 | 117 | 5.84 | Roger Pavlik, Tex | 1994 | 50.1 | 43 | 7.69 |
| Buck Ross, PhiA | 1936 | 200.2 | 130 | 5.83 | Scott Aldred, Min | 1997 | 77.1 | 66 | 7.68 |
| Jack Kramer, StLA | 1939 | 211.2 | 137 | 5.83 | King Cole, ChC-Pit | 1912 | 68.0 | 58 | 7.68 |
| Early Wynn, Was | 1948 | 198.0 | 128 | 5.82 | Kevin Jarvis, Cin-Min-Det | 1997 | 68.0 | 58 | 7.68 |
| Jeff Juden, Mil-Ana | 1998 | 178.1 | 115 | 5.80 | Hal Elliott, PhiN | 1930 | 117.1 | 100 | 7.67 |
| Terry Mulholland, SF | 1995 | 149.0 | 96 | 5.80 | Chris Nabholz, Cle-Bos | 1994 | 53.0 | 45 | 7.64 |
| Vern Kennedy, Det-StLA | 1939 | 212.2 | 137 | 5.80 | Bunky Stewart, Was | 1954 | 50.2 | 43 | 7.64 |
| Jaime Navarro, CWS | 1997 | 209.2 | 135 | 5.79 | George Turbeville, PhiA | 1935 | 63.2 | 54 | 7.63 |
| Jim Bivin, PhiN | 1935 | 161.2 | 104 | 5.79 | Roxie Lawson, Cle | 1931 | 55.2 | 47 | 7.60 |
| Phil Huffman, Tor | 1979 | 173.0 | 111 | 5.77 | Claude Willoughby, PhiN | 1930 | 153.0 | 129 | 7.59 |
| General Crowder, 2Tm | 1934 | 167.1 | 107 | 5.75 | Edwin Correa, Tex | 1987 | 70.0 | 59 | 7.59 |
| Bill Dietrich, 3Tm | 1936 | 162.2 | 104 | 5.75 | Danny Jackson, StL-SD | 1997 | 67.2 | 57 | 7.58 |
| Rick Sutcliffe, Bal | 1993 | 166.0 | 106 | 5.75 | Dick Such, Was | 1970 | 50.0 | 42 | 7.56 |
| Gordon Rhodes, PhiA | 1936 | 216.1 | 138 | 5.74 | Les Tietje, StLA | 1938 | 62.0 | 52 | 7.55 |
| Doug Drabek, CWS | 1997 | 169.1 | 108 | 5.74 | Jeff Russell, Tex | 1985 | 62.0 | 52 | 7.55 |

## How Many Records Did Orosco Set in 1999? (p. 127)

### Fewest Innings Per Game—Season (minimum 40 G)

| Pitcher, Team | Year | G | IP | IP/G | Pitcher, Team | Year | G | IP | IP/G |
|---|---|---|---|---|---|---|---|---|---|
| Jesse Orosco, Bal | 1999 | 65 | 32.0 | .492 | Jesse Orosco, Mil | 1992 | 59 | 39.0 | .661 |
| Tony Fossas, Bos | 1992 | 60 | 29.2 | .494 | Eddie Guardado, Min | 1997 | 69 | 46.0 | .667 |
| John Candelaria, LA | 1992 | 50 | 25.1 | .507 | Jim Poole, Phi-Cle | 1999 | 54 | 36.1 | .673 |
| Larry Thomas, CWS | 1996 | 57 | 30.2 | .538 | Yorkis Perez, Fla | 1995 | 69 | 46.2 | .676 |
| Tony Fossas, 3Tm | 1998 | 41 | 22.2 | .553 | Paul Assenmacher, Cle | 1998 | 69 | 47.0 | .681 |
| Larry Casian, ChC | 1995 | 42 | 23.1 | .556 | Mike Munoz, Col | 1995 | 64 | 43.2 | .682 |
| Tony Fossas, Bos | 1993 | 71 | 40.0 | .563 | Dan Plesac, Tor | 1997 | 73 | 50.1 | .689 |
| John Candelaria, LA | 1991 | 59 | 33.2 | .571 | Bob Patterson, ChC | 1996 | 79 | 54.2 | .692 |
| Sean Runyan, Det | 1998 | 88 | 50.1 | .572 | Dan Plesac, Tor-Ari | 1999 | 64 | 44.1 | .693 |
| Mike Holtz, Ana | 1998 | 53 | 30.1 | .572 | Alan Embree, Atl | 1997 | 66 | 46.0 | .697 |
| Al Osuna, Hou | 1993 | 44 | 25.1 | .576 | Steve Frey, SF | 1994 | 44 | 31.0 | .705 |
| Mike Myers, Mil | 1999 | 71 | 41.1 | .582 | Jesse Orosco, Bal | 1997 | 71 | 50.1 | .709 |
| Rick Honeycutt, Tex | 1994 | 42 | 25.0 | .595 | Mike Munoz, Col | 1997 | 64 | 45.2 | .714 |
| Paul Assenmacher, Cle | 1999 | 55 | 33.0 | .600 | Mike Myers, Mil | 1998 | 70 | 50.0 | .714 |
| Buddy Groom, Oak | 1999 | 76 | 46.0 | .605 | Rick Honeycutt, Oak | 1992 | 54 | 39.0 | .722 |
| Mike Myers, Det | 1997 | 88 | 53.2 | .610 | Tony Fossas, StL | 1996 | 65 | 47.0 | .723 |
| Vic Darensbourg, Fla | 1999 | 56 | 34.2 | .619 | Pedro Borbon, LA | 1999 | 70 | 50.2 | .724 |
| Vince Horsman, Oak | 1993 | 40 | 25.0 | .625 | Alvin Morman, Cle-SF | 1998 | 40 | 29.0 | .725 |
| Tony Fossas, StL | 1995 | 58 | 36.2 | .632 | Bob McClure, Cal-StL | 1991 | 45 | 32.2 | .726 |
| Joe Klink, Fla | 1993 | 59 | 37.2 | .638 | Tony Fossas, StL | 1997 | 71 | 51.2 | .728 |
| Dan Plesac, Tor | 1998 | 78 | 50.0 | .641 | Lance Painter, StL | 1998 | 65 | 47.1 | .728 |
| Scott Radinsky, StL | 1999 | 43 | 27.2 | .643 | Mike Munoz, Det | 1992 | 65 | 48.0 | .738 |
| Scott Aldred, TB | 1998 | 48 | 31.1 | .653 | Paul Assenmacher, Cle | 1996 | 63 | 46.2 | .741 |
| Paul Assenmacher, Cle | 1997 | 75 | 49.0 | .653 | Yorkis Perez, Fla | 1996 | 64 | 47.2 | .745 |
| Mike Holtz, Ana | 1997 | 66 | 43.1 | .657 | Vince Horsman, Oak | 1992 | 58 | 43.1 | .747 |

### Most Middle Relief Appearances—Career

| Pitcher | Relief G | GF | Middle Relief | Pitcher | Relief G | GF | Middle Relief |
|---|---|---|---|---|---|---|---|
| Jesse Orosco | 1,086 | 473 | 613 | Darold Knowles | 757 | 417 | 340 |
| Paul Assenmacher | 883 | 275 | 608 | Greg Harris | 605 | 266 | 339 |
| Mike Jackson | 828 | 377 | 451 | Mike Munoz | 446 | 107 | 339 |
| Eric Plunk | 673 | 234 | 439 | Lindy McDaniel | 913 | 577 | 336 |
| Larry Andersen | 698 | 267 | 431 | Clay Carroll | 703 | 373 | 330 |
| Dan Plesac | 808 | 386 | 422 | Mark Eichhorn | 556 | 226 | 330 |
| Tony Fossas | 567 | 149 | 418 | Jim Poole | 408 | 85 | 323 |
| Rob Murphy | 597 | 181 | 416 | Buddy Groom | 394 | 74 | 320 |
| Kent Tekulve | 1,050 | 638 | 412 | Jeff Nelson | 461 | 141 | 320 |
| Rick Honeycutt | 529 | 118 | 411 | Grant Jackson | 609 | 291 | 318 |
| Chuck McElroy | 562 | 163 | 399 | Willie Hernandez | 733 | 419 | 314 |
| Mike Stanton | 610 | 214 | 396 | Gene Garber | 922 | 609 | 313 |
| Bob McClure | 625 | 233 | 392 | Pedro Borbon | 589 | 278 | 311 |
| Scott Radinsky | 554 | 180 | 374 | Bob Miller | 595 | 290 | 305 |
| Steve Reed | 480 | 106 | 374 | Dennis Lamp | 476 | 173 | 303 |
| Tom Burgmeier | 742 | 370 | 372 | Greg Cadaret | 416 | 120 | 296 |
| Hoyt Wilhelm | 1,018 | 651 | 367 | Frank DiPino | 508 | 216 | 292 |
| Don McMahon | 872 | 506 | 366 | Roger McDowell | 721 | 430 | 291 |
| Craig Lefferts | 651 | 286 | 365 | Bob Locker | 576 | 288 | 288 |
| Paul Lindblad | 623 | 258 | 365 | Greg Minton | 703 | 415 | 288 |
| Rich Rodriguez | 483 | 119 | 364 | Xavier Hernandez | 456 | 169 | 287 |
| Bob Patterson | 538 | 175 | 363 | Jeff Parrett | 480 | 195 | 285 |
| Dennis Cook | 427 | 82 | 345 | Goose Gossage | 965 | 681 | 284 |
| Juan Agosto | 541 | 198 | 343 | Stan Belinda | 529 | 246 | 283 |
| Gary Lavelle | 742 | 399 | 343 | Tony Castillo | 397 | 114 | 283 |
| Mark Guthrie | 459 | 119 | 340 | Eddie Fisher | 627 | 344 | 283 |

## Which Pitchers Mop up the Most? (p. 129)

### Most Appearances With Team Trailing by Four-Plus Runs—1999

| Pitcher, Team | Mop | Pitcher, Team | Mop | Pitcher, Team | Mop |
| --- | --- | --- | --- | --- | --- |
| Dan Serafini, ChC | 21 | Mike DeJean, Col | 14 | Archie Corbin, Fla | 11 |
| Sean Lowe, CWS | 20 | S Hasegawa, Ana | 14 | Alan Embree, SF | 11 |
| Rodney Myers, ChC | 19 | Mike Magnante, Ana | 14 | Bryce Florie, Det-Bos | 11 |
| Onan Masaoka, LA | 18 | Chuck McElroy, 2Tm | 14 | Mike Grace, Phi | 11 |
| Mike Myers, Mil | 18 | Mike Trombley, Min | 14 | Todd Jones, Det | 11 |
| Carlos Reyes, SD | 18 | Matt Whisenant, KC-SD | 14 | Steve Kline, Mon | 11 |
| Benj Sampson, Min | 18 | Rigo Beltran, NYM-Col | 13 | Pat Mahomes, NYM | 11 |
| Rick White, TB | 18 | Willie Blair, Det | 13 | Mike Mohler, StL | 11 |
| Masao Kida, Det | 17 | Ken Cloude, Sea | 13 | Alvin Morman, KC | 11 |
| Curtis Leskanic, Col | 17 | Tom Davey, Tor-Sea | 13 | Scott Sanders, ChC | 11 |
| Al Levine, Ana | 17 | Brian Edmondson, Fla | 13 | Scott Schoeneweis, Ana | 11 |
| Danny Patterson, Tex | 17 | Wayne Gomes, Phi | 13 | Makoto Suzuki, Sea-KC | 11 |
| Brad Rigby, Oak-KC | 17 | Guillermo Mota, Mon | 13 | Gabe White, Cin | 11 |
| Felix Rodriguez, SF | 17 | Mike Porzio, Col | 13 | Rod Beck, ChC-Bos | 10 |
| Paul Spoljaric, Phi-Tor | 17 | Steve Schrenk, Phi | 13 | Ricky Bones, Bal | 10 |
| Amaury Telemaco, 2Tm | 17 | Bill Simas, CWS | 13 | Carlos Castillo, CWS | 10 |
| Scott Aldred, TB-Phi | 16 | J.D. Smart, Mon | 13 | John Frascatore, Ari-Tor | 10 |
| Mike Duvall, TB | 16 | Paul Assenmacher, Cle | 12 | Mike Holtz, Ana | 10 |
| Braden Looper, Fla | 16 | Scott Eyre, CWS | 12 | Joe Mays, Min | 10 |
| Mike Maddux, Mon-LA | 16 | Felix Heredia, ChC | 12 | C.J. Nitkowski, Det | 10 |
| Dan Naulty, NYY | 16 | Doug Jones, Oak | 12 | Dan Perkins, Min | 10 |
| Scott Sauerbeck, Pit | 16 | David Lee, Col | 12 | Jim Poole, Phi-Cle | 10 |
| Bob Wells, Min | 16 | Dan Miceli, SD | 12 | Roberto Ramirez, Col | 10 |
| Carlos Almanzar, SD | 15 | Julian Tavarez, SF | 12 | Dennys Reyes, Cin | 10 |
| Bobby Ayala, Mon-ChC | 15 | Dave Wainhouse, Col | 12 | Rafael Roque, Mil | 10 |
| Mark Guthrie, Bos-ChC | 15 | Bryan Ward, CWS | 12 | Mike Venafro, Tex | 10 |
| Rich Rodriguez, SF | 15 | Brian Williams, Hou | 12 | John Wasdin, Bos | 10 |
| Jerry Spradlin, Cle-SF | 15 | Rick Aguilera, Min-ChC | 11 | | |
| Anthony Telford, Mon | 15 | Hector Carrasco, Min | 11 | | |
| Tim Worrell, Oak | 15 | Brad Clontz, Pit | 11 | | |

### Most Appearances With Team Trailing by Four-Plus Runs—1987-99

| Pitcher | Mop | Pitcher | Mop | Pitcher | Mop |
| --- | --- | --- | --- | --- | --- |
| Tony Fossas | 109 | Carlos Reyes | 74 | Bob Patterson | 62 |
| Rich Rodriguez | 104 | Heathcliff Slocumb | 74 | Jeff Shaw | 62 |
| Mike Munoz | 103 | Darren Holmes | 73 | Jim Acker | 61 |
| Chuck McElroy | 99 | Dwayne Henry | 72 | Curtis Leskanic | 61 |
| Eric Plunk | 99 | Jose Bautista | 71 | Rich Monteleone | 61 |
| Joe Boever | 98 | Mike Fetters | 71 | Rick Aguilera | 60 |
| Paul Assenmacher | 94 | Donn Pall | 71 | Mark Guthrie | 60 |
| Jesse Orosco | 93 | Buddy Groom | 70 | Mike Magnante | 60 |
| Mark Eichhorn | 91 | Ken Patterson | 70 | Mark Williamson | 60 |
| Mike Maddux | 91 | Scott Bailes | 69 | Les Lancaster | 59 |
| Dan Plesac | 91 | Mitch Williams | 69 | Scott Radinsky | 59 |
| Doug Jones | 90 | Hector Carrasco | 65 | Steve Reed | 59 |
| Greg Cadaret | 87 | Steve Frey | 65 | Eric Gunderson | 58 |
| Rob Murphy | 81 | John Habyan | 65 | Dave Veres | 58 |
| Xavier Hernandez | 80 | Gary Wayne | 65 | Eddie Guardado | 57 |
| Juan Agosto | 79 | Terry Leach | 64 | Jeff Innis | 57 |
| Jeff Parrett | 79 | Dennis Cook | 62 | Alan Mills | 57 |
| Paul Gibson | 76 | Jim Corsi | 62 | Terry Mathews | 56 |
| Greg Harris | 76 | Chuck Crim | 62 | Turk Wendell | 56 |
| Willie Blair | 75 | Jeff Montgomery | 62 | Lee Guetterman | 55 |
| Jim Poole | 75 | Mike Myers | 62 | Brian Holton | 55 |
| Mike Jackson | 74 | Gregg Olson | 62 | Matt Whiteside | 55 |

# Who's Toughest to Pull? (p. 131)

## Pitcher Pull Percentages—Listed Alphabetically
## (minimum 400 batters faced in 1999)

| Pitcher, Team | T | Hit | Pull | Pct | Pitcher, Team | T | Hit | Pull | Pct |
|---|---|---|---|---|---|---|---|---|---|
| Acevedo, StL | R | 338 | 126 | 37.3 | Finley, Ana | L | 589 | 194 | 32.9 |
| Alvarez W, TB | L | 473 | 175 | 37.0 | Foulke, CWS | R | 248 | 90 | 36.3 |
| Anderson B, Ari | L | 426 | 139 | 32.6 | Garcia F, Sea | R | 603 | 210 | 34.8 |
| Appier, KC-Oak | R | 675 | 285 | 42.2 | Gardner, SF | R | 441 | 150 | 34.0 |
| Arrojo, TB | R | 438 | 157 | 35.8 | Glavine, Atl | L | 763 | 177 | 23.2 |
| Ashby, SD | R | 650 | 278 | 42.8 | Gooden, Cle | R | 358 | 128 | 35.8 |
| Astacio, Col | R | 689 | 245 | 35.6 | Graves, Cin | R | 326 | 118 | 36.2 |
| Avery, Cin | L | 285 | 131 | 46.0 | Guzman J, Bal-Cin | R | 595 | 256 | 43.0 |
| Aybar, StL | R | 302 | 119 | 39.4 | Halama, Sea | L | 569 | 218 | 38.3 |
| Baldwin, CWS | R | 654 | 236 | 36.1 | Halladay, Tor | R | 499 | 147 | 29.5 |
| Batista, Mon | R | 434 | 142 | 32.7 | Hamilton, Tor | R | 338 | 115 | 34.0 |
| Belcher, Ana | R | 479 | 192 | 40.1 | Hampton, Hou | L | 678 | 270 | 39.8 |
| Benes A, Ari | R | 634 | 272 | 42.9 | Harnisch, Cin | R | 620 | 243 | 39.2 |
| Benson, Pit | R | 596 | 213 | 35.7 | Hawkins, Min | R | 627 | 189 | 30.1 |
| Bergman, Hou-Atl | R | 370 | 143 | 38.6 | Haynes, Oak | R | 462 | 150 | 32.5 |
| Blair, Det | R | 464 | 181 | 39.0 | Helling, Tex | R | 689 | 249 | 36.1 |
| Boehringer, SD | R | 301 | 98 | 32.6 | Hentgen, Tor | R | 661 | 224 | 33.9 |
| Bohanon, Col | L | 647 | 261 | 40.3 | Heredia G, Oak | R | 684 | 302 | 44.2 |
| Bottenfield, StL | R | 600 | 227 | 37.8 | Hermanson, Mon | R | 686 | 245 | 35.7 |
| Brock, SF | R | 341 | 132 | 38.7 | Hernandez L, Fla-SF | R | 639 | 224 | 35.1 |
| Brown, LA | R | 707 | 266 | 37.6 | Hernandez O, NYY | R | 628 | 231 | 36.8 |
| Burba, Cle | R | 637 | 240 | 37.7 | Hershiser, NYM | R | 582 | 244 | 41.9 |
| Burkett, Tex | R | 489 | 219 | 44.8 | Hill, Ana | R | 400 | 132 | 33.0 |
| Byrd, Phi | R | 653 | 287 | 44.0 | Hitchcock, SD | L | 595 | 214 | 36.0 |
| Carpenter, Tor | R | 491 | 153 | 31.2 | Holt, Hou | R | 519 | 193 | 37.2 |
| Clemens, NYY | R | 542 | 202 | 37.3 | Hudson, Oak | R | 368 | 158 | 42.9 |
| Clement, SD | R | 553 | 255 | 46.1 | Irabu, NYY | R | 538 | 195 | 36.2 |
| Colon, Cle | R | 592 | 206 | 34.8 | Jimenez, StL | R | 517 | 248 | 48.0 |
| Cone, NYY | R | 526 | 212 | 40.3 | Johnson J, Bal | R | 368 | 120 | 32.6 |
| Cordova, Pit | R | 505 | 206 | 40.8 | Johnson R, Ari | L | 624 | 217 | 34.8 |
| Daal, Ari | L | 641 | 263 | 41.0 | Jones B, Col | L | 374 | 164 | 43.9 |
| Dempster, Fla | R | 432 | 154 | 35.6 | Jones D, Oak | R | 328 | 129 | 39.3 |
| Dreifort, LA | R | 534 | 185 | 34.6 | Karl, Mil | L | 695 | 255 | 36.7 |
| Edmondson, Fla | R | 309 | 115 | 37.2 | Kile, Col | R | 629 | 227 | 36.1 |
| Elarton, Hou | R | 338 | 123 | 36.4 | Leiter A, NYM | L | 629 | 311 | 49.4 |
| Erickson, Bal | R | 759 | 289 | 38.1 | Lieber, ChC | R | 612 | 225 | 36.8 |
| Escobar, Tor | R | 561 | 219 | 39.0 | Lima, Hou | R | 769 | 358 | 46.6 |
| Estes, SF | L | 618 | 233 | 37.7 | Loaiza, Tex | R | 383 | 130 | 33.9 |
| Farnsworth, ChC | R | 436 | 158 | 36.2 | Lowe D, Bos | R | 322 | 137 | 42.5 |
| Fassero, Sea-Tex | L | 542 | 202 | 37.3 | Lowe S, CWS | R | 284 | 110 | 38.7 |
| Fernandez, Fla | R | 442 | 137 | 31.0 | Maddux G, Atl | R | 738 | 242 | 32.8 |

| Pitcher, Team | T | Hit | Pull | Pct | Pitcher, Team | T | Hit | Pull | Pct |
|---|---|---|---|---|---|---|---|---|---|
| Martinez P, Bos | R | 460 | 184 | 40.0 | Rose, Bos | R | 326 | 128 | 39.3 |
| Mays, Min | R | 548 | 223 | 40.7 | Rueter, SF | L | 623 | 237 | 38.0 |
| Meadows, Fla | R | 631 | 240 | 38.0 | Rupe, TB | R | 436 | 162 | 37.2 |
| Mendoza, NYY | R | 410 | 176 | 42.9 | Saberhagen, Bos | R | 372 | 141 | 37.9 |
| Mercker, StL-Bos | L | 423 | 153 | 36.2 | Sanders, ChC | R | 309 | 106 | 34.3 |
| Millwood, Atl | R | 606 | 194 | 32.0 | Schilling, Phi | R | 516 | 172 | 33.3 |
| Milton, Min | L | 603 | 222 | 36.8 | Schmidt, Pit | R | 679 | 229 | 33.7 |
| Mlicki, LA-Det | R | 654 | 260 | 39.8 | Schourek, Pit | L | 351 | 151 | 43.0 |
| Moehler, Det | R | 662 | 240 | 36.3 | Sele, Tex | R | 646 | 257 | 39.8 |
| Morgan, Tex | R | 505 | 194 | 38.4 | Silva, Pit | R | 303 | 104 | 34.3 |
| Moyer, Sea | L | 712 | 305 | 42.8 | Sirotka, CWS | L | 701 | 285 | 40.7 |
| Mulholland, ChC-Atl | L | 583 | 244 | 41.9 | Smith, Mon | R | 279 | 107 | 38.4 |
| Mussina, Bal | R | 593 | 194 | 32.7 | Smoltz, Atl | R | 521 | 191 | 36.7 |
| Nagy, Cle | R | 679 | 310 | 45.7 | Snyder, CWS | R | 467 | 191 | 40.9 |
| Navarro, CWS | R | 574 | 195 | 34.0 | Sparks S, Ana | R | 508 | 202 | 39.8 |
| Neagle, Cin | L | 339 | 141 | 41.6 | Springer D, Fla | R | 676 | 257 | 38.0 |
| Nomo, Mil | R | 505 | 212 | 42.0 | Stottlemyre, Ari | R | 316 | 112 | 35.4 |
| Nunez, Ari-Fla | R | 299 | 115 | 38.5 | Sullivan, Cin | R | 323 | 113 | 35.0 |
| Ogea, Phi | R | 576 | 259 | 45.0 | Suppan, KC | R | 699 | 288 | 41.2 |
| Olivares, Ana-Oak | R | 698 | 278 | 39.8 | Suzuki, Sea-KC | R | 364 | 153 | 42.0 |
| Oliver, StL | L | 607 | 208 | 34.3 | Tapani, ChC | R | 465 | 171 | 36.8 |
| Oquist, Oak | R | 461 | 167 | 36.2 | Telford, Mon | R | 311 | 88 | 28.3 |
| Ortiz R, SF | R | 603 | 216 | 35.8 | Thompson J, Det | L | 470 | 152 | 32.3 |
| Park, LA | R | 572 | 189 | 33.0 | Thurman, Mon | R | 464 | 190 | 40.9 |
| Parque, CWS | L | 590 | 220 | 37.3 | Tomko, Cin | R | 520 | 203 | 39.0 |
| Parris, Cin | R | 381 | 142 | 37.3 | Trachsel, ChC | R | 658 | 255 | 38.8 |
| Pavano, Mon | R | 336 | 129 | 38.4 | Valdes, LA | R | 635 | 222 | 35.0 |
| Perez C, LA | L | 318 | 136 | 42.8 | Vazquez, Mon | R | 480 | 176 | 36.7 |
| Perez O, Atl | L | 280 | 100 | 35.7 | Villone, Cin | L | 414 | 151 | 36.5 |
| Perkins, Min | R | 315 | 131 | 41.6 | Wakefield, Bos | R | 433 | 211 | 48.7 |
| Person, Tor-Phi | R | 408 | 152 | 37.3 | Weathers, Mil | R | 286 | 76 | 26.6 |
| Pettitte, NYY | L | 619 | 241 | 38.9 | Weaver J, Det | R | 507 | 203 | 40.0 |
| Ponson, Bal | R | 691 | 239 | 34.6 | Wells D, Tor | L | 727 | 252 | 34.7 |
| Portugal, Bos | R | 523 | 218 | 41.7 | White R, TB | R | 353 | 122 | 34.6 |
| Powell J, Mon | R | 325 | 130 | 40.0 | Williams W, SD | R | 645 | 273 | 42.3 |
| Radke, Min | R | 725 | 277 | 38.2 | Witasick, KC | R | 522 | 186 | 35.6 |
| Rapp, Bos | R | 454 | 175 | 38.5 | Witt, TB | R | 577 | 190 | 32.9 |
| Reed R, NYM | R | 465 | 157 | 33.8 | Wolf, Phi | L | 348 | 115 | 33.0 |
| Rekar, TB | R | 324 | 119 | 36.7 | Woodard, Mil | R | 621 | 285 | 45.9 |
| Reynolds, Hou | R | 705 | 294 | 41.7 | Wright J, Col | R | 306 | 113 | 36.9 |
| Reynoso, Ari | R | 561 | 224 | 39.9 | Wright J, Cle | R | 420 | 152 | 36.2 |
| Ritchie, Pit | R | 537 | 214 | 39.9 | Yoshii, NYM | R | 536 | 200 | 37.3 |
| Rogers, Oak-NYM | L | 621 | 250 | 40.3 | **MLB Totals** | | | | **37.7** |
| Rosado, KC | L | 640 | 242 | 37.8 | | | | | |

## Which Pitchers Scored the Highest? (p. 133)

### Highest Game Scores—1999

| Pitcher, Team | Date | Opp | W/L | IP | H | R | ER | BB | SO | Score |
|---|---|---|---|---|---|---|---|---|---|---|
| Martinez P, Bos | 9/10 | @NYY | W | 9.0 | 1 | 1 | 1 | 0 | 17 | 98 |
| Milton, Min | 9/11 | Ana | W | 9.0 | 0 | 0 | 0 | 2 | 13 | 98 |
| Cone, NYY | 7/18 | Mon | W | 9.0 | 0 | 0 | 0 | 0 | 10 | 97 |
| Millwood, Atl | 8/28 | @StL | ND | 10.0 | 2 | 0 | 0 | 1 | 9 | 96 |
| Vazquez, Mon | 9/14 | @LA | W | 9.0 | 1 | 0 | 0 | 1 | 10 | 94 |
| Rupe, TB | 5/23 | Ana | ND | 9.0 | 1 | 0 | 0 | 0 | 8 | 93 |
| Jimenez, StL | 6/25 | @Ari | W | 9.0 | 0 | 0 | 0 | 2 | 8 | 93 |
| Reed R, NYM | 10/2 | Pit | W | 9.0 | 3 | 0 | 0 | 0 | 12 | 93 |
| Martinez P, Bos | 6/4 | Atl | W | 9.0 | 3 | 1 | 1 | 2 | 16 | 91 |
| Jimenez, StL | 7/5 | Ari | W | 9.0 | 2 | 0 | 0 | 1 | 9 | 91 |
| Martinez P, Bos | 9/21 | Tor | W | 9.0 | 3 | 0 | 0 | 2 | 12 | 91 |
| Harnisch, Cin | 8/19 | Pit | W | 8.0 | 1 | 0 | 0 | 2 | 12 | 90 |
| Martinez P, Bos | 9/4 | @Sea | W | 8.0 | 2 | 0 | 0 | 3 | 15 | 90 |
| Brown, LA | 9/4 | @ChC | W | 9.0 | 2 | 0 | 0 | 1 | 8 | 90 |
| Smoltz, Atl | 4/30 | Cin | W | 9.0 | 1 | 0 | 0 | 1 | 5 | 89 |
| Wells D, Tor | 7/11 | @Mon | W | 9.0 | 2 | 0 | 0 | 1 | 7 | 89 |
| Astacio, Col | 8/10 | @Mil | ND | 9.0 | 2 | 1 | 0 | 1 | 9 | 89 |
| Oliver, StL | 8/3 | SD | W | 9.0 | 4 | 0 | 0 | 2 | 11 | 88 |
| Lieber, ChC | 9/25 | Pit | W | 9.0 | 3 | 1 | 1 | 0 | 11 | 88 |
| Schilling, Phi | 5/29 | Col | W | 9.0 | 4 | 0 | 0 | 1 | 9 | 87 |
| Milton, Min | 7/31 | @Ana | W | 9.0 | 3 | 0 | 0 | 1 | 7 | 87 |
| Rogers, NYM | 9/6 | SF | W | 9.0 | 4 | 0 | 0 | 1 | 9 | 87 |
| Johnson R, Ari | 5/25 | SD | W | 9.0 | 6 | 0 | 0 | 1 | 12 | 86 |
| Witt, TB | 6/27 | Tor | W | 9.0 | 3 | 0 | 0 | 3 | 8 | 86 |
| Anderson B, Ari | 8/17 | ChC | W | 9.0 | 3 | 0 | 0 | 0 | 5 | 86 |
| Martinez P, Bos | 8/24 | @Min | W | 8.0 | 4 | 1 | 0 | 1 | 15 | 86 |
| Garcia F, Sea | 8/24 | Det | W | 9.0 | 6 | 0 | 0 | 1 | 12 | 86 |
| Leiter A, NYM | 10/4 | @Cin | W | 9.0 | 2 | 0 | 0 | 4 | 7 | 86 |
| Schilling, Phi | 4/27 | Cin | ND | 9.0 | 5 | 0 | 0 | 1 | 9 | 85 |
| Martinez P, Bos | 5/7 | Ana | W | 8.0 | 6 | 0 | 0 | 0 | 15 | 85 |
| Finley, Ana | 5/12 | @NYY | W | 8.0 | 3 | 0 | 0 | 2 | 11 | 85 |
| Johnson R, Ari | 6/25 | StL | L | 9.0 | 5 | 1 | 1 | 2 | 14 | 85 |
| Villone, Cin | 6/30 | Ari | W | 8.0 | 1 | 0 | 0 | 2 | 7 | 85 |
| Mays, Min | 7/17 | @ChC | W | 9.0 | 3 | 0 | 0 | 3 | 7 | 85 |
| Hampton, Hou | 7/18 | Cle | W | 9.0 | 4 | 0 | 0 | 2 | 8 | 85 |
| Sele, Tex | 8/7 | Tor | W | 9.0 | 6 | 0 | 0 | 0 | 10 | 85 |
| Bohanon, Col | 8/28 | Phi | W | 9.0 | 4 | 0 | 0 | 4 | 10 | 85 |
| Estes, SF | 9/14 | Fla | W | 9.0 | 4 | 0 | 0 | 2 | 8 | 85 |
| Carpenter, Tor | 4/15 | TB | W | 9.0 | 2 | 1 | 1 | 0 | 5 | 84 |
| Thompson J, Det | 4/22 | Bos | W | 8.0 | 2 | 0 | 0 | 1 | 7 | 84 |
| Hampton, Hou | 5/10 | Pit | W | 9.0 | 5 | 0 | 0 | 0 | 7 | 84 |
| Finley, Ana | 5/23 | @TB | W | 9.0 | 3 | 0 | 0 | 4 | 7 | 84 |
| Pavano, Mon | 6/13 | TB | W | 9.0 | 3 | 0 | 0 | 3 | 6 | 84 |
| Hudson, Oak | 7/10 | @Ari | W | 8.1 | 3 | 0 | 0 | 2 | 9 | 84 |
| Lorraine, ChC | 8/6 | Hou | W | 9.0 | 3 | 0 | 0 | 1 | 4 | 84 |
| Garcia F, Sea | 8/7 | NYY | L | 9.0 | 3 | 1 | 1 | 3 | 10 | 84 |
| Abbott P, Sea | 8/23 | Cle | W | 8.0 | 3 | 0 | 0 | 4 | 12 | 84 |
| Oliver, StL | 8/28 | Atl | ND | 9.0 | 4 | 0 | 0 | 1 | 6 | 84 |
| Maddux G, Atl | 9/6 | StL | W | 9.0 | 3 | 1 | 1 | 0 | 7 | 84 |

## Who Are the High-Quality Starters? (p. 135)

### Quality Start Percentage—Listed Alphabetically (minimum 15 GS in 1999)

| Pitcher, Team | GS | QS | Pct |
|---|---|---|---|
| Abbott J, Mil | 15 | 4 | 26.7 |
| Alvarez W, TB | 28 | 15 | 53.6 |
| Anderson B, Ari | 19 | 8 | 42.1 |
| Appier, KC-Oak | 34 | 18 | 52.9 |
| Arrojo, TB | 24 | 10 | 41.7 |
| Ashby, SD | 31 | 17 | 54.8 |
| Astacio, Col | 34 | 18 | 52.9 |
| Avery, Cin | 19 | 8 | 42.1 |
| Baldwin, CWS | 33 | 16 | 48.5 |
| Batista, Mon | 17 | 9 | 52.9 |
| Belcher, Ana | 24 | 9 | 37.5 |
| Benes A, Ari | 32 | 16 | 50.0 |
| Benson, Pit | 31 | 16 | 51.6 |
| Bergman, Hou-Atl | 16 | 9 | 56.3 |
| Blair, Det | 16 | 3 | 18.8 |
| Bohanon, Col | 33 | 12 | 36.4 |
| Bottenfield, StL | 31 | 16 | 51.6 |
| Brock, SF | 19 | 9 | 47.4 |
| Brown, LA | 35 | 25 | 71.4 |
| Burba, Cle | 34 | 19 | 55.9 |
| Burkett, Tex | 25 | 9 | 36.0 |
| Byrd, Phi | 32 | 19 | 59.4 |
| Carpenter, Tor | 24 | 14 | 58.3 |
| Clark, Tex | 15 | 3 | 20.0 |
| Clemens, NYY | 30 | 16 | 53.3 |
| Clement, SD | 31 | 16 | 51.6 |
| Colon, Cle | 32 | 19 | 59.4 |
| Cone, NYY | 31 | 18 | 58.1 |
| Cordova, Pit | 27 | 13 | 48.1 |
| Daal, Ari | 32 | 21 | 65.6 |
| Dempster, Fla | 25 | 12 | 48.0 |
| Dreifort, LA | 29 | 11 | 37.9 |
| Eiland, TB | 15 | 6 | 40.0 |
| Elarton, Hou | 15 | 8 | 53.3 |
| Eldred, Mil | 15 | 5 | 33.3 |
| Erickson, Bal | 34 | 16 | 47.1 |
| Escobar, Tor | 30 | 9 | 30.0 |
| Estes, SF | 32 | 14 | 43.8 |
| Farnsworth, ChC | 21 | 7 | 33.3 |
| Fassero, Sea-Tex | 27 | 9 | 33.3 |
| Fernandez, Fla | 24 | 10 | 41.7 |
| Finley, Ana | 33 | 18 | 54.5 |
| Garcia F, Sea | 33 | 16 | 48.5 |
| Gardner, SF | 21 | 5 | 23.8 |
| Glavine, Atl | 35 | 19 | 54.3 |
| Gooden, Cle | 22 | 5 | 22.7 |
| Guzman J, Bal-Cin | 33 | 20 | 60.6 |
| Halama, Sea | 24 | 13 | 54.2 |
| Halladay, Tor | 18 | 11 | 61.1 |
| Hamilton, Tor | 18 | 7 | 38.9 |
| Hampton, Hou | 34 | 27 | 79.4 |
| Harnisch, Cin | 33 | 16 | 48.5 |
| Hawkins, Min | 33 | 9 | 27.3 |
| Haynes, Oak | 25 | 11 | 44.0 |
| Helling, Tex | 35 | 15 | 42.9 |
| Hentgen, Tor | 34 | 16 | 47.1 |
| Heredia G, Oak | 33 | 19 | 57.6 |
| Hermanson, Mon | 34 | 21 | 61.8 |
| Hernandez, Fla-SF | 30 | 14 | 46.7 |
| Hernandez O, NYY | 33 | 23 | 69.7 |
| Hershiser, NYM | 32 | 14 | 43.8 |
| Hill, Ana | 22 | 12 | 54.5 |
| Hitchcock, SD | 33 | 18 | 54.5 |
| Holt, Hou | 26 | 15 | 57.7 |
| Hudson, Oak | 21 | 13 | 61.9 |
| Irabu, NYY | 27 | 14 | 51.9 |
| Jimenez, StL | 28 | 13 | 46.4 |
| Johnson J, Bal | 21 | 9 | 42.9 |
| Johnson R, Ari | 35 | 29 | 82.9 |
| Jones B, Col | 20 | 3 | 15.0 |
| Karl, Mil | 33 | 14 | 42.4 |
| Kile, Col | 32 | 12 | 37.5 |
| Leiter A, NYM | 32 | 21 | 65.6 |
| Lieber, ChC | 31 | 17 | 54.8 |
| Lima, Hou | 35 | 25 | 71.4 |
| Lincoln, Min | 15 | 4 | 26.7 |
| Loaiza, Tex | 15 | 10 | 66.7 |
| Maddux G, Atl | 33 | 19 | 57.6 |
| Martinez P, Bos | 29 | 24 | 82.8 |
| Mays, Min | 20 | 10 | 50.0 |
| Meadows, Fla | 31 | 11 | 35.5 |
| Meche, Sea | 15 | 9 | 60.0 |
| Mercker, StL-Bos | 23 | 9 | 39.1 |
| Millwood, Atl | 33 | 25 | 75.8 |
| Milton, Min | 34 | 14 | 41.2 |
| Mlicki, LA-Det | 31 | 16 | 51.6 |
| Moehler, Det | 32 | 16 | 50.0 |
| Morgan, Tex | 25 | 8 | 32.0 |
| Moyer, Sea | 32 | 21 | 65.6 |
| Mulholland, 2Tm | 24 | 16 | 66.7 |
| Mussina, Bal | 31 | 17 | 54.8 |
| Nagy, Cle | 32 | 16 | 50.0 |
| Navarro, CWS | 27 | 10 | 37.0 |
| Neagle, Cin | 19 | 11 | 57.9 |
| Nomo, Mil | 28 | 17 | 60.7 |
| Ogea, Phi | 28 | 11 | 39.3 |
| Olivares, Ana-Oak | 32 | 16 | 50.0 |
| Oliver, StL | 30 | 16 | 53.3 |
| Oquist, Oak | 24 | 8 | 33.3 |
| Ortiz R, SF | 33 | 21 | 63.6 |
| Park, LA | 33 | 17 | 51.5 |
| Parque, CWS | 30 | 10 | 33.3 |
| Parris, Cin | 21 | 11 | 52.4 |
| Pavano, Mon | 18 | 9 | 50.0 |
| Perez C, LA | 16 | 2 | 12.5 |
| Perez O, Atl | 17 | 5 | 29.4 |
| Person, Tor-Phi | 22 | 11 | 50.0 |
| Pettitte, NYY | 31 | 15 | 48.4 |
| Ponson, Bal | 32 | 19 | 59.4 |
| Portugal, Bos | 27 | 11 | 40.7 |
| Powell J, Mon | 17 | 8 | 47.1 |
| Pulsipher, Mil | 16 | 3 | 18.8 |
| Radke, Min | 33 | 21 | 63.6 |
| Rapp, Bos | 26 | 12 | 46.2 |
| Reed R, NYM | 26 | 13 | 50.0 |
| Reynolds, Hou | 35 | 20 | 57.1 |
| Reynoso, Ari | 27 | 15 | 55.6 |
| Ritchie, Pit | 26 | 16 | 61.5 |
| Rogers, Oak-NYM | 31 | 16 | 51.6 |
| Rosado, KC | 33 | 19 | 57.6 |
| Rose, Bos | 18 | 7 | 38.9 |
| Rueter, SF | 33 | 17 | 51.5 |
| Rupe, TB | 24 | 14 | 58.3 |
| Saberhagen, Bos | 22 | 10 | 45.5 |
| Schilling, Phi | 24 | 13 | 54.2 |
| Schmidt, Pit | 33 | 20 | 60.6 |
| Schourek, Pit | 17 | 5 | 29.4 |
| Sele, Tex | 33 | 13 | 39.4 |
| Sirotka, CWS | 32 | 19 | 59.4 |
| Smith, Mon | 17 | 5 | 29.4 |
| Smoltz, Atl | 29 | 18 | 62.1 |
| Snyder, CWS | 25 | 9 | 36.0 |
| Sparks S, Ana | 26 | 10 | 38.5 |
| Springer D, Fla | 29 | 13 | 44.8 |
| Stottlemyre, Ari | 17 | 9 | 52.9 |
| Suppan, KC | 32 | 17 | 53.1 |
| Tapani, ChC | 23 | 10 | 43.5 |
| Thompson J, Det | 24 | 13 | 54.2 |
| Thurman, Mon | 27 | 12 | 44.4 |
| Tomko, Cin | 26 | 12 | 46.2 |
| Trachsel, ChC | 34 | 12 | 35.3 |
| Valdes, LA | 32 | 20 | 62.5 |
| Vazquez, Mon | 26 | 10 | 38.5 |
| Villone, Cin | 22 | 9 | 40.9 |
| Wakefield, Bos | 17 | 6 | 35.3 |
| Weaver J, Det | 29 | 13 | 44.8 |
| Wells D, Tor | 34 | 14 | 41.2 |
| Williams W, SD | 33 | 19 | 57.6 |
| Witasick, KC | 28 | 12 | 42.9 |
| Witt, TB | 32 | 13 | 40.6 |
| Wolf, Phi | 21 | 9 | 42.9 |
| Woodard, Mil | 29 | 17 | 58.6 |
| Wright J, Col | 16 | 7 | 43.8 |
| Wright J, Cle | 26 | 8 | 30.8 |
| Yoshii, NYM | 29 | 20 | 69.0 |
| **MLB Average** |  |  | **46.3** |

## Whose Heater Is Hottest? (p. 137)

### Strikeouts Per Nine Innings—Listed Alphabetically
### (minimum 162 IP for starters, 50 IP for relievers in 1999)

| Pitcher, Team | SO | IP | SO/9 | Pitcher, Team | SO | IP | SO/9 |
|---|---|---|---|---|---|---|---|
| Abbott P, Sea | 68 | 72.2 | 8.4 | Daal, Ari | 148 | 214.2 | 6.2 |
| Acevedo, StL | 52 | 102.1 | 4.6 | Davey, Tor-Sea | 59 | 65.0 | 8.2 |
| Adams, ChC | 57 | 65.0 | 7.9 | DeJean, Col | 31 | 61.0 | 4.6 |
| Aguilera, Min-ChC | 45 | 67.2 | 6.0 | Dipoto, Col | 69 | 86.2 | 7.2 |
| Aldred, TB-Phi | 41 | 56.2 | 6.5 | Dreifort, LA | 140 | 178.2 | 7.1 |
| Alfonseca, Fla | 46 | 77.2 | 5.3 | Edmondson, Fla | 58 | 94.0 | 5.6 |
| Appier, KC-Oak | 131 | 209.0 | 5.6 | Elarton, Hou | 121 | 124.0 | 8.8 |
| Arnold, LA | 26 | 69.0 | 3.4 | Embree, SF | 53 | 58.2 | 8.1 |
| Ashby, SD | 132 | 206.0 | 5.8 | Erickson, Bal | 106 | 230.1 | 4.1 |
| Astacio, Col | 210 | 232.0 | 8.1 | Escobar, Tor | 129 | 174.0 | 6.7 |
| Ayala, Mon-ChC | 79 | 82.0 | 8.7 | Estes, SF | 159 | 203.0 | 7.0 |
| Aybar, StL | 74 | 97.0 | 6.9 | Finley, Ana | 200 | 213.1 | 8.4 |
| Baldwin, CWS | 123 | 199.1 | 5.6 | Florie, Det-Bos | 65 | 81.1 | 7.2 |
| Batista, Mon | 95 | 134.2 | 6.3 | Foulke, CWS | 123 | 105.1 | 10.5 |
| Benes A, Ari | 141 | 198.1 | 6.4 | Frascatore, Ari-Tor | 37 | 70.0 | 4.8 |
| Benitez, NYM | 128 | 78.0 | 14.8 | Fussell, KC | 37 | 56.0 | 5.9 |
| Benson, Pit | 139 | 196.2 | 6.4 | Fyhrie, Ana | 26 | 51.2 | 4.5 |
| Blair, Det | 82 | 134.0 | 5.5 | Garcia F, Sea | 170 | 201.1 | 7.6 |
| Boehringer, SD | 64 | 94.1 | 6.1 | Glavine, Atl | 138 | 234.0 | 5.3 |
| Bohanon, Col | 120 | 197.1 | 5.5 | Gomes, Phi | 58 | 74.0 | 7.1 |
| Borbon, LA | 33 | 50.2 | 5.9 | Grace, Phi | 28 | 55.0 | 4.6 |
| Bottalico, StL | 66 | 73.1 | 8.1 | Graves, Cin | 69 | 111.0 | 5.6 |
| Bottenfield, StL | 124 | 190.1 | 5.9 | Grimsley, NYY | 49 | 75.0 | 5.9 |
| Brocail, Det | 78 | 82.0 | 8.6 | Guthrie, Bos-ChC | 45 | 58.2 | 6.9 |
| Brown, LA | 221 | 252.1 | 7.9 | Guzman J, Bal-Cin | 155 | 200.0 | 7.0 |
| Burba, Cle | 174 | 220.0 | 7.1 | Halama, Sea | 105 | 179.0 | 5.3 |
| Byrd, Phi | 106 | 199.2 | 4.8 | Halladay, Tor | 82 | 149.1 | 4.9 |
| Charlton, TB | 45 | 50.2 | 8.0 | Hampton, Hou | 177 | 239.0 | 6.7 |
| Chen, Atl | 45 | 51.0 | 7.9 | Harnisch, Cin | 120 | 198.1 | 5.4 |
| Clemens, NYY | 163 | 187.2 | 7.8 | Hasegawa, Ana | 44 | 77.0 | 5.1 |
| Clement, SD | 135 | 180.2 | 6.7 | Hawkins, Min | 103 | 174.1 | 5.3 |
| Cloude, Sea | 35 | 72.1 | 4.4 | Helling, Tex | 131 | 219.1 | 5.4 |
| Colon, Cle | 161 | 205.0 | 7.1 | Hentgen, Tor | 118 | 199.0 | 5.3 |
| Cone, NYY | 177 | 193.1 | 8.2 | Heredia F, ChC | 50 | 52.0 | 8.7 |
| Cook, NYM | 68 | 63.0 | 9.7 | Heredia G, Oak | 117 | 200.1 | 5.3 |
| Coppinger, Bal-Mil | 56 | 58.1 | 8.6 | Hermanson, Mon | 145 | 216.1 | 6.0 |
| Cormier, Bos | 39 | 63.1 | 5.5 | Hernandez L, Fla-SF | 144 | 199.2 | 6.5 |
| Crabtree, Tex | 54 | 65.0 | 7.5 | Hernandez O, NYY | 157 | 214.1 | 6.6 |
| Croushore, StL | 88 | 71.2 | 11.1 | Hernandez R, TB | 69 | 73.1 | 8.5 |
| Cruz, Det | 46 | 66.2 | 6.2 | Hershiser, NYM | 89 | 179.0 | 4.5 |

| Pitcher, Team | SO | IP | SO/9 | Pitcher, Team | SO | IP | SO/9 |
|---|---|---|---|---|---|---|---|
| Hitchcock, SD | 194 | 205.2 | 8.5 | Mendoza, NYY | 80 | 123.2 | 5.8 |
| Hoffman, SD | 73 | 67.1 | 9.8 | Mesa, Sea | 42 | 68.2 | 5.5 |
| Holt, Hou | 115 | 164.0 | 6.3 | Miceli, SD | 59 | 68.2 | 7.7 |
| Howry, CWS | 80 | 67.2 | 10.6 | Mills, LA | 49 | 72.1 | 6.1 |
| Irabu, NYY | 133 | 169.1 | 7.1 | Millwood, Atl | 205 | 228.0 | 8.1 |
| Isringhausen, NYM-Oak | 51 | 64.2 | 7.1 | Milton, Min | 163 | 206.1 | 7.1 |
| Jackson, Cle | 55 | 68.2 | 7.2 | Mlicki, LA-Det | 120 | 199.0 | 5.4 |
| Jimenez, StL | 113 | 163.0 | 6.2 | Moehler, Det | 106 | 196.1 | 4.9 |
| Johns, Bal | 50 | 86.2 | 5.2 | Montgomery J, KC | 27 | 51.1 | 4.7 |
| Johnson R, Ari | 364 | 271.2 | 12.1 | Montgomery S, Phi | 55 | 64.2 | 7.7 |
| Johnstone, SF | 56 | 65.2 | 7.7 | Morman, KC | 31 | 53.1 | 5.2 |
| Jones D, Oak | 63 | 104.0 | 5.5 | Mota, Mon | 27 | 55.1 | 4.4 |
| Jones T, Det | 64 | 66.1 | 8.7 | Moyer, Sea | 137 | 228.0 | 5.4 |
| Kamieniecki, Bal | 39 | 56.1 | 6.2 | Mulholland, ChC-Atl | 83 | 170.1 | 4.4 |
| Karl, Mil | 74 | 197.2 | 3.4 | Munoz, Tex | 27 | 52.2 | 4.6 |
| Karsay, Cle | 68 | 78.2 | 7.8 | Munro, Tor | 38 | 55.1 | 6.2 |
| Kida, Det | 50 | 64.2 | 7.0 | Murray H, SD | 25 | 50.0 | 4.5 |
| Kile, Col | 116 | 190.2 | 5.5 | Mussina, Bal | 172 | 203.1 | 7.6 |
| Kline, Mon | 69 | 69.2 | 8.9 | Myers R, ChC | 41 | 63.2 | 5.8 |
| Koch, Tor | 57 | 63.2 | 8.1 | Nagy, Cle | 126 | 202.0 | 5.6 |
| Langston, Cle | 43 | 61.2 | 6.3 | Nen, SF | 77 | 72.1 | 9.6 |
| Leiter A, NYM | 162 | 213.0 | 6.8 | Nitkowski, Det | 66 | 81.2 | 7.3 |
| Leskanic, Col | 77 | 85.0 | 8.2 | Nomo, Mil | 161 | 176.1 | 8.2 |
| Levine, Ana | 37 | 85.0 | 3.9 | Nunez, Ari-Fla | 86 | 108.2 | 7.1 |
| Lieber, ChC | 186 | 203.1 | 8.2 | Ogea, Phi | 77 | 168.0 | 4.1 |
| Lima, Hou | 187 | 246.1 | 6.8 | Olivares, Ana-Oak | 85 | 205.2 | 3.7 |
| Lloyd, Tor | 47 | 72.0 | 5.9 | Oliver, StL | 119 | 196.1 | 5.5 |
| Loaiza, Tex | 77 | 120.1 | 5.8 | Olson, Ari | 45 | 60.2 | 6.7 |
| Looper, Fla | 50 | 83.0 | 5.4 | Ortiz R, SF | 164 | 207.2 | 7.1 |
| Lopez, TB | 37 | 64.0 | 5.2 | Painter, StL | 56 | 63.1 | 8.0 |
| Lowe D, Bos | 80 | 109.1 | 6.6 | Paniagua, Sea | 74 | 77.2 | 8.6 |
| Lowe S, CWS | 62 | 95.2 | 5.8 | Park, LA | 174 | 194.1 | 8.1 |
| Maddux G, Atl | 136 | 219.1 | 5.6 | Parque, CWS | 111 | 173.2 | 5.8 |
| Maddux M, Mon-LA | 45 | 59.2 | 6.8 | Patterson, Tex | 43 | 60.1 | 6.4 |
| Magnante, Ana | 44 | 69.1 | 5.7 | Percival, Ana | 58 | 57.0 | 9.2 |
| Mahomes, NYM | 51 | 63.2 | 7.2 | Perkins, Min | 44 | 86.2 | 4.6 |
| Mantei, Fla-Ari | 99 | 65.1 | 13.6 | Petkovsek, Ana | 43 | 83.0 | 4.7 |
| Martinez P, Bos | 313 | 213.1 | 13.2 | Pettitte, NYY | 121 | 191.2 | 5.7 |
| Masaoka, LA | 61 | 66.2 | 8.2 | Plunk, Mil | 63 | 75.1 | 7.5 |
| Mathews T, Oak | 42 | 59.0 | 6.4 | Ponson, Bal | 112 | 210.0 | 4.8 |
| Mays, Min | 115 | 171.0 | 6.1 | Powell J, Hou | 77 | 75.0 | 9.2 |
| McElroy, Col-NYM | 44 | 54.0 | 7.3 | Radke, Min | 121 | 218.2 | 5.0 |
| McGlinchy, Atl | 67 | 70.1 | 8.6 | Reed S, Cle | 44 | 61.2 | 6.4 |
| Meadows, Fla | 72 | 178.1 | 3.6 | Rekar, TB | 55 | 94.2 | 5.2 |

| Pitcher, Team | SO | IP | SO/9 | Pitcher, Team | SO | IP | SO/9 |
|---|---|---|---|---|---|---|---|
| Remlinger, Atl | 81 | 83.2 | 8.7 | Suppan, KC | 103 | 208.2 | 4.4 |
| Reyes A, Mil-Bal | 67 | 65.2 | 9.2 | Suzuki, Sea-KC | 68 | 110.0 | 5.6 |
| Reyes C, SD | 57 | 77.1 | 6.6 | Swindell, Ari | 51 | 64.2 | 7.1 |
| Reyes D, Cin | 72 | 61.2 | 10.5 | Tavarez, SF | 33 | 54.2 | 5.4 |
| Reynolds, Hou | 197 | 231.2 | 7.7 | Taylor, Oak-NYM | 52 | 56.1 | 8.3 |
| Reynoso, Ari | 79 | 167.0 | 4.3 | Telemaco, Ari-Phi | 43 | 53.0 | 7.3 |
| Rhodes, Bal | 59 | 53.0 | 10.0 | Telford, Mon | 69 | 96.0 | 6.5 |
| Rigby, Oak-KC | 36 | 83.2 | 3.9 | Timlin, Bal | 50 | 63.0 | 7.1 |
| Ritchie, Pit | 107 | 172.1 | 5.6 | Tomko, Cin | 132 | 172.0 | 6.9 |
| Rivera M, NYY | 52 | 69.0 | 6.8 | Trachsel, ChC | 149 | 205.2 | 6.5 |
| Rocker, Atl | 104 | 72.1 | 12.9 | Trombley, Min | 82 | 87.1 | 8.5 |
| Rodriguez F, SF | 55 | 66.1 | 7.5 | Urbina, Mon | 100 | 75.2 | 11.9 |
| Rodriguez F, Sea | 47 | 73.1 | 5.8 | Valdes, LA | 143 | 203.1 | 6.3 |
| Rodriguez R, SF | 44 | 56.2 | 7.0 | Venafro, Tex | 37 | 68.1 | 4.9 |
| Rogers, Oak-NYM | 126 | 195.1 | 5.8 | Veres, Col | 71 | 77.0 | 8.3 |
| Roque, Mil | 66 | 84.1 | 7.0 | Wagner B, Hou | 124 | 74.2 | 14.9 |
| Rosado, KC | 141 | 208.0 | 6.1 | Wakefield, Bos | 104 | 140.0 | 6.7 |
| Rueter, SF | 94 | 184.2 | 4.6 | Wall, SD | 53 | 70.1 | 6.8 |
| Sampson, Min | 56 | 71.0 | 7.1 | Wasdin, Bos | 57 | 74.1 | 6.9 |
| Sanchez, Fla | 62 | 76.1 | 7.3 | Watson, NYM-Sea-NYY | 64 | 77.0 | 7.5 |
| Sanders, ChC | 89 | 104.1 | 7.7 | Weathers, Mil | 74 | 93.0 | 7.2 |
| Santana J, Bos | 34 | 55.1 | 5.5 | Weaver J, Det | 114 | 163.2 | 6.3 |
| Sauerbeck, Pit | 55 | 67.2 | 7.3 | Wells B, Min | 44 | 87.1 | 4.5 |
| Schilling, Phi | 152 | 180.1 | 7.6 | Wells D, Tor | 169 | 231.2 | 6.6 |
| Schmidt, Pit | 148 | 212.2 | 6.3 | Wendell, NYM | 77 | 85.2 | 8.1 |
| Schrenk, Phi | 36 | 50.1 | 6.4 | Wetteland, Tex | 60 | 66.0 | 8.2 |
| Seanez, Atl | 41 | 53.2 | 6.9 | Whisenant, KC-SD | 37 | 54.1 | 6.1 |
| Sele, Tex | 186 | 205.0 | 8.2 | White G, Cin | 61 | 61.0 | 9.0 |
| Serafini, ChC | 17 | 62.1 | 2.5 | White R, TB | 81 | 108.0 | 6.8 |
| Service, KC | 68 | 75.1 | 8.1 | Wickman, Mil | 60 | 74.1 | 7.3 |
| Shaw, LA | 43 | 68.0 | 5.7 | Wilkins, Pit | 44 | 51.0 | 7.8 |
| Shuey, Cle | 103 | 81.2 | 11.4 | Williams B, Hou | 53 | 67.1 | 7.1 |
| Silva, Pit | 77 | 97.1 | 7.1 | Williams M, Pit | 76 | 58.1 | 11.7 |
| Simas, CWS | 41 | 72.0 | 5.1 | Williams W, SD | 137 | 208.1 | 5.9 |
| Sirotka, CWS | 125 | 209.0 | 5.4 | Williamson, Cin | 107 | 93.1 | 10.3 |
| Slocumb, Bal-StL | 60 | 62.0 | 8.7 | Witt, TB | 123 | 180.1 | 6.1 |
| Smart, Mon | 21 | 52.0 | 3.6 | Woodard, Mil | 119 | 185.0 | 5.8 |
| Smoltz, Atl | 156 | 186.1 | 7.5 | Worrell, Oak | 62 | 69.1 | 8.0 |
| Spoljaric, Phi-Tor | 73 | 73.1 | 9.0 | Yan, TB | 46 | 61.0 | 6.8 |
| Spradlin, Cle-SF | 54 | 61.0 | 8.0 | Yoshii, NYM | 105 | 174.0 | 5.4 |
| Springer D, Fla | 83 | 196.1 | 3.8 | Zimmerman J, Tex | 67 | 87.2 | 6.9 |
| Stanton, NYY | 59 | 62.1 | 8.5 | **MLB Average** | | | **6.5** |
| Sullivan, Cin | 78 | 113.2 | 6.2 | | | | |

## Who Were 1999's Most Overpowering Pitchers? (p. 140)

### Highest Strikeout/Hit Ratios—Listed Alphabetically
### (minimum 162 IP in 1999)

| Pitcher, Team | SO | H | SO/H | Pitcher, Team | SO | H | SO/H |
|---|---|---|---|---|---|---|---|
| Appier, KC-Oak | 131 | 230 | 0.57 | Maddux G, Atl | 136 | 258 | 0.53 |
| Ashby, SD | 132 | 204 | 0.65 | Martinez P, Bos | 313 | 160 | 1.96 |
| Astacio, Col | 210 | 258 | 0.81 | Mays, Min | 115 | 179 | 0.64 |
| Baldwin, CWS | 123 | 219 | 0.56 | Meadows, Fla | 72 | 214 | 0.34 |
| Benes A, Ari | 141 | 216 | 0.65 | Millwood, Atl | 205 | 168 | 1.22 |
| Benson, Pit | 139 | 184 | 0.76 | Milton, Min | 163 | 190 | 0.86 |
| Bohanon, Col | 120 | 236 | 0.51 | Mlicki, LA-Det | 120 | 219 | 0.55 |
| Bottenfield, StL | 124 | 197 | 0.63 | Moehler, Det | 106 | 229 | 0.46 |
| Brown, LA | 221 | 210 | 1.05 | Moyer, Sea | 137 | 235 | 0.58 |
| Burba, Cle | 174 | 211 | 0.82 | Mulholland, ChC-Atl | 83 | 201 | 0.41 |
| Byrd, Phi | 106 | 205 | 0.52 | Mussina, Bal | 172 | 207 | 0.83 |
| Clemens, NYY | 163 | 185 | 0.88 | Nagy, Cle | 126 | 238 | 0.53 |
| Clement, SD | 135 | 190 | 0.71 | Nomo, Mil | 161 | 173 | 0.93 |
| Colon, Cle | 161 | 185 | 0.87 | Ogea, Phi | 77 | 192 | 0.40 |
| Cone, NYY | 177 | 164 | 1.08 | Olivares, Ana-Oak | 85 | 217 | 0.39 |
| Daal, Ari | 148 | 188 | 0.79 | Oliver, StL | 119 | 197 | 0.60 |
| Dreifort, LA | 140 | 177 | 0.79 | Ortiz R, SF | 164 | 189 | 0.87 |
| Erickson, Bal | 106 | 244 | 0.43 | Park, LA | 174 | 208 | 0.84 |
| Escobar, Tor | 129 | 203 | 0.64 | Parque, CWS | 111 | 210 | 0.53 |
| Estes, SF | 159 | 209 | 0.76 | Pettitte, NYY | 121 | 216 | 0.56 |
| Finley, Ana | 200 | 197 | 1.02 | Ponson, Bal | 112 | 227 | 0.49 |
| Garcia F, Sea | 170 | 205 | 0.83 | Radke, Min | 121 | 239 | 0.51 |
| Glavine, Atl | 138 | 259 | 0.53 | Reynolds, Hou | 197 | 250 | 0.79 |
| Guzman J, Bal-Cin | 155 | 194 | 0.80 | Reynoso, Ari | 79 | 178 | 0.44 |
| Halama, Sea | 105 | 193 | 0.54 | Ritchie, Pit | 107 | 169 | 0.63 |
| Hampton, Hou | 177 | 206 | 0.86 | Rogers, Oak-NYM | 126 | 206 | 0.61 |
| Harnisch, Cin | 120 | 190 | 0.63 | Rosado, KC | 141 | 197 | 0.72 |
| Hawkins, Min | 103 | 238 | 0.43 | Rueter, SF | 94 | 219 | 0.43 |
| Helling, Tex | 131 | 228 | 0.57 | Schilling, Phi | 152 | 159 | 0.96 |
| Hentgen, Tor | 118 | 225 | 0.52 | Schmidt, Pit | 148 | 219 | 0.68 |
| Heredia G, Oak | 117 | 228 | 0.51 | Sele, Tex | 186 | 244 | 0.76 |
| Hermanson, Mon | 145 | 225 | 0.64 | Sirotka, CWS | 125 | 236 | 0.53 |
| Hernandez L, Fla-SF | 144 | 227 | 0.63 | Smoltz, Atl | 156 | 168 | 0.93 |
| Hernandez O, NYY | 157 | 187 | 0.84 | Springer D, Fla | 83 | 231 | 0.36 |
| Hershiser, NYM | 89 | 175 | 0.51 | Suppan, KC | 103 | 222 | 0.46 |
| Hitchcock, SD | 194 | 202 | 0.96 | Tomko, Cin | 132 | 175 | 0.75 |
| Holt, Hou | 115 | 193 | 0.60 | Trachsel, ChC | 149 | 226 | 0.66 |
| Irabu, NYY | 133 | 180 | 0.74 | Valdes, LA | 143 | 213 | 0.67 |
| Jimenez, StL | 113 | 173 | 0.65 | Weaver J, Det | 114 | 176 | 0.65 |
| Johnson R, Ari | 364 | 207 | 1.76 | Wells D, Tor | 169 | 246 | 0.69 |
| Karl, Mil | 74 | 246 | 0.30 | Williams W, SD | 137 | 213 | 0.64 |
| Kile, Col | 116 | 225 | 0.52 | Witt, TB | 123 | 213 | 0.58 |
| Leiter A, NYM | 162 | 209 | 0.78 | Woodard, Mil | 119 | 219 | 0.54 |
| Lieber, ChC | 186 | 226 | 0.82 | Yoshii, NYM | 105 | 168 | 0.63 |
| Lima, Hou | 187 | 256 | 0.73 | **MLB Average** | | | **0.69** |

## Who Gets the Easy Saves—And Who Toughs It Out? (p. 142)

### Easy, Regular and Tough Saves—Listed Alphabetically
### (minimum 5 Total Save Opportunities in 1999)

| Pitcher, Team | Easy Sv/Opp | Regular Sv/Opp | Tough Sv/Opp | Pitcher, Team | Easy Sv/Opp | Regular Sv/Opp | Tough Sv/Opp |
|---|---|---|---|---|---|---|---|
| Acevedo, StL | 2/3 | 2/3 | 0/0 | Olson, Ari | 9/12 | 4/8 | 1/3 |
| Adams, ChC | 6/7 | 7/8 | 0/3 | Paniagua, Sea | 1/1 | 2/4 | 0/7 |
| Aguilera, Min-ChC | 10/11 | 4/7 | 0/3 | Percival, Ana | 17/19 | 14/18 | 0/2 |
| Alfonseca, Fla | 13/13 | 7/9 | 1/3 | Powell J, Hou | 0/0 | 4/6 | 0/1 |
| Aybar, StL | 0/0 | 3/4 | 0/1 | Rhodes, Bal | 2/3 | 1/2 | 0/0 |
| Beck, ChC-Bos | 5/6 | 5/9 | 0/0 | Rivera M, NYY | 26/26 | 16/19 | 3/4 |
| Benitez, NYM | 7/7 | 12/16 | 3/5 | Rocker, Atl | 24/25 | 13/16 | 1/4 |
| Bottalico, StL | 5/6 | 13/19 | 2/3 | Sanders, ChC | 1/1 | 1/1 | 0/3 |
| Brantley, Phi | 3/4 | 1/1 | 1/1 | Sauerbeck, Pit | 1/1 | 1/2 | 0/2 |
| Christiansen, Pit | 2/2 | 1/3 | 0/0 | Seanez, Atl | 1/2 | 1/4 | 1/2 |
| Cook, NYM | 1/1 | 1/2 | 1/3 | Service, KC | 6/9 | 2/4 | 0/2 |
| Croushore, StL | 0/0 | 2/3 | 1/7 | Shaw, LA | 21/22 | 11/14 | 2/3 |
| Edmondson, Fla | 0/0 | 1/3 | 0/3 | Shuey, Cle | 2/3 | 4/6 | 0/3 |
| Foulke, CWS | 3/3 | 5/8 | 1/2 | Silva, Pit | 1/1 | 3/4 | 0/0 |
| Franco, NYM | 15/15 | 4/5 | 0/1 | Simas, CWS | 0/0 | 1/2 | 1/3 |
| Gomes, Phi | 4/4 | 12/14 | 3/6 | Stanton, NYY | 0/0 | 0/3 | 0/2 |
| Gordon, Bos | 7/8 | 4/5 | 0/0 | Sullivan, Cin | 1/1 | 2/2 | 0/2 |
| Graves, Cin | 13/15 | 11/14 | 3/7 | Taylor, Oak-NYM | 12/14 | 13/17 | 1/3 |
| Hasegawa, Ana | 1/1 | 0/2 | 1/2 | Telford, Mon | 0/1 | 2/5 | 0/3 |
| Heredia F, ChC | 0/1 | 1/3 | 0/3 | Timlin, Bal | 16/18 | 10/12 | 1/6 |
| Hernandez R, TB | 22/23 | 19/21 | 2/3 | Trombley, Min | 9/10 | 11/14 | 4/6 |
| Hoffman, SD | 23/24 | 14/16 | 3/3 | Urbina, Mon | 27/29 | 8/12 | 6/9 |
| Howry, CWS | 18/21 | 9/12 | 1/1 | Veres, Col | 17/20 | 12/17 | 2/2 |
| Isringhausen, NYM-Oak | 3/3 | 5/5 | 1/1 | Wagner B, Hou | 19/19 | 15/16 | 5/7 |
| Jackson, Cle | 25/25 | 14/18 | 0/0 | Wakefield, Bos | 6/7 | 6/8 | 3/3 |
| Johnstone, SF | 0/0 | 3/6 | 0/1 | Wall, SD | 0/0 | 0/4 | 0/2 |
| Jones D, Oak | 1/1 | 7/10 | 2/5 | Wasdin, Bos | 0/0 | 2/2 | 0/3 |
| Jones T, Det | 21/22 | 8/11 | 1/2 | Weathers, Mil | 1/1 | 1/4 | 0/1 |
| Koch, Tor | 12/12 | 19/22 | 0/1 | Wells B, Min | 0/0 | 1/2 | 0/3 |
| Lloyd, Tor | 1/1 | 2/6 | 0/2 | Wendell, NYM | 0/0 | 2/3 | 1/3 |
| Lowe D, Bos | 3/3 | 11/14 | 1/3 | Wetteland, Tex | 25/25 | 13/20 | 5/5 |
| Mantei, Fla-Ari | 21/25 | 10/11 | 1/1 | Whisenant, KC-SD | 0/0 | 0/2 | 1/3 |
| Mathews T, Oak | 1/1 | 2/3 | 0/1 | Wickman, Mil | 21/21 | 14/19 | 2/5 |
| Mendoza, NYY | 0/1 | 3/4 | 0/1 | Williams M, Pit | 12/12 | 8/10 | 3/6 |
| Mesa, Sea | 19/19 | 12/16 | 2/3 | Williamson, Cin | 6/6 | 12/17 | 1/3 |
| Mills, LA | 0/0 | 0/3 | 0/2 | Worrell, Oak | 0/0 | 0/1 | 0/4 |
| Montgomery J, KC | 8/10 | 3/5 | 1/4 | Zimmerman J, Tex | 2/2 | 0/1 | 1/4 |
| Nen, SF | 26/28 | 11/14 | 0/4 | **MLB Totals** | **599/665** | **530/793** | **88/350** |

# *If You Hold the Fort, Will You Soon Be Closing the Gate? (p. 145)*

## Most Holds—1999

| Pitcher, Team | Hld | Pitcher, Team | Hld | Pitcher, Team | Hld | Pitcher, Team | Hld |
|---|---|---|---|---|---|---|---|
| Johnstone, SF | 28 | Montgomery S, Phi | 11 | Wallace J, Pit | 7 | Beck, ChC-Bos | 3 |
| Groom, Oak | 27 | Nitkowski, Det | 11 | Yan, TB | 7 | Boehringer, SD | 3 |
| Zimmerman J, Tex | 24 | Radinsky, StL | 11 | Aldred, TB-Phi | 6 | Bones, Bal | 3 |
| Brocail, Det | 23 | Rincon, Cle | 11 | Cabrera, Hou | 6 | De Paula, Cle | 3 |
| Embree, SF | 22 | Rodriguez R, SF | 11 | Cordero, Det | 6 | Florie, Det-Bos | 3 |
| Foulke, CWS | 22 | Sanchez, Fla | 11 | Hasegawa, Ana | 6 | Kim, Ari | 3 |
| Lloyd, Tor | 22 | Spradlin, Cle-SF | 11 | Lowe S, CWS | 6 | Levine, Ana | 3 |
| Lowe D, Bos | 22 | Whisenant, KC-SD | 11 | Mecir, TB | 6 | Loiselle, Pit | 3 |
| Remlinger, Atl | 21 | Ayala, Mon-ChC | 10 | Mohler, StL | 6 | Mathews T, KC | 3 |
| Stanton, NYY | 21 | Byrdak, KC | 10 | Reyes A, Mil-Bal | 6 | Morman, KC | 3 |
| Wendell, NYM | 21 | Darensbourg, Fla | 10 | Reyes C, SD | 6 | Mota, Mon | 3 |
| Cook, NYM | 19 | Frascatore, Ari-Tor | 10 | Alfonseca, Fla | 5 | Pittsley, KC-Mil | 3 |
| Shuey, Cle | 19 | Maddux M, 2Tm | 10 | Cunnane, SD | 5 | Pote, Ana | 3 |
| Swindell, Ari | 19 | Munoz, Tex | 10 | Elarton, Hou | 5 | Ramirez R, Col | 3 |
| Venafro, Tex | 19 | Nelson, NYY | 10 | Masaoka, LA | 5 | Rodriguez F, SF | 3 |
| Mills, LA | 18 | Painter, StL | 10 | McElroy, Col-NYM | 5 | Rodriguez F, Sea | 3 |
| Seanez, Atl | 18 | Sauerbeck, Pit | 10 | Perez Y, Phi | 5 | Schoeneweis, Ana | 3 |
| Telford, Mon | 18 | Clontz, Pit | 9 | Ramirez H, Mil | 5 | Telemaco, Ari-Phi | 3 |
| Wall, SD | 18 | Coppinger, Bal-Mil | 9 | Rhodes, Bal | 5 | Trombley, Min | 3 |
| Benitez, NYM | 17 | DeJean, Col | 9 | Rigby, Oak-KC | 5 | Ward, CWS | 3 |
| Mathews T, Oak | 17 | Edmondson, Fla | 9 | Serafini, ChC | 5 | White G, Cin | 3 |
| Plunk, Mil | 17 | Gomes, Phi | 9 | Slocumb, Bal-StL | 5 | Almonte, Fla | 2 |
| Wells B, Min | 17 | Karsay, Cle | 9 | Tavarez, SF | 5 | Arnold, LA | 2 |
| Kline, Mon | 16 | Miceli, SD | 9 | Williamson, Cin | 5 | Belinda, Cin | 2 |
| Paniagua, Sea | 16 | Olson, Ari | 9 | Worrell, Oak | 5 | Bullinger, Bos | 2 |
| Powell J, Hou | 16 | Weathers, Mil | 9 | Acevedo, StL | 4 | Fassero, Sea-Tex | 2 |
| Borbon, LA | 15 | Bottalico, StL | 8 | Aguilera, Min-ChC | 4 | Fetters, Bal | 2 |
| Charlton, TB | 15 | Grimsley, NYY | 8 | Busby, StL | 4 | Garces, Bos | 2 |
| Cormier, Bos | 15 | Leskanic, Col | 8 | Cruz, Det | 4 | Halladay, Tor | 2 |
| Dipoto, Col | 15 | Looper, Fla | 8 | Davey, Tor-Sea | 4 | Henry D, Hou | 2 |
| Guardado, Min | 15 | Miller T, Min | 8 | Hansell, Pit | 4 | Karchner, ChC | 2 |
| Plesac, Tor-Ari | 15 | Myers R, ChC | 8 | Holmes, Ari | 4 | King R, ChC | 2 |
| Crabtree, Tex | 14 | Quantrill, Tor | 8 | Kida, Det | 4 | Lee D, Col | 2 |
| Croushore, StL | 14 | Reed S, Cle | 8 | Magnante, Ana | 4 | Mays, Min | 2 |
| Guthrie, Bos-ChC | 14 | Roque, Mil | 8 | Mendoza, NYY | 4 | Molina, Bal | 2 |
| Myers M, Mil | 14 | Service, KC | 8 | Miller T, Hou | 4 | Osuna, LA | 2 |
| Reyes D, Cin | 14 | Springer R, Atl | 8 | Mulholland, 2Tm | 4 | Pena J, CWS | 2 |
| Sullivan, Cin | 13 | Wilkins, Pit | 8 | Munro, Tor | 4 | Silva, Pit | 2 |
| Aybar, StL | 12 | Assenmacher, Cle | 7 | Nunez, Ari-Fla | 4 | Sinclair, Tor-Sea | 2 |
| Heredia F, ChC | 12 | Carrasco, Min | 7 | Patterson, Tex | 4 | Spoljaric, Phi-Tor | 2 |
| Lopez, TB | 12 | Chouinard, Ari | 7 | Santiago, KC | 4 | Strickland, Mon | 2 |
| Orosco, Bal | 12 | Christiansen, Pit | 7 | Vosberg, SD-Ari | 4 | Wasdin, Bos | 2 |
| Petkovsek, Ana | 12 | Corsi, Bos-Bal | 7 | White R, TB | 4 | Watson, 3Tm | 2 |
| Poole, Phi-Cle | 12 | Johns, Bal | 7 | Abbott P, Sea | 3 | Williams B, Hou | 2 |
| Simas, CWS | 12 | McGlinchy, Atl | 7 | Adams, ChC | 3 | Zimmerman J, Sea | 2 |
| Jones D, Oak | 11 | McMichael, 2Tm | 7 | Almanza, Fla | 3 | | |
| Kamieniecki, Bal | 11 | Sanders, ChC | 7 | Anderson M, Det | 3 | | |

## Who Knows How to Handle Their Inheritance? (p. 148)

### Inherited Runners Scoring Percentage—Listed Alphabetically (minimum 23 IR in 1999)

| Pitcher, Team | IR | SC | Pct | Pitcher, Team | IR | SC | Pct | Pitcher, Team | IR | SC | Pct |
|---|---|---|---|---|---|---|---|---|---|---|---|
| Aldred, TB-Phi | 46 | 19 | 41.3 | Lee D, Col | 24 | 5 | 20.8 | Reyes C, SD | 41 | 20 | 48.8 |
| Alfonseca, Fla | 25 | 6 | 24.0 | Leskanic, Col | 48 | 19 | 39.6 | Reyes D, Cin | 53 | 14 | 26.4 |
| Anderson M, Det | 26 | 13 | 50.0 | Levine, Ana | 44 | 16 | 36.4 | Rigby, Oak-KC | 48 | 20 | 41.7 |
| Arnold, LA | 27 | 11 | 40.7 | Lloyd, Tor | 50 | 13 | 26.0 | Rincon, Cle | 42 | 5 | 11.9 |
| Assenmacher, Cle | 43 | 10 | 23.3 | Looper, Fla | 51 | 23 | 45.1 | Rivera M, NYY | 27 | 5 | 18.5 |
| Ayala, Mon-ChC | 40 | 20 | 50.0 | Lopez, TB | 27 | 7 | 25.9 | Rocker, Atl | 27 | 10 | 37.0 |
| Aybar, StL | 26 | 8 | 30.8 | Lowe D, Bos | 45 | 14 | 31.1 | Rodriguez F, SF | 31 | 16 | 51.6 |
| Benitez, NYM | 30 | 6 | 20.0 | Lowe S, CWS | 59 | 20 | 33.9 | Rodriguez R, SF | 55 | 11 | 20.0 |
| Bones, Bal | 23 | 7 | 30.4 | Magnante, Ana | 48 | 19 | 39.6 | Roque, Mil | 30 | 8 | 26.7 |
| Borbon, LA | 37 | 8 | 21.6 | Mahomes, NYM | 25 | 5 | 20.0 | Sampson, Min | 24 | 10 | 41.7 |
| Bottalico, StL | 27 | 11 | 40.7 | Masaoka, LA | 31 | 10 | 32.3 | Sanchez, Fla | 44 | 19 | 43.2 |
| Brocail, Det | 30 | 7 | 23.3 | Mathews T, Oak | 41 | 14 | 34.1 | Sanders, ChC | 40 | 12 | 30.0 |
| Byrdak, KC | 29 | 17 | 58.6 | McElroy, Col-NYM | 39 | 23 | 59.0 | Santiago, KC | 37 | 17 | 45.9 |
| Carrasco, Min | 26 | 11 | 42.3 | McGlinchy, Atl | 37 | 11 | 29.7 | Sauerbeck, Pit | 57 | 17 | 29.8 |
| Charlton, TB | 27 | 13 | 48.1 | McMichael, 2Tm | 24 | 7 | 29.2 | Schoeneweis, Ana | 25 | 8 | 32.0 |
| Chouinard, Ari | 24 | 5 | 20.8 | Mendoza, NYY | 26 | 4 | 15.4 | Seanez, Atl | 32 | 8 | 25.0 |
| Clontz, Pit | 37 | 9 | 24.3 | Mesa, Sea | 32 | 10 | 31.3 | Serafini, ChC | 23 | 9 | 39.1 |
| Cloude, Sea | 27 | 12 | 44.4 | Miceli, SD | 28 | 10 | 35.7 | Service, KC | 50 | 19 | 38.0 |
| Cook, NYM | 54 | 11 | 20.4 | Miller T, Min | 40 | 7 | 17.5 | Shuey, Cle | 31 | 15 | 48.4 |
| Cormier, Bos | 51 | 17 | 33.3 | Miller T, Hou | 39 | 9 | 23.1 | Simas, CWS | 57 | 25 | 43.9 |
| Crabtree, Tex | 63 | 17 | 27.0 | Mills, LA | 41 | 15 | 36.6 | Slocumb, Bal-StL | 27 | 11 | 40.7 |
| Croushore, StL | 50 | 21 | 42.0 | Mohler, StL | 36 | 10 | 27.8 | Spoljaric, Phi-Tor | 34 | 10 | 29.4 |
| Cruz, Det | 24 | 12 | 50.0 | Montgomery J, KC | 25 | 12 | 48.0 | Spradlin, Cle-SF | 49 | 11 | 22.4 |
| Darensbourg, Fla | 52 | 20 | 38.5 | Morman, KC | 49 | 14 | 28.6 | Springer R, Atl | 29 | 4 | 13.8 |
| Davey, Tor-Sea | 34 | 15 | 44.1 | Mota, Mon | 28 | 8 | 28.6 | Stanton, NYY | 62 | 15 | 24.2 |
| DeJean, Col | 24 | 6 | 25.0 | Munoz, Tex | 39 | 11 | 28.2 | Sullivan, Cin | 50 | 16 | 32.0 |
| Dipoto, Col | 32 | 4 | 12.5 | Munro, Tor | 29 | 11 | 37.9 | Swindell, Ari | 37 | 9 | 24.3 |
| Duvall, TB | 45 | 20 | 44.4 | Myers M, Mil | 78 | 12 | 15.4 | Tavarez, SF | 38 | 13 | 34.2 |
| Edmondson, Fla | 40 | 14 | 35.0 | Myers R, ChC | 38 | 12 | 31.6 | Telford, Mon | 44 | 17 | 38.6 |
| Embree, SF | 47 | 12 | 25.5 | Naulty, NYY | 29 | 8 | 27.6 | Timlin, Bal | 30 | 11 | 36.7 |
| Florie, Det-Bos | 25 | 10 | 40.0 | Nelson, NYY | 36 | 8 | 22.2 | Trombley, Min | 41 | 14 | 34.1 |
| Foulke, CWS | 23 | 3 | 13.0 | Nitkowski, Det | 50 | 16 | 32.0 | Urbina, Mon | 37 | 11 | 29.7 |
| Frascatore, Ari-Tor | 46 | 16 | 34.8 | Olson, Ari | 23 | 9 | 39.1 | Venafro, Tex | 69 | 24 | 34.8 |
| Gomes, Phi | 30 | 5 | 16.7 | Orosco, Bal | 73 | 16 | 21.9 | Wall, SD | 30 | 9 | 30.0 |
| Graves, Cin | 44 | 9 | 20.5 | Painter, StL | 40 | 7 | 17.5 | Wallace J, Pit | 27 | 3 | 11.1 |
| Grimsley, NYY | 43 | 11 | 25.6 | Paniagua, Sea | 58 | 21 | 36.2 | Ward, CWS | 39 | 9 | 23.1 |
| Groom, Oak | 69 | 20 | 29.0 | Patterson, Tex | 41 | 18 | 43.9 | Wasdin, Bos | 33 | 14 | 42.4 |
| Guardado, Min | 54 | 12 | 22.2 | Pena J, CWS | 23 | 7 | 30.4 | Weathers, Mil | 28 | 11 | 39.3 |
| Guthrie, Bos-ChC | 32 | 15 | 46.9 | Percival, Ana | 25 | 11 | 44.0 | Wells B, Min | 67 | 21 | 31.3 |
| Hansell, Pit | 29 | 11 | 37.9 | Petkovsek, Ana | 58 | 23 | 39.7 | Wendell, NYM | 46 | 12 | 26.1 |
| Hasegawa, Ana | 52 | 10 | 19.2 | Plesac, Tor-Ari | 62 | 17 | 27.4 | Whisenant, KC-SD | 54 | 19 | 35.2 |
| Heredia F, ChC | 60 | 19 | 31.7 | Plunk, Mil | 52 | 21 | 40.4 | White G, Cin | 26 | 11 | 42.3 |
| Holmes, Ari | 28 | 7 | 25.0 | Poole, Phi-Cle | 46 | 15 | 32.6 | White R, TB | 62 | 30 | 48.4 |
| Jones D, Oak | 55 | 21 | 38.2 | Powell J, Hou | 30 | 11 | 36.7 | Williams B, Hou | 32 | 15 | 46.9 |
| Kamieniecki, Bal | 27 | 6 | 22.2 | Quantrill, Tor | 30 | 13 | 43.3 | Williamson, Cin | 27 | 9 | 33.3 |
| Karsay, Cle | 29 | 10 | 34.5 | Radinsky, StL | 37 | 15 | 40.5 | Worrell, Oak | 49 | 25 | 51.0 |
| Kida, Det | 37 | 7 | 18.9 | Reed S, Cle | 44 | 20 | 45.5 | Yan, TB | 31 | 7 | 22.6 |
| Kline, Mon | 65 | 11 | 16.9 | Remlinger, Atl | 27 | 5 | 18.5 | Zimmerman J, Tex | 40 | 12 | 30.0 |
| Langston, Cle | 27 | 8 | 29.6 | Reyes A, Mil-Bal | 41 | 15 | 36.6 | **MLB Average** | | | **33.2** |

# Which Relievers Prevent the Most Runs? (p. 150)

## Runs Prevented—1999
### (minimum 50 IP and more relief appearances than starts)

| Pitcher, Team | RP | Pitcher, Team | RP | Pitcher, Team | RP |
|---|---|---|---|---|---|
| Abbott P, Sea | 5.6 | Kida, Det | -6.0 | Rodriguez F, SF | 3.0 |
| Acevedo, StL | -0.2 | Kline, Mon | 18.8 | Rodriguez F, Sea | -6.6 |
| Adams, ChC | 2.6 | Koch, Tor | 9.1 | Rodriguez R, SF | 4.2 |
| Aguilera, Min-ChC | 12.0 | Langston, Cle | 2.2 | Roque, Mil | 3.7 |
| Aldred, TB-Phi | -3.2 | Leskanic, Col | 0.4 | Sampson, Min | -6.0 |
| Alfonseca, Fla | 16.5 | Levine, Ana | 14.8 | Sanchez, Fla | -8.4 |
| Arnold, LA | -1.5 | Lloyd, Tor | 10.8 | Sanders, ChC | -5.7 |
| Ayala, Mon-ChC | 0.5 | Looper, Fla | 1.6 | Santana J, Bos | -0.3 |
| Aybar, StL | 0.2 | Lopez, TB | 0.6 | Sauerbeck, Pit | 19.6 |
| Batista, Mon | -2.9 | Lowe D, Bos | 32.2 | Schrenk, Phi | 9.1 |
| Benitez, NYM | 29.3 | Lowe S, CWS | 14.8 | Seanez, Atl | 13.7 |
| Blair, Det | 7.4 | Maddux M, Mon-LA | 2.6 | Serafini, ChC | -13.5 |
| Boehringer, SD | 7.7 | Magnante, Ana | 10.2 | Service, KC | -11.3 |
| Borbon, LA | 3.6 | Mahomes, NYM | 11.2 | Shaw, LA | 15.4 |
| Bottalico, StL | -8.9 | Mantei, Fla-Ari | 16.3 | Shuey, Cle | 6.0 |
| Brocail, Det | 26.5 | Masaoka, LA | 2.1 | Silva, Pit | 10.6 |
| Charlton, TB | -0.2 | Mathews T, Oak | 5.1 | Simas, CWS | 0.4 |
| Chen, Atl | -1.7 | Mays, Min | -10.8 | Slocumb, Bal-StL | 5.3 |
| Cloude, Sea | -10.6 | McElroy, Col-NYM | -13.3 | Smart, Mon | -2.0 |
| Cook, NYM | 11.2 | McGlinchy, Atl | 16.2 | Spoljaric, Phi-Tor | 8.2 |
| Coppinger, Bal-Mil | 0.8 | Mendoza, NYY | 7.0 | Spradlin, Cle-SF | -1.8 |
| Cormier, Bos | 15.8 | Mesa, Sea | 0.5 | Stanton, NYY | 5.5 |
| Crabtree, Tex | 7.8 | Miceli, SD | -0.5 | Sullivan, Cin | 26.8 |
| Croushore, StL | 0.2 | Mills, LA | 6.4 | Suzuki, Sea-KC | -11.4 |
| Cruz, Det | 2.0 | Montgomery J, KC | -12.1 | Swindell, Ari | 16.9 |
| Davey, Tor-Sea | 1.0 | Montgomery S, Phi | 16.8 | Tavarez, SF | -4.3 |
| DeJean, Col | -20.1 | Morman, KC | 7.7 | Taylor, Oak-NYM | 1.3 |
| Dipoto, Col | 11.6 | Mota, Mon | 8.1 | Telemaco, Ari-Phi | -6.4 |
| Edmondson, Fla | -6.0 | Munoz, Tex | 10.0 | Telford, Mon | 4.4 |
| Elarton, Hou | 13.7 | Munro, Tor | -0.1 | Timlin, Bal | 10.4 |
| Embree, SF | 12.2 | Murray H, SD | 2.5 | Trombley, Min | 1.9 |
| Florie, Det-Bos | -2.7 | Myers R, ChC | 4.1 | Urbina, Mon | 9.7 |
| Foulke, CWS | 38.2 | Nen, SF | 3.8 | Venafro, Tex | 12.7 |
| Frascatore, Ari-Tor | 3.0 | Nitkowski, Det | 2.0 | Veres, Col | -4.6 |
| Fussell, KC | -1.0 | Nunez, Ari-Fla | 12.8 | Wagner B, Hou | 29.1 |
| Fyhrie, Ana | 1.1 | Olson, Ari | 3.1 | Wakefield, Bos | 8.3 |
| Gomes, Phi | 4.7 | Painter, StL | 4.6 | Wall, SD | 11.3 |
| Grace, Phi | -9.2 | Paniagua, Sea | 3.7 | Wasdin, Bos | 1.3 |
| Graves, Cin | 33.3 | Patterson, Tex | -3.0 | Watson, NYM-Sea-NYY | 6.4 |
| Grimsley, NYY | 12.3 | Percival, Ana | 1.0 | Weathers, Mil | -1.7 |
| Guthrie, Bos-ChC | -4.6 | Perkins, Min | 5.0 | Wells B, Min | 12.8 |
| Hasegawa, Ana | 8.1 | Petkovsek, Ana | 7.1 | Wendell, NYM | 21.7 |
| Heredia F, ChC | -1.2 | Plunk, Mil | 4.9 | Wetteland, Tex | 9.1 |
| Hernandez R, TB | 16.5 | Powell J, Hou | 7.9 | Whisenant, KC-SD | -1.0 |
| Hoffman, SD | 25.1 | Reed S, Cle | -5.6 | White G, Cin | -2.4 |
| Howry, CWS | 9.9 | Rekar, TB | -2.3 | White R, TB | 5.7 |
| Isringhausen, NYM-Oak | 8.3 | Remlinger, Atl | 31.7 | Wickman, Mil | 10.2 |
| Jackson, Cle | 8.4 | Reyes A, Mil-Bal | -5.7 | Wilkins, Pit | 0.2 |
| Johns, Bal | -1.6 | Reyes C, SD | 6.5 | Williams B, Hou | -2.0 |
| Johnstone, SF | 18.2 | Reyes D, Cin | 10.4 | Williams M, Pit | -4.9 |
| Jones D, Oak | 15.7 | Rhodes, Bal | -2.1 | Williamson, Cin | 24.5 |
| Jones T, Det | 11.2 | Rigby, Oak-KC | -1.8 | Worrell, Oak | -5.6 |
| Kamieniecki, Bal | 10.0 | Rivera M, NYY | 25.6 | Yan, TB | -2.0 |
| Karsay, Cle | 13.4 | Rocker, Atl | 13.9 | Zimmerman J, Tex | 29.3 |

## Who Gets the Red Barrett Trophy? (p. 154)

### Fewest Pitches in a Nine-Inning Complete Game—1999

| Pitcher, Team | Date | Score | Opp | W/L | IP | H | R | ER | BB | SO | Pit | Time |
|---|---|---|---|---|---|---|---|---|---|---|---|---|
| Cone, NYY | 7/18 | 6-0 | Mon | W | 9.0 | 0 | 0 | 0 | 0 | 10 | 88 | 2:16 |
| Wells D, Tor | 7/17 | 6-1 | Fla | W | 9.0 | 6 | 1 | 1 | 0 | 6 | 92 | 2:22 |
| Baldwin, CWS | 5/29 | 7-1 | @Det | W | 9.0 | 5 | 1 | 1 | 0 | 7 | 95 | 2:30 |
| Lima, Hou | 6/2 | 9-1 | @Mil | W | 9.0 | 4 | 1 | 1 | 0 | 8 | 98 | 2:26 |
| Wells D, Tor | 6/20 | 2-1 | KC | W | 9.0 | 4 | 1 | 1 | 0 | 7 | 98 | 2:26 |
| Fernandez, Fla | 8/6 | 9-1 | Col | W | 9.0 | 3 | 1 | 1 | 0 | 2 | 98 | 2:26 |
| Woodard, Mil | 5/15 | 7-2 | Fla | W | 9.0 | 4 | 2 | 2 | 1 | 6 | 99 | 2:28 |
| Mlicki, Det | 6/26 | 0-1 | Min | L | 9.0 | 6 | 1 | 1 | 1 | 4 | 99 | 2:27 |
| Anderson B, Ari | 8/17 | 4-0 | ChC | W | 9.0 | 3 | 0 | 0 | 0 | 5 | 99 | 2:01 |
| Suppan, KC | 9/16 | 7-1 | Ana | W | 9.0 | 6 | 1 | 1 | 1 | 5 | 99 | 2:23 |
| Olivares, Ana | 5/2 | 6-3 | CWS | W | 9.0 | 5 | 3 | 2 | 1 | 3 | 101 | 2:22 |
| Schilling, Phi | 5/12 | 8-4 | @StL | W | 9.0 | 7 | 4 | 4 | 0 | 5 | 101 | 2:25 |
| Rogers, Oak | 5/27 | 6-1 | KC | W | 9.0 | 6 | 1 | 1 | 1 | 3 | 101 | 2:13 |
| Jimenez, StL | 6/25 | 1-0 | @Ari | W | 9.0 | 0 | 0 | 0 | 2 | 8 | 101 | 2:10 |
| Erickson, Bal | 7/17 | 2-1 | Mon | W | 9.0 | 6 | 1 | 1 | 3 | 2 | 101 | 2:23 |
| Moyer, Sea | 9/3 | 2-1 | Bos | W | 9.0 | 3 | 1 | 1 | 1 | 5 | 101 | 2:39 |
| Brown, LA | 9/4 | 6-0 | @ChC | W | 9.0 | 2 | 0 | 0 | 1 | 8 | 101 | 2:25 |
| Maddux G, Atl | 9/18 | 3-4 | Mon | L | 9.0 | 8 | 4 | 0 | 1 | 8 | 101 | 2:14 |
| Lieber, ChC | 10/1 | 3-2 | @StL | W | 9.0 | 7 | 2 | 2 | 0 | 7 | 101 | 2:27 |
| Cordova, Pit | 7/7 | 4-1 | ChC | W | 9.0 | 5 | 1 | 1 | 0 | 7 | 102 | 2:11 |
| Schmidt, Pit | 7/25 | 6-1 | @Mon | W | 9.0 | 4 | 1 | 1 | 0 | 4 | 102 | 2:37 |
| Dreifort, LA | 8/18 | 7-0 | Fla | W | 9.0 | 7 | 0 | 0 | 0 | 4 | 102 | 2:13 |
| Arrojo, TB | 8/22 | 2-1 | KC | W | 9.0 | 6 | 1 | 1 | 1 | 5 | 102 | 2:05 |
| Woodard, Mil | 4/23 | 9-1 | @Pit | W | 9.0 | 8 | 1 | 1 | 1 | 5 | 103 | 2:33 |
| Smoltz, Atl | 4/30 | 3-0 | Cin | W | 9.0 | 1 | 0 | 0 | 1 | 5 | 103 | 2:13 |
| Bergman, Hou | 4/30 | 8-1 | @Fla | W | 9.0 | 9 | 1 | 1 | 0 | 5 | 103 | 2:49 |
| Schilling, Phi | 5/7 | 8-1 | @Col | W | 9.0 | 7 | 1 | 1 | 2 | 4 | 103 | 2:35 |
| Wells D, Tor | 7/11 | 1-0 | @Mon | W | 9.0 | 2 | 0 | 0 | 1 | 7 | 103 | 2:14 |
| Batista, Mon | 4/14 | 15-1 | Mil | W | 9.0 | 6 | 1 | 1 | 0 | 6 | 104 | 2:40 |
| Astacio, Col | 5/16 | 5-1 | @Ari | W | 9.0 | 7 | 1 | 0 | 0 | 5 | 104 | 2:20 |
| Maddux G, Atl | 9/6 | 4-1 | StL | W | 9.0 | 3 | 1 | 1 | 0 | 7 | 104 | 2:04 |
| **MLB Average** | | | | | | | | | | | 116 | |

### Most Pitches in a Game—1999

| Pitcher, Team | Date | Score | Opp | W/L | IP | H | R | ER | BB | SO | Pit | Time |
|---|---|---|---|---|---|---|---|---|---|---|---|---|
| Astacio, Col | 6/6 | 10-5 | Mil | W | 7.2 | 9 | 5 | 5 | 4 | 10 | 153 | 3:07 |
| Person, Phi | 8/20 | 5-8 | LA | ND | 8.2 | 3 | 4 | 4 | 5 | 11 | 144 | 3:29 |
| Alvarez W, TB | 8/29 | 6-4 | @Cle | W | 8.0 | 8 | 4 | 3 | 2 | 6 | 144 | 3:23 |
| Johnson R, Ari | 7/25 | 1-2 | LA | L | 7.0 | 8 | 2 | 2 | 1 | 11 | 143 | 2:53 |
| Moyer, Sea | 9/19 | 1-2 | Min | L | 9.0 | 6 | 2 | 2 | 2 | 6 | 143 | 2:44 |
| Bottenfield, StL | 8/24 | 4-8 | @Mon | L | 7.2 | 11 | 8 | 8 | 5 | 1 | 142 | 2:42 |
| Johnson R, Ari | 4/25 | 5-3 | @SD | ND | 8.0 | 5 | 3 | 3 | 3 | 11 | 141 | 3:23 |
| Hernandez L, Fla | 6/12 | 4-5 | NYY | L | 7.2 | 6 | 5 | 5 | 5 | 5 | 141 | 3:19 |
| Ortiz R, SF | 7/10 | 4-2 | StL | W | 8.2 | 2 | 2 | 2 | 2 | 10 | 141 | 2:38 |
| Hernandez L, SF | 8/9 | 4-5 | @Fla | ND | 7.2 | 8 | 3 | 3 | 2 | 4 | 141 | 3:15 |
| Wright J, Col | 9/3 | 5-2 | @NYM | ND | 8.0 | 10 | 2 | 2 | 3 | 4 | 141 | 3:25 |
| Hitchcock, SD | 7/26 | 0-2 | Ari | L | 8.0 | 7 | 2 | 2 | 3 | 8 | 140 | 2:47 |
| Ortiz R, SF | 10/1 | 9-4 | @Col | W | 9.0 | 7 | 4 | 2 | 3 | 3 | 140 | 2:50 |
| Garcia F, Sea | 8/24 | 5-0 | Det | W | 9.0 | 6 | 0 | 0 | 1 | 12 | 139 | 2:30 |
| Schilling, Phi | 5/23 | 4-5 | @NYM | L | 8.2 | 12 | 5 | 5 | 1 | 7 | 138 | 2:48 |
| Alvarez W, TB | 6/25 | 11-4 | Tor | W | 9.0 | 6 | 4 | 4 | 0 | 11 | 138 | 2:46 |
| Arrojo, TB | 8/27 | 1-2 | @Cle | L | 8.0 | 9 | 2 | 2 | 4 | 6 | 138 | 2:35 |
| Clemens, NYY | 8/27 | 8-0 | Sea | W | 8.0 | 4 | 0 | 0 | 3 | 9 | 138 | 3:15 |
| Johnson R, Ari | 9/10 | 3-1 | Phi | W | 9.0 | 6 | 1 | 1 | 3 | 7 | 138 | 2:25 |

## Which Pitchers Have Misleading ERAs? (p. 156)

**Predicted ERA vs. Actual ERA—1999**
(minimum 100 IP for starters, 50 IP for relievers; difference of 0.40)

| Pitcher, Team | Pred ERA | Act ERA | Diff | Pitcher, Team | Pred ERA | Act ERA | Diff |
|---|---|---|---|---|---|---|---|
| Gardner, SF | 4.99 | 6.47 | -1.49 | Helling, Tex | 5.24 | 4.84 | 0.40 |
| Jimenez, StL | 4.49 | 5.85 | -1.37 | Ortiz R, SF | 4.22 | 3.81 | 0.41 |
| Whisenant, KC-SD | 4.27 | 5.63 | -1.36 | Graves, Cin | 3.49 | 3.08 | 0.41 |
| Pavano, Mon | 4.30 | 5.63 | -1.33 | Alvarez W, TB | 4.64 | 4.22 | 0.42 |
| DeJean, Col | 7.13 | 8.41 | -1.28 | Karl, Mil | 5.20 | 4.78 | 0.42 |
| Kida, Det | 5.05 | 6.26 | -1.22 | Plunk, Mil | 5.44 | 5.02 | 0.42 |
| Rhodes, Bal | 4.39 | 5.43 | -1.04 | Mesa, Sea | 5.41 | 4.98 | 0.42 |
| Haynes, Oak | 5.36 | 6.34 | -0.98 | Stottlemyre, Ari | 4.51 | 4.09 | 0.43 |
| Wright J, Cle | 5.12 | 6.06 | -0.94 | Trombley, Min | 4.76 | 4.33 | 0.43 |
| Urbina, Mon | 2.77 | 3.69 | -0.92 | Carpenter, Tor | 4.83 | 4.38 | 0.45 |
| Villone, Cin | 3.33 | 4.23 | -0.89 | Valdes, LA | 4.44 | 3.98 | 0.46 |
| Trachsel, ChC | 4.68 | 5.56 | -0.88 | McElroy, Col-NYM | 5.96 | 5.50 | 0.46 |
| Aybar, StL | 4.60 | 5.47 | -0.88 | Ayala, Mon-ChC | 3.97 | 3.51 | 0.46 |
| Sampson, Min | 7.29 | 8.11 | -0.82 | Maddux G, Atl | 4.04 | 3.57 | 0.47 |
| Vazquez, Mon | 4.20 | 5.00 | -0.81 | Crabtree, Tex | 3.93 | 3.46 | 0.47 |
| Hawkins, Min | 5.86 | 6.66 | -0.80 | Looper, Fla | 4.28 | 3.80 | 0.48 |
| Tavarez, SF | 5.14 | 5.93 | -0.78 | Mussina, Bal | 3.98 | 3.50 | 0.48 |
| Smart, Mon | 4.24 | 5.02 | -0.78 | Wetteland, Tex | 4.17 | 3.68 | 0.48 |
| Gooden, Cle | 5.49 | 6.26 | -0.77 | Ritchie, Pit | 4.00 | 3.50 | 0.50 |
| Johnson J, Bal | 4.69 | 5.46 | -0.77 | Montgomery S, Phi | 3.85 | 3.34 | 0.51 |
| Lopez, TB | 3.89 | 4.64 | -0.75 | Lloyd, Tor | 4.15 | 3.63 | 0.53 |
| Telemaco, Ari-Phi | 5.04 | 5.77 | -0.73 | Bottalico, StL | 5.46 | 4.91 | 0.55 |
| Milton, Min | 3.77 | 4.49 | -0.72 | White G, Cin | 4.99 | 4.43 | 0.56 |
| Blair, Det | 6.14 | 6.85 | -0.71 | Radke, Min | 4.31 | 3.75 | 0.57 |
| Borbon, LA | 3.38 | 4.09 | -0.71 | Guzman J, Bal-Cin | 4.31 | 3.74 | 0.57 |
| Johns, Bal | 3.77 | 4.47 | -0.70 | Maddux M, Mon-LA | 4.34 | 3.77 | 0.57 |
| Percival, Ana | 3.12 | 3.79 | -0.67 | Mercker, StL-Bos | 5.38 | 4.80 | 0.57 |
| Snyder, CWS | 6.10 | 6.68 | -0.58 | Jones T, Det | 4.38 | 3.80 | 0.58 |
| Irabu, NYY | 4.26 | 4.84 | -0.58 | Dipoto, Col | 4.89 | 4.26 | 0.64 |
| Guthrie, Bos-ChC | 4.81 | 5.37 | -0.56 | White R, TB | 4.73 | 4.08 | 0.64 |
| Kile, Col | 6.05 | 6.61 | -0.56 | Reed S, Cle | 4.89 | 4.23 | 0.66 |
| Dreifort, LA | 4.25 | 4.79 | -0.54 | Simas, CWS | 4.41 | 3.75 | 0.66 |
| Escobar, Tor | 5.17 | 5.69 | -0.52 | Wickman, Mil | 4.07 | 3.39 | 0.68 |
| Embree, SF | 2.87 | 3.38 | -0.50 | Saberhagen, Bos | 3.64 | 2.95 | 0.69 |
| Belcher, Ana | 6.23 | 6.73 | -0.50 | Arrojo, TB | 5.90 | 5.18 | 0.71 |
| Tapani, ChC | 4.34 | 4.83 | -0.49 | Bottenfield, StL | 4.69 | 3.97 | 0.71 |
| Finley, Ana | 3.95 | 4.43 | -0.48 | Alfonseca, Fla | 3.97 | 3.24 | 0.72 |
| Wells D, Tor | 4.34 | 4.82 | -0.47 | Lowe S, CWS | 4.41 | 3.67 | 0.75 |
| Edmondson, Fla | 5.37 | 5.84 | -0.47 | Karsay, Cle | 3.73 | 2.97 | 0.76 |
| Spoljaric, Phi-Tor | 5.79 | 6.26 | -0.47 | Wendell, NYM | 3.81 | 3.05 | 0.76 |
| Heredia G, Oak | 4.35 | 4.81 | -0.46 | Slocumb, Bal-StL | 4.55 | 3.77 | 0.77 |
| Mathews T, Oak | 3.37 | 3.81 | -0.45 | Remlinger, Atl | 3.14 | 2.37 | 0.78 |
| Patterson, Tex | 5.23 | 5.67 | -0.44 | Levine, Ana | 4.23 | 3.39 | 0.84 |
| Fassero, Sea-Tex | 6.77 | 7.20 | -0.43 | Halladay, Tor | 4.78 | 3.92 | 0.86 |
| Seanez, Atl | 2.93 | 3.35 | -0.42 | Myers R, ChC | 5.26 | 4.38 | 0.88 |
| Jackson, Cle | 3.64 | 4.06 | -0.42 | Watson, NYM-Sea-NYY | 4.47 | 3.51 | 0.96 |
| Spradlin, Cle-SF | 4.45 | 4.87 | -0.41 | Parris, Cin | 4.46 | 3.50 | 0.97 |
| Estes, SF | 4.52 | 4.92 | -0.40 | Swindell, Ari | 3.51 | 2.51 | 1.01 |
| | | | | McGlinchy, Atl | 3.87 | 2.82 | 1.05 |
| | | | | Frascatore, Ari-Tor | 4.86 | 3.73 | 1.13 |
| | | | | Mota, Mon | 4.14 | 2.93 | 1.21 |
| | | | | Morman, KC | 5.40 | 4.05 | 1.35 |
| | | | | Mills, LA | 5.18 | 3.73 | 1.44 |
| | | | | Sauerbeck, Pit | 3.54 | 2.00 | 1.55 |

## Does Pudge Intimidate the Best Basestealers? (p. 160)

**SB Success vs. Ivan Rodriguez by Top Basestealers—1995-99**
(minimum 25 SB in 1995 or 30 SB in all other seasons;
minimum one game started vs. Rodriguez during that year)

| Player, Team | Year | vs. Rodriguez | | | | | vs. Other Catchers | | | | |
|---|---|---|---|---|---|---|---|---|---|---|---|
| | | GS | Att | SB | Att/GS | Pct | GS | Att | SB | Att/GS | Pct |
| Roberto Alomar, Tor | 1995 | 10 | 1 | 1 | .10 | 100.0 | 118 | 32 | 29 | .27 | 90.6 |
| Roberto Alomar, Cle | 1999 | 9 | 2 | 2 | .22 | 100.0 | 146 | 41 | 35 | .28 | 85.4 |
| Brady Anderson, Bal | 1995 | 5 | 1 | 1 | .20 | 100.0 | 135 | 32 | 25 | .24 | 78.1 |
| Brady Anderson, Bal | 1999 | 11 | 1 | 0 | .09 | 0.0 | 132 | 42 | 36 | .32 | 85.7 |
| Barry Bonds, SF | 1997 | 4 | 1 | 1 | .25 | 100.0 | 154 | 44 | 36 | .29 | 81.8 |
| Homer Bush, Tor | 1999 | 7 | 1 | 0 | .14 | 0.0 | 118 | 39 | 32 | .33 | 82.1 |
| Vince Coleman, KC-Sea | 1995 | 11 | 5 | 2 | .45 | 40.0 | 99 | 51 | 38 | .52 | 74.5 |
| Chad Curtis, Det | 1995 | 9 | 3 | 0 | .33 | 0.0 | 135 | 39 | 27 | .29 | 69.2 |
| Johnny Damon, KC | 1999 | 8 | 3 | 3 | .38 | 100.0 | 136 | 39 | 33 | .29 | 84.6 |
| Ray Durham, CWS | 1996 | 8 | 2 | 2 | .25 | 100.0 | 137 | 31 | 28 | .23 | 90.3 |
| Ray Durham, CWS | 1997 | 9 | 1 | 0 | .11 | 0.0 | 145 | 48 | 33 | .33 | 68.8 |
| Ray Durham, CWS | 1998 | 9 | 2 | 1 | .22 | 50.0 | 147 | 43 | 35 | .29 | 81.4 |
| Ray Durham, CWS | 1999 | 6 | 1 | 0 | .17 | 0.0 | 145 | 44 | 34 | .30 | 77.3 |
| Juan Encarnacion, Det | 1999 | 7 | 2 | 1 | .29 | 50.0 | 120 | 43 | 32 | .36 | 74.4 |
| Tom Goodwin, KC | 1995 | 11 | 3 | 1 | .27 | 33.3 | 118 | 64 | 48 | .54 | 75.0 |
| Tom Goodwin, KC | 1996 | 9 | 0 | 0 | .00 | — | 121 | 83 | 63 | .69 | 75.9 |
| Tom Goodwin, KC-Tex | 1997 | 8 | 8 | 7 | 1.00 | 87.5 | 134 | 56 | 43 | .42 | 76.8 |
| Shawn Green, Tor | 1998 | 9 | 3 | 3 | .33 | 100.0 | 138 | 44 | 32 | .32 | 72.7 |
| Rickey Henderson, Oak | 1995 | 6 | 4 | 1 | .67 | 25.0 | 101 | 38 | 31 | .38 | 81.6 |
| Rickey Henderson, 2Tm | 1997 | 2 | 0 | 0 | .00 | — | 105 | 53 | 45 | .50 | 84.9 |
| Rickey Henderson, Oak | 1998 | 8 | 1 | 0 | .13 | 0.0 | 136 | 77 | 65 | .57 | 84.4 |
| Brian Hunter, Det | 1997 | 10 | 4 | 1 | .40 | 25.0 | 152 | 88 | 73 | .58 | 83.0 |
| Brian Hunter, Det | 1998 | 6 | 0 | 0 | .00 | — | 131 | 53 | 41 | .40 | 77.4 |
| Brian Hunter, Det-Sea | 1999 | 9 | 1 | 1 | .11 | 100.0 | 120 | 51 | 43 | .43 | 84.3 |
| Damian Jackson, SD | 1999 | 3 | 2 | 1 | .67 | 50.0 | 102 | 36 | 29 | .35 | 80.6 |
| Stan Javier, Oak | 1995 | 8 | 2 | 1 | .25 | 50.0 | 103 | 39 | 35 | .38 | 89.7 |
| Derek Jeter, NYY | 1998 | 11 | 1 | 0 | .09 | 0.0 | 137 | 35 | 30 | .26 | 85.7 |
| Lance Johnson, CWS | 1995 | 8 | 2 | 2 | .25 | 100.0 | 124 | 43 | 37 | .35 | 86.0 |
| Chuck Knoblauch, Min | 1995 | 8 | 3 | 1 | .38 | 33.3 | 128 | 61 | 45 | .48 | 73.8 |
| Chuck Knoblauch, Min | 1996 | 10 | 4 | 3 | .40 | 75.0 | 141 | 55 | 42 | .39 | 76.4 |
| Chuck Knoblauch, Min | 1997 | 10 | 1 | 1 | .10 | 100.0 | 146 | 71 | 61 | .49 | 85.9 |
| Chuck Knoblauch, NYY | 1998 | 10 | 1 | 0 | .10 | 0.0 | 140 | 42 | 31 | .30 | 73.8 |
| Kenny Lofton, Cle | 1995 | 5 | 1 | 0 | .20 | 0.0 | 110 | 66 | 52 | .60 | 78.8 |
| Kenny Lofton, Cle | 1996 | 11 | 3 | 2 | .27 | 66.7 | 142 | 89 | 73 | .63 | 82.0 |
| Kenny Lofton, Cle | 1998 | 10 | 2 | 2 | .20 | 100.0 | 140 | 61 | 51 | .44 | 83.6 |
| Raul Mondesi, LA | 1997 | 3 | 1 | 1 | .33 | 100.0 | 154 | 46 | 31 | .30 | 67.4 |
| Raul Mondesi, LA | 1999 | 3 | 0 | 0 | .00 | — | 152 | 45 | 36 | .30 | 80.0 |

|  |  | vs. Rodriguez | | | | | vs. Other Catchers | | | | |
| --- | --- | --- | --- | --- | --- | --- | --- | --- | --- | --- | --- |
| Player, Team | Year | GS | Att | SB | Att/GS | Pct | GS | Att | SB | Att/GS | Pct |
| Otis Nixon, Tor | 1996 | 8 | 2 | 0 | .25 | 0.0 | 117 | 65 | 54 | .56 | 83.1 |
| Otis Nixon, Tor-LA | 1997 | 7 | 1 | 1 | .14 | 100.0 | 137 | 70 | 58 | .51 | 82.9 |
| Otis Nixon, Min | 1998 | 8 | 1 | 1 | .13 | 100.0 | 98 | 43 | 36 | .44 | 83.7 |
| Jose Offerman, KC | 1998 | 8 | 0 | 0 | .00 | — | 149 | 57 | 45 | .38 | 78.9 |
| Eric Owens, SD | 1999 | 2 | 0 | 0 | .00 | — | 96 | 37 | 30 | .39 | 81.1 |
| Alex Rodriguez, Sea | 1998 | 9 | 1 | 1 | .11 | 100.0 | 152 | 58 | 45 | .38 | 77.6 |
| Reggie Sanders, SD | 1999 | 3 | 1 | 0 | .33 | 0.0 | 125 | 48 | 36 | .38 | 75.0 |
| Shannon Stewart, Tor | 1998 | 7 | 2 | 2 | .29 | 100.0 | 118 | 65 | 47 | .55 | 72.3 |
| Shannon Stewart, Tor | 1999 | 10 | 3 | 0 | .30 | 0.0 | 134 | 48 | 37 | .36 | 77.1 |
| Quilvio Veras, SD | 1997 | 3 | 0 | 0 | .00 | — | 131 | 45 | 33 | .34 | 73.3 |
| Quilvio Veras, SD | 1999 | 3 | 1 | 1 | .33 | 100.0 | 115 | 46 | 29 | .40 | 63.0 |
| Omar Vizquel, Cle | 1995 | 7 | 3 | 1 | .43 | 33.3 | 128 | 37 | 28 | .29 | 75.7 |
| Omar Vizquel, Cle | 1996 | 12 | 3 | 1 | .25 | 33.3 | 137 | 40 | 33 | .29 | 82.5 |
| Omar Vizquel, Cle | 1997 | 9 | 3 | 2 | .33 | 66.7 | 140 | 52 | 41 | .37 | 78.8 |
| Omar Vizquel, Cle | 1998 | 10 | 1 | 1 | .10 | 100.0 | 139 | 48 | 36 | .35 | 75.0 |
| Omar Vizquel, Cle | 1999 | 9 | 3 | 3 | .33 | 100.0 | 131 | 48 | 39 | .37 | 81.3 |
| Larry Walker, Col | 1997 | 3 | 0 | 0 | .00 | — | 145 | 41 | 33 | .28 | 80.5 |
| Tony Womack, Ari | 1999 | 6 | 1 | 1 | .17 | 100.0 | 136 | 84 | 71 | .62 | 84.5 |
| Eric Young, Col-LA | 1997 | 5 | 2 | 2 | .40 | 100.0 | 146 | 57 | 43 | .39 | 75.4 |
| Eric Young, LA | 1998 | 1 | 0 | 0 | .00 | — | 113 | 55 | 42 | .49 | 76.4 |
| Eric Young, LA | 1999 | 3 | 0 | 0 | .00 | — | 113 | 73 | 51 | .65 | 69.9 |
| **Totals** |  | **424** | **101** | **59** | **.24** | **58.4** | **7,542** | **2,981** | **2,357** | **.40** | **79.1** |

*Baseball Scoreboard*

## Which Catchers Catch Thieves? (p. 163)

The chart below lists the runners each catcher caught stealing (**CCS**), the stolen bases (**SB**) while he was behind the plate, the caught stealing percentage (**CS%**), the runners he picked off (**CPk**), the stolen bases allowed per 9 innings (**SB/9**), and the runners caught stealing (**PCS**) and picked off (**PPk**) by his pitchers.

### Catcher Caught Stealing Percentages—Listed Alphabetically
### (minimum 500 innings caught in 1999)

| Catcher, Team | CCS | SB | CS% | CPk | SB/9 | PCS | PPk |
|---|---|---|---|---|---|---|---|
| Ausmus, Det | 32 | 59 | 35.2 | 0 | 0.49 | 3 | 5 |
| Bako, Hou | 18 | 35 | 34.0 | 2 | 0.57 | 1 | 1 |
| Blanco, Col | 37 | 59 | 38.5 | 0 | 0.77 | 2 | 2 |
| Castillo A, StL | 27 | 35 | 43.5 | 0 | 0.48 | 9 | 2 |
| Davis B, SD | 17 | 45 | 27.4 | 1 | 0.64 | 3 | 2 |
| Diaz E, Cle | 38 | 72 | 34.5 | 3 | 0.66 | 1 | 0 |
| Eusebio, Hou | 18 | 39 | 31.6 | 0 | 0.46 | 2 | 1 |
| Fabregas, Fla-Atl | 26 | 37 | 41.3 | 4 | 0.54 | 4 | 4 |
| Flaherty, TB | 49 | 78 | 38.6 | 2 | 0.71 | 3 | 3 |
| Fletcher, Tor | 22 | 79 | 21.8 | 0 | 0.76 | 7 | 3 |
| Fordyce, CWS | 17 | 61 | 21.8 | 0 | 0.68 | 10 | 2 |
| Girardi, NYY | 15 | 56 | 21.1 | 0 | 0.91 | 4 | 1 |
| Hinch, Oak | 10 | 42 | 19.2 | 0 | 0.67 | 5 | 3 |
| Hundley, LA | 23 | 107 | 17.7 | 0 | 1.10 | 9 | 6 |
| Johnson C, Bal | 36 | 62 | 36.7 | 3 | 0.51 | 2 | 1 |
| Johnson M, CWS | 14 | 36 | 28.0 | 0 | 0.56 | 5 | 4 |
| Kendall, Pit | 25 | 39 | 39.1 | 0 | 0.54 | 5 | 7 |
| Kreuter, KC | 30 | 68 | 30.6 | 0 | 0.80 | 6 | 1 |
| Lieberthal, Phi | 27 | 66 | 29.0 | 2 | 0.50 | 4 | 4 |
| Macfarlane, Oak | 24 | 36 | 40.0 | 0 | 0.61 | 1 | 0 |
| Marrero, StL | 24 | 41 | 36.9 | 1 | 0.53 | 5 | 4 |
| Mayne, SF | 23 | 69 | 25.0 | 0 | 0.80 | 8 | 1 |
| Miller, Ari | 29 | 67 | 30.2 | 0 | 0.84 | 7 | 7 |
| Nilsson, Mil | 19 | 104 | 15.4 | 2 | 1.23 | 8 | 3 |
| Perez E, Atl | 21 | 52 | 28.8 | 0 | 0.62 | 2 | 1 |
| Piazza, NYM | 30 | 115 | 20.7 | 0 | 0.89 | 7 | 8 |
| Posada, NYY | 21 | 75 | 21.9 | 1 | 0.76 | 8 | 2 |
| Redmond, Fla | 25 | 46 | 35.2 | 0 | 0.63 | 3 | 2 |
| Reed, Col-ChC | 22 | 79 | 21.8 | 2 | 1.18 | 2 | 0 |
| Rodriguez I, Tex | 38 | 34 | 52.8 | 10 | 0.25 | 3 | 3 |
| Santiago, ChC | 23 | 42 | 35.4 | 0 | 0.45 | 2 | 2 |
| Steinbach, Min | 15 | 47 | 24.2 | 1 | 0.52 | 0 | 3 |
| Stinnett, Ari | 22 | 69 | 24.2 | 0 | 0.88 | 8 | 5 |
| Taubensee, Cin | 15 | 97 | 13.4 | 0 | 0.90 | 2 | 7 |
| Valentin J, Min | 19 | 25 | 43.2 | 0 | 0.41 | 2 | 2 |
| Varitek, Bos | 42 | 124 | 25.3 | 0 | 0.97 | 4 | 4 |
| Walbeck, Ana | 27 | 59 | 31.4 | 0 | 0.74 | 3 | 6 |
| Widger, Mon | 26 | 101 | 20.5 | 0 | 1.02 | 3 | 6 |
| Wilson D, Sea | 19 | 78 | 19.6 | 2 | 0.71 | 6 | 3 |
| **MLB Average** | | | 27.2 | | 0.71 | | |

## Can We Improve Zone Ratings? (p. 165)

### Highest Ultimate Zone Rating—1999
### (minimum 500 innings)

| First Basemen | UZR | | | | |
|---|---|---|---|---|---|
| Kevin Young, Pit | 26.15 | Jose Offerman, Bos | 10.76 | Gary Gaetti, ChC | -0.39 |
| John Olerud, NYM | 25.35 | Ron Belliard, Mil | 10.53 | Travis Fryman, Cle | -1.02 |
| Rico Brogna, Phi | 20.13 | Edgardo Alfonzo, NYM | 10.47 | Ken Caminiti, Hou | -2.49 |
| Tino Martinez, NYY | 16.15 | Mark McLemore, Tex | 8.45 | Chipper Jones, Atl | -3.29 |
| Mark Grace, ChC | 15.62 | Carlos Febles, KC | 6.54 | Matt Williams, Ari | -3.87 |
| Tony Clark, Det | 15.11 | Marlon Anderson, Phi | 5.19 | Todd Zeile, Tex | -6.43 |
| Eric Karros, LA | 14.96 | Warren Morris, Pit | 2.33 | Vinny Castilla, Col | -6.89 |
| Doug Mientkiewicz, Min | 14.74 | Quilvio Veras, SD | 0.74 | Michael Barrett, Mon | -9.22 |
| Darin Erstad, Ana | 14.01 | Delino DeShields, Bal | 0.40 | Fernando Tatis, StL | -10.23 |
| Ron Coomer, Min | 8.85 | Mickey Morandini, ChC | -4.55 | Ed Sprague, Pit | -12.12 |
| Jim Thome, Cle | 8.64 | Jeff Kent, SF | -4.56 | Dean Palmer, Det | -12.96 |
| Jeff Conine, Bal | 8.57 | Miguel Cairo, TB | -4.64 | Joe Randa, KC | -13.66 |
| Wally Joyner, SD | 2.59 | Eric Young, LA | -4.69 | Wade Boggs, TB | -15.68 |
| Carlos Delgado, Tor | 1.75 | Ray Durham, CWS | -4.77 | Tony Fernandez, Tor | -21.97 |
| Mo Vaughn, Ana | 1.01 | David Bell, Sea | -7.91 | Greg Norton, CWS | -23.33 |
| Kevin Millar, Fla | 0.08 | Roberto Alomar, Cle | -9.00 | Russ Davis, Sea | -34.94 |
| Will Clark, Bal | -1.20 | Damion Easley, Det | -16.88 | **Shortstops** | **UZR** |
| Paul Konerko, CWS | -2.90 | Jose Vidro, Mon | -19.88 | Rey Sanchez, KC | 56.75 |
| Travis Lee, Ari | -4.01 | Luis Castillo, Fla | -21.69 | Rey Ordonez, NYM | 46.40 |
| Sean Casey, Cin | -5.50 | Bret Boone, Atl | -24.06 | Omar Vizquel, Cle | 25.19 |
| Jeff Bagwell, Hou | -5.65 | Todd Walker, Min | -32.05 | Mike Benjamin, Pit | 21.78 |
| Todd Helton, Col | -6.07 | Chuck Knoblauch, NYY | -40.58 | Royce Clayton, Tex | 17.56 |
| Lee Stevens, Tex | -8.15 | **Third Basemen** | **UZR** | Tony Batista, Ari-Tor | 16.66 |
| Ryan Klesko, Atl | -8.65 | Robin Ventura, NYM | 45.66 | Orlando Cabrera, Mon | 15.53 |
| J.T. Snow, SF | -9.12 | Adrian Beltre, LA | 33.57 | Damian Jackson, SD | 12.92 |
| Mike Sweeney, KC | -9.44 | Scott Rolen, Phi | 22.51 | Mike Bordick, Bal | 12.42 |
| Brad Fullmer, Mon | -10.13 | Aaron Boone, Cin | 16.71 | Barry Larkin, Cin | 11.18 |
| Mike Stanley, Bos | -12.06 | John Valentin, Bos | 16.63 | Miguel Tejada, Oak | 9.19 |
| Fred McGriff, TB | -15.02 | Kevin Orie, Fla | 12.76 | Jose Hernandez, ChC-Atl | 5.02 |
| Jason Giambi, Oak | -16.92 | Corey Koskie, Min | 11.72 | Nomar Garciaparra, Bos | 4.77 |
| David Segui, Sea-Tor | -16.93 | Scott Brosius, NYY | 10.54 | Andy Fox, Ari | 3.72 |
| Mark McGwire, StL | -20.40 | Troy Glaus, Ana | 10.14 | Edgar Renteria, StL | 2.76 |
| **Second Basemen** | **UZR** | Shane Andrews, 2Tm | 9.98 | Chris Gomez, SD | 2.08 |
| Pokey Reese, Cin | 56.28 | Eric Chavez, Oak | 5.68 | Mark Grudzielanek, LA | 0.93 |
| Homer Bush, Tor | 24.93 | Bill Spiers, Hou | 4.74 | Mike Caruso, CWS | 0.71 |
| Craig Biggio, Hou | 20.27 | Mike Lowell, Fla | 3.38 | Deivi Cruz, Det | 0.59 |
| Randy Velarde, Ana-Oak | 17.81 | Bill Mueller, SF | 3.25 | Neifi Perez, Col | 0.37 |
| Jay Bell, Ari | 16.10 | Phil Nevin, SD | 2.74 | Gary DiSarcina, Ana | -0.76 |
| Joe McEwing, StL | 12.17 | Cal Ripken Jr., Bal | 0.91 | Andy Sheets, Ana | -2.16 |
| | | Jeff Cirillo, Mil | 0.46 | Kevin Stocker, TB | -2.48 |

*Baseball Scoreboard*

| Player | UZR |
|---|---|
| Desi Relaford, Phi | -3.89 |
| Alex Rodriguez, Sea | -4.23 |
| Tim Bogar, Hou | -4.44 |
| Ricky Gutierrez, Hou | -11.32 |
| Mark Loretta, Mil | -13.93 |
| Alex Gonzalez, Fla | -14.60 |
| Jose Valentin, Mil | -17.33 |
| Alex Arias, Phi | -17.68 |
| Cristian Guzman, Min | -19.95 |
| Derek Jeter, NYY | -21.03 |
| Walt Weiss, Atl | -21.48 |
| Rich Aurilia, SF | -43.41 |
| **Left Fielders** | **UZR** |
| Geoff Jenkins, Mil | 32.35 |
| Darin Erstad, Ana | 27.99 |
| Ray Lankford, StL | 24.89 |
| Johnny Damon, KC | 21.33 |
| Luis Gonzalez, Ari | 16.47 |
| B.J. Surhoff, Bal | 15.14 |
| Ricky Ledee, NYY | 12.17 |
| Brian Hunter, Sea | 10.72 |
| Ron Gant, Phi | 10.21 |
| Rondell White, Mon | 9.67 |
| Juan Encarnacion, Det | 9.33 |
| Reggie Sanders, SD | 8.91 |
| Cliff Floyd, Fla | 6.96 |
| Troy O'Leary, Bos | 6.62 |
| Bruce Aven, Fla | 6.39 |
| Gerald Williams, Atl | 5.10 |
| Richard Hidalgo, Hou | 4.28 |
| David Justice, Cle | 1.67 |
| Greg Vaughn, Cin | 0.54 |
| Rusty Greer, Tex | -1.48 |
| Carlos Lee, CWS | -5.54 |
| Henry Rodriguez, ChC | -6.71 |
| Shannon Stewart, Tor | -7.51 |
| Barry Bonds, SF | -7.84 |
| Rickey Henderson, NYM | -13.30 |
| Al Martin, Pit | -13.82 |
| Gary Sheffield, LA | -21.04 |
| Ben Grieve, Oak | -22.36 |
| Chad Allen, Min | -30.35 |
| Dante Bichette, Col | -30.37 |
| **Center Fielders** | **UZR** |
| Andruw Jones, Atl | 44.72 |
| Mike Cameron, Cin | 35.82 |
| Gabe Kapler, Det | 32.23 |
| Ruben Rivera, SD | 28.65 |
| Chris Singleton, CWS | 22.84 |
| Jacque Jones, Min | 17.12 |
| Marvin Benard, SF | 12.63 |
| Kenny Lofton, Cle | 10.97 |
| Darren Lewis, Bos | 10.59 |
| Jose Cruz, Tor | 9.70 |
| Ryan Christenson, Oak | 8.24 |
| Torii Hunter, Min | 7.85 |
| Lance Johnson, ChC | 7.30 |
| Damon Buford, Bos | 7.27 |
| Garret Anderson, Ana | 5.89 |
| Carl Everett, Hou | 5.56 |
| Brady Anderson, Bal | 5.24 |
| Carlos Beltran, KC | 1.37 |
| Tom Goodwin, Tex | 0.84 |
| Brian Giles, Pit | 0.51 |
| Doug Glanville, Phi | -0.47 |
| J.D. Drew, StL | -0.54 |
| Steve Finley, Ari | -3.31 |
| Manny Martinez, Mon | -5.25 |
| Randy Winn, TB | -6.69 |
| Rondell White, Mon | -9.91 |
| Devon White, LA | -9.93 |
| Ken Griffey Jr., Sea | -14.74 |
| Darryl Hamilton, Col-NYM | -16.26 |
| Bernie Williams, NYY | -23.17 |
| Preston Wilson, Fla | -24.88 |
| Marquis Grissom, Mil | -29.44 |
| Brian McRae, 3Tm | -41.03 |
| **Right Fielders** | **UZR** |
| Shawn Green, Tor | 28.78 |
| Mark Kotsay, Fla | 26.54 |
| Jermaine Dye, KC | 19.36 |
| Tony Womack, Ari | 15.59 |
| Sammy Sosa, ChC | 14.67 |
| Brian Jordan, Atl | 13.83 |
| Vladimir Guerrero, Mon | 12.46 |
| Trot Nixon, Bos | 11.79 |
| Magglio Ordonez, CWS | 10.81 |
| Manny Ramirez, Cle | 9.73 |
| Jeromy Burnitz, Mil | 9.44 |
| Tim Salmon, Ana | 3.15 |
| Bob Higginson, Det | 3.02 |
| Roger Cedeno, NYM | 2.71 |
| Dmitri Young, Cin | 0.90 |
| Michael Tucker, Cin | 0.49 |
| Derek Bell, Hou | -4.37 |
| Juan Gonzalez, Tex | -7.97 |
| Tony Gwynn, SD | -8.29 |
| Raul Mondesi, LA | -8.84 |
| Jay Buhner, Sea | -9.14 |
| Paul O'Neill, NYY | -9.58 |
| Jose Guillen, Pit-TB | -10.24 |
| Larry Walker, Col | -10.80 |
| Matt Lawton, Min | -11.69 |
| Ellis Burks, SF | -14.16 |
| Dave Martinez, TB | -15.39 |
| Bobby Abreu, Phi | -16.51 |
| Matt Stairs, Oak | -28.31 |
| Albert Belle, Bal | -33.48 |

## Who's Best in the Infield Zone? (p. 174)

### Infield Zone Ratings—1999
### (minimum 1,000 defensive innings)

| FIRST BASE | | 1999 | | | 1997-99 | | |
|---|---|---|---|---|---|---|---|
| Player, Team | Innings | In Zone | Outs | Zone Rating | In Zone | Outs | Zone Rating |
| Young K, Pit | 1,358.2 | 280 | 256 | .914 | 701 | 617 | .880 |
| Grace, ChC | 1,379.2 | 261 | 233 | .893 | 827 | 721 | .872 |
| Clark T, Det | 1,147.2 | 225 | 200 | .889 | 730 | 635 | .870 |
| Olerud, NYM | 1,385.2 | 257 | 226 | .879 | 828 | 722 | .872 |
| Martinez T, NYY | 1,342.0 | 299 | 262 | .876 | 796 | 675 | .848 |
| Stevens, Tex | 1,151.0 | 233 | 201 | .863 | 383 | 321 | .838 |
| Brogna, Phi | 1,352.1 | 277 | 238 | .859 | 786 | 669 | .851 |
| Karros, LA | 1,302.1 | 261 | 223 | .854 | 782 | 663 | .848 |
| Bagwell, Hou | 1,401.2 | 261 | 222 | .851 | 802 | 683 | .852 |
| Delgado C, Tor | 1,305.0 | 235 | 199 | .847 | 711 | 603 | .848 |
| Giambi J, Oak | 1,208.2 | 214 | 181 | .846 | 576 | 475 | .825 |
| Casey, Cin | 1,297.0 | 225 | 190 | .844 | 360 | 305 | .847 |
| Snow, SF | 1,344.1 | 250 | 207 | .828 | 696 | 571 | .820 |
| Helton, Col | 1,310.0 | 277 | 227 | .819 | 603 | 504 | .836 |
| McGwire, StL | 1,257.2 | 238 | 193 | .811 | 774 | 630 | .814 |
| McGriff, TB | 1,065.2 | 211 | 170 | .806 | 657 | 537 | .817 |
| **MLB Average** | | | | **.846** | | | **.841** |

| SECOND BASE | | 1999 | | | 1997-99 | | |
|---|---|---|---|---|---|---|---|
| Player, Team | Innings | In Zone | Outs | Zone Rating | In Zone | Outs | Zone Rating |
| Reese, Cin | 1,222.2 | 411 | 372 | .905 | 440 | 398 | .905 |
| Alfonzo, NYM | 1,380.2 | 442 | 378 | .855 | 449 | 385 | .857 |
| Biggio, Hou | 1,351.1 | 471 | 402 | .854 | 1,461 | 1,246 | .853 |
| Velarde, Ana-Oak | 1,358.1 | 530 | 452 | .853 | 680 | 576 | .847 |
| Alomar, Cle | 1,306.1 | 500 | 426 | .852 | 1,341 | 1,118 | .834 |
| McLemore, Tex | 1,158.2 | 469 | 395 | .842 | 1,103 | 920 | .834 |
| Offerman, Bos | 1,096.2 | 379 | 317 | .836 | 1,145 | 939 | .820 |
| Kent, SF | 1,125.0 | 360 | 301 | .836 | 1,236 | 1,040 | .841 |
| Castillo L, Fla | 1,068.1 | 381 | 317 | .832 | 681 | 573 | .841 |
| Morris W, Pit | 1,215.2 | 463 | 385 | .832 | 463 | 385 | .832 |
| Boone B, Atl | 1,296.2 | 473 | 390 | .825 | 1,344 | 1,093 | .813 |
| Bell D, Sea | 1,307.2 | 468 | 385 | .823 | 895 | 726 | .811 |
| Bell J, Ari | 1,297.0 | 381 | 313 | .822 | 427 | 352 | .824 |
| Belliard, Mil | 1,007.2 | 354 | 290 | .819 | 354 | 290 | .819 |
| Veras Q, SD | 1,003.0 | 367 | 299 | .815 | 1,265 | 1,058 | .836 |
| Febles, KC | 1,066.0 | 408 | 327 | .801 | 430 | 344 | .800 |
| Easley, Det | 1,229.0 | 481 | 383 | .796 | 1,438 | 1,123 | .781 |
| Durham, CWS | 1,263.2 | 472 | 374 | .792 | 1,413 | 1,125 | .796 |
| Knoblauch, NYY | 1,316.2 | 519 | 404 | .778 | 1,447 | 1,164 | .804 |
| **MLB Average** | | | | **.827** | | | **.824** |

## THIRD BASE

| Player, Team | Innings | 1999 In Zone | Outs | Zone Rating | 1997-99 In Zone | Outs | Zone Rating |
|---|---|---|---|---|---|---|---|
| Ventura, NYM | 1,356.0 | 421 | 343 | .815 | 989 | 794 | .803 |
| Beltre, LA | 1,320.2 | 365 | 289 | .792 | 544 | 425 | .781 |
| Boone A, Cin | 1,110.0 | 347 | 268 | .772 | 520 | 399 | .767 |
| Brosius, NYY | 1,150.2 | 334 | 257 | .769 | 998 | 792 | .794 |
| Cirillo, Mil | 1,338.1 | 438 | 334 | .763 | 1,298 | 1,027 | .791 |
| Williams M, Ari | 1,358.0 | 419 | 318 | .759 | 1,206 | 934 | .774 |
| Castilla, Col | 1,351.1 | 410 | 309 | .754 | 1,308 | 972 | .743 |
| Glaus, Ana | 1,344.0 | 394 | 292 | .741 | 521 | 383 | .735 |
| Zeile, Tex | 1,354.1 | 425 | 314 | .739 | 1,187 | 865 | .729 |
| Palmer, Det | 1,212.0 | 350 | 253 | .723 | 1,026 | 723 | .705 |
| Jones C, Atl | 1,381.0 | 353 | 254 | .720 | 1,064 | 806 | .758 |
| Tatis, StL | 1,278.2 | 381 | 274 | .719 | 952 | 699 | .734 |
| Randa, KC | 1,355.1 | 480 | 337 | .702 | 1,121 | 819 | .731 |
| Sprague, Pit | 1,144.1 | 393 | 273 | .695 | 989 | 706 | .714 |
| Davis R, Sea | 1,058.2 | 310 | 213 | .687 | 1,011 | 694 | .686 |
| Fernandez T, Tor | 1,108.2 | 317 | 217 | .685 | 417 | 292 | .700 |
| **MLB Average** | | | | .745 | | | .746 |

## SHORTSTOP

| Player, Team | Innings | 1999 In Zone | Outs | Zone Rating | 1997-99 In Zone | Outs | Zone Rating |
|---|---|---|---|---|---|---|---|
| Ordonez R, NYM | 1,316.2 | 443 | 396 | .894 | 1,258 | 1,092 | .868 |
| Sanchez, KC | 1,128.2 | 478 | 425 | .889 | 792 | 704 | .889 |
| Larkin, Cin | 1,372.2 | 434 | 381 | .878 | 994 | 870 | .875 |
| Bordick, Bal | 1,355.0 | 543 | 471 | .867 | 1,479 | 1,287 | .870 |
| Vizquel, Cle | 1,214.1 | 442 | 381 | .862 | 1,404 | 1,226 | .873 |
| Batista, Ari-Tor | 1,207.2 | 473 | 405 | .856 | 765 | 651 | .851 |
| Grudzielanek, LA | 1,028.0 | 333 | 285 | .856 | 1,367 | 1,134 | .830 |
| Perez N, Col | 1,369.2 | 518 | 438 | .846 | 1,221 | 1,039 | .851 |
| Rodriguez A, Sea | 1,114.2 | 434 | 366 | .843 | 1,365 | 1,163 | .852 |
| Cruz D, Det | 1,300.1 | 510 | 430 | .843 | 1,464 | 1,245 | .850 |
| Renteria, StL | 1,258.0 | 463 | 389 | .840 | 1,323 | 1,111 | .840 |
| Clayton, Tex | 1,149.1 | 463 | 386 | .834 | 1,457 | 1,257 | .863 |
| Jeter, NYY | 1,395.2 | 430 | 358 | .833 | 1,388 | 1,169 | .842 |
| Aurilia, SF | 1,281.0 | 452 | 376 | .832 | 910 | 764 | .840 |
| Tejada, Oak | 1,377.1 | 528 | 438 | .830 | 981 | 799 | .814 |
| Caruso, CWS | 1,114.2 | 416 | 341 | .820 | 844 | 697 | .826 |
| Hernandez J, ChC-Atl | 1,054.0 | 436 | 356 | .817 | 589 | 487 | .827 |
| Garciaparra, Bos | 1,171.2 | 423 | 344 | .813 | 1,421 | 1,174 | .826 |
| Gonzalez A, Fla | 1,144.1 | 387 | 310 | .801 | 450 | 362 | .804 |
| Guzman C, Min | 1,069.0 | 435 | 340 | .782 | 435 | 340 | .782 |
| **MLB Average** | | | | .837 | | | .842 |

## Who Can Turn the Pivot? (p. 178)

### Pivot Percentages—Active Players, Listed Alphabetically
### (minimum 15 Opp, 1995-99)

| Player | Opp | DP | Pct | Player | Opp | DP | Pct |
|---|---|---|---|---|---|---|---|
| Abbott K | 74 | 34 | .459 | Hernandez J | 20 | 9 | .450 |
| Alexander | 79 | 51 | .646 | Hocking | 30 | 19 | .633 |
| Alfonzo | 129 | 86 | .667 | Howard D | 54 | 30 | .556 |
| Alicea | 272 | 166 | .610 | Huson | 43 | 30 | .698 |
| Alomar | 388 | 223 | .575 | Jordan K | 54 | 30 | .556 |
| Anderson M | 56 | 27 | .482 | Kelly P | 109 | 61 | .560 |
| Baerga | 316 | 183 | .579 | Kent | 314 | 190 | .605 |
| Batista | 49 | 32 | .653 | King | 56 | 28 | .500 |
| Bell Da | 210 | 125 | .595 | Knoblauch | 434 | 246 | .567 |
| Bell J | 93 | 45 | .484 | Lansing | 385 | 225 | .584 |
| Belliard | 70 | 44 | .629 | Ledesma | 29 | 15 | .517 |
| Benjamin | 50 | 29 | .580 | Lewis M | 182 | 95 | .522 |
| Berg | 25 | 17 | .680 | Lockhart | 134 | 93 | .694 |
| Biggio | 509 | 269 | .528 | Lopez L | 38 | 20 | .526 |
| Blauser | 16 | 6 | .375 | Loretta | 65 | 43 | .662 |
| Boone B | 383 | 238 | .621 | Martin N | 47 | 26 | .553 |
| Bournigal | 74 | 48 | .649 | Martinez RE | 18 | 16 | .889 |
| Bush | 84 | 42 | .500 | McEwing | 50 | 28 | .560 |
| Cairo | 188 | 116 | .617 | McLemore | 354 | 211 | .596 |
| Canizaro | 16 | 10 | .625 | Merloni | 18 | 9 | .500 |
| Castillo L | 167 | 101 | .605 | Morandini | 378 | 224 | .593 |
| Castro J | 26 | 18 | .692 | Mordecai | 28 | 19 | .679 |
| Catalanotto | 22 | 9 | .409 | Morris W | 83 | 50 | .602 |
| Cedeno D | 84 | 49 | .583 | Offerman | 245 | 130 | .531 |
| Cirillo | 17 | 12 | .706 | Perez N | 41 | 29 | .707 |
| Cordero | 25 | 13 | .520 | Phillips T | 56 | 32 | .571 |
| Counsell | 97 | 62 | .639 | Polanco | 38 | 25 | .658 |
| Cromer | 18 | 9 | .500 | Randa | 27 | 12 | .444 |
| DeShields | 321 | 175 | .545 | Reboulet | 51 | 29 | .569 |
| Doster | 28 | 14 | .500 | Reese | 83 | 51 | .614 |
| Durham | 457 | 277 | .606 | Sadler | 17 | 10 | .588 |
| Durrington | 22 | 14 | .636 | Sanchez | 94 | 60 | .638 |
| Easley | 317 | 212 | .669 | Scarsone | 59 | 38 | .644 |
| Febles | 91 | 53 | .582 | Sheets | 20 | 6 | .300 |
| Fernandez T | 113 | 58 | .513 | Shumpert | 43 | 24 | .558 |
| Fonville | 34 | 16 | .471 | Sojo | 80 | 47 | .588 |
| Fox | 55 | 29 | .527 | Spiezio | 171 | 103 | .602 |
| Franco J | 17 | 10 | .588 | Stynes | 33 | 20 | .606 |
| Frye | 189 | 107 | .566 | Valentin Jos | 65 | 40 | .615 |
| Garcia C | 166 | 103 | .620 | Velarde | 222 | 133 | .599 |
| Gates | 145 | 83 | .572 | Veras Q | 351 | 202 | .575 |
| Giovanola | 27 | 16 | .593 | Vidro | 84 | 46 | .548 |
| Gomez | 17 | 8 | .471 | Vina | 324 | 239 | .738 |
| Graffanino | 77 | 46 | .597 | Vizcaino | 91 | 62 | .681 |
| Grebeck | 81 | 43 | .531 | Walker T | 127 | 71 | .559 |
| Guerrero W | 97 | 46 | .474 | Womack | 222 | 113 | .509 |
| Hairston Jr. | 40 | 23 | .575 | Young Eri | 342 | 196 | .573 |
| Hansen J | 34 | 22 | .647 | **MLB Average** | | | **.586** |
| Harris | 28 | 14 | .500 | | | | |

*Baseball Scoreboard*

## Who's Best in the Outfield Zone? (p. 180)

### Outfield Zone Ratings—1999
### (minimum 1,000 defensive innings)

#### LEFT FIELD

| Player, Team | Innings | 1999 In Zone | Outs | Zone Rating | 1997-99 In Zone | Outs | Zone Rating |
|---|---|---|---|---|---|---|---|
| Gant, Phi | 1,118.2 | 276 | 260 | .942 | 727 | 673 | .926 |
| Jenkins, Mil | 1,012.1 | 271 | 251 | .926 | 397 | 366 | .922 |
| Damon, KC | 1,148.2 | 311 | 288 | .926 | 402 | 370 | .920 |
| Gonzalez L, Ari | 1,321.2 | 301 | 274 | .910 | 876 | 774 | .884 |
| Vaughn G, Cin | 1,191.1 | 297 | 265 | .892 | 772 | 690 | .894 |
| Martin A, Pit | 1,104.2 | 224 | 199 | .888 | 599 | 522 | .871 |
| Surhoff, Bal | 1,269.0 | 319 | 282 | .884 | 889 | 782 | .880 |
| Stewart, Tor | 1,207.0 | 277 | 243 | .877 | 511 | 455 | .890 |
| Allen, Min | 1,114.0 | 313 | 269 | .859 | 313 | 269 | .859 |
| Sheffield, LA | 1,222.1 | 276 | 237 | .859 | 276 | 237 | .859 |
| Greer, Tex | 1,267.1 | 347 | 287 | .827 | 1,037 | 875 | .844 |
| O'Leary, Bos | 1,357.2 | 370 | 301 | .814 | 769 | 641 | .834 |
| Bichette, Col | 1,233.0 | 315 | 241 | .765 | 858 | 689 | .803 |
| MLB Average | | | | .873 | | | .874 |

#### CENTER FIELD

| Player, Team | Innings | 1999 In Zone | Outs | Zone Rating | 1997-99 In Zone | Outs | Zone Rating |
|---|---|---|---|---|---|---|---|
| Rivera, SD | 1,023.0 | 345 | 314 | .910 | 378 | 343 | .907 |
| Cameron, Cin | 1,260.2 | 414 | 376 | .908 | 1,080 | 987 | .914 |
| Beltran, KC | 1,352.2 | 434 | 394 | .908 | 482 | 438 | .909 |
| Jones A, Atl | 1,447.1 | 548 | 494 | .901 | 1,149 | 1,047 | .911 |
| Singleton, CWS | 1,036.1 | 398 | 355 | .892 | 398 | 355 | .892 |
| Anderson B, Bal | 1,102.0 | 330 | 291 | .882 | 975 | 837 | .858 |
| Finley, Ari | 1,347.2 | 453 | 397 | .876 | 1,213 | 1,087 | .896 |
| Grissom, Mil | 1,285.0 | 433 | 378 | .873 | 1,205 | 1,055 | .876 |
| White D, LA | 1,065.0 | 313 | 273 | .872 | 895 | 796 | .889 |
| Anderson G, Ana | 1,011.2 | 392 | 341 | .870 | 480 | 419 | .873 |
| Glanville, Phi | 1,267.2 | 447 | 388 | .868 | 917 | 810 | .883 |
| Griffey Jr., Sea | 1,315.0 | 451 | 386 | .856 | 1,353 | 1,184 | .875 |
| Hamilton, Col-NYM | 1,085.1 | 357 | 304 | .852 | 988 | 847 | .857 |
| Benard, SF | 1,056.0 | 342 | 291 | .851 | 367 | 313 | .853 |
| Williams B, NYY | 1,354.2 | 454 | 384 | .846 | 1,079 | 954 | .884 |
| MLB Average | | | | .878 | | | .886 |

#### RIGHT FIELD

| Player, Team | Innings | 1999 In Zone | Outs | Zone Rating | 1997-99 In Zone | Outs | Zone Rating |
|---|---|---|---|---|---|---|---|
| Jordan B, Atl | 1,281.0 | 325 | 298 | .917 | 627 | 574 | .915 |
| Ordonez M, CWS | 1,341.1 | 361 | 331 | .917 | 716 | 653 | .912 |
| Abreu, Phi | 1,267.2 | 291 | 262 | .900 | 689 | 613 | .890 |
| Nixon T, Bos | 1,025.2 | 233 | 209 | .897 | 247 | 221 | .895 |
| Burnitz, Mil | 1,109.1 | 296 | 265 | .895 | 857 | 779 | .909 |
| Mondesi, LA | 1,378.2 | 351 | 314 | .895 | 831 | 759 | .913 |
| O'Neill, NYY | 1,303.1 | 330 | 295 | .894 | 974 | 883 | .907 |
| Dye, KC | 1,358.2 | 409 | 365 | .892 | 751 | 682 | .908 |
| Sosa S, ChC | 1,220.0 | 364 | 323 | .887 | 1,107 | 972 | .878 |
| Green S, Tor | 1,333.2 | 385 | 341 | .886 | 762 | 665 | .873 |
| Guerrero V, Mon | 1,378.1 | 380 | 335 | .882 | 912 | 808 | .886 |
| Ramirez M, Cle | 1,225.1 | 308 | 270 | .877 | 925 | 823 | .890 |
| Gonzalez J, Tex | 1,113.2 | 259 | 224 | .865 | 665 | 563 | .847 |
| Bell D, Hou | 1,105.0 | 225 | 194 | .862 | 724 | 639 | .883 |
| Belle, Bal | 1,340.0 | 316 | 254 | .804 | 316 | 254 | .804 |
| Stairs, Oak | 1,209.2 | 309 | 246 | .796 | 409 | 334 | .817 |
| MLB Average | | | | .874 | | | .878 |

# Which Outfielders Know How to Hold 'Em? (p. 183)

## Outfield Advance Percentage—1999
### (minimum 30 baserunner opportunities to advance)

| Right Field | | | | Center Field | | | | Left Field | | | |
|---|---|---|---|---|---|---|---|---|---|---|---|
| Player, Team | Opp | XB | Pct | Player, Team | Opp | XB | Pct | Player, Team | Opp | XB | Pct |
| Brown A, Pit | 42 | 14 | 33.3 | Barker G, Hou | 32 | 9 | 28.1 | Encarnacion, Det | 104 | 22 | 21.2 |
| Abreu, Phi | 135 | 46 | 34.1 | Brumfield, 2Tm | 41 | 12 | 29.3 | Ledee, NYY | 53 | 12 | 22.6 |
| Ochoa, Mil | 31 | 12 | 38.7 | Jones A, Atl | 208 | 81 | 38.9 | Erstad, Ana | 56 | 13 | 23.2 |
| Mondesi, LA | 141 | 56 | 39.7 | Owens, SD | 35 | 15 | 42.9 | Hidalgo, Hou | 96 | 23 | 24.0 |
| Lewis D, Bos | 35 | 14 | 40.0 | Singleton, CWS | 175 | 80 | 45.7 | Ochoa, Mil | 37 | 9 | 24.3 |
| Dye, KC | 188 | 76 | 40.4 | Griffey Jr., Sea | 226 | 105 | 46.5 | Sanders R, SD | 76 | 19 | 25.0 |
| Garcia K, Det | 42 | 17 | 40.5 | Anderson G, Ana | 144 | 68 | 47.2 | Williams G, Atl | 79 | 20 | 25.3 |
| Walker L, Col | 113 | 47 | 41.6 | Cruz J, Tor | 124 | 60 | 48.4 | Justice, Cle | 61 | 16 | 26.2 |
| Ramirez M, Cle | 124 | 52 | 41.9 | Everett, Hou | 115 | 56 | 48.7 | Palmeiro O, Ana | 61 | 16 | 26.2 |
| Kotsay, Fla | 133 | 57 | 42.9 | Glanville, Phi | 170 | 84 | 49.4 | Anderson G, Ana | 34 | 9 | 26.5 |
| Guerrero V, Mon | 191 | 82 | 42.9 | Bragg, StL | 50 | 25 | 50.0 | O'Leary, Bos | 123 | 34 | 27.6 |
| Ordonez, CWS | 130 | 56 | 43.1 | Mateo, Tex | 40 | 20 | 50.0 | Hunter B, 2Tm | 123 | 34 | 27.6 |
| Echevarria, Col | 30 | 13 | 43.3 | Winn, TB | 113 | 58 | 51.3 | Surhoff, Bal | 114 | 32 | 28.1 |
| Young D, Cin | 45 | 20 | 44.4 | Bartee, Det | 33 | 17 | 51.5 | Gant, Phi | 123 | 36 | 29.3 |
| Martinez D, TB | 91 | 41 | 45.1 | Rivera, SD | 124 | 64 | 51.6 | Sorrento, TB | 64 | 19 | 29.7 |
| Howard T, StL | 33 | 15 | 45.5 | Sosa S, ChC | 42 | 22 | 52.4 | Trammell, TB | 64 | 19 | 29.7 |
| Jordan B, Atl | 132 | 60 | 45.5 | Jones J, Min | 97 | 51 | 52.6 | Lee C, CWS | 110 | 33 | 30.0 |
| Lawton, Min | 93 | 44 | 47.3 | Beltran, KC | 209 | 110 | 52.6 | Vaughn G, Cin | 103 | 31 | 30.1 |
| Gonzalez J, Tex | 128 | 61 | 47.7 | Grissom, Mil | 185 | 98 | 53.0 | Gonzalez L, Ari | 128 | 39 | 30.5 |
| Sosa S, ChC | 123 | 59 | 48.0 | White D, LA | 109 | 58 | 53.2 | Stewart, Tor | 137 | 42 | 30.7 |
| Womack, Ari | 75 | 36 | 48.0 | Lofton, Cle | 152 | 81 | 53.3 | Jenkins, Mil | 112 | 36 | 32.1 |
| Higginson, Det | 88 | 43 | 48.9 | White R, Mon | 71 | 38 | 53.5 | Allen, Min | 130 | 42 | 32.3 |
| Cedeno R, NYM | 61 | 30 | 49.2 | Encarnacion, Det | 37 | 20 | 54.1 | Curtis, NYY | 40 | 13 | 32.5 |
| Tucker, Cin | 54 | 27 | 50.0 | Cameron, Cin | 107 | 58 | 54.2 | Polonia, Det | 30 | 10 | 33.3 |
| Nixon T, Bos | 105 | 53 | 50.5 | Johnson L, ChC | 82 | 45 | 54.9 | Owens, SD | 30 | 10 | 33.3 |
| Salmon, Ana | 85 | 43 | 50.6 | Anderson B, Bal | 138 | 76 | 55.1 | Sexson, Cle | 40 | 14 | 35.0 |
| Guillen J, Pit-TB | 83 | 42 | 50.6 | Lewis D, Bos | 96 | 53 | 55.2 | Aven, Fla | 54 | 19 | 35.2 |
| Bell D, Hou | 112 | 57 | 50.9 | Finley, Ari | 152 | 84 | 55.3 | Vander Wal, SD | 34 | 12 | 35.3 |
| O'Neill, NYY | 154 | 79 | 51.3 | Christenson, Oak | 94 | 52 | 55.3 | Martin A, Pit | 113 | 40 | 35.4 |
| Green S, Tor | 142 | 73 | 51.4 | Goodwin T, Tex | 119 | 66 | 55.5 | Grieve, Oak | 123 | 44 | 35.8 |
| Gwynn, SD | 76 | 40 | 52.6 | Barry, Col | 54 | 30 | 55.6 | Lankford, StL | 111 | 40 | 36.0 |
| Davis E, StL | 34 | 18 | 52.9 | Lowery, TB | 43 | 24 | 55.8 | Floyd, Fla | 61 | 22 | 36.1 |
| Belle, Bal | 136 | 72 | 52.9 | Williams B, NYY | 197 | 110 | 55.8 | Greer, Tex | 168 | 62 | 36.9 |
| Stairs, Oak | 130 | 69 | 53.1 | Giles, Pit | 122 | 69 | 56.6 | Bonds, SF | 75 | 28 | 37.3 |
| Bragg, StL | 32 | 17 | 53.1 | Martinez M, Mon | 111 | 63 | 56.8 | White R, Mon | 66 | 25 | 37.9 |
| Buhner, Sea | 83 | 45 | 54.2 | McRae, 3Tm | 102 | 59 | 57.8 | Sheffield, LA | 108 | 41 | 38.0 |
| Brown B, Pit | 35 | 19 | 54.3 | Hunter T, Min | 110 | 64 | 58.2 | Rodriguez, ChC | 113 | 43 | 38.1 |
| McGee, StL | 30 | 17 | 56.7 | Drew, StL | 91 | 53 | 58.2 | Damon, KC | 174 | 67 | 38.5 |
| Mabry, Sea | 30 | 17 | 56.7 | Buford, Bos | 83 | 49 | 59.0 | Bichette, Col | 151 | 59 | 39.1 |
| Burnitz, Mil | 114 | 67 | 58.8 | Edmonds, Ana | 54 | 32 | 59.3 | Henderson, NYM | 70 | 28 | 40.0 |
| Burks, SF | 76 | 46 | 60.5 | Hamilton, 2Tm | 136 | 81 | 59.6 | Javier, SF-Hou | 46 | 19 | 41.3 |
| **MLB Average** | | | **47.6** | Santangelo, SF | 56 | 34 | 60.7 | Klesko, Atl | 32 | 14 | 43.8 |
| | | | | Clemente, Col | 46 | 28 | 60.9 | Merced, Mon | 41 | 19 | 46.3 |
| | | | | Dunwoody, Fla | 54 | 33 | 61.1 | **MLB Average** | | | **32.2** |
| | | | | Benard, SF | 144 | 89 | 61.8 | | | | |
| | | | | Roberts, Cle | 42 | 26 | 61.9 | | | | |
| | | | | Martinez D, TB | 53 | 33 | 62.3 | | | | |
| | | | | Kapler, Det | 150 | 94 | 62.7 | | | | |
| | | | | Becker, Mil-Oak | 49 | 31 | 63.3 | | | | |
| | | | | Wilson P, Fla | 130 | 83 | 63.8 | | | | |
| | | | | Goodwin C, 2Tm | 63 | 41 | 65.1 | | | | |
| | | | | Phillips T, Oak | 30 | 20 | 66.7 | | | | |
| | | | | McDonald J, Oak | 42 | 28 | 66.7 | | | | |
| | | | | **MLB Average** | | | **54.1** | | | | |

## Which Fielders Have the Best Defensive Batting Average? (p. 186)

The MLB average in each category at each position is .280.

### Highest Defensive Batting Averages—1999
### (minimum 500 defensive innings)

| First Basemen | ZR | FP | PR | OA | DBA |
|---|---|---|---|---|---|
| Erstad, Ana | .350 | .327 | — | — | .344 |
| Coomer, Min | .324 | .309 | — | — | .320 |
| Grace, ChC | .318 | .292 | — | — | .311 |
| Conine, Bal | .318 | .282 | — | — | .309 |
| Young K, Pit | .337 | .213 | — | — | .306 |
| Clark T, Det | .314 | .270 | — | — | .303 |
| Martinez T, NYY | .303 | .297 | — | — | .302 |
| Olerud, NYM | .306 | .287 | — | — | .301 |
| Mientkiewicz, Min | .290 | .312 | — | — | .296 |
| Clark W, Bal | .291 | .298 | — | — | .293 |
| Vaughn M, Ana | .289 | .299 | — | — | .291 |
| Stevens, Tex | .291 | .287 | — | — | .290 |
| Brogna, Phi | .288 | .296 | — | — | .290 |
| Thome, Cle | .283 | .289 | — | — | .285 |
| Bagwell, Hou | .280 | .293 | — | — | .283 |
| Lee T, Ari | .272 | .310 | — | — | .282 |
| Joyner, SD | .276 | .297 | — | — | .281 |
| Casey, Cin | .275 | .299 | — | — | .281 |
| Giambi J, Oak | .276 | .294 | — | — | .281 |
| Karros, LA | .284 | .263 | — | — | .278 |
| Delgado C, Tor | .277 | .255 | — | — | .272 |
| Snow, SF | .260 | .302 | — | — | .271 |
| Klesko, Atl | .275 | .243 | — | — | .267 |
| Konerko, CWS | .256 | .297 | — | — | .267 |
| Helton, Col | .253 | .283 | — | — | .260 |
| Millar, Fla | .247 | .296 | — | — | .259 |
| Stanley, Bos | .254 | .236 | — | — | .250 |
| Segui, Tor | .234 | .296 | — | — | .250 |
| McGwire, StL | .245 | .253 | — | — | .247 |
| McGriff, TB | .241 | .243 | — | — | .241 |
| Fullmer, Mon | .228 | .260 | — | — | .236 |
| Sweeney M, KC | .225 | .180 | — | — | .214 |
| **Second Basemen** | ZR | FP | PR | OA | DBA |
| Reese, Cin | .369 | .322 | .295 | — | .343 |
| Alfonzo, NYM | .312 | .333 | .342 | — | .323 |
| Velarde, Oak | .309 | .286 | .322 | — | .309 |
| Alomar, Cle | .308 | .328 | .280 | — | .304 |
| McLemore, Tex | .297 | .287 | .331 | — | .304 |
| Biggio, Hou | .310 | .297 | .282 | — | .301 |
| McEwing, StL | .318 | .273 | .263 | — | .297 |
| Morandini, ChC | .270 | .325 | .299 | — | .285 |
| Anderson M, Phi | .307 | .270 | .239 | — | .285 |
| Morris W, Pit | .285 | .271 | .290 | — | .284 |
| Young E, LA | .293 | .290 | .254 | — | .283 |
| Castillo L, Fla | .286 | .253 | .288 | — | .281 |
| Kent, SF | .290 | .291 | .245 | — | .279 |
| Bell D, Sea | .275 | .262 | .295 | — | .278 |
| Belliard, Mil | .271 | .264 | .300 | — | .277 |
| Veras Q, SD | .266 | .276 | .301 | — | .276 |
| Boone B, Atl | .277 | .281 | .269 | — | .276 |
| Bush, Tor | .275 | .294 | .267 | — | .276 |
| Cairo, TB | .249 | .300 | .317 | — | .274 |
| Easley, Det | .245 | .315 | .310 | — | .272 |
| Offerman, Bos | .291 | .252 | .216 | — | .266 |
| Febles, KC | .251 | .268 | .293 | — | .264 |
| Vidro, Mon | .247 | .284 | .272 | — | .259 |
| DeShields, Bal | .264 | .260 | .243 | — | .258 |
| Bell J, Ari | .274 | .217 | .240 | — | .257 |
| Durham, CWS | .241 | .247 | .292 | — | .254 |
| Walker T, Min | .232 | .293 | .247 | — | .245 |
| Knoblauch, NYY | .225 | .197 | .248 | — | .226 |
| **Third Basemen** | ZR | FP | PR | OA | DBA |
| Ventura, NYM | .329 | .332 | — | — | .330 |
| Nevin, SD | .308 | .336 | — | — | .319 |
| Orie, Fla | .335 | .294 | — | — | .319 |
| Rolen, Phi | .329 | .293 | — | — | .315 |
| Koskie, Min | .313 | .297 | — | — | .307 |
| Fryman, Cle | .303 | .310 | — | — | .306 |
| Williams M, Ari | .289 | .325 | — | — | .303 |
| Mueller, SF | .308 | .290 | — | — | .301 |
| Chavez, Oak | .299 | .295 | — | — | .298 |
| Lowell, Fla | .274 | .333 | — | — | .298 |
| Cirillo, Mil | .292 | .305 | — | — | .297 |
| Brosius, NYY | .296 | .296 | — | — | .296 |
| Boone A, Cin | .299 | .288 | — | — | .294 |
| Gaetti, ChC | .291 | .296 | — | — | .293 |
| Valentin J, Bos | .300 | .281 | — | — | .292 |
| Castilla, Col | .285 | .282 | — | — | .284 |
| Spiers, Hou | .279 | .289 | — | — | .283 |
| Beltre, LA | .312 | .237 | — | — | .282 |
| Glaus, Ana | .276 | .281 | — | — | .278 |
| Tatis, StL | .261 | .289 | — | — | .272 |
| Zeile, Tex | .275 | .255 | — | — | .267 |
| Jones C, Atl | .261 | .274 | — | — | .266 |
| Ripken Jr., Bal | .284 | .239 | — | — | .266 |
| Andrews, 2Tm | .277 | .247 | — | — | .265 |
| Palmer, Det | .263 | .265 | — | — | .264 |
| Randa, KC | .248 | .277 | — | — | .260 |
| Davis R, Sea | .238 | .291 | — | — | .259 |
| Caminiti, Hou | .259 | .238 | — | — | .251 |
| Fernandez T, Tor | .236 | .252 | — | — | .242 |
| Boggs, TB | .222 | .258 | — | — | .236 |
| Norton, CWS | .243 | .219 | — | — | .233 |
| Sprague, Pit | .243 | .215 | — | — | .232 |
| Barrett, Mon | .212 | .260 | — | — | .231 |
| **Shortstops** | ZR | FP | PR | OA | DBA |
| Ordonez R, NYM | .342 | .336 | — | — | .341 |
| Sanchez, KC | .337 | .308 | — | — | .331 |
| Cabrera O, Mon | .331 | .303 | — | — | .325 |
| Larkin, Cin | .325 | .300 | — | — | .320 |
| Bordick, Bal | .314 | .324 | — | — | .316 |
| Vizquel, Cle | .308 | .296 | — | — | .305 |
| Bogar, Hou | .306 | .297 | — | — | .304 |
| Batista, Tor | .301 | .296 | — | — | .300 |
| Grudzielanek, LA | .301 | .289 | — | — | .299 |

| Name | ZR | FP | PR | OA | DBA |
|---|---|---|---|---|---|
| Perez N, Col | .290 | .308 | — | — | .293 |
| Cruz D, Det | .287 | .311 | — | — | .292 |
| Gomez, SD | .300 | .261 | — | — | .292 |
| DiSarcina, Ana | .298 | .264 | — | — | .292 |
| Rodriguez A, Sea | .287 | .298 | — | — | .289 |
| Benjamin, Pit | .284 | .309 | — | — | .289 |
| Jeter, NYY | .276 | .300 | — | — | .280 |
| Renteria, StL | .284 | .257 | — | — | .279 |
| Tejada, Oak | .272 | .289 | — | — | .276 |
| Relaford, Phi | .284 | .240 | — | — | .275 |
| Clayton, Tex | .277 | .260 | — | — | .273 |
| Aurilia, SF | .275 | .252 | — | — | .270 |
| Stocker, TB | .273 | .251 | — | — | .268 |
| Arias A, Phi | .253 | .323 | — | — | .267 |
| Gutierrez, Hou | .261 | .284 | — | — | .265 |
| Hernandez J, Atl | .258 | .278 | — | — | .262 |
| Fox, Ari | .264 | .254 | — | — | .262 |
| Garciaparra, Bos | .255 | .286 | — | — | .261 |
| Jackson D, SD | .272 | .213 | — | — | .260 |
| Caruso, CWS | .262 | .251 | — | — | .260 |
| Sheets, Ana | .257 | .271 | — | — | .259 |
| Weiss, Atl | .252 | .265 | — | — | .254 |
| Gonzalez A, Fla | .241 | .247 | — | — | .243 |
| Valentin J, Mil | .251 | .205 | — | — | .242 |
| Guzman C, Min | .220 | .256 | — | — | .227 |
| Loretta, Mil | .201 | .319 | — | — | .224 |

| **Left Fielders** | ZR | FP | PR | OA | DBA |
|---|---|---|---|---|---|
| Erstad, Ana | .335 | .325 | — | .327 | .332 |
| Gant, Phi | .324 | .310 | — | .290 | .315 |
| Lankford, StL | .337 | .297 | — | .258 | .315 |
| Encarnacion, Det | .301 | .263 | — | .335 | .302 |
| Sanders R, SD | .305 | .260 | — | .317 | .301 |
| Jenkins, Mil | .313 | .272 | — | .279 | .300 |
| Damon, KC | .313 | .297 | — | .247 | .297 |
| Gonzalez L, Ari | .302 | .289 | — | .288 | .297 |
| Williams G, Atl | .291 | .285 | — | .309 | .294 |
| Surhoff, Bal | .283 | .325 | — | .302 | .293 |
| Vaughn G, Cin | .289 | .295 | — | .290 | .290 |
| Hunter B, Sea | .283 | .292 | — | .301 | .288 |
| Ledee, NYY | .292 | .206 | — | .329 | .287 |
| White R, Mon | .308 | .233 | — | .242 | .284 |
| Stewart, Tor | .278 | .284 | — | .290 | .281 |
| Hidalgo, Hou | .256 | .325 | — | .324 | .280 |
| Justice, Cle | .260 | .279 | — | .312 | .273 |
| Martin A, Pit | .286 | .226 | — | .264 | .273 |
| Aven, Fla | .276 | .296 | — | .234 | .271 |
| Allen, Min | .265 | .274 | — | .280 | .270 |
| Lee C, CWS | .258 | .285 | — | .284 | .267 |
| Floyd, Fla | .279 | .225 | — | .262 | .267 |
| Bonds, SF | .266 | .291 | — | .246 | .266 |
| Rodriguez H, ChC | .267 | .272 | — | .248 | .264 |
| Sheffield, LA | .265 | .267 | — | .249 | .262 |
| O'Leary, Bos | .233 | .312 | — | .301 | .258 |
| Henderson, NYM | .251 | .301 | — | .237 | .256 |
| Grieve, Oak | .243 | .298 | — | .258 | .254 |
| Greer, Tex | .242 | .290 | — | .253 | .252 |
| Bichette, Col | .198 | .225 | — | .243 | .211 |

| **Center Fielders** | ZR | FP | PR | OA | DBA |
|---|---|---|---|---|---|
| Jones A, Atl | .305 | .266 | — | .358 | .315 |
| Kapler, Det | .370 | .283 | — | .225 | .313 |
| Singleton, CWS | .293 | .296 | — | .327 | .304 |
| Cruz J, Tor | .297 | .294 | — | .321 | .304 |
| Johnson L, ChC | .312 | .291 | — | .272 | .297 |
| Rivera, SD | .316 | .248 | — | .287 | .297 |
| Everett, Hou | .296 | .265 | — | .313 | .297 |
| Cameron, Cin | .313 | .262 | — | .283 | .296 |
| Hunter T, Min | .306 | .321 | — | .261 | .295 |
| Lewis D, Bos | .297 | .304 | — | .279 | .293 |
| Christenson, Oak | .317 | .224 | — | .278 | .291 |
| Beltran, KC | .313 | .234 | — | .277 | .290 |
| Anderson G, Ana | .265 | .304 | — | .323 | .288 |
| Anderson B, Bal | .280 | .323 | — | .281 | .287 |
| Lofton, Cle | .278 | .295 | — | .284 | .282 |
| Finley, Ari | .273 | .317 | — | .280 | .282 |
| Drew, StL | .308 | .236 | — | .251 | .280 |
| Giles, Pit | .276 | .306 | — | .265 | .277 |
| Glanville, Phi | .263 | .265 | — | .308 | .277 |
| Grissom, Mil | .269 | .288 | — | .282 | .276 |
| White D, LA | .268 | .284 | — | .279 | .274 |
| Griffey Jr., Sea | .248 | .256 | — | .328 | .273 |
| Goodwin T, Tex | .261 | .295 | — | .278 | .271 |
| Jones J, Min | .263 | .250 | — | .296 | .271 |
| Buford, Bos | .282 | .278 | — | .245 | .270 |
| Winn, TB | .244 | .316 | — | .292 | .269 |
| Martinez M, Mon | .277 | .220 | — | .263 | .264 |
| White R, Mon | .257 | .238 | — | .279 | .261 |
| Hamilton, NYM | .242 | .335 | — | .247 | .258 |
| Williams B, NYY | .235 | .290 | — | .273 | .255 |
| Benard, SF | .241 | .288 | — | .233 | .246 |
| McRae, Tor | .219 | .317 | — | .255 | .244 |
| Wilson P, Fla | .253 | .248 | — | .215 | .241 |

| **Right Fielders** | ZR | FP | PR | OA | DBA |
|---|---|---|---|---|---|
| Abreu, Phi | .305 | .301 | — | .354 | .321 |
| Ordonez M, CWS | .319 | .308 | — | .294 | .309 |
| Womack, Ari | .325 | .311 | — | .282 | .308 |
| Jordan B, Atl | .319 | .305 | — | .291 | .307 |
| Dye, KC | .298 | .287 | — | .323 | .305 |
| Mondesi, LA | .300 | .279 | — | .322 | .304 |
| Kotsay, Fla | .300 | .278 | — | .308 | .300 |
| Young D, Cin | .303 | .268 | — | .302 | .297 |
| Tucker, Cin | .303 | .300 | — | .282 | .295 |
| Ramirez M, Cle | .284 | .258 | — | .321 | .293 |
| Higginson, Det | .307 | .284 | — | .275 | .292 |
| Green S, Tor | .292 | .326 | — | .253 | .284 |
| Sosa S, ChC | .294 | .261 | — | .277 | .283 |
| Nixon T, Bos | .302 | .236 | — | .270 | .281 |
| O'Neill, NYY | .299 | .255 | — | .262 | .280 |
| Guerrero V, Mon | .289 | .175 | — | .309 | .279 |
| Cedeno R, NYM | .270 | .294 | — | .282 | .278 |
| Gonzalez J, Tex | .274 | .282 | — | .279 | .277 |
| Gwynn, SD | .275 | .315 | — | .258 | .275 |
| Lawton, Min | .264 | .273 | — | .285 | .273 |
| Bell D, Hou | .272 | .289 | — | .266 | .272 |
| Salmon, Ana | .274 | .278 | — | .260 | .269 |
| Burnitz, Mil | .300 | .279 | — | .218 | .268 |
| Walker L, Col | .231 | .279 | — | .302 | .263 |
| Martinez D, TB | .228 | .280 | — | .292 | .258 |
| Buhner, Sea | .245 | .312 | — | .245 | .255 |
| Burks, SF | .268 | .306 | — | .206 | .252 |
| Belle, Bal | .221 | .290 | — | .258 | .244 |
| Guillen J, TB | .225 | .212 | — | .267 | .238 |
| Stairs, Oak | .215 | .276 | — | .254 | .238 |

*Baseball Scoreboard*

## Who Were the Winningest Players of the 1990s? (p. 192)

### Highest Team Winning Percentage in Starts—1990-99
### (minimum 500 decisions)

| Player | W-L | Pct | Player | W-L | Pct |
|---|---|---|---|---|---|
| Chipper Jones | 478-285 | .626 | Rey Ordonez | 298-257 | .537 |
| Javy Lopez | 362-218 | .624 | Fred McGriff | 782-676 | .536 |
| Ryan Klesko | 426-264 | .617 | Jeff Bagwell | 693-600 | .536 |
| Derek Jeter | 386-249 | .608 | Sandy Alomar Jr. | 434-376 | .536 |
| Mark Lemke | 514-338 | .603 | Brady Anderson | 654-567 | .536 |
| Manny Ramirez | 491-333 | .596 | Joey Cora | 449-390 | .535 |
| Jim Thome | 517-359 | .590 | Brian Jordan | 386-336 | .535 |
| Jeff Blauser | 596-424 | .584 | Rusty Greer | 411-358 | .534 |
| Paul O'Neill | 777-555 | .583 | Roberto Alomar | 737-644 | .534 |
| David Justice | 677-492 | .579 | Mark McLemore | 502-439 | .533 |
| Moises Alou | 483-359 | .574 | Otis Nixon | 531-467 | .532 |
| Jose Lind | 384-287 | .572 | Barry Larkin | 673-592 | .532 |
| Bernie Williams | 619-463 | .572 | Chris Hoiles | 435-383 | .532 |
| Darryl Strawberry | 328-247 | .570 | Mike Stanley | 477-420 | .532 |
| Mike Gallego | 347-264 | .568 | Eddie Murray | 539-475 | .532 |
| Kenny Lofton | 605-462 | .567 | Joe Girardi | 450-397 | .531 |
| Tim Raines | 542-414 | .567 | John Olerud | 690-609 | .531 |
| Darrin Fletcher | 437-344 | .560 | Brent Mayne | 297-263 | .530 |
| Troy O'Leary | 386-305 | .559 | Ellis Burks | 568-504 | .530 |
| Ozzie Guillen | 565-448 | .558 | Edgardo Alfonzo | 312-278 | .529 |
| Ron Karkovice | 343-274 | .556 | Mariano Duncan | 410-366 | .528 |
| Luis Alicea | 364-294 | .553 | Rafael Palmeiro | 793-708 | .528 |
| Tony Pena | 372-303 | .551 | Mike Greenwell | 404-361 | .528 |
| Pat Kelly | 319-260 | .551 | Luis Sojo | 296-266 | .527 |
| Barry Bonds | 771-629 | .551 | Raul Mondesi | 466-419 | .527 |
| Omar Vizquel | 697-572 | .549 | Steve Finley | 706-636 | .526 |
| Ron Gant | 640-528 | .548 | Ivan Rodriguez | 586-530 | .525 |
| Marquis Grissom | 730-603 | .548 | Reggie Sanders | 465-421 | .525 |
| Terry Pendleton | 553-457 | .548 | Craig Biggio | 772-699 | .525 |
| Mike Piazza | 512-424 | .547 | Lance Johnson | 624-565 | .525 |
| Andy Van Slyke | 357-296 | .547 | Greg Vaughn | 663-601 | .525 |
| Sean Berry | 328-273 | .546 | Frank Thomas | 711-646 | .524 |
| Julio Franco | 438-365 | .545 | Chuck Knoblauch | 676-615 | .524 |
| Walt Weiss | 585-488 | .545 | Andres Galarraga | 600-547 | .523 |
| Darren Lewis | 485-408 | .543 | Ken Caminiti | 669-610 | .523 |
| Robin Ventura | 732-619 | .542 | Leo Gomez | 284-259 | .523 |
| Tino Martinez | 595-504 | .541 | John Valentin | 494-451 | .523 |
| Manuel Lee | 288-244 | .541 | Mike Lansing | 438-400 | .523 |
| Wade Boggs | 630-538 | .539 | Larry Walker | 624-570 | .523 |
| Greg Gagne | 543-464 | .539 | Felix Jose | 318-291 | .522 |
| Jim Leyritz | 347-298 | .538 | George Bell | 284-260 | .522 |
| Scott Fletcher | 293-252 | .538 | Albert Belle | 692-634 | .522 |
| Bret Boone | 486-418 | .538 | Tony Fernandez | 612-561 | .522 |

| Player | W-L | Pct | Player | W-L | Pct |
|---|---|---|---|---|---|
| Wally Joyner | 602-552 | .522 | Chili Davis | 595-585 | .504 |
| Jose Canseco | 583-536 | .521 | Ozzie Smith | 367-361 | .504 |
| Bill Spiers | 350-322 | .521 | Jose Vizcaino | 437-431 | .503 |
| Juan Gonzalez | 625-575 | .521 | J.T. Snow | 447-442 | .503 |
| Darryl Hamilton | 540-497 | .521 | Joe Carter | 646-639 | .503 |
| Tim Naehring | 262-242 | .520 | Hal Morris | 472-467 | .503 |
| Wil Cordero | 375-347 | .519 | Mike Blowers | 310-307 | .502 |
| Danny Tartabull | 402-373 | .519 | Alex Rodriguez | 317-314 | .502 |
| Dave Winfield | 350-325 | .519 | Shane Mack | 320-317 | .502 |
| Eddie Taubensee | 337-313 | .518 | Scott Servais | 335-332 | .502 |
| Lee Stevens | 270-251 | .518 | Greg Colbrunn | 252-250 | .502 |
| Lenny Dykstra | 328-305 | .518 | Joe Oliver | 420-417 | .502 |
| Rickey Henderson | 609-567 | .518 | Quilvio Veras | 281-279 | .502 |
| Derek Bell | 492-459 | .517 | Brian Harper | 287-286 | .501 |
| Cal Ripken Jr. | 762-711 | .517 | Pete Incaviglia | 293-292 | .501 |
| Scott Brosius | 415-388 | .517 | Jay Bell | 723-721 | .501 |
| Royce Clayton | 524-492 | .516 | Mike Devereaux | 390-389 | .501 |
| Andujar Cedeno | 297-279 | .516 | Brett Butler | 491-490 | .501 |
| Steve Buechele | 323-304 | .515 | Eric Karros | 577-576 | .500 |
| Pat Borders | 360-339 | .515 | Delino DeShields | 594-593 | .500 |
| Devon White | 632-596 | .515 | Jim Edmonds | 331-331 | .500 |
| Will Clark | 632-596 | .515 | Edgar Martinez | 635-636 | .500 |
| Darrin Jackson | 274-260 | .513 | Tim Wallach | 435-436 | .499 |
| Mark McGwire | 600-570 | .513 | Bernard Gilkey | 474-476 | .499 |
| Tony Phillips | 660-629 | .512 | Kevin Seitzer | 432-434 | .499 |
| Chris Sabo | 336-321 | .511 | Spike Owen | 283-285 | .498 |
| Tom Pagnozzi | 360-344 | .511 | Mike Bordick | 612-617 | .498 |
| Dan Wilson | 356-341 | .511 | Ray Lankford | 583-588 | .498 |
| Harold Baines | 571-548 | .510 | Willie McGee | 389-393 | .497 |
| Dave Hollins | 446-429 | .510 | John Jaha | 362-366 | .497 |
| Mickey Tettleton | 481-463 | .510 | Roberto Kelly | 517-524 | .497 |
| Luis Gonzalez | 595-573 | .509 | Mike Macfarlane | 430-437 | .496 |
| Don Mattingly | 375-362 | .509 | Jose Valentin | 330-336 | .495 |
| B.J. Surhoff | 635-613 | .509 | Reggie Jefferson | 266-271 | .495 |
| Carlos Baerga | 596-576 | .509 | Ray Durham | 357-365 | .494 |
| Greg Myers | 296-287 | .508 | Jody Reed | 476-487 | .494 |
| Jeff Kent | 499-484 | .508 | Henry Rodriguez | 344-352 | .494 |
| Brian McRae | 641-622 | .508 | Kevin McReynolds | 257-263 | .494 |
| Eric Davis | 375-364 | .507 | Chris Gomez | 356-365 | .494 |
| Matt Williams | 663-644 | .507 | Ken Griffey Jr. | 687-705 | .494 |
| Billy Hatcher | 263-256 | .507 | Dave Valle | 262-269 | .493 |
| Lenny Harris | 285-278 | .506 | George Brett | 274-282 | .493 |
| Mo Vaughn | 582-569 | .506 | Vinny Castilla | 441-454 | .493 |
| Bobby Bonilla | 633-619 | .506 | Orlando Merced | 413-426 | .492 |
| Paul Sorrento | 461-451 | .505 | Todd Zeile | 692-714 | .492 |
| Kent Hrbek | 278-273 | .505 | Robin Yount | 273-282 | .492 |
| Rick Wilkins | 282-277 | .504 | Carlos Delgado | 303-313 | .492 |

**Baseball Scoreboard**

| Player | W-L | Pct | Player | W-L | Pct |
|---|---|---|---|---|---|
| John Kruk | 317-328 | .491 | Rondell White | 296-325 | .477 |
| Ruben Sierra | 508-526 | .491 | Ed Sprague | 484-532 | .476 |
| Sammy Sosa | 630-653 | .491 | Lou Whitaker | 282-310 | .476 |
| Jay Buhner | 559-580 | .491 | Andre Dawson | 317-349 | .476 |
| Dave Nilsson | 369-383 | .491 | Glenallen Hill | 392-432 | .476 |
| Kevin Mitchell | 296-308 | .490 | Chad Curtis | 433-478 | .475 |
| Robby Thompson | 345-360 | .489 | Brad Ausmus | 327-364 | .473 |
| Garret Anderson | 344-359 | .489 | Juan Samuel | 265-295 | .473 |
| Tom Goodwin | 319-333 | .489 | Shawon Dunston | 376-419 | .473 |
| Shawn Green | 310-324 | .489 | Kevin Young | 291-326 | .472 |
| Alex Gonzalez | 284-297 | .489 | Al Martin | 372-417 | .471 |
| Ricky Gutierrez | 270-283 | .488 | Mickey Morandini | 484-545 | .470 |
| Charles Johnson | 286-300 | .488 | Tim Salmon | 442-498 | .470 |
| Jose Offerman | 527-553 | .488 | Benito Santiago | 441-498 | .470 |
| Paul Molitor | 603-634 | .487 | Stan Javier | 374-423 | .469 |
| Billy Ripken | 246-259 | .487 | Todd Hundley | 366-416 | .468 |
| Dante Bichette | 618-651 | .487 | Gary Sheffield | 543-621 | .466 |
| Gary DiSarcina | 513-541 | .487 | Edgar Renteria | 243-278 | .466 |
| Travis Fryman | 639-675 | .486 | Rico Brogna | 301-345 | .466 |
| Kirby Puckett | 414-438 | .486 | Harold Reynolds | 294-337 | .466 |
| Howard Johnson | 272-288 | .486 | Jason Giambi | 293-336 | .466 |
| Jim Eisenreich | 345-366 | .485 | Carlos Garcia | 253-291 | .465 |
| Jeromy Burnitz | 282-300 | .485 | Brent Gates | 264-306 | .463 |
| Geronimo Berroa | 288-307 | .484 | Eric Anthony | 232-270 | .462 |
| Darren Daulton | 371-396 | .484 | Gregg Jefferies | 543-633 | .462 |
| Dean Palmer | 520-556 | .483 | Derrick May | 243-284 | .461 |
| Jeff Reed | 243-260 | .483 | Felix Fermin | 287-339 | .458 |
| Gary Gaetti | 569-609 | .483 | Damion Easley | 350-414 | .458 |
| Randy Velarde | 384-411 | .483 | Alvaro Espinoza | 235-274 | .458 |
| Dave Magadan | 376-404 | .482 | Jeff Conine | 398-471 | .458 |
| Terry Steinbach | 530-570 | .482 | Rey Sanchez | 327-388 | .457 |
| Tony Gwynn | 595-641 | .481 | Charlie O'Brien | 255-306 | .455 |
| Jeff King | 503-542 | .481 | Jeff Cirillo | 324-390 | .454 |
| Fernando Vina | 241-260 | .481 | Phil Plantier | 229-278 | .452 |
| Mark Grudzielanek | 312-337 | .481 | Johnny Damon | 265-323 | .451 |
| Brian L. Hunter | 299-323 | .481 | Vince Coleman | 253-311 | .449 |
| David Segui | 455-492 | .480 | Joe Orsulak | 270-340 | .443 |
| Dave Martinez | 441-477 | .480 | Mark Lewis | 290-366 | .442 |
| Bip Roberts | 416-450 | .480 | Pat Meares | 320-404 | .442 |
| Ryne Sandberg | 428-464 | .480 | Alan Trammell | 239-303 | .441 |
| Luis Polonia | 376-408 | .480 | Kevin Stocker | 313-397 | .441 |
| Mark Whiten | 386-419 | .480 | John Flaherty | 247-325 | .432 |
| Eric Young | 388-423 | .478 | Bob Higginson | 269-359 | .428 |
| Cecil Fielder | 590-644 | .478 | Tony Clark | 248-332 | .428 |
| Charlie Hayes | 555-607 | .478 | Joe Randa | 214-287 | .427 |
| Kirt Manwaring | 380-416 | .477 | Marty Cordova | 257-349 | .424 |
| Mark Grace | 691-758 | .477 | | | |

## Are the Late-1990s Yankees the Most Dominant Postseason Team Ever? (p. 195)

**Best Postseason Overall Record, Four-Year Span—1903-99**
**(minimum 3 years in postseason during span)**

| Span | Team | Years | Total W-L | Pct | Series W-L | Pct |
|---|---|---|---|---|---|---|
| 1937-40 | Yankees | 3 | 12-1 | .923 | 3-0 | 1.000 |
| 1938-41 | Yankees | 3 | 12-1 | .923 | 3-0 | 1.000 |
| 1936-39 | Yankees | 4 | 16-3 | .842 | 4-0 | 1.000 |
| 1935-38 | Yankees | 3 | 12-3 | .800 | 3-0 | 1.000 |
| 1948-51 | Yankees | 3 | 12-3 | .800 | 3-0 | 1.000 |
| 1996-99 | Yankees | 4 | 35-10 | .778 | 9-1 | .900 |
| 1910-13 | Athletics | 3 | 12-4 | .750 | 3-0 | 1.000 |
| 1915-18 | Red Sox | 3 | 12-4 | .750 | 3-0 | 1.000 |
| 1947-50 | Yankees | 3 | 12-4 | .750 | 3-0 | 1.000 |
| 1925-28 | Yankees | 3 | 11-4 | .733 | 2-1 | .667 |
| 1926-29 | Yankees | 3 | 11-4 | .733 | 2-1 | .667 |
| 1949-52 | Yankees | 4 | 16-6 | .727 | 4-0 | 1.000 |
| 1973-76 | Reds | 3 | 16-6 | .727 | 4-1 | .800 |
| 1950-53 | Yankees | 4 | 16-7 | .696 | 4-0 | 1.000 |
| 1995-98 | Yankees | 4 | 26-12 | .684 | 6-2 | .750 |
| 1905-08 | Cubs | 3 | 10-5 | .667 | 2-1 | .667 |
| 1906-09 | Cubs | 3 | 10-5 | .667 | 2-1 | .667 |
| 1968-71 | Orioles | 3 | 17-9 | .654 | 4-2 | .667 |
| 1969-72 | Orioles | 3 | 17-9 | .654 | 4-2 | .667 |
| 1987-90 | Athletics | 3 | 17-9 | .654 | 4-2 | .667 |
| 1988-91 | Athletics | 3 | 17-9 | .654 | 4-2 | .667 |
| 1970-73 | Orioles | 3 | 15-8 | .652 | 3-2 | .600 |
| 1907-10 | Cubs | 3 | 9-5 | .643 | 2-1 | .667 |
| 1939-42 | Yankees | 3 | 9-5 | .643 | 2-1 | .667 |
| 1994-97 | Braves | 3 | 25-14 | .641 | 6-2 | .750 |
| 1951-54 | Yankees | 3 | 12-7 | .632 | 3-0 | 1.000 |
| 1995-98 | Braves | 4 | 30-18 | .625 | 7-3 | .700 |
| 1920-23 | Giants | 3 | 11-7 | .611 | 2-1 | .667 |
| 1928-31 | Athletics | 3 | 11-7 | .611 | 2-1 | .667 |
| 1929-32 | Athletics | 3 | 11-7 | .611 | 2-1 | .667 |
| 1993-96 | Braves | 3 | 22-14 | .611 | 5-2 | .714 |
| 1989-92 | Athletics | 3 | 14-9 | .609 | 3-2 | .600 |
| 1940-43 | Yankees | 3 | 9-6 | .600 | 2-1 | .667 |
| 1941-44 | Yankees | 3 | 9-6 | .600 | 2-1 | .667 |
| 1994-97 | Yankees | 3 | 15-10 | .600 | 3-2 | .600 |
| 1990-93 | Blue Jays | 3 | 17-12 | .586 | 4-1 | .800 |
| 1991-94 | Blue Jays | 3 | 17-12 | .586 | 4-1 | .800 |
| 1971-74 | Athletics | 4 | 21-15 | .583 | 6-1 | .857 |
| 1972-75 | Athletics | 4 | 21-15 | .583 | 6-1 | .857 |
| 1973-76 | Athletics | 3 | 14-10 | .583 | 4-1 | .800 |
| 1977-80 | Yankees | 3 | 14-10 | .583 | 4-1 | .800 |
| 1958-61 | Yankees | 3 | 11-8 | .579 | 2-1 | .667 |
| 1959-62 | Yankees | 3 | 11-8 | .579 | 2-1 | .667 |
| 1992-95 | Braves | 3 | 19-14 | .576 | 4-2 | .667 |
| 1975-78 | Yankees | 3 | 17-13 | .567 | 5-1 | .833 |
| 1976-79 | Yankees | 3 | 17-13 | .567 | 5-1 | .833 |
| 1941-44 | Cardinals | 3 | 9-7 | .563 | 2-1 | .667 |

| | | | | | | |
|---|---|---|---|---|---|---|
| 1942-45 | Cardinals | 3 | 9-7 | .563 | 2-1 | .667 |
| 1921-24 | Giants | 4 | 14-11 | .560 | 2-2 | .500 |
| 1972-75 | Reds | 3 | 15-12 | .556 | 3-2 | .600 |
| 1978-81 | Yankees | 3 | 15-12 | .556 | 4-2 | .667 |
| 1952-55 | Yankees | 3 | 11-9 | .550 | 2-1 | .667 |
| 1953-56 | Yankees | 3 | 11-9 | .550 | 2-1 | .667 |
| 1996-99 | Braves | 4 | 26-22 | .542 | 6-4 | .600 |
| 1994-97 | Indians | 3 | 20-17 | .541 | 4-3 | .571 |
| 1911-14 | Athletics | 3 | 8-7 | .533 | 2-1 | .667 |
| 1963-66 | Dodgers | 3 | 8-7 | .533 | 2-1 | .667 |
| 1995-98 | Indians | 4 | 25-22 | .532 | 5-4 | .556 |
| 1922-25 | Giants | 3 | 9-8 | .529 | 1-2 | .333 |
| 1956-59 | Yankees | 3 | 11-10 | .524 | 2-1 | .667 |
| 1980-83 | Phillies | 3 | 13-12 | .520 | 3-2 | .600 |
| 1970-73 | Athletics | 3 | 14-13 | .519 | 4-1 | .800 |
| 1943-46 | Cardinals | 3 | 9-9 | .500 | 2-1 | .667 |
| 1955-58 | Yankees | 4 | 14-14 | .500 | 2-2 | .500 |
| 1971-74 | Pirates | 3 | 10-10 | .500 | 2-2 | .500 |
| 1978-81 | Phillies | 3 | 10-10 | .500 | 2-2 | .500 |
| 1996-99 | Indians | 4 | 18-19 | .486 | 3-4 | .429 |
| 1970-73 | Reds | 3 | 12-13 | .480 | 2-3 | .400 |
| 1960-63 | Yankees | 4 | 11-12 | .478 | 2-2 | .500 |
| 1961-64 | Yankees | 4 | 11-12 | .478 | 2-2 | .500 |
| 1954-57 | Yankees | 3 | 10-11 | .476 | 1-2 | .333 |
| 1957-60 | Yankees | 3 | 10-11 | .476 | 1-2 | .333 |
| 1969-72 | Pirates | 3 | 9-10 | .474 | 2-2 | .500 |
| 1970-73 | Pirates | 3 | 9-10 | .474 | 2-2 | .500 |
| 1971-74 | Orioles | 3 | 9-10 | .474 | 1-3 | .250 |
| 1977-80 | Phillies | 3 | 9-10 | .474 | 2-2 | .500 |
| 1989-92 | Blue Jays | 3 | 10-12 | .455 | 2-2 | .500 |
| 1990-93 | Braves | 3 | 15-18 | .455 | 2-3 | .400 |
| 1991-94 | Braves | 3 | 15-18 | .455 | 2-3 | .400 |
| 1952-55 | Dodgers | 3 | 9-11 | .450 | 1-2 | .333 |
| 1953-56 | Dodgers | 3 | 9-11 | .450 | 1-2 | .333 |
| 1977-80 | Royals | 3 | 8-10 | .444 | 1-3 | .250 |
| 1989-92 | Pirates | 3 | 8-12 | .400 | 0-3 | .000 |
| 1990-93 | Pirates | 3 | 8-12 | .400 | 0-3 | .000 |
| 1920-23 | Yankees | 3 | 7-11 | .389 | 1-2 | .333 |
| 1921-24 | Yankees | 3 | 7-11 | .389 | 1-2 | .333 |
| 1962-65 | Yankees | 3 | 7-11 | .389 | 1-2 | .333 |
| 1978-81 | Royals | 3 | 6-10 | .375 | 1-3 | .250 |
| 1975-78 | Royals | 3 | 5-9 | .357 | 0-3 | .000 |
| 1976-79 | Royals | 3 | 5-9 | .357 | 0-3 | .000 |
| 1928-31 | Cardinals | 3 | 6-11 | .353 | 1-2 | .333 |
| 1910-13 | Giants | 3 | 6-12 | .333 | 0-3 | .000 |
| 1911-14 | Giants | 3 | 6-12 | .333 | 0-3 | .000 |
| 1906-09 | Tigers | 3 | 4-12 | .250 | 0-3 | .000 |
| 1907-10 | Tigers | 3 | 4-12 | .250 | 0-3 | .000 |
| 1972-75 | Pirates | 3 | 3-9 | .250 | 0-3 | .000 |
| 1975-78 | Phillies | 3 | 2-9 | .182 | 0-3 | .000 |
| 1976-79 | Phillies | 3 | 2-9 | .182 | 0-3 | .000 |
| 1996-99 | Astros | 3 | 2-9 | .182 | 0-3 | .000 |
| 1996-99 | Rangers | 3 | 1-9 | .100 | 0-3 | .000 |

## Which Teams Were 1999's Biggest Overachievers And Underachievers? (p. 198)

### Pythagorean Winning Percentages—1999

| Team | W-L | Pct | Pyth W | Pyth Pct | +/- |
|---|---|---|---|---|---|
| Rangers | 95-67 | .586 | 88.7 | .548 | 6.3 |
| White Sox | 75-86 | .466 | 71.4 | .444 | 3.6 |
| Indians | 97-65 | .599 | 93.8 | .579 | 3.2 |
| Braves | 103-59 | .636 | 100.0 | .618 | 3.0 |
| Cubs | 67-95 | .414 | 64.4 | .397 | 2.6 |
| Mariners | 79-83 | .488 | 76.8 | .474 | 2.2 |
| Tigers | 69-92 | .429 | 67.2 | .418 | 1.8 |
| Athletics | 87-75 | .537 | 85.4 | .527 | 1.6 |
| Devil Rays | 69-93 | .426 | 67.5 | .417 | 1.5 |
| Rockies | 72-90 | .444 | 70.8 | .437 | 1.2 |
| Giants | 86-76 | .531 | 84.9 | .524 | 1.1 |
| Angels | 70-92 | .432 | 68.9 | .426 | 1.1 |
| Blue Jays | 84-78 | .519 | 82.9 | .512 | 1.1 |
| Mets | 97-66 | .595 | 96.2 | .590 | 0.8 |
| Expos | 68-94 | .420 | 67.2 | .415 | 0.8 |
| Red Sox | 94-68 | .580 | 93.2 | .575 | 0.8 |
| Padres | 74-88 | .457 | 73.3 | .452 | 0.7 |
| Yankees | 98-64 | .605 | 97.6 | .603 | 0.4 |
| Brewers | 74-87 | .460 | 73.8 | .458 | 0.2 |
| Astros | 97-65 | .599 | 96.9 | .598 | 0.1 |
| Marlins | 64-98 | .395 | 64.3 | .397 | -0.3 |
| Twins | 63-97 | .394 | 63.6 | .397 | -0.6 |
| Reds | 96-67 | .589 | 97.3 | .597 | -1.3 |
| Pirates | 78-83 | .484 | 79.8 | .496 | -1.8 |
| Cardinals | 75-86 | .466 | 77.7 | .482 | -2.7 |
| Phillies | 77-85 | .475 | 80.5 | .497 | -3.5 |
| Diamondbacks | 100-62 | .617 | 104.2 | .643 | -4.2 |
| Dodgers | 77-85 | .475 | 81.6 | .504 | -4.6 |
| Orioles | 78-84 | .481 | 84.5 | .522 | -6.5 |
| Royals | 64-97 | .398 | 74.6 | .463 | -10.6 |

# Glossary

## Batting Average (Avg)
Hits divided by At-Bats.

## Career Assessments
Once known as the Favorite Toy, this method is used to estimate a player's chance of achieving a specific goal. In the following example, we'll say 3,000 hits. Four things are considered:

1. Need Hits, the number of hits needed to reach the goal. (Of course, this also could be Need Home Runs, Need Doubles, etc.)

2. Years Remaining. The number of years remaining to meet the goal is estimated by (42 minus Age) divided by two. This formula assigns a 20-year-old player 11.0 remaining seasons, a 25-year-old player 8.5 remaining seasons, a 30-year-old player 6.0 remaining seasons, and a 35-year-old player 3.5 remaining seasons. Any active player is assumed to have at least half a season remaining, regardless of his age. Additionally, if a player is coming off a year with at least 100 hits *and* an offensive winning percentage of at least .500, he's assumed to have at least 1.5 remaining seasons. And if a player is coming off a year with at least 100 hits *or* an offensive winning percentage of at least .500, he's assumed to have at least 1.0 remaining seasons.

3. Established Hit Level. For 1999, the established hit level would be found by adding 1996 Hits, (1997 Hits multiplied by two) and (1998 Hits multiplied by three), then dividing by six. A player can't have an established performance level that is less than 80 percent of his most recent performance. In other words, a player who had 200 hits in 1998 can't have an established hit level less than 160.

4. Projected Remaining Hits. This is found by multiplying Years Remaining by the Established Hit Level.

Once you get the projected remaining hits, the chance of getting to the goal is figured by dividing Projected Remaining Hits by Need Hits, then subtracting .5. Thus if Need Hits and Projected Remaining Hits are the same, the chance of reaching the goal is 50 percent. A player's chance of continuing to progress toward a goal can't be more than .97 raised to the power of Years Remaining. This prevents a player from figuring to have a 148 percent chance of reaching a goal.

## Component ERA (ERC)
A statistic that estimates what a pitcher's ERA should have been, based on his pitching performance. The steps in calculating an ERC are:

1. Subtract Home Runs from Hits.
2. Multiply step 1 by 1.255.
3. Multiply Home Runs Allowed by 4.
4. Add steps 2 and 3 together.
5. Multiply step 4 by .89.
6. Add Walks and Hit Batsmen.
7. Multiply step 6 by .475.
8. Add steps 5 and 7 together.

This yields the pitcher's total base estimate (PTB), which is:

$$(((H - HR) \times 1.255) + (HR \times 4)) \times .89) + ((BB + HB) \times .475)$$

If intentional walk data is available, adjust the formula as follows:

$$(((H - HR) \times 1.255) + (HR \times 4)) \times .89) + ((BB + HB - IBB) \times .56)$$

9. Add Hits and Walks and Hit Batsmen.
10. Multiply step 9 by PTB.
11. Divide step 10 by Batters Facing Pitcher. If BFP data is unavailable, approximate it by multiplying Innings Pitched by 2.9, then adding step 9.
12. Multiply step 11 by 9.
13. Divide step 12 by Innings Pitched.
14. Subtract .56 from step 13.

This is the pitcher's ERC, which is:

$$(((((H + BB + HB) \times PTB) / BFP) \times 9) / IP) - .56$$

If the result after step 13 is less than 2.24, adjust the formula as follows:

$$(((((H + BB + HB) \times PTB) / BFP) \times 9) / IP) \times .75$$

## Defensive Batting Average (DBA)

A composite statistic incorporating the standard deviations of various defensive statistics to arrive at a number akin to batting average. The statistics used for each position are as follows:

| Pos | Statistics |
|---|---|
| 1B | Zone Rating (75%), Fielding Percentage (25%) |
| 2B | Zone Rating (60%), Pivot Percentage (25%), Fielding Percentage (15%) |
| 3B | Zone Rating (60%), Fielding Percentage (40%) |
| SS | Zone Rating (80%), Fielding Percentage (20%) |
| LF | Zone Rating (65%), Outfield Advance Percentage (20%), Fielding Percentage (15%) |
| CF | Zone Rating (55%), Outfield Advance Percentage (30%), Fielding Percentage (15%) |
| RF | Zone Rating (50%), Outfield Advance Percentage (35%), Fielding Percentage (15%) |

## Earned Run Average (ERA)

Earned Runs multiplied by nine, divided by Innings Pitched.

## Fielding Percentage

(Putouts plus Assists) divided by (Putouts plus Assists plus Errors).

## Game Score

A tool that quantifies how well a starting pitcher performed in a single game. To calculate, start with 50. Add one point for each out recorded, two points for each inning completed after the fourth and one point for each strikeout. Subtract one point for each walk, two points for each hit, four points for each run and two points for each unearned run. A score of 50 is about average. Anything above 90 is outstanding. Kerry Wood's 105 game score for his 20-strikeout one-hitter against the Astros in 1998 is the record for a nine-inning game.

## Go-Ahead RBI (GARBI)

Any RBI which gives a player's team the lead.

### Go-Ahead RBI Opportunities

The total of a player's Go-Ahead RBI and the number of times he made an out with the go-ahead run in scoring position.

### Holds

A Hold is credited any time a relief pitcher enters a game in a Save Situation, records at least one out and leaves the game never having relinquished the lead. A pitcher can't finish the game and receive credit for a hold, nor can he earn a hold and a save in the same game.

### Inherited Runner (IR)

Any runner on base when a reliever enters a game is considered inherited by that pitcher.

### Offensive Winning Percentage (OWP)

A player's offensive winning percentage equals the percentage of games a team would win with nine of that player in its lineup, given average pitching and defense. The formula is the square of Runs Created per 27 Outs, divided by the sum of the square of Runs Created per 27 Outs and the square of the league average of runs per game.

### On-Base Percentage (OBP)

(Hits plus Walks plus Hit by Pitch) divided by (At-Bats plus Walks plus Hit by Pitch plus Sacrifice Flies).

### On-Base Plus Slugging Percentage (OPS)

On-Base Percentage plus Slugging Percentage.

### Outfield Advance Percentage

A statistic used to evaluate an outfielder's throwing arm. It's computed by dividing extra bases taken by baserunners by the number of opportunities. For example, if a single is hit to center field with men on first and second, and one man scores while the other stops at second, that's one extra base taken on two opportunities, a 50.0 advance percentage.

### Park Index

A method of measuring the extent to which a given ballpark influences a given statistic. Using home runs as an example, here's how the index is calculated (using intraleague games only):

1. Add Home Runs and Opponent Home Runs in home games.
2. Add At-Bats and Opponent At-Bats in home games. (If At-Bats are unavailable, use home games.)
3. Divide step 1 by step 2.
4. Add Home Runs and Opponent Home Runs in road games.
5. Add At-Bats and Opponent At-Bats in road games. (If At-Bats are unavailable, use road games.)
6. Divide step 4 by step 5.
7. Divide step 3 by step 6.
8. Multiply step 7 by 100.

An index of 100 means the park is completely neutral. A park index of 118 for home runs indicates that games played in the park feature 18 percent more home runs than the average park.

## Pivot Percentage

The number of Double Plays turned by a second baseman as the pivot man, divided by the number of Double Play Opportunities. A Double Play Opportunity is any situation with a runner on first and less than two out, where a groundball is hit to an infielder and the second baseman takes the throw.

## Plate Appearances (PA)

At-Bats plus Walks plus Hit By Pitch plus Sacrifice Hits plus Sacrifice Flies plus Times Reached on Defensive Interference.

## Predicted ERA

Opponent On-Base Percentage multiplied by Opponent Slugging Percentage multiplied by 31.

## Pythagorean Theory

A formula for determining the expected winning percentage for a team. The formula is the square of Runs, divided by the sum of the square of Runs and the square of Opponent Runs.

## Quality Start (QS)

Any start in which a pitcher works six or more innings while allowing three or fewer earned runs.

## Range Factor

If Defensive Innings are available, use (Putouts plus Assists) multiplied by 9, divided by Defensive Innings. If not, use (Putouts plus Assists) divided by Games.

## RBI Opportunities

The number of RBI a hitter would have accumulated if he had hit a home run every time up, given the total number of men that were on base when he batted. No RBI Opportunities are charged if the batter reaches base via a walk, hit by pitch or defensive interference, unless a runner scores as a result of the play.

## Relativity Index

A method of comparing the effectiveness of a player versus his league. For hitters, the most common relativity index is Runs Created per 27 Outs multiplied by 100, then divided by league runs per game. For pitchers, it's Component ERA multiplied by 100, then divided by league ERA. A relativity index of 100 indicates a league-average player. An index greater than 100 indicates an above-average player.

## Runs Created (RC)

Bill James has devised 24 different Runs Created formulas, depending on the statistics available in a given year. The current method is as follows:

1. Add Hits plus Walks plus Hit by Pitch.
2. Subtract Caught Stealings and Grounded Into Double Plays from step 1. This is the A Factor.
3. Add Unintentional Walks plus Hit by Pitch.
4. Multiply step 3 by .24.
5. Multiply Stolen Bases by .62.
6. Add Sacrifice Hits plus Sacrifice Flies.
7. Multiply step 6 by .5.
8. Add Total Bases plus step 4 plus step 5 plus step 7.
9. Multiply Strikeouts by .03.

10. Subtract step 9 from step 8. This is the B Factor.
11. Add At-Bats plus Walks plus Hit by Pitch plus Sacrifice Hits plus Sacrifice Flies. This is the C Factor.

To summarize:

$$A = H + BB + HBP - CS - GDP$$

$$B = ((BB - IBB + HBP) \times .24) + (SB \times .62) + ((SH + SF) \times .5) + TB - (SO \times .03)$$

$$C = AB + BB + HBP + SH + SF$$

Each player's Runs Created is determined as if he were operating in a context of eight other players of average skill. The final steps are:

12. Multiply C by 2.4.
13. Add A plus step 12.
14. Multiply C by 3.
15. Add B plus step 14.
16. Multiply step 13 by step 15.
17. Multiply C by 9.
18. Divide step 16 by step 17.
19. Multiply C by .9.
20. Subtract step 19 from step 18.

Expressed as an equation, that's:

$$(((( C \times 2.4) + A) \times ((C \times 3) + B)) / (C \times 9)) - (C \times .9)$$

Where home runs with men on base and batting average with runners in scoring position are available, we make further adjustments. First, figure out the player's home-run percentage by dividing his home runs by his at-bats. Then multiply that number by his at-bats with men on base to find his expected home runs in that situation. Subtract the expected total from the real total, and add the result to his Runs Created. For example, a player with 20 homers in 600 overall at-bats who hit 10 homers in 150 at-bats with men on base would get an extra five Runs Created because he would have been expected to hit five. If he hit three homers in 150 at-bats with men on base, he would lose two Runs Created.

The runners-in-scoring-position adjustment works in similar fashion. Multiply a player's batting average by his at-bats with runners in scoring position to determine his expected hits in that situation. Subtract the expected number from the real number, and again add the result to his Runs Created. A .300 hitter who batted .350 in 200 at-bats with runners in scoring position would get 10 extra Runs Created (70 hits minus 60 expected hits). If he batted .280 in that situation, he would lose four Runs Created (56 hits minus 60 expected hits).

The second-to-last step is to round a player's Runs Created to the nearest integer. Finally, once all of a team's individual players' Runs Created have been calculated, compare their total to the team's Runs Scored and reconcile the difference proportionally. For instance, if a team's players created 700 runs and the club scored 728 runs, increase each player's Runs Created by 4 percent (728 / 700 = 1.04) and round each off to the nearest integer once again. Repeat if necessary until the two totals are equal.

### Runs Created Per 27 Outs (RC/27)

This statistic estimates how many runs per game a team made up of nine of the same player would score. The name is actually a misnomer, however, because Bill James has based his revised formula on the number of league outs per team game rather than 27. The calculation is Runs Created multiplied by League Outs per Team Game, divided by

Outs Made (the sum of a player's At-Bats plus Sacrifice Hits plus Sacrifice Flies plus Caught Stealings plus Grounded Into Double Plays, less his Hits), or:

((RC x ((3 x LgIP) / (2 x LgG))) / (AB - H + SH + SF + CS + GDP)

## Runs Prevented

A linear-weights system that measures how many runs a reliever prevents, by estimating the difference between the opposition's scoring potential when he enters and exits the game and subtracting any runs allowed while he was on the mound. The scoring potential depends on the number of outs, the number of men on base and the bases they occupy, and any subsequent errors. The Run Expectation for each situation is:

| Runners | 0 Outs | 1 Outs | 2 Outs |
|---|---|---|---|
| None | .55 | .29 | .11 |
| 1st | .94 | .56 | .24 |
| 2nd | 1.19 | .71 | .34 |
| 3rd | 1.43 | .99 | .37 |
| 1st & 2nd | 1.55 | .96 | .47 |
| 1st & 3rd | 1.86 | 1.20 | .52 |
| 2nd & 3rd | 2.05 | 1.42 | .59 |
| Loaded | 2.33 | 1.63 | .79 |

(based on MLB, 1995-99)

Runs Prevented are calculated as follows:

1. Determine the Run Expectation when reliever enters the game. This is the Initial Run Expectation Value (IREV).
2. Subtract one run from step 1 for every run that scores while the pitcher is on the mound, regardless of whether the run is charged to him.
3. If an error is made while the reliever is in the game, find the Run Expectation for the situation that results.
4. Reconstruct that play as if the error hadn't occurred, as the official scorer would do when determining runs. Find the Run Expectation for that hypothetical situation.
5. Subtract step 4 from step 3. This is the Error Run Expectation Value (EREV).
6. Add step 2 and step 5.
7. Determine the Run Expectation when the reliever either finishes the inning (in which case it would be zero) or leaves the mound. This is the Final Run Expectation Value (FREV).
8. Subtract step 7 from step 6.
9. Repeat this process for each inning the reliever pitches.

To summarize, Runs Prevented = IREV - R + EREV - FREV. For example, assume a reliever enters the game in the eighth inning with a runner on second and one out. His IREV is .71. If his shortstop boots the next play, putting runners on the corners with one out instead of a runner on second and two out, the EREV is 1.19 - .34 = .85. If the reliever gets out of the inning and allows one run, his Runs Prevented = .71 - 1 + .85 - 0, which means he prevented .56 runs. If he pitches a scoreless ninth as well, he would get another .54 Runs Prevented and finish with 1.1 for the game.

## Saves (Sv)

A relief pitcher is credited with a save if he:

1. Finishes a game won by his team, and
2. Isn't the winning pitcher, and
3. Qualifies under one of three conditions: a) he enters the game with a lead of

no more than three runs and pitches at least one inning; b) he enters the game with the potential tying run on base, at bat or on deck; or c) he pitches effectively, in the opinion of the official scorer, for at least three innings.

### Saves: Easy, Regular and Tough

These distinctions are made to gauge the difficulty of a save. An Easy Save occurs when the first batter faced doesn't represent the tying run and the reliever pitches one inning or less. A Tough Save occurs if the reliever enters with the tying run anywhere on base. A Regular Save is one that doesn't fall into the Easy or Tough category.

### Save Opportunities/Situations

A relief pitcher is in a Save Opportunity (or Save Situation) if he enters the game with the club leading, isn't the pitcher of record and qualifies under one of three conditions: a) he has a lead of no more than three runs and the potential to pitch at least one inning; b) the potential tying run is on base, at bat or on deck; or c) he pitches effectively, in the opinion of the official scorer, for at least three innings and is credited with a save.

### Save Percentage

Saves divided by Save Opportunities.

### Secondary Average (Sec)

A way to look at a player's extra bases gained, independent of his Batting Average. The formula is (Total Bases minus Hits plus Walks plus Stolen Bases minus Caught Stealing) divided by At-Bats.

### Similarity Score

A method of measuring the degree of similarity of two statistical lines for a player or a team. Two identical stat lines would generate a score of 1,000.

### Slugging Percentage (Slg)

Total Bases divided by At-Bats.

### Total Bases (TB)

Hits plus Doubles plus (Triples multiplied by two) plus (Home Runs multiplied by three).

### Winning Percentage (Pct)

Wins divided by (Wins plus Losses).

### Zone Rating

A Zone Rating is an estimate of a player's efficiency in fielding balls hit into his typical defensive zone, as measured by STATS reporters. Picture the playing field as a piece of pie. Fair territory is sliced up into 22 equal and rather narrow parts, extending from home plate to the outfield fence. The first slice, running along the left-field line, is Zone C. Like any piece of pie, it grows wider as you approach the "crust" (in this case, the outfield fence). Zone C is about six or seven feet wide at the third-base bag, and about 20 feet wide at a distance of 300 feet from the plate. The next 21 Zones extend from Zone C to the edge of the right-field line, which is Zone X. The dividing line between Zones M and N runs over second base, splitting the field in half. (Zones A, B, Y and Z are in foul territory.)

The first baseman is responsible for covering Zones V through X, the three rightmost zones on the field. This includes all grounders hit within approximately 20 feet of the right-field line, as well as all bunts that travel more than 40 feet.

The second baseman is responsible for Zones O through T. Remember, the left boundary of Zone N is midfield. The right boundary of Zone N, where it meets Zone O, is the left edge of the second baseman's territory. It lies about eight feet to the right of second base. The second baseman's area runs through Zone T, and the first baseman's area begins at Zone V. Zone U, in between, belongs to neither fielder.

The respective areas of responsibility for the third baseman and shortstop are mirror images of the first and second baseman's zones. The third baseman is responsible for Zones C through F, and the shortstop is assigned Zones H through L. Zone G lies in between and belongs to neither fielder. The two middle zones, M and N, lay between the second baseman and shortstop and also are unassigned.

An infielder's Zone Rating is equal to the number of balls he converts into outs divided by the number of balls hit into the player's zone. Only groundballs are considered when Zone Rating is calculated. Line drives, popups and flyballs are ignored. An infielder is credited with an out made for every ball fielded that is turned into an out. When a player fields a ball outside his zone and turns it into an out, it is counted as a ball in his zone for the purposes of calculating his Zone Rating. Infielders no longer get credit for two outs when they start a double play.

Each outfielder is given two separate zones, one for flyballs and popups another one for line drives. Because liners remain in the air for a shorter amount of time, outfielders are assigned a smaller zone for them. For a batted ball to be assigned to an outfielder, it must travel a certain distance. Corner outfielders are responsible for all line drives in their area that travel between 280 and 340 feet. They also are responsible for all flyballs and popups that travel over 200 feet. The center fielder is responsible for all liners between 300 and 370 feet, and all flies and pops over 200 feet.

The left fielder's area covers Zones F through H on line drives and Zones C through I on flyballs and popups.

The right fielder's zones are the mirror image of the left fielders: Zones S through U on liners and Zones R through X on flies and pops.

The center fielder is responsible for Zones L through O on liners and Zones K through P on flies and pops.

An outfielder's Zone Rating equals the balls hit into his zone which don't result in hits, divided by the number of balls hit into his zone. As with infielders, an outfielder who catches a ball outside of his zone is credited with both an out and a ball in his zone for purposes of calculation his Zone Rating.

Any defender's ability to get to balls outside his zone can boost his Zone Rating. Therefore, Zone Rating shouldn't be interpreted simply as the percentage of balls hit into a player's zone that the fielder was able to turn into outs.

# Index

## A

Hank Aaron
    chances of HR record being broken ............ 76

Bobby Abreu
    .300 Avg, .400 OBP, .500 Slg and 25 SB
        at age 25 or younger ................................. 65

Age
    .300 Avg, .400 OBP, .500 Slg and 25 SB
        at age 25 or younger ................................. 65
    .300 Avg, 40 HR and 120 RBI at age 23
        or younger................................................. 79
    2,000 hits and 350 HR through age 34 ........ 36
    career wins for pitchers with a no-hitter
        through age 24 ......................................... 25
    highest winning pct., through season
        reaching 200 decisions, ages 29-32 ......... 9
    hits after age 39, all-time hit leaders ............ 71
    hitters after missing previous season,
        age 36-plus ............................................ 42
    most consecutive .320-plus seasons,
        age 33 or older ....................................... 71
    most home runs for original team when
        traded before age 30 ............................... 19
    most home runs through age 30, Brewers ... 58
    most strikeouts per nine innings,
        age 35 or older ..................................... 114
    winning pct., leagues' youngest teams ........ 15

Also-rans
    highest batting average, No. 2 in league
        two straight seasons ............................... 45
    lowest ERA, No. 2 in league two straight
        seasons .................................................. 45
    most home runs, No. 2 in league two
        straight seasons ..................................... 45
    most RBI, No. 2 in league two straight
        seasons .................................................. 45
    most strikeouts, No. 2 in league two
        straight seasons ..................................... 45
    most wins, No. 2 in league two straight
        seasons .................................................. 45

American League MVP Award
    ERA, RC/27 comparisons to league,
        candidates.............................................. 12
    team record with/without, candidates.......... 12

## B

Ballparks
    Bank One Ballpark indexes........................ 40
    Coors Field effects on Vinny Castilla,
        Jeff Cirillo.............................................. 50
    first-year winning pct. in new parks............ 73
    Safeco Field indexes.................................. 31
    Wrigley Field dimensions ........................ 200

Bank One Ballpark
    ballpark indexes........................................ 40
    ballpark indexes by roof status.................... 40

Bases loaded
    highest batting average.............................. 81
    most RBI per plate appearance................... 81

Batting average
    highest, bases loaded ................................ 81
    highest, No. 2 in league two straight years . 45
    most consecutive .320-plus seasons,
        age 33 or older ....................................... 71
    most runs per game, .260 or lower ............ 29

Carlos Beltran
    highest RC/27 index, rookies ..................... 22
    rookies with 20 HR, 100 R, 100 RBI.......... 22

Craig Biggio
    most doubles, two-year span ..................... 54
    most runs created, 1995-99 ....................... 54

Kevin Brown
    15-plus wins for most teams...................... 56
    lowest ERA, four-plus teams over
        five-year span ........................................ 56

Bunts
    base-hit percentage .................................. 104
    sacrifice percentage ................................. 104

Jeromy Burnitz
    highest career slugging percentage,
        Brewers................................................. 58
    most home runs through age 30, Brewers... 58

## C

Career assessments
    chances at 756 home runs........................... 76

chances at 2,298 RBI .................................... 76
chances at 3,000 hits .................................... 76

Vinny Castilla
   compared to Jeff Cirillo .............................. 50

Luis Castillo
   highest groundball-flyball ratio ................... 52

Catchers
   caught-stealing percentage ................ 163, 204
   stolen-base success against Ivan
      Rodriguez by top basestealers ............. 160
   stolen-base success against Ivan
      Rodriguez by top basestealing teams ... 160

Chicago White Sox
   winning pct., leagues' youngest teams ........ 15

Cincinnati Reds
   relievers working 90-plus innings ............... 48

Jeff Cirillo
   compared to Vinny Castilla .......................... 50

Cleveland Indians
   largest victory margin, division winners ..... 17

Component ERA
   highest component ERA index ................. 110

Coors Field
   effects on Vinny Castilla, Jeff Cirillo .......... 50

# D

Defense
   catcher caught-stealing percentage .... 163, 204
   defensive batting average .......................... 186
   fewest infield errors, team ............................ 62
   highest infield fielding percentage, team..... 62
   infield zone ratings .................................... 174
   outfield advance percentage ...................... 183
   outfield assists ............................................ 183
   outfield zone ratings .................................. 180
   pivot ratings ............................................... 178
   STATS Gold Gloves .................................. 204

Doubles
   most, two-year span ..................................... 54

# E

ERA
   highest ....................................................... 125
   highest index ............................................. 110
   lowest, four-plus teams over five-year
      span ........................................................ 56

lowest, No. 2 in league two straight years .. 45
predicted ................................................... 156
relievers with increases in four straight
   seasons ...................................................... 6

# F

Fouls
   percentage on swings with two strikes........ 86

# G

Andres Galarraga
   hitters after missing previous season,
      age 36-plus .............................................. 42

Game scores .................................................. 133

Brian Giles
   35 HR, 100 RBI and 1.000 OPS in first
      season as batting qualifier ...................... 67
   Pirates hitters with 1.000 OPS..................... 67

Go-ahead RBI .......................................... 93, 204

Juan Gonzalez
   most home runs for original team when
      traded before age 30 ............................... 19

Groundball-flyball ratio .................................. 52

Vladimir Guerrero
   .300 Avg, 40 HR and 120 RBI at age 23
      or younger.............................................. 79
   similarity scores ........................................... 79

Tony Gwynn
   hits after age 39, all-time hit leaders ........... 71
   most consecutive .320-plus seasons,
      age 33 or older ....................................... 71

# H

Mike Hampton
   most pitching wins plus batting hits .......... 120

Hearts of the order ........................................ 102

Hits
   after age 39, all-time hit leaders .................. 71
   chances at 3,000 ......................................... 76
   most pitching wins plus batting hits .......... 120

Hitters
   chances at 756 home runs ........................... 76
   chances at 2,298 RBI .................................. 76
   chances at 3,000 hits.................................... 76
   go-ahead RBI ..................................... 93, 204

hearts of the order ........................................ 102
highest batting average, bases loaded .......... 81
highest groundball-flyball ratio ................... 52
longest home runs ...................................... 107
most doubles, two-year span ....................... 54
most losses in starts, 1990-99 ..................... 192
most RBI per PA, bases loaded ................... 81
most runs created, 1995-99 .......................... 54
most wins in starts, 1990-99 ...................... 192
offensive winning percentage ...................... 89
percentage of fouls on swings with two
 strikes ..................................................... 86
percentage of swings in hitters' counts ....... 83
pitchers as hitters ....................................... 123
production in hitters' counts ....................... 83
RBI per opportunity ............................ 96, 204
runs created ................................................. 89
secondary average ....................................... 91
swings and misses ..................................... 100
winning percentage in starts, 1990-99 ....... 192

Hitters' counts
 percentage of swings in ............................. 83
 production in ............................................. 83

Holds .................................................... 145, 204

Home runs
 chances at 756 ........................................... 76
 longest ..................................................... 107
 most for original team when traded
  before age 30 ......................................... 19
 most, No. 2 in league two straight seasons .. 45
 most through age 30, Brewers .................. 58
 teams with four players who hit 30
  the year before ..................................... 34

Hottest heaters ..................................... 137, 204

Human air conditioners ............................... 100

## I

Infielders
 fewest errors, team .................................... 62
 highest fielding percentage, team ............. 62
 zone ratings ............................................. 174

Inherited runners scoring percentage ........... 148

## J

Randy Johnson
 most strikeouts per nine innings,
  age 35 or older .................................... 114

## K

Billy Koch
 most saves, rookies .................................... 38

## L

Leadoff men
 on-base percentage .................................... 98

Losses
 most by hitters in starts, 1990-99 ............. 192

## M

Pedro Martinez
 ERA compared to league ............................ 12
 highest component ERA index ................. 110
 highest ERA index ................................... 110
 highest strikeout-baserunner ratio ............ 110
 highest strikeout-walk ratio ..................... 110
 team record with/without ........................... 12

Mark McGwire
 chances of hitting 756 homers ................... 76
 projections had he stayed healthy .............. 69

Eric Milton
 career wins for pitchers with a no-hitter
  through age 24 ...................................... 25

Milwaukee Brewers
 highest career slugging percentage ............ 58
 most home runs through age 30 ................ 58

Mop-up appearances .................................... 129

Mike Mussina
 highest winning percentage, career ............. 9
 highest winning pct., through season
  reaching 200 decisions, ages 29-32 .......... 9

## N

New York Mets
 fewest infield errors ................................... 62
 highest infield fielding percentage ............. 62

New York Yankees
 championships by decade ........................... 27
 highest postseason winning percentage,
  four-year span .................................... 195
 sports franchises of the century ................. 27

No-hitters
 career wins for pitchers with, through
  age 24 .................................................. 25

*310*  *Baseball Scoreboard*

## O

Oakland Athletics
   highest secondary average, teams ................ 29
   most runs per game, .260 or lower
      batting average ........................................ 29

Offensive winning percentage ....................... 89

On-base percentage
   leadoff men ................................................ 98

On-base plus slugging percentage
   Pirates hitters with 1.000 OPS ..................... 67

Jesse Orosco
   fewest innings per game ........................... 127
   most middle-relief appearances, career ..... 127

Outfielders
   advance percentage .................................... 183
   assists ....................................................... 183
   zone ratings .............................................. 180

Overachieving teams ................................... 198

## P

Pacific Bell Park
   first-year winning pct. in new parks ............ 73

Rafael Palmeiro
   2,000 hits and 350 HR through age 34 ........ 36

Troy Percival
   relievers with ERA increases in four
      straight seasons ......................................... 6

Pitch counts
   1999 .................................................. 154, 204
   estimated .................................................. 204

Pitchers
   15-plus wins for most teams ........................ 56
   as hitters .................................................... 123
   fewest innings per game ........................... 127
   highest component ERA index .................. 110
   highest ERA .............................................. 125
   highest ERA index .................................... 110
   highest strikeout-baserunner ratio ............. 110
   highest strikeout-walk ratio ....................... 110
   highest winning percentage, career ............... 9
   most pitching wins plus batting hits .......... 120
   predicted ERAs ......................................... 156
   pull percentage .......................................... 131
   strikeout-hit ratio ....................................... 140
   strikeouts per nine innings ................. 137, 204

Pittsburgh Pirates
   hitters with 1.000 OPS ................................ 67

Pivot ratings ................................................. 178

Postseason
   highest winning pct., four-year span ......... 195
   performance of division winners with
      largest margin of victory ........................ 17

Predicted ERAs ............................................ 156

Pull percentage ............................................. 131

Pythagorean theorem ................................... 198

## Q

Quality starts ................................................ 135

## R

RBI
   chances at 2,298 .......................................... 76
   go-ahead RBI ...................................... 93, 204
   most, No. 2 in league two straight seasons . 45
   most per plate appearance, bases loaded ..... 81
   per opportunity .................................... 96, 204

Reader questions and comments ................. 212

Red Barrett Trophy .............................. 154, 204

Relievers
   easy, regular and tough saves .................... 142
   ERA increases in four straight seasons ......... 6
   holds .............................................. 145, 204
   inherited runners scoring percentage ........ 148
   mop-up appearances .................................. 129
   most middle-relief appearances, career ..... 127
   runs prevented values ............................... 150
   working 90-plus innings .............................. 48

Ivan Rodriguez
   stolen-base success against by top
      basestealers ........................................... 160
   stolen-base success against by top
      basestealing teams ................................ 160

Rookies
   highest RC/27 index .................................... 22
   most saves, rookies ..................................... 38
   saves in rookie season, all-time save
      leaders ..................................................... 38
   with 20 HR, 100 runs, 100 RBI ................... 22

Runs
   most per game, .260 or lower average ........ 29

*Baseball Scoreboard*

Runs created
  most, 1995-99 .............................................. 54
  most, 1999 ..................................................... 89

Runs created per 27 outs
  highest index, rookies ................................. 22

Runs prevented values ................................ 150

# S

Safeco Field
  ballpark indexes ........................................... 31

Saves
  easy, regular and tough ............................. 142
  in rookie season, all-time save leaders ........ 38
  most, rookies ................................................. 38

Second basemen
  pivot ratings ............................................... 178

Secondary average
  hitters ............................................................ 91
  teams ............................................................. 29

Similarity scores
  Vladimir Guerrero ........................................ 79

Slidin' Billy Trophy ............................... 98, 204

Sammy Sosa
  most home runs, No. 2 in league two
    straight seasons ....................................... 45

Slugging percentage
  highest career, Brewers ................................ 58

Starting pitchers
  game scores ................................................ 133
  pitch counts ........................................ 154, 204
  quality starts .............................................. 135

STATS awards ............................................ 204

STATS FlatBat ................................... 104, 204

STATS Gold Gloves .................................... 204

Stolen bases
  catcher caught-stealing percentage .... 163, 204
  stolen-base success against Ivan
    Rodriguez by top basestealers ............. 160
  stolen-base success against Ivan
    Rodriguez by top basestealing teams ... 160

Strikeouts (pitchers)
  highest strikeout-baserunner ratio ............. 110
  highest strikeout-walk ratio ....................... 110

  most, No. 2 in league two straight seasons . 45
  most per nine innings, age 35 or older ...... 114
  per nine innings ................................. 137, 204
  strikeout-hit ratio ....................................... 140

Swings and misses......................................... 100

# T

Tampa Bay Devil Rays
  teams with four players who hit 30 HR
    the year before ........................................ 34

# U

Underachieving teams ................................. 198

# W

Walks
  winning percentage, teams ranking last ...... 60

Winning percentage
  by hitters in starts, 1990-99 ...................... 192
  first year in new parks ................................. 73
  highest, career................................................. 9
  highest, postseason in four-year span........ 195
  highest, through season reaching 200
    decisions, ages 29-32 ................................ 9
  leagues' youngest teams............................... 15
  teams ranking last in walks ......................... 60

Wins
  15-plus for most teams ................................ 56
  most by hitters in starts, 1990-99 .............. 192
  most, No. 2 in league two straight seasons . 45
  most pitching wins plus batting hits .......... 120

Wrigley Field
  dimensions.................................................. 200

# Z

Zone ratings
  explanation ................................................ 165
  infield......................................................... 174
  outfield....................................................... 180
  ultimate ..................................................... 165

# About STATS, Inc.

STATS, Inc. is the nation's leading sports information and statistical analysis company, providing detailed sports services for a wide array of commercial clients. In January 2000, STATS was purchased by News Digital Media, the digital division of News Corporation. News Digital Media engages in three primary activities: operating FOXNews.com, FOXSports.com, FOXMarketwire.com and FOX.com; developing related interactive services; and directing investment activities and strategy for News Corporation, as they relate to digital media.

As one of the fastest growing companies in sports, STATS provides the most up-to-the-minute sports information to professional teams, print and broadcast media, software developers and interactive service providers around the country. STATS was recently recognized as "One of Chicago's 100 most influential technology players" by *Crain's Chicago Business* and has been one of 16 finalists for KPMG/Peat Marwick's Illinois High Tech Award for three consecutive years. Some of our major clients are Fox Sports, the Associated Press, America Online, *The Sporting News*, ESPN, Electronic Arts, MSNBC, SONY and Topps. Much of the information we provide is available to the public via STATS On-Line. With a computer and a modem, you can follow action in the four major professional sports, as well as NCAA football and basketball and other professional and college sports. . . as it happens!

STATS Publishing, a division of STATS, Inc., produces 12 annual books, including the *Major League Handbook*, *The Scouting Notebook*, the *Pro Football Handbook*, the *Pro Basketball Handbook* and the *Hockey Handbook*. In 1998, we introduced two baseball encyclopedias, the *All-Time Major League Handbook* and the *All-Time Baseball Sourcebook*. Together they combine for more than 5,000 pages of baseball history. Also available is *From Abba Dabba to Zorro: The World of Baseball Nicknames*, a wacky look at monikers and their origins. A new football title was launched in 1999, the *Pro Football Scoreboard*. These publications deliver STATS' expertise to fans, scouts, general managers and media around the country.

In addition, STATS offers the most innovative—and fun—fantasy sports games around, from Bill James Fantasy Baseball and Bill James Classic Baseball to STATS Fantasy Football and our newest game, Diamond Legends Internet Baseball. Check out our immensely popular Fantasy Portfolios and our great new web-based product, STATS Fantasy Advantage.

Information technology has grown by leaps and bounds in the last decade, and STATS will continue to be at the forefront as both a vendor and supplier of the most up-to-date, in-depth sports information available. For those of you on the information superhighway, you always can catch STATS in our area on America Online or at our Internet site.

For more information on our products or on joining our reporter network, contact us on:

America Online — Keyword: STATS

Internet — www.stats.com

Toll-Free in the USA at 1-800-63-STATS (1-800-637-8287)

Outside the USA at 1-847-470-8798

Or write to:

STATS, Inc.
8130 Lehigh Ave.
Morton Grove, IL 60053

# About the Authors

STATS co-founder and CEO John Dewan has co-authored all 11 editions of the *STATS Baseball Scoreboard*, as well as serving as editor of the annual *STATS Scouting Notebook*. Dewan's "Stat of the Week" segment has been a staple on Chicago sports radio's "The Mike Murphy Show" for a number of years.

Don Zminda is Vice President of Publishing Products for STATS, Inc. and a nationally-known expert on sports statistics. He is co-editor of the annual *STATS Scouting Notebook* and author of *From Abba Dabba to Zorro: the World of Baseball Nicknames*.

Associate Editor Jim Callis serves as editor of the *STATS Scouting Notebook* and the *STATS Minor League Scouting Notebook*. He also was an associate editor on the *STATS All-Time Major League Handbook* and the *STATS All-Time Baseball Sourcebook*. Prior to arriving at STATS, Jim worked at *Baseball America* for nine years, including four as managing editor. While at *Baseball America*, he established himself as the nation's leading authority on amateur and college baseball, winning USA Baseball's 1995 media award for increasing the awareness of college and amateur baseball.

# STATS All-Time Major League Handbook

**Item #ATHB, $79.95**

**Available April!**

*Second Edition*

*Updated Through the 1999 Season!*

***STATS All-Time Major League Handbook,*** updated through the 1999 season, is the ONLY baseball register featuring complete year-by-year career statistics for EVERY major league batter, pitcher and fielder in baseball history. In-depth position-by-position fielding stats and hitting stats for pitchers round out the most comprehensive register ever compiled.

### Coming This year!
Keep an eye out for ***Win Shares***, the newest addition to the STATS library. Written by the legendary Bill James, ***Win Shares*** will take a revolutionary look at exactly how much individual players contribute to their teams' wins. It's the best tool ever developed to evaluate baseball performance.

### Order From STATS Today!
1-800-63-STATS   847-470-8798   www.stats.com

**Free First-Class Shipping for Books Over $10**
**Order form in back of this book**

# STATS Power Hitters

Bill James Presents:
## STATS Major League Handbook 2000

- Career stats for every 1999 major leaguer
- Bill James' & STATS' exclusive player projections for 2000
- Complete fielding stats for every player at every position
- Expanded and exclusive leader boards
- Managerial performances and tendencies

"STATS consistently provides a thorough and innovative analysis of the game of baseball."
  Ron Schueler, GM, Chicago White Sox

### Item #HB00, $19.95, Available Now!
### Comb-bound #HC00, $24.95. Available Now!

## The Scouting Notebook 2000

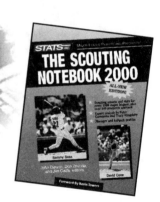

- Extensive scouting reports on over 650 major league players
- Evaluations of more than 400 minor league prospects
- Expert analysis from nationally-known writers
- Manager profiles evaluate skipper styles and strategies

"A phenomenal resource!"
  Jayson Stark, *Philadelphia Inquirer/ESPN*

### Item #SN00, $19.95, Available Now!
### Comb-bound #SC00, $24.95. Available Now!

## Order From STATS Today!
1-800-63-STATS     847-470-8798     www.stats.com

**Free First-Class Shipping for Books Over $10**
**Order form in back of this book**

# Rounding Out STATS' Starting Lineup

## STATS Player Profiles 2000

**Extensive season and five-year breakdowns including:**
- Lefty-righty splits for hitters and pitchers
- Breakdowns for clutch situations
- Home vs. road, day vs. night, grass vs. turf
- Batting in different lineup spots for hitters
- Pitching after various days of rest

"*Player Profiles* is my companion on all road trips."
Rod Beaton, *USA Today*

### Item #PP00, $19.95, Available Now!
### Comb-bound, $24.95, Available Now!

Bill James Presents:
## STATS Batter Versus Pitcher Match-Ups! 2000

- Career stats for pitchers vs. batters
- Leader boards with best and worst match-ups
- Batter and pitcher performances for each major league ballpark
- Stats for all 1999 major league players

"No other book delivers as much info that's so easy to use."
Peter Gammons, *Boston Globe/ESPN*

### Item #BVSP, $24.95, Available Now!

## Order From STATS Today!
1-800-63-STATS    847-470-8798    www.stats.com

**Free First-Class Shipping for Books Over $10**
**Order form in back of this book**

# Major League Coverage of the Minor Leagues

Bill James Presents:
## STATS Minor League Handbook 2000

- Career data for all Double-A and Triple-A players
- Bill James' exclusive Major League Equivalences
- Complete 1999 Class-A and Rookie statistics

"The place to check for info on up-and-coming players."
-Bill Koenig, *Baseball Weekly*

Item #MH00, $19.95, Available Now!
Comb-bound #MC00, $24.95, Sold Out!

## STATS Minor League Scouting Notebook 2000

- Evaluations of every organization's top prospects
- Essays, stat lines and grades for more than 1,200 prospects
- Author John Sickels' exclusive list of baseball's top 50 prospects
- Recap of the 1999 amateur draft

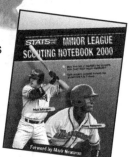

"*STATS Minor League Scouting Notebook* is a valuable tool that serves as an excellent complement to our scouting reports."
Greg Smith, Director of Scouting, Detroit Tigers

Item #MN00, $19.95, Available Now!

Order From STATS Today!
1-800-63-STATS     847-470-8798     www.stats.com

**Free First-Class Shipping for Books Over $10**
**Order form in back of this book**

# A Fantasy Player's Fantasies Come True!

The choice is yours. You can **just play** or you can **play to win**. If you play to win, make sure *Player Projections Update* is sitting by the phone in your GM's office.

## STATS Player Projections Update 2000

- The most up-to-the-minute information available
- Projections featuring players in new ballparks
- Forecasts that account for spring and winter trades
- More accurate playing-time projections
- Coverage of injury developments

### Item #PJUP, $9.95, Available March 2000!

# An Intriguing Look at Baseball!

## STATS Diamond Chronicles 2000

- Essays, debates and discussions from the 1999 season and offseason
- In-depth, often-heated dialogue between well-known baseball analysts
- Learn what experts think of trades, managerial strategies, etc.
- Statistical charts to reinforce opinions

### Item #CH00, $19.95, Available March 2000!

Order From **STATS INC.** Today!
1-800-63-STATS    847-470-8798    www.stats.com

**Free First-Class Shipping for Books Over $10
Order form in back of this book**

# Hard-Hitting Action!

## STATS Pro Football Handbook 2000

- A complete season-by-season register for every active NFL player
- Numerous statistical breakdowns for hundreds of NFL players
- Leader boards in both innovative and traditional categories
- Exclusive evaluations of offensive linemen
- Kicking, punting and defensive breakdowns

"*STATS Pro Football Handbook* is informative and easy to use."
-Will McDonough, *Boston Globe*

### Item #FH00, $19.95, Available April!
### Comb-bound #FC00, $24.95, Available April!

## STATS Pro Football Scoreboard 2000

- STATS answers football's hottest questions
- Creative essays on every team, the league and the game in general
- Coach and team profiles, draft coverage

This unique book is a must-have for all football fans!
### Item #SF00, $19.95, Available July!

**Look For Our Newest Football Publication:
Typical STATS Coverage, Typical STATS depth.**

### STATS Pro Football Sourcebook 2000

- Perfect Fantasy tool!
- Multi-year situational statistics
- Up-to-date draft and free-agent analysis
- Extensive team stats

### Item #PF00, $19.95, Available July!

**NEW**

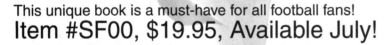

### Order From STATS INC. Today!
1-800-63-STATS        847-470-8798        www.stats.com

**Free First-Class Shipping for Books Over $10
Order form in back of this book**

# Hot Coverage of the Winter Sports

## STATS Hockey Handbook 2000-2001

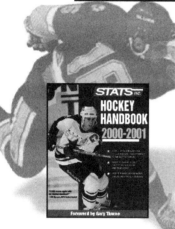

- Career stats for every NHL player who made an appearance in 1999-2000
- In-depth player profiles identifying strengths and weaknesses
- Leader boards for forwards, defensemen and goaltenders
- Team game logs

"STATS scores again with the **Hockey Handbook**."
Bill Clement, *ESPN* Hockey Analyst

### Item #HH01, $19.95, Available August

## STATS Pro Basketball Handbook 2000-2001

- Career stats for every player who logged minutes during the 1999-2000 season
- Team game logs with points, rebounds, assists and much more
- Leader boards from points per game to triple-doubles
- 1999-2000 and five-year player splits

"A great guide for the dedicated NBA fan."
Rick Telander, *ESPN Magazine*

### Item #BH01, $19.95, Available Sept.

## Order From STATS Today!

1-800-63-STATS     847-470-8798     www.stats.com

**Free First-Class Shipping for Books Over $10**
**Order form in back of this book**

# One of a Kind STATS!

## From Abba-Dabba To Zorro: The World of Baseball Nicknames

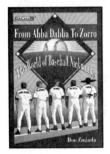

- STATS reveals the unusual and funny stories behind player nicknames
- Who are "Skoonj," "Big Six" and "The Tabasco Kid"?
- The All-Food Team, All-Body Parts Team, and many more
- Baseball celebrities including Bob Costas, Ernie Harwell, and Jim Palmer pick their favorite baseball nicknames

### Item #ABBA, $9.95, Available Now!

## STATS Baseball's Terrific 20

- Perfect for fans ages 7-12
- Featuring Mark McGwire, Ken Griffey Jr, Sammy Sosa and more
- Awesome color action photos of kids' favorite players
- Children will love the Triple Play Trivia Game

### Item #KID1, $9.95, Available Now!

## STATS Ballpark Sourcebook: Diamond Diagrams

- Analytical essays and historical summaries for more than 100 major and minor league parks
- Extensive playing characteristics for each field
- Anecdotes and accounts of memorable players and events at each park
- Photos, charts and diagrams detail every featured ballpark

### Item #BSDD, $24.95, Available Now!
(1st Printing Sold out!)

## Order From STATS INC. Today!

1-800-63-STATS    847-470-8798    www.stats.com

**Free First-Class Shipping for Books Over $10**
**Order form in back of this book**

# The Web Comes Alive!

BASEBALL'S PAST COMES ALIVE

Introducing Diamond Legends Internet Baseball Simulation game. It's the state-of-the-art baseball simulation that will blow you away! Diamond Legends is the first Web-based game to actually transport you back in time.

Featuring all the greats of the game and even some of the more recent baseball heroes like Don Mattingly and Kent Hrbek. Diamond Legends is the latest must-play gem in the STATS arsenal of fantasy sports.

STATS INC. FANTASY SPORTS

## www.diamondlegends.com

## Bill James Classic Baseball

Introducing the most realistic, fun, baseball simulation game ever created...

Now available at www.stats.com

### As owner and GM you'll be able to...

- "Buy" your team of up to 25 players from our catalog of over 2,400 historical players (You'll receive $1 million to buy your favorite players)
- Choose the park your team will call home– current or historical, 84 in all
- Rotate batting lineups for a right or left-handed starting pitcher
- Change your pitching rotation for each series
- Alter in-game strategies, including stealing frequency, holding runners on base, hit-and-run, and much more
- Select your best pinch-hitter and late-inning defensive replacements

*The Classic Game* uses players from all eras of major league baseball, at all performance levels — not just the stars. You'll see Honus Wagner, Josh Gibson, Carl Yastrzemski, Bob Uecker, and Billy Grabarkewitz.

Claim your team today!

www.stats.com
1-800-63-STATS

## Bill James Fantasy Baseball

Bill James Fantasy Baseball enters its 12th season of offering baseball fans the most unique, realistic and exciting game fantasy sports has to offer.

You draft a 26-player roster and can expand to as many as 28. Players aren't ranked like in rotisserie leagues - you'll get credit for everything a player does, like hitting homers, driving in runs, turning double plays, pitching quality outings and more!

Now available at www.stats.com

### Unique Features Include:

Live fantasy experts — available seven nights a week

The best weekly reports in the business — detailing who is in the lead, win-loss records, MVPs, and team strengths and weaknesses

Incredibly detailed boxscores of every game your team plays, including umpires and game attendance

Now playable by phone/mail or at *www.stats.com*

Sign up today!

www.stats.com
1-800-63-STATS

## Books (Free first-class shipping for books over $10)

| Qty | Product Name | Item Number | Price | Total |
|---|---|---|---|---|
| | STATS Major League Handbook 2000 | HB00 | $ 19.95 | |
| | STATS Major League Handbook 2000 (Comb-bound) | HC00 | $ 24.95 | |
| | The Scouting Notebook 2000 | SN00 | $ 19.95 | |
| | The Scouting Notebook 2000 (Comb-bound) | SC00 | $ 24.95 | |
| | STATS Minor League Handbook 2000 | MH00 | $ 19.95 | |
| | STATS Minor League Handbook 2000 (Comb-bound) | MC00 | **Sold Out** | |
| | STATS Player Profiles 2000 | PP00 | $ 19.95 | |
| | STATS Player Profiles 2000 (Comb-bound) | PC00 | $ 24.95 | |
| | STATS Minor League Scouting Notebook 2000 | MN00 | $ 19.95 | |
| | STATS Batter Vs. Pitcher Match-Ups! 2000 | BP00 | $ 24.95 | |
| | STATS Ballpark Sourcebook: Diamond Diagrams | BSDD | $ 24.95 | |
| | STATS Baseball Scoreboard 2000 | SB00 | $ 19.95 | |
| | STATS Diamond Chronicles 2000 | CH00 | $ 19.95 | |
| | STATS Pro Football Handbook 2000 | FH00 | $ 19.95 | |
| | STATS Pro Football Handbook 2000 (Comb-bound) | FC00 | $ 24.95 | |
| | STATS Pro Football Scoreboard 2000 | SF00 | $ 19.95 | |
| | STATS Pro Football Sourcebook 2000 | PF00 | $ 19.95 | |
| | STATS Hockey Handbook 1999-2000 | HH00 | $ 19.95 | |
| | STATS Pro Basketball Handbook 1999-2000 | BH00 | $ 19.95 | |
| | STATS All-Time Major League Handbook, 2nd Edition | ATHB | $ 79.95 | |
| | | | Total | |

## Books Under $10 (Please include $2.00 S&H for each book/magazine)

| | Product Name | Item Number | Price | Total |
|---|---|---|---|---|
| | From Abba Dabba to Zorro: The World of Baseball Nicknames | ABBA | $ 9.95 | |
| | STATS Baseball's Terrific 20 | KID1 | $ 9.95 | |
| | STATS Player Projections Update 2000 | PJUP | $ 9.95 | |
| | | | Total | |

## Previous Editions (Please Circle appropriate years and include $2.00 S&H for each book)

| | Product Name | Years | Price | Total |
|---|---|---|---|---|
| | STATS Major League Handbook | '91 '92 '93 '94 '95 '96 '97 '98 '99 | $ 9.95 | |
| | The Scouting Notebook/Report | '94 '95 '96 '97 '98 '99 | $ 9.95 | |
| | STATS Player Profiles | '93 '94 '95 '96 '97 '98 '99 | $ 9.95 | |
| | STATS Minor League Handbook | '92 '93 '94 '95 '96 '97 '98 '99 | $ 9.95 | |
| | STATS Minor League Scouting Notebook | '95 '96 '97 '98 '99 | $ 9.95 | |
| | STATS Batter Vs. Pitcher Match-Ups! | '94 '95 '96 '97 '98 '99 | $ 9.95 | |
| | STATS Diamond Chronicles | '97 '98 '99 | $ 9.95 | |
| | STATS Baseball Scoreboard | '92 '93 '94 '95 '96 '97 '98 '99 | $ 9.95 | |
| | Pro Football Revealed: The 100-Yard War | '94 '95 '96 '97 '98 | $ 9.95 | |
| | STATS Pro Football Handbook | '95 '96 '97 '98 '99 | $ 9.95 | |
| | STATS Pro Football Scoreboard | '99 | $ 9.95 | |
| | STATS Hockey Handbook | '96-97 '97-98 '98-99 | $ 9.95 | |
| | STATS Pro Basketball Handbook | '93-94 '94-95 '95-96 '96-97 '97-98 '98-99 | $ 9.95 | |
| | All-Time Major League Handbook (Slightly dinged) | First Edition | $ 45.00 | |
| | All-Time Major League Sourcebook (Slightly dinged) | First Edition | $ 45.00 | |
| | | | Total | |

| | Product Name | Item Number | Price | Total |
|---|---|---|---|---|
| | Bill James Classic Baseball | BJCB | $ 129.95 | |
| | Bill James Fantasy Baseball | BJFB | $ 89.95 | |
| | STATS Fantasy Football | SFF | $ 49.95 | |
| | | | Total | |

**TOTAL** [ ]

**1st Fantasy Team Name** (ex. Colt 45's):_____
Which Fantasy Game is the team for?_____

**2nd Fantasy Team Name** (ex. Colt 45's):_____
Which Fantasy Game is the team for?_____

Note: $1.00/player is charged for all roster moves and transactions.

**Mail:**
STATS, Inc.
8130 Lehigh Avenue
Morton Grove, IL 60053

**Phone:**
1-800-63-STATS
(847) 677-3322

**Fax:**
(847) 470-9140

**Bill To:**
Company_____
Name_____
Address_____
City_____State_____Zip_____
Phone (    )_____Ext.____Fax (    )_____
E-mail Address_____

**Ship To:** *(Fill in this section if shipping address differs from billing address)*
Company_____
Name_____
Address_____
City_____State_____Zip_____
Phone (    )_____Ext.____Fax (    )_____
E-mail Address_____

**Method of payment:**
**All prices stated**
**in U.S. Dollars**

❑ **Charge to my** *(circle one)*
  Visa
  MasterCard
  American Express
  Discover

❑ **Check or Money Order**
  *(U.S. funds only)*

Please include credit card number
and expiration date with charge orders!

☐☐☐☐☐☐☐☐☐☐☐☐☐☐☐☐

Exp. Date  ☐ / ☐
     Month  Year

X_____
  Signature *(as shown on credit card)*

| Totals for STATS Products: | | |
|---|---|---|
| **Books** | | ☐ |
| **Books Under $10**  * | | ☐ |
| **Prior Book Editions**  * | | ☐ |
| order 2 or more books/subtract:  $1.00/book *(Does not include prior editions)* | | ☐ |
| Illinois residents add 8.5% sales tax | | ☐ |
| | **Sub Total** | ☐ |
| **Shipping Costs** | | |
| Canada | Add $3.50/book | ☐ |
| * All books under $10 | Add $2.00/book | ☐ |
| **Fantasy Games** | | ☐ |
| | **Grand Total** | ☐ |
| | *(No other discounts apply)* | |

*(Orders subject to availability)*

# Free First-Class Shipping for Books Over $10